MARINE TECHNOLOGY, OCEAN DEVELOPMENT, AND THE LAW OF THE SEA

Emerging technologies such as autonomous vessels, artificial intelligence, and alternative fuels are revolutionizing the way we operate at sea. This volume examines how advancements in information technology and biotechnology are influencing the evolution of ocean law and policy. These technologies, including blockchain, satellite and submarine cable communications, nuclear power at sea, seabed mining, underwater archaeology, marine genetics, and decarbonization, are changing the architecture of ocean governance. This volume explores both the opportunities and the challenges these advancements pose to the law of the sea, which is evolving to adapt to ever-accelerating rates of global change. Looking forward, the book considers the role of the law of the sea in the future of ocean governance. This title is also available as open access on Cambridge Core.

James Kraska is Charles H. Stockton Chair of International Maritime Law at US Naval War College and Visiting Professor of Law and John Harvey Gregory Lecturer on World Organization at Harvard Law School. His research focuses on emerging and disruptive marine technologies, the law of the sea, and the law of naval warfare.

Khanssa Lagdami is ITF Seafarers' Trust Associate Professor at World Maritime University. She specializes in maritime labor law, human rights at sea, maritime security, and the future of work. With extensive international research, consultancy, and project leadership experience, she advances legal, policy, and capacity-building initiatives, particularly in developing regions.

Marine Technology, Ocean Development, and the Law of the Sea

Edited by

JAMES KRASKA
US Naval War College

KHANSSA LAGDAMI
World Maritime University

CAMBRIDGE
UNIVERSITY PRESS

CAMBRIDGE
UNIVERSITY PRESS

Shaftesbury Road, Cambridge CB2 8EA, United Kingdom

One Liberty Plaza, 20th Floor, New York, NY 10006, USA

477 Williamstown Road, Port Melbourne, VIC 3207, Australia

314–321, 3rd Floor, Plot 3, Splendor Forum, Jasola District Centre, New Delhi – 110025, India

Cambridge University Press is part of Cambridge University Press & Assessment, a department of the University of Cambridge.

We share the University's mission to contribute to society through the pursuit of education, learning and research at the highest international levels of excellence.

www.cambridge.org
Information on this title: www.cambridge.org/9781009760188

DOI: 10.1017/9781009760171

First published 2026

Cover image: Global Logistics international delivery concept / GreenOak / Shutterstock

A catalogue record for this publication is available from the British Library

Library of Congress Cataloging-in-Publication Data
NAMES: Kraska, James editor | Lagdami, Khanssa editor
TITLE: Marine technology, ocean development and the law of the sea / James Kraska, Khanssa Lagdami.
DESCRIPTION: New York : Cambridge University Press, 2026. | Includes bibliographical references and index.
IDENTIFIERS: LCCN 2025051223 (print) | LCCN 2025051224 (ebook) | ISBN 9781009760188 hardback | ISBN 9781009760225 paperback | ISBN 9781009760171 epub
SUBJECTS: LCSH: Law of the sea | Marine engineering–Law and legislation | Ships–Automation–Law and legislation | Artificial intelligence–Law and legislation | Marine resources conservation–Law and legislation
CLASSIFICATION: LCC KZA1145 .M37 2026 (print) | LCC KZA1145 (ebook)
LC record available at https://lccn.loc.gov/2025051223
LC ebook record available at https://lccn.loc.gov/2025051224

ISBN 978-1-009-76018-8 Hardback
ISBN 978-1-009-76022-5 Paperback

Contents

Notes on Contributors

Ceren Cerit Dindar is an assistant professor at Ankara Yildirim Beyazit University, where she is head of the Maritime Law Department and coordinator of the LLM program in maritime law. She earned her LLB from Ankara University and her LLM and PhD from Swansea University, where her research focused on legal issues concerning the delivery and redelivery of the vessel in time charters. Dr. Dindar is a dedicated senior researcher at DEHUKAM, having previously served as a research assistant at the Institute of International Shipping and Trade Law. Her recent studies are primarily concerned with maritime decarbonization. She coordinated a project titled "Legal Problems Relating to the Autonomous Vessels in Turkiye and Potential Solutions," which was funded by the Scientific and Technological Research Council of Turkey. Dr. Dindar has presented papers at various conferences and has published articles in journals, including the *Journal of International Maritime Law*.

Marc Fialkoff is a member of the nuclear security research staff at Oak Ridge National Laboratory, where his work supports countries developing transport security regulations for nuclear and other radioactive materials. Dr. Fialkoff also serves as a subject matter expert to the International Atomic Energy Agency and member States in the development of transport security regulations. His research investigates the intersection of nuclear security and maritime security with respect to floating nuclear power plants and civil nuclear propulsion, having published on this topic in the *Tulane Maritime Law Journal* and the *Journal of Maritime Law and Commerce*. Dr. Fialkoff serves as an adjunct professor of law at the College of Law of the University of Tennessee, Knoxville, where he teaches courses on nuclear law and national security law. He earned his PhD from Virginia Polytechnic Institute and State University in planning, governance, and globalization, and his JD from Roger Williams University School of Law, focusing on maritime law. Dr. Fialkoff was a

Fulbright scholar to the UK, earning his master's degree in sustainability (transport) from the Institute for Transport Studies at the University of Leeds.

Maral Javidbakht is a PhD candidate in the Faculty of Law at the University of Hamburg. Having defended her LLM thesis on international legal mechanisms for countering maritime terrorism in the Indian Ocean region, she joined the law faculty of Hamburg University as a scholarship holder in the Albrecht Mendelssohn Bartholdy Graduate School of Law. Her doctoral dissertation addresses the safety of MASS navigation in the higher levels of autonomy and the role of the flag State in this regard. Javidbakht's research interests concern the international law of the sea, especially with regard to maritime security, the impact of technological developments on the current law of the sea framework, and the protection of the marine environment.

Richard L. Kilpatrick, Jr. is Visiting Professor of Law at William H. Bowen School of Law of the University of Arkansas at Little Rock, where he teaches courses in contract law, international commercial law, and maritime law. He also serves as an academic fellow at the Centre for Maritime Law of the National University of Singapore. Having earned his JD from Tulane University Law School, he has practiced maritime law and taught at universities in Illinois and South Carolina. Professor Kilpatrick has published journal articles, book chapters, and essays covering a broad range of maritime and international commercial law issues. He is a member of the Illinois Bar and an academic member of the Maritime Law Association of the United States.

James Kraska is Charles H. Stockton Chair of International Maritime Law and Department Chair of the Stockton Center for International Law at the US Naval War College, and Visiting Professor of Law and John Harvey Gregory Lecturer on World Organization at Harvard Law School, where he teaches a popular course on the international law of the sea. Professor Kraska's research is focused on the law of the sea, maritime security law and policy, and the law of naval warfare. He has served as a visiting professor at the College of Law of the University of the Philippines, a distinguished visiting professor of law at Gujarat National Law University, and a visiting professor of law at the University of Maine School of Law. He was Mary Derrickson McCurdy Visiting Scholar at Duke University Marine Laboratory of the Nicholas School of the Environment, and Office of the Chief of Naval Research Fellow at the Marine Policy Center of Woods Hole Oceanographic Institution. His most recent books are *Disruptive Technology and the Law of Naval Warfare* (with Raul Pedrozo; 2022), *Emerging Technology and the Law of the Sea* (with Young Kil Park; 2022), and *Cultural Influences on the Law of the Sea* (with Jessie Ryou-Ellison; 2025). Professor Kraska has served for over twenty years as a US Navy judge advocate, with extensive service in the Indo-Pacific region, including assignments as legal adviser and international law attorney for naval, joint, and interagency task forces; as Oceans Law and Policy Adviser to the Pentagon; and as Director of International Negotiations on the Joint Staff, where he was also a member of the US delegation to the International Maritime Organization.

Khanssa Lagdami is ITF Seafarers' Trust Associate Professor in Maritime Labor Law and Policy at the World Maritime University (WMU) in Malmö, Sweden. She also serves as Academic Coordinator of WMU's Professional Development Program in Maritime Welfare (MARI-WEL), which delivers a comprehensive overview of topics and issues related to seafarers' welfare, bringing together world-leading experts on seafarers' rights, maritime regulations, and welfare issues. In addition, she is a lead member of the Future of Work Program at WMU. Dr. Lagdami's strengths lie in maritime labor law, human rights at sea, maritime security, and the future of work in the maritime sector. Her research and academic interests involve project creation, project management, capacity-building, and training (especially for developing countries). Dr. Lagdami has taught international public law, the law of the sea, and maritime law at the Faculty of Law of the University of Nantes in France. She earned her doctorate in maritime law from the University of Nantes. Her multi-disciplinary profile includes an MSc in Maritime Affairs Management and an LLM in International Comparative Law from the University of Perpignan in France.

Raul (Pete) Pedrozo (Captain, USN, Ret.) is Howard S. Levie Chair on the Law of Armed Conflict at the Stockton Center for International Law of the US Naval War College. Prior to his retirement from active duty after thirty-four years of service, he has held numerous positions advising senior military and civilian defense officials, including as Special Assistant to the Under Secretary of Defense for Policy and as Senior Legal Adviser to the Commander, US Pacific Command. Professor Pedrozo has lectured extensively at military and civilian academic institutions and participated in numerous multilateral and bilateral negotiations, including at the International Maritime Organization, the Transnational Organized Crime Convention, and the International Civil Aviation Organization. He is the coauthor of *International Maritime Security Law* (2013), *The Free Sea: The American Fight for Freedom of Navigation* (2018), *Emerging Technology and the Law of the Sea* (2022), "The Newport Manual on the Law of Naval Warfare" (in *International Law Studies* 101, 2023), and the "Annotated Supplement to the Commander's Handbook on the Law of Naval Operations" (in *International Law Studies* 102, 2024). Professor Pedrozo has an LLM in International and Comparative Law from Georgetown University Law Center and a JD from the Ohio State University College of Law.

Natalia Perez is a 2025 John A. Knauss MIT Marine Policy Fellow with the Office of Law Enforcement of the National Oceanic and Atmospheric Administration. Prior to the fellowship, she completed an internship with the Commission for the Conservation of Antarctic Marine Living Resources in Hobart, Tasmania, where she worked with the Fisheries Monitoring and Compliance team. She holds an MA in

Law and Diplomacy from Fletcher School at Tufts University, where she specialized in marine policy and international communication and technology. Her graduate studies centered on marine conservation in the polar regions, monitoring of at-sea transshipment, and marine wildlife trafficking. Throughout graduate school, she has worked as a graduate research assistant with the Shared Waters Lab, contributing to the creation of the Transboundary Freshwater Diplomacy Database. She graduated from Arcadia University in 2019 with a BA in International Studies, and her research focused on maritime zones in the Mediterranean Sea and human rights at sea. In 2018, she spent a semester in Rome, interning with a human rights legal clinic that focused on migration by sea. In 2021, she participated in the Rhodes Academy of Oceans Law and Policy and volunteered with the New England Aquarium and Oceanic Global for the United Nations World Oceans Day in 2022. She is a term member of the Explorers Club and a member of the Task Force for the Conservation of Deep-Ocean Biodiversity with the Deep-Ocean Stewardship Initiative. Her research interests center on the connection between international affairs, ocean governance, international maritime law, and marine environmental protection.

Sindhura Polepalli is a maritime legal consultant at the Directorate General of Shipping in the Ministry of Ports, Shipping, and Waterways of the Government of India. Her work focuses on the development and implementation of the law of the sea and the international law of shipping at the national level, including the protection and preservation of the marine environment; decarbonization and climate change in shipping; illegal, unregulated, and unreported fishing; and seafarers' rights and human rights law. Polepalli is engaged in national maritime legislation and policy drafting and international maritime cooperation for India, including at the International Maritime Organization. She is a member of a national committee to implement Maritime India Vision 2030, signed by the prime minister. Previously, she has served in the legal office of the International Tribunal for the Law of the Sea in Hamburg. Polepalli is engaged as a coauthor of the third UN World Ocean Assessment and is a member of the Pool of Experts for the UN Regular Process for Global Reporting and Assessment of the State of the Marine Environment. She is a fisheries global and regional processes specialist for the UN Food and Agriculture Organization. Polepalli has served as a visiting lecturer on international laws on maritime safety for the MA program in Maritime Studies at the University of Mumbai. She graduated from the Summer Academy of the International Foundation for the Law of the Sea (Germany), the Rhodes Academy of Oceans Law and Policy (Greece), and the Yeosu Academy of the Law of the Sea (Republic of Korea). Polepalli is a law graduate from the Government Law College, Mumbai, and has earned an LLM with distinction from the IMO International Maritime Law Institute in Malta, where she was awarded the Maltese Government Prize for Best Performance in the Law of the Sea.

Digvijay Rewatkar is a research associate at the Centre for International Law at the National University of Singapore. His work is focused on the role of the law of the sea in climate change discourses. Specifically, Rewatkar aims to develop a responsibility-centric paradigm for resource governance concerning minerals extracted through deep-seabed mining to facilitate a rapid green transition. Previously, he has worked at the National Security University of India on issues relating to national security and international law. Simultaneously, he has worked with the UN International Law Commission, where his research focused on issues such as sea level rise in relation to international law and the succession of States in respect of State responsibility. Rewatkar has also worked with the International Committee of the Red Cross in Geneva, developing policy on the intersection of climate change and conflict. He has attended the International Foundation of the Law of the Sea Summer Academy at the International Tribunal for the Law of the Sea, and the Yeosu Academy of the Law of the Sea, securing a magna cum laude diploma. Rewatkar completed his advanced master's degree in public international law at Leiden University, specializing in peace, justice, and development. In his free time, he can be found playing chess.

Murat Sümer is Nippon Foundation Lecturer in International Maritime Law at the IMO International Maritime Law Institute (IMLI), where he lectures on the public aspects of international maritime law and coordinates courses on the law of ports, the peaceful settlement of maritime disputes, and the delimitation of maritime boundaries. Dr. Sümer holds a PhD in public international law from Maastricht University. He has master's degrees from both IMLI and the National Defence Institute. Before joining IMLI, Dr. Sümer served as a career diplomat at the Turkish Ministry of Foreign Affairs, including as Alternate Permanent Representative to the IMO in London and as Head of the Maritime Section in Ankara. He has published numerous articles on the public aspects of international maritime law in peer-reviewed journals. Dr. Sümer is a member of the UN Division for Ocean Affairs and the Law of the Sea Pool of Experts; the OceanExpert directory of the Intergovernmental Oceanographic Commission of UNESCO; the IMO Roster of Experts; the Maritime Law Association (Turkey); and the Turkish Bar Association.

Krisztina Tilinger is a space lawyer and an expert in international maritime law. She is an adviser to the Institute of Aerospace and Telecommunications Law at the Ludovika University of Public Service in Budapest and a PhD candidate at the Doctoral School of Law and Political Sciences of Széchenyi István University in Győr, Hungary. Tilinger attended the University of Pécs in Hungary, the Comillas Pontifical University in Madrid, the UniSpace interdisciplinary program in Hungary, and the summer school on high-tech IP issues at Stanford University in California. For ten years, she has served as a contract agent for the EU's Public Administration (Brussels and Alicante), dealing with IP law and working on the quality of EU legislation. An experienced commercial and regulatory lawyer,

Tilinger is currently engaged in academia. Her research focuses on the analogy in space law, maritime law, and air law. She regularly teaches space law, organizes national and international conferences, and mentors young talents in the fields of space, maritime law, and security.

Youri van Logchem is Associate Professor of Law (Law of the Sea and Environmental Law) at the Norwegian Centre for the Law of the Sea in UiT The Arctic University of Norway, where he is also Academic Director of the LLM program on the Law of the Sea. Previously, he was a senior lecturer at the Institute of International Shipping and Trade Law at Swansea University and a PhD fellow at the Netherlands Institute for the Law of the Sea at Utrecht University. Dr. van Logchem has published widely on law of the sea issues, including a monograph titled *The Rights and Obligations of States in Disputed Maritime Areas* (2021). His work has been cited before international courts and tribunals. Dr. van Logchem is a recipient of the Rhodes Academy Submarine Cables Award.

Foreword

The oceans have long been the conduit of commerce, culture, and connectivity. Today, they are frontiers of unprecedented scientific discovery, strategic challenges, and transformative technological innovation.

I am pleased to introduce this comprehensive volume on the dynamic intersections of technology and the law of the sea, a subject of ever-growing importance in our increasingly complex and interconnected maritime domain. This book, through its diverse and in-depth chapters contributed by leading experts and scholars, offers a timely exploration of how cutting-edge technologies – from floating nuclear power plants and blockchain, to autonomous vessels, cyber navigation threats, deep-seabed mining, and artificial intelligence – are reshaping the legal landscape governing our seas.

This important work is the product of collaborative workshops jointly organized by the World Maritime University, the US Naval War College, and the Transport General Administration of the Kingdom of Saudi Arabia. Such a transcontinental partnership underscores the value of international cooperation among academic institutions and government agencies in addressing the multifaceted challenges arising at the nexus of maritime law, security, and technology.

As the global community strives to balance economic development, environmental stewardship, security, and human welfare, this work provides critical insights into the evolving governance frameworks needed to address novel challenges. The United Nations Convention on the Law of the Sea (UNCLOS) remains a remarkable foundation, yet, as these chapters illustrate, the rapid pace of technological advances forces us to rethink traditional legal principles, State responsibilities, and mechanisms of international cooperation.

Particularly noteworthy are the analyses of emerging issues, such as the implications of marine genetic resources for national security, the integration of artificial intelligence within maritime operations, and the persistent cyber threats confronting international shipping. These topics demonstrate the complexity of maintaining safe, secure, and sustainable oceans for present and future generations.

Beyond identifying challenges, this volume also highlights promising solutions – reflecting on how science and technology can be harnessed responsibly to advance ocean governance, protect marine biodiversity, and facilitate a just transition toward decarbonized shipping.

The contributors' multidisciplinary perspectives offer invaluable guidance for policymakers, academics, legal practitioners, and maritime professionals. This insightful work reflects the ethos of the World Maritime University's commitment to advancing knowledge, fostering innovation, and promoting sustainable maritime development worldwide.

I offer my profound thanks to the editors and authors for their visionary scholarship and dedication. They deserve praise and commendation for pushing knowledge further by publishing in this critical field. It is my hope that this book will serve not only as an academic resource in support of policy formulation but also as an inspiration for continued collaboration to adapt international maritime law to the realities of the twenty-first century, a century already marked by both extraordinary challenges and extraordinary promise for the governance of our oceans.

Professor Maximo Mejia, Jr.
President, World Maritime University

Preface

This volume helps policymakers, lawyers, and scholars understand the relationship between technology, the law of the sea, and ocean governance. Emerging technologies are revolutionizing international shipping, how we approach marine resources, marine science, efforts to protect the marine environment, and naval operations. These efforts are advancing quickly with innovation in a range of information and industrial technologies, including autonomous vessels and AI, fuel technology, cyber communications, deepwater operations, and blockchain.

The book is a companion to *Emerging Technology and the Law of the Sea*, edited by James Kraska and Young Kil Park (Cambridge University Press, 2022), and it continues to explore the interactions between new technologies and the law of the sea. The research is based on a workshop held in June 2024 at the World Maritime University in Malmö, Sweden, and the Stockton Center for International Law of the US Naval War College in Newport, RI. The World Maritime University, the US Naval War College, and the Korea Maritime Institute in Busan, Korea, generously supported this research. The Transport General Administration of the Kingdom of Saudi Arabia sponsored the workshop and funded open access to disseminate the findings to scholars and policymakers worldwide. All views of the editors and contributors are personal and do not reflect the official policy or position of their institutions or governments.

Abbreviations

AAWA	– Advanced Autonomous Waterborne Applications Initiative
ABMT	– Area-Based Management Tool
ACPPNM	– Amendment to the Convention on the Physical Protection of Nuclear Material (or Advanced Convention on the Physical Protection of Nuclear Material)
AI	– Artificial Intelligence
AIS	– Automatic Identification System
BAT	– Best Available Techniques
BBNJ	– Biodiversity Beyond National Jurisdiction (or Marine Biological Diversity of Areas Beyond National Jurisdiction)
BCT	– Blockchain Technology
BEP	– Best Environmental Practice
CBDR	– Common But Differentiated Responsibility
CBDR-RC	– Common But Differentiated Responsibilities and Respective Capabilities
CBTT	– Capacity-Building and Technology Transfer
CDEM	– Construction, Design, Equipment, and Manning
CIA	– Confidentiality, Integrity, and Availability (in cybersecurity context)
CII	– Carbon Intensity Indicator
CITES	– Convention on International Trade in Endangered Species of Wild Fauna and Flora
CLCS	– Commission on the Limits of the Continental Shelf
COLREG	– International Regulations for Preventing Collisions at Sea (COLREGS)

COP	– Conference of the Parties
CPPNM	– Convention on the Physical Protection of Nuclear Material
CPUCH	– Convention on the Protection of the Underwater Cultural Heritage
CRMG	– Cyber Risk Management Guidelines (IMO interim guidelines for maritime cuyber risk management)
CSI	– Container Security Initiative
DEHUKAM	– Turkish Centre for Maritime and Global Strategy (Denizcilik ve Küresel Strateji Merkezi)
DHS	– Department of Homeland Security
DNA	– Deoxyribonucleic Acid
DOC	– Document of Compliance
DOD	– Department of Defense
DOT	– Department of Transportation
DSI	– Digital Sequence Information
EEZ	– Exclusive Economic Zone
EEDI	– Energy Efficiency Design Index
EEXI	– Energy Efficiency Existing Ship Index
EIA	– Environmental Impact Assessment
EIS	– Environmental Impact Statement
EMMP	– Environmental Management and Monitoring Plan
EPRI	– Electric Power Research Institute
ECTS	– European Credit Transfer and Accumulation System
EU	– European Union
FAA	– Federal Aviation Administration
FCC	– Federal Communications Commission
FNPP	– Floating Nuclear Power Plant
GATT	– General Agreement on Tariffs and Trade
GHG	– Greenhouse Gas
GNSS	– Global Navigation Satellite System
GPS	– Global Positioning System
G77	– Group of 77
IAEA	– International Atomic Energy Agency
ICJ	– International Court of Justice
ICU	– Intensive Care Unit
IMO	– International Maritime Organization
IMU	– Inertial Measurement Unit
ILO	– International Labour Organization
INSDC	– International Nucleotide Sequence Database Collaboration
IPR	– Intellectual Property Rights

IRGC	– Islamic Revolutionary Guard Corps
ISA	– International Seabed Authority
ISM	– International Safety Management (Code)
ITF	– International Transport Workers' Federation
ITLOS	– International Tribunal for the Law of the Sea
JET	– Just Energy Transition
JWG	– Joint Working Group
LDCs	– Least Developed Countries
LRIT	– Long-Range Identification and Tracking
MARI-WEL	– Maritime Welfare (Professional Development Program)
MARPOL	– International Convention for the Prevention of Pollution from Ships
MASS	– Maritime Autonomous Surface Ship
MEPC	– Marine Environment Protection Committee
MFN	– Most Favoured Nation
MGR	– Marine Genetic Resources
MIT	– Massachusetts Institute of Technology
MJTTF	– Multi-Jurisdictional Task Force
MLC	– Maritime Labour Convention, 20026 as amended
MoU	– Memorandum of Understanding
MSR	– Marine Scientific Research
NASA	– National Aeronautics and Space Administration
NATO	– North Atlantic Treaty Organization
NAVCEN	– Navigation Center
NDC	– Nationally Determined Contribution
NIST	– National Institute of Standards and Technology
NOAA	– National Oceanic and Atmospheric Administration
NPT	– Treaty on the Non-Proliferation of Nuclear Weapons
NSF	– National Science Foundation
NWS	– National Weather Service
NYPE	– New York Produce Exchange (time charter party form)
OSH	– Occupational Safety and Health
OTA	– Office of Technology Assessment
PNT	– Positioning, Navigation, and Timing
PSC	– Port State Control
RNA	– Ribonucleic Acid
ROC	– Remote Operations Centre
ROV	– Remotely Operated Vehicle
SDGs	– Sustainable Development Goals
SDT	– Special and Differential Treatment

SEEMP	– Ship Energy Efficiency Management Plan
SIDS	– Small Island Developing States
SMART	– Sensor Monitoring and Reliable Telecommunications
SNC	– Single National Communication
SOLAS	– International Convention for the Safety of Life at Sea
STCW	– International Convention on Standards of Training, Certification and Watchkeeping for Seafarers
TRIPS	– Trade-Related Aspects of Intellectual Property Rights
UCH	– Underwater Cultural Heritage
UAV	– Unmanned Aerial Vehicle
UKMTO	– United Kingdom Maritime Trade Operations
UN	– United Nations
UNCLOS	– United Nations Convention on the Law of the Sea
UNGA	– United Nations General Assembly
US	– United States
USCG	– United States Coast Guard
USV	– Unmanned Surface Vehicle
VMS	– Vessel Monitoring System
WMU	– World Maritime University
WTO	– World Trade Organization

Introduction

This book examines some of the most pressing issues at the intersection of emerging and disruptive technologies, ocean governance, and the law of the sea. There is so much change in marine technology, and the velocity of change is increasing so quickly that it is challenging to scope the entire landscape.[1] We have selected leading thinkers and emerging scholars to contribute to this volume, exploring how some of the most significant technologies intersect with ocean law and governance.

The first collaboration in this area, which focused on emerging technologies and the law of the sea, was edited by James Kraska and Young Kil Park (Cambridge University Press, 2022).[2] That book was titled Emerging Technology and Law of the Sea and brought together two institutions focused on ocean development and the law of the sea: the Stockton Center for International Law at the US Naval War College and the Korea Maritime Institute. Similarly, this collaboration united efforts between the World Maritime University in Malmö, Sweden, and the US Naval War College, returning to some of the most compelling issues in marine technology, ocean governance, and the law of the sea. This book is an outgrowth of the findings and research questions explored by the contributors to this volume during a workshop at the World Maritime University in June 2024. The workshop was supported by the Transport General Authority of the Kingdom of Saudi Arabia and the Korea Maritime Institute.

Understanding how new technologies intersect with the law of the sea is important for implementing and progressively developing the rules that govern 71 percent of the planet. The relationship between technology and the law of the sea is dynamic, making any assessment perishable over time. The technology involves interpreting information related to the law of the sea, such as the widespread agreement that remote sensing by satellites in outer space does not constitute

1 Iryna Bursuk, "Dive into the Top 10 Maritime Trends and Innovations in 2025," StartUSinsight, March 26, 2025, www.startus-insights.com/innovators-guide/maritime-trends/.

2 James Kraska and Young Kil Park, *Emerging Technology and the Law of the Sea* (Cambridge: Cambridge University Press, 2022), www.cambridge.org/core/books/emerging-technology-and-the-law-of-the-sea/8CA0A0BF79157E52F1BFE50E0EBB21DB.

"marine scientific research" subject to the consent of coastal States under Article 246 of the Law of the Sea Convention. Likewise, the law of the sea is also shaping our approach to marine technology, distinguishing between those technologies that are developed and those that are not pursued. For example, the likelihood that the nascent seabed mining industry may finally become a reality is driving innovation in deep-sea operations and the protection of the marine environment.

Marine technologies are transforming virtually every aspect of humankind's use and presence in the oceans, from how we think about protecting the marine environment and conducting marine scientific research, to fisheries and nonliving resource exploitation and conservation, as well as the role of the oceans in multipolar geopolitics. The integration of AI is revolutionizing maritime operations by automating decision-making processes and replacing human judgment with autonomous decisions.

The optimum crew for a ship may be remote and not physically present on board. Machines are enabling long-distance navigation, facilitating maintenance, predicting equipment failure, and reducing vessel source pollution, including greenhouse gas emissions. Despite funding enormous, manned warships, naval forces are racing to put to sea a vast fleet of distributed, networked drone warships that dispense with even an occasional human presence ("optionally manned") on board.[3] Sensors are multiplying on vessels to feed data into these predictive models. Orca AI, for example, markets an infrared SeaPod system that captures thermal video through fog to supplement radar and identify collision risks.[4] As automation increases, the workload required of the crew during underway transit is expected to decline. The master and crew operating either remotely or on the water will harness AI to process data at a scale and speed beyond human capabilities. As the ocean environment is becoming a busier and more complex operating space, AI will provide previously unattainable fidelity, depth, and speed. AI will enable autonomous ships.

Maritime autonomous surface ships are already operating with minimal human intervention, especially for predictable routes. The sensors and real-time data can feed an AI model to enhance safe navigation, reducing human error and operating costs. In the naval domain, States are leveraging the vast potential for autonomous and unmanned subsurface, surface, and aerial vehicles to operate within the dangerous weapon engagement zone without putting humans at risk.

Marine robotics – including unmanned aerial vehicles (UAVs), unmanned surface vessels (USVs), and unmanned underwater vehicles (UUVs) – comprises a universe of drones and autonomous and sometimes expendable marine instruments that may be used to enhance inspection, maintenance, and surveillance for operations.

[3] Sam LaGrone, "Navy Moving Away from 'Optionally Manned' Vessels as Service Mulls Unmanned Future," USNI News, August 15, 2025, https://news.usni.org/2025/08/15/navy-moving-away-from-optionally-manned-vessels-as-service-mulls-unmanned-future.

[4] "Orca AI Launches Next-Gen SeaPod Watchkeeping Unit," Orca AI, January 10, 2024, www.orca-ai.io/resource/orca-ai-launches-next-gen-seapod-watchkeeping-unit/.

Machines are replacing humans, as human error accounts for 75–96 percent of maritime accidents.[5] The US Navy is developing robotic crawlers to detect and neutralize marine mines.[6]

New technologies are also aiding the drive for decarbonization, increasing the adoption of low-carbon fuels such as liquefied natural gas, hydrogen, ammonia, and biofuels. Wind-assisted propulsion is also gaining traction.[7] Wind has propelled traders across the oceans for millennia. During the nineteenth century, steam power gradually displaced wind power, followed by the advent of combustion engines. To reduce atmospheric pollution, the International Maritime Organization has established a goal to reduce emissions by 20 percent by 2030, a 70 percent cut by 2040, and full-scale decarbonization by about 2050. Wind-assisted propulsion systems (WAPS) have refined the traditional wind sail into an effective auxiliary power system that can contribute as much as one-third of the propulsion needed. This assistance can significantly reduce fuel consumption and atmospheric emissions while also extending the life of diesel engines. Bound4blue has an innovative eSAIL that can generate up to seven times the thrust of conventional rigid sails of the same size.[8]

Ocean sensing, monitoring, and operations are also experiencing the same Internet of Things (IoT) that is occurring on land. These connections require high-speed, low-latency connectivity to facilitate real-time data transmission between ship and shore. Maritime IoT is connected through 5G with real-time links between vessels and virtual reality collaboration tools.

We know that we have only scratched the surface of the issues connecting marine technology with the ocean governance and the law of the sea. The field is changing rapidly, and much more work lies ahead.

5 Joachim Rosenoegger, "Maritime Innovations: April 2024," Maritime Innovations, April 26, 2025, https://maritime-innovations.com/april-2025-maritime-innovations-autonomous-navigation-advanced-robotics/.

6 Michael Peck, "The US Navy Wants a Robotic Crawler to Eliminate the Most Dangerous Underwater Threat: Sea Mines," *Business Insider*, March 8, 2025, www.businessinsider.com/us-navy-underwater-robot-threat-sea-mines-2025-3.

7 Bound4Blue, "Blow by Blow: A Guide to Wind Assisted Propulsion Systems," December 14, 2024, https://bound4blue.com/a-guide-to-wind-assisted-propulsion-systems/.

8 Ibid.

PART I

Autonomous Shipping

1

Port State Jurisdiction and Remotely Controlled Ships

Murat Sümer

1.1 INTRODUCTION

Maritime transport handles around 80 percent of international trade, a figure that rises even higher for many developing States. An integral part of shipping, ports enable nations to engage in global trade and contribute to their prosperity and welfare. In this context, ports are fundamental gateways to international shipping for ensuring uninterrupted supply chains (ICS n.d.; UNCTAD 2023; World Bank Group n.d.).

Ports are indeed crucial, given that they act as gateways for goods carried by ships to enter a State's landmass, making them strategic points for control. Therefore, port performance and the facilitation of international trade are essential for the success of shipping. On the other hand, delays in maritime transport demonstrate the inefficiencies at ports. Enhancing digital infrastructure and adopting advanced technologies are critical for increasing the reliability of global supply chains, thus improving clearance efficiency and reducing delays. Digitalization plays a central role in enhancing port performance. By the integration of novel technologies, such as interactive data exchanges and artificial intelligence, ports can become more efficient. Indeed, technological progress can further enhance port operations (IMO n.d.b; UNCTAD 2023, ch. 4).

The current regulatory framework requires States to assume various jurisdictional roles, such as coastal, flag, and port States. While the 1982 United Nations Convention on the Law of the Sea (UNCLOS)[1] delineates the jurisdiction, in essence the International Maritime Organization (IMO) elaborates on the practical application of these jurisdictions to international shipping. Within the framework provided by UNCLOS, the IMO enhances jurisdiction by equipping States with the necessary regulatory tools. The IMO rightly maintains that the effective regulation of shipping necessitates a combination of efforts from flag, coastal, and port States. It is

[1] UNCLOS, December 10, 1982, 1833 UNTS 397.

also acknowledged that such regulation can only be effective when guided by uniform and universally enforced international standards. In this context, Chircop aptly observes that the IMO has supported the UNCLOS regime by developing norms that set the standards for the jurisdictional roles of the States (Balkin 2018, 23–24; Chircop 2018, 199–200).

Pursuant to IMO Conventions, governments bear the ultimate responsibility for ensuring compliance with international regulations. Typically, ships on the high seas have been under the exclusive jurisdiction of their flag State. However, this exclusivity is not absolute and is subject to several exceptions, such as coastal and port State jurisdictions. While flag State jurisdiction (FSJ) applies regardless of a ship's location, other forms of jurisdiction are contingent on the vessel's location. While much attention has been paid to their role as flag States, the ever-increasing obligations and responsibilities of port States are equally crucial (Barchue 2018, 252; Sumer 2023b, 117, 122).

Ports serve as pivotal locations in international logistical networks, where the safety of navigation is critical for the port/coastal States. Given the considerable risks present in the shipping activities around ports, it is incumbent upon port authorities to ensure navigational safety. This need for safety is indeed a legitimate concern, considering the growing number of vessels that navigate into, dock, visit, undock, exit, and maneuver within port areas (Agripino de Castro and Pasold 2016, 423). Port call operations, at both arrival and departure, involve numerous stakeholders, such as the port authority, pilots, tug operators, mooring personnel, terminal operators, stevedores, and other service providers (IMO 2023a).

The increase in substandard vessels over time and the severe consequence of several tragic maritime disasters have compelled coastal States, in their capacity as port States, to recognize the dire need to address the shortcomings in the enforcement capabilities of flag States (Yu et al. 2018, 87–88). In this regard, ports serve as critical checkpoints for inspecting and verifying whether visiting foreign ships comply with specific national or international technical standards and to ensure that they adhere to both national and international maritime regulations. When a merchant ship voluntarily enters a foreign port, she submits to the port State jurisdiction (PSJ). Therefore, a foreign-flagged ship must comply with the port State's regulations concerning navigation safety, customs, immigration, sanitation, national security, and environmental protection (Molenaar 2006, 2021; Sumer 2023b, 125–126).

Usually, IMO standards have demonstrated considerable flexibility in adapting to technological advancements. Moreover, the development of new technologies has always been encouraged for safer shipping. On the other hand, such innovations have also led to the creation of new legal norms and prompted the development of the IMO's compliance mechanisms (Luchenko et al. 2023, 23). Currently, shipping is in the stage of revolutionary transformation, perhaps similar to the transition from sailing to steam power. Petrig aptly highlights that Maritime Autonomous Surface

Ships (MASS) are no longer a futuristic scenario given that technology is progressing swiftly. Indeed, the right question is no longer if MASS will happen but rather how quickly and in what form it will unfold. Hence, the advent of MASS necessitates revisiting well-established jurisdictional roles of the States (IMO 2024d; Petrig 2021, 23). The current technological developments create considerable tension with the existing legal frameworks as regards the jurisdictional roles of States. Obviously, the architects of these jurisdictional frameworks did not anticipate the emergence of MASS during their drafting exercise.

1.2 PORT STATES AND MASS

The term "ports" refers to safe locations where vessels are loaded and unloaded. Notably, ports are integral to the territory of a State, which exercises full sovereignty over them. It is not one of the main characteristics of UNCLOS to offer definitions for its numerous terms. Unsurprisingly, this is also the case for "port" and "port State" although these terms are mentioned several times throughout the Convention (Articles 11, 18(1), and 129). Nevertheless, the concept of a port State becomes evident when foreign vessels visit other ports. The port State can exercise jurisdiction in the same way it would in any other part of its territory. Therefore, port States play a crucial role in ensuring compliance with international shipping standards. Yet, it is also incumbent on port States not to unnecessarily delay or hamper international shipping (Kopela 2016, 93–94; Marten 2014, 20–21; Molenaar 2021, paras. 3, 5).

Evidently, enforcement measures are more practicable in ports. Inspections at ports, rather than in open seas, are more convenient as they require fewer resources, and ships encounter fewer navigational obstacles (Coelho 2015, 273). Port State enforcement measures can include a variety of actions, such as denial of access to ports, prohibition on the loading and unloading of cargo, denial of the use of port services, inspection of vessels, detention, and fines (Molenaar 2006, 197). Against this backdrop, it may be safe to note that the successful integration of MASS operations into international shipping essentially depends on their ability to use the web of foreign ports like their conventional counterparts. Otherwise, their technological capabilities and legal capacity to navigate would not be meaningful for the industry's commercial usage.

1.2.1 *Historical Background*

As early as 1919, the Treaty of Versailles hinted at a general desire[2] for an international instrument regulating the regime of ports. In this respect, the 1923

[2] Article 379: "Without prejudice to the special obligations imposed on her by the present Treaty for the benefit of the Allied and Associated Powers, Germany undertakes to adhere to any

Convention and Statute on the International Régime of Maritime Ports[3] is a landmark development in the global regulation of ports. It primarily addresses the issue of equality of treatment concerning freedom of access to ports, the use of ports, and availing of benefits regarding the navigation and commercial operation and use of port facilities (see Article 2). In this respect, Article 2 of the Convention's Statute requires the contracting parties to ensure equal treatment of vessels from other State parties regarding the freedom of entry to ports. Although PSJ is not explicitly mentioned, it also refers to the general competence of port authorities (Articles 3 and 4).

Before the 1970s, in the absence of a directly applicable clear treaty rule, port States exercised restricted jurisdiction over foreign vessels under customary law, which was mainly in the form of denying entry to their ports or imposing specific conditions on foreign vessels. It is submitted that the concept of PSJ emerged in the 1970s. In particular, the 1973 Inter-Governmental Maritime Consultative Organisation (IMCO) Conference on Marine Pollution and the 1974 Conference of the International Law Association (British Branch Committee on the Law of the Sea) appear to be early examples. At the IMCO Conference, the US proposed a draft that would allow port States to ensure compliance with global regulations. However, the proposal was not accepted (Marten 2014, 33–35; Qi and Zhang 2021, 19–21). Over time, it became evident that the international shipping regulations set out in the IMO's major instruments[4] could only be enforced by expanding the powers of port States (Özçayir 2004, 74–77).

Significant developments in the evolution of PSJ occurred in the 1980s, particularly with the adoption of UNCLOS and the Paris Memorandum.[5] Notably, port States have assumed a critical role in ensuring compliance through various regional port State control agreements. UNCLOS (see Article 218) implicitly recognizes PSJ without providing an explicit definition, and it acknowledges the port State's authority to set conditions for foreign ships to have access to ports. Additionally, UNCLOS enables port States to physically inspect if a ship's actual conditions do not match its documentation. The evolution of PSJ was further enhanced in

General Conventions regarding the international regime of transit, waterways, ports or railways which may be concluded by the Allied and Associated Powers, with the approval of the League of Nations, within five years of the coming into force of the present Treaty."

3 Convention and Statute on the International Régime of Maritime Ports, December 9, 1923, 58 UNTS 285.

4 For example, International Convention for the Prevention of Pollution from Ships, November 2, 1973, 1340 UNTS 184, as amended by the Protocol of 1978 relating to the International Convention for the Prevention of Pollution from Ships, 1973, February 17, 1978, 1340 UNTS 61 (MARPOL); International Convention for the Safety of Life at Sea, November 1, 1974, 1184 UNTS 2, as amended by the Protocol of 1978 relating to the International Convention for Safety of Life at Sea, 1974, February 17, 1978, 1226 UNTS 213 (SOLAS); International Convention on Standards of Training, Certification, and Watchkeeping for Seafarers, July 7, 1978, 1361 UNTS 2 (STCW).

5 Paris Memorandum of Understanding on Port State Control, January 26, 1982.

1984 with the entry into force of the International Convention on Standards of Training, Certification, and Watchkeeping for Seafarers (STCW),[6] which grants port States the authority to detain ships until any deficiencies posing risks to people, property, or the environment are addressed. The evolution of PSJ has continued at both the regional and global levels; for instance, the IMO adopted the first version of Resolution A.472(18) in 1993, which set procedures for port State control (Marten 2014, 2–3, 2016, 471; Özçayir 2004, 74–77; Qi and Zhang 2021, 25–26). Over time, the myriad of IMO legal instruments enhanced the PSJ regime. Finally, the "no more favourable treatment" clause, which is usually incorporated into IMO Conventions, further consolidated PSJ vis-à-vis FSJ.

1.2.2 *Legal Basis of PSJ*

Port States possess regulatory and enforcement authority over foreign ships in their ports. As a fundamental principle, a port State, therefore, can necessitate compliance with its national regulations for foreign vessels, provided these do not pertain to aspects entirely internal to the ship. In this context, PSJ refers to the authority of a State over ships that voluntarily visit its ports (Ringbom 2011, 620–623). As a public law concept, PSJ is a direct extension of the principle of State sovereignty and is primarily a form of territorial jurisdiction, though it encompasses additional aspects.[7] Over time, PSJ has transformed from a voluntary application in specific areas to a more comprehensive and obligatory implementation largely through IMO instruments and their broadening reach to new areas (IMO 2023c, 9–10; Kopela 2016, 93–94; Marten 2014, 1, 7, 20–21; Molenaar 2006, 208–209; Sumer 2023b, 117).

PSJ is broadly viewed as allowing port States to exercise significant regulatory authority over foreign-flagged ships. In a nutshell, PSJ provides a mechanism for corrective action if flag States fail to meet their obligations. Although its significance has faded due to the expanding PSJ, FSJ remains a foundational mechanism for maintaining legal order at sea, especially on the high seas. However, over time, in response to the inadequacies of flag States in ensuring compliance of their ships, port States had to step in, and indeed, they have increasingly taken on a supplementary, if not leading, role (Derrig 2022, 534–536; Qi and Zhang 2021, 8–9).

While UNCLOS predominantly upholds FSJ over vessels, it also recognizes the growing significance of port States in ensuring adherence to international rules and standards. Indeed, the notion of the port State as a separate jurisdictional entity gained importance with the adoption of UNCLOS. However, UNCLOS, as an umbrella instrument, does not codify the scope of PSJ comprehensively.

6 See note 4 *above*.

7 For example, Article 218 of UNCLOS grants port States the authority to exercise extraterritorial jurisdiction over violations of IMO rules related to discharges from vessels that occur outside their maritime zones.

Nonetheless, it provides a legal basis, particularly in Article 218, "Enforcement by port States" (see also Articles 211(3) and 219), which also points to the IMO as the competent international organization (CIO). Acting as the secretariat for UNCLOS, the UN Division for Ocean Affairs and the Law of the Sea compiled a table elucidating the implications for the "competent or relevant international organizations" in relation to UNCLOS for ocean governance. That document, which was published in the *Law of the Sea Bulletin* No. 31, also confirms that the IMO is the CIO in the context of Article 218 (IMO 2014, 7–8; Marten 2014, 2–3; OECD 2001, 28; Sumer 2023b, 125–126; United Nations 1996).

The authority of a port State on foreign-flagged ships docked at its ports is crucial to the routine operations of international shipping. Although States have historically exercised territorial sovereignty over their ports, the concept of the port State as a distinct jurisdictional entity was formally established by UNCLOS. In establishing the legal framework for the rights and obligations of port States, UNCLOS heavily relies on the international rules developed at the CIO. By incorporating the IMO's regulations through rules of the reference system, UNCLOS indeed grants a significant role to the standards adopted under the auspices of the organization (Marten 2015, 5–6, 109–112; Sumer 2023b, 139–140).

Given that UNCLOS is relatively silent on PSJ, any limitations regarding the subject matter or scope of regulations in this context must be sought outside of the Convention. This is supported by the preamble of UNCLOS, which emphasizes that matters not explicitly regulated by the Convention continue to be governed by the general international law (Marten 2015, 109–112).

UNCLOS serves as the primary international legal framework, establishing the rights and obligations of States. States assume their roles as coastal, flag, and port States based on various factors, such as their geographical location, sovereignty, boundaries, and functions, as well as the treaties to which they are parties. Typically, a coastal State's authority diminishes as the distance from the shore increases (Beckman 2007, 326; Mansell 2009; Wolfrum 2014). Article 8 of UNCLOS establishes that waters on the landward side of the baselines are part of internal waters. This recognition affirms the sovereignty of port States over the waters in their ports. Furthermore, Article 25 reaffirms the right to regulate access to internal waters, including ports. Moreover, UNCLOS strengthens the powers of port States in protecting the marine environment, allowing them to regulate the access of vessels into their ports, inspect vessels for compliance with port entry requirements, and deny access to noncompliant vessels (Galani 2021, 609). In general, Articles 211, 218, and 219 address PSJ. Article 211(3) primarily sets the foundation for the State's jurisdiction to adopt domestic rules. On the other hand, Articles 218 and 219 specifically outline the port State's enforcement authority. In essence, while Article 211 focuses on the authority to legislate, Article 218 addresses the authority to enforce such legislation (Keselj 1999, 131–135; Özçayir 2004, 80–81).

As a framework convention, the UNCLOS emphasized general principles of the law of the sea, leaving broader discretion to States rather than restricting interpretation or hindering technological development. It was undoubtedly drafted for crewed ships. However, this does not mean that the drafters intended to exclude new types of vessels (Sumer 2023b, 138; Veal et al. 2019). Indeed, the UNCLOS regime is designed to evolve and address emerging issues that could not possibly have been foreseen during the adoption of UNCLOS. Therefore, it is suggested that the norms and principles regulating conventional manned vessels may apply to MASS with the necessary adjustments. In this context, Kraska aptly opines that the current legal framework for the law of the sea already offers a fundamental structure for regulating MASS (Kraska 2010, 44–45).

1.3 THE IMO'S REGULATORY MANDATE AND PORT STATES

In the pre-UNCLOS period, ensuring compliance with the technical, manning, and operational standards stipulated by the International Convention for the Safety of Life at Sea (SOLAS),[8] the International Convention for the Prevention of Pollution from Ships (MARPOL),[9] and the STCW proved to be challenging for flag States. Moreover, while port authorities were permitted to inspect certificates, they lacked the legal authority to board vessels to verify whether a ship's certificates accurately reflected compliance with international standards (Blanco-Bazan 2018, 42–44).

The IMO's mandate is rooted in multiple sources, notably beginning with the 1948 Convention on the International Maritime Organization[10] and various legal instruments adopted by the IMO after its inception. Although the IMO predates UNCLOS, the adoption of the Convention significantly enhanced its mandate as the CIO. UNCLOS introduces a system of "rules of reference" as a mechanism for its adaptation, requiring States to comply with the IMO's Generally Accepted International Regulations, Procedures, and Practices (GAIRS; Librando 2014, 579, 589–590; Sumer 2023b, 61–62). The active involvement of 176 IMO member States, along with that of numerous relevant stakeholders, and the broad adherence level to IMO Conventions support the argument that these rules and standards are indeed GAIRS (IMO 2023c, 7–8).

UNCLOS functions as an umbrella treaty, meaning that it can be enforced through specific regulations developed by the CIO (Librando 2014, 580–582). The IMO, which serves as the global standard-setting authority for international shipping, aims to adopt global regulations that are uniformly applied. Its mission is to promote safe, secure, environmentally sound, efficient, and sustainable shipping

[8] See note 4 *above*.
[9] See note 4 *above*.
[10] Convention on the International Maritime Organization, March 6, 1948, 289 UNTS 48.

through international cooperation. This goal could only be achieved by adopting the highest practical standards for maritime safety and security, navigational efficiency, and pollution control from ships (IMO 2023c, 4).

In this respect, IMO treaty instruments outline the way in which jurisdiction should be exercised to ensure adherence to its regulations. Similarly to UNCLOS, while the primary responsibility for enforcing these regulations falls to the flag State in the IMO context, a significant development in the IMO's efforts over the past decades has been the progressive strengthening of PSJ. This enhancement essentially aims to address noncompliance with IMO regulations by foreign ships that voluntarily visit ports. Such voluntary access to ports indeed indicates the foreign ship's consent to PSJ (Hughes 2018, 210–211).

Given that the IMO lacks enforcement powers, a core principle of its regulatory role is that State parties – whether as flag, coastal, or port States – are eventually responsible for ensuring compliance with international standards. (Balkin 2018, 22–23; IMO 2014, 12–13).

Initially, the IMO focused solely on maritime safety issues, but over time its responsibilities expanded as the environmental impact of shipping became apparent in the face of a dramatic increase in global oil transportation after the 1960s. As the IMO increasingly focused on the human element, the extent of regulatory controls broadened to encompass the entire operation of a ship. The International Safety Management Code (ISM Code) best illustrates this expansion for the safe operation of ships and for pollution prevention. Subsequently, UNCLOS and major IMO Conventions marked a shift toward enhancing the enforcement responsibilities of port States (Gavouneli 2007, 46–49; Marten 2014, 44–46). The IMO Assembly adopted its first resolution regarding the procedures for controlling ships at the end of 1981 (IMO 1981). Over time, that resolution has undergone numerous amendments to accommodate the developments in the industry (Özçayir 2009, 210–211).

Last but not least, the key IMO Conventions include provisions that govern PSJ[11] and detail the scope of its application. Pursuant to these instruments, for instance, port States are authorized to verify the authenticity of certificates issued by flag States. Furthermore, they grant port States the right to inspect ships if the certificates are found to be in disorder, if there is substantial evidence suggesting that a ship or its equipment does not match the details in the certificates, or if the certificates are not accurately maintained (IMO 2014, 19; Librando 2014, 592–594).

[11] Such as the International Convention on Load Lines, April 5, 1966, 640 UNTS 1333, as amended by the Protocol of 1988 relating to the International Convention on Load Lines, 1966, November 11, 1988, 2 UNTS 102; MARPOL; International Convention on Tonnage Measurement of Ships, June 23, 1969, 1291 UNTS 3; SOLAS; and STCW.

1.4 INTEGRATION OF REMOTELY CONTROLLED SHIPS TO INTERNATIONAL SHIPPING

The IMO defined the term "MASS" as ships capable of operating with varying degrees of human involvement and acknowledged that MASS could encompass a range of automation levels even in a single journey. To prevent confusion by employing different terms during its regulatory scoping exercise (RSE), the IMO has identified four degrees of autonomy. The said classification, particularly for degree four, although it was considered useful during the RSE, was not immune from criticism. Fortunately, a recent and more appropriate understanding has been developed at the IMO, which ensures that a remote master is required for degree four as well (Sumer 2023a). This study aims to address remotely controlled ships (RCS), which are classified as MASS degrees two and three.

Scholars generally concur that an RCS can be characterized as a ship under UNCLOS. In this regard, early research and deliberations at the IMO seem to suggest that the classification of an RCS as a ship should be at the discretion of the flag State. Indeed, Article 91 offers a wide discretion for flag States to fix conditions for granting nationality to ships. It follows that if a flag State designates an RCS as a ship, then the relevant provisions of UNCLOS would apply to it. Consequently, RCS should be able to use navigational rights and receive treatment similarly to their traditional crewed peers in the coastal waters and port areas (Dong et al. 2024, 2).

Having said that, until the IMO authoritatively clarifies the relationship between MASS and port States, there could be significant challenges for RCS operations. This uncertainty may deter port States from allowing such vessels to grant access to their ports. If a flag State registers an RCS but a port State does not recognize its status as a ship, then conflicts may arise, as the port State might view the RCS as noncompliant with the State's requirements. According to this scenario, conflicting State practices can emerge, which will cause defragmentation of international maritime law. Moreover, this can disrupt international shipping as well. Although such discrepancies may eventually be resolved through the IMO's GAIRS, these issues could prove particularly challenging during the initial period before global regulations are established. To prevent any gaps in the legal status of RCS, it is indeed imperative for the IMO to act swiftly. Given the express delegation of authority by the UNCLOS regime to the IMO, the CIO must fulfill its role in resolving uncertainties as regards port States and defining the specific requirements necessary to integrate RCS effectively (Gabay et al. 2023, 411; Sumer 2023b, 139–140).

1.4.1 *Construction, Design, Equipment, and Manning Standards*

The primary regulatory approach to enhance the safety of shipping and to control pollution from ships involves setting standards pertinent to the construction, design, equipment, and manning of ships (CDEM standards), as in the example of SOLAS and MARPOL (Churchill 2016, 443). This particularly merits closer scrutiny, given the varying qualifications of MASS compared to traditional ships.

In accordance with relevant IMO Conventions, States may adopt measures that require vessels to adhere to CDEM standards as both entry criteria and rules to be followed while in ports. The application of prescriptive jurisdiction regarding CDEM standards that extend beyond international legal requirements causes issues due to their extraterritorial effect. Naturally, vessels must meet these standards as a continuous activity throughout their journey, even before approaching port. Thus, CDEM requirements need to be met on the high seas before and after the port visit, suggesting an exercise of extraterritorial jurisdiction. Nevertheless, it is submitted that the extraterritorial impact of these measures is merely incidental, not the primary objective of the port State's domestic laws. Such static features are attributes that remain consistent regardless of a ship's location, meaning that a ship either complies or does not comply with them wherever it is, whether in port or not. Since these features cannot easily be modified during a voyage, they are often seen as the most intrusive in relation to a ship's navigational rights. Nonetheless, ships have the option of visiting a port. But, if they choose to do so, then, naturally, they must adhere to the CDEM standards set by the port State (Churchill 2016, 454–556; Kopela 2016, 95–96; Marten 2016, 472–473; Ringbom 2011, 620–623).

Port States have the authority to set CDEM standards for foreign ships intending to have access to their ports. It follows that port States can enforce these CDEM standards within their ports. Given that PSJ is fundamentally territorial, it stands to reason that a port State can, in principle, require foreign MASS that call at its ports to adhere to CDEM standards. The IMO Conventions often mandate port States to adopt and enforce such standards. A port State may also opt to avoid stringent CDEM measures if it values the economic benefits derived from foreign ships, including MASS, such as port fees and charges for services, and wishes to maintain its attractiveness as a port of call (Churchill 2016, 446–448, 467–469).

Given that ports are considered part of a State's territory, port States have the authority to set CDEM standards for vessels calling at their ports. They may set more stringent CDEM standards than IMO standards unless there exist specific IMO Conventions or unless international laws stop them. Essentially, PSJ is subject to three key limitations with regard to CDEM standards. First, port States must respect the immunity of foreign warships and government-owned ships engaged in non-commercial activities. Second, various treaties mandate that States should not discriminate between ships based on nationality. And, finally, pursuant to Article 211(3) of UNCLOS, port States are obliged to provide due publicity to CDEM measures (Churchill 2016, 467–469).

Vessels can choose to ignore a port State's regulations by not entering its ports. However, by deciding to visit a port, vessels implicitly agree to comply with the entry conditions, even if these conditions concern activities that occurred outside the port

State's territorial jurisdiction. In light of the foregoing, skeptical port States can indeed prescribe CDEM standards to deny access to MASS, unless the IMO's GAIRS (see UNCLOS, Article 21(2)) restrict this power. Indeed, a key limitation is that a port State cannot establish CDEM standards that conflict with IMO Conventions that it has ratified, as doing so would breach its treaty obligations (Churchill 2016, 450–452; Ringbom 2011, 626–628).

1.4.2 *The Location of the Remote Operation Centers*

According to the draft MASS Code, remote control involves operating the MASS or certain of its functions from a remote operation center (ROC). Under the Code, "ROC" means a distant location from the MASS that can control some or all aspects of the MASS functions. In this vein, the draft code defines a "Remote Operator" as a qualified person who is employed or engaged in operating some or all aspects of the MASS functions from a ROC. And, notably, "Remote Master" is a master in a ROC (IMO 2024b, annex I, 11).

The said new actors and terms cause some legal ambiguities. In particular, the location of a ROC can lead to intricate legal challenges concerning jurisdiction and the responsibilities of the flag State. For instance, customarily on the high seas, ships have been subject to the exclusive FSJ based on the view that vessels are essentially extensions of a flag State's territory. But this reasoning would be difficult to follow for ROCs, which are hosted in another State, due to the overlap between the territorial jurisdiction of the State hosting the ROC and the jurisdiction of the flag State. There can be several related issues if the ROC is situated in a country other than the flag State with regard to ensuring the effective FSJ requirement under Article 94 of UNCLOS. Evidently, the legal tension will be less if a ROC is in the territory of the flag State. Although, at first sight, it seems plausible to ensure that ROCs are located only in the flag States, there is no such obligation in the law of the sea regime (Ishii 2023, 268–269). Therefore, the legal status of ROCs is likely to become a contentious issue until the IMO clarifies the issue by developing a common understanding between flag and port States (Yoo and Shan 2019, 563).

Once registered, the flag State is bound under Article 94 to exercise effective jurisdiction and control to ensure that the registered vessel complies with the IMO's GAIRS. However, a critical issue arises with MASS: how the flag State can effectively oversee the remote operators to fulfil these obligations. Unlike manned ships, where the flag State can exert jurisdiction over both the vessel and the individuals on board, ROCs present unique legal complexities due to the absence of onboard crew and their presence elsewhere. Hence, the location of the ROC introduces intricate jurisdictional challenges. Notably, there may be overlapping jurisdictions between the State where the ROC is situated and the flag State. This issue can be further exacerbated depending on the legal characterization of the State in which the RCS is operated. For instance, the host State can be either a port or a coastal State, or both. Furthermore, the host State can be a landlocked State as well. Should this be the case, perhaps analogously to the presence of the dry ports, landlocked host States can arguably be considered as port States. There can be some legal creativity to address the issue in this manner, but, on the other hand, it is clearly not within the IMO's mandate to come up with a new jurisdictional role, such as host State and/or ROC State jurisdiction, given that there is no such concept under UNCLOS. Evidently, when the ROC is within the flag State's territory, it can exercise both prescriptive and enforcement jurisdiction. In contrast, if it is in the territory of a different State, then the flag State's jurisdiction and reach are significantly limited, preventing it from enforcing its laws against the individual in the foreign jurisdiction without that State's consent (Dong et al. 2024, 2).

As a corollary to this, there seem to be increasing concerns about enforcing regulations against ROCs abroad. Considering the legal complexities of a ROC situated in a different State from the flag State, some delegations at the IMO suggested that discussions should focus on scenarios where the ROC is within the flag State's territorial jurisdiction. However, other delegations argued that restricting the discussions in this way would impose an impractical limitation. The MASS Joint Working Group (JWG) subsequently agreed that the jurisdictional issue, including the conditions concerning a ROC located outside the flag State, should be reviewed by the IMO's Legal Committee (LEG; IMO 2024h).

Indeed, in the absence of bilateral arrangements or the IMO's GAIRS, flag States may face considerable limitations in meeting their international obligations when the ROCs are in different countries. For instance, the flag State may struggle to acquire necessary data for investigations due to a lack of cooperation or restrictions imposed by the State where the ROC is located (Ishii 2023, 281–284). Despite the abovementioned challenges, this is probably not a deal-breaker or a game-changing development hindering the integration of MASS. Indeed, the current legal architecture, including the trends toward stronger PSJ to ensure compliance, permits flexibility to address FSJ issues, as will be explained later.

1.4.3 *Ship as a Unit Concept*

It is a truism that the definition of "ship" varies depending on the subject matter and context of the convention in which it is mentioned. The terms "ship" and "vessel" are defined differently in various conventions adopted by the IMO, according to their scope of application and their objectives. At times, drafters of the legal instruments even attempted to avoid definitions so as not to confine the treaty texts to limited maneuverability spaces, as in the example of UNCLOS. Indeed, considering that UNCLOS aims to regulate all issues relating to the law of the sea, a single definition of "ship" would be neither feasible nor beneficial. On the definition issue in relation to the MASS concept, Kraska rightly observes a common aspect: that human control versus autonomous/remote control does not determine what constitutes a ship. Indeed, pursuant to Article 91 of UNCLOS, States have the discretion to fix the conditions for the granting of their nationality to vessels. In this regard, Kraska also maintains that registration of MASS is subject to national law (Kraska and Pedrozo 2023, 41–44; Petrig 2023, 83–84).

The International Tribunal for the Law of the Sea (ITLOS) has firmly refined the definition of a ship in a few cases, including the *M/V "Saiga" (No. 2)* case,[12] the *M/V "Virginia G"* case,[13] and the *M/V "Norstar"* case (Preliminary Objections).[14] In each of these cases, the respondent raised multiple objections regarding the admissibility of the flag State's claims, particularly focusing on the nationality of the claims. In all instances, ITLOS dismissed the objections and proceeded to evaluate the merits of the case. Through these rulings, ITLOS emphasized the distinct identity of a ship as a single unit, highlighting the flag State's right to pursue compensation on behalf of crew members who are not its nationals and underscoring the broader implications for maritime law. For instance, in countering the argument that a flag State cannot seek redress for crew members who are not its nationals, the Tribunal in *M/V "Saiga" (No. 2)*, upon reviewing UNCLOS, clarified that (Heidar 2024):

> 106. . . . [T]he Convention considers a ship as a unit, as regards the obligations of the flag State with respect to the ship and the right of a flag State to seek reparation for loss or damage caused to the ship by acts of other States and to institute proceedings under article 292 of the Convention. Thus the ship, every thing on it, and every person involved or interested in its operations are treated as an entity linked to the flag State. The nationalities of these persons are not relevant.
>
> 107. The Tribunal must also call attention to an aspect of the matter which is not without significance in this case. This relates to two basic characteristics of modern maritime transport: the transient and multinational composition of ships' crews and the multiplicity of interests that may be involved in the cargo on board a single ship. A container vessel carries a large number of containers, and the persons with interests in them may be of many different nationalities. This may also be true in relation to cargo on board a breakbulk carrier. Any of these ships could have a crew comprising persons of several nationalities. If each person sustaining damage were obliged to look for protection from the State of which such person is a national, undue hardship would ensue.

ITLOS reaffirmed its jurisprudence in the *M/V "Virginia G"* case:

> 127. The Tribunal finds that the *M/V Virginia* G is to be considered as a unit and therefore the *M/V Virginia* G, its crew and cargo on board as well as its owner and

[12] *M/V "Saiga" (No. 2) (St. Vincent v. Guinea)*, Case No. 2, Judgment of July 1, 1999, ITLOS Rep. 1999.

[13] *M/V "Virginia G" (Panama/Guinea-Bissau)*, Case No. 19, Judgment of April 14, 2014, ITLOS Rep. 2014.

[14] *M/V "Norstar" (Panama v. Italy)*, Case No. 25, Preliminary Objections, November 4, 2016, ITLOS Rep. 2016.

> every person involved or interested in its operations are to be treated as an entity linked to the flag State.

ITLOS reached these decisions by considering the practical elements that reflect modern maritime practices, such as the multinational and temporary composition of ship crews and the diverse interests associated with the cargo carried by a single vessel (Heidar 2024). Although it may be too early to consider that the ship as a unit concept can be extended to ROCs, nonetheless, it may be a useful tool to mitigate the legal tension with Article 94. Indeed, given the fact that ROCs are expected to be inherently crucial in the steering of RCS, this necessarily follows the line of thought that ROCs can perhaps be considered under the "unity principle," even if they are located in other States (Ishii 2023, 268–269). However, this does not necessarily mean that there would be effective compliance mechanisms for ROCs in practice. In this context, in addition to treating ROCs as inherent parts of single units, equivalent to ship bridges, they could arguably be subject to more robust PSJ and constant port State control inspections, which would alleviate the inadequacy of flag States.

1.4.4 *Latest Developments at the IMO*

The IMO's Maritime Safety Committee (MSC), the LEG, and the Facilitation Committee (FAL) conducted an RSE for the IMO Conventions under their remit to analyze the compliance issues. The RSE of the MSC and the LEG was concluded in 2021 and that of the FAL in 2022. The RSE is regarded as an important milestone in paving the way for further regulatory action with a view to adopt a goal-based MASS Code (IMO 2021).

In 2023, the MASS JWG aptly agreed that a human master should always be in charge of a MASS and should be able to reassume control when needed, irrespective of its degree of autonomy. Moreover, depending on the technology used on the MASS, the human master may not need to be on the vessel, which suggests that the human master can be a remote master located in the ROC (IMO 2024h). This is, indeed, noteworthy, as it practically corrects the shortcomings of degree four.

Currently, the development of the nonmandatory goal-based MASS Code has been limited to MASS cargo vessels (IMO 2024h, 8). The draft preamble of the MASS Code notes that specific operational functions may be controlled from a remote location and addresses necessary aspects of ROCs (4). To prevent discrepancies and ease the legal tension of the new MASS Code with UNCLOS and international law, particularly given the novel nature of the subject matter, the following text is suggested for inclusion in the MASS Code:

> The Code and the use of MASS are required to conform to the relevant rules of international law, including the United Nations Convention on the Law of the Sea (UNCLOS), and generally accepted international regulations, procedures and

> practices developed by the International Maritime Organization (IMO) as the competent international organization for global shipping. (IMO 2024g, 2)

Notably, the current draft Code obliges flag States for the certification and verification of ROCs. It stipulates that every vessel to which the Code applies should have a valid MASS Certificate (para. 6.1). Similarly, every ROC needs to be issued a MASS ROC Certificate (para. 6.2). Moreover, the draft Code states that every administration notified by a company of its intent to operate a MASS should, as it finds practical and necessary, either independently or in collaboration with other contracting governments provide its requirements, procedures, and guidelines for incorporation of the ROC in the verification and certification process of the Document of Compliance (DoC) and Safety Management Certificate (SMC). The process for issuing the DoC is expected to include at least one assessment of the ROC during the DoC's validity period. This assessment should be conducted by the flag State administration, a recognized organization (RO), or another contracting government at the administration's request. The DoC should only be valid for MASS if explicitly stated in the DoC. According to the draft Code, the SMC should be issued in line with SOLAS (Chapter IX, Regulation 4.3) and the ISM Code (Part B, paras. 13–15). The SMC should specify the type of ship, indicate that it is operated as a MASS, and identify the ROC, if applicable, involved in the operation of the MASS (IMO 2024h, annex 1, 19–22).

The draft Code also has provisions on Minimum Safe Manning Document (MSMD), for MASS and ROC, in accordance with IMO Resolution A.1047(27) (IMO 2011), as amended, and to the satisfaction of the administration. In this respect, the MSMD for the MASS may show a total manning number of zero linked to specific MASS and reference personnel training and certification requirements as specified in the Code (IMO 2024h, annex 1, 19–22).

It is noteworthy that several IMO member States (Belgium, Liberia, and the Republic of Korea) recently proposed that the MSC consider the following principles for the drafting of the MASS Code: the flag State of the MASS should determine and be responsible for the verification, survey, and certification of the MASS and its ROC; an oversight system, similar to the ISM Code, should be applied to the management certification of ROCs and MASS; the responsible ISM company for the MASS should retain its responsibilities and be certified in accordance with the ISM Code; and the management of remote operations should align with the duties and responsibilities of ISM companies. Cosponsors also proposed a system called "Remote Operations Management" (ROM), with ROM being the management structure for ROCs established by the MASS Code. In this regard, it is proposed that a ROC should be operated by a ROM company holding a ROM DoC. Moreover, MASS should be operated by a ROC holding a ROC Management Certificate. One ROM company could operate one or more ROCs under one ROM DoC, which should be issued by the administration, by an RO, or at the request of the administration by another contracting government in line with the principles of the ISM Code (IMO 2024a).

Furthermore, Belgium and the Republic of Korea, in their joint document submitted to the LEG, endorsed the previous proposal by noting that the ROM system aims to ensure the completion of tasks and responsibilities specific to ROCs. Within this framework, the flag State would verify that a ROM company complies with its safety and security regulations. Like the ISM model, a ROM company could be granted a DoC, and a ROC could be awarded a ROC Management Certificate. The system is flexible enough to allow ISM companies to operate their own ROCs, thereby functioning as ROM companies. Although not directly tackling jurisdictional and ensuing compliance challenges, the ROM concept appears to provide a practical path forward for mitigating FSJ issues (IMO 2024c).

Remarkably, the current version of the MASS Code, which is drafted by the MSC, appears to presume that the duties of flag States would be applicable to MASS. The initial version of the MASS Code draws upon the framework established in SOLAS and the ISM Code for the survey and certification of ROCs. In this regard, it specifically mandates that flag States carry out the survey of ROCs. When a MASS is remotely controlled from an onshore ROC, given that remote operators will replace the traditional master or crew on board, the flag State must oversee these ROCs to ensure proper performance, particularly if they are within the flag State's territory. For instance, pursuant to the ISM Code, to ensure an international standard for the safe management and operation of ships and for pollution prevention, flag States must conduct surveys and verify companies irrespective of their location. According to paragraph 13 of the ISM Code, vessels should be operated by a company that has been issued with a DoC as evidence that the company is capable of complying with the requirements of the ISM Code (paras. 13, 14). That DoC is issued either by the administration or by an RO, or, at the request of the administration, by another contracting government to the Convention to any company complying with the requirements of the Code. However, the flag State may certainly encounter challenges in overseeing ROCs located in other countries (IMO 2024d).

Japan submitted a paper to the MASS JWG with a view to stimulating further discussion on the scenario where a flag State conducts an inspection to certify and verify a ROC located in other jurisdictions. Such an action, if it is conducted with the consent of the State where the ROC is located and adheres to the provisions outlined in the new MASS Code concerning ROCs, is posited not to encroach upon the sovereignty of the State. Indeed, according to SOLAS, it is broadly recognized that a flag State's inspection to certify and verify a ship management company under the ISM Code and SOLAS does not violate the sovereignty of the State that hosts the ship management company as a SOLAS State party. In light of the above, Japan observed that a flag State's certification and verification of a ROC under the MASS Code would not infringe upon the sovereignty of the State where the ROC is operating (IMO 2024d).

During the previous LEG meeting, IMO member States engaged in an extensive discussion on whether the potential arrangements for ROCs, especially those located in a territory different from the flag State of the MASS, fulfill the obligation laid down in Article 94 of UNCLOS. There have also been diverging positions among the IMO delegates during the discussions. For instance, the Argentinian delegation, which seems to have had a more cautious approach to MASS, expressed significant concerns regarding whether the freedom of navigation under the law of the sea regime extends to vessels with higher levels of autonomy. Remarkably, Argentina emphasized its right to regulate the entry of MASS into its jurisdictional waters. In this context, notably, Argentina also referred to Article 25 of UNCLOS, which grants the authority to States to impose restrictions on the entry of foreign ships into their ports or territorial sea (IMO 2024f).

During the subsequent discussion, several member States expressed their concerns about the ability to meet the standards for the effective exercise of FSJ when MASS are controlled by ROCs situated in countries other than the flag State. Delegates raised several notable points: UNCLOS does not allow the transfer of flag State responsibility to ROCs located in other countries; if the ROC operating a MASS is situated outside of its flag State, significant questions arise regarding the flag State's capacity to maintain effective control over the ROC; the host State, which may have territorial jurisdiction over the ROC but no related obligations under UNCLOS, might not have a clear role; these jurisdictional uncertainties create ambiguity for flag, port, and coastal States about which country exercises jurisdiction over a MASS; this could dilute the flag State's responsibilities to a more symbolic level, inconsistent with UNCLOS; ROCs located outside the flag State would not fall under the flag State's effective jurisdiction; flag States might not have adequate access to ROCs situated in other countries; and applying the ISM Code model may not be sufficient to ensure effective access and oversight, thus necessitating bilateral or multilateral agreements.

Conversely, several States argued that locating a ROC abroad does not inherently weaken the jurisdictional connection. They claimed that such an arrangement is already grounded in existing maritime practices and legal frameworks. They supported the application of the ISM Code model to MASS operations through ROCs by noting that existing IMO instruments[15] already provide the framework for flag State oversight. Moreover, those States further expressed that currently international shipping operates efficiently with minimal physical ties to a flag State's territory; flag States frequently oversee the operation of their ships by establishing offices in different parts of the world; and, as international law does not require the physical presence of a vessel or its associated entities within a flag State's territory, it would be

[15] For example, SOLAS, the Code for Recognized Organizations, the Instruments Implementation Code, and the ISM Code.

unusual to claim that ROCs must be located solely within the territory of the flag State (IMO 2024f).

Notwithstanding the positive approach of some member States that are also expected to be the leading MASS technology providers, uninterrupted shipping requires a broader consensus, including port States.

1.5 MASS ACCESS TO PORTS

UNCLOS does not have specific provisions that directly address the entry of foreign ships into ports, leaving detailed rules on access to port States and other relevant international agreements (Mbiah 2020, 507). Under UNCLOS, maritime areas located landward of the baseline are considered internal waters, over which coastal States have full and absolute sovereignty. Legally speaking, internal waters are treated as the coastal State's land territory. Internal waters include features such as ports. Article 11 states that the outermost parts of harbor works are considered part of the coast. This effectively makes them part of the baseline, placing ports within internal waters. Hence, the foreign-flagged vessels do not have a right of access to internal waters beyond the baseline where ports are located. Consequently, subject to a few exceptions, foreign vessels do not have a general right to enter internal waters without prior authorization from the coastal State (Kraska 2011; Kraska and Pedrozo 2023, 69).

Indeed, for a vessel to fall under PSJ, it must visit the port voluntarily rather than seeking shelter due to distress or force majeure. In the doctrine, it is mostly acknowledged that port States should limit their authority over vessels that have entered their ports out of distress and avoid strictly imposing national laws on such vessels (Marten 2014, 27–28). Therefore, foreign-flagged ships do not have a right to enter ports unless specific international obligations dictate otherwise. Moreover, in port, these vessels must adhere to the laws of the port State. Port States possess residual territorial jurisdiction, allowing them to implement more stringent measures than those outlined in IMO Conventions, unless such instruments explicitly prohibit these further measures (Ryngaert and Ringbom 2016, 382).

PSJ enables the port State to implement jurisdictional measures over ships in line with the provisions of UNCLOS. According to Article 211(3), a port State can refuse entry to a vessel if it does not meet the State's specific requirements related to CDEM standards under certain conditions outlined in that provision. Additionally, Article 218 grants port States the power to investigate and initiate proceedings against foreign vessels that are suspected of committing discharge violations. Remarkably, this includes not only violations within the jurisdiction of the port State, such as in its internal waters, territorial sea, and EEZ, but also violations that occur on the high seas, marking a significant expansion of the port State's jurisdictional capabilities (Keselj 1999, 128).

As a matter of fact, international law recognizes a port State's broad discretion in exercising jurisdiction over its ports. In the *Nicaragua* case, the International Court of Justice acknowledged the discretionary right of port States. The Court noted that coastal States, through their sovereignty, have the authority to regulate access to their ports.[16] UNCLOS also confirmed the vast discretionary right of port States (Articles 25(2), 211(3), and 255).

Since ports fall under the sovereignty of the port State, that State can set specific requirements for foreign vessels entering its ports, provided that the requirements have been adequately publicized and communicated to the IMO (Beckman and Sun 2017, 223–226; Kopela 2016, 94–95). Moreover, port States can designate which ports are open to foreign vessels and can close ports to those vessels based on their national interests (Swan 2016, 396). Therefore, unless bound by specific obligations, hypothetically, a port State, by setting entry requirements that exceed international standards, can refuse RCS access to its ports.

In line with the existing legal framework, States appear to have the right to deny RCS access to their ports. Pursuant to Articles 25(2) and 211(3) of UNCLOS, States have the right to refuse ships access to their ports and to impose specific regulations on port calls by foreign ships. This could create a general barrier to the operation of MASS if port States are categorically against them. However, entry requirements set by port States must adhere to the principles of good faith and nonabuse of rights under Article 300 of UNCLOS, which involve considerations of jurisdictional reasonableness, nondiscrimination, proportionality, and respect for the rights of other States (see Articles 24(1), 25(3), 119(3), and 227). Consequently, achieving international consensus on the regulatory requirements for RCS is crucial to ensure that they are not confined to national waters where maritime authorities have a favorable stance on these vessels (Danish Maritime Authority 2017, 16, 40–41; Jordan 2020, 296–297; Kopela 2016, 105).

1.5.1 *International Trade Law on Port States and MASS*

As discussed earlier, port States can impose stricter standards than IMO norms as conditions for foreign ships to enter their ports. These high standards can regulate the behavior of foreign ships within the port area and may naturally extend to their actions outside the port before entering. Thus, through domestic laws, port States can indirectly establish extraterritorial jurisdiction over foreign ships, which is critical in the context of MASS. This can hinder MASS operations and may eventually lead to hidden trade barriers and discriminatory practices (Chen 2023).

Even though port States usually have broad discretion under IMO and International Labour Organization instruments, this discretion can be considerably

16 *Military and Paramilitary Activities in and against Nicaragua (Nicaragua v. United States)*, Merits, Judgment, 1986 ICJ Rep. 14, para. 213 (June 27).

limited by bilateral or multilateral trade law treaties to which a particular port State might be a party. The most significant limitations to PSJ may originate from international trade law rather than UNCLOS. International trade treaties under the World Trade Organization (WTO) can impose restrictions on PSJ. Since PSJ can restrict international trade, particularly in goods, it could potentially conflict with WTO law – specifically the General Agreement on Tariffs and Trade,[17] which includes the principles of freedom of transit (Molenaar 2006, 202; Ringbom 2011, 632–637; Ryngaert and Ringbom 2016, 386–388).

1.5.2 *Facilitation Committee*

For the operation of RCS, technology is expected to be increasingly responsible for information sharing with the flag, coastal, or port State authorities. Indeed, remote operation requires accurate, up-to-date data and reliable communication systems. The IMO's Facilitation Committee (FAL), which is tasked with addressing the facilitation of international shipping, concluded its RSE at the Facilitation Convention (FAL 46) in 2022 (IMO n.d.-a).

The outcome of the FAL's RSE noted that a new type of certification and identification for MASS operations would be required for the new duties. In this respect, it is indeed important to take the procedures for declarations made on arrival and departure into account. FAL also identified certificates and other documents and the sharing of information as high-priority cross-cutting issues. Regarding the requirements for the arrival, stay, and departure of ships to and from ports, shipowners must present their certificates and other documents related to registration, measurement, safety, manning, and similar matters to public authorities. Hence, the relevant certificates, documents, and data may need to be amended if new certification requirements for RCS are developed (IMO 2022, 2024d). The future work of FAL can be instrumental in mitigating the concerns of port States, as well as facilitating the operation of RCS.

1.6 PILOTAGE FOR MASS AS AN INCENTIVE FOR SKEPTICAL PORT STATES

1.6.1 *Definition*

The conditions that ships encounter in the high seas naturally differ significantly from those in port areas. In ports, there is usually high traffic density. Additionally, tides, shallow waters, and other unique port characteristics can present higher navigational hazards than in open seas. Therefore, pilotage is indeed necessary, as

[17] Marrakesh Agreement Establishing the World Trade Organization, April 15, 1994, 1867 UNTS 3, Annex 1A (General Agreement on Tariffs and Trade 1994), Articles V(3), XI.

it offers local knowledge. Essentially, a pilot possesses specialized knowledge of local conditions and navigational hazards and is typically brought aboard a vessel at a specific location to navigate or guide the ship through a particular channel or river, or enclosed waters, to or from a port. A "pilot" is defined as an individual who possesses specialized knowledge of local navigation conditions and potential hazards (Agripino de Castro 2016, 423; Aucoin 2024, 22–23).

1.6.2 *Interplay between Pilotage and MASS*

Pilotage services, while often seen as specialized services for shipping, also function as public services due to the significant potential risk of accidents and groundings. The success of pilotage service rests on effective communication and information exchange among the pilot and the master. At times, pilots already provide guidance remotely from shore via radio communications as well. Regardless of the method, MASS integration is likely to significantly transform the nature of pilotage operations. But, in any event, it is clear that an RCS would greatly benefit from a pilot's insights; moreover, pilotage can serve as a reassurance for port States. The extent and direction of these changes will largely depend on technological advancements in this field. Regardless of these developments, the value of a local guide remains clear; a remote master will undoubtedly benefit from the expertise of a pilot familiar with the local maritime environment (Aro and Heiskari 2018, 28–29; Uğurlu et al. 2017; Van Hooydonk 2014, 416).

Notably, the pilotage service is not exclusively governed by an international instrument, making the legal landscape complex. The legal status of pilots and the performance of pilotage services are regulated by domestic laws. Therefore, guidance should be sought from domestic laws until the situation changes. Typically, such laws grant local ports the authority to regulate and establish pilotage requirements at a local level. Consequently, even in a single country, different ports may have distinct pilotage requirements. Such local regulations often vary and may not be consistent even at the national level, let alone regionally or internationally. Ehlers notes that these services are thus far typically provided within national waters, especially in internal waters. Hence, the international law of the sea has only occasionally influenced pilotage in specific cases (Black 2020, 12–13; Ehlers 2024).

According to the UK Pilotage Act 1987, pilot means any person not belonging to a ship who has control of the ship. Under the Maltese Maritime Pilotage Regulations, "pilotage" means the act performed by a licensed pilot to assist the master during navigation and maneuvering when entering, departing, or shifting in port areas (Article 3). The Danish Pilotage Act allows shore-based pilotage. It defines "pilotage" as navigational advice regardless of whether the advice is provided to the master on board the vessel or by means of communication from a distant location (Davies 2020, 281–282).

Remote pilotage is applicable to any ship but is particularly pertinent to MASS. These vessels are likely unable to utilize traditional pilotage services – where a pilot physically boards the ship to provide navigational advice – due to physical and technical constraints. For degree two ships, which have onboard crews, complying with local pilotage requirements will be a straightforward task due to the presence of crew. Degrees three and four ships, which operate without any onboard crew, present unique challenges for pilotage. For these vessels, pilotage options may need to include shore-based pilotage, where a pilot remotely guides the ship from land (Danish Maritime Authority 2017, 21; Davies 2020, 284–286). Indeed, there is no legal requirement for the pilot to be physically on board the vessel to which they are rendering their services. Besides, it would be impractical for a pilot to board an RCS unless necessitated by urgent circumstances or domestic regulations. For these types of vessels, pilotage services are likely to be provided remotely. For instance, Finland has recently enacted legislation that permits pilotage to be conducted remotely (Soyer et al. 2022, 12–13).

The IMO Assembly, in 2003, adopted a resolution on "Recommendations on Training and Certification and on Operational Procedures for Maritime Pilots Other Than Deep-Sea Pilots." This nonbinding resolution acknowledges the crucial role of pilots in enhancing maritime safety and protecting the marine environment. In particular, the IMO underscores that pilotage areas require highly specialized local knowledge and experience of various specific port areas and waterways. The IMO had earlier highlighted that it does not intend to be involved with the member States' pilotage systems (IMO 2003). As early as 1968, it recommended that States organize pilotage services in areas where they enhance navigational safety more effectively than other measures. Chapter V of SOLAS (see Regulation 23) notes that vessels engaged on voyages during which pilots may be employed are required to have pilot transfer arrangements to ensure the safety of pilots. In line with SOLAS, there is an obligation for State parties to establish various maritime safety services, including aids to navigation, hydrographic, meteorological, search and rescue, and vessel traffic services. However, pilotage services are not specifically mentioned among such mandatory services. Ehlers opines that this likely stems from the absence of a perceived need for international regulation of pilotage services to date (Ehlers 2024, 4). Although the IMO, thus far rightly, avoided regulating pilotage issues comprehensively because of strong reference to varying local conditions, this may need to change, in part, in the era of MASS.

1.6.3 *Compulsory Pilotage*

A "compulsory" pilot is one required by national laws. Conversely, a "voluntary" pilot is one whom a ship owner chooses to employ without any legal obligation (Force 2004, 149). Pursuant to the Convention and Statute on the International Régime of Maritime Ports (see Article 11), State parties have the authority to administer pilotage, including the establishment of compulsory pilotage. Given the sovereignty exercised by coastal States over their internal waters and ports, there are generally no limitations under international law on the imposition of compulsory pilotage in these areas (Ehlers 2024, 9–10).

Yet, unlike the authority to designate sea lanes or traffic separation schemes, UNCLOS does not expressly specify the procedures to establish compulsory pilotage in coastal waters. Thus, the rules of the reference system also do not point out to the IMO. Moreover, State practice is also not clear in this area. Nevertheless, a few examples show the possible competence of coastal States to implement quasi-compulsory pilotage within their territorial seas, as seen, for example, in the Strait of Messina, the Great Barrier Reef, and around Svalbard Island. The adoption of such pilotage systems depends on the unique characteristics of each area, including the reliability of the system, the availability of qualified pilots, and the cost of services, and, more importantly, the nonhampering of the innocent passage (Solski 2021, 411–414).

For pilotage services offered within internal waters, including port areas, there is generally no issue, as the coastal State exercises unrestricted sovereignty therein. Nevertheless, beyond internal waters, the legality of establishing pilotage services depends on whether such services impair the existing rights of navigation in the respective maritime zones. This consideration is crucial in maintaining the balance between enhancing safety through pilotage and upholding the principle of freedom of navigation as prescribed by international law (Ehlers 2024, 5–6). Notably, one should be cautious considering that Australian efforts to impose compulsory pilotage as a protective measure in the Particularly Sensitive Sea Area of the Torres Strait have faced strong opposition from flag States underscoring their transit passage rights under international law. The eventual compromise involved enforcing compulsory pilotage in the Torres Strait exclusively for vessels entering Australian ports (Kopela 2016, 101–102).

However, despite the limitations, Article 21(1)(a) and (f) of UNCLOS allows coastal States to implement regulations aimed at enhancing maritime safety and environmental protection. This framework arguably enables coastal States to mandate pilotage in these waters as a measure to ensure the safety of navigation and safeguard the marine environment in relation to RCS operations while still respecting the principle of innocent passage. However, any national regulations related to pilotage must not only pursue safety and environmental protection but also adhere strictly to established international norms. In light of this, the compulsory pilotage for MASS arguably would not be seen as an interference with the navigational passage rights. Therefore, compulsory pilotage, when implemented to enhance navigational safety and environmental protection, does not contravene Articles 24 (1) and 211(4) and can be regarded as necessary and proportionate. Moreover, the compulsory pilotage in port approach waters beyond internal waters can be justified, especially when ships are bound to enter internal waters or ports, as coastal States can set conditions for entry to their ports based on Article 25(2). Indeed, this provision allows the coastal State to enforce regulations such as compulsory pilotage to prevent breaches of entry conditions into its waters (Ehlers 2024, 9–13).

Arguably, the coastal States seem to have the discretion to mandate compulsory pilotage for RCS as a condition for port entry. For instance, while pilotage through the Turkish Straits remains optional during peace times for merchant vessels under the 1936 Montreux Convention (Articles 2 and 4),[18] Türkiye can impose obligatory pilotage services in the straits if there is an imminent threat of war (Article 6). Significantly, this situation differs for ships that are calling at a Turkish port within the straits area, where compulsory pilotage can be established as a port entry requirement. Pilotage services for RCS to alleviate the concerns of port States, and even of coastal States, should be established and elucidated under the IMO's MASS Code to enhance the safety of navigation and environmental protection. Concurrently, the conditions under which States can mandate compulsory pilotage for MASS beyond internal waters need to be clarified to ensure consistent application and understanding. This may be contingent upon the consent of IMO member States, like existing regulations for ship routing and ship reporting services (Ehlers 2024, 18–24).

1.7 PORT STATE CONTROL

According to Beckman, the IMO since its inception has focused on compliance with international conventions from the perspectives of both flag and port States. The IMO initially recognized that flag States should have comprehensive and continuous control over their ships. To facilitate this, the IMO has developed guidelines to help flag States implement its instruments. In addition, the IMO system strongly depends on port State control (PSC) to address deficiencies in flag State compliance (Beckman and Sun 2017, 228).

PSC entails the practical implementation by port States of administrative authority to ascertain whether the documentation and condition of a foreign vessel adhere to their national legislation, as well as international regulations and standards ratified by port States. The overall objective of PSC is to supplement flag State responsibilities and tackle substandard ships (Bang 2013, 116–117). Port States are only authorized to conduct PSC for those conventions that they have ratified and incorporated into their domestic laws (IMO 2023b).

Naturally, PSJ encompasses a broader scope than PSC. PSJ is the legal basis of PSC. It includes the authority to carry out control inspections and extends to prescriptive and enforcement jurisdiction over foreign-flagged ships in their ports based on national or international law. Molenaar observes that PSC is most

[18] Convention regarding the Regime of the Straits, July 20, 1936, 173 UNTS 213 (Montreux Convention).

effectively understood within the context of the regional PSC agreements. These regional agreements were established in response to deficiencies in flag State performance and the prevalence of "ports of convenience." They involve harmonized and coordinated PSC procedures, along with commitments to conduct inspections and primarily enforce corrective measures (Molenaar 2021, para. 6). Legally speaking, although memoranda of understanding (MOUs) are not treaties, they are important regional arrangements designed for collaboration between maritime administrations to enhance the implementation of international regulations and to prevent unfair competition among ports within the same region. By joining regional memoranda, States commit their ports to harmonize their procedures. The regional MOU systems have brought several benefits: they enhance predictability by standardizing regional inspection procedures, increase awareness among their members through robust information sharing, and boost efficiency by preventing duplicated inspections (Blanco-Bazan 2018, 45; Molenaar 1996, 241–242; Whomersley 2020, 333–334; Yu et al. 2018, 87–88).

Notwithstanding its role as an enforcement mechanism for international standards, PSC ultimately relies on the sovereignty of the port State and its corresponding jurisdiction (Coelho 2015, 272). The bottom line is that the PSC regime grants the authority to board, inspect, and, if deemed necessary, detain a foreign vessel (Hare 1997). PSC has the potential not only to serve the national interest but also to advance the broader interests of the international community at large. The evolution of PSC in the framework of PSJ has seen significant developments through the inclusion of relevant provisions in all pertinent IMO and ILO instruments. By conducting inspections to assess both the physical condition of visiting ships and their certifications, PSC ensures adherence to international safety and environmental standards. Thus, PSC practice involves the inspection of vessels while in port to ensure that they comply with globally agreed standards. PSJ has grown gradually more complex, not merely due to updates to relevant international instruments but also because of its continual expansion into new subject areas. Initially, PSC inspections primarily focused on CDEM standards. During the 1990s, the focus within the IMO shifted toward the "human element." More recently, this evolution has expanded to include issues such as vessel-source air pollution, maritime security, ballast water management, and ship scrapping. Each of these areas includes components that enhance the scope of PSJ through PSCs (Balkin 2018, 23–24; Derrig 2022, 534–536; Marten 2014, 4–5; Molenaar 2006, 202–205).

PSC constitutes a crucial and evolving component of international shipping regulation. Despite still being seen as supplementary to FSJ, the evolution of PSC in the context of PSJ remains significant, as it signifies a gradual shift away from the notion of flag States bearing primary responsibility for ensuring vessel standards. A noteworthy example of this shift is the application of PSC to all vessels visiting foreign ports, as demonstrated by the "no more favorable treatment" principle, by means of which port States have the authority to enforce IMO regulations and standards on foreign-flagged vessels visiting their ports, irrespective of whether a flag State is a party to a specific IMO Convention or not (Marten 2014, 46–49). PSC is a globally agreed practice but also an evolving concept. As the IMO adopts new conventions, the PSC framework will also adapt to reflect these developments (Mbiah 2020, 517–521).

In the context of RCS, it is noteworthy that ships are required to carry several certificates on board in their international navigation in compliance with international conventions. Therefore, for degrees three and four, where seafarers do not physically onboard the vessel, handling certificates, record books, and other necessary documents pose challenges. Consequently, there is a pressing need for explicit regulations managing the use of appropriate digital documents. Additionally, in the practical execution of inspections, particularly PSC for MASS, the development of specialized guidelines and regulations is imperative. Since there are seafarers on board in degree two RCS, there is no issue in following the current regulations. However, in the absence of crew members for degree three RCS, a possible solution would be to relocate the required certificates to ROCs together with the crew. Or, the digitization of the certificates can also be a solution. FAL 42 endorsed guidelines for the adoption of electronic certificates (IMO 2016), urging State parties to transition to electronic certificates (Jo et al. 2020). Furthermore, foreign ROCs located in port States should arguably be subject to PSC.

1.8 CONCLUSION

The advent of RCS marks a revolutionary transformation in international shipping. However, it also leads to thorny legal questions, particularly in the context of State jurisdiction and ensuring safety of navigation. As this study has explored, the integration of RCS into the global merchant fleet poses unique challenges for flag States and new roles for port States due to the peculiar nature and location of ROCs. The law of ports grants States significant discretion in exercising jurisdiction over their ports. In this context, the ever-increasing trend of port States in ensuring compliance in general may also be instrumental in alleviating legal tension stemming from remote operations.

In addition to the operation of RCS, the location of ROCs is also legally sensitive. In this regard, flag States may perhaps choose to prohibit the operation of ROCs in other countries. However, this cannot be the ultimate solution, as there is no such corresponding obligation for flag States under the UNCLOS regime. On the other hand, it is equally true that FSJ alone may be insufficient, especially for ROCs located in territories other than flag States. Therefore, to ensure compliance of RCS, the measures taken by port States need to be significantly reinforced. While it remains crucial for flag States to uphold their international responsibilities, port States can certainly play a pivotal role for ROCs and RCS.

Arguably, remote shipping heralds and necessitates a broader role for port States. Although the IMO traditionally does not regulate ports, this may also need to be reconsidered in light of the transformation of shipping. Perhaps this could be in the context of special port arrangements for ROCs. Analogically, ROCs can be considered as ships visiting ports. PSC can be conducted especially at the beginning of each new voyage entailing remote operation through the ROCs. Since there is no jurisdiction as host State in the law of the sea regime, port States can increasingly continue to be the ultimate safety net and could ensure that foreign ROCs are fully compliant with IMO norms. It may be safe to argue that port States will play a critical role in the transition and successful realization of RCS operations.

Finally, given that ports are under the sovereignty of port States, port entry for RCSs is not a right but rather a privilege that is subject to domestic law. Thus, port States can impose stricter standards than international norms as conditions for foreign RCS to enter their ports. Port States therefore have the right to deny RCS access to their ports, as they would with conventional manned ships, until the IMO develops relevant GAIRS. But this would probably not be in the interests of port States, as they also depend on international shipping and generating income from their ports. Having said that, conflicting State practices may emerge due to diverging interests and priorities or to policy reasons, as well as due to the different legal interpretations. At least for the safety apprehensions, compulsory pilotage for RCS in the port approach waters may significantly alleviate the potential concerns of port States. Therefore, it may be advisable to establish an obligation to request pilotage services in areas where local conditions necessitate it under the IMO's MASS Code.

REFERENCES

Agripino de Castro, Osvaldo, Jr., and Cesar Luiz Pasold. 2016. "Law of Harbours and Pilotage." In *Shipping Law*, edited by David Joseph Attard, Malgosia Fitzmaurice, Norman Martinez, Ignacio Arroyo, and Elda Belja. Vol. 2 of *The IMLI Manual on International Maritime Law*. Oxford University Press.

Aro, Tommi, and Lauri Heiskari. 2018. "Challenges of Unmanned Vessels: Technical Risks and Legal Problems." Bach. Deg. Thesis, Novia University of Applied Sciences.

Aucoin, Emma. 2024. "Pilotage Law: Jack of All Trades, Master of None." *Loyola Maritime Law Journal* 23 (1): 19–38.

Balkin, Rosalie P. 2018. "The IMO and Global Ocean Governance: Past, Present, and Future." In *IMO and Global Ocean Governance*, edited by David Joseph Attard, Rosalie P. Balkin, and Donald W. Greig. Vol. 3 of *The IMLI Treatise on Global Ocean Governance*. Oxford University Press.

Bang, Ho-Sam. 2013. "Recommendations for Polices on Port State Control and Port State Jurisdiction." *Journal of Maritime Law and Commerce* 44 (1): 115–133.

Barchue, Lawrence, Sr. 2018. "The IMO, the Audit Scheme, and Its Role in Global Ocean Governance." In *IMO and Global Ocean Governance*, edited by David Joseph

Attard, Rosalie P. Balkin, and Donald W. Greig. Vol. 3 of *The IMLI Treatise on Global Ocean Governance*. Oxford University Press.

Beckman, Robert C. 2007. "PSSAs and Transit Passage: Australia's Pilotage System in the Torres Strait Challenges the IMO and UNCLOS." *Ocean Development and International Law* 38 (4): 325–357.

Beckman, Robert, and Zhen Sun. 2017. "The Relationship between UNCLOS and IMO Instruments." *Asia-Pacific Journal of Ocean Law and Policy* 2 (2): 201–246.

Black, Declan. 2020. "Uncrewed Vessel Port Entry." Master's thesis, Novia University of Applied Sciences.

Blanco-Bazan, Agustin. 2018. "The IMO: Working within the UNCLOS Framework and Global Ocean Governance." In *IMO and Global Ocean Governance*, edited by David Joseph Attard, Rosalie P. Balkin, and Donald W. Greig. Vol. 3 of *The IMLI Treatise on Global Ocean Governance*. Oxford University Press.

Chen, Linlin. 2023. "Research on the Modern Maritime Supervision Mechanism from the Perspective of Global Maritime Governance." *China Legal Science* 3: 11–31.

Chircop, Aldo. 2018. "The IMO's Work on Environmental Protection and Global Ocean Governance." In *IMO and Global Ocean Governance*, edited by David Joseph Attard, Rosalie P. Balkin, and Donald W. Greig. Vol. 3 of *The IMLI Treatise on Global Ocean Governance*. Oxford University Press.

Churchill, Robin. 2016. "Port State Jurisdiction Relating to the Safety of Shipping and Pollution from Ships: What Degree of Extra-Territoriality?" *International Journal of Marine and Coastal Law* 31 (3): 442–469.

Coelho, Nelson F. 2015. "Extraterritoriality from the Port: EU's Approach to Jurisdiction over Ship-Source Pollution." *SYbIL* 19: 269–284.

Danish Maritime Authority. 2017. *Analysis of Regulatory Barriers to the Use of Autonomous Ships: Final Report*. Ramboll and CORE Advokatfirma.

Davies, Martin. 2020. "Pilotage of Autonomous and Remotely-Controlled Ships." In *Autonomous Ships and the Law*, edited by Henrik Ringbom, Erik Røsæg, and Trond Solvang. Routledge.

Derrig, Ríán. 2022. "Inspecting Ships Autonomously under Port State Jurisdiction: Towards Sustainability and Biodiversity in the EU." *International Journal of Marine and Coastal Law* 37: 529–551.

Dong, Bingying, Lowell Bautista, and Ling Zhu. 2024. "Navigating Uncharted Waters: Challenges and Regulatory Solutions for Flag State Jurisdiction of Maritime Autonomous Surface Ships under UNCLOS." *Marine Policy* 161: 106039.

Ehlers, Peter. 2024. "Maritime Pilotage from the Perspective of the International Law of the Sea." *International Journal of Marine and Coastal Law* 39 (4): 661–684.

Force, Robert. 2004. *Admiralty and Maritime Law*. Federal Judicial Center.

Gabay, Danielle, Roee Furman, and Dov Greenbaum. 2023. "Autonomous Ships: Engines of Environmental Protection." *Tulane Maritime Law Journal* 47: 403.

Galani, Sofia. 2021. "Port Closures and Persons at Sea in International Law." *International and Comparative Law Quarterly* 70 (3): 605–633.

Gavouneli, Maria. 2007. *Functional Jurisdiction in the Law of the Sea*. Martinus Nijhoff.

Hare, John. 1997. "Port State Control: Strong Medicine to Cure a Sick Industry." *Georgia Journal of International and Comparative Law* 26 (3): 571–594.

Heidar, Tomas. 2024. "The Contribution of ITLOS to the Progressive Development of International Law." *IMLI*, April 8.

Hughes, Edmund. 2018. "The IMO: Ship-Sourced Emissions, Climate Change, and Global Ocean Governance." In *IMO and Global Ocean Governance*, edited by David Joseph Attard, Rosalie P. Balkin, and Donald W. Greig. Vol. 3 of *The IMLI Treatise on Global Ocean Governance*, edited by David Joseph Attard. Oxford University Press.

ICS (International Chamber of Shipping). n.d. "Shipping and World Trade: Driving Prosperity." www.ics-shipping.org/shipping-fact/shipping-and-world-trade-driving-prosperity/.

IMO (International Maritime Organization). 1981. "Procedures for the Control of Ships." A XII/Res. 466 (March 19, 1982).

2003. "Recommendations on Training and Certification and on Operational Procedures for Maritime Pilots Other Than Deep-Sea Pilots." A 23/Res.960 (December 5, 2003).

2011. "Principles of Minimum Safe Manning." A 27/Res.1047 (December 20, 2011).

2014. "Implications of the United Nations Convention on the Law of the Sea for the International Maritime Organization." LEG/MISC.8 (January 30, 2014).

2016. "Guidelines for the Use of Electronic Certificates." FAL.5/Circ.39/Rev.2 (April 20, 2016).

2021. "Autonomous Ships: Regulatory Scoping Exercise Completed." May 25. www.imo.org/en/MediaCentre/PressBriefings/pages/MASSRSE2021.aspx.

2022. "Outcome of the Regulatory Scoping Exercise and Gap Analysis of the FAL Convention with Respect to Maritime Autonomous Surface Ships (MASS)." FAL.5/Circ.49 (June 1, 2022).

2023a. "Guidelines for Setting Up a Maritime Single Window." FAL.5/Circ.42/Rev.3 (March 31, 2023).

2023b. "Sub-Committee on Implementation of IMO Instruments." III 9/WP.6 (August 3, 2023).

2023c. "Written Statement of the International Maritime Organization." International Tribunal for the Law of the Sea, Case No. 31 (June 16, 2023).

2024a. "Concepts on the Management of Remote Operations." Submitted by Belgium, Liberia, and the Republic of Korea. MSC 108/4/2 (February 13, 2024).

2024b. "Development of a Goal-Based Instrument for Maritime Autonomous Surface Ships (MASS)." MSC 108/4 (February 13, 2024).

2024c. "Information on the Management of Remote Operations." Submitted by Belgium and the Republic of Korea. LEG 111/10/8 (February 16, 2024).

2024d. "Joint MSC-LEG-FAL Working Group on MASS (MASS-JWG)." Submitted by Japan. MASS-JWG 3/3/2 (March 26, 2024).

2024e. "Legal Committee." LEG 111/10/1 (February 16, 2024).

2024f. "Legal Committee." LEG 111/WP.1 (April 26, 2024).

2024g. "Proposal to Ensure the Regulation of MASS Within the Framework of International Law." Submitted by United Arab Emirates. LEG 111/10/5 (February 16, 2024).

2024h. "Report of the MSC-LEG-FAL Joint Working Group on MASS on Its Second Session. Note by the Secretariat." LEG 111/10 (January 19, 2024).

n.d.-a. "Facilitation Committee (FAL 46), 9 to 13 May 2022." www.imo.org/en/MediaCentre/MeetingSummaries/Pages/FAL-46th-Session.aspx.

n.d.-b. "Maritime Single Window." www.imo.org/en/OurWork/Facilitation/Pages/MaritimeSingleWindow-default.aspx.

Ishii, Yurika. 2023. "Attacks on Commercial Maritime Autonomous Surface Ships at Sea." *Asia-Pacific Journal of Ocean Law and Policy* 8 (2): 266–286.

Jo, M. C., A. R. Lee, Y. D. Kim, and J. S. Seo. 2020. "Study on the Potential Gaps and Themes Identified by IMO Regulatory Scoping Exercise (RSE) for the Use of Maritime Autonomous Surface Ships (MASS)." *IOP Conference Series: Materials Science and Engineering* 929 (1): 012014.

Jordan, Samantha. 2020. "Captain, My Captain: A Look at Autonomous Ships and How They Should Operate Under Admiralty Law." *Indiana International and Comparative Law Review* 30 (2): 283–317.

Keselj, Tatjana. 1999. "Port State Jurisdiction in Respect of Pollution from Ships: The 1982 United Nations Convention on the Law of the Sea and the Memoranda of Understanding." *Ocean Development and International Law* 30 (2): 127–160.

Kopela, Sophia. 2016. "Port-State Jurisdiction, Extraterritoriality, and the Protection of Global Commons." *Ocean Development and International Law* 47 (2): 89–130.

Kraska, James. 2010. "The Law of Unmanned Naval Systems in War and Peace." *Journal of Ocean Technology* 5 (3): 44–68.

2011. *Maritime Power and the Law of the Sea*. Oxford University Press.

Kraska, James, and Paul Pedrozo. 2023. The Newport Manual on the Law of Naval Warfare. *International Law Studies* 101 (1): n.pag.

Librando, Gaetano. 2014. "The International Maritime Organization and the Law of the Sea." In *The Law of the Sea*, edited by David Joseph Attard, Malgosia Fitzmaurice, and Norman A. Martínez Gutiérrez. Vol. 1 of *The IMLI Manual on International Maritime Law*. Oxford University Press.

Luchenko, Dmytro, Iurii Georgiievskyi, and Maryna Bielikova. 2023. "Challenges and Developments in the Public Administration of Autonomous Shipping." *Lex Portus* 9 (1): 20–36.

Mansell, John N. K. 2009. *Flag State Responsibility: Historical Development and Contemporary Issues*. Springer.

Marten, Bevan. 2014. *Port State Jurisdiction and the Regulation of International Merchant Shipping*. Springer.

2015. "Port State Jurisdiction, International Conventions, and Extraterritoriality: An Expansive Interpretation." In *Jurisdiction over Ships: Post-UNCLOS Developments in the Law of the Sea*, edited by Henrik Ringbom. Brill Nijhoff.

2016. "Port State Jurisdiction over Vessel Information: Territoriality, Extra-Territoriality and the Future of Shipping Regulation." *International Journal of Marine and Coastal Law* 31 (3): 470–498.

Mbiah, Emmanuel Kofi. 2020. "Coastal, Flag and Port State Jurisdictions: Powers and Other Considerations Under UNCLOS." In *Maritime Law in Motion*, edited by Proshanto K. Mukherjee, Maximo Q. Mejia Jr., and Jingjing Xu. WMU Studies in Maritime Affairs. Springer.

Molenaar, Erik J. 1996. "The EC Directive on Port State Control in Context." *International Journal of Marine and Coastal Law* 11 (2): 241–287.

2006. "Port State Jurisdiction: Towards Mandatory and Comprehensive Use." In *The Law of the Sea: Progress and Prospects*, edited by David Freestone, Richard Barnes, and David M. Ong. Oxford University Press.

Molenaar, Erik J. 2021. "Port State Jurisdiction." *Max Planck Encyclopedia of Public International Law*. https://opil.ouplaw.com/display/10.1093/law:epil/9780199231690/law-9780199231690-e2052.

OECD (Organisation for Economic Co-operation and Development). 2001. *Regulatory Issues in International Maritime Transport*.

Özçayir, Z. Oya. 2004. *Port State Control*. 2nd ed. Routledge.

2009. "The Use of Port State Control in Maritime Industry and Application of the Paris MOU." *Ocean and Coastal Law Journal* 14 (2): 210–239.

Petrig, Anna. 2021. "Autonomous Offender Ships and International Maritime Security Law." In *Autonomous Ships and the Law*, edited by in Henrik Ringbom, Erik Røsæg, and Trond Solvang. Routledge.

2023. "Maritime Security in the Age of Autonomous Ships." In *Autonomous Vessels in Maritime Affairs: Law and Governance Implications*, edited by Tafsir Matin Johansson, Jonatan Echebarria Fernández, Dimitrios Dalaklis, Aspasia Pastra, and Jon A. Skinner. Palgrave Macmillan.

Qi, Jiancuo, and Pengfei Zhang. 2021. "Enforcement Failures and Remedies: Review on State Jurisdiction over Ships at Sea." *Journal of East Asia and International Law* 14 (1): 7–34.

Ringbom, Henrik. 2011. "Global Problem: Regional Solution? International Law Reflections on an EU CO_2 Emissions Trading Scheme for Ships." *International Journal of Marine and Coastal Law* 26 (4): 613–641.

Ryngaert, Cedric, and Henrik Ringbom. 2016. "Introduction: Port State Jurisdiction: Challenges and Potential." *International Journal of Marine and Coastal Law* 31: 379–394.

Solski, Jan Jakub. 2021. "The 'Due Regard' of Article 234 of UNCLOS: Lessons from Regulating Innocent Passage in the Territorial Sea." *Ocean Development & International Law* 52 (4): 398–418.

Soyer, B, A. Tettenborn, and G. Leloudas. 2022. *Remote Controlled and Autonomous Shipping: UK Based Case Study*. Swansea University, Institute of International Shipping and Trade Law.

Sumer, Murat. 2023a. "Applicability of the Right of Innocent Passage to Maritime Autonomous Surface Ships: Exploring the Potential Role of Advisory Opinions." In *Maritime Security, New Technology and Ethics. Vol. 3 of Ascomare Yearbook on the Law of the Sea*, edited by Pierandrea Leucci and Ilaria Vianellovol. Luglio Editore.

2023b. "Overcoming the Legal Challenges of Maritime Autonomous Surface Ships (MASS) and Compliance with UNCLOS and SOLAS: Designation of a Remote Master to Assume the Safety Duties of a Master." PhD diss., Maastricht University. https://doi.org/10.26481/dis.20230411ms.

Swan, Judith. 2016. "Port State Measures: From Residual Port State Jurisdiction to Global Standards." *International Journal of Marine and Coastal Law* 31 (3): 395–421.

Uğurlu, Özkan, Mehmet Kaptan, Serdar Kum, and Serdar Yildiz. 2017. "Pilotage Services in Turkey: Key Issues and Ideal Pilotage." *Journal of Marine Engineering and Technology* 16 (2): 51–60.

UN (United Nations). 1996. *Law of the Sea Bulletin* No. 31. Division for Ocean Affairs and the Law of the Sea, Office of Legal Affairs.

UNCTAD (UN Trade and Development). 2023. "Review of Maritime Transport." https://unctad.org/topic/transport-and-trade-logistics/review-of-maritime-transport.

Van Hooydonk, Eric. 2014. "The Law of Unmanned Merchant Shipping: An Exploration." *Journal of International Maritime Law* 20: 403–423.

Veal, Robert, Michael Tsimplis, and Andrew Serdy. 2019. "The Legal Status and Operation of Unmanned Maritime Vehicles." *Ocean Development and International Law* 50 (1): 23–48.

Whomersley, Chris. 2020. "The Principle of Exclusive Flag State Jurisdiction: Is It Fit for Purpose in the Twenty-First Century?" *Asia-Pacific Journal of Ocean Law and Policy* 5 (2): 330–347.

Wolfrum, Rüdiger. 2014. "Freedom of Navigation: New Challenges." Statement, International Tribunal for the Law of the Sea.

World Bank Group. n.d. “Sustainable Development in Shipping and Ports.” November 22. www.worldbank.org/en/topic/transport/brief/sustainable-development-in-shipping-and-ports.

Yoo, Jinho, and Desai Shan. 2019. “Legal Status of an Onshore Remote Controller of Maritime Autonomous Surface Ships (‘MASS’) Under the Canadian Maritime Law and IMO International Conventions.” Canadian Transportation Research Forum 54th Annual Conference, May 26–29: 562–569.

Yu, Yaodong, Yue Zhao, and Yen-Chiang Chang. 2018. “Challenges to the Primary Jurisdiction of Flag States over Ships.” *Ocean Development and International Law* 49 (1): 85–102.

2

Autonomous Ships and Time Charterparties

Ceren Cerit Dindar

2.1 INTRODUCTION

The form of a ship has been subject to considerable change and development, both structurally and technically, throughout the centuries, but one factor has always remained constant: "the human element" (Sözer 2024). The crew has always been on board the ship and has remained responsible for the operation, maintenance, navigation, and safety of the ship and its cargo. However, technological developments in shipbuilding and automation systems, such as AI and robotics, have in the past few years started to switch, or indeed promote, the shipping industry to a new level, which has been termed "autonomous shipping" – a distinguishing feature of which is the belief that the presence of the crew on board the ship should no longer be looked upon as an elementary condition, although some have submitted their concerns about this profound shift in the industry and asserted that the operation of autonomous ships on the sea is merely utopian and does not seem possible or viable when today's technology is taken into regard (Karlis 2018, 120).[1] The *Yara Birkeland*,[2] *Shortfall of Gravitas*,[3] *Mayflower*,[4]

[1] Hunter has pointed out the twofold perception of autonomous ships: some believe that they could operate commercially, while others argue that we are many decades away from being able to operate autonomous ships in international trade, as the existing rule of law will need to be reviewed and revised (Hunter 2021, 207).

[2] The *Yara Birkeland* is the result of a project that began in 2017 as a partnership between environmentally focused Norwegian agricultural company Yara and Finland-based global maritime technology company Kongsberg, with the aim of building the world's first autonomous, fully battery-powered, zero-emissions container ship. See further Yara (2023).

[3] The *Shortfall of Gravitas* (SOG) was introduced by SpaceX in July 2021 as an autonomous spaceport ship that is fully automated and capable of moving to the recovery area without a tug (SpaceX 2021).

[4] The *Mayflower*, an AI-driven and radar-sensor-deployed marine research boat, is engineered to traverse the Atlantic without a crew. The main motivation for starting this project was the belief that critical data for ocean protection could be collected more cheaply with autonomous research ships than with traditional research ships. See further Mayflower 400 UK n.d.

and *Zhi Fei*[5] are good examples to illustrate where the shipping sector is at the moment.

Considering their economic and environmental benefits and the prospects of better navigational safety compared to their human-controlled counterparts (AAWA 2016, 4; Burmeister et al. 2014, 5; Cain and Turner 2018; Coraddu et al. 2020, 1–2; Kretschmann et al. 2017, 78; Sözer 2024, 23–27; Tettenborn 2020, 118n17), it is likely that these unmanned ships, which can be partially or fully autonomous, will soon be widely operational. Despite the perceived benefits, the use of autonomous ships also poses certain risks. Indeed, one of the most challenging aspects of the proliferation of autonomous ships is widely considered to be the potential legal problems associated with their use. This is mainly because the current maritime legal framework was designed and developed for ships that are wholly controlled by a crew on board the ship. Therefore, to what extent the present laws and regulations are compatible with autonomous ships is a question to be answered conclusively. Many projects on autonomous ships have been developed over the past ten years[6] in different parts of the world, especially in major shipping countries such as Finland, Norway, and the UK. Some of these projects have been dedicated to the applicability of the existing legal rules to autonomous ships at the national and international levels,[7] such as the Maritime Unmanned Navigation through Intelligence Networks (MUNIN) project,[8] the Advanced Autonomous Waterborne Applications Initiative (AAWA),[9] and the Comité Maritime International Working Group on Maritime Autonomous Surface Ships.[10] Since 2017, the International Maritime Organization (IMO) has addressed the potential legal issues concerning the introduction of autonomous ships (IMO

5 The *Zhi Fei*, China's first autonomous and electric container ship, which has a capacity of 300 containers, began its regular voyages between the Chinese ports of Qingdao and Dongjiakou in April 2022 (Marine Industry News 2022).

6 It should be noted that research projects conducted on autonomous ships are not limited to the past decade. For example, the Intelligent Ship Project, the first research initiative on autonomous shipping, was initiated in Japan in the 1980s. The project examined the possibility of operating a ship without human support and intervention (Infomaritime 2018). For a recent autonomous ship project in Japan, the MEGURI 2040, see Inoue and Mori (2021); Nippon Foundation (n.d.).

7 Although others are technical R&D projects concentrating on the construction and operation of these types of ships. The principal objective of this group of projects is the production of a model that can pass actual sea trials (Soyer 2020, 105).

8 The MUNIN project developed a concept for unmanned merchant vessels, focusing on the operation of a dry bulk carrier in intercontinental trade, using a hybrid system combining autonomous technology with shore-based monitoring. The project assessed its technical, economic, and legal feasibility, showing commercial viability and safety improvements, while highlighting legal challenges concerning manning and liability attribution. See MUNIN (2016).

9 Funded by Tekes, AAWA is a project analyzing the feasibility of autonomous merchant ship navigation, the applicability of current technology, and the risks the industry will face: see Rolls-Royce (2016a).

10 In 2015, the Comité Maritime International (CMI) established the International Working Group on Maritime Autonomous Surface Ships (MASS) to address legal issues related to

2017b). The IMO's Regulatory Scoping Exercise for the Use of Maritime Autonomous Surface Ships (MASS) concluded in 2021 (IMO 2021, annex). The Maritime Safety Committee, during its 105th session, approved a separate code for autonomous ships and commenced drafting the MASS Code (IMO 2022b, 37). The nonmandatory Code[11] was set to be formally adopted in May 2026, with the effective date for adoption being July 1, 2030 (IMO 2024b).[12]

So far, the steps being taken to address the potential legal problems associated with autonomous ships are mostly focused on IMO instruments, as well as the United Nations Convention on the Law of the Sea (UNCLOS)[13] and the Civil Liability Convention[14] (Hunter 2021, 209). However, the concerns of industry in relation to autonomous ships should also be addressed.[15] This chapter reviews the standard forms of charterparties as a significant part of the overall study of rules, regulations, and civil liability (219). Following this review, the chapter turns to how the concept of time charterparty finds applicability to this new generation of ships, how the fundamental obligations of shipowners and charterers under the standard time charter forms will be affected, and to what extent the current standard contractual framework for time charter forms needs to be changed. Since English law is predominant in the field of charterparties, the analysis is derived from that perspective. It is also noted that charterparty relations are mainly conducted through standard charterparty forms.[16] These forms have been designed with types of trade, the needs of the charter industry, and developments in law in mind. There are

autonomous vessel operations and to assess international legal approaches. A questionnaire was circulated to CMI members, covering national law; liability; IMO conventions; the UNCLOS, December 10, 1982, 1833 UNTS 397; the International Convention for the Safety of Life at Sea, November 1, 1974, 1184 UNTS 2 (as amended) (SOLAS); the Convention on the International Regulations for Preventing Collisions at Sea, October 20, 1972, 1050 UNTS 16 (COLREGS); and the International Convention on Standards of Training, Certification, and Watchkeeping for Seafarers, July 7, 1978, 1361 UNTS 2 (STCW). Twenty-three associations responded and their answers were published on the CMI website. For the questionnaire, see CMI (2023).

11 At the 105th session, it was agreed that the finalization of nonmandatory guidelines will take place in the first half of 2024, with the adoption of a mandatory code targeted for entry into force in 2028 (IMO 2022a).

12 For more detail on the progress of the IMO's regulatory work on MASS, see Tunfors (2022).

13 UNCLOS, December 10, 1982, 1833 UNTS 397.

14 International Convention on Civil Liability for Oil Pollution Damage, November 29, 1969, 973 UNTS 3.

15 Those concerns faced by autonomous ships primarily revolve around issues of liability, insurance, safety standards, and gaps in the regulatory framework that have created hesitation among industry stakeholders, limiting investments in this technology and raising concerns about its practical implementation.

16 That such a practice is developed can be explained on the ground that it reduces the workload of the parties. Since the clauses are standardized, the parties do not need to think about the main obligations and rights of the parties; they only need to fill in details as to charterparty relations, such as the names of the parties, the ship's name, the delivery time, and the duration of the charter. See Plomaritou and Papadopoulos (2017, 234).

various standard time charter forms in current usage.[17] The New York Produce Exchange (NYPE) form is one of the shipping industry's most widely used dry-cargo time charterparties (BIMCO 2015; Plomaritou and Papadopoulos 2017, 235).[18] The analysis in this chapter is limited to the most recent version, NYPE 2015.[19]

2.2 AUTONOMOUS SHIPS GENERALLY

2.2.1 *Definition of Autonomous Ships and Analysis of Levels of Automation in Ship Operation*

The notion of autonomous vessels remains notably elusive, with no singular, universally recognized definition to command the field of discourse. However, the definition posited by the IMO is one of the most widely acknowledged and frequently cited. The IMO opts for the term "Maritime Autonomous Surface Ship" (MASS), meaning "a ship which, to a varying degree, can operate independently of human interaction" (IMO 2021, annex, 3, 2018a). The IMO further refines this definition by categorizing MASS into four distinct classes, gradated according to the extent to which automation permeates the operational functions of the vessel.[20] In this categorization,[21] with ships in the first degree of autonomy, the crew is on board for the purpose of providing the ship's direction and management. However, there is automation in some operations and the seafarer can intervene when necessary. A ship in this group is referred to as a "ship with automated process and decision support." Ships with a second degree of autonomy can be controlled and operated remotely. However, the crew continues to be on board to make interventions when necessary. The ships that will bring about the most radical change in the

[17] These include NYPE 46, NYPE 92, NYPE 2015, Baltime, Gentime, Asbatime, BPTime 3, and Shelltime 3 and 4 forms. Factors such as the purpose of the vessel, the type and specification of the vessel, the trading opportunities and restrictions, the cargoes to be carried, and the parties involved have a role in determining the form of charter chosen (Plomaritou and Papadopoulos 2017, 217).

[18] The authors of the book *Time Charters* indicated that the 1946 version of the NYPE form continues to be regarded as the most significant standard form within the dry cargo sector (Coghlin et al. 2014, para. I.2). As Professor Baughen elucidates, the detailed prescriptions in NYPE 46 concerning the obligations of shipowners and charterers, hire, vessel performance, and maintenance have rendered it an indomitable fixture (Baughen 2019, 315).

[19] The first draft of the document was produced by American broker interests in 1913. NYPE 2015, the sixth version, is the result of a joint authorship by the Association of Shipbrokers and Agents, the Baltic and International Maritime Council (BIMCO), and the Singapore Maritime Foundation (BIMCO 2015).

[20] In addition to the IMO's categorization, there are other automation levels suggested by organizations such as Lloyd's Register, DNV, Burea Veritas, Nippon Kaiji Kyokai, and the American Bureau of Shipping. For more on these classifications, see Fukuto (2021, 40–48); Sözer (2024, 46–49); Wright (2020, 37–44).

[21] Explanations regarding the categorization of autonomous ship are made considering IMO (2018b, annex I, 1). This categorization was later endorsed by the committee (IMO 2018c, 36).

maritime industry are those with the third and fourth degrees of autonomy, due to the absence of a crew on board the ship. In third-degree ships, the crew is not on board; it is accepted that the ship is operated and managed remotely by personnel in a center established on land or on shore. A ship in this category is a "remotely controlled ship without seafarers on board," or a semi-autonomous ship. Finally, ships with a fourth degree of autonomy, or "fully autonomous ships," have no crew on board and no active control by personnel from the remote operation center. Through AI systems integrated into the system, the ship determines its movement by evaluating the current situation and conditions and making the necessary decisions regarding the operation of the ship without the need for human support. In spite of the self-operation feature of this group of ships, remote operation centers still exist,[22] but the role of center personnel is limited to monitoring the actions of the system and decision-making process in case of system failure (IMO 2017a, 6). Whatever the method of operation and the level of autonomy, there should be a person in charge of the autonomous ship, either on board or in a remote operation center, who has the authority to intervene, performing the duties of the master (IMO 2023e, 42, 2023b, 4). Regarding the relationship between these accepted degrees, the IMO suggests that the levels do not represent a hierarchical order (IMO 2018b, annex 1, 1, 2021, annex, 4).

Based on these autonomy levels, theoretically, in a particular case, a ship may operate at just one level. There may be no expectation that the ship's autonomy level will change; the ship is assumed to operate at a fixed autonomy level throughout the voyage, or to maintain a "static autonomy level" (Barber et al. 2000, 145). However, it is also possible to design systems where the autonomy level changes during the voyage, based on different conditions or operations. For example, a ship may be designed to operate autonomously while sailing on the high seas, but the design might also enable control to transfer to the operator or crew during specific phases of the voyage, such as passing through a busy strait, entering a port, or performing docking or loading operations (AAWA 2016, 30; Ringbom and Collin 2021, 14–15). A ship's autonomy level may change multiple times during the voyage (Barber et al. 2000, 130; Sözer 2024, 45). This is referred to as a "dynamic autonomy level" in ship operation. Autonomous ships will transition freely between different levels of autonomy during a particular voyage (AAWA 2016, 6–7; Fukuto 2021, 47; Maritime UK 2022, 20–21; Ringbom and Collin 2021, 14–15; Yang et al. 2020). The operation and design of autonomous ships currently in service, such as the *Yara Birkeland*[23] and the *Prism Courage*,[24] support this submis-

[22] This can be inferred from the assumptions accepted for regulatory scoping exercise by the Maritime Safety Committee at its 103rd session (IMO 2021, annex, 6).

[23] The ship currently navigates autonomously under the supervision of a crew of three on board, but with mooring, for example, done manually (Yara 2024).

[24] The *Prism Courage* is an LNG ship currently in the testing period for a transoceanic voyage, designed to be operated under the fourth degree of autonomy. It has sailed for more than 300 hours without human intervention, except for the approval process. See IMO (2023c, 2).

sion.[25] The analysis in this chapter is approached through the prism of "dynamic autonomy." The term "autonomous ship" is used to refer to a ship operated without any crew on board.

2.2.2 *Remote Operation Center*

Unlike conventional ships, autonomous ships consist of two separate parts, the first of which has a classical appearance at sea. Because the crew is completely separated from the ship, its operation and monitoring involve a remote operation center.[26] That center is defined as "a location remote from the MASS that can operate some or all aspects of the functions of the MASS" (IMO 2023b, 6).[27] The center is also defined as a structure consisting of computer hardware, telecommunications equipment, and various high-tech tools arranged to perform a specific function, managed and operated by the relevant personnel (Sözer 2024, 84).[28] It is possible to list the functions of the center as monitoring the ship, ensuring the ship's direction and management, collecting data, and fulfilling certain legal obligations (Sözer 2024, 89–92). However, depending on the fact of each case, its main function may change during a particular voyage. Following the dynamic autonomy submission, for example, if the ship proceeds on the high seas, the main function of the center might be to monitor the ship. But, if the ship is sailing through a busy strait, the main function of the center might be to control the ship. Physical conditions and technical conditions may require such an active role change by the center during the voyage. It may not be technically possible to sail the ship remotely throughout the voyage – for example, where continuous data exchange and communication between the ship and the operation center, located either on land or aboard another vessel,[29] is not provided (AAWA 2016, 4). This communication would depend on the transmission of high-resolution and large-scale data collected by various sensors, cameras, radar, infrared technology, and the Automatic Identification System (AIS),

[25] For the explanations and citations given in this paragraph, the author is indebted to Dr. Selim Ciğer, whose recent submissions are summarized here (Ciğer 2024, 1152–1153).

[26] In 2022, the IMO updated its terminology, referring to what was previously known as a "shore control center" as a "remote operation center" (IMO 2023b, 6).

[27] The UK is among the first countries to specifically address remotely operated unmanned vessels in a code. Annex 2 of *The Workboat Code Edition 3* concerns remotely operated unmanned vessels. In the Code, the remote operation center is defined as "either a shore-based location which is permanent or mobile or a manned vessel from which a remotely operated unmanned vessel is operated" (MCA 2023, 26).

[28] For definitions as to remote operation centers in the literature, see Choi and Lee (2021, 448n11).

[29] Although these centers were referred to as shore centers when the concept of the center was first placed on the agenda, it was later suggested that they could be established not only on shore but also on land or at a location on the sea; for the first approach, see AAWA (2016); MUNIN (2016); for the second, see Sözer (2024, 85). The definition of a remote operation center in *The Workboat Code Edition 3* indicates that the center can be at any shore-based location or on manned ships (MCA 2023, 26).

ensuring that the operation center can maintain uninterrupted access to the ship's systems (Ciğer 2024, 1145).[30] The reliability of current technologies to facilitate such data transfer is debatable, particularly concerning potential risks arising from connection delays, as well as adverse factors such as weather and distance (1145).[31] Solutions may involve utilizing both technologies (remote operation and autonomous operation) in tandem (1146)[32] and active role changes at the remote operation center. The ship will be controlled through an interface in which the bridge is simulated in the center, which replicates camera and sensor systems on the ship, plus controls such as steering gear and joysticks for the remote operator.[33]

There are three main issues around the concept of the remote operation center. The first relates to the status of the remote operator.[34] The remote operator is responsible for monitoring the ship's condition, course, speed, and environmental factors during navigation in light of the information sent from the ship; supervising the decision held by the system; and, when necessary, taking direct operation and management of the ship (Ciğer 2024, 1149; Sözer 2024, 88–93). The Joint Working Group (JWG) has yet to explain fully the role of the remote operator, though it has provisionally affirmed that, irrespective of the level of autonomy, a human captain must preside over each autonomous ship (IMO 2023b, 4). In the report submitted by the International Federation of Shipmaster's Associations on the roles and responsibilities of the master, it is also emphasized that autonomous ships are ships by nature and that they need a master. Autonomous ships, like all ships, should be under the command and control of a master who has both situational awareness and sufficient maritime knowledge (IMO 2023a, 4). The role of the ship master will not disappear, but the execution of the role may be filled by a person on land who has the necessary qualifications and can exercise discretionary authority when necessary (4). A MASS ship master may be preferred over traditional manning (IMO 2023a, annex, 1). At this point, it should be mentioned that the UK was among the first countries to issue regulations on personnel working in remote operation centers. The Maritime and Coastguard Agency adopted the *Workboat Code Edition* 3 in December 2023. The technical requirements for the operation of ships remotely controlled are regulated within Annex 2. The Code is also important in terms of the definition of the remote operator. In Annex 2, the remote operator is defined as "any person, including the Master, with recognised or certifiable experience who is engaged in the remote operation of a [Remotely Operated Unmanned Vessel]" (MCA 2023, 27). The existence of a master in the remote operation center is also accepted by the

30 Ciğer cites AAWA (2016, 30–32); Ringbom and Collin (2021, 9): Ciğer (2024, 1145n51).

31 Ciğer cites AAWA (2016, 30–32); IMO (2024a, 4); Vartdal et al. (2018, 9–10): Ciğer (2024, 1145n52).

32 For similar submissions, see AAWA (2016, 13); IMO (2023d, annex, 9); Vartdal et al. (2018, 12).

33 For examples of these structures, see Rolls-Royce (2016a); for video, see Kongsberg (2021); Rolls-Royce (2016b).

34 For detailed analysis of the legal status of the remote operator, see Choi and Lee (2021).

JWG, which notes that the human master should have the means to intervene in ship operations when necessary, regardless of the mode of operation and the autonomy level (IMO 2023b, 4). Analysis held in the literature also demonstrates that the general trend is to treat the remote operator of the ship as a master while the application of master-related terms is evaluated. For example, the authors who analyze the application of Article 4(2)(a) of the Hague-Visby Rules[35] to autonomous ships submitted that a remote operator can be treated as the functional equivalent of a master in the context of the relevant article, so that the carrier can escape from liability for loss and damage arising due to the fault of the remote operator in the navigation or management of the autonomous ship (Baughen 2021, 87–88; Stevens 2020, 159, 161). The prevailing view, in essence, is to regard those entrusted with the control and operation of the ship – despite their absence from the ship's physical presence – as holding positions akin to master and crew.[36] It follows that personnel tasked with the governance of autonomous ships should be recognized in a capacity resembling that of the ship's master, bearing responsibilities comparable to those traditionally assigned to the master. This rationale, therefore, warrants the assertion that the relationship between the shore-based operational center staff and their autonomous vessels mirrors, in substance, the long-established association between the master and the time charterer.

The second issue regarding the remote operation center is whether each center and remote operator will be responsible for the operation of only one ship or more than one. The MUNIN project plans for up to ninety ships controlled from a remote center (Porathe et al. 2014, 2). The project also suggests that one operator may be responsible for monitoring and controlling up to six ships (Man et al. 2015, 2676). The possibility of a master being in charge of more than one ship was supported by the JWG (IMO 2023b, 5). It can be inferred from this approach that the general view of the JWG is that more than one ship can be controlled from one center. One of the currently active remote operation centers, Massterly in Horten, Norway, provides management and operation services for the *Yara Birkeland* and ASKO's electric barges MS *Marit* and MS *Therese*. This example also demonstrates the practical application of a single center controlling multiple ships (Massterly 2024; Wilhelmsen 2024). In fact, if it is accepted that each vessel will be controlled from a separate center, this will require a huge number of centers to be set up and staffed. From an economic perspective, this proposition appears to lack rationality, so probably the most effective approach would be to operate as many ships as possible from a single center.[37]

[35] International Convention for the Unification of Certain Rules of Law relating to Bills of Lading, August 25, 1924 (Hague Rules), as amended by the Protocol Amending the International Convention for the Unification of Certain Rules of Law Relating to Bills of Lading, February 23, 1968, 1412 UNTS 128.

[36] For a similar submission, see Choi and Lee (2021, 459); Soyer et al. (2022, 7); Stevens (2020, 148, 152).

[37] For the submissions that one operator can operate multiple ships, see Karlis (2018, 121); Soyer et al. (2022, 44); Stevens (2020, 148, 153).

The final issue is who will provide the remote operation service. It can be argued that the owner of an autonomous ship can construct its own center and staff it with personnel to monitor and operate the ship. However, these centers consist of computer hardware, telecommunications equipment, and various high-tech tools. The cost of establishing a remote operation center varies based on factors such as facility size, technology integration, and operational requirements. For example, while the cost of equipping and maintaining an autonomous bulker, inclusive of annual operational expenses and rental commitments, remains a matter of rough estimation, it is acknowledged that the investment for the development of the remote operation center lies between US$1 million and US$2.1 million, with annual operational outlay approximating US$0.87 million. The establishment of such a center entails a recurring cost of US$33,000 per vessel annually (Ziajka-Poznańska and Montewka 2021, 6–8), alongside the considerable infrastructure expenses, as exemplified by the KRISO research center's construction cost of 22.1 billion Korean won (approximately US$16 million) (KRISO n.d.). Following these values, the construction of an individual center by each owner may not be considered economically viable, especially if the shipowner operates a single ship. Since, as noted above, operating more than one ship from the center is a sensible choice, it could be argued that where the shipowner operates larger fleets, it could set up its own remote operation center and all its ships could be operated from the same center. Considering the fact that shipping companies even arrange special ports for their fleet,[38] this could also be done with respect to the operation center and it could be cost-effective. However, depending on the area it is traveling through, as the ship moves from one port to another it may be necessary for it to change the operation center (Sözer 2024, 85; see also Baughen 2021, 84),[39] such as the air traffic control area and the vessel traffic services system.[40] This may be due to the difficulty of transmitting information when the ship is at a great distance from the center (Sözer

38 For instance, the Mediterranean Shipping Company owns a terminal in Genoa port, which facilitates the seamless operation of its fleet (Combine Goodz 2021). Similarly, A. P. Moller-Maersk, through its subsidiary APM Terminals, operates numerous port facilities worldwide, including dedicated terminals in various countries (Maersk 2022). These strategic investments in port infrastructure enable shipping companies to exert greater control over their logistics operations, thereby reducing reliance on external port facilities and mitigating potential disruptions in their supply chains. For another recent example, see Berger (2024).

39 Professor Baughen, during his analysis on the seaworthiness obligation of the carrier, raises this question: "Will seaworthiness through the competence of the 'crew' attach at the time the voyage starts or will this be a moveable feast attaching each time the vessel passes into the orbit of a new set of [shore-based controllers]?" Behind these words, there might also be a thought that a new set of shore-based controllers might be an issue at the time each center is changed (Baughen 2021, 84).

40 Some academics point to similarities between the remote operation center and vessel traffic services. In this regard, see Carey (2017, 29–30); Soyer et al. (2022, 46). Air traffic control services are stated as the closest setup to a remote operation center (Sözer 2024, 95).

2024, 85; see also Carey 2019, 7).[41] When the ship goes outside the control area of the remote operation center, the owner of the ship might be required to connect with another center. Rather than the service of remote operation being provided by the shipowner and associated maritime centers throughout the entire voyage, third-party shipping management companies will usually be involved in the operation process. It is not uncommon for shipowners that do not have shipping knowledge and experience to contract with a company to provide technical, crew, and commercial management and ancillary services (Plomaritou and Papadopoulos 2017, 115). The company can provide a remote operations center and personnel to operate the ship, either onshore or on board, as well as serve as the technical managers of the ship (Hunter 2020).[42] Steps taken by the Baltic and International Maritime Council (BIMCO) actually reflect this view. The AUTOSHIPMAN agreement was recently adopted by BIMCO in view of the increasing number of remotely operated ships, with the aim of providing a contractual framework for third-party ship managers that deliver operational services for these ships. It contains terms regarding the obligations, responsibilities, and liabilities of the parties (BIMCO 2024b). The form is drafted considering the SHIPMAN 2024 agreement (BIMCO 2024a). In addition, the number of companies offering management and operation services for remotely operated and autonomous vessels is growing by the day (Massterly n.d.; Ocean Infinity 2022). The specialized nature of the capabilities and technology featured in these remote operation centers means that it is prudent to delegate ship responsibilities to specialized entities.

2.3 THE CONCEPT OF TIME CHARTERPARTY AND APPLICABILITY FOR AUTONOMOUS SHIPS

Time charters are simply contracts for the use of the ship and crew, under which the ship is manned by the shipowner and the charterer has the right to direct the commercial employment of the ship for an agreed period of time within the agreed trading limits in respect of geographical limitations and the type of cargo permissible in consideration of payment of hire, without obtaining possession of the ship

[41] In *Unmanned Ships and the Law* (Sözer 2024), Hans Ottosen, then CEO of Danelec Marine, pointed to the difficulty in transmitting constant vessel data due to satellite capacity and speed and suggested that operations of remote-controlled ships will be restricted to the area that is close to the shore with access to high bandwidth. Following this, it can also be said that where the ship is operated in a wider area, a practice could be developed that requires a change of center.

[42] Analysis of the AUTOSHIPMAN form shows that it is designed in a way that third-party managers provide technical management (box 6), crew management (box 7), and commercial management (box 8) of the ship, depending on the preference of the shipowner. The AUTOSHIPMAN form and permission to use it here have kindly been provided by BIMCO. It should be noted that BIMCO is the creator and copyright holder of the contract and any commercial use of the contract should be through BIMCO's contract editor, SmartCon.

(Baughen 2021, 93).[43] From the shipowner's standpoint, time charters are significant as they provide an opportunity for the shipowner to gain income for a particular period of time without worrying about operational costs. For charterers, this type of contract also serves an important purpose. As stipulated by Lord Wilberforce in *The "Nanfri"* case, "the nature and purpose of [a time charter] is to enable the charterers to use the vessels during the period of the charters for trading in whatever manner they think fit."[44] Most charterers are speculators who aim to gain from the fluctuations in the charter market (Plomaritou and Papadopoulos 2017, 226). From their perspective, time charters are a tool to maximize profits. Time charters are often used by traders who need transportation for their goods and wish to have maximum flexibility regarding the commercial usage of the ship (225). For example, for sellers who do not own a vessel but often sell their goods under a cost, insurance, and freight contract, time charters are a useful tool to perform their obligations under such sale contracts. There is, therefore, no doubt that time charters play a vital role in international trade.

The fact that a ship is autonomous does not change the significance of the time charter, but it may require a slight change in the definition. Indeed, one of the fundamental features of a time charter is that it gives the charterer the contractual right to direct the commercial employment of the ship within the agreed trading limits through the employment orders given to the master.[45] In the case of autonomous ships, since there is no crew on board to follow the charterer's employment orders, the ship is in fact chartered in a bare form – in other words, without crew. It is uncertain whether the concept of time charter will continue to exist or whether it will commence to be used as a form of bareboat charter.

A bareboat charter is a contractual arrangement whereby a ship is chartered by a third party without any crew on board. Under this agreement, possession of the ship and full authority over it pass to the charterer for an agreed period in return for a hire payment (Davies 2005, para. 1.1).[46] Bareboat charters are entered into not so much for the purpose of transporting goods but as part of a complicated financial arrangement. Often, the charterer will in due course become the owner of the ship.[47]

43 For explanations of the characteristics of the time charter, see *Skibsaktieselskapet Snefonn, Skibaksjeselskapet Bergehus and Sig Bergesen D.Y. & Company v. Kawasaki Kisen Kaisha Ltd. (The "Berge Tasta")* [1975] 1 Lloyd's Rep. 422, 424; *Scandinavian Trading Tanker Co. A.B. v. Flota Petrolera Ecuatoriana (The "Scaptrade")* [1983] 2 Lloyd's Rep. 253, 256–257.

44 *Federal Commerce & Navigation Co. Ltd. v. Molena Alpha Inc. (The "Nanfri")* [1979] AC 757, 777.

45 NYPE 2015, Clause 8(a) ("Performance of Voyages"), states in part: "The Master shall be conversant with the English language and (although appointed by the Owners) shall be under the orders and directions of the Charterers as regards employment and agency." That provision is commonly referred to as the employment clause, which will be discussed in more detail later in this chapter.

46 An explanation of the characteristics of the demise charter is given in the judgment of *The "Giuseppe di Vittorio"* [1998] 1 Lloyd's Rep. 136, 156.

47 A hire purchase agreement may, for instance, involve a bareboat charter arrangement. In a variant of this, a financial institution may extend a loan to facilitate the purchase of a vessel,

The contract in question may at first sight appear to be similar to a time charter, but with the difference that the bareboat charterer is obliged to provide its own crew, have the possession of the ship, and assume responsibility as "owner" for any liabilities arising during the operation of the ship.[48] Since the crew is employed by the charterer, any acts, omissions, or negligence committed by the crew are also considered to be the responsibility of the charterer under a bareboat charter.

Where the remote operation center and personnel working in the center are arranged by the time charterer in cases where there are no crew on board an autonomous ship, the concept of time chartering in the form of bareboat chartering is effectively beginning to be used (Baughen 2021, 97). However, the accuracy of this submission might change depending on whether – in the future, when autonomous ships are involved in time charter operations – the arrangement of remote operation centers and personnel provided by the time charterer will be the preferred method.

From the shipowner's point of view, this might at first sight seem to make sense. One of the shipowner's fundamental concerns under a time charter is that the orders given by the charterer during the charter period remain within the agreed trading limits and do not cause any unsafe situation for the ship, crew, and cargo. This concern in relation to the traditional ship is currently managed by the shipowner and its employee, the master. When the order is first given by the charterer, it is evaluated and a decision is then made to follow or reject it. With regard to autonomous ships, if trading limits in terms of geographical restrictions and the type of cargo permitted under the time charter and safety issues can be managed by the shipowner through an AI system, the shipowner may not need a person to protect its interests in the ship, crew, and cargo and may prefer not to deal separately with a remote operation center (Baughen 2021, 97). While this method makes the shipowner's work easier, it has two downsides. First, such an approach may give a harm to the nature of the time charter. The time charterer's right to use the ship is only limited with commercial employment of the ship. Arrangement of the remote operation center and personnel by the charterer in one sense means that navigational management of the ship is also transferred to the charterer. This transfer has the potential to disrupt established concepts under time charter. For example, in a case where the charterer fails to pay the charter hire on time, if the conditions arise, the shipowner has the right to suspend the charter service and withdraw the ship from the service.[49] While the control of the operation center is in the hands of the time charterer through personnel appointed by the charterer,

subsequently taking ownership of the ship while leasing it back on a bareboat charter to the borrower for the term of the loan. This arrangement permits the bank to mitigate both the operational expenses and the liabilities typically associated with the vessel's operation, which it would otherwise bear under a mortgage agreement. See the example in Williams (2013, 132).

48 The differences between bareboat charter and time charter were explained by MacKinnon L.J.: "There is all the difference between hiring a boat in which to row yourself about, in which case the boat is handed over to you, and contracting with a man on the beach that he shall take you for a row, in which case he merely renders services in rowing you about." *Sea and Land Securities v. William Dickinson* (1942) 72 Lloyd's Rep. 159, 163.

49 These rights of the shipowner are stipulated under Clause 11(c) and (d) of NYPE 2015.

how can the shipowner exercise these rights? It will not be physically possible for the shipowner to perform these rights without the cooperation of the charterer. The charterer can continue to use the ship, disregarding the shipowner's rights. Another example relates to the redelivery stage of the ship. It is well settled that under a time charter the charterer is obliged to redeliver the ship to the shipowner at the end of the charter duration (Coghlin et al. 2014, para. 4.30). However, where the control is in the hands of the charterer, although the shipowner does not want the ship to be delayed or redelivered early, the charterer can still send it to the most distant port by giving the orders to the personnel it has appointed, causing a late redelivery, or leave it earlier than the end of the duration. Thus, the arrangement of the center and personnel by the charterer might result in the charterer taking control of the ship in a manner that may conflict with the shipowner's interests under the time charter. With regard to the arrangements with the center made by the charterer, although the charterer does not have the ship physically, since he controls the ship remotely or autonomously, he can still be treated as having possession of the ship, and this will conflict with the nature of the time charter.[50] Second, considering the value of autonomous ships, which is likely to be higher than that of conventional ships, no shipowner is likely to trust the charterer to the extent that arrangements as to the remote operation of the ship are made by the charterer.[51]

Further, time charterers are mostly speculators who want to profit from the fluctuations in the charter market, or traders who need to transport their goods. Considering that the remote operation of ships and the selection of personnel for the center are areas that require more expertise than the management of traditional ships due to the high level of technology, they may have concerns about arranging for the remote operation center to take control of someone else's ship. In addition, assuming responsibility as "owner" for any liabilities arising during the operation of the vessel might carry additional risk. Therefore, in the future, it is more likely that the charterer will prefer not to be involved in the remote operation arrangement.

For these reasons, it is most likely that the shipowner will make arrangements for the center and personnel for the operation of the autonomous ships. The shipowner can make these arrangements itself or it may contract with third-party shipping management companies.[52] The latter is likely preferable because if the shipowner becomes the employer of the center personnel, there may be problems if several ships owned by different people are operated from the same center. Whatever the

[50] In instances where remote operation arrangements are undertaken by the charterer, since the shipowner loses the control of the ship and it can also be said that it loses the possession of the ship, it would be more precise to accept that the contract between the shipowner and the charterer is given a status of demise charter.

[51] A similar point is made when discussing who will be the employer of the remote operators under the demise charter: see Amaxilati (2022, 119).

[52] Under Clause 10 of the AUTOSHIPMAN form, the manager can be made responsible either for providing the remote operation center or for managing it, depending on the agreement of the parties. Crew management can also be left to the manager (see Clause 7).

preference, the autonomous ship is provided to the time charterer for a period of time with the remote operation center and personnel. In this case, the time charter will not take the form of a bareboat charter. The concept of time charter will continue to exist; the possession of the ship remains with the shipowner, but the definition needs to be broadened to indicate that the time charter is a contract to use the ship and "the arranged remote operation centers with personnel" for a specified period of time within the agreed trading limits. This outcome is based on the assumption that, under the time charter, the remote operation center and personnel are arranged by the shipowner or its appointed management company.

Following this model, the concept of time charter will continue to exist, but the relationship between shore-based personnel and the charterer, and between the shipowner and shore-based personnel, is added to the equation. It should be noted here that the charterparty agreement is operated under the freedom-of-contract principle. This means that contractual parties may freely decide the terms of their contract (Williams 2013, 131). They are not subject to any mandatory rules unless the charter contains a clause paramount.[53] Therefore, where time charters are made for autonomous ships in the future, it might be necessary for the contractual parties to make certain amendments related to contractual terms and their obligations and rights. In addition, the terms referring to the crew and master in the forms must be reconsidered. The remainder of this chapter is dedicated to those issues, with particular reference to NYPE 2015 and English case law.

2.4 ANALYSIS OF FUNDAMENTAL RIGHTS AND OBLIGATIONS OF SHIPOWNERS AND CHARTERERS UNDER TIME CHARTERS FOR AUTONOMOUS SHIPS

2.4.1. *The Shipowner's Obligation to Provide a Ship That Complies with the Charter Description at the Time of Delivery*

It is common to see a clause in time charters that describes features of the ship such as class, cargo capacity, nationality, speed, and bunker consumption. From the charterer's point of view, this clause is probably one of the most important parts of the time charter, as the charterer agrees to pay a fixed rent for an unknown vessel for

[53] The phrase "clause paramount" typically refers to clauses in contracts (such as bills of lading or charterparties) that identify certain governing rules – often those of a recognized international convention – that override the contractual terms in cases of conflict. These clauses ensure that the terms of international conventions like the Hague-Visby Rules or the Hamburg Rules supersede the contract's provisions on issues such as the limitation of liability, rights, and duties of the carrier, in the event of inconsistency. In *Homburg Houtimport B.V. v. Agrosin Private Ltd. ("The Starsin")* [2003] 1 Lloyd's Rep. 571, para. 35, the House of Lords emphasized the importance of the clause paramount in determining which international rules govern a contract of carriage.

the entire period of the charter, based solely on the contractual description of the vessel. The shipowner's obligation under the description clause is to provide a ship that conforms to the contractual description (Coghlin et al. 2014, para. I.33). Providing a ship that does not comply with the charter description is a breach of the charter, and the charterer is entitled to damages for the loss suffered, unless the charterparty contains a provision that excludes the shipowner's liability for its failure (para. 3.18). If the description in the charter indicates condition status,[54] such as the ship's class,[55] or an intermediate term status, such as the ship's speed and bunker consumption (Coghlin et al. 2014, para. 3.77),[56] the shipowner's failure to provide a ship that complies with the description can be considered a repudiatory breach, and the charterer has a right to terminate the charter. Under NYPE 2015, descriptions as to the ship are given in the preamble. In addition, the form contains Annex A ("Vessel Description") – a detailed vessel questionnaire that forms part of the charterparty. There is also Clause 12, under which speed and bunker consumption are stipulated.[57] When time charters are made for autonomous ships, the descriptive information given about the ship in the form needs to be extended.

Autonomous shipping possesses distinctive features that will facilitate functions such as mooring, berthing, and cargo handling without the need for human assistance. The *Yara Birkeland*, a ship that is currently expected to perform these operations, serves as a tangible example of this emerging technological development.[58] From the charterer's perspective, capabilities of the ship to perform these

[54] Under English law, contractual terms are classified as condition, warranty, and innominate terms depending on their importance for contractual parties. While the term "condition" is used to refer to the fundamental term of the contract and its breach gives the innocent party the right to terminate the contract (*Poussard v. Spiers* (1876) 1 QBD 410), the term "warranty" is used to express an immaterial term of the contract, the breach of which entitles the innocent party only to claim for damages (*Bettini v. Gye* (1876) QBD 183). The third category of the contractual term, an innominate term, is later added to the other two in *Hongkong Fir Shipping Company Ltd. v. Kawasaki Kisen Kaisha Ltd. (The "Hongkong Fir")* [1961] 2 Lloyd's Rep. 478. It can be said that this group of terms is somewhere in the middle of the two in terms of importance. The breach of it entitles the innocent party to claim damages, but in order that the right to terminate the contract is provided the breach must have "deprived [the innocent party] of substantially the whole benefit which it was intended that he should obtain from the contract": *The "Hongkong Fir,"* 494.

[55] *Routh v. MacMillan* (1863) 9 LT 541; *Cosmos Bulk Transport Inc. v. China National Foreign Trade Transportation Corporation (The "Apollonius")* [1978] 1 Lloyd's Rep. 53, 61.

[56] See *Dolphin Hellas Shipping S.A. v. Itemslot Ltd. (The "Aegean Dolphin")* [1992] 2 Lloyd's Rep. 178.

[57] For detailed analysis of Clause 12 of NYPE 2015, see Dindar (2017).

[58] During the construction and trial process of the *Yara Birkeland*, various sources pointed to the ship's ability to berth, moor, and handle cargo autonomously. (In this regard, see, for example, Ship Technology 2017.) After two years of operation, it is currently known that the ship is able to berth without any human support. However, mooring is still done manually, since the ship's robotic mooring arms remain in the testing process (Yara 2024). With regard to the cargo-handling capabilities of the *Yara Birkeland*, the author is unaware of any source that refers to this at the present time.

operations, especially cargo handling, might be important. Under Clause 8 of NYPE 2015, "charterers shall perform all cargo handling, including but not limited to loading, stowing, trimming, lashing, securing, dunnaging, unlashing, discharging, and tallying, at their risk and expense, under the supervision of the Master." If the ship is capable of performing cargo-handling autonomously, this provision will be inapplicable. Since the charterer is not the one who has the right of ownership or possession of the chartered ship, it would not be reasonable to hold it liable for cargo-handling, which is performed by the ship under remote or autonomous operation without involvement of the charterer. In such a case, it will be more proper to impose this obligation on the shoulders of the shipowner. Thus, an autonomous ship's cargo-handling capability requires a profound shift in terms of the liability. Therefore, if the autonomous ship has such a capability, the charterer will want to be aware of this information, so the description clause should be extended by making this information a part of the ship's description.

It might also be important for the charterer to know the location of the remote operation center. Although the remote operation center and the ship are separate elements, without the center the ship will not have any meaning for the charterer. Therefore, the time charter is now a contract for the use of the ship with an associated remote operation center and personnel. This author suggests that information related to the capacity of potential remote operation centers arranged for the ship can be made a part of the ship's description. For example, if the shipowner prefers an operation center that has limited capacity and only allows the ship to be used within the geographical limit of a particular region due to data transmission difficulties and if the shipowner does not have any intention to arrange another center that extends the employment area of the ship outside of the specified region, this information should be given as part of a description clause and/or under Clause 1(b) as part of the trading limits.[59] It is important that the charterer knows this beforehand, because the information is relevant to plan future employment. If its intention is to use the ship outside of the designated area, it might not enter into the charter agreement for that ship. There might also be some cases in which the shipowner changes the remote operation center during the period of charter. The reason behind this may be due to problems the shipowner encounters with the remote operation center or its closure. The shipowner should be careful about such a change. One of the implied obligations imposed on the shipowner under the time charter is that the shipowner will not, at any stage of the charter, make any alterations to the ship that may (or potentially will) affect the services to be provided.[60] Following this, if the remote operation center is changed during the

[59] NYPE 2015, Clause 1(b) ("Trading limits") states: "The Vessel shall be employed in such lawful trades between safe ports and safe places within the following trading limits [text to be entered here] as the Charterers shall direct."

[60] *Isaacs v. McAllum* (1921) 6 Ll. L. Rep. 289, 291.

charter period, the shipowner must arrange a center that has at least the same capabilities as the previous one. If we consider this in terms of the geographical area in which the operation center can provide the service, the center that limits the charterer's area of operation compared to the previous center should not be chosen by the shipowner. Otherwise, this will be a breach of the shipowner's implied obligation, and the charterer is entitled to damages. If it is proved that this alteration goes to the root of the contract, the charterer may also be entitled to terminate the charter.[61] Some information as to personnel in the remote operation center can also be important for the charterer to evaluate the seaworthiness of the autonomous ship. However, this information is more accurately considered under the clause dealing with the seaworthiness of the ship rather than under the description clause.

Under NYPE 2015, some changes might also be needed related to the description given to warranties for speed and bunker consumption (performance). These warranties are usually subject to weather conditions.[62] This means that the shipowner warrants that the ship will be able to achieve the described speed and bunker consumption only if good weather conditions exist. Good weather is commonly defined in time charters referring to the Beaufort[63] and Douglas scales.[64] For example, Clause 12(a) of NYPE 2015 refers to both scales to describe good weather as "wind up to and including Force four (4) as per the Beaufort Scale and sea state up to and including Sea State three (3) as per the Douglas Sea Scale."[65] In a particular case where the time charterer asserts that the ship underperformed during the voyage, the burden of proof rests on the charterer. In order to clear this hurdle, the charterer needs to show that, although good weather conditions existed, the ship underperformed. To prove this, the chartering party normally relies on a report of the ship's performance prepared by a weather routing company (WRC). Clause 12 (b) of NYPE 2015, which states that "the Charterers shall have the option of using their preferred weather routing service," provides an option to the charterer. It is made clear later, in Clause 12(d) of NYPE 2015, that the charterer can rely on this report to support its claim for underperformance. On the other hand, the ship's

[61] This conclusion is reached considering the comments by the authors of the *Time Charters* book on how the changes of elements of the ship's description affect the contractual relations (Coghlin et al. 2014, para. 3.15).

[62] See line 9 of NYPE 46, line 18 of NYPE 93, and lines 11–12 of the Baltime form.

[63] The Beaufort scale is a system for measuring wind speeds. Used both at sea and on land, it provides a scale of wind force ranging from 0 to 12. For a detailed description of each force, see Met Office (2023).

[64] The Douglas sea scale is a tool used to measure the conditions of the sea and swell. It comprises ten degrees, ranging from 0 to 9. For a description of each degree, see OceanWave Sail (n.d.); see also London Club (2001).

[65] NYPE 2015, Clause 12(a) states: "Upon delivery and throughout the duration of this Charter Party the Vessel shall be capable of speed and daily consumption rates as stated in Appendix A in good weather on all sea passages with wind up to and including Force four (4) as per the Beaufort Scale and sea state up to and including Sea State three (3) as per the Douglas Sea Scale (unless otherwise specified in Appendix A)."

logbook prepared by the master is preferred by the shipowner as a main source of evidence to rebut the chartering party's underperformance claims in a particular case.[66] Since they are prepared by different parties, there are often inconsistencies between weather and sea conditions recorded in a WRC report and the ship's logbook. Generally, the records maintained by the master in a logbook are given greater credence than those recorded in a WRC report. This perspective appears to be logical, given the master's status as a trained weather observer recognized by the World Meteorological Organization. The master's presence on board the vessel during the entire charter period, observing weather and sea conditions firsthand, further substantiates the credibility of these records (Harris 2014, 4). This conventional view also supports the ship's logbook by pointing out that the WRC report is prepared by using satellite imagery, which is just a snapshot of weather and sea conditions, and so that may not capture the local impact of weather and sea conditions, such as currents, on the ship's performance (4). Furthermore, data for the preparation of the report is collected only once or twice a day (Alexander 2013). Where autonomous ships are used, the traditional view will lose its dominance because information in a ship's logbook entries[67] on the effect of sea and weather conditions on the ship's performance will no longer be recorded by the master who is on board the ship but by a person in the remote operation center, or perhaps by AI using shipboard sensors. When autonomous ships are operated under time charter, there will be no difference between the ship's remote operation center logbook[68] and the WRC report in terms of the way data is collected. Both will be done remotely, but the first will be more reliable as it will be collected by an advanced system of autonomous ships and during the actual voyage. There may even be no need for the charterer's WRC arrangement. Autonomous ships will reduce the charterer's main concern that the master may exaggerate the sea and wind conditions and make inaccurate logbook entries to the shipowner's advantage. Even if the records are kept by personnel working at the center arranged by the shipowner, and there may be some contractual relationship between them and the shipowner or between them and a third-party manager arranged by the shipowner, the center personnel or its AI systems will make entries in the ship's logbook based on data collected continuously from the ship. Therefore, even if the charterer has concerns about the records, it can easily request that their accuracy be validated by the shipboard sensors.

[66] Clause 12(e) of NYPE 2015 also indicates that this will be the main source of the shipowner against the underperformance claims.

[67] A logbook is still kept in the case of autonomous ships. This submission can be supported by the recent regulatory work in the UK. Under Annex 2, para. 2.2.2 of the *Workboat Code Edition 3*, it is stipulated that all remotely operated unmanned vessels shall have a working log or equivalent which is completed and kept at the control position (MCA 2023).

[68] As the logbook is no longer kept on board the ship, this terminology may be preferred. Given the level of technology and autonomy involved in operating an autonomous vessel, this book is most likely to be kept electronically by personnel at the operation center.

Following these explanations, it can be said that the description as to the capability of the autonomous ship to record the sea and weather conditions might also be made a part of the ship's description under NYPE 2015, so that the charterer might not need to worry about the records and the WRC arrangement indicated under Clause 12(d). Further consideration might also be needed as to Clause 12(e) of NYPE 2015. The clause indicates that where the ship fails to perform as agreed in the charter, the parties may refer the dispute to "an independent expert or alternative weather service by mutual agreement." These experts resolve disputes over underperformance claims arising from a discrepancy between the parties' evidence. This clause might be changed for autonomous ships, to state that data collected through the ships will prevail.

2.4.2 *The Shipowner's Obligation to Provide a Seaworthy Ship*

Under time charters, for the delivery of the ship to be valid and for the charter period to commence, it is important that the ship meets certain delivery requirements relating to delivery time, the place of delivery, and the condition of the ship, which are commonly set out in the charterparty. These requirements are deemed to be conditions precedent to delivery unless the terms of the contract provide otherwise. Therefore, if the ship does not comply with these requirements, the charterer may reject the ship (Coghlin et al. 2014, para. 8.3). In the context of the operation of autonomous ships, a consideration of the requirements stipulated in time charter forms indicates that those relating to the time and place of delivery may not require reevaluation. However, a more thorough analysis is necessary regarding the requirements concerning the ship's condition.

Standard time charter forms contain terms that specify how the condition of the ship should be at the time of delivery.[69] Most of the forms require the ship to be seaworthy at the time of delivery.[70] The shipowner's seaworthiness obligation under NYPE 2015 is defined in Clause 2(b):

> The Vessel on delivery shall be seaworthy and in every way fit to be employed in the intended service, having water ballast and with sufficient power to operate all cargo handling gear simultaneously, and, with full complement of Master, officers and ratings who meet the Standards for Training, Certification and Watchkeeping for Seafarers (STCW) requirements for a vessel of her tonnage.

Even if the charter does not refer to any express seaworthiness requirement in this regard, this is implied by law.[71] The classic test for seaworthiness at common law is expressed by Scrutton L.J. as follows:

69 Some of these terms are very detailed, such as Clause 1 of Shelltime 4, while others describe the condition of the ship very briefly, such as lines 25–26 of Baltime.

70 See, for example, lines 21–24 of NYPE 46, Clause 2 of NYPE 93 and 2015, Clause 1 of Baltime, Clause 2.1 of BPTime 3, and Clause 1(b) of Shelltime 4.

71 *Kopitoff v. Wilson* (1876) 1 QBD 602.

> The ship must have that degree of fitness which an ordinary careful owner would require his vessel to have at the commencement of her voyage having regard to all the probable circumstances of it. Would a prudent owner have required that it should be made good before sending his ship to sea, had he known of it?[72]

If this question is answered in the affirmative in a particular case, then it can be said that the ship is unseaworthy. The concept of seaworthiness, in relation to traditional ships, enters the analysis mainly under three groups: (1) physical defects of the ship and inadequate and insufficient equipment; (2) inadequacy and insufficiency of the crew; and (3) inadequacy of documentation.[73] The legal principles in this regard are well established, and a substantial body of literature has already been written on this topic (Coghlin et al. 2014, ch. 8; Girvin 2011, 383–399; Kassem 2006; Zhan and Zang 2023). The shipowner's obligation to provide a seaworthy ship will continue, but these three groups should be reinterpreted and subject to potential change for autonomous ships, considered below.[74]

2.4.2.1 Physical Defects of the Ship and Inadequate and Insufficient Equipment

The traditional ship is a single object, the body, called a hull, which contains the machinery, the equipment, and the operation center that holds the crew members. Unlike traditional ships, autonomous ships are composed of two parts: a sea module and a land module. Although these two modules are separated physically, they have an operational and functional connection. Imagine that the sea part of the autonomous ship is working properly, collecting large-scale data through various sensors, cameras, and radar systems. However, there is a regular failure in the transmission of the collected data due to a communication problem related to the center. In such a case, the ship may not be able to operate unless it proceeds autonomously.[75] Defects in the operation center, such as those relating to the cyber risk management system, may also render the ship unseaworthy. Due to this distinctive feature of autonomous ships, two different concepts have been proposed as a new category of seaworthiness: "communication worthiness," which is the ability of the center to maintain continuous connectivity and provide services remotely (Sözer 2024, 85, 88), and "cyber-worthiness," which gauges the efficiency and quality of measures taken against

[72] *F. C. Bradley & Sons Ltd. v. Federal Steam Navigation Co.* (1926) 24 Ll. L. Rep. 446, 454.

[73] These three groups of categorizations are emphasized in *Papera Traders Co. Ltd. v. Hyundai Merchant Marine Co. Ltd. (The "Eurasian Dream")* [2002] 1 Lloyd's Rep. 719, 736–737.

[74] If it is accepted that such an obligation will not be an issue, this will give a harm to the essence of the contractual relations since in such a case the charterer will not be able to use the ship efficiently.

[75] While seaworthiness analysis is made in respect of Hague/Hague-Visby Rules, Professor Baughen and Professor Williams also reached the conclusion that seaworthiness analysis now extends to landward and covers issues related to remote operation centers (Baughen 2021, 83; Williams 2021, 224–225).

cyber-attacks (Sözer 2021, 99–110). Time should tell whether these concepts will enter widespread use.

Furthermore, seaworthiness is a relative term.[76] The concept includes the type and age of the ship, the type of voyage planned, the nature of the cargo, and various other factors (Girvin 2017, 17; Kassem 2006, 25–26; Wilson 2010, 181). Therefore, depending on an autonomous ship's navigational, technical, and operational characteristics, the standard expected from a particular operation center is dynamic and subject to change.

2.4.2.2 Inadequacy and Insufficiency of the Crew

Scholars accept that the inadequacy and insufficiency of the crew for seaworthiness evaluation should extend to personnel in the operation center (Baughen 2021; Stevens 2020, 148; Williams 2021, 226–227). This conclusion is sensible because of the strong functional and operational links between the ship and the operation center. If seaworthiness analysis were not extended to land-based personnel, the charterer's right to use the ship might be harmed fundamentally, undermining the essence of the time charterer. Therefore, the duty to provide adequate and sufficient personnel for the operation center should be imposed on the shipowner as part of its seaworthiness obligation. The most challenging question is how personnel in the operation center are deemed to be adequate or sufficient.

Clause 2(b) of NYPE 2015, regarding the traditional ship, incorporates the International Convention on Standards of Training, Certification, and Watchkeeping for Seafarers (STCW)[77] as a benchmark to assess the crew's situation. The applicability of STCW is regulated in Article III(1), which states that the Convention "shall apply to seafarers serving on board seagoing vessels entitled to fly the flag" of a State party. Following this wording, the application of the Convention directly to personnel in the center so as to evaluate their adequacy and sufficiency might not be possible due to the requirement of working on board and to the qualifications of seafarers (Eder 2019, 55; Soyer 2021, 171; Veal and Tsimplis 2017, 322). However, the absence of specific standards regarding personnel staffing an operation center should not be interpreted as indicating they lack appropriate qualifications. Although personnel will not be present on board, the general approach adopted is to hold their position akin to that of master and crew members.[78] The persons responsible for monitoring and operating the ship from the operation center should have certain qualifications. If these standards are not established, the capability of personnel

[76] *Eridania S.P.A. v. Rudolf A. Oetker (The "Fjord Wind")* [1999] 1 Lloyd's Rep. 307, 315 (Lord Justice Clarke approved this in the Court of Appeal: [2000] 2 Lloyd's Rep. 191, 197). See also Girvin (2011, 384); Stevens (2020, 148, 150).

[77] International Convention on Standards of Training, Certification, and Watchkeeping for Seafarers, July 7, 1978, 1361 UNTS 2 (STCW).

[78] See Section 2.2.2.

working in each center will be different, with the result that the risks to which each ship is exposed during its voyage will vary according to the qualifications of the center's personnel. This can even affect insurance. Determining the required qualifications and competences of personnel in the center may not be easy. First, although the deployment of these personnel will be from land and not from sea, it may still be possible to take into account some of the standards that should be met in relation to seafarers for these personnel. The STCW Appendix to Regulation II/2 contains regulations on the minimum knowledge required for the certification of the masters and chief mates of ships weighing 200 gross registered tons or more:

> A master has ultimate responsibility for the safety of the ship, its passengers, crew and cargo, and that a chief mate shall be in a position to assume that responsibility at any time, examination in these subjects shall be designed to test their ability to assimilate all available information that affects the safety of the ship.

Since personnel working in the center will also be responsible for the safe navigation of the ship and its cargo, it will be appropriate to seek the qualifications and characteristics of the master and chief mate stated in this regulation for personnel working in the operation center, rather than associating them directly with the seafarers on board the ship. For example, the information that personnel in the center may need includes radar devices, meteorology and oceanography, ocean current systems, ship maneuvering and handling, and maritime law. One might think that when a ship with a fourth degree of autonomy is operating autonomously, these skills might not be needed because the ship is capable of performing all functions independently. But that assertion may not be entirely accurate. The ship may start its voyage under full autonomy, but, when it needs human support and remote control, personnel with these skills could have a significant effect.

In addition, the STCW is within the scope of Regulation II/2, the mandatory minimum requirements for being certified as master and first mate on ships weighing over 200 gross tons. Masters and chief mates of ships weighing 1,600 or more gross tons will be required to have an appropriate certificate. To obtain this certificate, each candidate must comply with the conditions set by the flag State administration in terms of health, especially vision and hearing. In addition, for certification as master, at least thirty-six months is needed; however, this period may be reduced to at least twenty-four months if at least twelve months of seagoing service has been performed as a chief mate or if the administration requires special training that is considered equivalent to this service. The health condition required under this regulation can be explained by the ability to fulfil the task effectively, and the condition of having served for a certain period of time before can be explained by the experience requirement of the work to be performed. At this point, similar conditions should also be required from personnel at the center, given the nature of the work to be performed by them.

Following this analysis, to some extent the qualifications required by the STCW can apply to personnel working in the center.[79] Two recent legal steps – the AUTOSHIPMAN form[80] and the UK *Workboat Code Edition* 3[81] – also show that qualifications expressed in the STCW will continue to be applicable. However, the pursuit of the qualifications in the STCW alone will not be sufficient for these personnel due to the distinguishing feature of remote operations. For example, although Clause 5(a) of AUTOSHIPMAN references the STCW, other qualifications also apply: "The Managers shall provide suitably qualified Crew who shall comply with the requirements of the Applicable Laws (including but not limited to the STCW)."[82] Such an approach is sensible because, while personnel in the center ensure the safe navigation of the ship, this navigation is carried out by systems with a high degree of autonomy. This specialized work has particular requirements (Choi and Lee 2021, 461; Williams 2021, 227; Wright 2020, 91).[83] For example, personnel receive training in software, communication technology, and special protocols regarding autonomous ship operation (Veal and Tsimplis 2017, 323). The existing regime regulating the training and certification standards for vessel traffic system personnel (IMO 1997) can be applied to training and certification standards for personnel working in the center (Amaxilati 2022, 120).

In conclusion, with regard to crew-related requirements set out in NYPE 2015, reference to the STCW is necessary but insufficient in terms of an autonomous ship's operation. Additional requirements should be incorporated into the clause. The common position of the JWG regarding personnel capabilities is that training, certification, and competency requirements will be addressed under the MASS Code using the STCW requirement as a basis (IMO 2023b, 5).

2.4.2.3 Adequacy of Documentation

Documentation is the third focus for the seaworthiness analysis of autonomous ships. The governing law of the contract, the law of the flag, or the law of the port

79 For a similar view, see Choi and Lee (2021, 456).

80 AUTOSHIPMAN, Clause 5(a) states: "The Managers shall provide suitably qualified Crew who shall comply with the requirements of the Applicable Laws (including but not limited to STCW)."

81 The *Workboat Code Edition* 3 provides: "Training and certification requirements for manned vessels are applicable to operators of Remotely Operated Unmanned Vessels" (MCA 2023, annex 2, para. 7.2.4).

82 Similarly, Clause 7.2.5 of the *Workboat Code Edition* 3 provides: "A remote operator shall … be appropriately trained and qualified for the remote operation of all vessels they are required to operate" (MCA 2023).

83 For submissions that the STCW and new requirements as to shore-based personnel should found application side by side for cases where a dynamic autonomy level (see Section 2.2.1) from onboard operation to remote control became an issue, and that while the first continues to be applicable for seafarers on board, new requirements are sought for personnel in the center: see Amaxilati (2022, 121); Carey (2017).

may legally require documentation (Girvin 2019, 450; Wilson 2010, 11). Documents relating to cargo, navigational charters, and documents required under the International Safety Management Code and the International Ship and Port Facility Security Code are included in seaworthiness analysis (Kassem 2006, 45). Where the autonomous ship has started to be used, especially for the carriage of goods internationally, documents related to safety management, emergency plans, and documents that show autonomous features of the ship might be required to test compliance of the ship with the relevant port features.

2.4.2.4 Timing for Seaworthiness Analysis

Is the wording in NYPE 2015 regarding the point in time considered for the seaworthiness analysis applicable to the operation of an autonomous ship under time charter? Unlike its predecessors, which required the ship to be in a seaworthy condition and ready to receive cargo at the time of delivery,[84] NYPE 2015 separates the shipowner's obligation to deliver the ship in a seaworthy condition from its obligation to deliver the ship in a cargoworthy condition.[85] The reason for this change is that in practice the first port of loading is usually different from the place of delivery specified in the charterparty.[86] It seems unreasonable to expect the shipowner to provide a vessel capable of carrying cargo when there is no cargo at the place of delivery. Following this separation of the two obligations, Clause 2(c) of NYPE 2015 now gives the parties the right to choose the time at which the shipowner is obliged to provide a cargoworthy vessel. That time can be either at delivery or at the first port of loading, as agreed between the parties. Where time charters are made for an autonomous ship, the wording adopted in NYPE 2015 for cargoworthiness can remain. However, with regard to the analysis of the seaworthiness of an autonomous ship, the author suggests that restricting the shipowner's obligation regarding seaworthiness to the time of delivery may not serve the purpose of the obligation and might significantly affect the charterer's right to use the autonomous ship under the time charter. As explained at the beginning of this chapter, a change in the location of the remote operation center can be an issue during the voyage. If this becomes a regular practice, it might be preferable to provide the opportunity to test the seaworthiness of the ship each time it remotely connects to another remote operation center and to analyze each center following the three criteria set forth above as to seaworthiness. Otherwise, the shipowner may not demonstrate due diligence in choosing a new operation center. In addition, even if the operation center is not changed, a change of personnel working in the

[84] See NYPE 46, lines 21–24; NYPE 1993, lines 33–36.
[85] See NYPE 2015, Clause 2(b)–(c).
[86] See NYPE 2015, Time Charterparty Explanatory Notes, 4.

center may be an issue.[87] Change of a crew is not something that is regularly done during the voyage, as the ship is in the middle of the sea. However, personnel in the operation center may come and go at will. In this sense, autonomous ships are different from traditional ships. This difference might be considered as reasonable grounds for transforming the seaworthiness obligation to a continuous one. Although this approach is not adopted in most time charter forms and the obligation of the shipowner is heavily extended, such a change may be made in the future.

In the context of the operation of autonomous ships, analysis as to delivery requirements stipulated in NYPE 2015 shows that those relating to the time and place of delivery may not require reevaluation. However, a more thorough analysis is necessary with regard to the requirements concerning the condition of the ship – in other words, its seaworthiness.

2.4.3 *The Shipowner's and Master's Obligation to Comply with the Charterer's Orders*

In the context of a time charter, the shipowner, in consideration of payment of hire, grants the charterer the right to exploit the ship's earning capacity[88] and undertakes to provide a specified charter service. Consequently, the time charterer is entitled to provide instructions to the master about how the vessel is used. Almost all time charter forms contain a provision commonly referred to as an employment clause, which delineates the scope of the charterer's authority to issue directives to the master concerning the employment of the ship.[89] For example, Clause 8(a) of NYPE 2015 provides: "The Master … (although appointed by the Owners) shall be under the orders and directions of the Charterers as regards employment and agency." In the absence of an express stipulation in this regard, the obligation is implied because it is necessary to ensure that the contract efficiently works. It should be noted that the master is not obliged to comply with every single order given by the charterer. Under a time charter, the master is obliged to comply with the charterer's instructions as to employment, but does not have such an obligation if the instructions affect the navigation or safety of the ship. This is a well-established principle of English jurisprudence.[90] The distinctions between employment and navigation are articulated by Lord Hobhouse in *The "Hill Harmony"* case: "'Employment'

87 This was also pointed out by Professor Baughen, who submitted that during a particular voyage, different shore-based controllers will be employed at different stages of the ship's operation. Baughen posed the question of when the seaworthiness analysis should be made in such a case (Baughen 2021, 84).

88 *Whistler International Ltd. v. Kawasaki Kisen Kaisha Ltd. (The "Hill Harmony")* [2001] 1 Lloyd's Rep. 147, 156.

89 NYPE 46, Clause 8; NYPE 1993, Clause 8(a); NYPE 2015, Clause 8(a); Baltime, Clause 9; BPTime 3, Clause 10; Shelltime 4, Clause 13(a).

90 For details of this principle, see *Whistler International Ltd. v. Kawasaki Kisen Kaisha Ltd. (The "Hill Harmony")* [2001] 1 Lloyd's Rep. 147; Coghlin et al. (2014, ch. 19).

embraces the economic aspect – the exploitation of the earning potential of the vessel. 'Navigation' embraces matters of seamanship" (at 159). Since the charterer's order regarding the selection of the ports of loading and discharge and orders relating to loading, carriage, and delivery of the cargo embrace an economic aspect, in an ordinary case these must be regarded as lawful employment orders (unless they affect the navigation or safety of the ship, cargo, or crew). Therefore, the master has a duty to follow these orders. Orders that affect the navigation and safety of the ship are left outside the charterer's right to use, as these are "matters falling within the specialized professional maritime expertise of the master" (at 152).

When this obligation of the master is considered in relation to an autonomous ship, the first question is who (in the absence of any master on board the ship) will be responsible for analyzing whether the order given by the charterer has the status of an employment order that the master is obliged to follow, or affects the navigation and safety of the ship, which the master may disregard. This function can be performed by remote operators.[91] It has also been suggested that the word "master" in the abovementioned employment clause of NYPE 2015 should be replaced by "the owners and/or the person or persons operating the vessel" (Baughen 2021, 95). Considering that an autonomous ship is operated under a dynamic level of autonomy,[92] such an approach seems sensible. In a particular case, even if the ship is operated fully autonomously during service at the time of charter, when the order is given by the charterer, the level of autonomy can be reduced to remote operation. The controller can evaluate orders given in terms of safety and navigation and then decide how to proceed. In other words, here the remote operator has started to act in the capacity of the master in assessing the orders,[93] and the remote operator's "professional maritime expertise" is brought into the assessment. In such a case, there might be no need for further analysis of this obligation, as the established rules relating to the master's assessment of the employment orders may also apply to remote operators. For example, when the order is given, it is not expected that the master is obliged to comply with every order immediately. There may be some

[91] Professor Baughen considered Clause 8 of NYPE 2015 regarding the wording that the master shall be under the orders and directions of the charterers and submitted that this function could be performed by a shore-based controller (SBC; Baughen 2021, 95). Although Baughen prefers to use the term "SBC" in his paper, "remote operator" is used throughout this chapter.

[92] For an explanation of a dynamic level of autonomy approach, see Section 2.2.2.

[93] Similarly, for example, it has been submitted that the "reasonable judgment" of the risk to the ship by the master assumes that the master is the person "on the spot" and in a good position to assess the risk to the ship, crew, and cargo. In the third degree of autonomy, the ship is unmanned but remotely controlled, so the "controller" may act in the capacity of the master in assessing the risk. These comments were made on the emphasized wording in the war risks clause (Clause 17(d)) of GENCON 1994: "If at any stage of the voyage after the loading of the cargo commences, it appears that, *in the reasonable judgement of the Master and/or the Owners*, the Vessel, her cargo, crew or other persons on board the Vessel may be, or are likely to be, exposed to War Risks ... and there is another longer route to the discharging port, the Owners shall give notice to the Charterers that this route will be taken." See Hunter (2021, 211).

orders that require further consideration. In such cases, the master has the right to evaluate the order for a reasonable period of time.[94] For an autonomous ship, such time is also provided to the remote operator. Similarly, in terms of a traditional ship, if compliance with the order in question does not fall within the scope of the charter, such as the charterer's last voyage order, causing delay, the master has the right to refuse to comply with it and to ask the charterer for a new order.[95] This can also be applied in a similar way to autonomous ships. In such cases, the remote operator can ask the charterer for a new order.

However, considering that the remote operator is expected to be responsible for the operation and monitoring of more than one ship, it might not be practical that the autonomy level during a particular voyage is reduced and then every single order of the charterer is evaluated by the remote operator. Therefore, it might be useful to leave some place for the independent decision-making ability of the ship under full autonomy. It will be evaluated below to what extent the autonomous ship may itself evaluate the charterer's orders under three groups without human support.

The first group comprises employment orders, with which the master is under an obligation to comply. Unless it affects the safety and navigation of the ship, it is expected that the autonomous system also complies with these orders. It is unclear whether the system is capable of making such an assessment. At this point, it might be useful to mention how these systems are to be operated.

AI applications mimic human cognitive and decision-making processes, achieving navigation safety on par with, if not exceeding, vessels manned by humans. In doing so, human-induced risks may be eliminated altogether. AI systems do not merely execute preprogrammed instructions, although it is impossible to program a system to account for every potential problem and solution. Rather, these systems must be capable of adapting to dynamic conditions, much like the crew members they aim to replace, and be able to resolve unforeseen issues (Porathe et al. 2018, 422). As such, it is highly probable that machine-learning methods will be predominantly employed in the management of these ships (Ringbom and Collin 2021, 10; Vartdal et al. 2018, 10). During machine-learning processes involving technology that enables computers to perform complex tasks by learning from examples, data, and experience (Royal Society 2017, 16), humans can play an active role, either by categorizing or labeling the data for the machine to analyze or, in a more limited capacity, by correcting the machine's erroneous predictions or selections (Wright 2020, 54–55).[96]

94 *Midwest Shipping Company Ltd. Inc. v. D. I. Henry (Jute) Ltd. (The "Anastasia")* [1971] 1 Lloyd's Rep. 375, 379; *Kuwait Petroleum Corporation v. I & D Oil Carriers Ltd. (The "Houda")* [1994] 2 Lloyd's Rep. 541.

95 *Torvald Klaveness A/S v. Arni Maritime Corporation (The "Gregos")* [1995] 1 Lloyd's Rep. 1; *The Alma Shipping Corporation of Monrovia v. Mantovani (The "Dione")* [1975] 1 Lloyd's Rep. 115, 118.

96 For the explanations and citations given in this paragraph, the author is indebted to Dr. Selim Ciğer (Ciğer 2024, 1142–1143).

In some cases, the ship itself may be capable of evaluating the employment status of the charterer's order. For example, if the charterer's order is to depart from the port at a certain time, as that time approaches, the ship itself can evaluate the order in terms of safety, using data on weather and sea conditions collected by the ship's sensors. The system can then determine the most appropriate response to these conditions. Similarly, when the charterer orders the ship to slow steam or to proceed with full speed, the ship can evaluate whether it is required to comply or whether the order should be refused for safety or navigational reasons in accordance with the algorithm, engine capacity of the ship, and charterparty performance warranties. Recall, however, that time charters, by their very nature, rely on continuous adaptability to accommodate instructions from the charterer, and each order introduces potential unanticipated occurrences. Therefore, if the order given is the one that the ship itself cannot evaluate and make a decision about within its algorithm, human support might be needed. In such a case, the autonomy level can be reduced swiftly to remote operation, and the remote operator's approval, or final decision, can proceed based on the charterer's orders.

The second group comprises the orders that the master has a right to refuse. These are the orders that fall outside the scope of the agreed charter. If the effect of the employment order given by the charterers is to require the master to do something outside that scope of the agreed charter, the order requires the shipowner to provide services that it has not agreed to provide at the beginning. The master has a right to refuse this order. When the vessel is operated fully autonomously, it may be possible for the ship to evaluate these orders, taking into account the geographical and time restrictions of the charterparty. When the order is given, the autonomous system of the ship without any human support can consider algorithms related to agreed limitations and then refuse to comply with the order on the ground that it is outside the scope of the agreed charter terms. For example, if the last voyage order exceeds the agreed charter period given by the charterer, the system can calculate the length of the proposed voyage and then refuse it. Similarly, if the order causes the ship to proceed to a port outside the agreed geographical limits, the system can refuse to comply with the order. The system can correctly analyze the situation and refuse these orders on the ground that they are outside the scope of the charter. The master has a right to refuse the second group of orders. However, the master may also prefer to comply with this group of orders even though they exceed the limits of the charter. If an autonomous ship makes a decision that the shipowner does not like, a remote operator could come into an active position to overrule it.

Lastly, the master is under an obligation to refuse the third group of orders. These are orders that cause illegal and fraudulent acts (Williams 2013, 148).[97] The common

97 Professor Williams also indicates the orders that subject the ship and crew to danger as orders that the master is obliged to refuse. The role of safety in the assessment of an employment order has been considered previously and will not be revisited here.

example relates to a bill of lading. For example, after the cargo has been loaded on board the ship, the charterer may ask the master to sign the date of the bill earlier than the actual date. Such an order is particularly likely to be given if the charterer has entered into a sales contract under which it, as the seller, is obliged to complete the loading of the cargo on the specified date. In order not to breach its obligation under the contract of sale, the terms insist that the master signs the bill of lading as an ante-date bill of lading. Similarly, the charterer may also order the master to sign the date of charter later than the actual date (that is, postdate the bill of lading). In some cases, the charterer might also order the master to record the goods as being in apparent good order and condition, although the goods are not in such a state.[98] Since the purpose of such orders by the charterer is to defraud the consignee, the master is obliged to refuse them. The master is also under an obligation to refuse the charterer's order to deliver the cargo to a person who does not have a right to receive it, unless there is an express term to the contrary in this regard.[99]

Following this information, the question is whether the autonomous system can evaluate this type of order. Even if the ship is eligible to perform loading and discharging operations autonomously, given that a paper bill of lading is still required, since there will be no crew on board the ship, the evaluation of these types of orders can only be possible if there is involvement of a shipowner's land-based personnel. This is not something that can be done by the autonomous system or by the remote operator from another center. In terms of autonomous ship operations, if the electronic bill of lading is an issue, the author believes that land-based personnel support is still needed, but signing the bill of lading as ante or postdate can be prevented by the autonomous system.

Continuous reference to human oversight for routine operations would undermine the intended efficiency of autonomous systems. Even if the autonomous system has a role in the assessment of the charterer's order, it cannot be fully delegated to technology. An autonomous ship should do what it can to the extent of its capabilities, but if it encounters unforeseen risks or conditions that fall outside the scope of its programming and machine-learning process, it becomes essential to rely on the approvals and decisions of remote operators as to the status of the charterer's order. Following this, it is now clear that Clause 8(a), the employment clause, of NYPE 2015 should be redrafted and the obligation to comply with the charterer's order should be imposed on "the owners and/or the person or persons operating the ship and/or the autonomous system itself."

98 See *Naviera Mogor S.A. v. Société Metallurgique de Normandie (The "Nogar Marin")* [1988] 1 Lloyd's Rep. 412. This is actually not a time charter case: voyage charterers presented an inaccurate bill of lading (although the goods were not in good condition, the bill of lading contained a statement that they were shipped in apparent good order and condition).

99 See *Enichem Anic S.p.A. v. Ampelos Shipping Co. Ltd. (The "Delfini")* [1990] 1 Lloyd's Rep. 252.

Where the time charterer's orders have been assessed by the ship's independent decision-making ability, in some cases legal issues may also arise as to the indemnity right of the shipowner. Indemnity is normally implied when the shipowner suffers loss or liability because of complying with the charterer's orders, unless the shipowner has agreed in the charter to bear the loss, damage, or liability in question (Coghlin et al. 2014, para. 19.32), or unless the order in question is one that the master is under an obligation to refuse (para. 19.19). The principle of causation is integral to indemnity claims. For shipowners to recover under implied indemnities, there must be an unbroken chain of causation between the instructions of the charterers and the loss suffered.[100] The advent of autonomous systems seems to challenge this direct causation paradigm. For example, if an autonomous ship grounds at an ostensibly safe port, as in *The "Erechthion"* case,[101] causation might not be straightforward. Was the grounding due to defective programming, erroneous input data, the inherent unsafety of the port, or the charterer's order? The court's finding in *The "Erechthion"* – that the grounding was proximately caused by compliance with charterers' orders – could be difficult to transpose onto autonomous scenarios. Moreover, *The "Island Archon"*[102] demonstrates that liability flows from charterers' orders when risks are not contractually assumed by the owners. It was held by the Court of Appeal that an indemnity was to be implied, since the risk of incurring liability for dubious cargo claims was one that, under the charter, the owners had not agreed to bear. An analogous argument could arise with autonomous ships where programming errors exacerbate port risks. The legal system must address whether such errors constitute an extension of the charterers' orders or an independent navigation failure.

2.4.4 *The Charterer's Obligation to Use the Ship between the Safe Ports*

The advent of autonomous ships also plants a flag on a reevaluation of traditional principles, such as the safe port obligation. The charterer's obligation to send ships only to ports that can accommodate them safely is one of the key aspects of a time charterparty. This obligation is expressly stipulated under standard charter forms.[103]

[100] *A/B Helsingfors Steamship Company Ltd. v. Rederiaktiebolaget Rex (The "White Rose")* [1969] 2 Lloyd's Rep. 52, 59; *Royal Greek Government v. Minister of Transport (The "Ann Stathatos")* (1949) 83 Ll. L. Rep. 228.

[101] *New A Line v. Erechthion Shipping Co. S.A. (The "Erechthion")* [1987] 2 Lloyd's Rep. 180.

[102] *Triad Shipping Co. v. Stellar Chartering & Brokerage Inc. (The "Island Archon")* [1993] 2 Lloyd's Rep. 388; appeal in [1994] 2 Lloyd's Rep. 227.

[103] NYPE 46, lines 27–35; NYPE 93, Clause 5; Baltime, Clause 2; Shelltime 4, Clause 4(c). In the absence of any express provision regarding trading of the vessel between safe ports, the court may imply a term in this regard if this is necessary to give business efficiency to the contract. See *Vardinoyannis v. The Egyptian General Petroleum Corporation (The "Evaggelos Th.")* [1971] 2 Lloyd's Rep. 200; *Atkins International H.A. v. Islamic Republic of Iran Shipping Lines (The "APJ Priti")* [1987] 2 Lloyd's Rep. 37, 42.

Clause 1(b) of NYPE 2015 states: "The Vessel shall be employed in such lawful trades between safe ports and safe places within the following trading limits [text to be entered here] as the Charterers shall direct." The existence of such a provision primarily requires the charterer to direct the ship to a prospectively safe port.[104] This kind of provision is also construed to mean that if the port becomes unsafe later due to a change of circumstances while the ship is still en route, the charterer then has a secondary obligation to cancel its previous order and provide a new, prospectively safe port for the vessel.[105] The reason behind imposing a secondary obligation on the charterer regarding unsafe ports is mainly to protect the shipowner and also the crew and any third-party interests.

The automation and digitization of ships and ports redefines what constitutes the well-established general principle of a "safe port" and, particularly, the meaning of "safety." Therefore, the principle in question, rooted in protecting vessel integrity, requires recalibration to address the uniqueness posed by autonomous ships. The notion is intricately linked with the master's responsibility to navigate the ship safely and the charterer's obligation to nominate safe ports. This recalibration can be made through reference to the earlier decisions embodied in case law, as stated in *The "Mary Lou"*: points of law could arise that were not covered by the general principles, and it might then be helpful to consult earlier authorities, albeit that the conclusion of the court on such points of law should be consistent with those general principles.[106] The seminal definition of a safe port was articulated by Sellers L.J. in *The "Eastern City"*:

> A port will not be safe unless, in the relevant period of time, the particular ship can reach it, use it and return from it without, in the absence of some abnormal occurrence, being exposed to danger which cannot be avoided by good navigation and seamanship.[107]

The question of whether a port is safe for a particular vessel at a particular time is a subjective one, and the answer depends on the particular circumstances of each case. As English case law developed over time, various modalities emerged to define the concept. These include the identification of dangers as either temporary or persistent, the establishment of monitoring and reporting systems, the consideration of delays and inordinate duration, the evaluation of local warnings and departure systems, the adequacy of warning systems, the analysis of deficient berthing and mooring facilities, the evaluation of navigational aids, and the assessment of safety in

[104] *Kodros Shipping Corporation v. Empresa Cubana De Fletes (The "Evia" (No 2))* [1982] 2 Lloyd's Rep. 307, 320.
[105] *The "Evia" (No 2)*, 320.
[106] *Transoceanic Petroleum Carriers v. Cook Industries Inc. (The "Mary Lou")* [1981] 2 Lloyd's Rep. 272, 276.
[107] *Leeds Shipping Company Ltd. v. Société Française Bunge (The "Eastern City")* [1958] 2 Lloyd's Rep. 127, 131.

departure. Considering these modalities, this analysis will first focus on the meaning of safe ports. Such an analysis is necessary to decide whether the charterer is in breach of its obligation to nominate a safe port under the time charter in the case of autonomous ships. The charterer's duty to nominate a safe port must extend beyond mere physical hazards to encompass the burgeoning risks associated with cybersecurity. In this regard, digital resilience is an integral component of the "safe port" doctrine (Shazi 2024, 3, 14).

2.4.4.1 The Meaning of Safety in the Light of Modalities

TYPES OF DANGERS. Temporary dangers described in English case law are those that arise sporadically or unpredictably and that do not inherently define the port's characteristics. Temporary dangers for autonomous ships may include weather events, systemic failures in AI navigation due to disrupted satellite signals, and unplanned latency in V2X (Vehicle-to-Everything) communication. Regarding the impact of temporary dangers on the concept of safe port, it is submitted that purely temporary dangers will not make a port unsafe. But temporary dangers may be an important element in a lack of safety, particularly if the existence of the danger is not known to the master of the ship.[108] We may infer that the temporary danger might also make the port unsafe in some circumstances.

Temporary risks, manageable through navigation, do not render a port unsafe. As Teare J. noted in *The "Ocean Victory"*: "The measure of safety is not what is 'reasonable' but whether any dangers in a port can be avoided by good navigation and seamanship."[109] The legal principles articulated in cases such as *The "Evia" (No. 2)* emphasize that charterers are not liable for a lack of safety arising from "unexpected and abnormal events" that are transient in nature. Lord Roskill clarified this principle:

> If those characteristics are such as to make that port or place prospectively safe in this way, I cannot think that in spite of them, some unexpected and abnormal event thereafter suddenly occurs, which creates conditions of unsafety where conditions of safety have previously existed and as a result the ship is delayed, damaged or destroyed, that contractual promise extends to making the Charterer liable for any resulting loss or damage, physical or financial.[110]

Following this, if the temporary danger in the port might be accounted as an unexpected and abnormal event, the charterer might escape liability. Yet temporary dangers like weather events could be handled by real-time adjustments in the ship's

[108] *Independent Petroleum Group Ltd. v. Seacarriers Count Pte. Ltd. (The "Count")* [2008] 1 Lloyd's Rep. 72, para. 22.

[109] *Gard Marine & Energy Ltd. v. China National Chartering Co. Ltd. (The "Ocean Victory")* [2014] 1 Lloyd's Rep. 59, para. 100.

[110] *The "Evia" (No. 2)*, 315.

course or speed, if it is assumed that the system is equipped to respond. In addition, temporary dangers might be set aside, requiring advanced systems capable of real-time data processing for autonomous ships. These ships must rely on continuous environmental monitoring and data analytics to mitigate short-term hazards, such as adverse weather or sudden navigational obstructions, that may otherwise jeopardize port safety.

Persistent dangers, such as silting, may render a port inherently unsafe. In contrast to temporary dangers, persistent threats are integral to the port's nature. For autonomous ships, structural issues with the port or a consistent failure in port systems can be considered as persistent dangers. In *The "Houston City,"* the absence of hauling-off buoys and a missing fender, both long-standing deficiencies, rendered the port inherently unsafe.[111] Such deficiencies are recognized as fundamental breaches of the charterer's obligations. Sellers L.J., in *The "Stork,"* affirmed that it is not enough that a danger merely exists: the danger must be of such a nature that it constitutes a characteristic of the port that renders it unsafe.[112] For autonomous ships, addressing persistent dangers entails integrating these known risks into the programming of navigation and decision systems. The importance of standardized digital infrastructures in ports, including cybersecurity protocols and the consistent maintenance of physical and digital systems, is needed to ensure that these dangers do not compromise vessel safety. Thus, the liability implications of algorithmic errors versus port deficiencies remain a contentious area. Persistent cyber vulnerabilities, for example, could be likened to the physical deficiencies in *The "Houston City"* if they are endemic to the port's infrastructure and might require that the port in question is accepted as an unsafe port.

PROPER SYSTEMS FOR MONITORING AND REPORTING. Ports must integrate predictive technology and redundancies to handle autonomous ships, ensuring that temporary dangers (such as a loss of network coverage) are managed. The absence of AI-compatible safety systems may render a port unsafe, even if traditional dangers (such as weather) are manageable. Modern jurisprudence increasingly emphasizes port systems and information dissemination over inherent physical risks: the focus of

[111] *Reardon Smith Line Ltd. v. Australian Wheat Board (The "Houston City")* [1956] 1 Lloyd's Rep. 1.

[112] *Compania Naviera Maropan S/A v. Bowater's Lloyd Pulp and Paper Mills Ltd. (The "Stork")* [1954] 2 Lloyd's Rep. 397; appeal in [1955] 1 Lloyd's Rep. 349. In *The "Stork,"* the key issue was whether Tommy's Arm was an unsafe port. The court found that it was unsafe because it had inherent characteristics – such as its small size and exposure to regular gales – that created a persistent and unavoidable risk to ships using it. Even though the master was aware of the potential danger and had been reassured by a pilot, the port was still deemed unsafe because the risk was inherent to the location itself and could not be mitigated by the ship's ordinary precautions. Thus, a port is not unsafe merely because a danger exists, but because the danger is an inherent feature of the port itself. Temporary, unusual, or avoidable hazards (such as an isolated act of negligence by a pilot) do not necessarily render a port unsafe unless they form part of the port's general characteristics.

unsafe port arbitrations is very often about the systems in place for dealing with known physical risks, as much as or more than physical risks.[113] For example, in *The "Marinicki,"*[114] a lack of proper systems for monitoring channel safety and reporting hazards rendered the port unsafe, even if the obstruction itself was temporary or minor. It is unclear whether autonomous ships can integrate real-time data and rely on existing port information systems, or whether ports must develop new systems that cater to their specific needs. Failure to provide this could make a port unsafe for autonomous ships under the standard set forth in *The "Marinicki."* Given this logic, ports are required to adopt cybersecurity measures that are certified in accordance with ISO standards to safeguard autonomous ships from external threats.

DELAYS. Delays at ports can transform a prospectively safe port into an unsafe one, particularly when the delay exposes the ship to additional risks. *The "Lucille"*[115] reflects the proposition that a port prospectively safe at the time of nomination can become unsafe due to congestion or other factors. This is exacerbated for autonomous ships, as they depend on digital optimization and predictive scheduling, leaving them particularly vulnerable to unforeseen delays. For example, without dynamic adjustment to traffic flows or access to real-time data on congestion, autonomous systems may fail to adequately reposition vessels to mitigate risks. Ports accommodating autonomous ships should have AI-integrated scheduling systems that minimize delays and offer automated contingency plans. The absence of such capabilities might render a port retrospectively unsafe, as autonomous ships lack the onboard human discretion to compensate for failures of external systems. However, the involvement of a remote operator might set aside potentially unsafe situations. Autonomous ships may also face difficulties in handling delays caused by unforeseen circumstances, such as cyberattacks, temporary infrastructure failures, or weather disruptions. The ability of an autonomous ship to respond to such delays may be affected by the sophistication of its navigational algorithms and the availability of alternatives for diversion. If delays lead to frustration of the voyage or inordinate duration, the port might be deemed unsafe.

LOCAL WARNINGS AND DEPARTURE SYSTEMS. The court in *The "Dagmar"*[116] emphasized the necessity of local warning systems to ensure that ships receive adequate notice to depart during adverse weather. This principle applies even more

[113] For cases that emphasize port systems, see, for example, the early case of *Smith v. Dart* (1884) 14 QBD 105 and the more recent case of *Maintop Shipping Company Ltd. v. Bulkindo Lines Pte. Ltd. (The "Marinicki")* [2003] 2 Lloyd's Rep. 655.

[114] *Maintop Shipping Company Ltd. v. Bulkindo Lines Pte. Ltd. (The "Marinicki")* [2003] 2 Lloyd's Rep. 655.

[115] *Uni-Ocean Lines Pte. Ltd. v. C-Trade S.A. (The "Lucille")* [1983] 1 Lloyd's Rep. 387.

[116] *Tage Berglund v. Montoro Shipping Corporation Ltd. (The "Dagmar")* [1968] 2 Lloyd's Rep. 563.

stringently to autonomous ships if they rely entirely on digital inputs and preset programming for decision-making. Local warning systems should interface with the vessel's autonomous operating system to trigger immediate adjustments in course or initiate departure sequences. *The "Khian Sea"*[117] demonstrates the need for ports to provide systems to ensure that vessels can depart promptly in emergencies. For autonomous ships, these systems should include automated departure protocols that integrate weather forecasts, traffic conditions, and berthing clearances into vessel operating systems. A port failing to provide digitally integrated warnings and departure mechanisms tailored for autonomous ships likely would breach its safe port obligation.

ADEQUACY OF WARNING SYSTEMS. The adequacy of warning systems directly relates to whether a port can mitigate risks prospectively. *The "Ocean Victory"* stressed the importance of a systematic approach where warnings must be part of a broader infrastructure capable of addressing the risks associated with navigation and berth safety. For autonomous ships, the adequacy test extends beyond traditional systems (such as weather alerts and meteorological data) to encompass cybersecurity protocols. Autonomous systems are vulnerable to cyberattacks that could distort critical warning data or disable the ship's response mechanisms. For instance, a port's warning system for autonomous ships should be capable of verifying the authenticity and accuracy of incoming data to prevent tampering. Systems such as blockchain-enabled communications and secure V2X protocols have emerged as benchmarks for adequacy. A failure to provide these safeguards would compromise the safe port doctrine, as autonomous ships are entirely dependent on reliable digital inputs.

DEFICIENT BERTHING AND MOORING FACILITIES. A port may be deemed unsafe if the mooring or berthing facilities are inadequate. The impact of deficient facilities for mooring or berthing, which are prerequisites for autonomous ships, may constitute unsafe conditions if they cannot accommodate the specific operational parameters of autonomous ships, such as automated docking systems. For example, in *The "Houston City,"* the ship was damaged in a northerly gale due to the absence of a hauling-off buoy and a section of fender. It was held that Geraldton was unsafe for the ship because of these deficiencies. The case demonstrates that even temporary or localized inadequacies in infrastructure, such as missing buoys or fenders, create foreseeable risks that can render a port unsafe. This principle translates to the autonomous shipping context by necessitating a reevaluation of infrastructure compatibility. Autonomous ships require berths equipped with automated docking systems, such as dynamic positioning fenders, automated mooring arms, and AI-

[117] *Islander Shipping Enterprises S.A. v. Empresa Maritima Del Estado S.A. (The "Khian Sea")* [1979] 1 Lloyd's Rep. 545.

driven berth allocation systems. The absence of facilities designed for autonomous operations, such as robotic line handlers or AI-guided fender positioning, may directly impact the vessel's ability to safely berth or unberth. Ports failing to provide these modernized systems could be deemed unsafe, particularly where the deficiencies foreseeably impair the vessel's autonomous systems, resulting in physical damage or delays.

NAVIGATIONAL AIDS. Navigational aids are critical to a port's safety and were addressed in *The "Saga Cob,"* which emphasized the role of navigational aids in neutralizing hazards such as properly lighted channels.[118] For autonomous ships, this requirement should extend to digital navigational aids such as real-time hydrographic updates, geofencing capabilities, and high-accuracy GPS. The failure to provide such aids would disproportionately affect autonomous ships that rely on machine-readable inputs. *The "Sussex Oak"*[119] noted that risks beyond the port's control, such as the presence of sea ice, require navigational aids to mitigate the ship's exposure. A port's failure to provide accurate digital aids, such as unreliable hydrographic surveys or poorly maintained electronic charts, may expose autonomous ships to navigation errors. These vulnerabilities can be mitigated by remote monitoring and operation, but the availability of robust navigational aids can still be considered essential to meeting the safe port standard. For example, ports utilizing augmented reality overlays for channel navigation have set new benchmarks, demanding that autonomous ships receive real-time guidance tailored to their specific draught and size. It is thought that the absence of these systems compromises the navigational safety of autonomous ships, particularly in ports with dynamic environmental conditions, such as siltation or shifting currents.

CYBERSECURITY RISKS. Even if the adequacy of port safety is provided through equipment and infrastructure, political and physical risks may also be present. For example, *The "Evaggelos Th."*[120] draws attention to political risks, such as confiscation or war, while *The "Saga Cob"* emphasizes that political threats must be an inherent characteristic of the port. In that regard, autonomous ships may introduce new threats to political safety, including State interference in digital systems (such as forced shutdowns and GPS spoofing) and risks tied to AI export controls and proprietary software regulations. Ports in politically volatile regions must demonstrate technological sovereignty and robust cybersecurity protocols to be deemed safe for autonomous ships. As per *The "Chemical Venture,"* charterers must exercise due

[118] *K/S Penta Shipping A/S v. Ethiopian Shipping Lines Corporation (The "Saga Cob")* [1992] 2 Lloyd's Rep. 545, 550.

[119] *G. W. Grace & Co Ltd. v. General Steam Navigation Company Ltd. (The "Sussex Oak")* [1949] 83 Ll. L. Rep. 297.

[120] *Vardinoyannis v. The Egyptian General Petroleum Corporation (The "Evaggelos Th.")* [1971] 2 Lloyd's Rep. 200.

diligence to assess political and physical safety.[121] In doing so, reasonable care includes evaluating the apparent degree of danger.[122] For autonomous ships, it can be said that due diligence requires assessing port compatibility with autonomous systems and cybersecurity certifications of the port. Failure to evaluate these risks can be considered a breach of due diligence obligations.

2.4.4.2 The Charterer's Defenses to Avoid Liability

The safe port obligation also allocates liability for losses resulting from an unsafe port to the charterer who nominates it.[123] However, as can be inferred from the definition of a safe port in *The "Eastern City"* case, the charterer can escape liability if the danger is avoidable by ordinary good navigation and seamanship, or if there is an abnormal event. At this point, it is important to look at how these two exceptions will be interpreted in terms of autonomous ship operations.

ABNORMAL OCCURRENCES. Abnormal occurrences (such as rare storms or collisions caused by third-party negligence) are those that do not render a port unsafe unless inherent in the port's characteristics.[124] In the author's view, for autonomous ships, cyberattacks or failures in digital traffic management are no longer "abnormal" but are predictable risks in technologically dependent ports. Abnormal occurrences, such as sudden algorithmic failures or external interference, must be anticipated in port risk assessments (Wróbel et al. 2017, 159, 166). Ports that fail to provide adequate risk mitigation protocols should not be considered safe. Autonomous ships require ports to ensure resilience against digital anomalies and redundancy in communication protocols. The traditional doctrine of "abnormal occurrences" should exclude cyber-related failures that may be anticipated. A port prone to frequent cyber threats would be inherently unsafe for an autonomous ship.

GOOD NAVIGATION AND SEAMANSHIP. It is also important to note that a port is only considered unsafe if the risk in question cannot be avoided by the exercise of good seamanship and navigation. This implies that the shipowner and the master of a ship cannot exonerate themselves from their responsibility to mitigate the consequences of risks that, with reasonable diligence, they could have circumvented (Coghlin et al. 2014, para. 10.46). In the event of loss occurring in such circumstances, the liability shall not fall upon the charterer.

[121] *Pearl Carriers Inc. v. Japan Line Ltd. (The "Chemical Venture")* [1993] 1 Lloyd's Rep. 508.
[122] *The "Saga Cob,"* 407–408.
[123] *St. Vincent Shipping Co. Ltd. v. Bock, Godeffroy & Co. (The "Helen Miller")* [1980] 2 Lloyd's Rep. 95.
[124] See *The "Mary Lou"* and *The "Ocean Victory."*

In *The "Polyglory,"* the test for safety rests on whether an ordinary prudent and skillful master can reasonably overcome the risks.[125] Yet, the paradigm shift introduced by autonomous ships necessitates a reevaluation of this doctrine. Autonomous systems, equipped with algorithm-driven navigation, now assume the role traditionally entrusted to the master. However, these systems cannot, in isolation, encompass the discretionary prudence that lies at the heart of good seamanship. Where dangers arise that extend beyond the predictive capabilities of an autonomous system – such as an unforeseen port hazard, digital anomaly, or operational complexity – the role of a remote operator must be considered. This hybrid model (a dynamic level of automation) recognizes that the principle of good seamanship in autonomous navigation cannot be reduced solely to AI performance. Instead, it is augmented by the oversight of a remote operator, whose intervention replicates – to the extent practicable – the judgment of a prudent and skillful master.

Autonomous ships are designed to perform navigational tasks with precision, but their programming can be inherently limited to programmed scenarios. For example, if a port experiences sudden cyber disruptions or physical hazards, the remote operator's ability to intervene and reassess the situation ensures that the ship's actions adhere to the principles of good seamanship. As noted in *The "Ocean Victory,"* "safety is not absolute, but the measure of safety is whether any dangers in a port can be avoided by good navigation and seamanship" (para. 100). This principle now applies equally to the collaborative functioning of AI systems and remote operators, so that all risks – whether physical or digital – are managed with prudence and skill. The fundamental inquiry remains, as articulated in *The "Ocean Victory,"* whether any dangers in a port can be avoided by good navigation and seamanship. For autonomous ships, it can be said that this inquiry incorporates two critical components: (1) AI's operational capacity, which is the primary executor of good seamanship in routine navigation – that is, whether the autonomous system, operating as programmed, can navigate safely within the anticipated parameters of port conditions; and (2) remote operator intervention, which acts as the secondary layer of decision-making, stepping in when the vessel's AI systems encounter risks outside its programmed parameters. To this end, as an adjunct to the vessel's navigation, the remote operator does not supplant the AI but ensures that its actions are aligned with maritime principles when faced with unforeseen events. A failure to recognize this dual structure would be to ignore the realities of modern navigation and, indeed, to leave the vessel bereft of the discretionary judgment required under the doctrine of good seamanship.

[125] *Kristiandsands Tankrederi A/S v. Standard Tankers (Bahamas) Ltd. (The "Polyglory")* [1977] 2 Lloyd's Rep. 353, 363. Similarly, it was pointed out in *The "Ocean Victory"* that the standard required is that "expected of the ordinary prudent and skilful master": para. 112.

2.4.4.3 Suggestions for the Application of the Safe Port Doctrine for Autonomous Ships

The available modalities for interpreting the "safe port" principle and the charterer's defense to avoid liability are interpreted above in the context of autonomous shipping. Since the safe port doctrine is mainly developed by case law, and the obligation of the charterer to use the ship only between safe ports is included in NYPE 2015 with the words "The Vessel shall be employed . . . between safe ports and safe places," this author does not propose any changes to the text. This wording is also applicable in terms of autonomous ships. However, in NYPE 2015, an autonomous ship can specifically be recognized, so the language should be amended to account explicitly for the safety requirements of technologically advanced vessels. For example, "safe port" should be redefined to include compatibility with autonomous ship infrastructure, such as sensor networks, automated berthing systems, and robust cybersecurity measures. More importantly, the meaning of safety and exceptions in the context of autonomous ships should be reinterpreted by case law. Globally recognized standards for smart port technologies should be adopted, ensuring consistency and reliability across international ports.

2.4.5 *The Charterer's Obligation to Payment of Hire-Off Hire*

The payment of hire by the charterer in consideration of the use of the ship is another obligation for consideration in relation to the autonomous ship. This obligation is expressly stipulated under Clause 17 of NYPE 2015. In the case of autonomous ships operating under time charter, it is important to acknowledge that the charterer's obligation remains unchanged. The expectation is that the remote operation services are arranged by the shipowner. In most cases, these services will be provided by third-party shipping management companies upon agreement with the shipowner, rather than the shipowner setting up its own center. Since the time charterer will be outside the contractual relationship between the shipowner and the center, the charterer should not be exposed to any further obligation as to payment made in consideration of remote and autonomous operation of the ship. This responsibility should remain with the shipowner. The author suggests that, in the context of autonomous ships engaged in time charter operations, the discussion surrounding payment of hire is likely to be predominantly focused on the concept of off-hire. An off-hire clause is a common feature of time charters.[126] While the exact wording of these clauses varies among charters, it serves to release the charterer from its obligation to pay the hire for a period during which the ship cannot be used due

[126] See NYPE 46, Clause 15; NYPE 93, Clause 17; NYPE 2015, Clause 17; Baltime, Clause 11(a); Shelltime 4, Clause 21(a); Shelltime 3, Clause 21; BPTime 3, Clause 19.

to circumstances beyond its control.[127] Clause 17 of NYPE 2015 contains two main parts. The latter part of the clause addresses the issue of loss of time resulting from a decrease in the ship's speed. This constitutes an alternative avenue for loss recovery for the charterer in cases of underperformance of the ship.[128] The section requiring further consideration in terms of an autonomous ship is the initial part of the clause, which refers to particular events:

> *In the event of loss of time from deficiency and/or default and/or strike of officers or ratings, or deficiency of stores, fire, breakdown of, or damage to hull, machinery or equipment, grounding, detention by the arrest of the Vessel, . . . or detention by Port State control or other competent, authority for Vessel deficiencies, or detention by average accidents to the Vessel or cargo, unless resulting from inherent vice, quality or defect of the cargo, drydocking for the purpose of examination, cleaning and/or painting of underwater parts and/or repair*, or by any other similar cause preventing the full working of the vessel, payment of hire and overtime, if any, shall cease for the time thereby lost. (emphasis added)

There are two potentially problematic issues surrounding the off-hire clause in NYPE 2015 regarding autonomous ships in time charters. The first is the impact of the text "preventing the full working of the ship." Although the clause quoted above is silent as to whether the charterparty must be completely interrupted or whether the partial loss of the service provided in a particular case is sufficient to accept that the full operation of the vessel is prevented, the NYPE off-hire clause is a net loss of time clause.[129] Therefore, a partial loss of the charterparty service is also accepted as sufficient for the charterer to benefit from the off-hire clause. Following this, if an autonomous ship operation is prevented partially, for example, it can still be said that the charterer benefits from the off-hire clause.

The second problematic issue is related to events that trigger the off-hire clause. It is accepted that the vessel will be off-hired if these specified events prevent the full operation of the ship. Some of the italicized text identifies events that may still have a role in terms of autonomous ship operations. For example, issues pertaining to the radar system or sensor of the autonomous ship can be interpreted under the

[127] *Mareva Navigation Co. Ltd. v. Canaria Armadora S.A. (The "Mareva A.S.")* [1977] 1 Lloyd's Rep. 368, 381.

[128] For how the second part of the clause has a role in underperformance claims, see Coghlin et al. (2014, paras. 25.78–25.81). Although comments in that book regarding the relevant subject focus on the wording (lines 99–100) in NYPE 46, the wording preferred in the second part of the off-hire clause in NYPE 2015 (lines 402–405) is not different. Therefore, it is submitted that the explanations offered are also valid for NYPE 2015.

[129] The authors of the *Time Charters* book, while evaluating the net loss of time status of the off-hire clause in NYPE 46, noted the wording "shall cease for the time thereby lost" in line 99 of NYPE 46. They submitted: "Clauses of this kind, which allow the charterers to deduct hire equivalent to the amount of time lost, rather than for the whole of a defined period, are called 'net loss of time'" (Coghlin et al. 2014, para. 25.56). Following this, since similar wording also exists in NYPE 2015, it can be said that clause 17 of NYPE 2015 is also a net loss of time clause.

"machinery or equipment" group. Although the first part of the events responds, to some extent, to the need for autonomous ship operations, the problems that may arise in relation to the remote operation center, such as a physical deficiency of the center preventing the full operation of the ship, do not fall under any of the events listed. This is normal because autonomous ship operations were not considered when the clause was drafted. It is also important to explore whether at least the second part of the events expressed in the clause under the wording of "by any other similar cause" prevent the full working of the vessel and its lash-up to the operation center.

At first sight, the text appears to cover all types of events that prevent the full operation of the vessel. It may be suggested that all types of events that occur during the operation of an autonomous ship and prevent the full working of the ship could fall under this group. Following this, during the operation of an autonomous ship, if there are any problems related to the remote operation center or personnel in the center, the charterer could benefit from the off-hire provision under this category. However, due to the existence of the word "similar," the text must be regarded as referring to the same types of causes as those previously mentioned in Clause 17.[130] The term therefore will only apply to other similar causes listed in the first part of the clause. When the events listed in the first part above are considered in terms of autonomous ship operations, none of them appear related to events that might arise at a remote operation center. Therefore, it is difficult to include the loss of time in relation to the operation center and personnel in the center in the "any other similar cause" wording. If the word "whatsoever" is inserted and the wording in the NYPE 2015 off-hire clause is redrafted as "any other cause whatsoever," there will be no need for the causes to be the same as those in the list to trigger the off-hire clause.[131] This approach underscores the dispositive effect of the word "whatsoever."[132] In such cases, problems relating to remote operation centers or personnel at the centers can

[130] It should be noted here that, contrary to the wording of NYPE 93 and NYPE 2015 ("any other similar cause"), the wording "any other cause" is preferred to express the second part of events under NYPE 46, so that the word "similar" is missing. However, it is submitted that this wording is also interpreted as covering the same types of causes as those previously mentioned in line 99 of NYPE 46 on grounds of a rule of construction known as the *ejusdem generis* rule: *Andre & Cie S.A. v. Orient Shipping (Rotterdam) B.V. (The "Laconian Confidence")* [1997] 1 Lloyd's Rep. 139, 150; see also Coghlin et al. (2014, paras. 25.37–25.41). Adding "similar" before "any other cause" under the off-hire clause in NYPE 93 and NYPE 2015 simply makes the *ejusdem generis* causes explicitly effective (Coghlin et al. 2014, para. 25.41).

[131] For examples of cases related to the interpretation of the "whatsoever" wording, see *Belcore Maritime Corporation v. F.LII. Moretti Cereali S.p.A. (The "Mastro Giorgis")* [1983] 2 Lloyd's Rep. 66; *Andre & Cie S.A. v. Orient Shipping (Rotterdam) B.V. (The "Laconian Confidence")* [1997] 1 Lloyd's Rep. 139, 151; *Cosco Bulk Carrier Co Ltd. v. Team-Up Owning Co Ltd. (The "Saldanha")* [2011] 1 Lloyd's Rep. 187, para. 36.

[132] *Belcore Maritime Corporation v. F.LII. Moretti Cereali S.p.A. (The "Mastro Giorgis")* [1983] 2 Lloyd's Rep. 66, 68.

fall within the second part of the events and the charterer can gain the benefit of the off-hire clause. However, inclusion of the phrase "whatsoever" will widen the scope of the off-hire clause considerably, so it will be challenging to convince the shipowner to accept this new text. Instead, the easier solution would be that, considering the nature of autonomous ship operation, the list of events given in the initial part of the clause is expanded to include new events sui generis to the remote operation center, such as a breakdown of the connection system, software issues, and data transmission problems. It should be noted that although these problems arise, in some cases this might not prevent the full operation of the ship and loss of time may not arise. For example, if the ship is operated remotely and its control and operation are lost due to a failure in data transmission, and the ship's autonomous operation feature comes into play (as a result of the dynamic autonomy of the ship) and the ship is still able to operate on its own, there will be no loss of time, so there will be no off-hire period. In addition, it is possible that the service provided in the operation center is disturbed due to fire, flood, earthquake, or other natural events, so that the full working of the ship is prevented. Such events might also be incorporated into the clause. As given above, the off-hire clause also refers to particular events related to the crew – such as deficiency, default, or labor strike – and those types of events might also arise at the center. Such a situation is, of course, more manageable than at sea, but might still cause loss of time for the charterer. Therefore, a deficiency, default, or labor strike of personnel in the center should be included in the clause.[133]

Given that the occurrence of some types of events, such as communications or software problems, may regularly disturb the operations of autonomous ships, the incorporation into the clause of a provision for de minimis events is sensible. Such a provision makes the activation of an off-hire clause conditional on the minimum period required by the clause to have been lost due to events specified in the clause.[134] For example, according to the de minimis provision in BPTime 3, the ship is not considered to be off-hire in a case in which the loss of time is less than three hours in any calendar month. Under that clause, the charterer is deemed to have calculated the time lost due to an off-hire event incorrectly if it takes into account a loss of time less than three hours. The addition of such a provision in NYPE 2015 could prevent the expected but common problems related to software and connection problems from causing legal issues between the parties if they occur for only a short period of time.

[133] Professor Baughen also draws attention to the fact that the phrase "deficiency and/or default and/or strike of officers" will have no meaning in relation to the autonomous operation of the ship. It has been suggested that this wording should be redrafted to refer to "servants or agents of the owners involved in the performance of the charter" to serve the purpose of the off-hire clause. See Baughen (2021, 96).

[134] See Shelltime 4, lines 346–348; BPTime 3, lines 352–353.

2.5 CONCLUSION

The integration of AI into the maritime shipping sector is advancing rapidly. While autonomous vehicle technology is nearing practical implementation on roads, with automotive manufacturers worldwide competing for dominance, similar developments are occurring in the maritime domain both domestically and internationally. Autonomous ships play a critical role in military missions, hydrographic surveys, and oil exploration. The shipping sector of the carriage of goods by sea has also started to benefit from autonomous ships, but this benefit is currently limited to domestic carriage. Moving AI into international seagoing vessels is challenging due to the lack of an international framework. Developing an AI regime for international shipping will be possible only after the MASS Code has been completed. However, the adoption of the Code may not be sufficient to enable autonomous ships to trade globally. Standard maritime contracts, such as charterparties and management contracts, should also be ready for this type of carriage. The latter are now in place, with the AUTOSHIPMAN form recently released by BIMCO. However, no steps have been taken to integrate autonomous shipping in the law governing charterparties. This chapter offered elements for a regime for time charters.

The analysis shows that the wording of NYPE 2015 is not flexible enough to accommodate the concept of autonomous shipping with regard to the fundamental obligations of the shipowner and charterer under time charters. These terms need to be reconsidered and the clauses dealing with these obligations under NYPE 2015 should be redrafted. Regarding the shipowner's obligation to provide a ship that complies with the charter description, it can simply be said that it is necessary to add new elements as part of the ship's description. The shipowner's obligation to provide a seaworthy ship should be reevaluated considering issues as to the remote operation center and personnel at the center so that the time charterer uses the ship efficiently during the period of charters. Time charters, by their very nature, rely on continuous adaptability to accommodate instructions from the charterer. Analysis of the shipowner's obligation to comply with the charterer's order shows that the assessment of the status of the charterer's orders, whether they are employment orders or not, by an AI system might not always be an issue. The remote operator is likely to be involved in the assessment process in some cases. This shows the importance of a dynamic autonomy level in ship operations, especially under time charters. With regard to the charterer's obligation to use the ship only between safe ports, it is imperative to reevaluate the concept of a safe port within the context of case law, taking into account features of the autonomous ships and their operational capabilities. Finally, the off-hire clause of NYPE 2015 needs to be redrafted to cover events relating to the remote operation center and personnel employed there, as these may cause the charterer to lose some level of service during the charter period. Although there is no separate analysis in this chapter regarding the wording of master and crew used in NYPE 2015, it can simply be said that this language should be replaced with the words "shipowner, remote operator, or personnel at the center," and the form should include a definition of what the remote operator and remote personnel mean in the context of the form.

REFERENCES

AAWA (Autonomous Waterborne Applications Initiative). 2016. "Remote and Autonomous Ships: The Next Steps." AAWA Position Paper.

Alexander, Leon. 2013. "Speed & Performance: Discrepancies between Ships' Data and Independent Weather Bureaus." *Clyde & Co Shipping Newsletter*, February 8.

Amaxilati, Zoumpoulia. 2022. "The Human Element in Autonomous Shipping." In *Disruptive Technologies, Climate Change and Shipping*, edited by Barış Soyer and Andrew Tettenborn. Informa Law.

Barber, K. Suzanne, Anuj Goel, and Cheryl E. Martin. 2000. "Dynamic Adaptive Autonomy in Multi-Agent Systems." *Journal of Experimental & Theoretical Artificial Intelligence* 12 (2): 129–147.

Baughen, Simon. 2019. *Shipping Law*. 6th ed. Routledge.

2021. "Unmanned Vessels and International Conventions for the Carriage of Goods by Sea." In *Artificial Intelligence and Autonomous Shipping: Developing the International Legal Framework*, edited by Barış Soyer and Andrew Tettenborn. Bloomsbury.

Berger, Paul. 2024. "DP World Is Seeking to Build a Trade Hub in Mexico." *Wall Street Journal*, September 25.

BIMCO (Baltic and International Maritime Council). 2015. "NYPE 2015." Accessed December 18, 2024. www.bimco.org/contracts-and-clauses/bimco-contracts/nype-2015.

2024a. "AUTOSHIPMAN Now Available." December 17. Accessed December 20, 2024. www.bimco.org/insights-and-information/contracts/20241217-autoshipman-now-available.

2024b. "BIMCO Approves First Management Agreement for Autonomous Ships." November 8. Accessed December 20, 2024. www.bimco.org/news/priority-news/2024 1009-autonomous-ships.

Burmeister, Hans-Christoph, Wilko Bruhn, Ørnulf Jan Rødseth, and Thomas Porathe. 2014. "Can Unmanned Ships Improve Navigational Safety?" *Transport Research Arena (TRA) 5th Conference: Transport Solutions from Research to Deployment*. Accessed January 25, 2025. https://publications.lib.chalmers.se/records/fulltext/198207/local_198207.pdf.

Cain, Fiona, and Matthew Turner. 2018. "Autonomous Ships: Are We Ready?" Hayes Boone, May 17. www.haynesboone.com/news/publications/cain-and-turner-on-autonomous-ships.

Carey, Luci. 2017. "All Hands Off Deck? The Legal Barriers to Autonomous Ships." CML Working Paper Series, No. 17/06.

2019. "Report on BIMCO Autonomous Ship Seminar." Report 19/01, National University of Singapore, Centre for Maritime Law.

Choi, Junghwan, and Sangil Lee. 2021. "Legal Status of the Remote Operator in Maritime Autonomous Surface Ships (MASS) under Maritime Law." *Ocean Development & International Law* 52 (4): 445–462.

Ciğer, Selim. 2024. "Yeni Tip Gemilerin İşleyiş Esasları Bakımından Otonomi Kavramı ve IMO'nun Otonom Gemi Kategorileri Üzerine Düşünceler." *İstanbul Hukuk Mecmuası* 82 (4): 1135–1183.

CMI (Comité Maritime International). 2023. "Maritime Law for MASS." Accessed December 20, 2024. https://comitemaritime.org/work/mass/.

Coghlin, Terence, Andrew W. Baker, Julian Kenny, John D. Kimball, and Thomas H. Belknap, Jr. 2014. *Time Charters*. 7th ed. Informa Law.

Combine Goodz. 2021. "Mediterranean Shipping Company." September 14. Accessed January 20, 2025. www.combinegoodz.com/blog/Mediterranean-Shipping-Company/.

Coraddu, Andrea, Luca Oneto, Beatriz Navas de Maya, and Rafet Kurt. 2020. "Determining the Most Influential Human Factors in Maritime Accidents: A Data-Driven Approach." *Ocean Engineering* 211: 107588.

Davies, Mark. 2005. *Bareboat Charters: A Practical Guide to the Legal and Insurance Implications*. 2nd ed. Informa Law.

Dindar, Ceren Cerit. 2017. "The Performance of the Chartered Ship: A Much Clearer Obligation under the NYPE 2015?" *Journal of International Maritime Law* 23 (6): 425–442.

Eder, Bernard. 2019. "Unmanned Vessels: Challenges Ahead." *Lloyd's Maritime and Commercial Law Quarterly* 25 (1): 47–56.

Fukuto, Junji. 2021. "Automation Levels of Automated/Autonomous Ships." *ClassNK Technical Journal* 4: 35–50.

Girvin, Stephen. 2011. *Carriage of Goods by Sea*. 2nd ed. Oxford University Press.

2017. "The Obligation of Seaworthiness: Shipowner and Charterer." CML Working Paper Series, No. 17/11.

2019. "The Carrier's Fundamental Duties to Cargo under the Hague and Hague-Visby Rules." *Journal of International Maritime Law* 25 (6): 443–462.

Harris, Graham. 2014. "Speed and Consumption." *Speed and Consumption Issues Conference*, London Shipping Law Centre, October 22.

Hunter, Grant. 2020. "First Ever Standard Form Contract for Autonomous Ship Operation Underway." BIMCO, November 6.

2021. "Standard Contracts for the MASS(es): Charterparties and Other Arrangements for Autonomous Ships." In *Ship Operations: New Risks, Liabilities and Technologies in the Maritime Sector*, edited by Barış Soyer and Andrew Tettenborn. Informa Law.

IMO (International Maritime Organization). 1997. "Guidelines for Vessel Traffic Services." A 20/Res.857 (December 3, 1997).

2017a. "Final Report: Analysis of Regulatory Barriers to the Use of Autonomous Ships." Submitted by Denmark. MSC 99/INF.3 (January 18, 2017).

2017b. "Scoping Exercise on Autonomous Vessels Put on Agenda." www.imo.org/en/MediaCentre/MeetingSummaries/Pages/MSC-98th-session.aspx.

2018a. "IMO Takes First Steps to Address Autonomous Ships." May 25. www.imo.org/en/MediaCentre/PressBriefings/Pages/08-MSC-99-MASS-scoping.aspx.

2018b. "Regulatory Scoping Exercise for the Use of Maritime Autonomous Surface Ships (MASS): Report of the Working Group." MSC 99/WP.9 (May 23, 2018).

2018c. "Report of the Maritime Safety Committee on Its Ninety-Ninth Session." MSC 99/22 (June 5, 2018).

2021. "Outcome of the Regulatory Scoping Exercise for the Use of Maritime Autonomous Surface Ships (MASS)." MSC.1/Circ.1638 (June 3, 2021).

2022a. "Development of a Goal-Based Instrument for Maritime Autonomous Surface Ships (MASS): Draft Road Map for Maritime Autonomous Surface Ships." MSC 105/7 (April 22–29, 2022).

2022b. "Report of the Maritime Safety Committee on Its 105th Session." MSC 105/20 (May 19, 2022).

2023a. "Common Issues Identified in the RSEs of the Three Committees and How Best to Address Them, Including Consideration of the Outcome of MSC 106, FAL 47 and LEG

110 and Any Documents Referred to MASS-JWG 2 by the Three Committees." Submitted by IFSMA. MASS-JWG 2/2/1 (March 8, 2023).

2023b. "Development of a Goal-Based Instrument for Maritime Autonomous Surface Ships (MASS): Report of the MSC-LEG-FAL Joint Working Group on Maritime Autonomous Surface Ships (MASS) on Its Second Session." MSC 107/5/1 (May 2, 2023).

2023c. "Development of a Goal-Based Instrument for Maritime Autonomous Surface Ships (MASS): Results of a Transoceanic Voyage Test with Autonomous Navigation System." Submitted by the Republic of Korea. MSC 107/INF.18 (March 28, 2023).

2023d. "Development of a Goal-Based Instrument for Maritime Autonomous Surface Ships (MASS): Study on the Definition and Organization of a Remote Control Centre (RCC) with a View to Its Certification." Submitted by Belgium. MSC 107/INF.14 (March 28, 2023).

2023e. "Report of the Maritime Safety Committee on Its 107th Session." MSC 107/20 (June 26, 2023).

2024a. "Consideration of Common Issues, Taking into Account Those Identified in the RSE and by FAL 47, LEG 110 and MSC 107." Network Governance Submitted by Liberia, Republic of Korea, and United Arab Emirates. MASS-JWG 3/3/3 (March 27, 2024).

2024b. "Maritime Safety Committee: 109th Session (MSC 109), December 2–6, 2024." Accessed January 20, 2025. www.imo.org/en/MediaCentre/MeetingSummaries/Pages/MSC-109th-session.aspx.

Infomaritime. 2018. "Timeline: Development of Autonomous Ships (1970s–2018)." June 8. http://infomaritime.eu/index.php/2018/06/08/timeline-development-of-autonomous-ships/.

Inoue, Soichiro, and Hideo Mori. 2021. "Development of Automated Ship Operation Technologies: MEGURI 2040 Unmanned Ship Demonstration Experiment Project." *ClassNK Technical Journal* 3: 59–66.

Karlis, Thanasis. 2018. "Maritime Law Issues Related to the Operation of Unmanned Autonomous Cargo Ships." *World Maritime University Journal* 17 (1): 119–128.

Kassem, Ahmad Hussam. 2006. "The Legal Aspects of Seaworthiness: Current Law and Development." PhD diss., Swansea University.

Kongsberg. 2021. "Kongsberg Maritime: Remote Operation Center." https://youtu.be/UPtdgiIrlJI?feature=shared.

Kretschmann, Lutz, Hans-Christoph Burmeister, and Carlos Jahn. 2017. "Analyzing the Economic Benefit of Unmanned Autonomous Ships: An Exploratory Cost-Comparison between an Autonomous and a Conventional Bulk Carrier." *Research in Transportation Business & Management* 25: 76–86.

KRISO. n.d. "Autonomous Ship Verification & Evaluation Research Center." Accessed January 20, 2025. https://kriso.re.kr/menu.es?mid=a20202070000.

London Club. 2001. "Weather-Wise Performance." *Stoploss Bulletin* 21 (February): 1.

Maersk. 2022. "A.P. Moller-Maersk Divests Its Share in Global Ports." August 29. www.maersk.com/news/articles/2022/08/29/maersk-divests-its-share-in-global-ports.

Man, Yemao, Monica Lundh, and Thomas Porathe. 2015. "From Desk to Field: Human Factor Issues in Remote Monitoring and Controlling of Autonomous Unmanned Vessels." *Procedia Manufacturing* 3: 2674–2681.

Marine Industry News. 2022. "China Launches Autonomous Container Ship Zhi-Fei." May 4. https://marineindustrynews.co.uk/china-launches-autonomous-container-ship-zhi-fei/.

Maritime UK. 2022. *Being a Responsible Industry: Maritime Autonomous Ship Systems (MASS) UK Industry Conduct Principles and Code of Practice*. Version 5.

Massterly. 2024. "Remote Operations Centre Opened." March 8. www.massterly.com/archives/blog-post-title-three-mrmsx.
n.d. "Massterly: Pioneering the Autonomous Shipping Industry." www.massterly.com.
Mayflower 400 UK. n.d. "The Mayflower Autonomous Ship." Accessed January 10, 2025. www.mayflower400uk.org/mayflower-autonomous-ship/.
MCA (Maritime and Coastguard Agency). 2023. *The Workboat Code Edition 3: The Safety of Small Workboats and Pilot Boats: A Code of Practice*.
Met Office. 2023. *Factsheet 6: The Beaufort Scale*. National Meteorological Library and Archive.
MUNIN (Maritime Unmanned Navigation through Intelligence Networks). 2016. "Final Report Summary: MUNIN (Maritime Unmanned Navigation through Intelligence in Networks)." https://cordis.europa.eu/project/id/314286/reporting.
Nippon Foundation. n.d. "The Nippon Foundation MEGURI2040 Fully Autonomous Ship Program." Accessed January 25, 2025. www.nippon-foundation.or.jp/en/what/projects/meguri2040.
Ocean Infinity. 2022. "Remote Control Centre Goes Live." February 15. https://oceaninfinity.com/remote-control-centre-goes-live/.
OceanWave Sail. n.d. "Douglas Sea Scale." Accessed January 25, 2025. https://oceanwavesail.com/explore-sailing/douglas-sea-scale/.
Plomaritou, Evi, and Anthony Papadopoulos. 2017. *Shipbroking and Chartering Practice*. 8th ed. Informa Law.
Porathe, Thomas, Nicole Costa, and Åsmund Tjora. 2014. *MUNIN D7.4: Organizational Layout of SOC*. MUNIN.
Porathe, T. Å. Home, Ø. Rødseth, K. Fjørtoft, and S. O. Johnsen. 2018. "At Least as Safe as Manned Shipping? Autonomous Shipping, Safety and 'Human Error.'" In *Safety and Reliability: Safe Societies in a Changing World*, edited by Stein Haugen, Anne Barros, Coen Gulijk, Trond Kongsvik, and Jan Erik Vinnem. CRC Press.
Ringbom, Henrik, and Fellix Collin. 2021. "Terminology and Concepts." In *Autonomous Ships and the Law*, edited by Henrik Ringbom, Erik Røsæg, and Trond Solvang. Routledge.
Rolls-Royce. 2016a. "Autonomous Ships: The Next Step." www.rolls-royce.com/~/media/Files/R/Rolls-Royce/documents/%20customers/marine/ship-intel/rr-ship-intel-aawa-8pg.pdf
Rolls-Royce. 2016b. "Rolls Royce Plans to Deploy Fully Autonomous Cargo Ships by 2020." Accessed January 25, 2025. https://youtu.be/yRwQ95vXVmM?feature=shared.
Royal Society. 2017. *Machine Learning: The Power and Promise of Computers That Learn by Example*. DES4702.
Shazi, Ntandokazi. 2024. "An Evaluation of the Safe Port Obligation in the Light of Smart and Autonomous Ships." NUS Law Working Paper 2024/005, NUS Centre for Maritime Law Working Paper 24/02.
Ship Technology. 2017. "YARA Birkeland Autonomous Container Vessel." October 5. www.ship-technology.com/projects/yara-birkeland-autonomous-container-vessel/?cf-view.
Soyer, Barış. 2020. "Autonomous Vessel and Third Party Liabilities: The Elephant in the Room." In *New Technologies, Artificial Intelligence and Shipping Law in the Twenty-first Century*, edited by Barış Soyer and Andrew Tettenborn. Informa Law.
2021. "The Future of Autonomous Shipping: The Regulatory Challenge." In *Artificial Intelligence and Autonomous Shipping: Developing the International Legal Framework*, edited by Barış Soyer and Andrew Tettenborn. Bloomsbury.

Soyer, B. A. Tettenborn, and G. Leloudas. 2022. *Remote Controlled and Autonomous Shipping: UK Based Case Study*. Swansea University, Institute of International Shipping and Trade Law.

Sözer, Bülent. 2021. "Seaworthiness within the Context of Cyber Risks: Cyberworthiness." In *Ship Operations: New Risks, Liabilities and Technologies in the Maritime Sector*, edited by Barış Soyer and Andrew Tettenborn. Informa Law.

2024. *Unmanned Ships and the Law*. Informa Law.

SpaceX. 2021. "A Shortfall of Gravitas." SpaceOFFSHORE, July. https://space-offshore.com/a-shortfall-of-gravitas/.

Stevens, Frank. 2020. "Carrier Liability for Unmanned Ships; Goodbye Crew, Hello Liability?" In *New Technologies, Artificial Intelligence and Shipping Law in the 21st Century*, edited by Barış Soyer and Andrew Tettenborn. Informa Law.

Tettenborn, Andrew. 2020. "Shipping: Product Liability Goes High-Tech." In *New Technologies, Artificial Intelligence and Shipping Law in the Twenty-first Century*, edited by Barış Soyer and Andrew Tettenborn. Informa Law.

Tunfors, Henrik. 2022. "Evolution of IMO's MASS: Through the Prism of the Chair." In *Autonomous Vessels in Maritime Affairs: Law and Governance Implications*, edited by Tafsir Matin Johansson, Jonatan Echebarria Fernández, Dimitrios Dalaklis, Aspasia Pastra, and Jon A. Skinner. Palgrave Macmillan.

Vartdal, Bjørn Johan, Rolf Skjong, and Asun Lera St. Clair. 2018. "Remote-Controlled and Autonomous Ships." DNV GL Maritime, Position Paper.

Veal, Robert, and Michael Tsimplis. 2017. "The Integration of Unmanned Ships into the *Lex Maritima*." *Lloyd's Maritime and Commercial Law Quarterly* 2: 303–335.

Wilhelmsen. 2024. "Massterly Launches Pioneering Remote Operation Centre in Horten." March 20. www.wilhelmsen.com/media-news-and-events/news/2024/massterly-launches-pioneering-remote-operation-centre-in-horten/.

Williams, Richard. 2013. *Gard Guidance on Maritime Claims and Insurance*. Gard.

2021. "Unmanned Ships: A Challenge to the Current International Regime Regulating the Carriage of Goods?" In *Ship Operations: New Risks, Liabilities and Technologies in the Maritime Sector*, edited by Barış Soyer and Andrew Tettenborn. Informa Law.

Wilson, John F. 2010. *Carriage of Goods by Sea*. 7th ed. Pearson Education.

Wright, Robin Glenn. 2020. *Unmanned and Autonomous Ships: An Overview of MASS*. Routledge.

Wróbel, Krzysztof, Jakub Montewka, and Pentti Kujala. 2017. "Towards the Assessment of the Potential Impact of Unmanned Vessels on Maritime Transportation Safety." *Reliability Engineering & System Safety* 165: 155–169.

Yang, Xue, Ingrid B. Utne, Stian S. Sandøy, Marilia A. Ramos, and Børge Rokseth. 2020. "A Systems-Theoretic Approach to Hazard Identification of Marine Systems with Dynamic Autonomy." *Ocean Engineering* 217: 107930.

Yara. 2023. "The Fully Autonomous, Battery-Powered Container Feeder." Accessed January 10, 2025. www.yara.com/news-and-media/media-library/press-kits/yara-birkeland-press-kit//.

Yara. 2024. "Yara Birkeland, Two Years On." April 28. www.yara.com/knowledge-grows/yara-birkeland-two-years-on/.

Zhan, Xiankai, and Pengfei Zhang. 2023. *Merchant Ships' Seaworthiness: Law and Practice*. Routledge.

Ziajka-Poznańska, Ewelina, and Jakub Montewka. 2021. "Costs and Benefits of Autonomous Shipping: A Literature Review." *Applied Sciences* 11 (1): 4553.

3

AI at Sea

Implications for Seafarers and Maritime Labor Law

Khanssa Lagdami

3.1 INTRODUCTION

Artificial intelligence (AI) is a branch of computer science focused on creating intelligent systems capable of performing tasks typically requiring human intelligence, such as reasoning, learning, problem-solving, visual perception, and language processing (Glover 2024). Unlike traditional data-processing methods, which tend to be less analysis-oriented, AI systems learn from data. The more data AI systems collect, the better they learn and perform tasks as humans do (Obschonka and Audretsch 2020). AI is recognized as an intelligent system capable of processing vast quantities of data known as big data and extracting relevant information from it. Big data and AI complement each other. This involves extensive sources of both structured and unstructured data from various origins, including sensors, social media, and transactions, and making sense of them. AI technologies employ machine learning, neural networks, and deep learning to identify patterns within big data, predict outcomes, and generate new knowledge. AI can undertake complex tasks that would otherwise require human effort, such as making decisions in uncertain situations, learning from experience to improve performance, and generating new data, as seen with generative AI models (Liu 2021).

The maritime industry, which is the backbone of global trade and the economy, is making tremendous efforts to adopt AI to enhance efficiency and safety and to fuel optimization, predictive maintenance, voyage optimization, and energy management (Durlik et al. 2024). Big data analytics platforms process vast amounts of ship performance and navigation data to support decision-making, ranging from logistics optimization to energy efficiency and safety improvements (Munim et al. 2023). A study by Zhang and Martinez indicates that approximately 35 percent of newly built merchant ships currently utilize AI-powered navigational systems (Zhang and Martinez 2023). The most notable applications in this area are automated identification systems supported by machine-learning capabilities, which allow for improved tracking and collision avoidance. These systems utilize inputs from various sources, such as radar, weather forecasts, and satellite imagery, to enhance the predictive accuracy of potential navigational hazards. Nevertheless, they still operate under human oversight rather than as fully autonomous solutions (Johannsen et al. 2024).

This technological advancement is expected to significantly impact the maritime workforce, including seafarers and shore-based personnel. Conventional skills may need to evolve alongside emerging technological competencies, demanding a paradigm shift in maritime education and training. Research conducted by the World Maritime University in 2023 revealed changes in seafarers' task performance, including the introduction of new roles and responsibilities, modifications to existing activities, adaptation to managing emerging technologies, and the need for diverse new vocational skills and knowledge (WMU 2023). A notable example is the evolution of navigational aids on a ship's bridge. The study highlighted the transitions occurring across various maritime professions. This transition is not limited to navigation but also extends to engineering and maintenance operations. AI-based technology is increasingly being used to redefine, predict, and optimize ship maintenance, helping to reduce corrective maintenance costs (Gupta 2024). However, this transformation may require engineers to develop new skills in data analysis and the management of systems that generate and process large volumes of data (WMU 2023).

The maritime industry has sought to address various disruptive changes while highlighting the emerging issues facing the maritime workforce. The International Maritime Organization (IMO) published an e-navigation strategy to facilitate the use of digital tools on board, as detailed in MSC 85/26 (IMO 2008). The circular outlines a vision for the future of navigation systems and vessel traffic information, aiming to establish harmonized data and communication frameworks to mitigate the increasing challenges associated with the safe and efficient operation of ships. In this context, the IMO conducted a scoping exercise for Maritime Autonomous Surface Ships (MASS) from 2017 to 2021 to assess the impacts of rising levels of automation on safety, security, and the environment, completing the e-navigation plan.

From the perspective of technology developers, integrating digitalization, information, and communication technologies, including AI, into the maritime industry and onboard ships is a high priority for enhancing safety and operational efficiency. Research reveals that while these advancements offer numerous benefits, they have also introduced various challenges, such as technostress and mental health concerns among seafarers (Lagdami 2024). Moreover, digitalization and ICT depend on reliable connectivity, which increases the risk of cyberattacks. Therefore, such advancements can sometimes be counterproductive and ineffective. As a result, the impact of these emerging technologies on growth and employment is more complex than traditionally perceived and heavily depends on the institutional and policy context (Aghion et al. 2019).

With the advancement of autonomous ships, scholars hold differing opinions on the future role of seafarers. Some seem to support the idea that automation may reshape rather than reduce employment opportunities (Fonseca et al. 2021), while others argue that the AI-driven revolution will not necessarily threaten jobs but is likely to lead to a more skilled workforce (Aghion et al. 2019). This latter perspective is backed by studies such as the one conducted by the Hamburg School of Business Administration (HSBA) for the International Chamber of Shipping, focusing on seafarers and digital disruption. That study indicates that the advent of autonomous ships would redefine rather than eliminate seafarers' roles, increasing the demand for skilled professionals, particularly marine officers, over the next twenty years. While crew size may adapt due to technological advancements on board, the maritime industry may also see significant additional shore-based job opportunities that require maritime expertise (HSBA 2018).

The preceding discussion highlights the apparent advantages perceived by all regarding the integration of AI in the maritime sector. However, a critical yet often overlooked aspect is the utilization of big data and algorithms associated with AI systems onboard ships, particularly concerning the surveillance and control responsibilities assigned to seafarers. Therefore, this chapter primarily examines the application of AI in the maritime sector and its potential impact on seafarers, given the currently limited use of AI on ships. It also analyzes the legal dimensions and their ramifications for the maritime sector, focusing specifically on the Maritime Labour Convention (MLC)[1] and other legal instruments regulating maritime labor, such as the International Convention on Standards of Training, Certification, and Watchkeeping for Seafarers (STCW).[2]

3.2 AI APPLICATIONS IN THE MARITIME INDUSTRY AND THE IMPLICATIONS FOR SEAFARERS

The application of AI in maritime operations has accelerated significantly since early 2020. The maritime industry has increasingly adopted AI-powered systems for autonomous shipping, predicting maintenance needs, enhancing safety through real-time monitoring, and conducting risk management, among other functions (Spire Maritime n.d.). These systems process vast amounts of data from sensors, historical trends, and real-time environmental conditions, integrating them into decision-making processes that were previously reliant solely on human judgment. This shift suggests a future where ships may operate independently without human

[1] Maritime Labour Convention, February 23, 2006, 2952 UNTS 3 (MLC).

[2] International Convention on Standards of Training, Certification, and Watchkeeping for Seafarers, July 7, 1978, 1361 UNTS 2, as amended (STCW). The STCW entered into force on April 28, 1984.

intervention, introducing challenges to traditional and conventional labor structures and frameworks.

3.2.1 *AI and Autonomous Shipping*

AI enables the operation of autonomous ships that can operate with few or no crew members on board, utilizing advanced technologies for navigation, safety, and efficiency. As classified by the IMO, MASS are divided into four degrees of autonomy: degree one (automated processes and decision support), degree two (remotely controlled ship with a crew on board), degree three (remotely controlled ship without a crew on board), and degree four (fully autonomous ship; Askari and Hossain 2022). AI is essential for MASS operations, including route optimization, collision avoidance, predictive maintenance, and autonomous decision-making. However, its integration also introduces challenges concerning crew roles, legal liability, and regulatory frameworks. Autonomous ships, especially at degrees three and four, lessen the requirement for onboard crew, potentially resulting in job losses or transitions to shore-based positions, igniting ongoing debates and discussions in the maritime industry regarding potential job displacement versus the preservation of traditional seafarer roles (Lee 2023).

One of the notable projects involving AI applications in maritime is Yara Birkeland, widely recognized as the world's first fully autonomous container ship. Developed by a fertilizer company with the support of Rolls-Royce, this container ship utilizes AI for navigation, collision avoidance, and energy management. The ship sails without a crew on board, relying on shore-based control, which is considered the third degree of autonomy (Youd 2022). Rolls-Royce's vision for autonomous vessels demonstrates just how powerful AI can be in achieving fully autonomous operations through ongoing trials (RINA 2018). Forecasts suggest that, by the mid-2030s, up to 3,000 autonomous or semi-autonomous ships will be deployed, necessitating the widespread adoption of AI, according to the HSBA 2018 report. A more recent study conducted by DNV and commissioned by the Maritime Just Transition Task Force predicts that as many as 800,000 seafarers will require additional training and upskilling by the mid-2030s to enable the shipping industry to transition toward alternative fuels and decarbonization (Kaspersen et al. 2022). This research highlights the challenges faced by the maritime sector in addressing the increasing uncertainties about the specific skills and profiles required for the future maritime workforce.

3.2.2 *Maritime Voyage Optimization*

Technologies based on AI systems are revolutionizing maritime voyage planning and route optimization. As one of the most advanced technologies, AI can efficiently process vast amounts of real-time data, such as fluctuations in weather conditions, changing ocean currents, and active ship traffic, to identify the most efficient and secure maritime routes (Riviera News 2022). One example of these technologies is OptiNav AI, a commercialized solution designed as an innovative maritime voyage-planning tool that heavily relies on big data. Powered by cutting-edge technology, this tool strategically utilizes key parameters of maritime operations, including adverse weather conditions, equipment efficiency, and potential security risks.[3] OptiNav AI, through the use of advanced algorithms, has continually achieved significant fuel savings, demonstrating that such solutions can navigate intelligently – optimizing vessel performance with cost efficiency – while safely navigating the open seas (True North Marine 2025).

AI algorithms also play an important role in conducting accurate energy-based performance analysis of maritime routes. By comparing features such as variable weather conditions, ocean currents, and fuel consumption ratios of ships, the algorithms can optimize energy-efficient routes for vessels (Unoks 2024). With these sophisticated systems, delivery operations can organize power more efficiently, ultimately affecting overall performance and reliability. This technology could simultaneously reduce the need for specific human roles, potentially leading to job displacement. This shift prompts significant debates and discussions about the onboard roles of seafarers, many of whom derive pride and fulfillment from their expertise at sea. However, the integration of AI may lead to the creation of new roles, requiring upskilling and adaptation. As with other emerging technologies, the resilience and adaptability of seafarers will be crucial in aiding navigation through this transformation of the industry.

As this type of technology automates the navigational routines of ships, its impact on seafarers must be carefully managed. The maritime industry should prioritize collaboration between humans and AI over complete automation to maintain human judgment, empathy, teamwork, and creativity.

3.2.3 *Predictive Maintenance*

AI is also transforming predictive maintenance within the maritime sector, providing substantial improvements in operational efficiency and safety. AI-driven predictive maintenance systems analyze real-time data from sensors installed on ship components, employing machine-learning algorithms to detect early signs of potential failures (Hamidah 2024). This approach enables ship operators to perform proactive and preventive maintenance, thereby minimizing unanticipated downtime and extending the ship's lifespan. Through continuous monitoring of equipment health and performance, AI algorithms can identify minor changes in vibration, temperature, or other parameters that may indicate emerging technical issues (Nautilus

3 For more information on this AI-driven voyage optimization solution, see the website of True North Marine at https://tnmservices.com.

Shipping 2024). This early detection allows maintenance personnel to address problems before they escalate into major failures, thereby reducing the risks of accidents and costly repairs. A significant advantage of AI-driven predictive maintenance is its ability to integrate and analyze extensive datasets swiftly and accurately, leading to more precise decision-making regarding maintenance schedules (Buzinkay 2023).

However, the impact of AI on maritime labor is complex. Although AI-driven predictive maintenance solutions can automate many routine tasks, they are not expected to completely replace crew members. Instead, these machines enhance human capabilities, allowing the crew to focus on more complex and critical responsibilities. By providing real-time data analytics and risk assessments, AI systems empower maritime professionals to make better, informed, and safety-centric decisions (Editorial Team 2024a). Nevertheless, the integration of AI in maritime operations presents challenges. Resistance to change may exist among crew members and other relevant maritime stakeholders, and ensuring data quality and reliability from various sources can be difficult (Durlik et al. 2024).

The deployment of AI systems requires significant investment in technology and training, which may create financial challenges for some maritime operators. Despite these hurdles, the potential benefits of AI in predictive maintenance for maritime work are substantial. By reducing unforeseen failures and improving maintenance schedules, AI helps to create safer conditions for seafarers onboard ships (Nautilus Shipping 2024). Additionally, AI can track the working hours and health indicators of crew members to prevent overexertion and fatigue, common factors in maritime accidents. Moreover, the growing integration of AI technologies in the maritime industry for predictive maintenance is expected to change the roles of the workforce onboard ships. While some tasks may become automated, new roles will arise, concentrated on supervising and evaluating AI-generated insights. This transformation will demand ongoing training and upskilling to ensure effective collaboration with AI systems (Editorial Team 2024a).

3.2.4 *Maritime Security and Risk Management*

AI applications in maritime security and risk management cover several areas, including predictive maintenance, route optimization, cybersecurity, and port operations. AI-driven sensors and machine-learning algorithms facilitate operations in turbulent seas.

The legal framework governing AI in maritime operations continues to evolve in order to address the unique challenges posed by this technology. The IMO has recognized the importance of cybersecurity in maritime operations and has released guidelines for protecting digital systems on ships. However, the implementation of these cybersecurity standards for MASS presents new challenges, as their reliance on AI and external communication systems increases their susceptibility to cyber threats.

A key legal concern is liability in mishaps utilizing AI-driven systems. The conventional notion of flag State responsibility, as outlined in the United Nations Convention on the Law of the Sea,[4] may need reassessment in relation to AI-operated vessels. For instance, if a system failure leads to a multi-vessel collision in international waters, establishing liability becomes complicated when several ships rely on the same machine-learning algorithms (Adnan 2023). The EU's Artificial Intelligence Act (AI Act),[5] currently in development, is anticipated to significantly impact the maritime sector. This legislation aims to regulate AI systems based on their risk levels, affecting all areas of the shipping industry. The AI Act underscores safety, data protection, transparency, and accountability tied to the use of AI systems, which will certainly shape the design and operation of autonomous vessels.

Incorporating AI into maritime operations offers advantages and challenges for seafarers. While AI can improve safety by minimizing human errors and offering real-time decision support, it raises concerns about job displacement. Automating maritime operations may result in considerable job displacement among seafarers, requiring a transformation in skills and roles within the industry.

The legal ramifications of AI in maritime security pertain to data protection and privacy. MASS produces and conveys substantial volumes of data, encompassing sensitive details regarding vessel operations and positioning. Securing this data is essential to avert unauthorized access and privacy violations. Therefore, a comprehensive legislative framework is essential to govern the collection, storage, and transfer of data from ships, emphasizing protection against cyberattacks.

3.2.5 *Use of AI in Employment Management*

While automation provides numerous advantages for managing seafarers' employment, it also presents notable challenges. The incorporation of process automation and AI into the maritime industry can greatly diminish labor demand, particularly for low-skilled positions. However, highly skilled roles, such as captains and engineers, are likely to be less impacted (WMU 2023).

To mitigate the impact of automation on employment, it is crucial to invest in training, upskilling, and reskilling seafarers while also ensuring their retention in the sector. Improving seafarer qualifications and training seafarers in emerging technologies are essential to help the workforce adapt to the sector's demands. At the

4 United Nations Convention on the Law of the Sea, December 10, 1982, 1833 UNTS 397.

5 Regulation (EU) 2024/1689 of the European Parliament and of the Council of June 13, 2024, laying down harmonized rules on artificial intelligence and amending Regulations (EC) No 300/2008, (EU) No 167/2013, (EU) No 168/2013, (EU) 2018/858, (EU) 2018/1139 and (EU) 2019/2144 and Directives 2014/90/EU, (EU) 2016/797 and (EU) 2020/1828 (Artificial Intelligence Act) (AI Act).

European level, for example, Recommendation (EU) 2024/236 of the European Commission emphasizes the importance of skill-based training.[6] This training should focus on knowledge, methodology, participation, and adapting workers' skills to new technologies and processes. Government training initiatives and the modernization of regulated vocational training are key tools in preparing maritime professionals for the automation era. This effort can transform challenges associated with automation into a productive advantage rather than a threat. AI-driven tools can further support the analysis of future skill needs and gaps at the national and industry levels and help individuals identify potential career paths and learning opportunities. These tools, which are already utilized by some public employment services (OECD 2022), can also offer opportunities for additional systemic solutions in various transportation sectors, not just maritime.

3.3 IMPLICATIONS OF AI ON THE DEVELOPMENT OF MARITIME LABOR LAWS

Multiple scientific papers have reported that the integration of AI in maritime shipping, particularly in the development of autonomous ships, is expected to reduce crew sizes on board, which may create fewer job opportunities. However, it could also generate new positions, such as remote operators that require specialized skills, advanced training, and technical competencies. These developments may necessitate revisions to labor laws to ensure clear and fair working conditions for the maritime workforce, including seafarers, while also addressing legal liability in accidents involving AI systems. The current legal framework, specifically the MLC, protects formal seafarers' rights on ships but does not clearly address how those rights apply to unmanned vessels, potentially necessitating legislative amendments to the Convention. Additionally, other key instruments, such as the STCW, also require revision and adaptation to the new paradigm of technology use in the maritime sector. As AI and automation technologies continue to reshape the maritime industry, legal and institutional structures must evolve accordingly to safeguard seafarers' rights, redefine new roles, and, importantly, establish clear accountability in AI-driven maritime operations.

3.3.1 *Ongoing Discussions and Future Outlook*

International organizations, including the IMO, are endeavoring to regulate autonomous vessels, taking into account labor law ramifications, including the definition of "crew" in the context of remote operations. The International Labor Organization (ILO), although not explicitly addressing autonomous ships, is examining the larger

[6] Commission Recommendation (EU) 2024/236 of November 29, 2023, on means to address the impact of automation and digitalization on the transport workforce, C/2023/8067.

labor implications of AI, which may guide the maritime sector adjustments. Upcoming modifications may entail revised training mandates and alterations to social security, mirroring the dynamic characteristics of maritime employment that are likely to influence different maritime legal instruments governing seafarers' rights.

3.3.1.1 Maritime Labor Instruments

The MLC, adopted by the ILO, is a comprehensive convention that sets minimum standards for the working and living conditions of seafarers. It entered into force on August 20, 2013, and includes aspects such as minimum age, medical certification, employment agreements, wages, hours of work and rest, leave, repatriation, social security, health and safety, accident prevention, and on-board medical care, among other fundamental labor rights for seafarers. Its primary goal is to ensure the fair employment of seafarers and equitable competition among shipowners, applying to ships entering the ports of ratifying States and those flying their flag. The MLC is not the only regulatory framework governing maritime labor. Other significant instruments adopted by the IMO, such as the STCW, address training and certification relevant to the emerging skill requirements in an AI-driven environment. The STCW was initially developed in 1978 in response to the Torrey Canyon disaster in 1967. The Convention has been continuously revised, with major amendments in 1995 and 2010 following diplomatic conferences. To date, 195 modifications have been introduced to the STCW Code. The Code outlines the basic competency levels for several maritime professions within a series of tables in its mandatory Part A; its nonbinding Part B offers recommendations for the effective implementation of the Convention.

Despite their significance in maritime labor law, these instruments do not yet address the complexity and challenges of the human elements associated with autonomous vessels. Challenges for maritime law regarding the integration of AI (primarily autonomous ships) include, but are not limited to, crew size reduction (and potential job loss), new roles and proficiencies, working conditions for remote operators, legal responsibility and liability, and social security and benefits.

POTENTIAL REDUCTION IN CREW SIZE AND JOB IMPLICATIONS. Autonomous ships could significantly reduce the need for onboard crew, leading to job displacement or transformation. A study conducted by Kretschmann et al. highlights the cost advantages of autonomous ships through decreased crew expenses, but also points out potential increases in port expenses and monitoring costs (Nguyen et al. 2022). Discussions in both industry and academia reflect this dual perspective. For instance, the World Maritime University report on the future of work indicates that whether autonomous ships will signal the end for seafarers' jobs or not, there will still be a need for seafarers to oversee and maintain these ships when necessary, with appropriate training and skills (WMU 2023). In contrast, as mentioned earlier, another study asserts that seafarers' jobs will continue to exist even with the increased development of autonomous or semi-autonomous ships, albeit in evolving and more complex capacities and roles (Nautilus International 2018). This controversy underscores the need for international and national labor regulations to address seafarers' employment security and retraining. In this context, the provisions regarding wages and employment agreements in the MLC may become less relevant for crewless ships, necessitating legislative amendments to support shore-based roles or alternative employment for maritime professionals adapting to the new technological landscape shaped by AI and automation.

NEW ROLES AND SKILLS. The impact of AI on maritime operations creates employment opportunities for remote operators who oversee autonomous ships from shore. The interim requirements for MASS trials established by the IMO and confirmed in 2019 underscore the essential need for a maritime workforce – which includes all maritime professionals operating on board, on shore, or remotely – to possess adequate qualifications and experience (IMO 2019). Such a shift necessitates revisions to the STCW, ensuring that training programs incorporate skills in AI system administration, as well as remote operations such as cybersecurity. Equipping seafarers with these skills will enable them to safely transition into these new roles. This transition is crucial not only to secure seafarers' employment but also to ensure that labor regulations serve a protective role in substance. In 2017, the IMO initiated a regulatory scoping exercise (RSE) to evaluate how the organization's legal instruments could support MASS operations. The RSE identifies the STCW and its Code as critical focus areas for the IMO, indicating that substantial efforts must be made to provide necessary clarifications and guidance before implementing MASS operations with advanced degrees of autonomy on a broader scale. The results of the RSE are documented in MSC.1/Circ.1638 (IMO 2021). The STCW outlines three primary components: (1) definitions and clarifications regarding the roles of the master, crew, and responsible individuals; (2) definitions and clarifications relating to remote control centers; and (3) definitions and clarifications concerning remote operators classified as seafarers. The RSE primarily stressed the importance of defining the new responsibilities of the crew onboard ships and remote operators. It emphasized the need to clarify the connection between remote operators and onboard personnel. However, the RSE did not specify the necessary capabilities for crew members or remote operators involved in MASS operations. Thus, modifications to the STCW and its Code should be evaluated with regard to new technologies or automated procedures. The organization's structure and the roles of different parties in implementing MASS, along with the required competencies to undertake these additional tasks, remain unclear. Consequently, the maritime community currently faces challenges in determining new training requirements due to the industry's limited expertise with MASS.

It is important to note that developing new educational and training programs requires significant time and resources. Training and education for seafarers are unique because they include a professional qualification, as outlined by the STCW Code, while also integrating an academic component, which in many countries is incorporated into the higher education system. This duality results in the attainment of a professional certification, specifically a Certificate of Competency, along with an academic degree upon successfully completing the relevant academic programs. Higher education institutions must justify any changes to their academic programs to provide relevant education. Given the considerable time gap between developing an academic program and the subsequent entry of graduates into the labor market, further discussions are essential regarding the curriculum of relevant academic programs and the methods of training and education. The STCW, in its current form, lacks the necessary training materials and organization required for the operation of MASS. In this regard, only a limited number of research projects have begun efforts to investigate the proper training requirements for maritime operations involving MASS ships and other emerging technologies.[7]

BEYOND TRAINING: CONTINUOUS PROFESSIONAL DEVELOPMENT FOR SEAFARERS. As ships evolve from manned to remotely operated or fully autonomous, the responsibilities of ship operators will shift from direct navigation to managing supervisory autonomy. The required expertise includes algorithmic interpretability, human–autonomy collaboration, and crisis response, which may become the primary training objectives. In the future, remotely operated and autonomous ships will need to coexist with conventional vessels, making the roles of masters and engineers crucial for operational continuity, safety, and regulatory compliance (Kim and Schröder-Hinrichs 2021). The diverse landscape of global shipping, characterized by the coexistence of autonomous, remotely operated, and crewed vessels in shared navigational areas, demands that maritime professionals possess both traditional seafaring skills and advanced technical competencies to manage effectively the interactions among these various types of vessels.

New roles are expected to emerge, including remote operation operators, AI ship engineers, and maritime cybersecurity managers, to align with future demands. The integration of AI, automation, and remote operations in shipping is expected to transform numerous professions in the maritime industry, transitioning career paths from conventional hazardous and labor-intensive positions to highly specialized and technology-driven roles. This will augment the intellectual and strategic sophistication of maritime vocations, boost welfare and working conditions, and elevate their status to a level commensurate with specialists in aerospace, robotics, and high-tech industries. In this context, conventional seafarer career trajectories, defined by a

7 For an example of such projects, see the REFRAME website at https://site.uit.no/reframe/.

hierarchical structure (that is, rank-based) and flexibility (that is, employment per voyage contract), are poised for transformation.

HEALTH, SAFETY, AND SOCIAL SECURITY PROTECTION. The transformation of crew structure due to AI-driven automation will impact social security and benefits. Seafarers are entitled to benefits if their employment terms are impacted by technological development or work performed onshore. However, according to the provisions of the MLC, their benefits, such as medical care and repatriation, may need to be reevaluated. Therefore, inclusive policies are necessary to ensure the welfare of seafarers in an AI-driven future (Kim and Schröder-Hinrichs 2021). The influence of AI on health and safety in maritime operations is substantial, particularly as autonomous ships reduce the need for onboard seafarers. Remote operators may experience isolation or stress due to constant surveillance, and onboard crews of semi-autonomous ships must contend with AI malfunctions, which increase the likelihood of accidents. The MLC's health and safety provisions, specifically accident prevention under Title 4, require modifications to address these issues, including extending coverage to cover shore-based roles. Social protection, including medical care and repatriation under the MLC, may need reassessment for reduced crew size or shore-based personnel. For its part, the STCW must ensure that seafarers are adequately trained to manage these new situations. Cybersecurity training, for instance, becomes crucial due to the digital nature of AI and other emerging technologies (IMO 2025b). Social protection may guide the STCW's long-term welfare objectives, ensuring that training includes emergency response for AI-related incidents and cyberattacks.

To address these challenges, tripartite collaboration among governments, shipowners, and representatives of seafarers is essential. In the maritime sector, this approach could influence not only the MLC, which is part of its functionality, but also revisions to the STCW. The IMO's 2021 regulatory scoping exercise for MASS identified gaps in labor law, including issues related to training and certification, suggesting that tripartite dialogue is necessary to define "crew" and "responsible person" for remote operations (IMO 2025a). For the STCW, tripartite engagement could establish new competency standards for AI interaction, data analysis, and cybersecurity. Social partners, such as the International Transport Workers Federation and Nautilus International, play a critical role in shaping training requirements and aligning them with industry needs and technological advancements.

LEGAL RESPONSIBILITY AND LIABILITY. Determining liability in accidents involving autonomous ships is a complex issue. Traditional labor regulations assign responsibility and accountability to the ship's master and crew, but with AI, these could shift to shipowners, AI technology developers, software developers, or remote operators. This uncertainty has implications for insurance providers, which must develop new models to cover the unique risks associated with AI. The IMO's legal committee scoping exercise, as part of the 2021 regulatory review, identifies gaps in liability and compensation treaties, suggesting a need for new frameworks (IMO 2025a). This affects labor law, particularly concerning compensation for injuries or incidents, potentially requiring amendments to the MLC's provisions on accident prevention and shipowner liability.

3.3.1.2 Working Conditions and Potential Control of Workers at Sea

Numerous studies have linked electronic or digital monitoring systems with various aspects of working conditions, considering factors such as employee performance, job duration, work rhythms, collaboration between employees and employers, skill development, and employee well-being. Human capital management and performance management are two primary human resources functions enhanced by AI, though they come with implications for occupational safety and health (OSH). "People analytics" solutions are recognized for improving the recruitment process by enabling informed decisions regarding potential employees, based on their access to relevant data. Certain types of systems allow employers to conduct video interviews to reduce specific biases during the interview process. They can also assess employee performance through performance-based compensation to aid in formulating corporate strategies for individual workers. Without human oversight and ethical considerations, this algorithmic decision-making tool has shown significant potential to create OSH issues, including increased structural, physical, and psychosocial risks such as stress and anxiety (Moore 2019, 93). Employees may be led to question the fairness, integrity, and accuracy of decisions made by their employers – such as job displacement and workplace restructuring – due to their lack of access to data derived from people analytics systems.

Workers may feel that they are being monitored if they think that people analytics data is used for performance management without appropriate oversight. This perception, along with the fear of layoffs resulting from performance evaluations, may drive them to increase their work effort excessively due to job loss anxiety, potentially leading to OSH concerns. The most urgent issues related to AI in workplaces stem from using people analytics to gather employee data for decision-making. Other AI systems in the workplace that have contributed to OSH concerns include cobots and chatbots. These AI-enhanced tools have been integrated into various industrial processes, causing psychosocial issues linked to the fear of job displacement due to automation. Different sectors, including automotive manufacturing, utilize cobots to perform tasks that would typically require significantly more human time. Robotic arms have replaced human hands, and AI has enhanced robots with cognitive abilities, allowing them to think like humans and effectively take over human intellect (Moore 2020).

A report indicates that using cobots has reduced OSH risks by lowering workers' exposure to hazardous ergonomic, physical, and chemical conditions (Moore 2019, 93). Conversely, another study has identified three primary categories of OSH issues arising from interactions among humans, cobots, and the environment: (1) collision hazards between robots and humans arising from unexpected robot behavior due to machine learning; (2) security vulnerabilities stemming from the robot's internet connectivity, which can compromise software integrity and expose the system to threats; and (3) environmental risks, where unpredictable human actions and sensor degradation in unstructured environments can lead to hazards (Moore 2019, 93). Moreover, AI has facilitated the integration of voice recognition and machine vision into chatbots, which is recognized to threaten both unskilled and skilled jobs due to the increasing automation of tasks traditionally performed by humans. For example, in a chemical firm that manufactures optical peripherals for machinery, an individual would spend numerous hours examining repetitive images of tiny machine chips to detect errors. AI has replaced human labor in this task, eliminating occupational health issues such as musculoskeletal disorders and visual strain. However, improperly utilized AI-augmented robots in factories may induce stress among workers. It is noted that integrating automation, algorithmic management, and digitalization can create a harmful system that may result in psychosocial problems, particularly when employees are expected to perform at a robotic pace instead of allowing robots to operate at a human pace. Occasionally, an employee monitors a single machine that sends notifications to their electronic devices, such as smartphones or computers. This can lead to other psychosocial problems, such as job overload, where individuals continue to work beyond their designated hours.

At sea, the ship is limited in space and vulnerable to navigational hazards. Employment onboard ships is influenced not only by potential accident risks but also by factors of movement and isolation. Life on board requires the integration of work and personal life in a single environment, highlighting the importance of work management along with the composition and size of the crew. Improving onboard working conditions relates to the quality of the ship's habitability and the safety of life at sea. Maritime surveillance may involve both security and control, as seafarers are required to follow the directives of the shipowner through the ship's master. As a result, surveillance techniques serve various purposes, including safety, security, regulatory compliance monitoring, and the enhancement of commercial operations. The tripartite objective of overseeing the vessel and its crew is a responsibility of shipowners established by international conventions set by the IMO and the ILO.

Emerging technologies such as AI onboard ships can also increase labor intensity through continuous surveillance and inconsistent scheduling (De Stefano 2018). In maritime operations, remote operators supervising autonomous vessels may face similar pressures as AI systems control duties and working hours. The MLC's provisions on work hours and rest for onboard seafarers may not directly apply to shore-based positions, necessitating new regulations to ensure fair treatment, including rights to disconnect and protection from excessive monitoring, in line with general labor regulation trends. Therefore, seafarers have the right to negotiate the use of algorithms and to oversee big data onboard ships. Seafarers' unions should advocate for safeguards against excessive surveillance of seafarers through various technologies and ensure equitable working conditions (Lagdami 2023).

Therefore, to ensure the responsible and ethical use of AI aboard ships, it is crucial to focus on four key areas. First, seafarers should have ownership and control over data produced during their work on ships. This principle recognizes the importance of individual privacy and data rights in an increasingly digital maritime environment. Allowing seafarers to control their data fosters trust and transparency in the application of emerging technologies at sea. Second, data generated from seafarers should only be used for purposes related to maritime safety and security. This information should be limited to protect the privacy and interests of maritime workers and to focus on enhancing safety and security in maritime activities. Clearly defining how the data will be used will help prevent its misappropriation or abuse. Third, international regulations should govern the use of AI on board, enshrining the principle of ultimate human responsibility for its impacts. Fourth, seafarers should be trained to address new challenges related to emerging technologies. Seafarers should be aware of the technical, legal, economic, and ethical issues associated with the use of AI-based tools (Lagdami 2023).

3.3.1.3 Cybersecurity and the Leakage of Seafarers' Personal Information

The integration of AI and big data in the maritime industry also increases vulnerability to cybersecurity breaches. As we transition more seriously into the digital era, cybersecurity breaches have surged, with operational technology attacks soaring by as much as 900 percent in the past three years (Akpan et al. 2022). Systems that rely on interconnected networks, cloud platforms, and real-time data exchange become prime targets for cyberattacks. Various threat actors could exploit these vulnerabilities to access information and manipulate or disrupt critical operations at sea. For instance, a cyberattack on an AI-powered navigation system could result in an incorrect route for vessels, thereby putting crew and cargo in dangerous situations. Likewise, a breach in big data systems can adversely affect operations at ports or disrupt global supply chains (Kanellopoulos 2024).

Notable incidents have been demonstrated in the outcomes of such breaches – for example, the ransomware attack on Maersk, the largest shipping company in the world, in 2017. This incident was essentially operational, except for the broader implications on data security; sensitive information and operational data were at risk of corruption during the rapid recovery process (Clavijo Mesa et al. 2024). Similarly, in 2020, the Mediterranean Shipping Company encountered a cyber-related incident involving unauthorized access to its customer database (Ben Farah et al. 2022). This breach disrupted container bookings and exposed sensitive data, undermining customer trust and necessitating expensive mitigation efforts. These incidents have underscored the growing need for robust cybersecurity measures to safeguard sensitive information – including seafarers' personal details – from theft and misuse.

By far the most concerning impact of such incidents is the leakage of seafarers' personal information in the era of digitalization onboard ships. In fact, with the increasing use of networked digital tools in everyday operations, seafarers are particularly at risk from hacking incidents (Finn 2020). In addition, current maritime education and training programs lack a proper element of cybersecurity, rendering seafarers poorly prepared while on the job to identify and neutralize any cyber threats (Heering 2020). Such cyber incidents put at risk sensitive information such as medical records, identity details, and financial data. In addition, such information may lead to identity theft, fraud involving financial transactions, and psychological trauma, among other impacts, which can further increase the issue of the criminalization of seafarers. Trust between seafarers and their employers is also undermined whenever inadequate steps have been taken to secure information. These incidents could also cause profound reputational harm to shipping companies, leading to possible legal liabilities, regulatory penalties, and the erosion of stakeholder confidence and trust. Therefore, maritime cybersecurity risks must be dealt with through robust regulatory frameworks and international cooperation to keep sensitive data secure and ensure the resilience of maritime operations.

3.4 THE AI ACT FROM A MARITIME LABOR PERSPECTIVE

The AI Act – which was adopted in June 2024, entered into force on August 1 of that year, and became fully applicable by August 2026 – is considered the first ever regulatory legal framework governing AI and its challenges and risks. Thus, it puts Europe at the forefront of international AI regulation.

The AI Act was developed based on a risk model; it in fact clusters AI systems according to the risks posed to humans and society (Kosinski and Scapicchio 2024). The Act categorizes AI systems into four risk levels: unacceptable risk (prohibited), high risk (strict requirements), limited risk (transparency obligations), and minimal or no risk (no specific obligations; European Parliament 2025). High-risk systems, such as those used in critical applications like medical devices or transportation, must comply with requirements including risk management, data governance, transparency, and human oversight (Meier and Spichiger 2024). The Act prohibits certain AI practices, imposes strict regulations on high-risk AI systems, and sets transparency requirements for limited-risk AI applications. This approach permits a nuanced application of rules, imposing stricter regulations that should be applied to high risk AI systems and less stringent rules for those deemed lower risks. The Act explicitly bans numerous AI methods, especially those that lever human behavior or exploit specific vulnerable groups. Thus, the AI Act complements the General Data

Protection Regulation (GDPR)[8] with its governance framework. It strengthens some of the principles of the GDPR, such as the lawfulness of processing personal data, purpose limitation, and transparency. The Act affirms that AI systems must comply with the same legal basis for processing information under the GDPR; thus, no data can be collected for wrongful purposes (Meier and Spichiger 2024). It also sets out specific rules for protecting personal data in AI systems. The Act permits the processing of sensitive personal data for bias detection and mitigation in high-risk AI systems, but only under stringent conditions (Hullen 2024). This is one of the conditions necessary to ensure nondiscrimination and fairness in AI applications. In addition, the Act emphasizes data minimization – requiring AI systems to use only the data necessary for the given purpose, which is aligned with the GDPR and reduces the risk of data breaches or misuse. In a move toward such a new legal environment, the European Commission launched the AI Pact, a voluntary scheme to encourage AI developers in and out of European geographies to implement key provisions of the Act in preparation for the legal timeline. In its first expression of interest in the AI Pact, in November 2023, over 550 organizations from various geographies, sectors, and sizes demonstrated a strong willingness to comply proactively.

3.4.1 *Intersection of the AI Act with the MASS Code*

Currently, the IMO is advancing the development of the MASS Code, which serves as a regulatory instrument for MASS capable of operating at various levels of autonomy, as discussed earlier. The nonmandatory MASS Code aims to ensure safety, security, and environmental protection, and it was expected to be adopted by May 2025. In contrast, a mandatory code could come into effect as early as July 2030, with enforcement potentially beginning in January 2032 (Editorial Team 2024c). This framework is essential as a wide range of sectors within the marine industry start to implement AI and automation, which could transform traditional roles and responsibilities.

The AI Act significantly affects the maritime industry, particularly in relation to MASS. The Act establishes a risk-based framework for AI regulation, which has real implications for autonomous ships where AI systems are responsible for navigation, collision avoidance, and other essential functions. This classification necessitates rigorous testing for compliance before these systems can be commercialized and for subsequent adherence to operational and safety standards for autonomous vessels. On a broader scale, the Act requires human oversight for high-risk AI systems, which could entail ensuring remote monitoring for fully autonomous MASS (degree four) when no crew members are present. The MASS Code, centered on safety, likely

[8] Regulation (EU) 2016/679 of the European Parliament and of the Council of April 27, 2016, on the protection of natural persons with regard to the processing of personal data and on the free movement of such data, and repealing Directive 95/46/EC (General Data Protection Regulation).

aligns by mandating human intervention capabilities, especially for higher levels of autonomy, to address risks such as cyberattacks or system failures (Kepesedi 2022).

The AI Act's requirements for high-risk AI systems will likely influence the MASS Code, particularly for MASS operating in or related to the EU. For degrees one and two, human oversight is clear, with seafarers on board providing direct control. However, for degree three, remote operators must ensure effective monitoring, aligning with the Act's transparency and oversight requirements. Degree four, which involves fully autonomous ships, presents a significant challenge, as the Act mandates human involvement, potentially requiring remote monitoring systems or contingency plans for human intervention (Lölfing 2023). As the MASS Code is still under development, it must incorporate these requirements to ensure compliance, potentially leading to provisions for remote operation centers and clear definitions of remote operator responsibilities (Editorial Team 2024b).

So far, there are no examples directly linked to the AI Act and MASS; however, parallels can be drawn from regulations on autonomous vehicles. For instance, the Act's influence on autonomous vehicles indicates that MASS providers might benefit from AI regulatory sandboxes, which would allow testing in controlled environments (Güçlütürk and Vural 2024). Trials of MASS conducted by companies in Korea, Japan, and Norway highlight the necessity for robust AI systems with human oversight, aligning with both frameworks.

3.4.2 *The AI Act's Potential Impact on Seafarers' Roles and Job Prospects*

As previously discussed, the AI Act requires human involvement for high-risk AI systems, including MASS, for navigation and decision-making. Even fully autonomous ships (degree four, with no crew on board) may need remote monitoring or intervention, shifting traditional seafaring roles to shore-based positions such as operators based in remote centers. For ships with lower autonomy (degrees one and two, with crew on board), seafarers will continue to oversee AI systems. Still, their roles may evolve to include more monitoring and less hands-on control. This change could reduce demand for on-board seafarers, potentially leading to job displacement, but it also creates new opportunities in remote operation centers. As a general fact, seafarers may need retraining and upskilling to adapt to these new roles, focusing on competencies such as remote monitoring, AI system management, and cybersecurity. This aligns with the AI Act's focus on a human-centric AI approach and may involve collaborations with training institutions both inside and outside Europe (Meier and Spichiger 2024).

3.4.3 *Potential Opportunities and Challenges*

The alignment of the MASS Code with the AI Act could enhance safety. However, it faces challenges – such as defining human oversight for fully autonomous ships, harmonizing regulatory frameworks, and addressing potential cyber threats – as highlighted in a UN Trade and Development report (Kepesedi 2022). Unlike conventional ships, where crew members can respond immediately to emergencies, remote operators must rely on robust communication systems and real-time data to make critical decisions. This dependence on technology introduces new vulnerabilities, such as cybersecurity risks and threats, along with the possibility of communication breakdowns, which could compromise the safety of the vessel, its cargo, and the marine environment. Solutions may include remote monitoring systems or innovative contingency plans. This intersection emphasizes the need for international cooperation, such as between IMO and EU bodies, and the development of codes of best practice for AI in maritime applications (Caroli 2025).

The future outlook suggests a balanced approach that ensures innovation while prioritizing safety and ethical considerations, with ongoing updates to the AI Act and MASS Code as technology evolves. This intersection also underscores the need for collaborative regulatory efforts to navigate the complexities of autonomous shipping and the use of emerging technologies, such as AI, onboard ships. The development of best practice codes for AI in maritime applications is another area where international cooperation could yield significant benefits. Such practice codes could standardize training requirements and define roles for seafarers involved in remote operations, ensuring a consistent approach across different jurisdictions (Wylie 2024). This standardization is crucial for building trust in the use of autonomous shipping technologies and facilitating their global adoption.

Last but not least, as the maritime industry navigates these uncharted waters, it is clear that successfully integrating emerging technologies such as AI into global shipping operations will require a delicate balance between technological innovation and regulatory oversight. The ongoing dialogue between regulatory bodies, industry stakeholders, and technology providers will be crucial in shaping a future where autonomous ships can operate safely and efficiently alongside conventional vessels.

3.5 CONCLUSION

AI is increasingly being integrated into the maritime domain, driving a profound shift across the operational efficiencies, technology, human element, and regulatory frameworks. Through maritime AI application solutions, including voyage optimization, significant improvements in safety, economic effectiveness, and environmental sustainability can be achieved. Such shifts, however, must be approached with caution, particularly their impact on seafarers and the legal frameworks governing their employment and responsibilities.

At the core of this transformation is the evolving nature of seafarers' roles and the competencies they must acquire and master. While concerns over job loss persist, research indicates that AI is more likely to transform seafarers' roles rather than eliminate them, which will increase the demand for new competencies such as data analysis, monitoring AI systems, and operating more complex systems. This shift necessitates a proactive approach to maritime education and training, ensuring that the maritime workforce is able to collaborate with AI systems in tasks and adapt to the changing demands of the industry.

The growing use of AI in maritime operations raises significant legal and ethical concerns. Solutions are needed to address concerns related to liability and accountability that arise from AI system accidents, along with continuing concerns over data privacy and cybersecurity and the need for global coherence among technical standards. Current legal frameworks, largely designed for traditional maritime operations, may not adequately address the unique challenges posed by AI, thus requiring careful scrutiny and realignment to ensure clarity and legal certainty.

The IMO has initiated key efforts to address these challenges, such as developing a strategy on e-navigation and working groups on MASS. These initiatives are essential to establishing a consistent regulatory framework. The initiatives call for more cooperation between different industry actors to develop regulations that balance the need to accelerate AI adoption in the maritime industry with the need for caution and prudence regarding how this technology may affect the global maritime workforce.

While AI-driven transformation represents unprecedented opportunities in the maritime industry, its ultimate success can be achieved only through a holistic solution that addresses human factor concerns and legal uncertainties and promotes multinational cooperation. Innovation in AI is only valuable in the maritime industry when it upholds fundamental principles of safety, security, and occupational health and well-being. The maritime industry must ensure that new technologies complement the work of maritime professionals rather than eliminate it. The responsible proliferation of AI in the maritime sector necessitates a continuous learning mindset, fostering an adaptability and knowledge-sharing culture. Furthermore, prioritizing ethical AI deployment is of prime importance. While ensuring regulatory clarity and workforce development, the maritime industry can efficiently leverage automation and AI's potential benefits to ensure sustainable and equitable technological advancement.

REFERENCES

Adnan, Zaria. 2023. "AI in Maritime Operations: Legal under War Law?" *DLP Forum*, November 1. www.dlpforum.org/2023/11/01/is-ai-in-maritime-operations-legal-under-war-law/.

Aghion, Philippe, Céline Antonin, and Simon Bunel. 2019. "Artificial Intelligence, Growth and Employment: The Role of Policy." *Economie et Statistique / Economics and Statistics* no. 510-511-512: 149–164.

Akpan, Frank, Gueltoum Bendiab, Stavros Shiaeles, Stavros Karamperidis, and Michalis Michaloliakos. 2022. "Cybersecurity Challenges in the Maritime Sector." *Network* 2: 123–138.

Askari, Humayun Rashid, and Mohammad Nazir Hossain. 2022. "Towards Utilizing Autonomous Ships: A Viable Advance in Industry 4.0." *Journal of International Maritime Safety, Environmental Affairs, and Shipping* 6 (1): 39–49.

Ben Farah, Mohamed Amine, Elochukwu Ukwandu, Hanan Hindy, David Brosset, Miroslav Bures, Ivan Andonovic, and Xavier Bellekens. 2022. "Review: Cyber Security in the Maritime Industry: A Systematic Survey of Recent Advances and Future Trends." *Information* 13 (1): 22.

Buzinkay, Mark. 2023. *Leveraging Predictive Maintenance: Transforming Maritime Operations.* Identec Solutions.

Caroli, Laura. 2025. "Talks on the EU AI Act Code of Practice at a Crucial Phase." Center for Strategic & International Studies, January 24. www.csis.org/analysis/talks-eu-ai-act-code-practice-crucial-phase.

Clavijo Mesa, Maria Valentina, Carmen Elena Patino-Rodriguez, and Fernando Jesus Guevara Carazas. 2024. "Cybersecurity at Sea: A Literature Review of Cyber-Attack Impacts and Defenses in Maritime Supply Chains." *Information* 15 (11): 710.

De Stefano, Valerio DS. 2018. "'Negotiating the Algorithm': Automation, Artificial Intelligence and Labour Protection." Employment Working Paper No. 246, ILO.

Durlik, Irmina, Tymoteusz Miller, Ewelina Kostecka, and Tomasz Tuński. 2024. "Artificial Intelligence in Maritime Transportation: A Comprehensive Review of Safety and Risk Management Applications." *Applied Sciences* 14: 8420.

Editorial Team. 2024a. "How AI Will Affect Future Workforce: Key Considerations for Shipping." SAFETY4SEA, August 12. https://safety4sea.com/cm-how-ai-will-affect-future-workforce-key-considerations-for-shipping/.

2024b. "IMO: A Human Will Be Responsible for MASS Regardless of Autonomy Level." SAFETY4SEA, April 16. https://safety4sea.com/imo-a-human-will-be-responsible-for-mass-regardless-of-autonomy-level/.

2024c. "IMO MSC 108 Paves the Way for MASS Implementation." SAFETY4SEA, May 29. https://safety4sea.com/msc-108-paves-the-way-for-mass-implementation/.

European Parliament. 2025. "EU AI Act: First Regulation on Artificial Intelligence." February 19. www.europarl.europa.eu/topics/en/article/20230601STO93804/eu-ai-act-first-regulation-on-artificial-intelligence.

Finn, Patrick. 2020. "Cyber Security Principles for Seafarers." *Thetius.* https://thetius.com/cyber-security-principles-for-seafarers/.

Fonseca, Tiago, Khanssa Lagdami, and Jens-Uwe Schröder-Hinrichs. 2021. "Assessing Innovation in Transport: An Application of the Technology Adoption (TechAdo) Model to Maritime Autonomous Surface Ships (MASS)." *Transport Policy* 114: 182–195.

Glover, Ellen. 2024. "What Is Artificial Intelligence (AI)?" Built In. https://builtin.com/artificial-intelligence?cartflows_flow = ai-tools&page = 2.

Güçlütürk, Osman Gazi, and Bahadir Vural. 2024. "Driving Innovation: Navigating the EU AI Act's Impact on Autonomous Vehicles." Holistic AI, March 20. www.holisticai.com/blog/driving-innovation-navigating-eu-ai-acts-impact-on-autonomous-vehicles.

Gupta, Manish. 2024. "VoyageX AI Elevating Onboard Ship Operations with Predictive Maintenance Solutions." VoyageX AI. https://voyagex.ai/predictive-maintenance-onboard-ships/.

Hamidah, Al Mar'atul. 2024. "AI-Based Predictive Maintenance for Ships: Enhancing Operational Efficiency and Reliability." iStow, September 24. https://istow.id/ai-based-predictive-maintenance-for-ships-enhancing-operational-efficiency-and-reliability/.

Heering, D. 2020. "Ensuring Cybersecurity in Shipping: Reference to Estonian Shipowners." *TransNav* 14 (2): 271–278.

HSBA (Hamburg School of Business Administration). 2018. *Seafarers and Digital Disruption: The Effect of Autonomous Ships on the Work at Sea, the Role of Seafarers and the Shipping Industry*. HSBA Hamburg School of Business Administration.

Hullen, Nils. 2024. "Top 10 Operational Impacts of the EU AI Act: Leveraging GDPR Compliance." IAPP25, November. https://iapp.org/resources/article/top-impacts-eu-ai-act-leveraging-gdpr-compliance/.

2008. "Strategy for the Development and Implementation of e-Navigation." MSC 85/26/Add.1 (January 6, 2009), Annex 20.

IMO (International Maritime Organization). 2019. "Interim Guidelines for MASS Trials." MSC.1/Circ.1604 (June 14, 2019).

2021. "Outcome of the Regulatory Scoping Exercise for the Use of Maritime Autonomous Surface Ships (MASS)." MSC.1/Circ.1638 (June 3, 2021).

2025a. "Autonomous Shipping." www.imo.org/en/MediaCentre/HotTopics/Pages/Autonomous-shipping.aspx.

2025b. "IMO e-Learning and Training." www.imo.org/en/OurWork/TechnicalCooperation/Pages/IMOe-LEARNING.aspx.

Johannsen, K., P. Smith, and M. Rodriguez. 2024. "AI-Enhanced Navigation Systems: Current Capabilities and Limitations." *International Journal of Maritime Engineering* 166 (1): 15–30.

Kanellopoulos, Anastasios-Nikolaos. 2024. "Enhancing Cyber Security and Counterintelligence in the Shipping Industry." *National Security and the Future* 25 (1): 137–154.

Kaspersen, Raymond Antoni, Henning Odeby Karlsen, Henrik Helgesen, Georg Giskegjerde, Christine Lagerstedt Krugerud, and Peter Nyegaard Hoffmann. 2022. *Insights into Seafarers Training and Skills Needed to Support a Decarbonized Shipping Industry*. DNV.

Kepesedi, Argyro. 2022. "Maritime Autonomous Surface Ships: A Critical 'MASS' for Legislative Review." UNCTAD, December 13. https://unctad.org/news/transport-newsletter-article-no-97-fourth-quarter-2022.

Kim, Tae-eun, and Jens-Uwe Schröder-Hinrichs. 2021. "Research Developments and Debates Regarding Maritime Autonomous Surface Ship: Status, Challenges and Perspectives." In *New Maritime Business: Uncertainty, Sustainability, Technology and Big Data*, edited by Byoung-Wook Ko and Dong-Wook Song. Springer Nature.

Kosinski, Matt, and Mark Scapicchio. 2024. "What Is the Artificial Intelligence Act of the European Union (EU AI Act)?" IBM, September 20. www.ibm.com/think/topics/eu-ai-act.

Lagdami, Khanssa. 2023. "Country Reports: Impact of Technology on Occupational Safety and Health of Seafarers." In *World Maritime University, Transport 2040: Automation, Technology, Employment, The Future of Work*. World Maritime University.

2024. "Technostress and the Future of Work at Sea." In *Human Factors in Design, Engineering, and Computing*, edited by Tareq Ahram and Waldemar Karwowski. AHFE International, vol. 159.

Lee, Kok Leong. 2023. "Will AI Sail Away with Jobs of Seafarers?" *Maritime Fairtrade*, July 17. https://maritimefairtrade.org/will-ai-sail-away-with-jobs-of-seafarers/.

Liu, Bin. 2021. "'Weak AI' Is Likely to Never Become 'Strong AI,' So What Is Its Greatest Value for Us?" *Arxiv*, March 29. https://arxiv.org/abs/2103.15294.

Lölfing, Nils. 2023. "Impact of the EU's AI Act Proposal on Automated and Autonomous Vehicles." Twobirds, April 12. www.twobirds.com/en/insights/2023/global/impact-of-the-eus-ai-act-proposal-on-automated-and-autonomous-vehicles.

Meier, Konrad, and Roger Spichiger. 2024. "The EU AI Act: What It Means for Your Business." EY, March 15. www.ey.com/en_ch/insights/forensic-integrity-services/the-eu-ai-act-what-it-means-for-your-business.

Moore, Phoebe V. 2019. "Artificial Intelligence in the Workplace: What Is at Stake for Workers?" In *Work in the Age of Data*. BBVA OpenMind Collection, No. 12.

2020. "The Mirror for (Artificial) Intelligence: In Whose Reflection?" In "Automation, Artificial Intelligence and Labour Protection," edited by Valerio De Stefano. Special issue, *Comparative Labor Law and Policy Journal* 41 (1): 47–67.

Munim, Ziaul Haque, Mariia Dushenko, Hyeran Raaness, and Tine Viveka Westerberg. 2023. "The Impact of Big Data Analytics Capabilities on the Sustainability of Maritime Firms." In *Data Analytics for Supply Chain Networks*, edited by Niamat Ullah Ibne Hossain. Springer.

Nautilus International. 2018. "Increase in Autonomous Ships Won't Mean a Shortage of Jobs for Seafarers." December 2. www.nautilusint.org/en/news-insight/telegraph/increase-in-autonomous-ships-wont-mean-a-shortage-of-jobs-for-seafarers/.

Nautilus Shipping. 2024. "The Role of Artificial Intelligence (AI) in Maritime Safety." www.nautilusshipping.com/the-role-of-artificial-intelligenceai-in-maritime-safety-3.

Nguyen, Gam Thi Hong, Daria Ruzaeva, Julio Cesar Góez, and Mario Guajardo. 2022. "Aspects Regarding the Adoption of Autonomous Vessels in Liner Shipping Networks." *Journal of Shipping and Trade* 7: article 12.

Obschonka, Martin, and David B. Audretsch. 2020. "Artificial Intelligence and Big Data in Entrepreneurship: A New Era Has Begun." *Small Business Economics* 55 (3): 529–539.

OECD (Organisation for Economic Co-operation and Development). 2022. "Policy Brief: Harnessing Digitalisation in Public Employment Services to Connect People with Jobs." www.oecd.org/employment/activation.htm.

RINA (Royal Institute of Naval Architects). 2018. "Collaboration Powers Rolls-Royce's Autonomous Vision." May 4. https://rina.org.uk/news/collaboration_powers_rolls-royces_autonomous_vision-html/.

Riviera News. 2022. "Yara Marine Adds Route Pilot AI to Voyage Optimisation Portfolio." September 8. www.rivieramm.com/news-content-hub/news-content-hub/yara-marine-adds-route-pilot-ai-to-voyage-optimisation-portfolio-72762.

Spire Maritime. n.d. "Maritime Artificial Intelligence & Machine Learning: Ultimate Guide." https://spire.com/maritime/maritime-artificial-intelligence-and-machine-learning/.

True North Marine. 2025. "West Africa's High-Risk Area: What's Changed & How AI Can Optimize Your Voyage." January 28. https://tnmservices.com/west-africas-high-risk-area-whats-changed-how-ai-can-optimize-your-voyages/.

Unoks. 2024. "AI Innovations Transforming the Maritime Industry." September 17. www.unoks.com/en/blog/artificial-intelligence-applications-in-the-maritime-industry.

WMU (World Maritime University). 2023. *Transport 2040: Automation, Technology, Employment, the Future of Work*. World Maritime University.

Wylie, Matt. 2024. "What Are the Safety Considerations for Maritime Autonomous Systems?" BMT, August 9. www.bmt.org/insights/what-are-the-safety-considerations-for-maritime-autonomous-systems/.

Youd, Frankie. 2022. "Crewless Cargo: The World's First Autonomous Electric Cargo Ship." Economic Development Board, February 24. www.ship-technology.com/features/crewless-cargo-the-worlds-first-autonomous-electric-cargo-ship/.

Zhang, L., and R. Martinez. 2023. "AI Adoption Rates in Commercial Maritime Operations." *Maritime Technology Review* 12 (3): 45–62.

4

Attribution of the Conduct of MASS Shipmasters to the Flag State

Maral Javidbakht

4.1 INTRODUCTION: THE NEXT AFTER GOD

Decades after the foresightful work of Schönknecht on ships and the shipping of tomorrow,[1] technological advancements in the shipping sector have finally reached the point of introducing Maritime Autonomous Surface Ships (MASS) and, with them, the shipmasters of tomorrow (Schönknecht and Bertholdt 1983).[2]

MASS are ships that enjoy variable degrees of the ability to operate independently from human interaction (IMO 2021, para. 3.3). The emergence of MASS is the outcome of the utilization of a range of technological advancements in the shipping sector that alters the level and the pattern of human involvement in the operation and navigation of a ship. As a result, many of those operational and navigational tasks that were to be performed by human beings on board a ship are now delegated to sensors, complex data processes, advanced algorithms, or AI-based systems. Therefore, the need for the presence of human beings on board a ship, or their involvement in its operation and navigation, is affected to variable degrees depending on the level of automation.[3]

The emergence of MASS has had a certain effect on the traditional concept of the shipmaster, which has evolved based on the authorities and responsibilities of the

[1] One of the early references to the utilization of technological developments in ship operations was made by Schönknecht, who predicted that in the future the shipmaster would not be obliged to be physically present on board, and that computers would take charge of the navigational tasks.

[2] The expression "next after God" in the title of this section refers to the shipmaster and highlights that great role and position regarding the operation and navigation of a ship during its voyage. References to the expression can be found in the early literature, including Barnes (1930).

[3] This chapter defines "automation" as functionality without human intervention. Accordingly, the term will be used whenever the ability to make relevant operational and navigational decisions is concerned. Therefore, the extent to which a ship is autonomous depends on its level of automation. Unmanned navigation is not equal to autonomous navigation. Depending on the level and extent of automation, an onboard shipmaster or crew may still be needed.

role. Those authorities and responsibilities can be traced back to ancient times, being rooted in the key navigational position of the shipmaster.[4] From a historical perspective, the salient position of the shipmaster regarding almost all matters concerning a ship and its voyage empowered them with a vast scope of authority and accordingly charged them with various responsibilities (Kay et al. 1894).

Modern technological advancements in the shipping sector have caused many of those traditional authorities and responsibilities of the shipmaster to pale into insignificance, but they have not completely eradicated the key position of the shipmaster due to the wide scope of the operational and navigational tasks that remain tied to the role.[5] The fact that these duties were unimaginable to be performed from a location rather than on board the ship, or by an entity rather than a human being, led to the formation of a presumption that the shipmaster is always a human being and performs their relevant duties with regard to the operation and navigation of the ship under their command on board. Based on this presumption, the very traditional concept of the shipmaster connotes a human being physically present on board.

However, along with the advancements in MASS-related technologies, the traditional concept of the shipmaster began to alter. This alteration is due to the possibility for MASS shipmasters to perform their duties from a remote location, typically called a remote operational center. It is also arguable that in the higher levels of ship autonomy – when great numbers of relevant operational or navigational tasks, each vast in scope, are to be performed autonomously – there will be no room left for a human shipmaster. Yet, at least from a legal perspective, this argumentation receives weak approvals.

The current International legal framework does not favor masterless navigation.[6] Many of the safety-related duties of the shipmaster, as codified under the relevant international instruments, imply that they are to be fulfilled by a human being as the shipmaster. An evident example is the overriding authority of the shipmaster, which enables them to proceed with their professional judgment in situations where the safety or security of navigation is endangered (see IMO 1980, 1993, Article 5(2)).[7] Due to the very aim of this duty, ensuring the safety of navigation, and taking into consideration that non–human-generated decisions are always accompanied by a

4 For an overview of the historical role and position of the shipmaster, see Ward (2009) and Toremar (2000).

5 For example, it is hard to assume the same authority for a modern shipmaster to sell the ship or its cargo as the representative of the shipowner. Yet the shipmaster is still in charge of the overall management of the cargo or passengers during the voyage.

6 See, for example, the mandates in Article 94 of the UNCLOS, December 10, 1982, 1833 UNTS 397.

7 This is comparable to the discretion of the shipmaster, as codified under the International Convention for the Safety of Life at Sea, November 1, 1974, 1184 UNTS 2, as amended by the Protocol of 1978 relating to the International Convention for Safety of Life at Sea, 1974, February 17, 1978, 1226 UNTS 213 (SOLAS), Chapter V, Regulation 34(1).

certain level of unpredictability, unreliability, and uncertainty, it is safe to assume that this role remains to be taken by human beings.[8]

Moreover, under many of the available national definitions of the term "shipmaster," emphasis has been added on the shipmaster as a "human" who retains the "command."[9] Thus, regardless of how advanced the level of autonomy in a MASS is, the national laws of several flag States require the overall command to be retained by a human as the shipmaster. In higher levels of ship autonomy, this overall command may be exercised through implementing decisions generated by autonomous systems or by supervising the system, always maintaining a way of intervention where deemed necessary. This position aligns with the view of the respondent flag States to a questionnaire conducted by the Comité Maritime International working group on unmanned ships, which unanimously expressed that the role of a shipmaster is to be taken by a natural person directly involved in the operation of MASS (CMI IWG 2017, 3).

Considering this, the chapter proceeds with the assumption that, even in the highest levels of autonomy, a human being must always be in overall command of the ship as the shipmaster. If a human retains the role of the shipmaster, their remote location is legally justifiable. Not only do most of the relevant definitions of shipmaster contain no indication of the necessity of the physical presence on board,[10] the current technological advancement makes room for a wide range of shipmaster's tasks to be done remotely. Yet, this finding does not imply that relocating the shipmaster from on board is unaccompanied by a range of legal issues.[11]

Retaining a human being in overall command of the ship is also what paves the way for assessing the applicability of the rules of attribution under the Draft Articles on Responsibility of States for Internationally Wrongful Acts (ARSIWA; ILC 2001)

8 A comparable argument is made by Ringbom and Veal with regard to a provision of the Convention on the International Regulations for Preventing Collisions at Sea, October 20, 1972, 1050 UNTS 16, which stated that the decision based on which rules of the Convention may be subject to deviation must be human-generated (Ringbom and Veal 2017).

9 Examples include, but are not limited to, 46 US Code §10101(1); the UK Merchant Shipping Act 1995, s. 313; the Maritime Commerce Law of the Republic of Panama of 2008, Ch. III, s. 1 (a), Article 29; the Maritime and Port Authority of Singapore Act 1996, as revised in 2020, Pt. 1; and the Italian Navigation Code of 1942, Article 292. See also Van Hooydonk (2014, 413n98).

10 There are indeed national definitions indicating a physical presence for the shipmaster on board the ship, including the definitions codified under the Dutch and German laws. See the Burgerlijk Wetboek of 1992, Verkeersmiddelen en Vervoer, 8:5–8:6; the Seearbeitsgesetz of 2013, §§3(1), 5(1).

11 Aside from the question of whether such relocation is accommodated by and in alignment with the current international regulations, it should be borne in mind that the relocation of the shipmaster from on board does not erase their duties concerning the operation and navigation of the ship. This becomes even more challenging when considering that many of these duties, as codified under the relevant international instruments, have revolved around the assumption that the shipmaster certainly has a physical presence on board the ship. An example is the duty of the shipmaster to render assistance to people in distress at sea, subject to Article 33 of SOLAS.

for the purpose of attribution of the conduct of a remote shipmaster to the flag State, as this chapter aims to do. According to the mandates of ARSIWA, there is no reliable ground for attribution of the conduct of a nonhuman to a State. With regard to MASS, it is vital to establish flag State responsibility that the wrongful conduct concerned can be traced back to a human being, here the shipmaster.[12]

Such an assessment also needs the term "shipmaster" to be defined. This is due to the vagueness of the concept, resulting from the lack of a comprehensive definition of the term despite the significance of the role and position. This vagueness, when accompanied by the alteration in the traditional concept of the shipmaster, as explained earlier, demands a clarification of the term "shipmaster."

Examples of a definition of the term under the relevant international instruments are not numerous.[13] Under several national maritime laws and regulations, the concept is defined and yet is referred to by different terms. For instance, the term "Captain" under the Dutch Civil Code or the German Maritime Labor Act is equivalent to the term "Master" under the UK Merchant Shipping Act or the Maritime and Port Authority of Singapore Act.[14]

To avoid terminological confusion, this chapter uses the term "shipmaster" to refer to the person who is in overall command of a ship and holds plenary responsibility for its operation and navigation (Cartner 2022, §§ 1.2.0, 1.2.1, 1.2.2). The approach of using distinguished terms for addressing such a person based on the ownership and utilization of the ship concerned, as is taken under US laws, is also avoided.[15]

This understanding of the term "shipmaster" not only reflects the significance of the shipmaster's position and their authority and responsibilities in the context of conventional navigation but also remains relevant and reliable when it comes to the operation and navigation of autonomous ships.

The main legal question the chapter addresses is whether relocating the shipmasters from on board has any effect on the attributability of their conduct as individuals to the flag State according to the rules of attribution codified under ARSIWA. In attempting to present a reliable answer to this question, the chapter raises various

[12] For a comprehensive discussion on the necessity of human conduct under the rules of ARSIWA, see Boutin (2023, 139–141).

[13] The International Convention on Standards of Training, Certification, and Watchkeeping for Seafarers defines "master" as the person who has the command of the ship: July 7, 1978, 1361 UNTS 2.

[14] See, for the Netherlands, the Burgerlijk Wetboek of 1992, Verkeersmiddelen en Vervoer, 8:5; for Germany, the Seearbeitsgesetz of 2013, §§3(1), 5(1); for the UK, the Merchant Shipping Act 1995, s. 313; and the Maritime and Port Authority of Singapore Act 1996, as revised in 2020, Pt. I.

[15] As explained by Cartner, naval ships under US laws do not have a master; rather, they have a commanding officer who is the ship's captain. In the case of commercial vessels, the master of the ship and the captain are equivalent and have the command of the ship (Cartner et al. 2009, 3–5). In his successive work, Cartner uses the term "Civil Commander" for the master of a commercial vessel (Cartner 2022).

subquestions: Is there a legal relationship between the shipmaster and the flag State? What are the legal grounds for the attribution of the conduct of the shipmaster to the flag State, based on the rules of ARSIWA, in the case of conventional ships? When, if ever, may these legal grounds be applicable to the remote shipmasters of MASS and their conduct?

The chapter next illustrates how the shipmaster and the flag State are legally and jurisdictionally bound to each other. Subsequently, the rules of ARSIWA on the attribution of the conduct of individuals to States come into play. Upon the evaluation of the application of the rules of attribution on the conduct of the shipmaster as a private person, the chapter further proceeds by illustrating the features that distinguish conventional shipmasters and MASS shipmasters to assess whether those features have any effect on the attributability of the conduct of MASS shipmasters to their flag State.

4.2 THE LEGAL RELATIONSHIP BETWEEN THE SHIPMASTER AND THE FLAG STATE

The question of attribution starts with mapping how the shipmaster and the flag State are linked to each other (ILC 2001, Article 8(1) commentary). Establishing a link between the shipmaster and the flag State, although it does not automatically make the conduct of the shipmaster attributable to the flag State, forms a basis for the application of rules of ARSIWA to the attribution of the conduct of a private person to a State.

Several potential grounds can be imagined for establishing a legal relationship between the flag State and the shipmasters of ships flying its flag. The appointment of the shipmaster to the role is usually based on a legal contract between the shipowner and the shipmaster, which is also a legal basis for the rights and duties of the shipmaster. An important instance is that to be eligible to enter into such a contract, the shipmaster must be sufficiently licensed and certified. As Cartner notes, the legal criteria and the process of obtaining the relevant licenses and certificates are determined and enforced in accordance with the laws of the flag State, taking into account the relevant international rules and standards to the extent ratified and adopted (Cartner et al. 2009, 98n108). In other words, it is the flag State that enables the shipmaster to enter the contract with the shipowner by warranting them.

When appointed, the shipmaster arguably acts as a conduit through which the flag State enforces its national laws on board the ship flying its flag (Cartner et al. 2009, 89). Many of these national laws are also international obligations codified under the relevant International law of the sea instruments, imposed either directly on the shipmaster or on the flag State to require the shipmaster to give effect to them. An example is the duty of the shipmaster to render assistance to people in distress at sea, as codified under the International Convention for the Safety of Life at Sea (SOLAS)[16] and the United Nations Convention on the Law of the Sea (UNCLOS).[17]

Furthermore, the shipmaster has traditionally been acting as the agent of the shipowner, safeguarding the common benefits of the ship and its cargo while voyaging on distant waters or berthing in foreign ports (Gold 2004, 57). Although the scope of such agency in the modern era has been subject to limitations, the agent status of the shipmaster is still relevant, especially when it comes to the commercial aspect of a voyage (58). This leads to the stimulating question of whether the shipmaster of a governmentally owned or operated ship acts as the agent of its flag State. Whether that is the case or not, it should be borne in mind that the scope and capacity of this agency are unlikely to be the same as the agency in the sense of the Articles on Responsibility of States for Internationally Wrongful Acts. Therefore, it cannot form, at least solely, a basis for attribution of conduct.

The flag State also has the competency to represent the shipmaster, as well as the right to institute a claim in the case of any loss or damage. As argued by Saint Vincent and the Grenadines in the case concerning the M/V *Saiga*, the rule of international law with regard to the right of States to protect their nationals is not applicable in cases where the claim concerns a ship flying its flag, things on board it, or all persons involved or interested in its operation. Therefore, the flag State enjoys the right to protect the shipmaster regardless of their nationality.[18]

The legal justification of this argument flows from the content of Article 91(1) of UNCLOS, where it is noted that ships hold the nationality of their flag State. Endowing nationality to a ship creates a jurisdictional link between the flag State and the ship (O'Connell 1984, 796; see also Guilfoyle 2017, Article 91, para. 1, 693). As the International Tribunal for the Law of the Sea (ITLOS) notes in its procedural rule, UNCLOS considers ships and all people involved in their operation as a single unit linked to the flag State.[19] Thus, the jurisdiction of the flag State over the ship flying its flag also expands itself to the shipmaster, not to mention that exercising such jurisdiction over the shipmaster and other crew members is the basis for the flag State to give effect to its obligations – for example, those codified under Articles 94 and 217 of UNCLOS.[20]

Nevertheless, the legal relationship between the shipmaster and the flag State as such cannot be a basis for the attribution of the conduct. The matter of attribution of the conduct of a private person or entity to a State is a matter of international law

[16] International Convention for the Safety of Life at Sea, November 1, 1974, 1184 UNTS 2, as amended by the Protocol of 1978 relating to the International Convention for Safety of Life at Sea, 1974, February 17, 1978, 1226 UNTS 213 (SOLAS), Annex V, Regulation 33.

[17] UNCLOS, December 10, 1982, 1833 UNTS 397, Article 98.

[18] *M/V "Saiga" (No. 2) Case (St. Vincent v. Guinea)*, Case No. 2, Judgment of July 1, 1999, ITLOS Rep. 1999, para. 104.

[19] *M/V "Saiga" (No. 2)*, para. 106.

[20] *M/V "Saiga" (No. 2)*, para. 104.

and, therefore, as noted by the International Law Commission, is to be exclusively settled by criteria provided by international law (ILC 2001, Chapter II commentary, para. 4).

What is considered applicable international law in this context is the mandate of the second chapter of ARSIWA on the rules of attribution. Although ARSIWA, by its nature, does not constitute a source of international law, its content has gained binding effect through customary international law. Thus, despite the existence of a relationship between the flag State and the shipmaster, the attributability of the conduct of a shipmaster as a private person to the flag State is to be assessed taking into consideration the mandates of ARSIWA.

4.3 ATTRIBUTION OF THE CONDUCT OF THE SHIPMASTER TO THE FLAG STATE

As noted under its rules of attribution, ARSIWA implies that, as a general principle, the conduct of private persons cannot be attributed to a State (ILC 2001, Chapter II commentary, para. 3). This general rule applies to the conduct of a shipmaster as an individual. However, exceptions to this general rule are also mentioned under ARSIWA.

According to Article 4 of ARSIWA, the conduct of organs of a State is attributable to the State. Individuals may be considered organs of a State, provided they have such status under the internal laws of that State. As prescribed by Article 4 of ARSIWA, whenever an organ status is established for an entity or individual, their conduct is considered the act of the State itself. A State and its organs are one. It cannot be assumed that the actions and intentions of an organ of a State are distinguished from the actions and intentions of the State, for the State functions and declares its intentions through its organs (Anzilotti 1912, 126; see also Sereni 1940, 639n5). In this regard, neither is there a difference in their function or their position, nor if they act as central organs of a government or local units (ILC 2001, Article 2 commentary, paras. 6–8).

Whether a shipmaster can be considered an organ of a flag State depends on whether the ship concerned is governmentally or privately operated. When the ship concerned is governmentally operated, the shipmaster is considered as a de jure organ of the flag State (De Vittor and Starita 2018, 84; Papastavridis 2016, 172). The shipmaster is designated by the flag State to take command of a ship that represents the government of the flag State.[21]

[21] See UNCLOS, Article 29, which, among other constitutive elements of the definition of "warship," includes being "under the command of an officer duly commissioned by the government of the State." Although not all governmentally operated ships are warships, this element is extendable to other types of governmentally operated ships.

This analysis is also inferred from the South China Arbitration Award, which notes that the actions of a government-operated ship are attributable to the state as actions of the government.[22] A ship is only an object and, therefore, cannot proceed with any actions on its own. It is the shipmaster, in their commanding position, who puts the ship into action. This finding is also in accordance with the procedural rule of the ship as a unit, as previously mentioned.

The internal law of a flag State also plays an important role in determining whether the shipmaster of a governmentally operated ship enjoys an organ status. However, even in cases where a direct indication of the recognition of an organ status for the shipmaster is absent under the internal laws of the flag State, the shipmaster of a governmentally operated ship may still be considered a de facto organ of the flag State, since the concept of de facto organ evolves on the fact that even when the internal laws of a state do not recognize an entity as an organ of the state, that entity enjoys organ status as long as it practices as an organ (Crawford 2013). According to ARSIWA, the term "organ" covers all those individual or collective entities that act on behalf of a State (ILC 2001, Article 4 commentary, para. 1). Given the representative status of governmentally operated ships, regardless of their function, it is safe to assume that their shipmasters act on behalf of the State.

When it comes to private ships, attributability of the conduct of the shipmaster to the flag State is not as straightforward as the case of governmentally operated ships, yet it is still feasible. One way of establishing attribution is using the mandates of Article 5 of ARSIWA, which prescribes that the conduct of a person who is not an organ of a State, but who exercises elements of governmental authority, shall be considered the act of the State.[23] Obviously, not all duties embedded in the role of the shipmaster are in fulfillment of governmental authorities. Thus, assessing the possibility of the attribution of the shipmaster's conduct based on Article 5 depends on the particulars of the certain obligation breached and accordingly requires a context.[24] For instance, under Article 98 of UNCLOS, the flag State is charged with an international obligation to require the shipmaster to render assistance to people in distress at sea. The wording of the regulation evidently addresses flag States and imposes an obligation on them. Yet the very subject of such an obligation affects and involves the shipmaster.

The obligation "to require," as codified under Article 98 of UNCLOS, resembles an obligation of result.[25] All that the first paragraph of this article requires from the

[22] *South China Sea Arbitration (Philippines v. China)*, Case No. 2013-19, Award, para. 703 (Perm. Ct. Arb. 2016), 33 RIAA 3.

[23] The seventh paragraph of the Commentaries on this article clearly notes that the entity or person concerned must be empowered by internal laws to exercise such governmental authority (ILC 2001).

[24] See Crawford (2013, 129), where it is argued that defining what exactly falls into the scope of governmental authority always depends on the particulars of each situation and society.

[25] Also noted by Papastavridis (2016, 164). For an opposing view on the content of the obligation of the flag State under Article 98 of UNCLOS, see Attard (2020, 44).

flag State is to require the shipmaster of the ship flying its flag to perform certain actions as described under its subparagraphs. The flag State performs this duty by enacting national legal provisions through its national legislative body (Guilfoyle 2017, Article 98, para. 7, 727). Thus, once such provisions are included in the national laws of the flag State, the result is achieved and, therefore, the obligation is fulfilled.[26]

Here, the shipmaster is indeed empowered by the national laws of the flag State to render assistance to people in distress at sea. The shipmaster, in this sense, enforces the national laws of the flag State, which demand that the shipmaster provide assistance (De Vittor and Starita 2018). However, it is unlikely that enforcing the laws of the flag State in this case can be considered an exercise of governmental authority.

The reason for this is simply that the very act of rendering assistance and rescuing is nothing but a humanitarian duty for the flag State (Papastavridis 2016, 172; Attard 2020, 263; Trevisanut 2017). In other words, no level of delegated governmental authority can be detected in this case, since the very act of rendering assistance cannot be branded governmental unless provided otherwise by the national laws of the flag State. As stated in the commentaries to Article 5: "The internal law in question must specifically authorize the conduct as involving the exercise of public authority" (ILC 2001, Article 5 commentary, para. 7).[27] Thus, the matter is up to the national laws of the flag State and the very position of the shipmaster in its legal framework. When the national laws of the shipmaster label a certain duty of the shipmaster governmental and empower the flag State with the authority to perform it, the conduct of the shipmaster with regard to that duty can be attributable to the flag State.

Another potential scenario for attributing the conduct of the shipmaster of a private vessel to the flag State is when the flag State instructs or controls the wrongful conduct of the shipmaster. This is to be inferred from the mandates of Article 8 of ARSIWA, which provides that the conduct of a person who is instructed, directed, or controlled by a State is considered the conduct of that State. It is crucial to note that, in cases of both instruction and control, establishing attribution based on the mandates of the article always requires a certain level of effectiveness in the control. Although the notion and content of "effective control" has been repeatedly addressed by international courts, there is no single way to formulate such control.

[26] What is demanded under Article 98 to be required from the shipmaster is still indeed to be performed by the shipmaster. In this sense, what binds the shipmaster are the national laws of the flag State. Hence, not giving effect to what is required by the laws of the flag State on board the ship may make the shipmaster subject to criminal responsibility for the shipmaster's own actions, but will not make the flag State subject to international responsibility.

[27] There are criteria for determining what constitutes governmental authority: the content of power, how the power is granted to the entity concerned, the purpose for exercising the power conferred, and the level and extent of the accountability of the entity concerned for exercising the power. For a full discussion, see Crawford (2013).

This is because the legal test for effective control varies among cases (Crawford 2013, 204). For instance, while the International Court of Justice in both the *Nicaragua* and *Genocide* cases held that the State must exercise effective control over each and every specific act involved in the wrongful conduct, the position of the International Criminal Tribunal for the former Yugoslavia was that an overall control of the State sufficed.[28]

Nevertheless, determining the existence of such control may be challenging when a privately operated ship is concerned.[29] As De Vittor and Starita suggest, the shipmaster as a human being always possesses some autonomy to refuse the wrongful instruction of a flag State (De Vittor and Starita 2018, 85). Therefore, establishing attribution based on the mandates of Article 8 of ARSIWA requires such a great level of control being exercised by the flag State as to practically leave the shipmaster with no option other than giving effect to the wrongful conduct ordered or controlled by the flag State.

The discussion above has concerned the legal grounds for attributing the conduct of the shipmaster to the flag State, taking into account the mandates of ARSIWA. A noteworthy observation is that for the purpose of establishing flag State responsibility, attribution is one of the undisputedly crucial elements. However, in cases where flag State responsibility is to be established based on the wrongful conduct of the shipmaster, what is attributable to the flag State may also be not the shipmaster's conduct but rather its own.

The flag State is obliged to ensure that what is required from the shipmaster is discharged by them. This duty is categorized as an obligation of conduct. Therefore, when the shipmaster of a privately operated ship avoids discharging their relevant duties, the matter should be settled through the channel of criminal responsibility of the shipmaster, unless it is evident that the flag State has not taken all necessary steps to prevent or punish such avoidance.

In an advisory opinion requested by the Sub-Regional Fisheries Commission, ITLOS determined that flag States are bound by the due diligence obligation concerning illegal, unreported, and unregulated fishing activities conducted by vessels flying their flags.[30] As Papastavridis maintains, a similar due diligence obligation can be assumed for the flag State in the context of rendering assistance and rescue operations as what is required from flag States under Article 98 of

[28] *Military and Paramilitary Activities in and against Nicaragua (Nicaragua v. United States of America)*, Merits, Judgment, 1986 ICJ Rep. 14, para. 115 (June 27); *Application of the Convention on the Prevention and Punishment of the Crime of Genocide (Bosnia and Herzegovina v. Serbia and Montenegro)*, Judgment, 2007 ICJ Rep. 43, paras. 400–413 (February 26); *Prosecutor v. Tadić*, Case No. IT-94-1-A, Appeals Chamber Judgment (ICTY, July 15, 1999), para. 137.

[29] This is generally far easier to be concluded when the case concerns a governmentally operated ship. See, for example, *Hirsi Jamaa v. Italy*, App. No. 27765/09 (February 23, 2012) (ECtHR).

[30] *Request for Advisory Opinion Submitted by the Sub-Regional Fisheries Commission*, Advisory Opinion of April 2, 2015, ITLOS Rep. 2015, para. 146.

UNCLOS, which includes a "level of vigilance in their enforcement" (Papastavridis 2016, 164). This is very well aligned with the position of the International Law Commission, which noted that "the different rules of attribution stated in chapter II have a cumulative effect, such that a State may be responsible for the effects of the conduct of private parties, if it failed to take necessary measures to prevent those effects" (ILC 2001, Chapter II commentary, para. 4).

Therefore, the conduct of the shipmaster of a private vessel may attract the responsibility of the flag State, if the flag State fails to ensure that the shipmaster discharges their duties and refrains from not giving effect to them. In this case, what is attributable to the flag State is not the conduct of the shipmaster but its failure to ensure that the performance of the shipmaster is in accordance with what is legally expected from them; and, if not, their wrongful performance is to be dealt with through effective punitive measures.

However, this may be challenging to establish due to the content of the obligation. As previously noted, the due diligence obligation of the flag State to prevent wrongful conduct of the shipmaster requires it to take all necessary steps to ensure that such conduct is prevented. Thus, establishing flag State responsibility is feasible only if it is proven that the flag State has indeed failed in making its best efforts to prevent the conduct concerned.

4.4 THE NEW SHIPMASTER AND THE FLAG STATE

When it comes to the context of autonomous shipping, the attributability of the conduct of the shipmaster to the flag State must be evaluated, taking into account elements that distinguish between the shipmasters of conventional ships and those of MASS – most importantly, their remote location.

Before proceeding further with this element, it is necessary to note that autonomous ships, regardless of their special features, enjoy the same characteristic as their conventional peers as "ship." The matter of what is considered a ship under the international law of the sea is beyond the scope of this chapter. However, it can generally be argued that as far as UNCLOS is concerned, the matter depends on the laws of flag States.[31]

Several national maritime laws do not exclude the special features of MASS in their definitions of the term "ship." In addition, autonomous ships meet the constitutive criteria based on which a vessel is recognized as a ship, as included in those definitions, such as the ability to float, having a hollow design, or being involved in navigation.[32]

[31] The same argument has been delivered in Veal et al. (2016, 10); see also Veal et al. (2019).

[32] Examples include but not limited to: In Australia, the Shipping Registration Act 1981 (Cth), Pt. I, s. 3; the Maritime Code of the People's Republic of China of 1992 (Zhao and Li 2017, 7); in the Netherlands, the Burgerlijk Wetboek of 1992, Verkeersmiddelen en Vervoer, 8:1 (Falkanger et al. 2017, 50–51); and in the UK, the Merchant Shipping Act 1995, s. 313.

The enjoyment of a ship's status is what makes autonomous ships equally subject to the same legal rules enshrined in the international law of the sea framework as their conventional peers. Thus, they must have a master at least in overall command (UNCLOS, Article 94). This role is always to be taken by a human being, regardless of their level of involvement in operational or navigational tasks or their location. Thus, the assessment of whether the same legal relationship can be assumed between the flag State and these "new" shipmasters hinges on whether that relationship flows from the physical location of the shipmaster on board the ship concerned.

Among the different factors that create a link between the shipmaster and the flag State, as previously discussed, the jurisdictional link is the one that may arguably be most affected by the relocation of the shipmaster from on board. Assuming that the jurisdiction of the flag State on the shipmaster flows from its jurisdiction on the ship, the procedural rule of the ship as a unit again comes into play.

As formulated by ITLOS, "every person involved or interested in [the ship's] operation is linked to the flag state."[33] The wording of that paragraph makes no reference to the physical location of "every person"; rather, their involvement in the ship's operation suffices to link them to the ship and, consequently, to the flag State, since the ship itself is linked to the flag State once it has been registered under its flag (UNCLOS, Article 91).

The most important element that distinguishes conventional and MASS shipmasters is their remote location, especially in higher degrees of ship autonomy. The new shipmaster who, as a result of the ship's automation, performs their relevant duties from a remote location is still, to a high degree, involved in the ship's operation. Thus, they retain their position linked to the ship and subsequently to the flag State. As argued by Yoo and Shan, it is crucial for remote shipmasters and crew that they are assumed to be an integral and inseparable part of the MASS, regardless of their location (Yoo and Shan 2019, 563). Otherwise, not only would they fall out of the scope of the relevant regulations under the international law of the sea framework, but also the ship itself would be exposed to unseaworthiness.

Furthermore, Article 94(2)(b) of UNCLOS explicitly notes that the flag State is obliged to assume jurisdiction over the ship flying its flag and its shipmaster under its internal laws. The answer to the question of how exactly the flag State must fulfill this obligation is closely bound to the content and nature of the obligation, as well as whether the remote location of the new shipmaster remains within the territorial jurisdiction of the flag State. This falls outside the scope of this chapter. Yet, nothing would diminish the importance of this obligation being fulfilled, as giving effect to various other international obligations imposed on the flag State is bound to such jurisdiction being effectively exercised (Nandan and Rosenne 1995, Article 94, para. 94.8(a)).

[33] *M/V "Saiga" (No. 2)*, para. 106.

Thus, not only does the remote location of the shipmaster have no effect on them being jurisdictionally linked to the flag State, but also the flag State is, in fact, bound by an international obligation to effectively exercise such jurisdiction over the remote shipmaster. Even in cases where the remote shipmaster does not have the nationality of the flag State and performs their duties from an ROC located outside the territory of the flag State, the flag State shall exercise its jurisdiction over the master. The ship as a unit is under the jurisdiction of the flag State, and this provides sufficient legal ground for the situation mentioned.

However, the effective implementation of this situation may need the flag State to cover sufficiently the matter under its national laws, since the situation would not fit into the common rules of allocation of jurisdiction. Nevertheless, it is important to note that attribution and jurisdiction are two separate concepts that may overlap, but do not necessarily do so. Assessment of the relationship between attribution and jurisdiction in the context of the international law of the sea is different from other contexts, such as human rights law.[34] When it comes to the international law of the sea, assuming jurisdiction by the flag State over the shipmasters of ships flying its flag is a basis for guaranteeing the enforcement of the laws of the flag State on board a ship. Moreover, this jurisdiction provides a legal basis on which the flag State can represent the shipmaster regardless of their nationalities or take punitive measures in cases where shipmasters refrain from performing their relevant duties.

Although the remote location of the shipmaster, especially in cases where the remote operational centers are located outside the territory of the flag State, poses challenges for the flag State to enforce its jurisdiction, it is unlikely that these challenges also attenuate grounds for attribution of the conduct of the shipmaster based on the rules of ARSIWA. This is simply because as far as the rules of attribution under ARSIWA are concerned, no indication of the necessity of jurisdiction for establishing attribution can be detected. In other words, ARSIWA does not require a jurisdictional link between the private person and the State for the purpose of attribution. Attribution can be established based on nationality or territoriality. This reasoning may extend further by relying on cases in which the conduct of a private person or entity was attributable to a State while they neither were nationals of that State nor had committed the wrongful conduct within its territorial jurisdiction. Instead, "control" was a basis for the attributability of conduct.[35]

It is arguable that in the context of the international law of the sea, jurisdiction, when effectively exercised, normally entails a certain level of control. When Article 94 of UNCLOS makes it an obligation for the flag State to effectively exercise its

[34] For an overall assessment of the relationship between jurisdiction and attribution, see in general Caflisch (2017), Jorritsma (2019), and Rooney (2015).

[35] See *Military and Paramilitary Activities in and against Nicaragua (Nicaragua v. United States of America)*, Merits, Judgment, ICJ Rep. 1986, paras. 105–115; *Application of the Convention on the Prevention and Punishment of the Crime of Genocide (Bosnia and Herzegovina v. Serbia and Montenegro)*, Judgment, ICJ Rep. 2007, paras. 391–406.

jurisdiction over the ship flying its flag, it seems that the ultimate goal is to ensure that the flag State retains a certain level of control over the vessel as a unit, which enables it to deliver its relevant duties with regard to the safety of navigation.

Given that exercising jurisdiction over the ship and its master is a duty imposed on the flag State under UNCLOS, it is safe to assume that the flag State must retain a consistent control over the ship flying its flag, as well as its master, officers, and crew (see Article 94(2)(b)). Whether such a control is effective enough to form a ground for attribution of the conduct of the shipmaster to the flag State is a matter that is to be evaluated on a case-by-case basis, taking into consideration the applicable rules of international law and the particulars of each case.

4.5 CONCLUSION

The advent of emerging technologies in the maritime sector has made it necessary for many of the current relevant regulations to be reconsidered, adjusted, modified, or even replaced. Many others, however, may retain their relevance and applicability. Rapid advancement in MASS results in many safety and security concerns, to which the current international regulations may not be fully respondent. This highlights the importance of the question of responsibility for their operation and navigation.

Among all parties involved in the operation of MASS, their flag States are at the forefront of ensuring the safety and security of their operation and navigation. Thus, it is crucial for the flag States willing to benefit from the advantages of MASS to be fully aware of their duties regarding their operation and navigation. This very well leads to the question of the international responsibility of the flag State for the operation of MASS flying their flag.

Establishing flag State responsibility is bound to the existence of constitutive elements of the international responsibility of States, including attribution of the wrongful conduct to the flag State. For MASS to identify as ships, they are subject to the same regulatory framework applicable to conventional ships. This, among other things, includes the rejection of masterless navigation as well as the unsuitability of appointing a nonhuman shipmaster. Yet, the special features of MASS have enabled the shipmaster to retain the overall command of the MASS concerned, performing a vast scope of relevant operational and navigational duties from a remote location, especially in higher levels of ship autonomy.

The relocation of the shipmaster from on board, although it is accompanied by a certain range of legal issues, has almost no impact on the applicability of the rules of attribution as codified under ARSIWA. Taking into consideration the relationship between the shipmaster and the flag State, along with the procedural rule of the "ship as a unit" as formulated by ITLOS, it becomes evident that what creates a link between the shipmaster and the flag State is not the physical location of the shipmaster. Rather, it is the legal position of the shipmaster, as well as the jurisdictional link between the shipmaster and the flag State that is created when the ship is endowed with the right to fly the flag of the State.

Exercising effective jurisdiction by the flag State over MASS flying its flag, and accordingly over their shipmasters, is one of the most significant legal challenges that must be addressed, especially in cases where the remote operational center is located outside of the territory of the flag State. The legal challenge, however, does not hinder the applicability of rules of attribution as formulated under ARSIWA.

Although jurisdiction, when effectively exercised, is indeed a legal basis for exercising control over the performance of the shipmaster and, accordingly, taking punitive measures against the wrongful conduct of the shipmaster, it cannot solely be a legal ground for establishing attribution. Attribution of the conduct of an individual to a State is a matter of international law and, therefore, is solely governed by the rules of international law, here the mandates of ARSIWA.

Thus, attribution of the conduct of the shipmaster to the flag State is to be assessed through Articles 4, 5, and 8 of ARSIWA. Elements such as MASS being governmentally or privately operated, whether the duty imposed on the shipmaster may be labeled governmental, whether the wrongful conduct of the shipmaster regarding that duty forms a breach, the role and the level of control of the flag State on prescribing the wrongful conduct, and the particulars of each case are among the factors that impact the applicability of those articles. It should also be borne in mind that flag States – those willing to endow the right to fly their flag to MASS – must clearly define the role and the position of MASS shipmasters in their national laws. This potentially plays a determinant role in the assessment of the applicability of rules of attribution with regard to the conduct of the shipmaster, as codified under ARSIWA.

REFERENCES

Anzilotti, Dionisio. 1912. *Corso di dritto internazionale*. Athenaeum.

Attard, Felicity G. 2020. *The Duty of the Shipmaster to Render Assistance at Sea Under International Law*. Brill Nijhoff.

Barnes, William Morris. 1930. *When Ships Were Ships and Not Tin Pots: The Seafaring Adventures of Captain William Morris Barnes*. Albert & Charles Boni.

Boutin, Bérénice. 2023. "State Responsibility in Relation to Military Applications of Artificial Intelligence." *Leiden Journal of International Law* 36 (1): 133–150.

Caflisch, Lucius. 2017. "Attribution, Responsibility and Jurisdiction in International Human Rights Law." *Anuario colombiano de derecho internacional* 10: 161–203.

Cartner, John A. C. 2022. *Cartner on the International Law of the Shipmaster: On the New Command at Sea*. Informa Law.

Cartner, John A. C., Richard Fiske, and Tara Leiter. 2009. *The International Law of the Shipmaster*. Informa Law.

CMI IWG (Comité Maritime International International Working Group). 2017. "Summary of Responses to the CMI Questionnaire on Unmanned Ships." CMI IWG Submission to the 99th Session of IMO's Maritime Safety Committee, Annex 1. https://comitemaritime.org/wp-content/uploads/2018/05/Summary-of-Responses-to-the-CMI-Questionnaire.docx.

Crawford, James. 2013. *State Responsibility: The General Part*. Cambridge University Press.

De Vittor, Francesca, and Massimo Starita. 2018. "Distributing Responsibility Between Shipmasters and the Different States Involved in SAR Disasters." *Italian Yearbook of International Law* 28 (1): 77–95.

Falkanger, Thor, Hans Jacob Bull, and Lasse Brautaset. 2017. *Scandinavian Maritime Law: The Norwegian Perspective*. 4th ed. Universitetsforlaget.

Gold, Edgar. 2004. "From Privilege to Peril: The Shipmaster's Current Legal Rights and Responsibilities." *WMU Journal of Maritime Affairs* 3: 51–66.

Guilfoyle, Douglas. 2017. "Part VII: High Seas: Articles 86–111." In *United Nations Convention on the Law of the Sea: A Commentary*, edited by Alexander Proelss. Nomos Verlagsgesellschaf.

ILC (International Law Commission). 2001. "Draft Articles on Responsibility of States for Internationally Wrongful Acts, with Commentaries." In *Yearbook of the International Law Commission 2001*, vol. II, pt. 2. United Nations.

IMO (International Maritime Organization). 1980. "Decisions of the Shipmaster with Regard to Maritime Safety and Marine Environment Protection." A XI/Res.443 (March 6, 1980).

1993. "International Safety Management Code for the Safe Operation of Ships and for Pollution Prevention (International Safety Management (ISM) Code)." A 18/Res.741 (November 17, 1993), as amended by MSC.104(73), MSC.179(79), MSC.195(80), and MSC.173(85).

2021. "Outcome of the Regulatory Scoping Exercise for the Use of Maritime Autonomous Surface Ships (MASS)." MSC.1/Circ.1638 (June 3, 2021).

Jorritsma, Remy. 2019. "Unravelling Attribution, Control and Jurisdiction: Some Reflections on the Case Law of the European Court of Human Rights." In *International Law and Litigation: A Look into Procedure*, edited by Hélène Ruiz Fabri. Nomos.

Kay, Joseph, John William Mansfield, and George William Duncan. 1894. *The Law Relating to Shipmasters and Seamen: Their Appointment, Duties, Powers, Rights, and Liabilities*. 2nd ed. Stevens and Haynes.

Nandan, Satya N., and Shabtai Rosenne, eds. 1995. *United Nations Convention on the Law of the Sea 1982: A Commentary*, vol. III. Martinus Nijhoff.

O'Connell, D. P. 1984. *The International Law of the Sea*, vol. 2. Clarendon Press.

Papastavridis, Efthymios. 2016. "Rescuing Migrants at Sea and the Law of International Responsibility." In *Human Rights and the Dark Side of Globalisation*, edited by Thomas Gammeltoft-Hansen and Jens Vedsted-Hansen. Routledge.

Ringbom, Henrik, and Robert Veal. 2017. "Unmanned Ships and the International Regulatory Framework." *Journal of International Maritime Law* 23 (2): 100–118.

Rooney, Jane M. 2015. "The Relationship between Jurisdiction and Attribution after *Jaloud v. Netherlands*." *Netherlands International Law Review* 62 (3): 407–428.

Schönknecht, Rolf, and J. Bertholdt. 1983. *Ships and Shipping of Tomorrow*. McGregor.

Sereni, Angelo Piero. 1940. "Agency in International Law." *American Journal of International Law* 34 (4): 638–660.

Toremar, Marcus. 2000. "The Legal Position of the Ship Master." Master's diss., Göteborg University.

Trevisanut, Seline. 2017. "Search and Rescue Operations at Sea." In *The Practice of Shared Responsibility in International Law*, edited by André Nollkaemper and Ilias Plakokefalos. Cambridge University Press.

Van Hooydonk, Eric. 2014. "The Law of Unmanned Merchant Shipping: An Exploration." *Journal of International Maritime Law* 20 (3): 403–423.

Veal, Robert, Michael Tsimplis, and Andrew Serdy. 2019. "The Legal Status and Operation of Unmanned Maritime Vehicles." *Ocean Development & International Law* 50 (1): 23–48.

Veal, Robert, Michael Tsimplis, Andrew Serdy, Alexandros Ntovas, and Simon Quinn. 2016. *Liability for Operations in Unmanned Maritime Vehicles with Differing Levels of Autonomy Deliverable: Final Report*. University of Southampton for the European Defence Agency, Ref. No: 14.CAT.OP.065.

Ward, Robin. 2009. *The World of the Medieval Shipmaster: Law, Business and the Sea, c.1350–c.1450*. Boydell & Brewer.

Yoo, Jinho, and Desai Shan. 2019. "Legal Status of an Onshore Remote Controller of Maritime Autonomous Surface Ships ('MASS') under the Canadian Maritime Law and IMO International Conventions." Canadian Transportation Research Forum 54th Annual Conference, May 26–29: 562–569.

Zhao, Liang, and Lianjun Li. 2017. *Maritime Law and Practice in China*. Informa Law.

PART II

Protection of the Marine Environment

5

Toward a Just and Equitable Transition to Decarbonization of the International Shipping Sector

Sindhura Polepalli

5.1 INTRODUCTION

Climate change is moving faster than we are . . . There is no more time to waste. (Guterres 2018; see also IPCC 2018; UNEP 2022)

On May 21, 2024, the Advisory Opinion[1] of the International Tribunal for the Law of the Sea (ITLOS) confirmed that climate change, including global warming and sea-level rise, poses an existential threat and raises human rights concerns (IPCC 2019b, 78, 2021a). This international judicial holding relies heavily on the scientific findings of the Intergovernmental Panel on Climate Change (IPCC) and specifically acknowledges the "unequivocal" role of human activities in driving climate change by increasing atmospheric greenhouse gas (GHG)[2] concentrations in the past two millennia (ITLOS Advisory Opinion, para. 48; IPCC 2023).

Anthropogenic GHG emissions hinder the ability of solar energy to escape the Earth's atmosphere, trapping heat therein and leading to its reabsorption into the Earth's surface (UNEP 2022). Also known as the greenhouse effect, this means that increased GHG emissions accelerate global warming, which is one of the key drivers of climate change (IPCC 2019a). The IPCC has warned that human-induced climate change is a global emergency that affects human and environmental health in multiple ways and that global warming is threatening its escalation (IPCC 2021b,

[1] *Request for an Advisory Opinion submitted by the Commission of Small Island States on Climate Change and International Law*, Advisory Opinion of May 21, 2024, ITLOS Case No. 31, paras. 47, 53, 54, 55, 57, 59, 66, 175, 388, 398 (hereinafter ITLOS Advisory Opinion).

[2] Greenhouse gases are those gaseous constituents of the atmosphere, both natural and anthropogenic, that absorb and reemit infrared radiation. See United Nations Framework Convention on Climate Change, May 9, 1992, 1771 UNTS 107 (UNFCCC), Article 1.5. The six GHGs are carbon dioxide (CO_2), methane (CH_4), nitrous oxide (N_2O), hydrofluorocarbons (HFCs), perfluorocarbons (PFCs), and sulfur hexafluoride (SF6). See Kyoto Protocol to the United Nations Framework Convention on Climate Change, December 11, 1997, 2303 UNTS 162 (Kyoto Protocol), Annex A.

2023, 89). In this context, the Advisory Opinion of ITLOS – an international judicial body established under the United Nations Convention on the Law of the Sea (UNCLOS),[3] which today has 171 State parties – serves as a major global legal endorsement of these scientific findings by reinforcing the scientific consensus and amplifying the call for decisive action.

The oceans are fundamental climate regulators (ITLOS Advisory Opinion, para. 55). There is no denying that the pressing need for deep reductions in GHG emissions summoned by the IPCC report, which was signed by the World Meteorological Organization and the United Nations Environment Programme (IPCC 2023, v), also warrants urgent sensitization of anthropogenic marine interactions. ITLOS has held that UNCLOS State parties have "specific obligations to take all necessary measures to prevent, reduce and control marine pollution from anthropogenic GHG emissions and to endeavour to harmonize their policies in this connection" (ITLOS Advisory Opinion, para. 441(3)(b)).

Despite such global clarity for the need to specifically address anthropogenic maritime GHG emissions, the case for relevant actions within the international shipping sector (hereinafter "the sector") is rather complex. The sector has been the backbone of global trade and economy due to its cost- and energy-efficient character in comparison to other modes of transport.[4] However, increased global maritime trade has resulted in a 62 percent increase in the sector's share of global anthropogenic GHG emissions over the past two decades, with estimates suggesting a 90–130 percent increase in emissions by 2050 compared to 2008 levels (IMO 2021a). Moreover, the sector's global nature, with diverse and multiple stakeholders across various jurisdictions, complicates the attribution of its emissions to any particular national economy. Therefore, the contemporary global goal of reducing GHG emissions in the sector requires a customized approach.

Against that backdrop, this chapter examines the existing approach to addressing GHG emissions within the sector and finds certain procedural and legal disparities toward achieving a "just and equitable transition" (JET). This finding is a culmination of components analyzed in Sections 5.2, 5.3, and 5.4 of this chapter. Section 5.2 highlights the multinational and multidimensional character of the sector and explores its interaction with the general international legal framework to address climate change, including the findings of the ITLOS Advisory Opinion. Section 5.3 traces the specialized measures adopted under the auspices of the International Maritime Organization (IMO) for addressing anthropogenic GHG emissions within the sector. Section 5.4 contextualizes the relevant measures in the sector with the

[3] United Nations Convention on the Law of the Sea, December 10, 1982, 1833 UNTS 397 (UNCLOS).

[4] The United Nations Conference on Trade and Development (UNCTAD) reports that over 80 percent of the volume of international trade in goods is carried by sea, and the percentage is even higher for most developing countries (UNCTAD n.d.).

consensus-driven goal for JET within the IMO. This exercise has helped identify gaps in the sector's practical and legal approaches toward JET.

5.2 THE INTERNATIONAL SHIPPING SECTOR AND THE INTERNATIONAL LEGAL FRAMEWORK TO ADDRESS CLIMATE CHANGE

Ships have facilitated oceanic navigation for thousands of years and have undergone significant technological transformation in their build and operation. The shipping sector has evidenced technological progress through a history of maritime enterprise – from ancient boats, canoes, rafts, kayaks, and floats progressively spanning materials from animal skins and timber to strong metals. Ships, which were once reliant on oceanic winds for navigation, eventually upgraded to steam-powered engines, coal-fired steamships, oil-powered vessels, and diesel engines (De Souza 2002, 7–42; Paine 2013, 526). These technological advancements have been instrumental in increased speed, capacity, time, and cost efficiency of the maritime trade (Paine 2013, 599). Today, the focus is on addressing the environmental tradeoffs from the sector's business-as-usual practices.

5.2.1 *Decarbonization*

Today, maritime transport largely relies on fossil fuels for sustained international shipping operations. Among the six GHGs, carbon dioxide (CO_2), emitted from burning fossil fuels in support of human activities, as in the case of maritime transport, has the most significant impact on global warming (IPCC 2005, 53). Hence, the imperative for specifically reducing anthropogenic CO_2 emissions has attained critical urgency in the sector. This goal is termed "decarbonization."[5] Essentially, it aims for the adoption of energy-efficient and climate-friendly methods to help slow the rate of global warming by stabilizing the Earth's temperature in line with the ultimate objective of the United Nations Framework Convention on Climate Change (UNFCCC).[6] It appears that the dominance of CO_2 emissions in the sector has led to the usage of "decarbonization" as a proxy term for GHG emissions reduction in the sector. Therefore, unsurprisingly, decarbonization in relation to the sector has been defined as "an overarching term that describes acts, pathways, or processes, by which countries, individuals or other entities aim to reduce and ultimately eliminate GHG emissions from human activities" (BIMCO 2023).

[5] Decarbonization is a process by which countries, individuals, or other entities aim to achieve zero fossil carbon existence. It typically refers to a reduction in the carbon emissions associated with electricity, industry, and transport (IPCC 2018, Annex I, Glossary, 546).

[6] United Nations Framework Convention on Climate Change, 9 May 1992, 1771 UNTS 107 (UNFCCC), Article 2.

In the past three decades, the world has acknowledged the need for globally coordinated and integrated responses to climate change, including through decarbonization. This global reinforcement comes from the near-universal membership of 198 State parties to the 1992 UNFCCC, which entered into force in 1994 (UNTC n.d.). The ultimate objective of the UNFCCC is to undertake time-frame-sufficient interventions to stabilize GHG concentrations in the atmosphere "at a level that would prevent dangerous anthropogenic interference with the climate system" (Article 2). The goal is to be executed in a manner that naturally enables ecosystems to adapt to climate change without threatening food production and by sustainably enabling economic development (Article 2).

Further, the UNFCCC serves as an umbrella mechanism, with an implementation operationalized through the 1997 Kyoto Protocol[7] and the 2015 Paris Agreement.[8] The Kyoto Protocol binds the developed world to meet emissions reduction and limitation commitments (Article 2). ITLOS has affirmed that the necessary measures to be taken by UNCLOS State parties under Article 194(1) to address marine pollution from anthropogenic GHG emissions must be determined by taking into account the Paris Agreement's "global temperature goal of limiting the temperature increase to 1.5°C above pre-industrial levels and the timeline for emission pathways to achieve that goal" (ITLOS Advisory opinion, para 441(3)(b)). The Paris Agreement, which has 195 parties and entered into force in 2016, commits all parties to prepare and communicate five-year climate action plans in the form of their nationally determined contributions (Article 4(2) and (9)). It further encourages the formulation of long-term low GHG emissions development strategies (Article 4(19)). These policy measures are expected to serve as the basis for pursuing domestic mitigation measures in line with the objects of the Paris Agreement (Article 4(2) and (19)).

5.2.2 *The Principle of Common but Differentiated Responsibilities and Respective Capabilities*

The UNFCCC approach is centered on the principles of intergenerational and intragenerational equity (Article 3(1)). It supports taking full account of the legitimate priority needs of developing countries with a view to avoiding adverse impacts on social and economic development (preamble). This approach is influenced by the proclamations of the 1972 Stockholm Declaration on the Human Environment (UN 1972). The UNFCCC recognizes that, historically, the largest share of global GHG emissions originated in developed countries, and that there will be a predictable growth of this share in developing countries to meet their social and development needs (preamble). This recognition is materialized through the formal

[7] Kyoto Protocol to the United Nations Framework Convention on Climate Change, December 11, 1997, 2303 UNTS 162 (Kyoto Protocol).

[8] Paris Agreement, December 12, 2015, 3156 UNTS 79, Article 2(a).

adoption of the principle of common but differentiated responsibilities and respective capabilities (CBDR-RC) (Articles 3(1) and 4(1)). The CBDR-RC is also reflected in Principle 7 of the 1992 Rio Declaration on Environment and Development (UNGA 1992). Applying this principle, the UNFCCC puts the onus on the developed world to take action specifically for sustainably protecting the climate system (Articles 3(4) and 4(1)).[9] For implementation purposes, the UNFCCC categorizes the developed country parties in Annexes I and II, while the developing countries are those that are not included in either Annex – that is, non-Annex parties (Article 4(2)). In addition to meeting their own commitments, the developed country parties are also obliged to promote, facilitate, and financially support, including for the transfer of technology, and extend assistance to, the developing country parties toward compliance with the obligations under the UNFCCC (Article 4(3), (4), and (5)).

ITLOS has also been mindful of incorporating this approach in its Advisory Opinion. It has been observed that some elements common to the principle of CBDR-RC are contained in the obligation under Article 194(1) of UNCLOS, which clarifies that the scope of measures to reduce anthropogenic GHG emissions causing marine pollution may differ between developed States and developing States (ITLOS Advisory Opinion, para. 229). While all States must make mitigation efforts in this regard, developed States should "continue taking the lead" (para. 229).

5.2.3 *The Obligation of Due Diligence and the Precautionary Approach*

Given the high risks of serious and irreversible harm to the marine environment from anthropogenic GHG emissions, ITLOS has held that UNCLOS State parties have an obligation to take necessary measures to prevent, reduce, and control marine pollution from such emissions with a "stringent standard of due diligence" (ITLOS Advisory Opinion, para. 441(3)(c)). Importantly, ITLOS has linked the obligation of due diligence with the precautionary approach (para. 242).

The UNFCCC applies the precautionary principle in cases of threats of serious or irreversible damage and lack of full scientific certainty by expressly requiring parties to "take precautionary measures to anticipate, prevent or minimize the causes of climate change and mitigate its adverse effects" (Article 3(3)). Similarly, Article 196 (1) of UNCLOS obliges State parties "to take all measures necessary to prevent, reduce and control pollution of the marine environment resulting from the use of

[9] Sustainable development is a process of change in which the exploitation of resources, the direction of investments, the orientation of technological development, and institutional change are all in harmony and enhance both current and future potential to meet human needs and aspirations: see UNGA (1987, Annex, para. 15).

technologies under their jurisdiction or control or the intentional or accidental introduction of species, alien or new, to a particular part of the marine environment, which may cause significant and harmful changes thereto." In this context, ITLOS has clarified that "scientific certainty" is not required for determining "necessary measures" and, in the absence of such certainty, the precautionary approach must be applied (ITLOS Advisory Opinion, para. 213). ITLOS has taken a progressive and impactful view that the precautionary approach is implicit in UNCLOS, even in the absence of explicit reference (para. 213). For instance, ITLOS interpreted that the use of the word "may" in Article 196(1) implies a precautionary approach and creates an obligation requiring the application of this approach (paras. 434, 441(4)(g)). Further, ITLOS also applied the precautionary approach to limit the margin of discretion of State parties for executing the obligation of environmental impact assessments under Article 206 of UNCLOS (paras. 361, 367).

5.2.4 *Polluter-Pays Principle*

The implementation of the obligation of due diligence may vary according to the capabilities and available resources of States. In practice, the application of the precautionary approach for undertaking the necessary measures to prevent, reduce, and control marine pollution comes with financial implications or costs. The Rio Declaration made significant progress in embodying a legal mechanism for allocating such costs. Principle 16 states that "national authorities should endeavour to promote the internalization of environmental costs and the use of economic instruments, taking into account the approach that the polluter should, in principle, bear the cost of pollution, with due regard to the public interest and without distorting international trade and investment." Popularly referred to as the "polluter-pays principle," it obliges the polluter to bear the cost of pollution.

Although the UNFCCC does not expressly refer to this principle and the ITLOS Advisory Opinion fails to account for it, the principle of CBDR-RC contains some common elements. Given that the principle of CBDR-RC creates differential obligations on parties based on their historical contributions to global GHG emissions and thereby to climate change, it can be suggested that this principle sets the appropriate stage for implementing the tenets of the polluter-pays principle. However, the application of the polluter-pays principle and the UNFCCC regime to the sector is not straightforward. This is because the application of the principle hinges on the identification of the polluter, while the sector continues to ask: Who is the polluter?

5.2.5 *Complexities of the International Shipping Sector*

The UNFCCC requires all parties – whether developed or developing – to develop, update, publish, and make available national anthropogenic GHG inventories (Article 4(1)(a)). This is intended to help evaluate the effectiveness of measures aimed at limiting emissions and enhancing removals of GHG. However, no explicit reference to the sector has been made in the UNFCCC (Article 4(1)(a)). The IPCC has clarified that emissions based upon fuel sold to ships engaged in international transport are not to be included in national totals but reported separately (IPCC 1996, I.3, 2006, 8.4). The reason for this segregation emerges from the sector's global nature. The sector witnesses a multitude of interactions by multinational and cross-jurisdictional stakeholders, which complicates the attribution of GHG emissions from international shipping to any national economy.

International shipping operations are not singular in character, where responsibilities are divested among more than one entity based on the type of charterparty or the applicable international commercial terms. For example, consider a ship flying the flag of State A, owned by a national of or a company established in State B, chartered by a national of or a company established in State C, manned by nationals belonging to States D, E, and F, and carrying the cargo from State G bound for States H, I, and J. As part of its operations, the ship is required to navigate not only through the high seas but also through the exclusive economic zones and/or territorial waters of coastal States K and L. In this case, the attribution of the anthropogenic GHG emissions from this ship not only transcends the confines of national or domestic law but also demonstrates the complication in identifying the polluter or responsible party operating across myriad jurisdictions for the emissions in question.

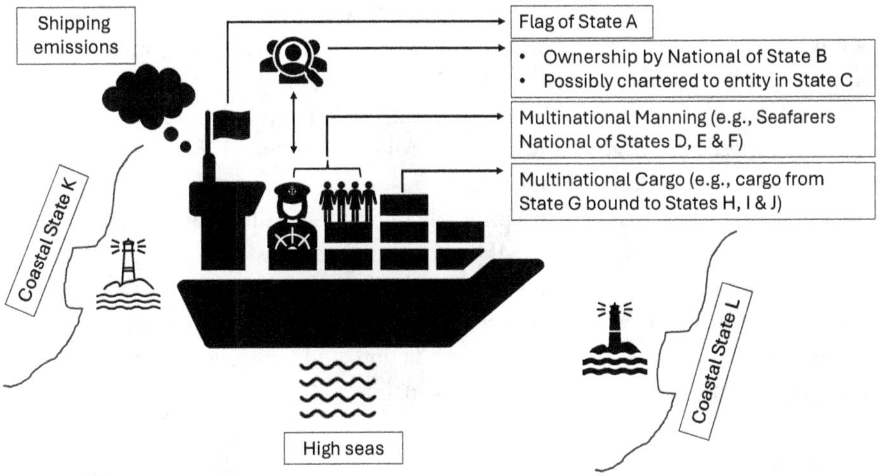

FIGURE 5.1 Simplified model illustrating the multinational and multidimensional nature of international commercial shipping operations and the associated GHG emissions from ships.

5.3 THE ROLE OF THE IMO IN REDUCING GHG EMISSIONS IN INTERNATIONAL SHIPPING

The multinational nature of the sector, as emphasized in Section 5.2, summons multilateral action. This is also reaffirmed under Part XII of UNCLOS for the protection and preservation of the marine environment from any source, including ship-source GHG emissions. Article 211 of UNCLOS centralizes the role of a "competent international organization or general diplomatic conference" in providing the basis for legislation and enforcement to prevent pollution from vessels. ITLOS has confirmed the understanding that the term "competent international organization" in this context refers to the IMO (ITLOS Advisory Opinion, para. 280). Besides, the Kyoto Protocol had already solidified the intent to separately regulate anthropogenic GHG emissions from the sector, rather than within the UNFCCC. With 192 parties, it expressly affirms that the limitation or reduction of GHG emissions from marine bunker fuels is to be pursued by working through the IMO (Article 2(2)). Therefore, with the urgency to reduce GHG emissions in the sector, the role of the IMO has become nonnegotiable.

The IMO is a specialized agency of the United Nations with a mission to promote safe, secure, environmentally sound, efficient, and sustainable shipping through cooperation (IMO n.d.-a; UNGA 1948). Through intergovernmental cooperation, it has adopted global measures for preventing marine and atmospheric pollution from ships, particularly in the form of the 1973 International Convention for the Prevention of Pollution from Ships, as modified by its 1978 protocol (MARPOL).[10] MARPOL, which entered into force in 1983, is a result of the IMO's focused approach toward marine environmental concerns that are specifically addressed by its Marine Environment Protection Committee (MEPC) – one of the five main committees of the IMO. It has 162 contracting States, reflecting approximately 99 percent of the gross tonnage of the world's merchant fleet (IMO 2024i; ITLOS Advisory Opinion, para. 280). With such strong global participation, the framework of MARPOL sets forth generally accepted rules and standards for the purposes of Article 211 of UNCLOS (IMO 1997, para. 6.1).

MARPOL champions the IMO principle of nondiscrimination and, accordingly, no more favorable treatment (NMFT) to nonparty ships. This is specifically to ensure that ships of parties are not disadvantaged against ships of nonparties, in line with the IMO's conventional purpose of promoting freedom of shipping and "to encourage removal of discriminatory action and unnecessary restrictions by Governments affecting shipping engaged in international trade so as to promote

[10] International Convention for the Prevention of Pollution from Ships, November 2, 1973, 1340 UNTS 184, as amended by the Protocol of 1978 relating to the International Convention for the Prevention of Pollution from Ships, 1973, February 17, 1978, 1340 UNTS 61 (MARPOL). See also Convention on the International Maritime Organization, March 6, 1948, 289 UNTS 48 (IMO Convention), Article 1.

the availability of shipping services to the commerce of the world without discrimination" (MARPOL, Article 5(4), IMO convention, Article 1(b)).[11] In practice, the application of these principles may include equivalent surveys or inspections of nonparty ships, as well as relevant sanctions under national law or possible detention of noncompliant ships visiting ports of a party (IMO 2022i).

5.3.1 *MARPOL and the Reduction of GHG Emissions from Ships*

MARPOL, as an umbrella instrument, regulates six forms of ship-source pollution: (1) pollution by oil (Annex I); (2) pollution by noxious liquid substances in bulk (Annex II); (3) pollution by harmful substances carried by sea in packaged form (Annex III); (4) pollution by sewage (Annex IV); (5) pollution by garbage (Annex V); and (6) pollution by air pollution from ships (Annex VI). However, the originally adopted MARPOL Annexes did not make regulations concerning CO_2 or other GHG emissions from ships. It was in 1997 that the MEPC recognized the significance of following those developments, even outside of the scope of IMO, such as in the UNFCCC (IMO 1997, para. 6.79).

The 1997 International Air Pollution Conference, which adopted MARPOL Annex VI, invited the IMO to cooperate with the UNFCCC for a twofold purpose: (1) to exchange information on GHG emissions; and (2) to undertake a study of CO_2 emissions from ships for establishing their amount and relative percentages as part of the global inventory of CO_2 emissions (MARPOL COP 1997, 96). To meet the first purpose, the IMO provides verbal and written updates on its progress and achievements to the multidisciplinary Subsidiary Body for Scientific and Technological Advice (SBSTA) established under the UNFCCC, which further reports to the Conference of Parties (COP) of the UNFCCC (IMO n.d.-d). Further, the details of the IMO's participation and the outcome of COP are submitted to the MEPC.

With respect to the latter purpose, four GHG studies were commissioned by the IMO, with reports published from 2000 to 2020 (IMO n.d.-e). At the 61st Session of the SBSTA held in November 2024, the IMO informed about ongoing considerations at the MEPC for commissioning a fifth IMO GHG Study to support evidence-based decision-making (IMO 2024f). Given that the four studies identified CO_2 emissions as the most important GHG from shipping in terms of the quantity and quality of global warming potential, the GHG emissions standard is proposed as a CO_2 emissions standard (IMO 2001a, para. 3, 2001b, para. 7, 2002, para. 4.21, 2009, 1). These studies indicate an over 62 percent increase in the anthropogenic CO_2 emissions contribution of the sector in the past two decades, as shown in Table 5.1.

Subsequent to the call from the global maritime community to consider feasible CO_2 reduction strategies (MARPOL COP 1997), the IMO affirmed its prerogative to lead the development of GHG limitation and reduction strategies and mechanisms

[11] See also IMO Convention, Article 1(b).

TABLE 5.1 *Shipping sector CO_2 emissions, 1996–2018.*

No. of IMO GHG study	Year of IMO GHG study	Percentage of global total anthropogenic CO_2 emissions	Year of calculation
First	2000	1.8	1996
Second	2009	2.7	2007
Third	2014	2.2	2012
Fourth	2020	2.89	2018

Source: IMO GHG Study Reports (IMO 2000, 2009, 2015, 2021a).

for international shipping through three measures: (1) technical; (2) operational; and (3) market-based (IMO 2004). The advocacy for market-based measures (MBMs) was based on the view that technical and operational measures had "a limited potential for contributing to reduced emissions from ships" and that there was a need for market pressures to incentivize this goal (IMO 2000, 8). However, the MBMs are contentious and continue to be deliberated for adoption. The relevant legal aspects are discussed in Section 5.4.

5.3.2 *Technical and Operational Energy-Efficient Measures for Ships*

In the years that followed, MEPC deliberations recognized that emissions reduction in the sector warranted measures to improve the energy efficiency of ships (IMO 2011a). To directly target the goal, the primary IMO action came through the implementation of technical and operational measures. This was partially achieved through the 2011 amendments to Annex VI of MARPOL that implemented the first ever mandatory global energy efficiency standard for an international industry sector (IMO 2011a). However, these regulations were only applicable to new ships,[12] and there was a requirement to develop the technical and operational energy efficiency of existing ships (IMO 2018d, para. 4.7.2). Besides, the 2018 IMO initial strategy on the reduction of GHG emissions from international shipping (Initial Strategy) outlined the need to reduce CO_2 emissions specifically with regard to transport work – that is, the carbon intensity of international shipping (IMO 2018d, para. 4.7.2). This goal called for a change of technical specification of ships or their operational practices or both and, therefore, the need for ship-specific targets (IMO 2020).

Deliberations also revealed the need to provide flexibility to shipowners for deciding the means or measures for carbon intensity reductions of their ships, which could only be possible by mandatory goal-setting rather than enlisting such means

[12] A "new ship" is a ship: (1) for which the building contract is placed on or after January 1, 2013; (2) in the absence of a building contract, the keel of which is laid or which is at a similar stage of construction on or after July 1, 2013; or (3) the delivery of which is on or after July 1, 2015: MARPOL Annex VI, Regulation 2.23.

and measures (IMO 2018b, paras. 7, 11, 2019d, para. 7.36.16). Therefore, MARPOL Annex VI seeks to reduce GHG emissions from international shipping through mandatory *goal-based* operational and technical measures (IMO 2021e). The technical measures comprise an Energy Efficiency Design Index (EEDI) and Energy Efficiency Existing Ship Index (EEXI). The operational measures are interconnected and consist of a Ship Energy Efficiency Management Plan (SEEMP), Data Collection System (DCS), and Carbon Intensity Indicator (CII) rating. While the DCS feeds data for the CII ratings of ships, the latter integrates into the SEEMP to continually enhance the operational efficiency of the ships. The scope of application, purpose, and manner of implementation of these measures are tabulated in Table 5.2.

The implementation of these technical and operational measures is supported by the IMO Roadmap, which takes a three-step approach: (1) data collection of ships' fuel oil consumption, specifying the fuel oil type and methods used for such data collection; (2) data analysis; and (3) decision on measures to enhance the energy efficiency of international shipping (MARPOL Annex VI, Regulation 22A; see also IMO 2016a, paras. 6.8, 7.7.1, 7.7.4, 7.7.6, 2016b). The third stage aimed for the adoption of the Revised Strategy for the reduction of GHG emissions from ships by the 80th Session of the MEPC in 2023 (IMO 2016b, 2). While this was achieved in principle (IMO 2023l), it has led to practical and interpretational ambiguity, as elaborated in Section 5.4.

In essence, the Revised Strategy is time-conscious and builds on the enlisted implementation of measures already elaborated in the Initial Strategy (IMO 2018d, para. 4). These measures have been specified for implementation in three phases: (1) short term between 2018 and 2023; (2) mid-term between 2023 and 2030; and (3) long term beyond 2030. Short-term measures largely seek to apply operational and technical measures on ships (IMO 2018d, para. 4.1.1). Among them, EEXI, EEDI, SEEMP, and DCS, technical cooperation, and transfer of technology aspects, as discussed above, are already incorporated into MARPOL Annex VI through amendments (IMO 2018d, para. 4.7). The 83rd session of the MEPC agreed on an IMO Net-Zero Framework comprising amendments to the MARPOL Annex VI and integrating an economic mechanism to incentivize JET, which were scheduled for adoption in October 2025 but was adjourned for one year (IMO 2025a).

5.4 JUST AND EQUITABLE TRANSITION OF THE INTERNATIONAL SHIPPING SECTOR

The Revised Strategy, like the Initial Strategy, is guided by the principles of implementation enshrined in the IMO conventions and the UNFCCC. The IMO principles of nondiscrimination and NMFT, which mandate equivalent treatment to all ships, are to be balanced against the UNFCCC principle of CBDR-RC, which encourages differential treatment based on considerations of

TABLE 5.2 *MARPOL Annex VI goal-based operational and technical measures.*

Type of measure	Name of measure	Application	Purpose of measure	Implementation
Technical	EEDI	New ships of 400 gross tonnage (GT) and above	These indices aim to promote energy-efficient ship design. They indicate a minimum energy efficiency level per capacity mile (e.g., tonne mile) for different ship types and size segments (regs. 20, 21; IMO n.d.-g).	For demonstrating energy efficiency, the EEDI attained in the case of a new ship, or the EEXI attained in the case of an existing ship, is verified against the required EEDI calculated in accordance with the manner provided in MARPOL Annex VI (regs. 24, 25; IMO n.d.-g).
	EEXI	Existing ships[a] of 400 GT and above		
Operational	SEEMP	Ships of 400 GT and above	This is a ship-specific mechanism to encourage actions to monitor and improve the ship and fleet's energy efficiency performance and carbon intensity over time (IMO 2022j, paras. 1.2.1, 1.3.1).	The SEEMP comprises plans for energy efficiency improvement, fuel oil consumption data collection, and operational carbon intensity (IMO 2022j, para. 1.3). It is executed by planning, implementation, monitoring, and self-evaluation and improvement. It is determined by the current state of ship energy efficiency and carbon intensity and the expected improvement through best measures (IMO 2022j, paras. 3.6, 4.1). These measures could include speed optimization, hull maintenance, retrofitting energy efficiency devices, and the use of alternative fuels (IMO 2022j, para. 4.1.2).

DCS	Ship of 5,000 GT and above	This is an annual data collection mechanism of the technical characteristics of the ships.	DCS includes details of fuel oil consumption and the power output of internal combustion engines. This data is to be transferred to the IMO DCS, with the purposes of data analysis as part of Part 2 of the IMO Roadmap.
CII rating	Ship of 5,000 GT and above	This is an annual measure to incentivize most energy-efficient ships.	The CII is built on fuel oil consumption from the IMO DCS (IMO n.d.-g). The attained annual operational CII must be documented and verified against the required annual operational CII. Based on this, Flag State Administration rates a ship as A (major superior), B (minor superior), C (moderate), D (minor inferior), or E (inferior performance level). A ship rated D for three consecutive years or rated E is required to develop a "plan of corrective actions," which is to be included in the revised SEEMP (reg. 28).

[a] An "existing ship" is a ship that is not a new ship: MARPOL Annex VI, Regulation 2.22.

socioeconomic circumstances. The interplay of these principles influences the decisions made for meeting the vision and ambition of the Revised Strategy. While these principles were also included in the Initial Strategy, the principle of CBDR-RC and the utility of its components appear to be strengthened in the Revised Strategy.

For instance, the Revised Strategy has significantly revised the earlier ambition of reducing 50 percent of the total annual GHG emissions by 2050 to reach net zero by 2050, all while accounting for different national circumstances (IMO 2023l, Annex, para. 3.3.4). Amid support to reach the highest level of GHG emissions from international shipping as soon as possible and phase them out by 2050, deliberations also reveal a preference for alignment with the UNFCCC by using the agreed language of the Glasgow Climate Pact – that is, "aim for achieving net-zero GHG emissions by or around mid-century, taking into account different national circumstances" (IMO 2023f, paras. 15, 16). This culminated in setting two key targets for reducing total annual GHG emissions from international shipping compared to 2008 levels: first, by at least 20 percent, aiming for 30 percent, by 2030; and second, by at least 70 percent, aiming for 80 percent, by 2040 (IMO 2023l, Annex, paras. 3.3.3, 3.4). A comparison of the ambitions of the Initial Strategy and the Revised Strategy is shown in Figure 5.2.

Further, while both versions of the IMO strategy continue to envision urgent reductions and the phasing-out of GHG emissions from international shipping in

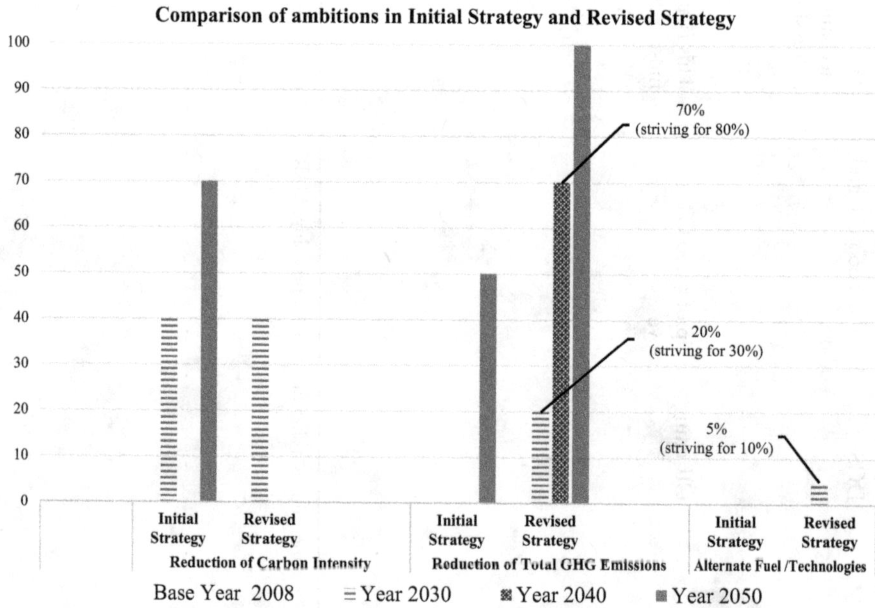

FIGURE 5.2 Comparison of ambitions in Initial Strategy and Revised Strategy.

this century, the Revised Strategy seeks to reach this vision while promoting JET (IMO 2018d, para. 2). What constitutes JET has not been specifically described or defined in the Revised Strategy. However, its character can be implied to some extent. The Revised Strategy guides that JET should have the impact of "leaving no country behind" (IMO 2023l, Annex, para. 5.3). Further, it asserts that the nature of the mid-term measures should be such that, while they promote and incentivize energy transition, they should also simultaneously contribute to a level-playing field within the sector (IMO 2023l, Annex, para. 4.5). The lack of an explicit definition, however, may be seen as an attempt to offer constructive ambiguity to account for different or broad-ranged circumstances. The *travaux préparatoires* suggest that the intention is to interpret it as being intrinsically linked to the principle of CBDR-RC (IMO 2023g, paras. 47, 50, 58).

Meanwhile, reference may also be made to the definition adopted by the International Labour Organization (ILO), which plays a critical role in regulating maritime labor concerns. According to the ILO, the term "just transition" means "greening the economy in a way that is as fair and inclusive as possible to everyone concerned, creating decent work opportunities and leaving no one behind" (ILO n. d.). Therefore, it would not be far-fetched to suggest that the possible indicators that contribute to JET for the sector could be derived from the means and factors that influence the IMO's decisions for addressing GHG emissions in international shipping – that is, matters concerning the IMO's decision-making procedures and the actors and stakeholders impacted by those decisions.

5.4.1 *Procedural Element*

Recent literature has identified that MEPC deliberations concerning GHG emissions reduction in shipping are steered by certain highly active State actors, such as Japan, Norway, and the US, while also noting the emergence and increased participation by intergovernmental organizations, such as the European Commission, and nongovernmental organizations, such as the Clean Shipping Coalition, in recent years (Baumann 2023). Moreover, it was also found that the developed countries or regional organizations, such as the European Union, exercise financial influence in promoting participation of the Small Island Developing States (SIDS) (Baumann 2023). Such voluntary initiatives by developed countries beyond the administrative purview of the IMO may be seen as a demonstration of their leadership in fostering inclusive deliberations. However, they also raise concerns about arbitrariness and the misuse of financial incentives in favor of vulnerable or less-capable countries to drive consensus at the IMO, potentially prioritizing the donor's agendas over genuine benefits.

Therefore, deliberations emphasize the need for procedural fairness for an equitable transition. This entails that representation, maritime mitigation, and the response to climate impacts are equitable while also being just for seafarers, and that disproportionately negative impacts are addressed (IMO 2023f, para. 10.5, 2023g, para. 39). These views seek to ensure a level-playing field and to safeguard the interests of developing countries – in particular, the Least Developed Countries (LDCs) and SIDS, which contribute very little to total global GHG emissions (IMO 2023f, para. 10.5, 2023g, para. 39). This approach also aligns with the suggestion for facilitating a transition that is "environmentally effective, procedurally fair, socially just, globally equitable, and technologically inclusive" (Shaw and De Beukelaer 2022). The culmination of these discussions resulted in the call of the Revised Strategy to consider the impacts of GHG reduction measures on the emerging needs of the developing world (IMO 2023l, Annex, para. 3.5.3). Moreover, the IMO's Strategic Plan for 2024–2029, which was adopted in 2023, also focuses on addressing the needs of the developing world through principles of respect, non-discrimination, inclusivity, and transparency, with specific regard to capacity development and emerging technologies (IMO 2023j, paras. 4, 21, 25).

Procedural fairness is key to achieving the smooth implementation of measures, as it is a critical tool for inclusivity in the global maritime sector. The maritime community's appreciation of the need for procedural fairness predates the adoption of the Revised Strategy or the 2024–2029 Strategic Plan. The IMO has attempted to facilitate diverse and equal representation in its GHG meetings through the establishment of a Voluntary Multi-Donor Trust Fund (VMTDF) to support participants from developing countries, particularly SIDS and LDCs (IMO 2023b, 2023c, n.d.-i). Concerns of equity were highlighted on the grounds that LDCs and SIDS were poorly represented, where deliberations reveal that financial support for participation in the decision-making process was integral for sustaining equitable efforts to reach the IMO's goals toward GHG emissions reduction from international ships (IMO 2018a, para. 1, 2018c, para. 7.7.5, 2019a, para. 6, 2019b, 2019c, para. 2, Annex). Although the VMTDF opened applications in February 2023, only twenty-five of the sixty-five LDCs and SIDS attended the fifteenth Intersessional Working Group on the reduction of GHG emissions from ships, which was instrumental in influencing the finalization and adoption of the Revised Strategy by the 80th Session of the MEPC (IMO 2023c, 2023e, 2023i, para. 7.22).

5.4.2 *Human Element*

Furthermore, it was also realized that decarbonizing the sector impacts the training and labor conditions of around 2 million seafarers globally, who would require upskilling with respect to the new and alternative fuel technologies (MJTTF 2022). Therefore, for a just and human-centered transition to net zero, the Maritime Just Transition Task Force (MJTTF) was launched at COP 26 in 2021 (IMO n.d.-h). The IMO supports the MJTTF, along with the International Chamber of Shipping, the International Transport Workers' Federation, the United Nations Global Compact, and the ILO (MJTTF 2022). Marking its first phase in 2022, a position paper of the

MJTTF was developed with a ten-point action plan in the context of "mapping a Just Transition for the global maritime workforce" (MJTTF 2022). The paper essentially recommends alignment with global maritime labor standards, championing gender and diversity and prioritizing health and safety onboard ships (MJTTF 2022). The influence of the MJTTF action plan echoes through the Revised Strategy, which – unlike the Initial Strategy – specifically acknowledges the effects on seafarers and other maritime professions (IMO 2023l, Annex, paras. 5.6, 5.11). To meet the ambition of the Revised Strategy while ensuring a just transition for the human element in the maritime sector, it urges the IMO to evaluate its instruments, guidance, and training standards and develop a seafarers' training and skills program (IMO 2023l, para. 3, Annex, paras. 5.6, 5.11).

5.4.3 *Technical Element*

The Revised Strategy emphasizes the importance of adopting technologies, fuels, and energy sources with zero or near-zero GHG emissions (IMO 2023l, para. 3, Annex, para. 3.3.3). It aims for these sustainable alternatives to account for a minimum of 5 percent, with a target of 10 percent, of the energy consumed by international shipping by 2030. Presently, 98.8 percent of the global fleet rely on conventional marine fuels,[13] which are produced from crude oil formed over millions of years from the remains of plants and animals that lived in the seas (UNCTAD 2023, 68). The transition to alternative fuels is still at a nascent stage (IMO 2023h, Annex; UNCTAD 2023, 68). Alternative fuels are nonconventional fuels, which are deemed to serve, at least partly, as a substitute for traditionally used fossil fuels in the energy supply and which have the potential to contribute to decarbonization (IMO 2023h, Annex, para. 1.4.2; BIMCO 2023).

Based on the terminologies used, it also appears that alternative fuels are further categorized as low-carbon fuels, near-zero carbon fuels, and absolute-zero carbon fuels. Since the term "near zero" describes reducing emissions to a level significantly lower than current levels and as close as possible to zero with available technologies, it would be consistent to derive that "low carbon" denotes emissions reductions below the current levels (BIMCO 2023). With respect to alternative low-carbon and zero-carbon fuels, there is no universally applicable and readily available solution today (UNCTAD 2023, 68). Alternative fuels include methanol, ammonia, hydrogen gas, liquified natural gas (LNG), and electrical energy, and it is apparent that the list of alternative fuels is not exhaustive (IMO 2023h, Annex, para. 1.4.2). UN Trade and Development (UNCTAD) reports that, in 2022, only 5.5 percent of the active fleet used alternative fuels, mainly LNG, and, to a lesser extent, battery/hybrid, liquified petroleum gas, and methanol (UNCTAD 2023, 69). The IMO

[13] Marine fuels are liquid fossil fuel oils such as heavy fuel oil (HFO) or light fuel oil (LFO) and gas oils such as marine gas oil (MGO) (Vermeire 2021, 3; Oiltanking n.d.).

reports that, in 2023, 92.53 percent of the fuels used by ships were conventional fuels comprising heavy fuel oil, light fuel oil, or diesel or gas oil, with increasing usage for alternative fuels (IMO 2024f, para. 17). Reports assume that these small quantities have been delivered mainly via small-scale terminals with truck-to-ship transfers (IMO 2023h, Annex, para. 5.1). The dominant usage of conventional fuels in the international shipping industry is owed to their established supply chains and infrastructure, and to their lower costs (UNCTAD 2023, 68, 72). There is another complexity to the required infrastructure development. It has been evaluated that not all alternative fuels will be able to use existing bunkering infrastructure, with some needing new infrastructure; this suggests that tailored infrastructure will be required based on each fuel's characteristics (IMO 2023h, Annex, para. 5.1).

Further, while vessel design technologies, such as optimized hull dimensions, had attained maturity for many new vessels, there are challenges, including lack of clarity, concerning the commercial maturity and readiness of various energy efficiency and reduction technologies, such as shore power (IMO 2023h, Annex, para. 4.1). For the uptake of alternative fuels and technologies for international shipping, it is imperative to ensure technological readiness, scalability, and regulatory certainty (UNCTAD 2023, 68, 72). Therefore, IMO measures at mid-term include the uptake of alternative low-carbon and zero-carbon fuels, operational enhancements, continued capacity-building efforts, and feedback mechanisms to address GHG emissions in shipping (IMO 2018d, para. 4.8).

The emphasis on the adoption of alternative technologies, fuels, and energy sources spotlights the need for the environmental effectiveness of this transition, which would require scientific, holistic, and robust development of an international framework to assess life-cycle GHG intensity and the sustainability of alternative low- and zero-emission fuels used by ships (IMO 2023k). Life-cycle analysis of marine fuels seeks to quantify the environmental impacts of a product over its entire life cycle (IMO 2023a, paras. 4, 9). Therefore, the Revised Strategy requires consideration of total GHG emissions produced throughout the entire life cycle of a marine fuel, from its extraction or production, that is, the "well," to its utility and combustion in a ship's engines, that is, the "wake" (IMO 2023l, Annex, para. 3.2, 2023k). To this end, the Revised Strategy propagates a goal-based marine fuel standard to reduce the GHG intensity of marine fuels progressively (paras. 4.3, 4.5.1). In this regard, the draft IMO Net-Zero Framework deliberated at the 81st Session of the MEPC considered a GHG marine fuel standard (GFS) as a component in the proposed amendments to MARPOL Annex VI (IMO 2024e, 1).

The GFS has been advocated to address the GHG intensity of energy consumed on ships from "well-to-wake," providing a predictable transition to low- and zero-emission fuels (IMO 2022b, para. 5, 2022c). This approach benefits both ship operators and fuel producers by providing a predictable timeline for implementation, leading to concrete actions to achieve emissions-reduction goals (IMO 2022c). Although the GFS takes a technology-neutral approach without preferring any specific fuel type, compliance is estimated to increase costs (IMO 2022b, para. 4, 2022c, paras. 23–25). However, the IMO has in the past pioneered a similar fuel standard with the implementation of the global sulfur cap of 0.50 percent m/m in 2020 to promote qualitative fuel standards (MARPOL Annex VI, Regulation 14). To facilitate the same, MARPOL Annex VI also prescribes obligations for ascertaining fuel oil availability and quality (reg. 18). This demonstrates the IMO's ability to implement global fuel standards effectively and create a level-playing field, which has been a referred guide for the potential application of GFS (IMO 2022c, paras. 23, 24, 25).

5.4.4 *Economic Element*

It is reiterated that the Revised Strategy's call for the uptake of alternative low-carbon and zero-carbon fuels can only be supported through demand, which is driven by technological and commercial readiness, scalability, and regulatory certainty (UNCTAD 2023, 68). Therefore, as firming the viability of alternative or low- or zero-carbon fuels continues to be a matter of research and development, which is accompanied by financial implications, it particularly impacts the economic capabilities of the developing world. In addition, the uptake of alternative fuels summons support from adequate infrastructure and technologies, including at ports (IMO 2023l, Annex, para. 4.9.7). In this relation, the legal challenges manifest in creating a just and equitable atmosphere for all States to be well positioned to implement these measures. While the IMO principles of nondiscrimination and NMFT advocate the application of energy-efficient measures for internationally plying ships of all States, there are practical challenges faced by developing States, particularly LDCs and SIDS, due to their differing national circumstances. These practical challenges create a disproportionate or inequitable effect on the developing world in contradiction to the UNFCCC principle of CBDR-RC.

Nevertheless, a 2023 study commissioned by the IMO on the readiness and availability of low- and zero-carbon ship technology and marine fuels found that with clear demand, the increased cost implications for candidate fuels were not a barrier to their uptake for the shipping industry. The study highlighted the prerogative of clear policy actions "to help unlock investment in candidate fuels and their associated infrastructure . . . needed to ensure the feasibility of this transition" (IMO 2023h, Annex, 26). Importantly, it supported complementary technical and economic measures to ensure the feasibility of the transition (26). The Revised Strategy supports this perspective by aiming to finalize a set of candidate mid-term measures that combine a technical component of a goal-based marine fuel standard discussed above with an economic component involving a maritime GHG emissions pricing mechanism (IMO 2023l, Annex, paras. 4.1.1, 4.5). In addition to the GFS, the draft IMO Net-Zero Framework proposes incorporation of an economic mechanism to incentivize the transition (IMO 2024e).

An economic element in the basket of IMO GHG reduction measures was considered pursuant to broad support over the years, including in the first IMO GHG study in 1997 (IMO 2000, 8). The 2023 IMO study found major gaps for decarbonization by 2050, due to the critical requirement for the full potential of energy efficiency measures and the availability of candidate fuels (IMO 2023h, Annex). Financial ability to unlock investment is key. To address this globally, an economic component was considered as a means to incentivize the reduction of GHG emissions from international shipping through mechanisms of an economic or market-based nature – that is, MBMs. The MBMs are expected to serve as financial incentives, or disincentives, to encourage shipping companies to reduce their carbon footprint. The notion is that assigning a cost to emissions will incentivize the shipping companies to assess whether it is more cost-effective to reduce emissions or to pay for them (IMO 2011b, Annex 1, 11). In essence, the concept resonates with the polluter-pays principle.

Over the years, various proposals have been progressively considered for a levy-based MBM, including a fund and reward system, to reduce or close the price gap between new low- and zero-carbon fuels and conventional fuels (IMO 2021b, 2022f, 2022g, 2022h). For instance, the IMO Maritime Sustainability Fund and Reward was conceptualized to collect funding contributions from ships with actual CO_2 emissions above the upper benchmark level and rewarding ships with CO_2 emissions below the lower benchmark level. The benchmark levels are set by utilizing the existing DCS and CII mechanisms in MARPOL Annex VI. This mechanism seeks to utilize the collected contributions to finance the capacity-building, mitigate negative impacts in developing countries, and support the acceleration of the research, development, and deployment of low- or zero-carbon marine fuels and technologies, and address issues concerning their accessibility by developing countries (IMO 2022e, 2022f, para. 4).

Further, the Zero Emission Vessels (ZEVs) Incentive Scheme or the "feebate mechanism" builds on incentivizing the early adopters of zero-carbon fuels and effectively deploying ZEVs (IMO 2022e, paras. 4, 6, 7). It proposes the payment of levies by ships using fossil fuels and the receipt of rebates by ships using zero-emission fuels, where the rates are to be determined by the IMO in an inclusive and transparent manner, based on considerations of the estimated costs of and demand for zero-emission fuels (IMO 2022e, paras. 11, 14). The Scheme proposes recycling the generated revenues to incentivize first movers and assist in the equitable transition toward maritime GHG reduction efforts in vulnerable States, in particular SIDS and LDCs (IMO 2022e, para. 18). Another proposal pertains to a universal GHG levy on the bunker or emissions of the entities responsible on the basis of the polluter-pays principle (IMO 2021c, para 19, IMO 2022d, para 3). The generated revenue is proposed for disbursement through separate funds for climate change mitigation and adaptation efforts in vulnerable countries, as well as to subsidize the research, development, and deployment of new technologies and fuels administrated under the IMO mandate (IMO 2021c, para. 20). The proposal of the Emission Cap-and-Trade System (ECTS) suggests the trade of allowances as Ship Emission Units (SEUs) for the GHG emitted during a calendar year (IMO 2021d, para. 32). The number of SEUs is proposed to be limited to the agreed emissions cap, which is gradually reduced toward the IMO's 2050 ambition (IMO 2021d, para. 33). During the finalization of the Revised Strategy, express opposition was witnessed for the ECTS (IMO 2023f, Annex 3, 14, 26).

Hybrid proposals have been tabled by the European countries to apply the technical measure of GFS with an economic measure characterized as either a levy or a cap-and-trade scheme to incentivize GHG emissions reduction through profitable measures and investments in energy efficiency (IMO 2022a, paras. 12, 17, 2022d). While they suggest the application of a "flag-neutral, transparent, effective, easy to implement, cost-effective" levy that is "enforceable to prevent fraud, in line with the 'polluter pays' principle," they fail to propose the manner for identification of a polluter amid complex international shipping operations (IMO 2022a, para. 12). At the 82nd Session of the MEPC held in 2024, Solomon Islands advocated for the combination of a universal contribution with a GFS as the "most efficient solution, and in the long term, the cheapest." It is argued that the required revenue for climate mitigation action and for the maritime transition of SIDS and LDCs would be met by imposing a high price on GHG emissions (IMO 2024d, para. 5).

Amid the multiplicity of proposals debated, the agreed IMO Net-Zero Framework incorporates a hybrid MBM combining a global emissions pricing mechanism with a tradable compliance credit system linked to fuel intensity targets (IMO 2025a). Pertinently, achieving JET also pivots on the manner of disbursement of the revenue generated from the proposed MBM. India has submitted that revenue disbursement is a key area for the application of CBDR-RC and the realization of JET in the sector (IMO 2024c, para 9). The proposed amendments to MARPOL Annex VI under this Framework determine that revenue shall be disbursed through the IMO Net-Zero Fund to: (1) reward the use of zero and near-zero emission technologies; (2) JET support activities such as research, development, and deployment of low-emission fuels, technologies, and infrastructure, enabling a just transition for seafarers and the maritime workforce, facilitating information-sharing, technology transfer, capacity-building, training, and technical cooperation, supporting the development and implementation of National Action Plans, and addressing disproportionately negative impacts on States, including on food security; and (3) cover the administration and operational costs of the Fund and its Governing Board (IMO 2025b, Annex, Regulation 41). This inclusion appears to build on proposals included in the IMO's previously commissioned Comprehensive Impact Assessment (CIA) of these mid-term measures, which marked the following seven categories for revenue disbursement: (1) research, development, and deployment; (2) capacity-building and negative impact mitigation; (3) addressing disproportionately negative impacts as appropriate; (4) reward for eligible fuels in general; (5) GHG mitigation and adaptation; (6) equitable transition; and (7) administration (IMO 2024g, Annex, 35).

The CIA, which assessed the impacts of the measures on shipping fleets and States, also advanced stakeholder analysis. However, its analysis is limited to selected commodities from only ten IMO member States (IMO 2024h). It also highlighted uncertainties for decarbonization pathways and embracing alternative fuels and technologies, with the main reasons being uncertain future fuel prices. From the projections in the CIA, India has interpreted a need for considerable sectoral infrastructure investment alongside green fuel supply chains for ships (IMO 2024c, para. 7). China, Saudi Arabia, and the United Arab Emirates have raised concerns regarding the CIA's assessment of impact on States on the grounds of misleading conclusions due to a lack of transparency, among other limitations (IMO 2024b).

5.4.5 *Obligation of Assistance*

ITLOS has implied the need for a level-playing field among nations with varying levels of ability and capacity to implement the IMO GHG reduction measures. It has manifestly found the existence of some elements of the principle of CBDR-RC in the obligation of assistance under Articles 202 and 203 of UNCLOS (ITLOS Advisory Opinion, para. 326). ITLOS has intensified the necessity for IMO decisions to facilitate assistance in favor of the developing world (para. 326). By synonymously using the terms "States with lesser capabilities" as a reference for the developing States and "States that are better placed" for developed States, ITLOS has clarified the purpose of CBDR-RC as being nested in the "obligation of assistance," which must be executed in acknowledgment of the contemporary inequalities in the capacity of States to meet environmental obligations (para. 326). Moreover, ITLOS has also asserted that the obligation of assistance is of a continuing nature, which is to extend until the developing States are enabled in the long term "to set up their own programmes to counter marine pollution from anthropogenic GHG emissions" (para. 332).

It can be argued that, lacking consensus at present over the terms of the economic measures as part of the IMO GHG reduction measures, the ITLOS Advisory Opinion forms a robust basis for developing maritime nations, particularly SIDS and LDCs, to assert in the upcoming MEPC deliberations that an economic measure must prioritize the "continuous" fulfillment of the obligation of assistance by the developed IMO member States until a level-playing field has been achieved. The fulfillment of this obligation of assistance can only be derived from crystallizing and connecting the purpose of these principles and the impact of each relevant IMO GHG reduction measure (Polepalli 2024).

The CIA was the first step in realizing the potential impact of the proposed IMO measures. The Revised Strategy calls for an impact assessment of IMO GHG reduction measures on States, with particular attention to the needs of developing countries, in particular LDCs and SIDS (IMO 2023l, Annex, paras. 4.10–4.14). Even prior to the CIA, the Revised Strategy acknowledges specific barriers concerning the development and global availability of zero and near-zero GHG emissions technologies, fuels, and/or energy sources, and associated port infrastructure. It highlights the significance of public–private partnerships, information-sharing, technology transfer, capacity-building activities, and technology cooperation for enabling a smoother transition (IMO 2023l, Annex, para. 5). To this end, the IMO has already initiated various supporting measures. Technical assistance for GHG emissions reduction in the sector has been rolled out through the IMO's Integrated Technical Cooperation Programme (ITCP) and other externally supported mechanisms, such as the establishment of a GHG Trust Fund (IMO n.d.-f), Global Maritime Technology Cooperation Centres (IMO n.d.-c), and projects run with the assistance of other IMO member States such as Norway, South Korea, and Saudi Arabia.[14] Appendix 2 of the Revised Strategy provides an overview of these initiatives. The externally supported technical assistance programs are based on voluntary cooperation and initiation among the IMO States.

The IMO's in-house ITCP, which aims to assist governments that lack the technical knowledge and resources for safe and efficient shipping operations, has had a dedicated program for GHG emissions reductions in the sector (IMO 2023l, Appendix 2). The approved ITCP budget for 2024–25 is £10.781 million (IMO 2024a, 2). The financial distribution from this budget for technical assistance under the ITCP is based on the present regional geographical distribution of countries. To this end, the ITCP is presently divided into five regions: (1) Africa region, which comprises thirty-seven IMO member States; (2) Arab States and the Mediterranean region, which comprises twenty-two IMO member States; (3) Asia and the Pacific region, which comprises twenty-two IMO member States and two IMO associate members; (4) Western Asia and Eastern Europe region, which comprises twenty-three IMO member States; and (5) Latin America and the Caribbean region, which comprises nineteen IMO member States (IMO n.d.-b). It can be observed that there is no uniform criteria for determining these geographic groupings, which invariably results in a disproportionate allocation of resources for the ITCP programs. For instance, the geographic grouping of Asia Pacific, as compared to other geographic groupings, may not be proportionate because the Asia region itself consists of the two most populous countries in the world. This also evidences that the present

[14] IMO GreenVoyage2050 is a project aiming to support implementation of the Revised Strategy, particularly by providing support to developing countries in their efforts to reduce GHG emissions from ships. The donors to this project are Finland, France, Germany, the Netherlands, and Norway: see GreenVoyage (2050 n.d.). The Future Fuels and Technology Project also supports the Revised Strategy with funding from the Republic of Korea: see IMO and Government of Korea (n.d.). The IMOCARES project is funded by Saudi Arabia specifically to help SIDS and LDCs identify suitable market-ready technology solutions that will help improve the efficiency of selected vessels and/or ports and to reduce operational costs and GHG emissions: see IMO CARES (2022).

geographic groupings at the IMO are not based on contemporary circumstances faced by IMO member States and may not align with the principles of CBDR-RC. India had made a written submission raising these concerns at the 129th Session of the IMO Council and advocating for the review and reconsideration of the existing geographic grouping countries in light of significant equitable factors, such as population in the region, per capita income, number of seafarers, coastline and navigable waterways, volume of cargo handled, vulnerabilities, and underrepresentation in the maritime sector (IMO 2023d, para. 12). However, this proposal failed to receive the required support, and for reasons not specified, the forty-member IMO Council decided on behalf of the 176 IMO member States that no such review was "necessary" (IMO 2023m, para. 4(b).3).

5.5 CONCLUSION

The IMO has assumed the stewardship to navigate the complex task of regulating GHG emissions in the sector. However, its attempts to holistically address this subject do not appear to dive deep beyond the ambit of technical and operational measures. The financial or economic component is integral to driving the goal for net zero in the sector by mid-century, as it is tied to the other elements to be accounted for JET – that is, the procedural, human, and technical elements detailed in Section 5.4. Considering the sector's complexity discussed in Section 5.2, an examination of the IMO's work in Section 5.3 and the legal aspects of JET in Section 5.4 reveals an imbalance in procedural aspects and legal focus within the IMO for achieving JET in the sector. The procedural aspects involve facilitation and consideration of the subject for comprehensive and focused decision-making, ensuring equitable representation in IMO decision-making and equitable access to technical assistance for JET. The legal aspects entail realization of the legal principles underpinning the Revised Strategy in the IMO measures for GHG emissions reduction in the sector.

Despite crossing the IMO Roadmap's Phase III of decision-making and the adoption of the Revised Strategy, the scope and nature of the proposed economic component for the sector remain unclear. The IMO decision-making process is consensus-driven, which is impacted by the divergent perspectives over the alignment of the proposed economic component with JET. Moreover, Section 5.4 surfaces an added complexity stemming from the undefined JET in the Revised Strategy, leading to interpretational ambiguity. It can therefore be argued that aligning the application of an economic component in the sector with JET necessitates a targeted legal examination. However, at present, the agenda of GHG emissions reduction in the sector is exclusively within the ambit of the MEPC, which may lack representatives with legal expertise, unlike the IMO Legal Committee. Including this subject on the Legal Committee's agenda may help bolster legal clarity on JET. Achieving this requires a procedural reform within the IMO.

Further, Section 5.4 has revealed that perspectives on the economic component vary according to the socioeconomic positions of IMO member States. While the developed IMO member States, such as the European countries, strongly propose levying a price on GHG emissions from ships (IMO 2022a), the SIDS, particularly the Pacific Island States, strongly advocate for the disbursement aspects of the economic component (IMO 2018c, 2024d). Developing IMO member States, such as India, China, the United Arab Emirates, Argentina, and Brazil, focus on alleviating the economic burden emanating from the proposed economic component (IMO 2022f). In this regard, the emergence of coalitions can be observed at the IMO to advocate their policy goals. Further studies can examine the character and role of such coalitions among IMO member States, actors, and stakeholders toward the interpretation and application of JET, particularly its procedural, human, technical, economic, and regulatory elements.

The legal disparities manifest in the inconsistent practical emphasis on the legal principles underpinning the Revised Strategy. While the need for balancing the IMO principles of NMFT and nondiscrimination with the UNFCCC principle of CBDR-RC has been acknowledged, the latter's realization within the sector remains elusive. Although proposals emphasize the application of the polluter-pays principle, the Revised Strategy and the proposed IMO Net-Zero Framework fail to reflect it. The polluter-pays principle is not just significant for the disbursement of revenue; as proposed in the 76th session of the MEPC (IMO 2021c), it is nonnegotiable for the stage of levying costs for emissions in the sector. Therefore, as the IMO Net-Zero Framework nears its potential adoption, there is an imminent need to examine it through the lens of environmental justice, both in theory and empirically, because the Framework's design and implementation will have profound implications for how the burdens and benefits of maritime decarbonization are distributed, whose voices are recognized in decision-making, and whether the transition reinforces or redresses existing inequities in the maritime sector.

Further, the ITLOS Advisory Opinion has confirmed that the principle of CBDR-RC entails the obligation of assistance, demanding leadership from the developed countries. However, the draft IMO Net-Zero Framework proposes embedding the economic component with the mandatory provisions of MARPOL Annex VI, relegating the obligation to assist to a voluntary and less significant role, thereby compromising the principle of CBDR-RC. Further, the concerns of unilateral voluntary financial aid to drive consensus at the IMO, as highlighted in Section 5.4, also need to be addressed. Moreover, even the voluntary disbursement of technical assistance funds under the IMO's ITCP is subject to the disproportionate regional geographic groupings within the IMO, as shown in Section 5.4.5. There is a strong need to bring geographic reforms to realize the principle of CBDR-RC within the IMO. The obligation to steward this goal, including by way of the relevant reforms proposed in this chapter, lies with the developed IMO member States. Such an obligation, as confirmed by ITLOS, shall continue until a level-playing field is achieved.

REFERENCES

Baumann, Jennifer. 2023. "Shifting to Sustainable Shipping: Actors and Power Shifts in Shipping Emissions in the IMO." *Sustainability* 15 (17): 12472.

BIMCO (Baltic and International Maritime Council). 2023. *Glossary of Climate Change Definitions in Relation to Shipping*. BIMCO.

De Souza, Philip. 2002. *Seafaring and Civilization: Maritime Perspectives on World History*. Profile Books.

GreenVoyage2050. n.d. "About IMO GreenVoyage2050." https://greenvoyage2050.imo.org/about-the-project/.

Guterres, António. 2018. "Secretary General's Remarks on Climate Change [as delivered]." United Nations, September 10. www.un.org/sg/en/content/sg/statement/2018-09-10/secretary-generals-remarks-climate-change-delivered.

ILO (International Labour Organization). n.d. "Green Jobs and a Just Transition in Eastern Europe and Central Asia." www.ilo.org/regions-and-countries/europe-and-central-asia/areas-work/enterprises-development/green-jobs-and-just-transition-eastern-europe-and-central-asia.

IMO (International Maritime Organization). 1997. "Report to the Marine Environment Protection Committee on Its Thirty-Ninth Session." MEPC 39/13 (April 25, 1997).

2000. "Study of Greenhouse Gas Emissions from Ships." https://wwwcdn.imo.org/localresources/en/OurWork/Environment/Documents/First%20IMO%20GHG%20study.pdf.

2001a. "Elements to Be Considered in a Possible Development of a GHG Emission Standard for Ships." Submitted by Norway, MEPC 47/4/1 (December 28, 2001).

2001b. "Proposal for Elements to Be Included in an IMO Strategy on Greenhouse Gases." Submitted by Norway, MEPC 46/10/1 (February 16, 2001).

2002. "Report to the Marine Environment Protection Committee on Its Forty-Seventh Session." MEPC 47/20 (March 18, 2002).

2004. "IMO Policies and Practices Related to the Reduction of Greenhouse Gas Emissions from Ships." A 23/Res.963 (March 4, 2004).

2009. *Second IMO GHG Study 2009*. IMO.

2011a. "Amendments to the Annex of the Protocol of 1997 to Amend the International Convention for the Prevention of Pollution from Ships, 1973, as modified by the Protocol of 1978 relating thereto." MEPC.203(62) (July 15, 2011).

2011b. "Two Studies on Market-Based Measures." Submitted by the Netherlands, 3rd Session, Intersessional Meeting of the Working Group on Reduction of GHG Emissions from Ships, GHG-WG 3/INF.2 (February 23, 2011).

2015. "Third IMO Greenhouse Gas Study 2014." www.imo.org/en/ourwork/environment/pages/greenhouse-gas-studies-2014.aspx.

2016a. "Report to the Marine Environment Protection Committee on Its Sixty-Ninth Session." MEPC 69/21 (May 13, 2016).

2016b. "Roadmap for Developing a Comprehensive IMO Strategy on Reduction of GHG Emissions from Ships." MEPC 70/18/Add.1, Annex 11 (November 11, 2016).

2018a. "Establishment of a GMN Voluntary Multi-Donor Trust Fund." Submitted by Cambodia, China, Ecuador, Georgia, Islamic Republic of Iran, Jamaica and Kenya, MEPC 73/7/4 (August 17, 2018).

2018b. "Possible Approaches to Improvement of SEEMP." Fourth Session of the Intersessional Meeting of the Working Group on Reduction of GHG Emissions from Ships, ISWG-GHG 4/2/14 (August 31, 2018).

2018c. "Report to the Marine Environment Protection Committee on Its Seventy-Third Session." MEPC 73/19 (October 26, 2018).
2018d. "Initial IMO Strategy on Reduction of GHG Emissions from Ships." MEPC 72/17/Add.1, Annex 11 (April 13, 2018).
2019a. "Comments on Document MEPC 74/7/1 on Possible Future Working Arrangements to Support the Follow-Up Actions of the IMO Strategy on Reduction of GHG Emissions from Ships." Submitted by Kiribati, Marshall Islands, Solomon Islands, and Tuvalu, MEPC 74/7/12 (March 22, 2019).
2019b. "Possible Future Working Arrangements to Support the Follow-Up Actions of the IMO Strategy on Reduction of GHG Emissions from Ships." Submitted by Belgium, Chile, Marshall Islands, Solomon Islands, and Tuvalu, C 122/9/1 (June 14, 2019).
2019c. "Proposal for a Draft Assembly Resolution on Financing and Partnership Arrangements to Enable the Active and Full Participation by SIDS and LDCs in the GHG Emissions Reduction Processes." Submitted by Kiribati, Marshall Islands, Solomon Islands, and Tuvalu, MEPC 74/7/13 (March 22, 2019),
2019d. "Report to the Marine Environment Protection Committee on Its Seventy-Fourth Session." MEPC 74/18 (June 9, 2019).
2020. "Proposal for a Mandatory Operational Goal-Based Short-Term Measure." Submitted by Denmark, France, and Germany, Seventh Session of the Intersessional Meeting of the Working Group on Reduction of GHG Emissions from Ships, ISWG-GHG 7/2/9 (February 7, 2020).
2021a. "Fourth IMO Greenhouse Gas Study 2020: Full Report." www.imo.org/en/ourwork/environment/pages/fourth-imo-greenhouse-gas-study-2020.aspx
2021b. "A Levy-Based MBM, per Tonne of CO_2 Emissions, to Expedite the Uptake and Deployment of Zero-Carbon Fuels." Submitted by ICS and INTERCARGO, Tenth Session, Intersessional Meeting of the Working Group on Reduction of GHG Emissions from Ships, ISWG-GHG 10/5/2 (September 3, 2021).
2021c. "Proposal for IMO to Establish a Universal Mandatory Greenhouse Gas Levy." Submitted by the Marshall Islands and Solomon Islands, 76th Session, Marine Environment Protection Committee, MEPC 76/7/12 (March 10, 2021).
2021d. "Proposal for Regulatory Mechanisms for the Effective Uptake of Sustainable Low-Carbon and Zero-Carbon Fuels." Submitted by Norway, Tenth Session, Intersessional Meeting of the Working Group on Reduction of GHG Emissions from Ships, ISWG-GHG 10/5/6 (September 3, 2021).
2021e. "Amendments to the Annex of the Protocol of 1997 to Amend the International Convention for the Prevention of Pollution from Ships, 1973, as Modified by the Protocol of 1978 relating thereto." MEPC 76/15/Add.1 (June 17, 2021).
2022a. "Consideration of a Combination of Different Types of Global Market-Based Measures with Technical Mid- and Long-Term Measures." Submitted by Austria et al., Twelfth Session, Intersessional Meeting of the Working Group on Reduction of GHG Emissions from Ships, ISWG-GHG 12/3/5 (March 30, 2022).
2022b. "Further Development of the Proposal for a GHG Fuel Standard." Submitted by Austria et al., Thirteenth Session, Intersessional Meeting of the Working Group on Reduction of GHG Emissions from Ships, ISWG-GHG 13/4/7 (October 21, 2022).
2022c. "Proposal for a GHG Fuel Standard." Submitted by Austria et al., TwelfthSession, Intersessional Meeting of the Working Group on Reduction of GHG Emissions from Ships, ISWG-GHG 12/3/3 (March 30, 2022).
2022d. "Proposal for a GHG Levy as a Component in a Basket of Measures Submitted by Marshall Islands and Solomon Islands." Thirteenth Session, Intersessional Meeting of

the Working Group on Reduction of GHG Emissions from Ships, ISWG-GHG 13/4/11 (October 21, 2022).

2022e. "Proposal on Market-based Measures (MBMs) to Incentivize GHG Emission Reduction and to Make Equitable Transition with an Overview of Mid- and Long-Term Measures." Submitted by Japan, Twelfth Session, Intersessional Meeting of the Working Group on Reduction of GHG Emissions from Ships, ISWG-GHG 12/3/17 (April 1, 2022).

2022f. "Proposal to Establish an International Maritime Sustainability Funding and Reward (IMSF&R) Mechanism as an Integrated Mid-Term Measure." Submitted by Argentina, Brazil, China, South Africa, and United Arab Emirates, Twelfth Session, Intersessional Meeting of the Working Group on Reduction of GHG Emissions from Ships, ISWG-GHG 12/3/9 (April 1, 2022).

2022g. "Refined Proposal on Zero-Emission Shipping Incentive Scheme (ZESIS) to Incentivize GHG Emission Reduction and to Make an Equitable Transition." Submitted by Japan, Thirteenth Session, Intersessional Meeting of the Working Group on Reduction of GHG Emissions from Ships, ISWG-GHG 13/4/6 (October 21, 2022).

2022h. "Refinements to IMSF&R (F&R) Proposal Using a Flat Rate Contribution System, for Consideration as a Mid-Term Measure Under Phase II of the Work Plan." Thirteenth Session, Intersessional Meeting of the Working Group on Reduction of GHG Emissions from Ships, ISWG-GHG 13/4/9 (October 21, 2022).

2022i. "Procedures for Port State Control." A 32/Res.1155 (January 28, 2022).

2022j. "2022 Guidelines for the Development of a Ship Energy Efficiency Management Plan (SEEMP)." MEPC 78/17/Add.1 (June 10, 2022).

2023a. "The Application of Life Cycle Assessment (LCA) Guidelines." Submitted by Austria et al., Fifteenth Session, Intersessional Meeting of the Working Group on Reduction of GHG Emissions from Ships, ISWG-GHG 15/3/3 (May 12, 2023).

2023b. "Call for Applications to the Voluntary Multi-Donor Trust Fund (VMDTF) for Financial Support to Participants from Developing Countries, Particularly Small Island Developing States (SIDS) and Least Developed Countries (LDCs) to Attend Meetings of the Marine Environment Protection Committee (MEPC 80) and the Intersessional Working Group on Greenhouse Gas Emissions (ISWG-GHG 15)." Circular Letter No. 4704, March 17.

2023c. "Establishment of Voluntary Multi-Donor Trust Fund to Facilitate the Participation of Developing Countries, Especially Small Island Developing States (SIDS) and Least Developed Countries (LDCs) to Attend Meetings of the Marine Environment Protection Committee (MEPC) and the Intersessional Working Group on Greenhouse Gas Emissions (ISWG-GHG)." Circular Letter No. 4703, March 16.

2023d. "Geographical Regions Used at IMO." Submitted by India, 129th Session, Council, C 129/4(b)/1 (May 19, 2023).

2023e. "List of Participants." Fifteenth Meeting of the Intersessional Working Group on Reduction of GHG Emissions from Ships, ISWG-GHG 15/INF.1 (July 12, 2023).

2023f. "Report of the Fifteenth Meeting of the Intersessional Working Group on Reduction of GHG Emissions from Ships (ISWG-GHG 15)." MEPC 80/WP.7 (June 30, 2023).

2023g. "Report of the Fourteenth Meeting of the Intersessional Working Group on Reduction of GHG Emissions from Ships (ISWG-GHG 14)." MEPC 80/WP.6 (April 3, 2023).

2023h. "Report on the Study on the Readiness and Availability of Low- and Zero-Carbon Ship Technology and Marine Fuels. Note by the Secretariat." 3 MEPC 80/INF.10 (April 3, 2023).

2023i. "Report to the Marine Environment Protection Committee on Its Eightieth Session." MEPC 80/17 (July 28, 2023).
2023j. "Strategic Plan for the Organization for the Six-Year Period 2024 to 2029." A 33/Res.1173 (December 11, 2023).
2023k. "Guidelines on Life Cycle GHG Intensity of Marine Fuels (LCA Guidelines)." MEPC 80/17/Add.1, Annex 14 (July 7, 2023).
2023l. "2023 IMO Strategy on Reduction of GHG Emissions from Ships." MEPC.377(80) (July 7, 2023).
2023m. "Summary of Decisions." 129th Session, Council, C 129/D (July 24, 2023).
2024a. "Budget Considerations for the 2024–2025 Biennium and Outline for the 2026–2027 – by the Secretary-General." 133rd Session, Council, C 133/5(b) (October 20, 2024).
2024b. "Comments on Document MEPC 82/7/4." Submitted by China, Saudi Arabia and United Arab Emirates, 82nd Session, Marine Environment Protection Committee, MEPC 82/7/16 (August 9, 2024).
2024c. "Comments on Document MEPC 82/7/4." Submitted by India, 82nd Session, Marine Environment Protection Committee, MEPC 82/7/12 (August 9, 2024).
2024d. "Financing a Just and Equitable Transition of Maritime Transport in Solomon Islands." Submitted by Solomon Islands. 82nd Session, Marine Environment Protection Committee, MEPC 82/7/7 (June 26, 2024).
2024e. "Illustration of a Draft Possible Outline of the 'IMO Net-Zero Framework.'" MEPC 81/16/Add.1, Annex 12 (April 10, 2024).
2024f. "Note by the IMO to the Sixty-First Session of the UNFCCC Subsidiary Body for Scientific and Technological Advice (SBSTA 61)." Agenda 14(b).
2024g. "Report of the Steering Committee on the Comprehensive Impact Assessment of the Basket of Candidate GHG Reduction Mid-Term Measures: Executive Summary of the Report on Task 2 (Impacts on the Fleet)." Submitted by the Secretariat, 82nd Session, Marine Environment Protection Committee, MEPC 82/7/4/Add.2 (July 26, 2024).
2024h. "Report of the Steering Committee on the Comprehensive Impact Assessment of the Basket of Candidate GHG Reduction Mid-Term Measures: Executive Summary of the Report on Task 4 (Stakeholder Analysis) Submitted by the Secretariat." 82nd Session, Marine Environment Protection Committee, MEPC 82/7/4/Add.4. (July 26, 2024).
2024i. "Status of IMO Treaties." November 20. wwwcdn.imo.org/localresources/en/About/Conventions/StatusOfConventions/Status%202024.pdf.
2025a. "IMO approves net-zero regulations for global shipping." 11 April. www.imo.org/en/MediaCentre/PressBriefings/pages/IMO-approves-netzero-regulations.aspx.
2025b. "Draft Revised MARPOL Annex VI." Circular Letter No. 5005, April 11. https://wwwcdn.imo.org/localresources/en/MediaCentre/HotTopics/Documents/Circular%20Letter%20No.5005%20-%20Draft%20Revised%20Marpol%20Annex%20Vi%20%28Secretariat%29.pdf.
n.d.-a. "Brief History of IMO." www.imo.org/en/About/HistoryOfIMO/Pages/Default.aspx.
n.d.-b. "Geographical Coverage." www.imo.org/en/OurWork/TechnicalCooperation/Pages/Geo-Coverage.aspx.
n.d.-c. "The Global MTCC Network." www.imo.org/en/OurWork/PartnershipsProjects/Pages/IMO-EuropeanUnionProject.aspx.
n.d.-d. "IMO and UNFCCC." www.imo.org/en/OurWork/Environment/Pages/IMO%20and%20UNFCCC.aspx.
n.d.-e. "IMO GHG Studies." www.imo.org/en/OurWork/Environment/Pages/IMO-GHG-studies.aspx.

n.d.-f. "IMO's Multi-Donor GHG Trust Fund." www.imo.org/en/OurWork/Environment/Pages/IMO's-Multi-donor-GHG-Trust-Fund.aspx.

n.d.-g. "Improving the Energy Efficiency of Ships." www.imo.org/en/OurWork/Environment/Pages/Improving%20the%20energy%20efficiency%20of%20ships.aspx.

n.d.-h. "Maritime Just Transition." www.imo.org/en/OurWork/HumanElement/Pages/Maritime-Just-Transition.aspx.

n.d.-i. "Voluntary Multi-Donor Trust Fund (VMDTF) for Financial Support to Attend IMO GHG Meetings." www.imo.org/en/OurWork/Environment/Pages/VMDTF.aspx.

IMO (International Maritime Organization) and Government of Korea. n.d. "About the Project: Supporting MEPC Decision-Making." Future Fuels and Technology Project. https://futurefuels.imo.org/home/about/.

IMO CARES. 2022. "The Project." https://imocares.imo.org/the-project/.

IPCC (Intergovernmental Panel on Climate Change). 1996. "Understanding the Common Reporting Framework." In *Greenhouse Gas Inventory Reporting Instructions*. Vol. 1 of *Revised 1996 IPCC Guidelines for National Greenhouse Gas Inventories*. IPCC.

2005. *IPCC Special Report on Carbon Dioxide Capture and Storage*. Cambridge University Press.

2006. *General Guidance and Reporting*. Vol. 1 of *2006 IPCC Guidelines for National Greenhouse Gas Inventories*. IPCC.

2018. *Global Warming of 1.5°C: An IPCC Special Report*. IPCC.

2019a. "IPCC Updates Methodology for Greenhouse Gas Inventories." May 13. www.ipcc.ch/2019/05/13/ipcc-2019-refinement/.

2019b. *The Ocean and Cryosphere in a Changing Climate: Special Report of the Intergovernmental Panel on Climate Change*. Cambridge University Press.

2021a. *Climate Change 2021: The Physical Science Basis*. IPCC.

2021b. "Climate Change Widespread, Rapid, and Intensifying – IPCC." August 9. www.ipcc.ch/2021/08/09/ar6-wg1-20210809-pr/.

2023. *Climate Change 2023: Synthesis Report*. IPCC.

MARPOL COP (Conference of Parties). 1997. "CO_2 Emissions from Ships." MP/CONF. 3/35 (October 22, 1997).

MJTTF (Maritime Just Transition Task Force). 2022. "Mapping a Maritime Just Transition for Seafarers." United Nations Global Compact, International Chamber of Shipping, and International Transport Workers' Federation Position Paper, November.

Oiltanking. n.d. "Marine Fuels (Bunker Fuels)." www.oiltanking.com/en/news-info/glossary/marine-fuels-bunker-fuels.html.

Paine, Lincoln. 2013. *The Sea and Civilization: A Maritime History of the World*. Alfred A. Knopf.

Polepalli, Sindhura. 2024. "The ITLOS Advisory Opinion and the Normative Future of IMO GHG Reduction Measures." *OpinioJuris*, July 22. https://opiniojuris.org/2024/07/22/the-itlos-advisory-opinion-and-the-normative-future-of-imo-ghg-reduction-measures/.

Shaw, Aly, and Christiaan De Beukelaer. 2022. "Why Should We Talk about a 'Just and Equitable' Transition for Shipping?" *UNCTAD Transport and Trade Facilitation Newsletter* no. 96: article no. 9. https://unctad.org/news/why-should-we-talk-about-just-and-equitable-transition-shipping.

UN (United Nations). 1972. "Report of the United Nations Conference on the Human Environment." Stockholm, June 5–16, A/CONF.48/14/Rev.1.

UNCTAD (UN Trade and Development). 2023. *Review of Maritime Transport 2023: Towards a Green and Just Transition*. UNCTAD.

n.d. "Review of Maritime Transport." https://unctad.org/topic/transport-and-trade-logistics/review-of-maritime-transport.

UNEP (United Nations Environment Programme). 2022. "How Do Greenhouse Gases Actually Warm the Planet?" January 5. www.unep.org/news-and-stories/story/how-do-greenhouse-gases-actually-warm-planet.

UNGA (United Nations General Assembly). 1948. "Agreement between the United Nations and the Inter-Governmental Maritime Consultative Organization." A/RES/204 (III) (November 18, 1948).

1987. "Report of the World Commission on Environment and Development." A/42/427 (August 4, 1987).

1992. "Report of the United Nations Conference on Environment and Development." Rio de Janeiro, June 3–14, A/CONF.151/26, vol. I (August 12, 1992).

UNTC (United Nations Treaty Collection). n.d. "Status of Treaties, United Nations Framework Convention on Climate Change." https://treaties.un.org/Pages/ViewDetailsIII.aspx?src=TREATY&mtdsg_no=XXVII-7&chapter=27&Temp=mtdsg3&clang=_en.

Vermeire, Monique B. 2021. *Everything You Need to Know about Marine Fuels*. Chevron Marine Products.

PART III

Maritime Cyber Safety and Security

6

Maritime Cyber Threats

Jamming and Spoofing of Commercial Vessels

Raul (Pete) Pedrozo

6.1 INTRODUCTION

The importance of high navigational standards for ships operating at sea goes without question. These standards ensure the safety of vessels, crews, and cargoes, as well as the protection of the marine environment. Ships rely heavily on types of the Global Navigation Satellite System (GNSS) – such as the NAVSTAR Global Positioning System (GPS), Global'naya Navigatsionnaya Sputnikovaya Sistema (GLONASS), BeiDou Navigation Satellite System (BDS), and Galileo[1] – for the safety of navigation. Position, navigation, and time (PNT) based on satellite input allow shipboard "receivers to determine location to a high degree of precision" (McCrystal 2018). Thus, GNSS as a source of PNT must be certain and protected from manipulation.

GNSS performance is assessed using four criteria: (1) accuracy, the difference between a receiver's measured and real position, speed, or time; (2) integrity, a system's capacity to provide a threshold of confidence and, in the event of an anomaly in the positioning data, an alarm; (3) continuity, a system's ability to function without interruption; and (4) availability, the percentage of time a signal fulfills the above accuracy, integrity, and continuity criteria (INTERTANKO 2019, 12).

The views expressed in this chapter are those of the author and do not represent the views of the Department of the Navy, the Department of Defense, or the US government.

[1] GPS (USA), GLONASS (Russia), BeiDou (China), and Galileo (EU) are all types of GNSS. GPS provides users with position, navigation, and time (PNT) services and has global coverage. The US Air Force develops, maintains, and operates the space and control segments. GLONASS is a "space-based satellite navigation system operating in the radionavigation-satellite service." It "provides an alternative to GPS and is the second navigational system in operation" with global coverage and comparable precision. BeiDou has been in operation in the Asia Pacific region since December 2012. Galileo provides "improved services relating to the use of dual frequency" (INTERTANKO 2019, 12–13).

While some interference with GNSS-type systems is unintentional, there is a growing threat to these systems by malign actors (such as China, Iran, and Russia) that can adversely affect their use for safe navigation. Blocking, jamming, or seriously degrading services that rely on radio waves (that is, harmful interference) threaten "critical infrastructure and safety services used every day, from commercial aviation to energy distribution to satellite navigation systems" (ITU News 2022). Protecting the GNSS is therefore critical for ensuring the safe and efficient operation of manned, unmanned, and autonomous ships at sea that rely on positioning and navigation systems.

GNSS-type systems, however, are vulnerable to attack. State and non-State actors can attack PNT data "through electronic warfare (EW) capabilities" that can result in significant damage to (inter alia) military operations, as well as everyday commercial shipping activities (C4ADS 2019). Thus, the proliferation of new technologies and methodologies to interfere with GNSS has emerged "as a viable, disruptive strategic threat" that could "endanger everything from global navigational safety to civilian finances, logistics, and communication systems" (C4ADS 2019).

This chapter will discuss the various threats to the GNSS and how States can mitigate against disruption of services caused by jamming and spoofing. It will discuss the efforts at the International Maritime Organization (IMO) to mitigate threats to the GNSS. It will also review various measures taken by the US to protect the US maritime transportation system from cyber threats.

6.2 TERMINOLOGY

GPS is the premier provider of PNT service. It is comprised of three segments: ground control, space, and user equipment. The constellation of satellites that make up the space segment continuously broadcasts GPS signals and is under the command and control of the ground control segment. The user equipment segment consists of cards and receivers used by military aircraft, ships, land vehicles, munitions, and handheld devices that derive PNT data from the satellite signals (GAO 2024). PNT allows for the "determination of location (positioning), the ability to traverse to a new location along a path (navigation), and the knowledge of the current time (timing), all with a high level of precision" (NSTC 2021).

GNSS satellites provide signals that "transmit positioning and timing data to GNSS receivers," which are used to determine location (INTERTANKO 2019, 4). Because GNSS signals have low power compared to other radio signals, even a weak interference source can cause a GNSS receiver to fail or produce misleading information. Interference occurs when RF waveforms overwhelm the satellite signal, thereby degrading or denying the GNSS receiver's ability to operate (NSTC 2021, 3–4).

Jamming is caused by interfering with signals at GNSS frequencies. When done intentionally, jamming overpowers the weak GNSS signal receiver. As a result, a vessel is unable to determine its exact location. Brute force jamming occurs "when an attacker generates noise-like signals at frequencies used by a GNSS system . . . to prevent GNSS receivers from tracking authentic signals" (C4ADS 2019, 9). Both military jammers and Personal Protection Devices (PPDs) can be used to jam GNSS receivers intentionally (INTERTANKO 2019).

GNSS spoofing attacks provide GNSS-like signals that are coded and transmitted locally to deceive a GNSS receiver "by broadcasting incorrect GNSS signals, structured to resemble a set of normal GNSS signals, or by rebroadcasting genuine signals captured elsewhere or at a different time" (INTERTANKO 2019, 5; C4ADS 2019, 9). Spoofed signals may be altered by the attacker to cause the GNSS receiver to think its position is "somewhere other than where it actually is" or where it really is "but at a different time" (INTERTANKO 2019, 5). Measurement spoofing creates "signals that cause the target receiver to produce incorrect measurements of time of arrival or frequency of arrival or their rates of change" (NSTC 2021, 4). Data spoofing applies "incorrect digital data to the target receiver for its use in processing of signals and the calculation of PNT" (3).

A common form of GNSS spoofing – a carry-off attack – begins by broadcasting synchronized signals with "genuine signals observed by the target receiver" (INTERTANKO 2019, 5). As the power of the counterfeit signals is gradually increased, the "vessel's GNSS receiver tracks the false signals," which are then "manipulated to report a different location to the genuine signals" (5). Spoofing attacks that are intended to remain undetected require military grade technology.

The International Telecommunication Union (ITU) Radio Regulations are the international treaty regulating the global use of the RF spectrum and satellite orbits. The Regulations provide that "all stations, whatever their purpose, must be established and operated in such a manner as not to cause harmful interference to the radio services or communications of other Members or of recognized operating agencies, or of other duly authorized operating agencies which carry on a radio service" (ITU 2020, 0.4). Harmful interference occurs when interference "endangers the functioning of a radionavigation service or of other safety services or seriously degrades, obstructs, or repeatedly interrupts a radiocommunication service operating in accordance with Radio Regulations" (1.169). Stations are prohibited from carrying out unnecessary transmissions or transmitting superfluous signals, false or misleading signals, or signals without identification (15.1).

6.2.1 *Jamming and Spoofing*

Cyberattacks against international shipping by State-sponsored hackers have risen dramatically over the past twenty years, increasing from zero in 2003 to three in 2013 to sixty-four in 2023. These attacks adversely affect safety at sea by interfering with a vessel's navigation and communication equipment. For example, an Automatic Identification System (AIS) can be easily spoofed to broadcast incorrect data. Over 80 percent of these attacks have originated in China, Iran, North Korea, and Russia (Telling 2024). Given that China and Russia operate their own GNSS (BeiDou and GLONASS), they are more likely to manipulate GNSS for tactical and strategic advantages.

In May 2017, the US Director of National Intelligence reported to Congress that "the global threat of electronic warfare (EW) attacks against space systems will expand in the coming years in both number and types of weapons" (Coats 2017). These developments will "focus on jamming capabilities against dedicated military satellite communications (SATCOM), Synthetic Aperture Radar (SAR) imaging satellites, and enhanced capabilities against GNSS, such as the US Global Positioning System (GPS)" (Coats 2017). Malign States will blend EW and cyber-attack capabilities to develop "sophisticated means to deny and degrade information networks" (Coats 2017). Chinese researchers are working on "methods to enhance robust jamming capabilities with new systems to jam commonly used frequencies," and Russia will "modernize its EW forces and field a new generation of EW weapons by 2020" (Coats 2017). Additionally, Iran and North Korea are "enhancing their abilities to disrupt military communications and navigation" (Coats 2017).

6.2.1.1 China

Systematic GPS manipulation occurred in at least twenty locations along the Chinese coast during 2019. The sites include both oil terminals and government installations in Shanghai and Qingdao. Although the reason for the manipulation is uncertain, it may be associated with China's illicit import of UN-sanctioned Iranian crude oil. The anomaly – GPS spoofing circles – was first detected by the M/V *Manukai* in July 2019. As the US-flagged container ship entered the port of Shanghai, its AIS[2] appeared to malfunction: "vessels on the navigation screen appeared and disappeared without explanation and appeared to move when they were in fact stationary" (Bergman 2019).

A closer analysis by the Center for Advanced Defense Studies determined that hundreds of AIS vessel locations from ships navigating on the Huangpu River were appearing at false locations. Notably, vessel GPS locations were jumping from the river "to a ring of positions appearing on land" (Bergman 2019). When vessels approached the area of interference, their AIS broadcast positions jumped from their true locations to a point on land where the false broadcasts occurred in a ring about "200 meters in diameter" (Bergman 2019). Vessel speeds within the circle ranged from 21 to 31 knots, and their course varied depending on their location within the circle. Once a vessel was affected by the anomaly, it would broadcast a

[2] AIS transponders are designed to provide position, identification, and other information about the ship to other ships and to coastal authorities automatically to enhance situational awareness and promote safety at sea.

random position within the ring "or from other high-speed positions scattered around it" (Bergman 2019). In all probability, the center of the ring marks the location of a GPS-disrupting device.

The locations affected by GPS manipulation were in six Chinese cities, with the focus (sixteen of the twenty) on oil terminals. Nonetheless, three government buildings in Shanghai and Qingdao were also affected – "the Industrial and Commercial Bank of China in Shanghai, the Qingdao tax administration office, and the Qingdao headquarters of the Qingjian industrial group" (Bergman 2019). Activation of the GPS-disrupting devices at these buildings was likely a security measure.

Deployment of GPS manipulation devices at oil terminals, however, may be an effort by China to mask imports of US-sanctioned Iranian crude oil. AIS tracking data indicates that Iranian tankers delivered oil to China in June and July and that Chinese tankers engaged in ship-to-ship transfers with Iranian tankers to circumvent US sanctions (Bergman 2019; Goward 2019; Sheppard et al. 2019; Singhi et al. 2019; Zeng Xiaojun 2021). For example, at an oil terminal east of Dalian, although the manipulation devices were unable to mask the position of all vessels approaching the terminal, their use "would make it impossible to reliably link a vessel's AIS track with satellite imagery of a vessel discharging crude at dock" (Bergman 2019; Goward 2019; Zeng Xiaojun 2021).

It is also not uncommon for Chinese vessels to disable their AIS or spoof their location to mask illegal, unreported, and unregulated fishing activities (Pedrozo 2022). In 2020, over 300 Chinese fishing vessels converged on the waters around the Galápagos Islands (a UNESCO World Heritage Site and an Ecuadorian national marine reserve) to fish for squid and other fish stocks. Although there is no direct evidence that any Chinese vessels entered the marine reserve, numerous ships went "dark" to conceal their actual location and identity (AFP 2020; Ramos Miranda 2020; Rust 2020).

A Virginia-based company – HawkEye 360 – did confirm that there were unidentified vessels operating within Ecuador's exclusive economic zone (EEZ) that coincided with Chinese fishing vessels going dark (Alberts 2020). Data collected between July 13 and August 13, 2020, reflects that Chinese fishing vessels turned off their AIS devices on forty-three occasions for an average of two days at a time (Alberts 2020). During that timeframe, HawkEye 360 determined that fourteen unidentified vessels were operating within the EEZ around the Galápagos, six of which were "immediately adjacent to the bulk of the Chinese DWF fleet, suggesting that they had broken away" from the main fleet and entered Ecuador's EEZ (Alberts 2020). Additionally, six Chinese vessels spoofed their true location, sending out false signals that "puts them between the Chatham Islands and New Zealand, about 10,000km away" (Satherley 2020). Satellite imagery was unable to confirm the presence of Chinese vessels in New Zealand's waters.

6.2.2.2 Iran

Iran has publicly stated that it has the capacity to spoof GPS signals, which it appears to have used to interfere with shipping in the Persian Gulf (Goward 2020). In May, the Iranian Revolutionary Guard Corps (IRGC) seized the UK-flagged *Stena Impero* and the Liberian-flagged *Mesdar* after the vessels experienced interference with their GPS (Browne and Starr 2019). The US Maritime Administration (MARAD) subsequently issued a warning in August 2019 regarding Iranian threats to commercial shipping operating in the Strait of Hormuz, the Persian Gulf, and the Gulf of Oman. The administration warned that vessels operating in the region may "encounter GPS interference, bridge-to-bridge communications spoofing, and/or other communications jamming with little to no warning" (MARAD 2019). The warning indicated that the *Stena Impero* and *Mesdar* had experienced GPS interference prior to their seizure. Additionally, the administration warned that there had been reports that unknown entities were falsely claiming to be US or coalition warships via bridge-to-bridge communications (MARAD 2019).

Officials at US Central Command stated that GPS jammers have been placed at "Abu Musa Island, which lies in the Persian Gulf close to the entrance of the Strait of Hormuz." The IGRC uses the jammers to disrupt "ship navigation systems, hoping ships … will mistakenly wander into Iranian waters" while their GPS systems are malfunctioning, giving the IRGC a pretext to seize them (Browne and Starr 2019). The IRGC is additionally using spoofed communications to disguise their boats as merchant ships instead of IRGC or Iranian Navy vessels (Browne and Starr 2019).

Like China, Iran has also engaged in "circle spoofing." In March 2020, a user in Iran reported testing a GPS device. After ten minutes, the device showed the correct time but not the correct location – it was "moving around a big circle in Tehran" at a speed of 35 km per hour (Goward 2020). The circle was located near the Iran Army's Command and Staff College. A second location was reported around a "government complex that houses offices for several defense and technology-related organizations" (Goward 2020). One theory is that Iran may be interfering with GPS signals to disrupt "surveillance systems in the vicinity of sensitive government facilities" (Goward 2020).

In 2023, MARAD issued two additional maritime advisories due to heightened tensions in the region for the Persian Gulf and Strait of Hormuz regarding (inter alia) navigation and communications disruptions. MSCI Advisory 2023-11 warned that vessels operating in these areas could "encounter GPS interference (see Advisory 2023-005), AIS spoofing, bridge-to-bridge communications spoofing, and/or other communications jamming" (MARAD 2023b). The advisory further warned that "vessels have also reported bridge-to-bridge communications from unknown entities falsely claiming to be U.S. or coalition warships" (MARAD 2023b). MARAD advised that "in addition to risks to navigation, confusion from such disruptions could be leveraged by bad actors to facilitate physical attacks," and that vessels should take additional precautions if they (or vessels in their vicinity) experience such disruptions (MARAD 2023b). US-flagged vessels were advised to notify the US Fifth Fleet Battle Watch immediately if they suspected that they were being "hailed from a source falsely claiming to be a U.S. or coalition naval vessel" or if they were "asked for positions or info on coalition military vessels or aircraft operating in the area" (MARAD 2023b). Any disruptions or anomalies regarding maritime GPS were to be reported immediately to the US Coast Guard (USCG) Navigation Center (NAVCEN).

MSCI Advisory 2023-005 similarly warned that there had been multiple instances of GPS interference reported in the Strait of Hormuz and that this interference could "result in lost or inaccurate GPS signals affecting bridge navigation, GPS-based timing, and communications equipment (including satellite communications equipment)" (MARAD 2023a). MARAD also advised that "AIS signals can be spoofed, resulting in or missing AIS data" because AIS operates on nonsecure VHF-FM channels using open, unencrypted, and unprotected radio systems (MARAD 2023a). Therefore, AIS "should never be solely relied upon for collision avoidance or navigational decision-making" (MARAD 2023a). Maritime GPS disruptions or anomalies should be reported immediately to the NAVCEN.

The UK Maritime Trade Operations (UKMTO) office has similarly reported on "electronic interference" incidents involving merchant ships in the Persian Gulf. For example, between April 2 and 3, 2024, the UKMTO received a report from a vessel that was experiencing disruption to its electronic navigation systems (GPS/AIS) 95 nautical miles east of Las Al Zour, Saudi Arabia (Schuler 2024).

6.2.2.3 Russia

Russia has the capability and technology to spoof GPS and may be assisting Iran in interfering with AIS transmissions in the Persian Gulf (Joffre 2019). Russia has also actively engaged in spoofing attacks in the Black Sea. In June 2020, more than twenty ships in the Black Sea, near Novorossiysk Commercial Sea Port, reported that their AIS was erroneously showing their position as Gelendzhik Airport, 32 km inland, and that the GPS considered the position to be safe within 100 m. MARAD issued a warning that GPS interference had been reported in the vicinity of 44-15.7N, 037-32.9E on June 22, 2017, and that ships should "exercise caution when transiting the area" (C4ADS 2019, 14; Goward 2017). Navigation experts concluded that the interference was a clear case of "spoofing or sending false signals to cause a receiver to provide false information" (Goward 2017). Although there was no official explanation for the disruption, it could be "attributed to Russian testing of satellite navigation spoofing technology" or to encourage the use of Russia's GLONASS instead of GPS (Goward 2017; Lo 2019).

In June 2020, the positioning data of two NATO warships – HMS *Defender* and HNLMS *Evertsen* – showed the ships to be off the Crimean coast near Sevastopol when they were, in fact, moored 180 miles away in Odesa. The British destroyer and the Dutch frigate arrived in Odesa on June 18 after conducting an exercise in the Black Sea. The ships' AIS showed them leaving Odesa just before midnight on June 18, and then sailing directly to Sevastopol, coming to within 2 nautical miles of the Russian Black Sea Fleet's headquarters. Evidence from live webcam feeds shows that the warships never left Odesa (Sutton 2021).

Ukrainian authorities have also warned shipowners sailing to Odesa that satellite communication systems are being disrupted in the Black Sea. In June 2024, at least forty ships in the Black Sea were broadcasting compromised AIS locations. Over 33 percent of the ships reporting incorrect positions were loading Russian coal (Quinn 2024).

A 2024 report prepared by the Center for Advanced Defense Studies indicates that Russia has developed "a comparative advantage in the targeted use and development of GNSS spoofing capabilities to achieve tactical and strategic objectives at home and abroad" (C4ADS 2019, 9). Russia is developing "a comprehensive suite of asymmetrical EW systems designed to deceive, degrade, and deny military and civilian GNSS receivers" and has the "capability to create large GNSS denial-of-service spoofing environments" without targeting a single GNSS satellite (13).

The report identified nearly 10,000 instances "across 10 locations that affected 1,311 civilian vessel navigation systems" between 2016 and 2018 (C4ADS 2019, 13, 16, 20–21). In some cases, the Russian Federal Protective Service (FSO) is using mobile systems to spoof GNSS to protect very important persons. In other cases, Russian GNSS spoofing is used to protect strategic facilities in Moscow and protected facilities off the coast of Russia and Crimea in the Black Sea. Finally, Russia is also using GPS spoofing in active combat zones such as Syria "for airspace denial purposes" (13, 23–24, 26–28, 31–33, 44–46).

Many of these instances occur over brief periods of time in isolated locations, suggesting that "at least some of the devices used to conduct GNSS disruptions are mobile and can be temporarily deployed to create local areas of effect."[3] During President Putin's visit to the Kerch Bridge on May 15, 2018, twenty-four vessels anchored near the bridge "reported spoofed GNSS positioning information at the Anapa Airport more than 65 kilometers away."[4] Similar incidents occurred in September 8, 2017, and September 11, 2018, when Putin visited the Zvezda

[3] For example, GNSS spoofing activities in proximity to the Kerch Bridge on September 15, 2016, and May 15, 2018, coincided with a visit by President Vladimir Putin "to oversee the progress and completion of the Kerch Bridge" (C4ADS 2019, 26).

[4] The vessels were probably spoofed by a transmitter on one of the FSO vehicles accompanying Putin (C4ADS 2019, 27).

Shipyard, which is "located near the remote Russian Far East town of Bolshoy Kamen," 30 km from the port city of Vladivostok.[5]

GNSS spoofing devices used to protect strategic government residences owned and operated by the FSO and other sensitive facilities are stationary. Spoofing incidents at these facilities occur more frequently, affect "a greater number of vessels," and "interfere with receivers over a greater distance" (C4ADS 2019, 31). Vessels affected by spoofing report their "positions at local civilian airports" (31). Nearly 8,000 of the GNSS spoofing events occurred beyond the Russian territorial sea in the Black Sea and potentially posed a risk to the safety of navigation. Given the geographic extent and the nature of the events, some of the instances of interference also violated Article 15 of the Radio Regulations, which prohibit harmful interference with RFs (25).

6.3 MITIGATING RISKS

The importance of ensuring reliable PNT has prompted the concept of "Resilient PNT." Resilient PNT merges traditional PNT technology "with non-traditional and emerging technology to improve the reliability, performance, and safety of mission-critical applications, where the discrepancy in data accuracy, availability, and stability can impact the safety, security and economic viability of vessels at sea" (McCrystal 2018). By detecting, protecting, and authenticating vulnerabilities in GNSS (such as jamming and spoofing), vessels can be offered alternatives to existing PNT sources and provided PNT information they can trust (McCrystal 2018).

6.3.1 *International Maritime Organization Initiatives*

6.3.1.1 Maritime Safety Committee Resolution MSC.428(98)

In 2017, the Maritime Safety Committee adopted Resolution MSC.428(98) to raise awareness of cyber risk threats and vulnerabilities to support safe and secure shipping and encourage all maritime industry stakeholders to expedite work toward safeguarding shipping from current and emerging cyber threats and vulnerabilities. The resolution (inter alia) affirmed that an approved safety management system should consider cyber risk management and encouraged administrations to ensure that cyber risks are appropriately addressed in safety management systems (IMO 2017c).

GUIDELINES ON MARITIME CYBER RISK MANAGEMENT. The Guidelines on Maritime Cyber Risk Management were first adopted in 2017 and have since been

5 A vessel moored at the Zvezda Shipyard "reported spoofed positioning information at the Vladivostok International Airport" (C4ADS 2019, 28).

revised twice (IMO 2017b).[6] They provide high-level recommendations on maritime cyber risk management to safeguard shipping from current and emerging cyber threats and vulnerabilities. The guidelines also include functional elements that support effective cyber risk management (IMO 2022).

A "maritime cyber risk" refers to a measure of the extent to which a technology asset is threatened by a potential circumstance or event that may result in shipping-related operational, safety, or security failures because of information or systems being corrupted, lost, or compromised (IMO 2022, para. 2.1.1). Stakeholders are encouraged to take the necessary steps to safeguard shipping from current and emerging threats and vulnerabilities related to the digitization, integration, and automation of processes and systems in shipping (para. 1.2).

The guidelines are predicated on the goal of supporting safe and secure shipping that is operationally resilient to cyber risks (IMO 2022, paras. 1.5, 3.2). Risk management is fundamental to safe and secure shipping operations, and greater reliance on digitization, integration, automation, and network-based systems creates an increasing need for cyber risk management in the shipping industry (para. 1.4).

Vulnerabilities created by accessing, interconnecting, or networking shipboard systems that are critical to the safety and security of shipping can result in cyber risks that must be addressed. Vulnerable shipboard systems include (inter alia) bridge systems, cargo handling and management systems, propulsion and machinery management and power control systems, access control systems, passenger servicing and management systems, passenger-facing public networks, administrative and crew welfare systems, and communication systems (IMO 2022, para. 1.4).

The guidelines emphasize that there is a distinction between information technology and operational technology systems and that consideration should be given to the protection of information and data exchange within these systems. "Information technology systems" focus on the use of data as information. "Operational technology systems" focus on the use of data to control or monitor physical processes. These technologies and systems present risks to critical systems and processes associated with the operation of systems integral to shipping. These risks may result from vulnerabilities arising from inadequate operation, integration, maintenance, and design of cyber-related systems, or from intentional and unintentional cyber threats. The exploitation of operational and/or information technology vulnerabilities raises safety issues, particularly where critical systems (such as bridge navigation or main propulsion systems) are compromised (IMO 2022, paras. 2.1.2, 2.1.3, 2.1.5).

"Cyber risk management" is the process of identifying, analyzing, assessing, and communicating a cyber-related risk and accepting, avoiding, transferring, or mitigating that risk to an acceptable level, considering the costs and benefits of actions

[6] A third revision was approved by the Maritime Safety Committee in September 2024 but has not yet been approved by the Facilitation Committee.

taken by stakeholders (IMO 2022, para. 3.1). Functional elements that support effective cyber risk management should be incorporated concurrently and continuously into a risk management framework. These elements include the following:

1 **Identify:** Define personnel roles and responsibilities for cyber risk management and identify the systems, assets, data, and capabilities that, when disrupted, pose risks to ship operations.
2 **Protect:** Implement risk control processes and measures, along with contingency planning, to protect against a cyber event and ensure the continuity of shipping operations.
3 **Detect:** Develop and implement the activities necessary to detect a cyber event in a timely manner.
4 **Respond:** Develop and implement activities and plans to provide resilience and to restore systems necessary for shipping operations or services impaired due to a cyber event.
5 **Recover:** Identify measures to back up and restore cyber systems necessary for shipping operations impacted by a cyber event (IMO 2022, para. 3.5).

These functional elements include activities and desired outcomes of effective cyber risk management across critical systems affecting maritime operations and information exchange. They establish an ongoing process with effective feedback mechanisms (IMO 2022, para. 3.6). For cyber risk management to be effective, there must be an appropriate level of awareness of cyber risks at all levels of the organization (para. 3.7).

In addition to these guidelines, States should refer to State and Flag Administration requirements, as well as relevant international and industry standards and best practices, including (inter alia) the following:

1 The Guidelines on Cyber Security Onboard Ships produced and supported by the International Chamber of Shipping, the International Union of Marine Insurance, the Baltic and International Maritime Council (BIMCO), the Oil Companies International Marine Forum, the International Association of Independent Tanker Owners (INTERTANKO), the International Association of Dry Cargo Shipowners (INTERCARGO), InterManager, the World Shipping Council, and the Superyatch Builders Association (SYBAss).
2 The consolidated IACS Recommendation on Cyber Resilience (No. 166).
3 ISO/IEC 27001: Information security, cybersecurity, and privacy protection – Information Security Management Systems – requirements.
4 The US National Institute of Standards and Technology's Framework for Improving Critical Infrastructure Cybersecurity.
5 The IAPH Cybersecurity Guidelines for Ports and Port Facilities (IMO 2022, paras. 4.1, 4.2).

PERFORMANCE STANDARDS FOR MULTI-SYSTEM SHIPBORNE RADIONAVIGATION RECEIVERS. In 2015, the IMO adopted performance standards for multi-system shipborne radionavigation receivers (IMO 2015) to allow for the combined use of current and future radionavigation, as well as augmentation systems,[7] for the provision of position, velocity, and time data within the maritime navigation system (para. 1.4). A multi-system receiver that uses navigation signals from two or more GNSS-type systems, with or without augmentation, provides improved position, velocity, and time data, as well as improved resistance to intentional and unintentional RF interference. This combined approach also provides redundancy to mitigate the loss of a single system (para. 1.5).

A multi-system shipborne radionavigation receiver equipment should include the following minimum components and capabilities:

1 antennas capable of receiving all radionavigation signals required to support the functionality of the receiver equipment;
2 receiver(s) and processor(s) capable of processing the radionavigation signals required to support the functionality of the receiver equipment;
3 means of accessing the computed position, velocity, and time (PVT) information;
4 interface for supplying data controlling/configuring the receiver;
5 display;
6 raw data output for the provision of additional information, such as range measurements and the GNSS's navigation data;
7 an indication of the quality and reliability of the computed and distributed PVT data to the user; and
8 an indication of radionavigation systems currently used for the PVT information to the user (IMO 2015, para. 2.1).

The system should be capable of mitigating interference from authorized out–of-band sources. It should provide a means of integrity monitoring for each PVT source employed and multi-source autonomous integrity monitoring (IMO 2015, para. 2.3).

The equipment should operate using civil access navigation signals of at least two independent GNSS-type systems, provide PVT data with the necessary level of resilience and integrity, and have the facilities to process augmentation data (IMO 2015, paras. 3.1, 3.2, 3.4). The system should also have the capability to operate using terrestrial radionavigation systems signals if the use of such signals is anticipated, as well as the ability to select or deselect radionavigation and augmentation signals (paras. 3.3, 3.5).

7 Augmentation systems use ground- or space-based transmitters to provide augmentation data to improve accuracy and integrity for specific service areas (such as harbor entrances, harbor approaches, and coastal waters) (IMO 2015, para. 1.3).

The equipment should additionally be able to provide a single PVT solution, including:

1 position information of the consistent common reference point in latitude and longitude, with coordinates in degrees and minutes to a precision reflective of the accuracy of the position information, up to four decimal places;
2 course over ground (COG) of the consistent common reference point in degrees to a precision reflective of the accuracy of the calculated course information, relative to true north, up to one decimal place;
3 speed over ground (SOG) of the consistent common reference point in knots to a precision reflective of the accuracy of the calculated speed information, up to two decimal places; and
4 time, referenced to Universal Coordinated Time (UTC), to one-tenth of one second (IMO 2015, para. 3.6).

In addition, the system should be capable of providing the PVT solution to the required accuracy within five minutes where there is no valid satellite almanac data (cold start), within one minute where there is valid satellite almanac data (warm start), and within two minutes when subjected to a power interruption or loss of signals of <60 s (IMO 2015, para. 3.7). It should also provide time in UTC and be capable of meeting the requirements for the phases of navigation outlined in Assembly Resolution A.1046(27) (IMO 2011, 2015, paras. 3.8, 3.9).

The equipment should be able to generate a new PVT solution at least once every half second for high-speed craft (HSC) and at least once every second for conventional vessels (IMO 2015, para. 3.10). It should also be able to assess whether the performance of the PVT solution (such as accuracy and integrity) meets the requirements for each phase of navigation and to provide an alert when such assessment cannot be determined (para. 3.11). If the equipment is unable to assess the current achieved performance (such as accuracy and integrity) with respect to each navigation phase, it should provide a caution after two seconds for HSC and three seconds for conventional vessels (para. 3.12). It should additionally provide a warning if (after five seconds for HSC or seven seconds for conventional vessels) new PVT data has not been calculated (para. 3.13).

If it is not possible to provide a new position update at the next scheduled update, the system should output the last plausible position, SOG, COG, and the time of the last valid fix, until position update is resumed (IMO 2015, para. 3.14). The equipment should also provide an indication of augmentation status, including the receipt of augmentation signals; the validity of the signals received; whether augmentation is applied to the position in the PVT solution; and the identification of the augmentation signals (para. 3.15). The following information should be provided, in alphanumerical form, for the final PVT solution and for each individual source when requested, to a local display (or a separate interfaced display):

(1) position; (2) COG and SOG; (3) time; (4) the PVT solution sources; (5) the assessment of the navigation phases for which performance requirements are supported; (6) the identification of the augmentation signals applied to the position solution; and (7) any alert information (para. 3.16).

In addition, the equipment should provide the following interfaces:

1 at least one interface from which the PVT solution should be available in the WGS 84;
2 at least one interface from which data from all available sources can be provided;
3 an interface for alert management (that is, with the Bridge Alert Management); and
4 facilities to accept the input of augmentation signals from at least one source (IMO 2015, para. 4.1).

The system should be capable of operating satisfactorily under normal interference conditions, consistent with the requirements of IMO Resolution A.694(17) (IMO 1991), taking into account the typical electromagnetic and RF spectrum environment on board and from outside a vessel and ensuring that no permanent damage can result from an accidental short circuit or grounding of the antenna or any of its input or output connections or any of the inputs or outputs (IMO 2015, paras. 4.2, 4.3). Documentation for the equipment should be provided, preferably in an electronic format (para. 5).

6.3.1.2 Guidelines for Shipborne PNT Data Processing

In June 2017, the Maritime Safety Committee approved guidelines for shipborne PNT data processing (PNT-DP) to enhance the safety and efficiency of navigation by improving the provision of PNT data to bridge teams (including pilots) and shipboard applications (for example, AIS and ECDIS) (IMO 2017a, para. 1). Shipborne PNT-DP[8] is the core repository for principles and functions used for the provision of reliable and resilient PNT data (para. 2).

The guidelines aim to establish a modular framework for the further enhancement of shipborne PNT data provision by supporting:

1 the consolidation and standardization of requirements on shipborne PNT data provision considering the diversity of ship types, nautical tasks,

[8] PNT-DP is defined as a set of functions facilitating: (1) multiple sources of data provided by PNT-relevant sensors and services (for example, GNSS receiver and DGNSS corrections) and further onboard sensors and systems (for example, radar, gyro, speed and distance measuring equipment (SDME), and echo-sounder providing real-time data) to exploit existing redundancy in the PNT-relevant input data; and (2) multi-system and multi-sensor-based techniques for enhanced provision of PNT data (IMO 2017a, para. 3).

nautical applications, and the changing complexity of situations up to customized levels of support;

2 the identification of dependencies between PNT-relevant data sources (sensors and services), applicable PNT data-processing techniques (methods and thresholds), and achievable performance levels of provided PNT data (accuracy, integrity, continuity, and availability);

3 the harmonization and improvement of onboard PNT data processing based on a modular approach to facilitate changing performance requirements in relation to nautical tasks, variety of ship types, and nautical applications, and under consideration of user needs (SN.1/Circ.274);

4 the consequent and coordinated introduction of data and system integrity as a smart means to protect PNT data generation against disturbances, errors, and malfunctions (safety), as well as intrusions by malicious actors; and

5 the standardization of PNT output data, including integrity and status data (IMO 2017a, para. 5).

The guidelines provide recommendations on how to handle differences regarding installed equipment, the current system in use, the feasibility of tasks and related functions, and the performance of data sources, as well as usability in specific regions and situations (IMO 2017a, para. 6). A structured approach for the stepwise introduction of integrity is developed to achieve resilient PNT data provision in relation to the application grades and supported performance levels (para. 7). The guidelines are designed to achieve standardized and integrity-tested PNT output data to enhance user awareness regarding the achieved performance level (para. 8).

The guidelines have a modular structure: (1) Module A, data input – sensors, services, and sources; (2) Module B, functional aspects; (3) Module C, operational aspects; (4) Module D, interfaces; and (5) Module E, documentation (IMO 2017a, para. 10). Definitions, abbreviations, and expected operational and technical requirements on PNT/Integrity (I) data output are contained in the three appendices (para. 11).

Shipborne PNT-DP comprises three functional blocks: (1) pre-processing; (2) main processing; and (3) post-processing (IMO 2017a, para. 15). The pre-processing function extracts, evaluates, selects, and synchronizes input (sensor and service) data (including the associated integrity data) to preselect the applicable techniques to determine PNT and integrity output data (para. 16). The main processing function generates the PNT output data and associated integrity and status data (para. 18). Finally, the post-processing function generates the output messages by coding the PNT output data (PNT, integrity, and status data) into specified data protocols (para. 19).

6.3.2 *Industry Initiatives*

Several maritime groups provide industry guidelines, standards, and best practices on cyber security onboard ship – for example, the International Chamber of Shipping, BIMCO, the Oil Companies International Marine Forum, INTERTANKO, INTERCARGO, InterManager, the World Shipping Council, and SYBAss.

The INTERTANKO guidelines, for example, provide "guidance on the various types of GNSS, an introduction to threats associated with these systems and guidance on how to mitigate against these threats" (INTERTANKO 2019, 1). Guidelines for the ship's navigator include:

1 using radar and Electronic Chart Display and Information Systems (ECDIS) interlay (overlay or underlay) to detect GPS spoofing and jamming when land is visible on the radar;
2 verifying position at appropriate intervals;
3 observing significant difference between dead reckoning (DR) position (arrived with Gyro Course steered and distance by speed log) and GNSS fix; and
4 observing and verifying using an echo sounder to compare the depths when sailing in suitable depth areas (INTERTANKO 2019, 6).

If jamming and spoofing are detected, the navigator should take immediate action:

1 Manually select a secondary position sensor.
2 Select other GNSS input if provided and use a "GNSS divergence" alarm to check any marginal difference between positioning sources.
3 If a secondary sensor is unable to provide a vessel's position and no other means are available to input position fixing, the navigator should select the DR or estimated position (EP) mode.
4 Manually plot the ship's position if near enough to shore and seek greater sea room, if possible.
5 Use AIS with extreme caution, since it will also be affected by the jamming and spoofing attack.
6 If unable to ascertain vessel position relative to navigational hazards, stop the vessel (INTERTANKO 2019, 6).

When the situation is somewhat stable:

1 Check the vessel's GNSS position frequently to detect when the service is available again.
2 Report GNSS disruptions or anomalies to the authorities listed in Appendix A.

3 Take note of critical information, such as the actual location (latitude/longitude), date/time, and duration of the outage or disruption.
4 When possible, provide photos or screenshots of equipment failures during a disruption to assist analysts with identifying a potential cause.
5 For vessels using paper charts, continue plotting with alternative position fixing or DR (INTERTANKO 2019, 7).

Ship owners/managers should ensure that the bridge navigation equipment complies with MSC.1/Circ.1575 (IMO 2017a; INTERTANKO 2019, 7). The ECDIS should have an alarm management function. A multi GNSS receiver will enhance the system, and the use of GNSS open signals that have Navigation Message Authentication will provide additional protection (INTERTANKO 2019, 7). Ship owners/managers should also consider using Loran/E-Loran receivers as a backup/part of the resilient system and a way to detect jamming and spoofing (7). Crew training should include regular GNSS failure drills to develop competency in the detection of GNSS jamming or spoofing and safe navigation practices that are independent of GNSS.

Multiple mitigation strategies are available to help overcome interference:

1 filter in the receiver;
2 aid the receiver with an inertial measurement unit (IMU);
3 use of an adaptive antenna array (such as controlled reception pattern antennas);
4 development of advanced mitigation techniques using wideband GNSS signals; and
5 use of E-Loran receivers as a backup (INTERTANKO 2019, 8).

With respect to jamming, various GNSS-type systems deliver different services at different frequencies. This will mitigate against an attack but does not mean that the system will work through it. An IMU and an appropriate alarm management plan can be used to aid the receiver/navigation equipment in detecting an attack (INTERTANKO 2019, 8).

Spoofing countermeasures include the use of array antennas, such as controlled reception pattern antennas (CRPA). Monitoring GNSS receiver KPIs (key performance indicators) – clock jumps, unusual or implausible signal-to-noise density ratios, or differences between code and carrier measurements – and cryptographic techniques can also be effective (INTERTANKO 2019, 8). Other countermeasures include:

1 use of an adaptive antenna array;
2 fly-wheel algorithms to prohibit the system from immediate jumps in location and time in the GNSS receiver (ECDIS or external PNT software);
3 limiting the jumps (location) – GNSS receiver;

4 aiding the receiver with an IMU (even a low-cost IMU would be very effective for this purpose); and
5 use of Loran/E-Loran receivers as a backup/part of the resilient system, where available (INTERTANKO 2019, 9).

Suspected jamming and spoofing attacks should be reported as soon as possible. The Interference Detection and Mitigation Task Force was established to coordinate international efforts regarding the detection and reporting of jamming and spoofing (INTERTANKO 2019, 10). Reports regarding degradations, disruptions, or other incidents or anomalies can also be sent to the NAVCEN. Before reporting an incident to the NAVCEN, the following steps should be taken:

1 Reset the device by cycling power to the unit.
2 Confirm the settings for the GPS unit or GPS application.
3 Refer to the equipment manual.
4 Update the equipment software or firmware and GPS-mapping software.
5 Contact the equipment manufacturer for additional assistance (INTERTANKO 2019, 10).

Reports can also be made to the European GNSS Service Centre. In addition, merchant ships and shipping companies can contact the NATO Shipping Centre.

6.3.3 *US Government Initiatives*

6.3.3.1 Executive Order 13905

In February 2020, then president Donald Trump issued Executive Order 13905, aimed at strengthening US PNT services.[9] Disruption or manipulation of PNT services can adversely affect US national and economic security. "PNT services" is defined as any system, network, or capability that provides a reference to calculate, or augment the calculation of, longitude, latitude, altitude, or transmission of time or frequency data, or any combination thereof (§2(a)). "Critical infrastructure" is defined as systems and assets, whether physical or virtual, so vital to the US that their incapacity or destruction would have a debilitating impact on national security, national economic security, national public health or safety, or any combination of those matters (§2(c)).

The executive order establishes US policy to ensure that the disruption or manipulation of PNT services does not undermine the reliable and efficient functioning of US critical infrastructure. The federal government is tasked with increasing national awareness of the extent to which critical infrastructure depends on, or is enhanced by, PNT services. The federal government is also tasked with ensuring

[9] Executive Order 13905, 85 Fed. Reg. 9359 (February 18, 2020).

that critical infrastructure can withstand the disruption or manipulation of PNT services (§3).

The Secretary of Commerce, in coordination with other relevant federal agencies and private sector users, was tasked with developing PNT profiles and making them available to the relevant agencies and private users. These PNT profiles will be used to identify systems, networks, and assets dependent on PNT services; identify appropriate PNT services; detect the disruption and manipulation of PNT services; and manage the associated risks to the systems, networks, and assets dependent on PNT services. PNT profiles will be reviewed and updated every two years (§4(a)). The PNT profiles created for the Defense, Transportation, and Homeland Security Departments will be used in updates to the Federal Radionavigation Plan (§4(b)). Relevant information from the PNT profiles will also be included in government contracts for products, systems, and services that integrate or utilize PNT services (§§4(d), 4(e)).

The Secretary of Homeland Security, in coordination with other relevant federal agencies, shall develop a plan to test the vulnerabilities of critical infrastructure systems, networks, and assets in the event of disruption and manipulation of PNT services and shall use the results of that test to inform updates to the PNT profiles (§4 (c)). Additionally, the Transportation, Energy, and Homeland Security Departments shall engage with critical infrastructure owners or operators to evaluate the responsible use of PNT services (§4(g)). Finally, the Director of the Office of Science and Technology Policy shall coordinate the development of a national plan for the research, development, and testing of additional, robust, and secure PNT services that are not dependent on GNSS (§4(h)).

6.3.3.2 Federal Radionavigation Plan (2021)

The Federal Radionavigation Plan reflects the federal government's official PNT policy and planning and covers both terrestrial- and space-based, common-use, federally operated PNT systems. It does not apply to systems used exclusively by the Department of Defense or systems used primarily to conduct surveillance and communications functions. Federal PNT systems are operated to enable safe transportation and to enable commerce within the US. PNT services are provided in a "resilient and cost-effective manner, balancing costs and needed safety, security, and efficient operational capabilities" (DoD et al. 2022, x).

The Department of Transportation is responsible "for ensuring safe and efficient transportation" (DoD et al. 2022, x). The Department of Defense is responsible for "maintaining aids to navigation required exclusively for national defense" and "providing for the sustainment and operation of GPS for peaceful civil, commercial, and scientific uses on a continuous, worldwide basis, free of direct user fees" (x). The Department of Homeland Security is responsible, in coordination with other federal agencies, for enhancing the security and resilience of US critical infrastructure and for the detection and mitigation of "sources of GPS interference within the United States" (x).

US GPS Standard Positioning Services (SPS) are available worldwide for continuous use on a nondiscriminatory basis by the international community free of direct user fees (DoD et al. 2022, §§3.2.2.1, 5.1). The US has committed to taking "all necessary measures for the foreseeable future to maintain the integrity, reliability, and availability of the GPS SPS" (§§3.2.2.1, 5.1). Protected Positioning Service (PPS) is available to authorized US and allied military users (§§3.2.2.2, 5.1).

GPS PPS signals are continuously monitored in near-real time, twenty-four hours a day, by satellite operators at the Schriever Air Force Base. SPS signals are not continuously monitored; however, PPS monitoring can detect "most anomalies in service, including user range errors, providing satellite operators the necessary information to take action and protect users from anomalous signals" (DoD et al. 2022, §3.2.5).

GPS users must plan for potential disruptions and take necessary steps to authenticate the reliability of the received GPS data and ranging signal. GPS users must be aware of the impact of GPS interference, should consider using GPS receivers designed to mitigate the effects of the jamming and spoofing of signals, and incorporate alternative PNT sources to ensure continued operations (DoD et al. 2022, §§3.2.10, 5.1.2). The Secretary of Transportation, in coordination with the Secretary of Homeland Security, is "responsible for the development, acquisition, operation, and maintenance of backup PNT capabilities that can support critical transportation, homeland security, and other critical civil and commercial applications" (§5.1.2).

The Secretary of Defense (SECDEF) is responsible for improving navigation warfare (NAVWAR) capabilities to deny hostile use of US "space-based PNT services, without unduly disrupting civil and commercial access to civil PNT services outside an area of military or homeland security operations" (DoD et al. 2022, §3.2.3).[10] SECDEF will also "develop, acquire, operate, realistically test, evaluate, and maintain NAVWAR" and other capabilities required to (1) effectively use "GPS services in the event of an adversary or other jamming, disruption, or manipulation"; (2) "develop effective measures to counter adversary efforts to deny, disrupt, or manipulate PNT services"; and (3) "identify, locate, and mitigate," in coordination with other federal agencies, "any intentional disruption or manipulation that adversely affects use of GPS for military operations" (§3.2.3). The NAVWAR program is designed to "ensure that the U.S. retains a military advantage in the area of conflict by protecting authorized use of GPS; preventing the hostile

[10] NAVWAR is defined as the deliberate defensive and offensive action to assure and prevent PNT information through the coordinated employment of space, cyberspace, and electronic warfare. Desired effects are generated through the coordinated employment of components within information, space, and cyberspace operations, including electronic warfare, space control, space force enhancement, and computer network operations.

use of GPS, its augmentations, or any other PNT service; and preserving peaceful civil GPS use outside an area of military operations" (§3.2.3).

The US has introduced three additional coded signals to support future civil applications. One of these (L1C) is at full operational capability for accuracy, integrity, continuity, and availability. The other two (L2C and L5) are operationally capable only for accuracy and integrity (DoD et al. 2022, §3.2.6.1). Military signals will be supplemented in the future with a next-generation GPS signal (M-code), which is encrypted and spectrally separated from civilian signals and other radio-navigation satellite service signals. This will significantly improve exclusivity of access and enhance NAVWAR operations. When tracking encrypted military signals, military GPS receivers are "much more resistant to interference than commercial GPS equipment" (§3.2.6.2).

The Department of Defense has been modernizing its use of GPS for the past twenty years with M-code, a more jam-resistant, encrypted, military-specific signal, which is essential to maintain GPS "effectiveness in the face of adversary threats" (DoD et al. 2022, §5.1.1; GAO 2024, 1). M-code is designed to meet military PNT information needs and will help military users overcome attempts by adversaries to jam GPS signals "by using a more powerful signal with a broader radio frequency range" (GAO 2024, 3). M-code will also protect against spoofing "by providing enhanced encryption for the signal" (4).

M-code modernization requires a "ground control system that can enable the launch and control of existing and new, more powerful satellites" (GAO 2024, 4). The first satellite able to broadcast the M-code signal was launched by the US Air Force in 2005. As of May 2024, twenty-four of thirty-one "satellites in the GPS constellation were M-code-capable" (5). The Department of Defense will also need to "upgrade existing weapon systems and platforms with M-code capable" GPS receivers (6). In short, GPS enhancement efforts continue to include modernizing ground control systems, upgrading satellites, and integrating user equipment with platforms to receive the M-code signal, but significant challenges remain for each segment (6).

6.3.3.3 National Research and Development Plan for PNT Resilience

Numerous systems used in multiple sectors of US critical infrastructure rely solely on GNSS/GPS for PNT services. Many of these systems are not designed or tested to respond effectively to the disruption and manipulation of PNT services and are therefore at an elevated risk of interference. Such interference "could compromise national security, increase the risk of loss of life, severely impact the economy, and disrupt the daily activities of the American people" (NSTC 2021, 3). Interference or loss of PNT services can also potentially impede mitigation and recovery efforts.

To be resilient, a PNT enterprise must (1) use multiple, diverse sources of PNT and data paths; (2) use an architecture that minimizes "attack opportunities and overlapping attack vectors that could reduce protections or result in single points of failure"; (3) apply defense-in-depth ("multiple layers of protections, mitigations, and responses"); and (4) integrate "modern cybersecurity principles into the greater PNT enterprise" (NSTC 2021, 3). The PNT enterprise must also be capable of (1) delivering and using PNT in "physically or electronically impeded environments"; (2) consistently providing "higher accuracy with greater assurance"; (3) providing "notification of degraded or misleading information"; (4) providing PNT services at high altitudes and in space; and (5) developing "adequate modeling and simulation capabilities, including capabilities to predict how PNT services are affected in urban environments" (NSTC 2021, 3).

The US R&D plan supports "three overarching goals for greater PNT service resilience and prioritizes fourteen R&D objectives for further R&D across these overarching goals" (NSTC 2021, 5). Agencies should:

1 characterize and model current and future PNT system and service capabilities, performance characteristics, vulnerabilities, and the projected future needs of PNT users (7–8);
2 work to improve and expand PNT services and capabilities across the enterprise by developing PNT equipment with better performance specifications (such as accuracy, availability, continuity, coverage, and integrity) to enable greater resilience, as well as innovations (such as size, weight, power consumption, and cost) to motivate its adoption (9–11); and
3 integrate and deploy resilient PNT architectures through the development of prototype systems and demonstrations (12–14).

6.3.3.4 Memorandum on Space Policy Directive 7

Space Policy Directive 7 provides implementation actions and guidance for US space-based PNT programs and activities for US national and homeland security, civil, commercial, and scientific purposes, including:

a the sustainment and modernization of the GPS and federally developed, owned, and operated systems used to augment or otherwise improve GPS;
b the implementation and operation of capabilities to protect US and allied access to and use of GPS for national, homeland, and economic security, and to deny adversaries from the use of US space-based PNT services; and
c US participation in international cooperative initiatives regarding foreign space-based PNT services and the foreign use of GPS and its augmentations (White House 2021).

The US will "improve and maintain GPS and its augmentations to meet growing national, homeland, and economic security requirements as well as other civil requirements, and to enable diverse commercial and scientific applications" (White House 2021, §3). It will also "improve capabilities to deny adversary access to space-based PNT services, particularly including services that are openly available and can be readily used by adversaries or terrorists, to threaten the security of the United States." In addition, the US will encourage the responsible use of PNT service "acquisition, integration, and deployment across critical infrastructure" (§3). Additionally, the US is developing "alternative approaches to PNT services and security that can incorporate new technologies and services . . ., such as quantum sensing, relative navigation and private or publicly owned and operated alternative PNT services" (§3).

To maintain US leadership in service provision and the responsible use of GPS and foreign systems, the US shall (inter alia):

a provide continuous worldwide access to US space-based GPS services and government-provided augmentations, free of direct user fees, and provide open, free access to information necessary to develop and build equipment to use these services;
b improve NAVWAR capabilities to deny the hostile use of US space-based PNT services, without unduly disrupting civil and commercial access to civil PNT services outside an area of military or homeland security operations;
c improve the performance of US space-based PNT services, including developing more robust signals that are more resistant to disruptions and manipulations consistent with US and allied national security, homeland security, and civil purposes;
d improve the cybersecurity of GPS, its augmentations, and US-owned GPS-enabled devices, and foster private sector adoption of cyber-secure GPS-enabled systems through system upgrades and the incorporation of cybersecurity principles for space systems, interface specifications, and other guidance that prescribes cybersecurity for user equipment;
e protect the spectrum environment that is currently used by GPS and its augmentations, and work with US industry to investigate additional areas of the radio spectrum that could increase GPS and PNT resilience;
f invest in domestic capabilities and support international activities to detect, mitigate, and increase resilience to the harmful disruption or manipulation of GPS, and identify and implement alternative sources of PNT for critical infrastructure, key resources, and mission-essential functions;
g maintain GPS and its augmentations for use by US critical infrastructure to enhance safety of life functions and operational efficiency;
h engage with international GNSS providers to ensure compatibility, encourage interoperability with likeminded nations, promote transparency in civil service provision, and enable market access for US industry;

i encourage foreign development of PNT services and systems based on GPS and the inclusion of GPS as an essential element in systems that integrate multiple PNT services;
j seek to ensure that all foreign systems are compatible with GPS and its augmentations, that they do not interfere with GPS military and civil signals, and that mutual security concerns are addressed to prevent the hostile use of US space-based PNT services;
k promote the responsible use of US space-based PNT services and capabilities; and
l promote US technological leadership in the provision of space-based PNT services and in the development of secure and resilient end-user equipment (White House 2021, § 4).

The Secretary of Defense is responsible for (inter alia) (1) developing, acquiring, operating, testing, evaluating, and maintaining NAVWAR capabilities and other capabilities to allow for the effective use of GPS services "in the event of an adversary or other jamming, disruption, or manipulation"; (2) developing "effective measures to counter adversary efforts to deny, disrupt, or manipulate PNT services"; and (3) identifying, locating, and mitigating (in coordination with other agencies) any "intentional disruption or manipulation that adversely affects use of GPS for military operations" (White House 2021, §7).

The Secretary of Commerce shall (inter alia), in cooperation with other agencies, "develop guidelines to improve the cybersecurity of PNT devices, including their capability to detect and reject manipulated or counterfeit signals, and promote the responsible use of space-based PNT services and capabilities for applications that support national security, economic growth, transportation safety, and homeland security" (White House 2021, §7). The Secretary of Transportation shall (inter alia), in coordination with the Secretaries of Defense and Homeland Security and other agencies, implement federal "capabilities to monitor, identify, locate, and attribute space-based PNT service disruption and manipulations within the US that adversely affect use of space-based PNT for transportation safety, homeland security, civil, commercial, and scientific purposes" (§7).

The Secretary of Homeland Security – in coordination with the Secretaries of Defense and Transportation, and in cooperation with the Secretary of Commerce – is responsible for (inter alia) (1) ensuring that "mechanisms are in place to monitor, identify, locate, and attribute space-based PNT service disruptions and manipulations within the US that can cause significant disruption to United States critical infrastructure and scientific purposes"; and (2) developing procedures to notify all stakeholders when space-based services have "anticipated disruptions or are deemed to be no longer reliable" (White House 2021, §7). The Secretary of Homeland Security shall also, in coordination with the Secretaries of Defense, Commerce, and Transportation, "develop and maintain capabilities, procedures, and techniques for, and routinely exercise, civil contingency responses to ensure continuity of operations in the event that access to GPS services are disrupted or manipulated" (§7). Additionally, the Secretary of Homeland Security shall, in coordination with the Secretaries of Defense and Transportation, and in cooperation with other agencies, "coordinate the use of existing and planned capabilities to identify, locate, and attribute any disruption or manipulation of GPS and its augmentations within the United States that significantly affects homeland security or critical infrastructure" (§7). Finally, the Secretary of Homeland Security is also responsible for notifying the interagency of any significant domestic or international disruption to or manipulation of US space-based PNT services "to enable appropriate investigation, notification, or enforcement action" (§7).

Any agency that detects or receives a report of harmful disruption or manipulation of US space-based PNT services shall provide a timely report to the Secretaries of Homeland Security, Defense, and Transportation, and to the Director of National Intelligence (White House 2021, §8). When notified, the Secretary of Commerce and the Chairman of the Federal Communications Commission (in cooperation with other federal agencies) shall take appropriate action to mitigate harmful disruption or manipulation of US space-based PNT services within the US. The Secretary of State is responsible for notifying foreign governments and international organizations when there is a harmful disruption or manipulation of US space-based PNT services caused by foreign government or commercial activities (§8).

6.3.3.5 National Security Memorandum NSM-22

The US is in an era of strategic competition with nations that target US critical infrastructure and enable malicious actions by non-State actors. If there is a crisis or conflict, US adversaries will increase their efforts to compromise critical infrastructure to undermine the will of the American public and threaten the projection of US military power. NSM-22 recognizes that the incapacity or destruction of US critical infrastructure will have a debilitating impact on national security, national economic security, and national public health or safety (White House 2024). The US will therefore increase its efforts to strengthen and maintain a secure, functioning, and resilient critical infrastructure.

Strengthening the security and resilience of America's critical infrastructure will be consistent with the following principles:

1. **Shared responsibility.** Safeguarding critical infrastructure is a shared responsibility among all stakeholders and requires public–private collaboration.
2. **Risk-based approach.** National efforts must be prioritized based on the relationship between specific infrastructure and national security, national economic security, national public health or safety, and the government's ability to perform essential functions and services. Risk assessments must consider all threats and hazards, likelihoods, vulnerabilities,

and consequences, including shocks and stressors – as well as the scope and scale of dependencies within and across critical infrastructure sectors, the immediate and long-term consequences, and the cascading effects.

3 **Minimum requirements.** All government entities are responsible for prioritizing the establishment and implementation of minimum requirements for risk management.
4 **Accountability.** Robust accountability and enforcement mechanisms from all government and private sector entities, as well as independent third parties, are essential for effective risk management for critical infrastructure.
5 **Information exchange.** The sharing of timely, actionable information among all stakeholders is essential for effective risk management, which will be facilitated by the federal government.
6 **Expertise and technical resources.** The federal government will leverage expertise and technical resources from all relevant federal departments and agencies to mature the capacity and capability of each federally led effort to manage sector-specific risk to secure US critical infrastructure.
7 **International engagement.** The federal government will work closely with international partners to strengthen the security and resilience of the international critical infrastructure on which the US depends.
8 **Policy alignment.** Efforts to safeguard critical infrastructure will be aligned with complementary federal policies and frameworks.

Objectives under the national effort to strengthen the security and resilience of US critical infrastructure include:

1 refine and clarify the roles and responsibilities of the federal government for critical infrastructure security, resilience, and risk management;
2 identify and prioritize critical infrastructure security and resilience based on risk and implement a coordinated national approach to assess and manage sector-specific and cross-sector risk;
3 establish minimum requirements and accountability mechanisms for the security and resilience of critical infrastructure, including through aligned and effective regulatory frameworks;
4 leverage federal government agreements, including grants, loans, and procurement processes, to require or encourage owners and operators to meet or exceed minimum security and resilience requirements;
5 enhance and improve the quality of intelligence collection and analysis pertaining to threats to critical infrastructure;
6 improve the real-time sharing of timely, actionable intelligence and information at the lowest possible classification level among federal,

State, local, Tribal, territorial, private sector, and international partners to facilitate risk mitigation to critical infrastructure;

7 promote timely and cost-effective investments in technologies and solutions that mitigate risk from evolving threats and hazards to critical infrastructure; and

8 strengthen the security and resilience of critical infrastructure by engaging international partners and allies to build situational awareness and capacity, facilitate operational collaboration, promote effective infrastructure risk management globally, and develop and promote international security and resilience recommendations.

The federal government will use a risk-based approach to reduce risk to critical infrastructure. Critical infrastructure risks will be assessed in terms of threats or hazards, vulnerability, and consequence. Risk management efforts will be prioritized by identifying the criticality of assets and systems within and across sectors. Nonfederal critical infrastructure owners and operators are primarily responsible for managing most risks to their operations and assets. The federal government shall support and guide the entities that own, operate, or otherwise control critical infrastructure assets and systems by providing these entities with the information, intelligence analysis, and other support to manage and mitigate asset-level risks.

The federal government, in coordination with owners and operators, will identify, assess, prioritize, mitigate, and monitor risks that may have a potentially debilitating impact on national security, national economic security, or public health or safety. These nationally significant risks may arise within and impact sectors or cut across multiple sectors. The federal government is responsible for identifying and mitigating national-level risk through a whole-of-government effort, led by the Department of Homeland Security in coordination with Sector Risk Management Agencies (SRMAs) and supported by other federal departments and agencies.

SRMAs are responsible for the day-to-day prioritization and coordination of efforts to mitigate risks within each sector, as part of the broader whole-of-government effort. The National Coordinator shall manage systemic and cross-sector risk by working with SRMAs, federal departments and agencies, and industry to identify, analyze, prioritize, and manage the most significant risks involving multiple sectors based on data provided by the SRMAs.

Effective risk management requires the adoption of minimum security and resilience requirements within and across critical infrastructure sectors. The Department of Homeland Security, including the National Coordinator, SRMAs, and regulators, shall coordinate to produce cross-sector and sector-specific guidance, performance goals and metrics, and requirements to adequately mitigate risk. SRMAs, in coordination with regulators, shall develop sector-specific minimum security and resilience requirements for each respective sector and a plan to use existing authorities or other tools to implement those requirements effectively. The National Coordinator shall review proposed sector-specific security and resilience guidance, performance goals, and requirements in coordination with SRMAs, and in consultation with regulators, to facilitate the harmonization of these directives and recommendations at the national and cross-sector level.

The federal government will collaborate with private-sector partners; State, local, Tribal, and territorial governments; community organizations; and international partners that can take actions that provide resilience and security benefits to owners and operators in the US and other countries.

Every two years, the Secretary of Homeland Security shall develop and submit to the president a National Infrastructure Risk Management Plan, which shall be informed by (1) individual sector-specific risk assessments and risk management plans; and (2) a cross-sector risk assessment. Each SRMA shall develop sector-specific risk assessments and sector-specific risk management plans based on strategic directions provided by the Secretary of Homeland Security. Sector-specific risk assessments will identify the most significant critical infrastructure risks to their sector, including key cross-sector risks and interdependencies.

Sector-specific risk management plans will be developed or refreshed every two years to leverage individual SRMA tools and authorities, as well as other federal tools and authorities, to safeguard critical infrastructure in each sector from all threats and hazards, considering national-level priorities and guidance from the Secretary of Homeland Security. The National Coordinator shall develop a cross-sector risk assessment in coordination with SRMAs identifying the most significant cross-sector risks to US critical infrastructure.

Based on the sector-specific risk assessments and risk management plans and the cross-sector risk assessment, the Secretary of Homeland Security shall develop and submit to the president, through the assistant to the president and the Homeland Security Advisor, the National Infrastructure Risk Management Plan to guide the federal effort to mitigate cross-sector and other national risks to critical infrastructure. The plan shall prioritize specific cross-sector risks, with a focus on new and emerging threats to critical infrastructure, and shall identify innovative approaches to limit the risks from these new and emerging threats, particularly risk mitigation strategies for increasingly interdependent and interconnected assets and systems.

The National Coordinator shall regularly identify organizations (Significantly Important Entities – SIEs) that own, operate, or otherwise control critical infrastructure that is prioritized based on the potential for its disruption or malfunction to cause nationally significant and cascading negative impacts to national security, national economic security, or national public health or safety. The SIE list shall inform the prioritization of federal activities, including the provision of risk mitigation information and other operational resources to nonfederal entities.

Critical infrastructure risk management requires those who own or operate infrastructure to be informed of a wide range of threats that are manmade or result from natural hazards, including by the actionable and timely intelligence and information available on those threats or hazards. To establish a comprehensive, integrated threat picture for US critical infrastructure, the Director of National Intelligence shall lead Intelligence Community efforts, in consultation with the Department of Homeland Security, including the National Coordinator, SRMAs, and relevant departments and agencies, to collect, integrate, analyze, and share information from intelligence reporting, data, and assessments to understand and identify threats to critical infrastructure and disseminate intelligence reports in an accessible, usable, and shareable format for nonfederal stakeholders.

The Director of National Intelligence shall also produce, receive, integrate, and share information, to include information from intelligence assessments and warnings, that enables federal department or agency leadership to consider the widest possible options for mitigating a risk or addressing a threat, including the coordinated balancing of national interests, stakeholder equities, and authorities. The Director of National Intelligence shall also establish, in coordination with the Department of Homeland Security and the Department of Justice, a process to ensure that Intelligence Community elements provide timely notification to appropriate federal elements, including the Federal Bureau of Investigation, the Cybersecurity and Infrastructure Security Agency, and relevant SRMAs, when Intelligence Community elements are aware of specific and credible threats to US critical infrastructure.

6.3.3.6 Maritime Administration Guidance

To mitigate GNSS interference, MARAD advises ships operating in the Persian Gulf and the Strait of Hormuz to review security measures, ensure that AIS is always transmitting, and monitor VHF Channel 16. US-flagged vessels are also encouraged to register with the UKMTO, the International Maritime Security Construct (IMSC), and US Fifth Fleet Naval Cooperation and Guidance for Shipping (NCAGS) Watch (if activated) when entering the Indian Ocean Voluntary Reporting Area. Additionally, vessels are advised to provide their transit plans for the Strait of Hormuz and the Persian Gulf to the UKMTO, the IMSC, and NCAGS Watch to include the time of entering or exiting the Strait of Hormuz Traffic Separation Scheme, an outline of the navigation plan for operating in the strait and the gulf, and speed restrictions or other constraints.

In the event of an incident or suspicious activity (such as being hailed from a source falsely claiming to be a US or coalition naval vessel), vessels should call the UKMTO, the IMSC, or the US Fifth Fleet Battle Watch and activate the Ship Security Alert System immediately. In addition, all suspicious activities, breaches of security, and transportation security incident events must be reported to the USCG National Response Center (MARAD 2023a, 2023b). Maritime GPS disruptions or anomalies should be reported immediately to the USCG NAVCEN (MARAD 2023a, 2023b).

Prior to getting underway, ships should review the NAVCEN and NATO Shipping Center websites, which contain information regarding safe navigation practices for vessels experiencing GPS interference. The websites also provide useful guidance on reporting disruptions, which will generate further discussion within the maritime industry about disruption mitigation practices and procedures. Incidents of disruption should be reported in real time, noting the location (latitude and longitude), date, time, and duration of the outage/disruption and providing photographs or screenshots of equipment failures experienced to facilitate analysis (MARAD 2023a).

6.3.4 *Alternative Mitigation Systems and Technologies*

Satellite Time and Location (STL) is an alternative navigation system that operates on the Iridium satellites and offers "an encrypted signal, 1000 times stronger than GNSS that resists jamming and spoofing" (McCrystal 2018). STL is not as accurate as GNSS, but "it provides 30–50 meter accuracy which can serve as a check to the GNSS indicated position or time" (McCrystal 2018). STL therefore provides ships with an "additional signal authenticating tool" that can be used to validate communication and network access (McCrystal 2018). Because it uses an encrypted signal, "the vessel has an irrefutable PNT source" that can be trusted to reflect that the "vessel was in a certain location at a certain time and that communications to and from the vessel are genuine" (McCrystal 2018). STL can also be "combined with an Inertial Navigation System (INS)," which provides "valuable range and Doppler updates to the inertial measurements, reducing drift and maintaining a proper navigation solution, even during extended periods of GNSS denial" (McCrystal 2018).

Navigation Protection Devices (NPDs) include "a monitoring component, such as Orolia's NPD Broad Shield, which monitors GNSS receptions, analyses the signals, and alerts the pilot on the bridge" (McCrystal 2018). The device "is independent of the vessel's navigation system and interfaces with the ECDIS display ... to give real time indication of alerts and positional discrepancies" (McCrystal 2018). Broad Shield is also capable of sending "alarms or warnings in other forms for vessels not equipped with an ECDIS" (McCrystal 2018).

If available, eLoran can provide an alternative signal for NPDs. GNSS and eLoran are at opposite ends of the spectrum – "low frequency instead of microwave; high-power pulse instead of low power spread spectrum; and terrestrial instead of space-based" (McCrystal 2018). Jammers used to block GNSS are different from those capable of blocking eLoran, thereby adding resiliency to navigation.

An NPD will activate if there are additional signals present in the GNSS band or there is an anomalous behavior of the signal; if the NPD determines that the "navigation solution does not match the ship's GNSS guidance solution due to equipment malfunction or malicious signals"; or if the NPD detects "that the navigation solution differs from the GNSS constellations and its alternatives sources, such as STL or eLoran" (McCrystal 2018).

Veripos GAJT-710MS, an anti-jamming technology developed by Hexagon Autonomy & Positioning, mitigates GPS interference by "creating nulls in the antenna gain pattern in the direction of the jammers" (Wingrove 2020). The hardened enclosure contains an antenna array and null-forming electronics and can be installed on a wide variety of vessels. Inertial instruments provide an additional alternative to GPS. Sonardyne International installed a Sprint-Nav hybrid inertial navigation instrument on a British Sea-Kit X-class unmanned surface vessel and tested it against local real-time kinematic GPS positioning.

A US company – Zephr – that specializes in developing tools to protect against GPS signal interference is conducting field tests in Ukraine using cell phones loaded with special software to locate Russian jamming equipment (Tucker 2024). The tests show that "by comparing the GPS reception of various phones" working together in a network, they could detect when one or more of the phones was being attacked (Tucker 2024). Zephr is also conducting field experiments to not only "detect jammers but triangulate their positions so the jammer can be avoided or eliminated" (Tucker 2024). The location of a jammer can be determined using three inputs:

1 localization by range inferred from power;
2 localization by area of effect; and
3 triangulation of jammers based on angle of arrival (Tucker 2024).

Laser can also be used to augment "GNSS services with measurements of range and bearing to a set of geographically referenced reflectors." The CyScan GeoLock sensor, produced by Wärtsilä's Guidance Marine, "provides position references without risk of spoofing, interference or loss of signal" by using lasers rather than satellites (Tucker 2024). The system is used to maneuver vessels in port, terminals, or offshore drilling rigs. As the ship approaches the port, the CyScan GeoLock sensor automatically starts tracking the vessel. The system then "compares the geometric pattern produced by its range and bearing measurements of detected reflectors with the corresponding geometric pattern of the surveyed reflectors in the configuration file" (Tucker 2024). Once a match is found, "the reflectors are accepted into the sensor's tracking solution" and the sensor produces a position reference (Tucker 2024).

The French are also experimenting with laser technology to mitigate against GPS jamming. In September 2024, a project funded by the French Defence Innovation Agency successfully used a laser to establish a stable link between a low-orbit nano satellite and an optical ground station for several minutes (Ruitenberg 2024). Lasers have the capability to transfer very large files (such as Earth images) quickly. Because of their point-to-point nature, lasers are "more secure than radio frequencies" and less susceptible to jamming (Ruitenberg 2024). Lasers have a low probability of detection and interception, so putting them on ships reduces the radio footprint of the ship that is normally associated with an RF antenna. The successful test will allow France to integrate the laser technology on its future military satellites and use space-based laser communications on "mobile, land-based, naval and airborne platforms" (Ruitenberg 2024). A Defense Ministry spokesperson explained:

> Advantages of the optical link over the usual radio link are its speed, discretion and independence from regulations that coordinate the use of radio waves. Even if ... [the] optical link can sometimes be perturbed by atmospheric turbulence, the ... satellite is able to circumvent them ... to achieve optimum transmission quality. (MacKenzie 2024)

China is also developing laser communication technology. In mid-September 2024, China successfully deployed a laser communication ground system with a 500-mm-caliber antenna, which will significantly enhance China's "capacity for massive satellite data transmission" (Xinhua 2024). Once the technology becomes fully operational, China will no longer have to rely "solely on microwave ground stations for satellite data reception" (Xinhua 2024). Satellite-to-ground laser communications have between ten and a thousand times wider bandwidth than microwave communications. The system is also smaller and lighter, and it consumes less power.

The Royal Navy and the US Department of Defense are conducting experiments to develop "quantum navigation." This new technology would allow for GPS-free navigation. Once perfected, quantum technologies will not be susceptible to spoofing or jamming, thus providing a 100 percent "resilient satellite-free capability" (MI News Network 2024; see also Advanced Navigation 2024; Tucker 2021; Vallance 2024).

An American company – SandboxAQ – has developed an AI-enabled navigation system (AQNav) that uses "quantum sensors to gather data from the Earth's crustal magnetic field" and AI algorithms that eliminate potential interference from jamming and spoofing.[11] This technology enables the system to "provide real-time navigation in areas where GPS signals are denied or unavailable" (Saballa 2024). AQNav can be installed on civilian or military air, land, and sea platforms and could be "used to improve autonomous vehicle control or aid in underground/underwater operations where GPS signals are unavailable" (Saballa 2024).

6.4 CONCLUSION

There is now a growing awareness of the vulnerability of GNSS, but it is not yet clear what to do about it. Although there is no single solution that can address all the vulnerabilities associated with GNSS, by combining several alternative methods, GNSS can be augmented and thereby "provide the resilience necessary for all critical operations" to include PNT for maritime navigation (McCrystal 2018).

[11] The Earth's crustal magnetic field is a "highly reliable data source for navigation" because it provides a persistent, passive external signal (Saballa 2024).

Resilient PNT receivers can identify and operate through jamming and spoofing attacks, adjust to an additional PNT source that is not experiencing interference, provide longer PNT solutions without receiving updates from trusted PNT services, and thus avoid unacceptable degradation in performance (NSTC 2021, 4).

A resilient PNT enterprise will use various sources of PNT and data paths. The PNT architecture must be able to minimize attack opportunities and attack vectors that degrade services or result in a single point of failure. Defense-in-depth (numerous layers of protection, mitigation, and response) is essential, as well as the integration of "modern cybersecurity principles into the greater PNT enterprise" (NSTC 2021, 3). Resilient PNT enterprises must be able to deliver and use PNT in physically or electronically degraded environments. They must also consistently provide "higher accuracy with greater assurance" and provide "notification of degraded or misleading information" (3).

As intentional interference by rogue States and non-State actors continues to increase, cyber security designed to mitigate the disruption of PNT services used by navigation and communication systems is more important than ever to ensure safety at sea. Conducting regular risk assessments can identify system vulnerabilities and prioritize mitigation strategies. Having a clear incident response plan in place can also help respond to cyberattacks and "minimize damage and expedite recovery" (Chua 2024). The use of intrusion detection and prevention systems "allows for real-time monitoring of network activity and enables the detection of suspicious activity." It will also be important to leverage and deploy new and emerging technologies – such as M-code, quantum navigation, anti-jamming technology, and lasers – as they become available to mitigate or eliminate the threat of cyberattacks more effectively.

REFERENCES

Advanced Navigation. 2024. "The Future of Inertial Navigation Is Classical-Quantum Sensor Fusion." June 7. www.advancednavigation.com/tech-articles/the-future-of-inertial-navigation-is-classical-quantum-sensor-fusion.

AFP (Agence France Presse). 2020. "Ecuador Says Chinese Trawlers Turned Off Tracking System Near Galapagos." *Barron's*, August 18. www.barrons.com/news/ecuador-says-chinese-trawlers-turned-off-tracking-system-near-galapagos-01597802704.

Alberts, Elizabeth Claire. 2020. "New Evidence Suggests China's 'Dark' Vessels Poached in Galápagos Waters." *Mongabay*, October 9. www.news.mongabay.com/2020/10/new-evidence-suggests-chinas-dark-vessels-poached-in-galapagos-waters.

Bergman, Bjorn. 2019. "Systematic GPS Manipulation Occurring at Chinese Oil Terminals and Government Installations." *SkyTruth*, December 12. https://skytruth.org/2019/12/systematic-gps-manipulation-occuring-at-chinese-oil-terminals-and-government-installations/.

Browne, Ryan, and Barbara Starr. 2019. "US Government Warns of Iranian Threats to Commercial Shipping, Including GPS Interference." *CNN*, August 7. https://edition.cnn.com/2019/08/07/politics/us-warns-of-iranian-threats-to-shipping/index.html.

C4ADS. 2019. "Above Us Only Stars: Exposing GPS Spoofing in Russia and Syria." https://c4ads.org/reports/above-us-only-stars/

Chua, Joey. 2024. "Navigating through the Storm: Cybersecurity and Its Stakeholders." *Maritime Executive*, April 23. https://maritime-executive.com/editorials/navigating-through-the-storm-cybersecurity-and-its-stakeholders.

Coats, Daniel R. 2017. "Statement for the Record: Worldwide Threat Assessment of the US Intelligence Community, Senate Select Committee on Intelligence." May 11. www.intelligence.gov/assets/documents/archive/SASC%202017%20ATA%20SFR%20-%20FINAL.PDF

DoD, DoT and DHS (US Department of Defense, Department of Transportation, and Department of Homeland Security). 2022. "2021 Federal Radionavigation Plan." www.navcen.uscg.gov/sites/default/files/pdf/2021_Federal_Rdionavigation_Plan.pdf.

GAO (US Government Accountability Office). 2024. *GPS Modernization: Delays Continue in Delivering More Secure Capability for the Warfighter*. Report to Congressional Committees, GAO-24-106841.

Goward, Dana. 2017. "Mass GPS Spoofing Attack in Black Sea?" *Maritime Executive*, July 11. https://maritime-executive.com/editorials/mass-gps-spoofing-attack-in-black-sea.

2019. "Chinese GPS Spoofing Circles Could Hide Iran Oil Shipments." *GPS World*, December 17. www.gpsworld.com/chinese-gps-spoofing-circles-could-hide-iran-oil-shipments/.

2020. "GPS Circle Spoofing Discovered in Iran." *GPS World*, April 21. www.gpsworld.com/gps-circle-spoofing-discovered-in-iran/.

IMO (International Maritime Organization). 1991. "General Requirements for Shipborne Radio Equipment Forming Part of the Global Maritime Distress and Safety System (GMDSS) and for Electronic Navigational Aids." A 17/Res.694 (November 25, 1991).

2011. "Worldwide Radionavigation System." A 27/Res.1046 (December 20, 2011).

2015. "Performance Standards for Multi-System Shipborne Radionavigation Receivers." MSC 95/22/Add.2, Annex 17 (June 8, 2015).

2017a. "Guidelines for Shipborne Position, Navigation, and Timing (PNT) Data Processing." MSC.1/Circ.1575 (June 16, 2017).

2017b. "Guidelines on Maritime Cyber Risk Management." MSC-FAL.1/Circ.3 (July 5, 2017).

2017c. "Maritime Cyber Risk Management in Safety Management Systems." MSC 98/23/Add.1, Annex 10 (June 16, 2017).

2022. "Guidelines on Maritime Cyber Risk Management." MSC-FAL.1/Circ.3/Rev.2 (June 7, 2022).

INTERTANKO. 2019. "Jamming and Spoofing of Global Navigation Satellite Systems (GNSS)." www.maritimeglobalsecurity.org/media/1043/2019-jamming-spoofing-of-gnss.pdf.

ITU (International Telecommunication Union). 2020. "Radio Regulations." www.itu.int/hub/2022/08/warning-harmful-interference-rnss/.

ITU News. 2022. "ITU Issues Warning on Interference with Radio Navigation Satellite Service." August 23. www.itu.int/hub/2022/08/warning-harmful-interference-rnss/.

Joffre, Tzvi. 2019. "U.S. Warns of GPS Interference, Communications Spoofing in Persian Gulf." *Jerusalem Post*, August 8. www.jpost.com/Middle-East/US-warns-of-GPS-interference-communications-spoofing-in-Persian-Gulf-597998.

Lo, Chris. 2019. "GPS Spoofing: What's the Risk for Ship Navigation?" *Ship Technology*, April 15. www.ship-technology.com/features/ship-navigation-risks/?cf-view.

MacKenzie, Cristina. 2024. "France Claims World's First Space-to-Earth Laser Comms." *Breaking Defense*, September 23. https://breakingdefense.com/2024/09/france-claims-worlds-first-space-to-earth-laser-comms/.

MARAD (US Maritime Administration). 2019. "MSCI Advisory 2019-012 – Persian Gulf, Strait of Hormuz, Gulf of Oman, Arabian Sea, Red Sea – Threats to Commercial Vessels by Iran and Its Proxies." www.maritime.dot.gov/msci/2019-012-persian-gulf-strait-hormuz-gulf-oman-arabian-sea-red-sea-threats-commercial-vessels.

2023a. "MSCI Advisory 2023-005 – Various – GPS Interference & AIS Spoofing." www.maritime.dot.gov/msci/2023-005-various-gps-interference-ais-spoofing.

2023b. "MSCI Advisory 2023-011 – Persian Gulf, Strait of Hormuz, Gulf of Oman, Arabian Sea, Gulf of Aden, Bab al Mandeb Strait, Red Sea, and Somali Basinx – Threats to Commercial Vessels." www.maritime.dot.gov/msci/2023-011-persian-gulf-strait-hormuz-gulf-oman-arabian-sea-gulf-aden-bab-al-mandeb-strait-red.

McCrystal, Sean. 2018. "Detecting and Defeating GPS Jamming." *Maritime Executive*, February 16. https://maritime-executive.com/blog/detecting-and-defeating-gps-jamming.

MI News Network. 2024. "Royal Navy Works on GPS-Free Technology for Advanced Navigation at Sea." *Marine Insight*, February 21. www.marineinsight.com/shipping-news/royal-navy-works-on-gps-free-technology-for-advanced-navigation-at-sea/.

NSTC (National Science and Technology Council). 2021. "National Research and Development Plan for Positioning, Navigation, and Timing Resilience." https://bidenwhitehouse.archives.gov/wp-content/uploads/2021/08/Position_Navigation_Timing_RD_Plan-August-2021-1.pdf.

Pedrozo, Raul (Pete). 2022. "China's IUU Fishing Fleet: Pariah of the World's Oceans." *International Law Studies* 99: 319–353.

Quinn, Áine. 2024. "Ukraine Warns Ships of Scrambled GPS Navigation in Black Sea." *gCaptain*, June 20. https://gcaptain.com/ukraine-warns-ships-of-scrambled-gps-navigation-in-black-sea/.

Ramos Miranda, Natalia A. 2020. "Chile Keeps Eye on Chinese Fishing Fleet along South American Coast." *Reuters*, October 8. www.reuters.com/article/uschile-fishing-china-idUSKBN26T3IL.

Ruitenberg, Rudy. 2024. "France Tests Space Lasers for Secure Satellite Downlink in World First." *Defense News*, September 13. www.defensenews.com/global/europe/2024/09/13/france-tests-space-lasers-for-secure-satellite-downlink-in-world-first.

Rust, Susanne. 2020. "Tensions Rise in Ecuador and Peru as Chinese Fishing Fleet Moves South from Galapagos." *Los Angeles Times*, September 23. www.latimes.com/environment/story/2020-09-23/tensions-rise-in-ecuador-and-peru-as-chinese-fishing-fleetmoves-south-from-galapagos.

Saballa, Joe. 2024. "US Firm Develops AI-Enabled, Anti-GPS Jamming Navigation System." *Defense Post*, June 27. https://thedefensepost.com/2024/06/27/us-ai-navigation-system/.

Satherley, Dan. 2020. "Chinese Fishing Flotilla in Galapagos Accused of Pretending to Be in New Zealand." *Stuff*, August 6. www.stuff.co.nz/nz-news/350543267/chinese-fishing-flotilla-in-galapagos-accused-of-pretending-to-be-in-new-zealand.

Schuler, Mike. 2024. "Vessel Reports 'Electronic Interference' Incident in Persian Gulf." *gCaptain*, April 3. https://gcaptain.com/vessel-reports-electronic-interference-incident-in-persian-gulf/.

Sheppard, David, Demetri Sevastopulo, and Lucy Hornby. 2019. "US Identifies Chinese Tankers Carrying Iranian Oil." *Financial Times*, August 4. www.ft.com/content/62220484-b37c-11e9-8cb2-799a3a8cf37b.

Singhi, Anjali, Edward Wong, and Denise Lu. 2019. "Defying U.S. Sanctions, China and Others Take Oil from 12 Iranian Tankers." *New York Times*, August 3. www.nytimes.com/interactive/2019/08/03/world/middleeast/us-iran-sanctions-ships.html.

Sutton, H. I. 2021. "Positions of Two NATO Ships Were Falsified Near Russian Black Sea Naval Base." *USNI News*, June 21. https://news.usni.org/2021/06/21/positions-of-two-nato-ships-were-falsified-near-russian-black-sea-naval-base.

Telling, Oliver. 2024. "Cyber Attacks on Shipping Rise amid Geopolitical Tension." *Financial Times*, July 28. www.ft.com/content/c05c9b21-77bd-4ddf-82e1-02356acf0899.

Tucker, Patrick. 2021. "Quantum Sensor Breakthrough Paves Way for GPS-Free Navigation." *Defense One*, November 2. www.defenseone.com/technology/2021/11/quantum-sensor-breakthrough-paves-way-gps-free-navigation/186578/.

2024. "In Ukraine, a US Firm Tests a Promising Tool against GPS Jammers: Cell Phones." *Defense One*, September 30. www.defenseone.com/technology/2024/09/group-ukraine-testing-newest-weapon-against-gps-jammers-cell-phones/399952/.

Vallance, Chris. 2024. "Unjammable Navigation Tech Gets First Airborne Test." *BBC*, May 13. www.bbc.com/news/articles/cz744gp1dpo.

White House. 2021. "Memorandum for the Vice President: Space Policy Directive 7, The United States Space-Based Positioning, Navigation, and Timing Policy." Trump White House, January 15. https://trumpwhitehouse.archives.gov/presidential-actions/memorandum-space-policy-directive-7/.

2024. "National Security Memorandum on Critical Infrastructure Security and Resilience." NSM-22 (April 30, 2004). https://bidenwhitehouse.archives.gov/briefing-room/presidential-actions/2024/04/30/national-security-memorandum-on-critical-infrastructure-security-and-resilience/.

Wingrove, Martyn. 2020. "How Shipping Mitigates GPS Jamming and Spoofing." *Riviera*, July 9. www.rivieramm.com/news-content-hub/news-content-hub/how-shipping-mitigates-gps-jamming-and-spoofing-60193.

Xinhua. 2024. "China Builds Laser Communication Ground Station for Massive Satellite Data Transmission." *Xinhua*, September 15. https://english.news.cn/20240915/2718ac48dea946ad9a9b6914ed02add3/c.html.

Zeng Xiaojun, Katie. 2021. "Background: GNSS Spoofing in China and Beyond." *Risk Intelligence*, June 29. www.riskintelligence.eu/background-and-guides/background-gnss-spoofing-in-china-and-beyond.

7

Vessel-Tracking Innovations

Promise and Peril

Richard L. Kilpatrick, Jr.

7.1 INTRODUCTION

Maritime law enforcement initiatives are increasingly dependent on tracking vessel movements at sea. Although some vessel operators engaged in nefarious activities – such as contraband trafficking, economic sanctions circumvention, piracy, and illegal fishing – attempt to operate without regulatory oversight, authorities are tapping into emerging technologies as a means of exposing those activities.[1] Running parallel to enforcement actions, regulators are also obliging legitimate commercial shipping participants to enhance compliance initiatives, which is further building reliance on sophisticated vessel-tracking products developed by third-party technology companies.[2] These innovations repackage vessel-tracking data collected to promote maritime safety and achieve search-and-rescue preparedness into computer applications that provide actionable recommendations designed for compliance monitoring. Notably, many of these market-leading vessel-tracking tools rely on Automatic Identification System (AIS) transmissions flowing from treaty obligations designed to protect the safety of life at sea.[3] By processing this data with cutting-edge advances in machine learning, advanced algorithms, and artificial intelligence, and cross-referencing this information with other sources of vessel location data, such as real-time high-resolution satellite imagery, vessel-tracking companies are offering regulatory authorities and compliance-attuned commercial actors the tools necessary to embrace a new era of maritime transparency.

[1] Other unlawful activities recently revealed by vessel-tracking technology include undersea cable sabotage and cargo laundering (Bockmann 2024a; Diakun 2023b; Lloyd's List 2025).

[2] The IMO has recently highlighted the safety, security, and environmental consequences of a "dark fleet" of vessels attempting to sidestep oversight by "intentionally taking measures to avoid ship detection" (IMO 2023).

[3] For instance, many of the vessel-tracking products rely substantially on the location transmissions flowing from compliance with the International Convention for the Safety of Life at Sea, November 1, 1974, 1184 UNTS 2, as amended (SOLAS 1974).

Public authorities are relying on these innovations to maintain maritime domain awareness as criminal actors double down on efforts to disguise their activities. Simultaneously, legitimate commercial actors are deploying these transparency tools both to match due-diligence obligations imposed by regulators and to protect themselves in the commercial disputes that flow from exposure to noncompliance. In this way, recent innovations in vessel tracking are serving multiple purposes: to strengthen law enforcement initiatives and to serve as commercial intelligence for legitimate actors aiming to avoid penalties, protect against contractual liabilities, and guard against the reputational harm associated with unlawful trades. But as vessel-tracking technology improves, this is also increasing the risks for the misuse of sensitive vessel location information. Just as enhanced vessel-tracking technology may be used for the commendable purposes of promoting the safety of life at sea, facilitating law enforcement initiatives, and bolstering private sector compliance efforts, the same information may also be commandeered by malign actors to target merchant vessels for piracy or politically motivated attacks. The risks associated with sophisticated vessel tracking are now starkly illustrated by the many recent attacks against merchant ships performed by Houthi militants occupying parts of Yemen. As merchant vessels have attempted to transit the Baab Al-Mandab Strait and the Red Sea for access to the Suez Canal, the Houthis have repeatedly targeted vessels after engaging in intelligence gathering of the vessels' trading histories and ownership links.[4] This alarming trend highlights the need to prevent emerging vessel-tracking technology from being abused by hostile actors (Mathews 2024; Sweeney 2024).

Examining that dichotomy of transparency and risk, this chapter explores the technological, strategic, and policy evolutions that developed over decades of monitoring vessel movements through technology. First, the chapter maps the evolving stages of vessel-tracking tools from the invention of the radio in the nineteenth century, to the treaty-mandated equipment and satellite-supported framework developed incrementally during the twentieth century, and finally to the technology-fueled present. It then explores the shifts that led to the tools originally adopted for the safety of life at sea to be repurposed into law enforcement and compliance mechanisms and analyzes how this approach has spawned unexpected vulnerabilities. Finally, the chapter discusses the future of vessel tracking by framing the emerging tools as critical to enhancing maritime transparency while also generating new responsibilities to counteract resulting risks.

7.2 VESSEL TRACKING: PAST, PRESENT, AND FUTURE

7.2.1 *Radio to GMDSS*

Before the advent of radio technology, ships operating at sea relied on visual and audible methods to signify their locations to other ships and to shore. Shipmasters

[4] These Houthi attacks on commercial shipping have been condemned by the UN Security Council (UNSC 2024a, 2024b).

and crews were confined to using rudimentary tools, such as flags, lamps, and flares, or bells, horns, and whistles, to communicate with other vessels and to shore for safety-of-navigation purposes and in the event of distress situations. These limitations substantially impacted the ability to react in the event of a maritime emergency demanding assistance. The invention of the radio during the late nineteenth century revolutionized opportunities for maritime communication that could span much longer distances. Equipping vessels with radio transmitters and antennas made it possible to transmit telegraphic messages through Morse code for many miles. During the early twentieth century, this radio technology was incorporated into the technical machinery of some ships, but this was not yet compulsory. In efforts to harmonize the use of the equipment and the communications methods, more than twenty nations agreed in 1906 to an International Radiotelegraph Convention[5] outlining commitments regarding radiotelegraph processes, including for maritime distress situations.

A technological leader in the field at the time was the Marconi Company, established by Italian inventor Guglielmo Marconi (Baker 1971). The Marconi Company outfitted many ships with equipment during the early twentieth century, including the infrastructure on the RMS *Titanic*, which had its own "Marconi Room" (Photo Museum Ireland n.d.). During the *Titanic*'s ill-fated voyage in 1912, Marconi Company technicians sent telegraphic messages on behalf of passengers as the vessel made its way from Southampton toward New York (Hersey 2012). After the vessel hit an iceberg hundreds of miles from the coast of Canada, the same radio technicians relayed a distress message, "CQD," which was received by several ships, resulting in a rescue response saving hundreds of passengers.[6] But more passengers may have been saved had there been a more coordinated response by additional vessels nearby.

The *Titanic* disaster mobilized significant changes in the way that ships at sea utilized radio technology to aid safe navigation, as the incident quickly led to international efforts to incorporate radio technologies into regulatory mandates. The 1914 Convention for the Safety of Life at Sea (SOLAS 1914)[7] codified for the first time an obligation for merchant shipmasters to monitor designated radio channels for distress alerts that might be relayed by nearby vessels. SOLAS 1914 required qualifying ships to be fitted with a "radiotelegraphic installation" capable of "clearly sending perceptible signals" covering at minimum 100 sea miles (Articles 31 and 35).

As innovations expanded, especially during the two World Wars, these tools were incorporated into new efforts to facilitate maritime safety on a global scale.[8] This was

5 International Radiotelegraphic Convention, November 29, 1906.

6 "CQD" was understood at the time to mean roughly "all stations distress." It was a form of distress message equivalent to "SOS" (*New York Times* 1912).

7 Convention for the Safety of Life at Sea, January 20, 1914 (SOLAS 1914).

8 SOLAS was updated in 1929 to reflect technological changes occurring during and after the First World War: International Convention for the Safety of Life at Sea, May 31, 1929, 136 LNTS 81.

aided by the postwar emergence of multilateral institutions, which provided the diplomatic infrastructure for negotiations of new treaties. In particular, the Intergovernmental Maritime Consultative Organization, the precursor to the International Maritime Organization (IMO), paved the way for the treaty-based measures designed to harmonize mandatory navigation information to be relayed and received by ships operating at sea (IMO n.d.). The advent of new space-based satellite equipment during the Cold War substantially strengthened these efforts as it became possible to relay radio messages by bouncing signals off satellites in continuous orbit, which enlarged the capability of sending and receiving distress messages from ships at sea, even those operating in remote locations.[9]

Incorporating these technological advancements, SOLAS was updated multiple times during the twentieth century.[10] The most recent wholesale revisions, reflected in SOLAS 1974,[11] contain explicit requirements for qualifying ships to utilize maritime monitoring equipment to facilitate data exchange and enhance communication between ships and to shore. SOLAS 1974 provisions required qualifying vessels to carry radio equipment capable of sending and receiving distress alerts across very-high-frequency (VHF) radio channels (Chapters IV–V). These included specific "shipborne navigational equipment," including various technologies of the era, such as radar and echo-sounding devices.

But telecommunications developed quickly in the years following SOLAS 1974, especially due to widespread advancements in satellite and space-based infrastructure. The SOLAS 1974 framework required further amendments to operationalize these technological developments. Having foreseen the likelihood of this need, the drafters of SOLAS 1974 included a flexible amendment procedure that allowed the IMO's Maritime Safety Committee (MSC) to update its provisions. In the following decades, fast-tracked changes facilitated regulatory dynamics to keep pace with evolving technologies (Article VIII).[12]

Among the most significant of the IMO's amendments to SOLAS 1974 is the establishment of the Global Maritime Distress and Safety System (GMDSS) in 1988 (Chapter IV, Regulation 4). The GMDSS amendments require qualifying ships to carry certain types of radio equipment that are capable of transmitting and receiving distress alerts and, at the push of a button, communicating a preformatted distress message to rescue coordination centers managed by State authorities (Bréhaut 2013). This GMDSS technology mandate requires the use of shipborne equipment

[9] These technological developments drove the establishment of an international framework governing the use of satellites to support maritime safety initiatives. See Convention on the International Maritime Satellite Organization, September 3, 1976, 1143 UNTS 105.

[10] For example, the International Convention for the Safety of Life at Sea, June 17, 1960, 536 UNTS 27.

[11] International Convention for the Safety of Life at Sea, November 1, 1974, 1184 UNTS 2 (SOLAS 1974).

[12] Under Article VIII of SOLAS 1974, amendments may be "referred to the Maritime Safety Committee of the Organization for consideration."

designed to interact with satellites and shore-based tools to create a comprehensive long-distance messaging framework.[13] The advent of the GMDSS was a revolution in the development of international legal rules governing vessel tracking. By mandating satellite-linked transmissions covering even remote sea areas, the GMDSS created a new apparatus to protect life at sea by delivering critical vessel location information to State-operated rescue coordination centers prepared to react promptly to distress alerts.[14]

7.2.2 *AIS and LRIT*

This GMDSS framework paved the way for enhanced vessel tracking after the turn of the new century. In 2000, the MSC adopted further amendments to SOLAS to enhance navigational safety through the use of automatic information exchanges relayed via shipborne equipment (IMO 2000b). These SOLAS amendments require qualifying vessels to carry AIS equipment, which continuously relays identifying information on a VHF radio band, including the vessel's identity, type, position, course, speed, and navigational status, along with other safety information.[15] This information transmitted from the AIS equipment is then collected by other ships' receivers and by shore-based facilities for the purpose of promoting the underlying interests driving the SOLAS framework – namely, the safety of life, the safety of navigation, and the protection of the marine environment.

Shortly after the AIS mandate was promulgated, the MSC issued Guidelines for the Onboard Operational Use of Shipborne Automatic Identification Systems (AIS Guidelines; IMO 2001). The Guidelines, which were updated in 2015 to clarify further its implementation (IMO 2015), explain that the AIS should relay static information, such as the vessel's IMO number, Maritime Mobile Service Identity number, and details regarding its type and size. In addition, the AIS should also include "dynamic" information, such as the vessel's position, speed, and intended destination (IMO 2015). Some of this information, such as the vessel's position and speed, is updated automatically by the equipment, but other information, such as the vessel's destination, requires manual input (IMO 2015).[16]

Both the SOLAS amendments establishing AIS and the AIS Guidelines make it clear that operators of qualifying vessels have an obligation to relay the AIS information continuously. Thus, the AIS "should always be in operations when ships are

[13] In particular, the GMDSS rules mandate vessels carry emergency position indicating radio beacons, search-and-rescue transponders for precise location determination, and navigational telex devices that allow for the automatic reception of safety messages (USCG n.d.).

[14] This GMDSS also ties into the rescue framework established by the International Convention on Maritime Search and Rescue, April 27, 1979, 1405 UNTS 97.

[15] This qualification depends on the vessel's gross tonnage and whether the vessel is "engaged on international voyages." See SOLAS 1974, as amended, Chapter V, Regulation 19.

[16] For a visual description of AIS functionality, see NATO (2021).

underway or at anchor" (IMO 2015). However, the Guidelines do indicate an important exception to this rule: "If the master believes that the continual operation of AIS may compromise the safety or security of his/her ship or where security incidents are imminent, the AIS may be switched off" (IMO 2015). In such unique security situations, the AIS Guidelines indicate that "the master should however restart the AIS as soon as the source of danger has disappeared" (IMO 2015).

The AIS requirement and its narrow security-based exception represent a critical moment in international regulation through vessel tracking, as the rules mandate continuous location and identity disclosures in the interests of safety at sea. But even at the time the rules were drafted, this transparency mandate and security exception was viewed as a necessary compromise. During the development of the AIS Guidelines, shipping industry organizations, including the International Chamber of Shipping (ICS) and the International Association of Independent Tanker Owners (INTERTANKO), expressed concern that the regulatory obligation requiring vessel operators to relay vessel locations continuously could ultimately create security risks. Although the ICS and INTERTANKO both submitted documents to the MSC in support of the adoption of the AIS requirements, the submissions also advocated for the shipmaster to retain the authority to turn off the transponder if the shipmaster believes that the safety of the ship could be affected by the transmission of its location (IMO 2000a, 2000c). This advocacy appears to have shaped the rule allowing shipmasters to switch off the AIS transponder at their discretion in the interests of maritime security.

An additional vessel-tracking amendment was made to SOLAS as part of a maritime security response to the 9/11 attacks. At that time, there was an urgent concern about the security vulnerabilities of maritime ports, which drove substantial regulation under IMO auspices, most notably the establishment of the International Ship and Port Facility Security Code (SOLAS 1974, Chapter XI; IMO 2012). In addition to these changes, to enhance vessel-tracking capabilities, the MSC updated SOLAS in 2006 to establish a Long-Range Identification and Tracking (LRIT) system to be carried out alongside the AIS requirements (IMO 2006). In some ways, the LRIT framework is similar to AIS and perhaps even redundant, but LRIT contrasts with AIS in that it relies on different technologies to relay a narrow scope of identifying information to a limited class of authorized audiences.[17]

The LRIT regulations require the automatic transmission of information: the ship's identity and position, along with the specific date and time of the messages (IMO 2006). The framework envisions the communication of vessel location data utilizing the same equipment already carried on ships to facilitate the original GMDSS program to cooperate with orbiting satellites and data collection facilities on shore (IMO 2006). Collectively, the equipment allows these tracking messages to be automatically relayed via a "digital select calling" process at six-hour intervals

[17] For a discussion of the policy arguments for the adoption of LRIT, see Krajewski (2008).

without any human intervention or manual inputs (IMO 2006). This information is collected by designated service providers and then sent to authorized State organizations entitled to review the data – namely, flag, port, and coastal States that may wish to use the information to enhance search-and-rescue capabilities and to establish maritime domain awareness (IMO 2006). Even with transparency and security driving the adoption of the LRIT, under its framework, governmental entities accessing this data must "recognize and respect the commercial confidentiality and sensitivity" of the information they receive (IMO 2006). Thus, the distribution of LRIT data is much more confined than its AIS counterpart.

Although the LRIT system does not rely on VHF radio signals, as does AIS, the equipment can still be switched off by the shipmaster. Even at the time the MSC adopted the amendments to implement the LRIT system, IMO documents explained that the equipment "shall be capable of being switched off" and cease distribution of the signal when an exceptional circumstance, in the view of the shipmaster, compromises the "safety and security of the ship" (IMO 2006, para. 7). Although it would appear that the security risks associated with unimpeded transmissions of LRIT information are reduced in comparison to AIS, given that LRIT data is only sent to State actors and is generally unavailable to the public (and, therefore, it is not accessible by malign private actors, such as pirates or terrorists), the security switch-off exception reflects the perceived sensitivity of the LRIT vessel-tracking information.

Since its implementation, the AIS framework has been improved by pairing it with newer technologies (Carson-Jackson 2012). In its original form, AIS relied on VHF radio signals that could only be received by equipment carried on vessels or shore-based facilities. This limited its functionality for vessel-tracking purposes. Technical reconfiguration through the use of satellite technology facilitated the collection of AIS signals regardless of whether the transmitting equipment was in relative proximity to the receiving equipment. In the modern era, satellite AIS systems receive, collect, and report vessel identification information, which can then be displayed publicly in highly digestible formats, such as those platforms used by popular ship-tracking websites used by hobbyist ship watchers and shipping industry participants.[18]

As AIS data has been made publicly available through these resources, it has also been incorporated into a range of scientific and economic studies (Armelloni et al. 2021; Dupont et al. 2020; Fournier et al. 2018; Serra-Sogas et al. 2021; Shelmerdine 2018; Svanberg et al. 2019). But AIS has also become an increasingly common source of vessel tracking for use across a range of law enforcement and legal compliance initiatives, often linked to national security concerns (Creech et al. 2003). These uses include repurposing AIS data to track vessels for the purposes of

[18] For instance, marinetraffic.com and vesseltracker.com are popular websites for tracking ships using publicly accessible AIS data.

counteracting piracy, drug trafficking, migrant smuggling, and illegal fishing.[19] Perhaps most of all, regulators have emphasized the use of AIS for the purposes of monitoring economic sanctions compliance at sea (Kilpatrick 2022). At the same time, there is widespread recognition that AIS is not always a reliable source of vessel-tracking data (Goudossis and Katsikas 2019; Harati-Mokhtari et al. 2007). Even satellite AIS is susceptible to technical dropout, given that it fundamentally depends on VHF transmissions. Furthermore, since AIS relies on manual inputs, it can also give rise to unintentional human error. Its dependency on unencrypted VHF channels also makes it vulnerable to external interference, including hacking, jamming, manipulation, and spoofing (Androjna et al. 2021; Wolsing et al. 2022).

Recognizing these vulnerabilities, law enforcement authorities have regularly cited suspicious AIS transmissions – or gaps in AIS signals – as evidence of unlawful activities. At present, one of the most common references to AIS and law enforcement in the compliance context is through an inference of nefarious activity when the vessel operator has switched off the AIS. In this way, rather than simply using AIS to monitor vessels engaging in malfeasance, law enforcement authorities are also analyzing irregularities in AIS signals, which have been referenced to demonstrate malintent. In part to follow regulatory guidance on the subject, commercial actors aiming to monitor the compliance of counterparties or third parties with a nexus to underlying transactions are also carefully monitoring AIS for switch-off or manipulation, which may also be used as an evidentiary source to justify contractual responses.[20]

Further illustrating regulatory interest in AIS gaps, a recent proposal in the US Senate to mobilize new technologies for the purpose of aiding law enforcement officials in tracking vessels, particularly in the sanctions space. For instance, the Vessel Tracking for Sanctions Enforcement Act of 2023 a legislative proposal aimed at requiring US agencies to "assess the feasibility and advisability of using big data analytics to identify and predict instances in which disabling or manipulating [AIS] on a vessel is an indicator that there is a high risk that the vessel is transporting goods in a manner that evades sanctions or export controls."[21]An explanatory document disseminated by the office of one of the Senators who proposed the bill indicates that the program might address the problem of "American law enforcement agencies sifting through huge amounts of data to try to identify bad actors and intervene" (Hassan 2023). As of early 2025, the bill has not moved forward, but it has attracted the attention of the international shipping media (Raanan 2023).

Remarkably, the technologically more reliable LRIT system has been less frequently mentioned in legislative proposals, regulatory guidance, and court documents

[19] Journalistic investigations have also used vessel-tracking technology to demonstrate cargo-laundering activities: see, for example, Diakun (2023a).

[20] Examples of this practice are discussed in Section 7.3.2.

[21] See 118th Congress, 1st Session, S.2248 (2023).

filed by law enforcement authorities seeking to demonstrate vessel involvement in unlawful activities.[22] LRIT data is also rarely deployed as a source of vessel-tracking information in academic studies.[23] The obvious reason for this is that under the LRIT framework, the ship-tracking data is not designed to be made publicly available. Nevertheless, despite these limitations in data distribution, a 2020 Advisory issued by US regulators regarding economic sanctions compliance in the maritime sector cites LRIT data as one factor for shipowners and charterers to consider when engaging in counterparty due diligence (Department of the Treasury et al. 2020, 18). This is an unusual recommendation, as the Advisory fails to acknowledge that LRIT data is not available for scrutiny by private shipping industry participants.

Perhaps in correction, more recent compliance Advisories on the subject either mention only AIS or narrow the LRIT monitoring recommendations to those public actors with access, such as flag States.[24] Emphasizing the role of States in addressing the fallout from vessel-tracking circumvention, a recent IMO Resolution addressing the problem of an expanding "dark fleet" or "shadow fleet" defines the phenomenon as ships that are "engaged in illegal operations" that include "intentionally taking measures to avoid ship detection such as switching off their AIS or LRIT transmissions or concealing the ship's actual identity when there is no legitimate safety or security concern to justify such action" (IMO 2023, para. 1.6).[25] Urging States to combat these practices, since these vessels may have "substandard maintenance, unclear ownership, lack of insurance coverage and disguise their cargoes' destination or origin," the Resolution recommends that port States "subject such ships to enhanced inspections" (IMO 2023, para. 5).

7.3 A NEW ERA IN MARITIME TRANSPARENCY

7.3.1 *Recent Technological Innovations*

In response to the commercial demand created by regulatory mandates and private compliance needs, technology companies have proliferated in efforts to analyze AIS,

[22] Examples of AIS references in law enforcement complaints are discussed in Kilpatrick (2022, 233–238).

[23] At least some academic studies have examined the implications of LRIT data for various purposes. See, for example, Vespe et al. (2015).

[24] See, for example, Price Cap Coalition 2024: "*If accessible, complement AIS Tracking with Long-Range Identification and Tracking ('LRIT')*. In instances of AIS outages or suspected AIS manipulation, stakeholders such as flagging registries that have access to LRIT should use it to determine the true location of vessels, including, where feasible, those leased to third parties. For those industry stakeholders who have access to LRIT, combining AIS and LRIT is a best practice for mitigating risk" (4, emphasis in original).

[25] The Resolution also recalls that "the long-range identification and tracking (LRIT) system can be used to identify ships up to 1,000 nautical miles from the coastal state": IMO (2023, para. 1.6).

LRIT, satellite imagery, and other vessel-tracking data. Described as part of a "transparency revolution" in shipping, the products are building capacity to process varied sources of vessel movement information to make judgments, predictions, and actionable recommendations to flag potentially unlawful behavior (Lloyd's List 2021). These products fall into several categories, including those that repackage AIS in user-friendly platforms, process LRIT or LRIT-analogous data, examine or cross-reference satellite imagery, and compare shipborne transmissions with photographic imagery from shore-based sources.

The market-leading products include those provided by UK-based Lloyd's List Intelligence. In marketing materials, the Lloyd's List program is described as "turning maritime data into actionable insights" (Lloyd's List Intelligence n.d.). This product includes using AI and advanced algorithmic tools to reframe vessel-tracking information collected from a range of sources, including AIS, as a means of assessing risk for legal exposure that can be used for counterparty know-your-customer analysis as required by regulatory mandates (Lloyd's List Intelligence n. d.). Other comparable offerings are provided by Israel-based company Windward, which markets its vessel-screening and fleet-monitoring technology to create predictive commercial intelligence fueled by "Maritime AI" (Windward n.d.). Like the Lloyd's List products, Windward's processes appear to rely on AIS data with operability enhanced through machine-learning analysis with integration into compliance-targeted and user-friendly systems.[26]

Other companies have focused predominantly on satellite imagery analysis. Firms operating in this space include Planet Labs and Maxar Technologies, both of which utilize optical sources to support a variety of surveillance activities, including maritime domain awareness (Maxar n.d.-b; Planet n.d.). Although satellite imagery carries its own limitations, including its high cost and the potential for obstruction by cloudy weather conditions, the variables are diminishing as technology improves. For instance, Maxar has marketed its products as leveraging "synthetic aperture radar" imagery that has the potential to function even in cloud cover (Maxar n.d.-a.).[27] Law enforcement agencies, media outlets, and private sector initiatives have referenced these imagery sources largely as a basis to fact-check AIS switch-off, manipulation, and spoofing. These imagery-based options have the potential to strengthen the credibility of vessel-tracking assessments depending on ship-borne AIS or LRIT data.

Nonsatellite imagery options are also emerging to cross-reference AIS and LRIT. A company called Tanker Trackers, for instance, relies in part on "shoreside photography" to cross-reference other sources of information, including AIS, for sanctions compliance purposes in the oil transport sector (TankerTrackers n.d.). Its findings have been widely shared on social media and through the reporting of

[26] Spire is another company configuring AIS data for compliance-focused tracking: Spire (n.d.).
[27] Other companies are also marketing similar satellite-based options: see ICEYE (n.d.).

major news outlets in investigative journalism on the "dark fleet" (Triebert et al. 2023). Other approaches relying on aerial – and perhaps even undersea – drones may offer similar compliance value as they have the capacity to capture real-time vessel data, particularly as vessels approach geographically narrow areas of navigational significance such as straits and ports (Adamopoulos 2019).[28]

A more controversial option is the commercial marketability of LRIT data. A UK firm called Pole Star is one company that administers LRIT data collection for use by State actors, such as flag States. But Pole Star has allegedly also offered LRIT-equivalent data for commercial compliance purposes (Bockmann 2020).[29] This has sparked contentious discussion within the maritime community because sharing LRIT data for private compliance processes would appear to run counter to the spirit of the IMO regulations that established LRIT for government eyes only. However, it does raise the possibility that the LRIT architecture could be reimagined to provide vessel-tracking information to a broader array of actors. LRIT utilizes equipment already carried on vessels, and it relays location-tracking transmissions automatically at scheduled intervals without any direct human intervention, which offers promise that these tools could be reconfigured potentially to sidestep dependence on the less secure and less reliable AIS. Whether LRIT can mimic the same broader scope of information relayed by AIS is an open technical question. If it is indeed possible to update the LRIT framework with the relatively minor reconfiguration of existing equipment, this could help promote vessel-tracking transparency reform by offering a stable and economically efficient solution that is derivative of the current IMO-mandated regime.

7.3.2 *Commercial Uses*

Motivated by regulatory guidance and the new technologies available on the market, industry organizations have developed contract clauses that seek to address the risks of switching off AIS transponders (BIMCO n.d.). Recent case law provides examples of the ways that commercial actors have relied on vessel-tracking tools and contract clauses to address compliance issues and grounds for termination due to unlawful activities. These cases provide practical endorsements of the vessel-tracking tools that have recently become available and demonstrate how commercial actors may need to rely on them to protect themselves from legal compliance risk.

One example is an arbitration award decided by the New York-based Society of Maritime Arbitrators resolving a charterparty dispute. In *Brujo Finance Company v. Sea Energy Company*, the parties agreed to a contract to perform consecutive voyages carrying gasoline from "Cristobal to Curacao or Aruba, with Charterer

28 Researchers have even relied on albatross patterns to track fishing vessels that have turned off vessel-tracking transponders to evade detection (Kornei 2020; Weimerkirch et al. 2019).

29 This controversy is discussed in more detail in Kilpatrick (2022, 242–243).

having the option of discharging the cargo by means of a ship-to-ship transfer."[30] In response to the charterer's request to perform a ship-to-ship (STS) transfer near Aruba, the shipowner sent a message to charter indicating concern that the STS transfer might involve sanctioned Venezuelan cargo. The message read: "Owners WILL NOT participate in any illegal trading. If the intention is to transship the cargo [STS] to move it to Venezuela same will not be done. Any vessel nominated for transshipment will be subject to strict anti-sanctions scrutiny." Then, the charterer informed the shipowner that the proposed STS transfer would involve a vessel called the MT *Beauty One*. In an attempt to assure the shipowner that the vessel would not be engaged in any kind of sanctions-busting trades, the charterer emphasized to the shipowner that the *Beauty One* was not on any US sanctions lists.

After being notified that the proposed STS transfer would involve the *Beauty One*, the shipowner obtained documents from an external "tracking service" indicating that the vessel had made several calls to Venezuelan ports during the previous year. On that basis, the shipowner noted that all parties involved in the transaction could become sanctioned by US authorities if the transaction involved a Venezuelan nexus. The shipowner then referenced the *Beauty One*'s "recent trading history exclusively in Venezuelan waters" as a basis to seek additional assurances of legal compliance. But the charterer did not provide additional assurances meeting the shipowner's standards, so the shipowner wrote back to the charterer explaining that "saying 'trust us'" is insufficient to provide assurances of compliance. The shipowner then invoked a sanctions clause in the charterparty on grounds that the charterers had failed to give assurances that the *Beauty One* would not perform an unlawful trade.

In the arbitration proceedings that followed, the Society of Maritime Arbitrators held in favor of the shipowner. The arbitral panel reasoned that there was sufficient evidence to determine that there was a "discernible risk" that facilitating the transaction with the *Beauty One* could trigger US sanctions. As evidence of this risk, the panel referenced the reported trading history of the *Beauty One* as a relevant consideration. Since the charterer did not provide any contrary evidence of the *Beauty One*'s previous trading history, this caused the panel to find that the shipowner properly invoked the sanctions clause by refusing the charterer's orders to engage in an STS transaction that "could expose" it to US sanctions.

Another recent case involving reference to vessel tracking is *Kuvera Resources Pte Ltd v. JPMorgan Chase Bank* NA, which was decided by the Court of Appeal of the Republic of Singapore (Kilpatrick 2023).[31] In that case, a Singaporean trading company was the beneficiary of letters of credit linked to transactions of coal that

[30] *Brujo Finance Company v. Sea Energy Company*, SMA 4388 (July 3, 2020). The quotations that follow are from this decision.

[31] *Kuvera Resources Pte Ltd v. JPMorgan Chase Bank* NA [2023] SGCA 28. The quotations that follow are from this decision.

had been moved from Indonesia to the Middle East. In attempts to collect under the letters of credit, the trading company went to the Singapore branch of US bank JPMorgan Chase and presented documents compliant with the letters of credit. When the bank performed its internal compliance check, it determined that a vessel that had moved coal in the underlying trade had previously used another name and had been beneficially owned by a Syrian national, which made it potentially subject to US sanctions. On that basis, the bank refused to pay on the letters of credit and invoked the sanctions clause that granted it the liberty to avoid payment if documents presented involved a "vessel" subject to sanctions.

The trial court held in favor of the bank on grounds that since the vessel was apparently previously owned by an actor subject to US sanctions, the name and registration change would have been viewed as an attempt to mask its true identity, which could expose the bank to sanctions if it paid on the letters of credit. The Court of Appeal reversed that decision, however, in part because it determined that the sanctions clauses in the letters of credit contained an implicit burden of proof that the bank did not meet. That burden of proof required the bank to demonstrate that the vessel was "Syrian-owned at all material times." It reasoned that due in part to commercially available vessel-tracking information, this was a fact that was "capable of objective determination." As evidence of this, the court referenced the Lloyd's List Intelligence database (discussed above), which apparently showed that during the relevant period, the vessel owner and various operating entities did not have a direct Syrian nexus.

7.3.3 *Security Risks*

The paradoxical challenge of promoting vessel location transparency while also maintaining maritime security has come into focus during the recent emergence of security threats for vessels moving through the Red Sea. Citing the deteriorating humanitarian conditions associated with the Israel–Hamas War and utilizing weapons apparently provided by Iran, Houthi militias occupying substantial territory in Yemen have attacked dozens of merchant ships in and around the Red Sea. These events have been so disruptive that they caused many ships to reroute around the Cape of Good Hope rather than risk transit through the Suez Canal. They also led to condemnations by a UN Security Council Resolution and coalition airstrikes inside Yemeni territory (UNSC 2024a).

Although these Houthi attacks have impacted vessels with a nexus to a broad range of national interests, according to statements made by Houthi leaders, there has been at least some attempt to target vessels with links to "enemy" States (Bockmann 2024b). The Houthis initially claimed to target vessels with an Israeli connection. But determining the Israeli nexus of merchant ships is a complicated endeavor that might involve layers of connections, including the vessel's flag, place of beneficial ownership, place of management, and ports of origin and discharge, as well as the trading history, the cargo carried on board, the place of the vessel's various insurers, and, of course, the nationalities of the seafarers on board. As an illustration of this complexity, ships operated by the Swiss-based Mediterranean Shipping Company have been targeted more than other container lines, apparently because one of the company's shareholders holds an Israeli passport (as well as Swiss and Italian passports); (Lloyd's List 2024).

In response to this threat, vessel operators in the region begin utilizing their vessel-tracking transponders to send messages to the Houthis indicating their lack of any Israeli connection and to indicate the presence of armed guards on board. According to media outlets, vessel operators have used their AIS signals to relay messages such as "NOLINKISRAEL," "ALL CHINESE CREW," "ALLRUSSIAN," and "RUSSIA+CHINA" (Maritime Executive 2023). Houthi leaders have even issued statements on social media addressed to "ministries of transport in all countries of the world and to international shipping companies," requesting vessel operators to utilize their vessel-tracking transponders to relay such information – including "no relationship to Israel" (Raanan 2024).

In attempts to ascertain these various factors, it appears that Houthis have been engaged in some level of investigation when determining whether to attack a given vessel. This is thought to have involved utilizing commercial vessel-tracking products, as well as more sophisticated intelligence gathering from State allies such as Iran (Bryen 2023; Faucon et al. 2023). But, despite attempts by vessel operators to communicate regarding any potential political risk associated with a vessel, and despite the Houthi "investigations" into vessel affiliations, the attacks on vessels with apparently neutral connections demonstrate the arbitrary nature of the Houthi strategy.

In part due to this risk, regulators have issued guidance indicating that vessels operating in the Red Sea should deactivate their vessel-tracking transponders to complicate the Houthis' ability to locate them. For instance, the US Maritime Administration issued an Advisory in March 2024 regarding threats to commercial vessels (MARAD 2024). It advises that "U.S.-flagged vessels transiting the Southern Red Sea, Bab el Mandeb Strait, and Gulf of Aden with AIS transponders on are at increased risk of targeting by adversarial actors" (MARAD 2024). Accordingly, the Advisory relays the position that vessel operators are "strongly advised to turn off their AIS transponders unless vessel Masters believe that doing so would compromise the safety of the vessel" (MARAD 2024). The Advisory explains that "while vessels have been attacked by the Houthis while transponders were on and while off, turning AIS off makes it more difficult to track and accurately target a vessel" (MARAD 2024). It then notes that "adherence to all flag state and international requirements and guidance regarding operation of AIS, and the safe navigation of the vessel, remains the responsibility of individual companies and vessel Masters" (MARAD 2024).[32]

[32] A sanctions compliance Advisory issued by the US regulators in September 2024 highlights this challenge of balancing transparency and risk: "There can be legitimate reasons for AIS to be

Simultaneously, UK authorities have made different recommendations on the basis that Houthis have attacked both vessels with AIS switched off and vessels with AIS switched on, indicating that they may have other means of tracking vessels. A February 2024 Advisory issued by UK Maritime Trade Operations (UKMTO) explains that "turning off AIS makes it marginally more difficult to track a ship but may also hinder the ability of the military to provide support or direct contact" (UKMTO 2024). The Advisory notes: "Limiting the information in AIS data fields or switching off AIS could make a ship harder to locate, but it is unlikely to prevent an attack. Limiting AIS data to the mandatory fields and omitting the next port of call (NPOC) could be considered" (UKMTO 2024).

Insurers, being critical stakeholders as they may be responsible for paying claims in the event of an attack, have also weighed in on what shipmasters should do to avoid risk in the Red Sea. Although war risk insurers have not publicly issued guidance indicating whether vessel operators should keep AIS switched off or on, protection and indemnity clubs have issued circulars on the matter. Swedish insurer Skuld, for instance, has explained that "some ships have been targeted despite having their AIS turned off, suggesting that the Houthis have alternative methods of identifying and tracking their targets" (Skuld 2024).

These regulatory and commercial best practices advocating for vessel operators to deactivate vessel-tracking transponders are a stark juxtaposition to the vessel transparency mandates provided by regulators and commercial actors reacting to other compliance concerns, especially in the sanctions context. Vessel operators are compelled through both regulation and contractual obligations to evaluate carefully the circumstances in which the vessel-tracking transponders should remain on or be switched off. These distinct risks demonstrate that such decisions cannot be made relying on a bare reading of SOLAS or the IMO Guidelines but instead require vessel operators to use holistic judgment depending on a range of legal compliance and security factors.

7.4 CONCLUSION

As vessel tracking is adopted for law enforcement and compliance initiatives, the technological standards for consistent and accurate monitoring capacity are growing exponentially. Although vessel-tracking tools have rapidly expanded in recent years, they still largely rely on voluntary shipborne transmissions the user or third-party interference can manipulate. Efforts to enhance vessel tracking beyond the status

turned off or 'go dark' (e.g., passage through waters at high-risk of piracy or due to other security considerations). In such situations, it is advisable for ships to turn off their AIS to evade threats, and thus should not be considered a red flag for illicit activity. However, ship registries, insurers, charterers, vessel owners, or port operators should consider investigating vessels that appear to have turned off their AIS transponders for extended periods or unknown reasons while operating in the Mediterranean and Red Seas" (OFAC 2024).

quo will require the implementation of new tools and techniques that rectify the vulnerabilities of current processes. These advances in machine learning, AI, satellite imagery, and aerial and undersea drones, along with other operational improvements, will undoubtedly facilitate the regulatory demand for maritime transparency. The success of these new models will be driven by the ingenuity of engineers and code-writers rather than policy analysts, but as capacity quickly builds, it may only be a matter of time before monitoring tools are able to track vessels without reliance on shipborne equipment at all. In reimagining a vessel-tracking standard, these new tools will create highly valuable insights that may facilitate the regulation of the "dark fleet" and its shadowy activities. But, as recent events tragically demonstrate, this unprecedented visibility may beget pronounced security risks.

REFERENCES

Adamopoulos, Anastassios. 2019. "Denmark Turns to Drones for Sulphur Compliance." *Lloyd's List*, April 15.

Androjna, Andrej, Marko Perkovič, Ivica Pavic, and Jakša Miškovič. 2021. "AIS Data Vulnerability Indicated by a Spoofing Case-Study." *Applied Sciences* 11 (11): 5015.

Armelloni, Enrico Nicola, Anna Nora Tassetti, Carmen Ferrà, Alessandro Galdelli, Martina Scanu, Adriano Mancini, Gianna Fabi, and Giuseppe Scarcella. 2021. "AIS Data, a Mine of Information on Trawling Fleet Mobility in the Mediterranean Sea." *Marine Policy* 129: 104571.

Baker, W. J. 1971. *A History of the Marconi Company*. St. Martin's Press.

BIMCO (Baltic and International Maritime Council). n.d. "AIS Switch Off Clause 2021." www.bimco.org/contracts-and-clauses/bimco-clauses/current/ais_switch_off_clause_2021.

Bockmann, Michelle Wiese. 2020. "Government-Only Vessel-Tracking Data Up for Sale 'with US Approval.'" *Lloyd's List*, June 19.

2024a. "Dark Fleet Tanker Reportedly Detained off Finland after Undersea Cable Cut." *Lloyd's List*, 26 December.

2024b. "Greece-Owned Ships Are Top Houthi Target." *Lloyd's List*, October 23.

Bréhaut, Denise. 2013. *GMDSS: A User's Handbook*. 5th ed. Bloomsbury.

Bryen, Stephen. 2023. "Iran-Houthis Tap AIS Tracking Tech for High Seas Attacks." *Asia Times*, December 25.

Carson-Jackson, J. 2012. "Satellite AIS: Developing Technology or Existing Capability?" *Journal of Navigation* 65 (2): 303–321.

Creech, Jay A., and Joseph F. Ryan. 2003. "AIS, The Cornerstone of National Security?" *Journal of Navigation* 56 (1): 31–44.

Diakun, Bridget. 2023a. "Shadowy Trade in 'Stolen' Grain from Russia-Occupied Azov Ramps Up." *Lloyd's List*, 8 September.

2023b. "US-Sanctioned Crimea Caller and Accused Grain Plunderer Renames." *Lloyd's List*, November 2.

Department of the Treasury, Department of State, and Coast Guard (United States). 2020. "Sanctions Advisory for the Maritime Industry, Energy and Metals Sectors, and Related Communities." May 14.

Dupont, Clement, Françoise Gourmelon, Catherine Meur-Ferec, Frédérick Herpers, and Christophe Le Visage. 2020. "Exploring Uses of Maritime Surveillance Data for Marine Spatial Planning: A Review of Scientific Literature." *Marine Policy* 117: 103930.

Faucon, Benoit, Dov Lieber, and Gordon Lubold. 2023. "Iranian Spy Ship Helps Houthis Direct Attacks on Red Sea Vessels." *Wall Street Journal*, December 22.

Fournier, Melanie, R. Casey Hilliard, Sara Rezaee, and Ronald Pelot. 2018. "Past, Present, and Future of the Satellite-Based Automatic Identification System: Areas of Applications (2004–2016)." *WMU Journal of Marine Affairs* 17: 311–345.

Goudossis, Athanassios, and Sokratis K Katsikas. 2019. "Towards a Secure Automatic Identification System (AIS)." *Journal of Marine Science and Technology* 24 (6): 410–423.

Harati-Mokhtari, Abbas, Alan Wall, Philip Brooks, and Jin Wang. 2007. "Automatic Identification Systems (AIS): Data Reliability and Human Error Implications." *Journal of Navigation* 60 (3): 373–389.

Hassan, Maggie. 2023. "Vessel Tracking for Sanctions Enforcement Act of 2023." www.dco.uscg.mil/Portals/9/DCO%20Documents/Proceedings%20Magazine/Archive/2012/Vol69_No2_Sum2012.pdf

Hersey, Joe. 2012. "Radio Communications from the Time of the Titanic." Proceedings (US Coast Guard), Summer. www.dco.uscg.mil/Portals/9/DCO%20Documents/Proceedings%20Magazine/Archive/2012/Vol69_No2_Sum2012.pdf.

ICEYE. n.d. "Maritime Domain Awareness." www.iceye.com/sar-data/use-cases/maritime-domain-awareness.

IMO (International Maritime Organization). 2000a. "Guidelines on Automatic Identification of Shipping (AIS) Operational Matters: Note by the International Chamber of Shipping (ICS)." MSC 72/10/12 (May 31, 2000).

2000b. "Adoption of Amendments to the International Convention for the Safety of Life at Sea, 1974, as Amended." MSC.99(73) (December 5, 2000).

2000c. "Revision of Chapter V of SOLAS: Transponders." Submitted by INTERTANKO. MSC 72/10/8 (March 14, 2000).

2001. "Guidelines for the Onboard Operational Use of Shipborne Automatic Identification Systems (AIS)." A 22/Res.917 (November 29, 2001).

2006. "Adoption of Amendments to the International Convention for the Safety of Life at Sea, 1974, as Amended." MSC.202(81) (May 19, 2006).

2012. *Guide to Maritime Security and the ISPS Code.*

2015. "Revised Guidelines for the Onboard Operational Use of Shipborne Automatic Identification Systems (AIS)." A 29/Res.1106 (December 14, 2015), Annex.

2023. "Urging Member States and All Relevant Stakeholders to Promote Actions to Prevent Illegal Operations in the Maritime Sector by the 'Dark Fleet' or 'Shadow Fleet.'" A 33/Res.1192 (December 11, 2023).

n.d. "Brief History of IMO." www.imo.org/en/About/HistoryOfIMO/Pages/Default.aspx.

Kilpatrick, Richard L., Jr., 2022. "Monitoring Sanctions Compliance at Sea." *Northwestern Journal of International Law and Business* 42 (2): 221–251.

2023. "Sanctions Clause Redux." *Journal of International Maritime Law* 29 (4): 199.

Kornei, Katherine. 2020. "They're Stealthy at Sea, but They Can't Hide from the Albatross." *New York Times*, January 29.

Krajewski, Jason M. 2008. "Out of Sight, Out of Mind? A Case for Long Range Identification and Tracking of Vessels on the High Seas." *Naval Law Review* 56: 219–249.

Lloyd's List. 2021. *Transparency in Shipping: A Special Report.* Informa.

2024. "Ships Should Not Be Attacked on the Basis of an Owner's Passport." *Lloyd's List*, May 10.

2025. "UK-Led Alliance Using AI to Monitor Threats to Undersea Cables." *Lloyd's List*, January 7.

Lloyd's List Intelligence. n.d. "About Us: Our Data." www.lloydslistintelligence.com/about-us/our-data.

MARAD (United States Maritime Administration). 2024. MSCI Advisory 2024-004: Southern Red Sea, Bab el Mandeb Strait, Gulf of Aden, Indian Ocean, Somali Basin, Arabian Sea, Gulf of Oman, Strait of Hormuz, and Persian Gulf – Threats to Commercial Vessels.

Maritime Executive. 2023. "Report: Ships Make Novel Use of AIS to Ward Off Attacks by Houthis." *Maritime Executive*, December 28.

Mathews, Sean. 2024. "How the Houthis Mined Commercial Intelligence to Sabotage Global Trade." *Middle East Eye*, September 5. www.middleeasteye.net/news/how-houthis-mined-commercial-intelligence-sabotage-global-trade.

Maxar. n.d.-a. "Crow's Nest." www.maxar.com/maxar-intelligence/products/crows-nest.

n.d.-b. "Near Real-Time Vessel Detection." https://explore.maxar.com/maritime-monitoring.html.

NATO (North Atlantic Treaty Organization). 2021. "AIS (Automatic Identification System) Overview." https://shipping.nato.int/nsc/operations/news/2021/ais-automatic-identification-system-overview.

New York Times. 1912. "Titanic Sinks Four Hours after Hitting Iceberg; 866 Rescued by Carpathia, Probably 1250 Perish; Ismay Safe, Mrs. Astor Maybe, Noted Names Missing." *New York Times*, April 15.

OFAC (United States Department of the Treasury, Office of Foreign Assets Control). 2024. "OFAC Advisory to the Maritime Petroleum Shipping Community: Sanctions Risks Related to Petroleum Shipments Involving Iran and Syria." September 11.

Photo Museum Ireland. n.d. "The Marconi Room, on Board the Titanic." https://timeline.photomuseumireland.ie/timeline/the-marconi-room-on-board-the-titanic/.

Planet. n.d. "Maritime and Coastal Monitoring from Planet." www.planet.com/industries/maritime/.

Price Cap Coalition. 2024. "Updated Price Cap Coalition Advisory for the Maritime Oil Industry and Related Sectors: Best Practices in Response to Recent Developments in the Maritime Oil Trade." October 21.

Raanan, Tomer. 2023. "US Lawmakers Mulling AIS-Spoofing Bill as Iran's Oil Export Surge." *Lloyd's List*, 31 August.

2024. "Houthi Leader Tells Ships to Deny Israel Links on AIS." *Lloyd's List*, January 8.

Serra-Sogas, Norma, Patrick D. O'Hara, Kim Pearce, Leh Smallshaw, and Rosaline Canessa. 2021. "Using Aerial Surveys to Fill Gaps in AIS Vessel Traffic Data to Inform Threat Assessments, Vessel Management, and Planning." *Marine Policy* 133: 104765.

Shelmerdine, Richard L. 2018. "Teasing Out the Detail: How Our Understanding of Marine AIS Data Can Better Inform Industries, Developments, and Planning." *Marine Policy* 54: 17–25.

Skuld. 2024. "Updated Threats to Shipping in the Red Sea." www.skuld.com/topics/port/piracy/updated-threats-to-shipping-in-the-red-sea/.

Spire. n.d. "Maritime AIS Data for Vessel Tracking." https://spire.com/maritime/.

Svanberg, Martin, Vendela Santén, Axel Hörteborn, Henrik Holm, and Christian Finnsgård. 2019. "AIS in Maritime Research." *Marine Policy* 106: 103520.

Sweeney, Michael. 2024. "'Darking' AIS: US and UK Maritime Agencies Split on Strategy to Protect Vessels in Red Sea." *Intelligence Online*, May 20. www.intelligenceonline.com/government-intelligence/2024/05/20/-darking–ais-us-and-uk-maritime-agencies-split-on-strategy-to-protect-vessels-in-red-sea,110227492-art.

TankerTrackers. n.d. "Tracking for a Transparent Oil Market." https://tankertrackers.com.

Triebert, Christiaan, Blacki Migliozzi, Alexander Cardia, Muyi Xiao, and David Botti. 2023. "Fake Signals and American Insurance: How a Dark Fleet Moves Russian Oil." *New York Times*, May 30.

UKMTO (United Kingdom Maritime Trade Operations). 2024. "Notice, Interim Industry Transit Advice, Southern Red Sea and Gulf of Aden." February 5.

UNSC (United Nations Security Council). 2024a. Resolution 2722. S/RES/2722 (January 10, 2024).

2024b. Resolution 2739. S/RES/2739 (June 27, 2024).

USCG (United States Coast Guard). n.d. "Global Maritime Distress and Safety System." Navigation Center. www.navcen.uscg.gov/global-maritime-distress-and-safety-system.

Vespe, Michele, Harm Greidanus, and Marlene Alvarez Alvarez. 2015. "The Declining Impact of Piracy on Maritime Transport in the Indian Ocean: Statistical Analysis of 5-Year Vessel Tracking Data." *Marine Policy* 59: 9–15.

Weimerkirch, Henri, Julien Collet, Alexandre Corbeau, Adrien Pajot, Floran Hoarau, Cédric Marteau, Dominique Filippi, and Samantha C. Patrick. 2019. "Ocean Sentinel Albatrosses Locate Illegal Vessels and Provide the First Estimate of the Extent of Nondeclared Fishing." *PNAS* 117 (6): 3006–3014.

Windward. n.d. "About Us." https://windward.ai/company/about-us/.

Wolsing, Konrad, Linus Roepert, Jan Bauer, and Klaus Wehrle. 2022. "Anomaly Detection in Maritime AIS Tracks: A Review of Recent Approaches." *Journal of Marine Science and Engineering* 10 (1): 112.

PART IV

Conservation and Use of Marine Resources

8

Blockchain and Protection Community Interests in the Law of the Sea

Krisztina Tilinger

8.1 SUPPORTING THE SUSTAINABLE DEVELOPMENT OF OCEAN GOVERNANCE

Oceans are the lungs of the Earth. They function as a respiratory system for our planet by producing oxygen and absorbing carbon dioxide. The amount of carbon dioxide absorbed by the oceans equals 23 percent of that emitted by all the human activities on Earth during a year. Protecting the healthy functioning of the oceans supports the mitigation of climate change. Because extreme environmental changes negatively influence the climate-sensitive species of the biosphere, the health of the oceans safeguards the biodiversity of our planet. It plays an extremely important role in greenhouse gas management. Marine biodiversity is especially sensitive and vulnerable to climate change: it is impossible for marine species to adapt to the extreme speed of ocean warming, oxygen loss, and acidification. With these issues in mind, the United Nations chose the protection of the seas and oceans as one of its Sustainable Development Goals (SDGs; UNDESA n.d.). SDG 14 is defined as a goal to "conserve and sustainably use the oceans, seas and marine resources for sustainable development." Ocean governance and the international law of the sea can do much to promote the SDGs, especially SDG 14. When setting up appropriate legal frameworks and implementing existing ones, focusing on SDG 14 is key not only to supporting the sustainable development of ocean governance but also to protecting the community interests at sea.

Under sustainable development, we understand the concept of seeking to protect the needs of the present population without compromising the ability to meet the needs of future generations. In this regard, regulatory efforts traditionally face the challenge of balancing the individual interests of States and the common interest of (hu)mankind in protecting the oceans and fostering the long-term sustainability of their use and exploitation. The preservation of the marine environment and the sustainable development of marine resources stand as the most critical elements of the entire international community (Zou and Chang 2023). This chapter analyzes three main elements of international cooperation that can protect the community interests at sea and contribute to the sustainable development of ocean governance: (1) the conservation of marine living resources; (2) the protection of the marine environment; and (3) the conservation of marine biological diversity. The chapter examines how blockchain technology (BCT), as the backbone of the technical revolution and the digital transformation in our century, can and should be introduced into ocean governance by taking into consideration its potential applications when implementing international treaties or other legal instruments under the umbrella of the law of the sea. In such a way, the chapter suggests, BCT can foster the implementation and acceleration of the SDGs.

Regardless of what model or doctrine of internalizing the international legal norms a particular State is following (dualist or monist, self-executing treaty doctrine, or necessity of ratification), the burden of bureaucracy, together with the potential lack of trust of the citizens in the administrative processes, is usually challenging. Consequently, when it comes to ocean governance or the implementation of international treaties, choosing the right management tools or processes strongly impacts the operational effectiveness of all international, regional (European Union), governmental, and local public administrations. Therefore, the two main purposes of applying new technologies in the implementation of international law (other advantages are detailed later in this chapter) are (1) to make the traditional, mainly paper-based and bureaucracy-burdened documentation and administrative processes speedier and more cost-effective; and, more importantly, (2) to strengthen public trust. Blockchain has been proclaimed as the greatest innovation since the invention of the internet. The technology has the ability to ensure that data stored in and shared through the blockchain is authentic. The process lacks the possibility of fraud, corruption, and human error. The importance and relevancy of BCT is reinforced by the fact that the United Nations has begun working on adapting and using BCT within its system (Dumitriu 2020). Petru Dumitriu recommends that "the governing bodies of the United Nations system organizations should ensure that, when applicable, the use of blockchain applications will be integrated, together with other digital technologies, into the innovation strategies and policies adopted by their respective organizations." Dumitriu also recommends that the executive heads of UN organizations, through the relevant coordination mechanisms and with support from the UN International Computing Centre, consider the adoption of a nonbinding interagency blockchain governance framework for use by interested organizations, with a view to ensuring coherent and consistent blockchain approaches across the system. He also refers to the distributed ledger technology as a key contributor for achieving SDG 14. Already the United Nations uses BCT for purposes including tracking commodities (cashmere and cocoa) from point of origin through to sale by the United Nations Development Programme; tracking food donations from retailers to a nongovernmental organization (NGO) that receives donations; a UNICEF Venture Fund that provides product and technical assistance, support for business growth, and access to a network of experts and partners; a cash-based intervention initiative by the World Food Programme and UN Women serving Syrian and Rohingya refugees in Jordan and Bangladesh to coordinate the determination and delivery of mutual assistance in refugee camps; another UN Women project involving a blockchain-based cash transfer test in the Kakuma refugee camp in Kenya; and the Blocks for Transport project of the World Food Programme in Ethiopia and Djibouti aiming to explore ways to improve the timely availability of shipping documents using blockchain (Dumitriu 2020).

A PricewaterhouseCoopers study estimates that BCT has the potential to boost global GDP by US$1.76 trillion over the next decade (PwC 2020), but there are already much higher forecasts available.[1] Measuring the financial implications of using BCT shows not only in its GDP-boosting potential but also in its cost-saving effect. It reduces overhead and transaction costs (IBM n.d.). Eliminating the necessity of third parties, multiple intermediaries, or repeated supervision or controlling activities not only saves related costs but also facilitates trust between citizens and the national or local government. The BCT can also automate and simplify administrative tasks and processes. Most spectacularly, it saves the costs of financial transactions. The data and information stored in the blockchain are accurate, authentic, and unalterable; therefore, applying the technology in public administration ensures transparency and traceability, consequently raising public trust. When the processes become more rapid, all stakeholders (employees and citizens) will be more satisfied. Ultimately, when – with the assistance of BCT – public administration at any level can reach or even exceed the results achieved by traditional processes, the resources will be used in a way that maximizes benefits and minimizes environmental impacts. That is the aim of the SDGs.

8.2 PROTECTION OF THE COMMUNITY INTERESTS AT SEA

Before we dive into the ideas and cases on how BCT can make the implementation of the international law of the sea more effective, it is worth considering the three main elements of the protection of the community interests at sea: the conservation of marine living resources, the protection of the marine environment, and the conservation of marine biological diversity.

8.2.1 *Conservation of Marine Living Resources*

The adverse natural and human events – pollution, climate change, and overfishing – pose risks to the sustainable use of marine living resources. According to the UN Food and Agriculture Organization (FAO), the fraction of fishery stocks within

[1] Gartner's forecasts estimate that blockchain's innovation business value add will exceed US$3.1 trillion by 2030 (Shoker 2021).

biologically sustainable levels decreased to 64.6 percent in 2019, which is 1.2 percent lower than in 2017. In contrast, the percentage of stocks fished at biologically unsustainable levels has been increasing since the late 1970s, from 10 percent in 1974 to 35.4 percent in 2019 (FAO 2022).

The United Nations Convention on the Law of the Sea (UNCLOS)[2] recognizes in its preamble the importance of the protection of marine living resources. Due to the lack of an agreed definition of what conservation means under UNCLOS, the author relies on Article 2 of the 1958 Geneva Convention on Fishing and Conservation of the Living Resources of the High Seas.[3] The Convention stipulates that the expression "conservation of the living resources of the high seas" means the aggregate of the measures rendering possible the optimum sustainable yield from those resources so as to secure a maximum supply of food and other marine products. UNCLOS imposes the necessity to protect the marine living resources on the parties to the Convention. Traditionally, the international law of the sea follows a "zonal management" approach for protecting the marine living resources. The coastal States are specifically obliged, under Article 61(2), to ensure that the maintenance of the living resources in the exclusive economic zone (EEZ) is not endangered by overexploitation. Within this obligation, States are obliged to determine the allowable catch of the living resources in the EEZ and the capacity to harvest them. In addition, UNCLOS stipulates that the freedom of fishing on the high seas is subject to conditions (Articles 116–120). Accordingly, in determining the allowable catch and establishing other conservation measures for the living resources in the high seas, States shall, along with other requirements, take measures to maintain or restore populations of harvested species at levels that can produce the "maximum sustainable yield." The international cooperation imposed on States by Article 118 is implemented through participation in regional fisheries organizations and on the basis of the relevant case law.[4] Noncompliance with the obligation to cooperate in the high seas regarding the conservation of living resources entails breaching Articles 117 and 118 (Tanaka 2019, 281–290). Consequently, the main elements of the conservation of marine living resources for the purpose of the present study are the process of determining the allowable catch and the capacity to harvest natural resources.

However, it must be noted that, according to Professor Yoshifumi Tanaka, the above-referenced traditional zonal management approach to the protection of marine living resources is limited by the ecological reality of marine species. Therefore, it is worth paying attention to the concepts more recently introduced into the international protection of natural resources. One of those is "sustainable

[2] UNCLOS, December 10, 1982, 1833 UNTS 397.

[3] Convention on Fishing and Conservation of the Living Resources of the High Seas, April 29, 1958, 559 UNTS 285.

[4] *Pulp Mills on the River Uruguay (Argentina v. Uruguay)*, 2010 ICJ Rep. 14 (April 20).

development," introduced by the Stockholm Declaration of the UN Conference on the Human Environment in 1972[5] and confirmed in the report of the World Commission on Environment and Development (WCED 1987). Even if the concept would be regarded only as soft law because these documents are nonbinding, during judicial interpretation of UNCLOS it can be taken into consideration when resolving legal conflicts in the field.

8.2.2 *The Protection of the Marine Environment*

The second element of the protection of the community interests at sea analyzed in this chapter is the protection of the marine environment. There is no need to argue that marine pollution endangers both the ecosystem and human health. The importance of the subject was highlighted by the 2024 UN Ocean Decade Conference,[6] which identified marine pollution as one of the Ocean Decade's ten challenges.[7] The main conference outcome – the Barcelona Statement – lists marine pollution monitoring and ocean observations as one of its three priorities.[8]

The international legal framework regarding marine pollution includes numerous international treaties, as well as nonbinding soft law instruments. UNCLOS expressly recognizes in its preamble the importance of the protection and preservation of the marine environment. Article 1(1)(4) defines marine pollution as "the introduction by man, directly or indirectly, of substances or energy into the marine environment, including estuaries, which results or is likely to result in such deleterious effects as harm to living resources and marine life, hazards to human health, hindrance to marine activities, including fishing and other legitimate uses of the sea, impairment of quality for use of sea water and reduction of amenities." The UNCLOS concept for the protection of the marine environment is based on six sources of marine pollution. Land-based marine pollution, together with pollution through or from the atmosphere, seemingly constitutes 80 percent of marine pollution (UNGA 2024, 29). These types of pollution cover industrial, agricultural, and municipal discharges, such as sewage. Vessel-sourced pollution includes any kind of pollution (such as oily residues and fumes) originating from the normal operation of ships, as well as pollution resulting from accidents. Marine pollution originating from seabed activities includes pollution as a result of mining, especially the toxic metals contained in the drilling mud. Continental-shelf drilling is another source of oil pollution. Dumping at sea is defined in Article 1(1)(5)(a) and, as Professor Tanaka

5 Declaration of the United Nations Conference on the Human Environment, June 16, 1972.

6 Held in Barcelona, April 10–12, 2024. In 2017, the UN General Assembly proclaimed the Decade of Ocean Science for Sustainable Development (2021–30).

7 Challenge 1 is to "understand and map land and sea-based sources of pollutants and contaminants and their potential impacts on human health and ocean ecosystems and develop solutions to remove or mitigate them" (UNESCO n.d.).

8 Barcelona Statement, April 12, 2024.

notes, does not include disposal from land, while dumping from vessels is distinguished from vessel-based marine pollution (Tanaka 2019, 324–329). UNCLOS not only contains detailed rules for preventing, reducing, and controlling the different types of marine pollution, but, as a general obligation in Article 192, it imposes a basic obligation of protecting and preserving the marine environment, where "marine environment" means the ocean as a whole, including the high seas. UNCLOS also prescribes for contracting parties the obligation to cooperate on a global basis and, as appropriate, on a regional basis – directly or through competent international organizations – in formulating and elaborating international rules, standards, and recommended practices and procedures, consistent with UNCLOS, for the protection and preservation of the marine environment. The International Maritime Organization plays an important role at the international level, especially in relation to pollution from vessels and pollution by dumping.

8.2.3 *The Conservation of Marine Biological Diversity*

The third element under analysis is the conservation of marine biological diversity. According to Article 2 of the 1992 Convention on Biological Diversity (CBD),[9] "biological diversity" means the variability among living organisms from all sources, including, inter alia, terrestrial, marine, and other aquatic ecosystems and the ecological complexes of which they are a part. This includes diversity within species, between species, and of ecosystems. Unsustainable use of the Earth's natural resources means that we jeopardize them in such a way that they can no longer regenerate. Naturally managed marine areas cannot resist pollution, climate change, and human disturbance and are threatened by fast-growing and nonnative microbes and diseases. Therefore, they offer less shelter for biodiversity. Pollution and the disturbance of larger areas entail hindering the renewal of the natural habitat, increasing the danger of loss of biodiversity. In dedicated reserve areas, which in the oceans are called marine protected areas (MPAs), the management and protection of natural resources, including genetic resources, is more successful. These reserves promote natural self-regulation and can predominate and help long-term sustainability.

UNCLOS has only two general provisions regarding the protection of marine biodiversity. Article 194(5) prescribes the preservation of rare and fragile ecosystems (including endangered species and other forms of marine life), while Article 196(1) places an obligation on States to prevent, reduce, and control pollution of the marine environment (Tanaka 2019, 409–430). The CBD contains general obligations for the conservation of biodiversity and for the sustainable use of its components, as well as fair and equitable sharing of the benefits arising out of the utilization of genetic resources. The provisions apply to the conservation not only of terrestrial

[9] Convention on Biological Diversity, June 5, 1992, 1760 UNTS 79 (CBD).

biodiversity but also of marine biological diversity. When we examine the relationship between these two international agreements, on the basis of Article 22 of the CBD,[10] we see that UNCLOS prevails, unless there is a serious damage or threat to the biodiversity. The most critical weak point of the CBD is that it is not effective for transboundary damages and in areas beyond national jurisdictions. The establishment of MPAs offers the solution of protecting the whole ecosystem of a certain area by taking into consideration the relevance of ecological interactions between marine species – and not only areas under national jurisdiction, but in the high seas as well. At the dawn of the Agreement on Marine Biological Diversity of Areas Beyond National Jurisdiction (High Seas Treaty),[11] the subject of MPAs and the protection of marine biological diversity is getting even more international attention. As evidence for that, the Second UN Ocean Conference, held in 2022, yielded as one of its fifty pledges an investment of at least US$1 billion to support the creation, expansion, and management of MPAs and Indigenous and locally governed marine and coastal areas by 2030 (Kosolapova and Wagner 2025).

After this analysis of the relevant legal framework containing the international obligations that are under research, the chapter introduces BCT, the tool recommended for use in implementing those obligations.

8.2.4 *What Is Blockchain and How Can International Law Benefit from It?*

Blockchain is a disruptive information technology that enables stakeholders to track transactions recorded in a public (or private) and secure, cryptographically verified database. Let's discuss the meaning of each element of the above definition. We call disruptive any solution that is new and innovative compared to an existing technological process or mechanism. Disruption can have many benefits for society, including improving public governance by reducing costs and the time burden of administrative processes. However, it is necessary to ensure that an increase in automation does not have a negative effect – for example, on employment – that might result in the introduction of new technology causing damage that undermines its benefits.

Cryptographic verification ensures the security and safety of records, ensuring that stakeholders can trust that the data introduced and stored in the system are authentic and that the events or transactions recorded are without the risk of fraud, error, or

[10] Article 22 provides: "(1) The provisions of this Convention shall not affect the rights and obligations of any Contracting Party deriving from any existing international agreement, except where the exercise of those rights and obligations would cause a serious damage or threat to biological diversity. (2) Contracting Parties shall implement this Convention with respect to the marine environment consistently with the rights and obligations of States under the law of the sea."

[11] Agreement under the United Nations Convention on the Law of the Sea on the Conservation and Sustainable Use of Marine Biological Diversity of Areas beyond National Jurisdiction, A/CONF.232/2023/4 (June 19, 2023) (High Seas Treaty).

inaccuracy and are, therefore, true. Blockchain is a type of distributed ledger technology by which transactions are stored in a chain of blocks and each block contains the same updated (live) information. In this way, each participant (node) of the system, having a copy of the whole ledger of the blockchain, can trust that the information contained therein is up-to-date and authentic. The so-called consensus protocol of the technology essentially refers to a decentralized agreement on the validity of the transaction. This protocol allows only correct blocks to be added to the ledger. In case of a malicious attempt to add a wrong block, the honest participants can refuse it. In this way, the authenticity of the ledger can be easily maintained.

On the basis of accessibility, we can differentiate four basic types of blockchain: public, private, hybrid, and consortium. Public blockchain is open to the public without any restriction. Any participant can act as a node and be part of the decision-making process. In these permissionless blockchains, anyone can verify transactions, and valid transactions cannot be changed, unless someone gains 51 percent or more of the computing power. The public blockchain is independent of any organization, and only computers connected to the blockchain are needed to see or share data on it. This type of blockchain is used mainly for cryptocurrencies, but it is also a perfect technical solution for real estate records or validating documents. Private blockchains are only open for certain individuals within a group, who will receive permission for participating in the given blockchain as nodes. They are usually controlled by only one entity and are typically used within the corporate environment, where they are usually applied in supply chain management or asset ownership control. Hybrid blockchains are a mixture of public and private, meaning that part of the blockchain is public, while the remainder is private. In this way, there is a possibility to keep confidential some chosen information within a public blockchain and give access to those data only to select persons. The confidential data are also verifiable. This concept is well suited to medical or real estate records. Consortium blockchain is also partly private and partly public. It differs from the hybrid blockchain in that in a consortium, multiple organizational members can collaborate on a decentralized network. Essentially a consortium blockchain is a private blockchain with limited access to a particular group, eliminating the risks that come with a single entity controlling the network on a private blockchain. This type of blockchain is widely used in banking and research activities.

The first product of BCT is Bitcoin, the well-known cryptocurrency, which was created in 2008. Since then, the technology has proved to be reliable and has found its way into other applications outside of the world of finance. Besides securing financial transactions, BCT is applied in, among other fields, healthcare (such as digital medical records), education, secure transactions, and data exchange. Governments are using BCT to set up reliable voting systems and for securing identification, while industry is using it in supply chain management and transportation. We have already seen smart contracts used for selling and buying real estate.

One of the largest achievements of BCT, from which international law can benefit, is its decentralized nature. The technology allows control over transactions, processes, and databases in a noncentralized way, as detailed above. It provides a secure and reliable record of activities and the exchange or sharing of information in a decentralized way, which ensures and increases trust, transparency, and reliability in the given system. The idea of using BCT for the implementation and execution of international treaties is grounded in the fact that, in the international community, there is no hierarchy among stakeholders, meaning that they act based on the same strategic framework as do the nodes in the blockchain. Nowadays, when the emphasis on the importance of digitalized information is shifting toward the cooperative and fruitful coexistence of humans and machines, it is more than necessary to look into the methods from which legal professionals can benefit and show not only acceptance but also highly useful exploitation of the technological developments in terms of the implementation of international agreements.

According to Koshzhanova Baktygul, the enforcement of international law could be accomplished through the blockchain. Taking that idea further, blockchain could strengthen the assurance that international law should not be a burden, as States might see it, and may actually be a tool for order in the world. When referring to the role of blockchain in international law, Baktygul cites the speech of Prince Albert at the 1851 International Exhibition in London: "Nobody who has paid any attention to the peculiar features of our present era will doubt for a moment that we are living a period of the most wonderful transition which tends rapidly to accomplish that great end to which indeed all history points – the realization of the unity of humankind." Baktygul argues that this is the exact change that is coming to life through blockchain and would bring authoritative power to international law. He states that, by being decentralized, blockchain perhaps allows itself to bypass domestic law, but international law could establish jurisdiction if States are able to reach agreement (Baktygul 2023). There is no better time for stepping forward with the application of BCT to the implementation of international treaties. At the time of writing, the international community is preparing for the *Our Ocean Conference 2025* to promote global actions for a sustainable ocean and to discuss "Ocean Digital," a concept that brings together the ocean industry and digital technology to serve as an implementation tool to achieve a sustainable ocean.

8.3 ADVANTAGES AND DISADVANTAGES OF USING BCT

There are numerous advantages in the application of BCT to the implementation of the international law of the sea and to ocean governance. The technology enables the recording of data and information in a ledger, safeguards the authenticity and security of such data, and ensures that the data are not corrupted or manipulated. In addition, the entries are time-stamped, which enables the traceability and tracking of transactions. The technology also ensures that all stakeholders can immediately access the data stored on the blockchain. The necessity of repeated key-in is avoided, making the processes based on BCT faster, cheaper, and more effective. The supervision and control of documents and processes by authorities are easier than with traditional paper-based solutions. When accidents or incidents do occur, information sharing can be immediate, enabling faster decision-making and reaction. BCT can improve the quality of supply and value chains. It can combat fraud and, with the involvement of local communities, offer incentives for environmentally friendly behaviors that can mitigate poverty. Considering all of these factors, BCT can accelerate the achievement of SDG 14.

Individuals and NGOs are already using BCT to protect the marine environment. It is now time for governments and international organizations to harness BCT and benefit from its potential to solve global challenges (Buckup and Waughray 2020). For this purpose, close cooperation between the sectors that already have experience with BCT and the governments and international organizations is required, together with the establishing of appropriate safeguards in order to build trust in the technology. From a technological point of view, the most important aspect of such cooperation is to harmonize the blockchain platforms to be used at an early-enough stage in order to avoid unnecessary costs, which are generated by using different platforms. A blockchain platform is the software on which the blockchain is built (for example, ethereum, solana, hyperledger fabric, and corda). Blockchain platforms differ in the consensus mechanism they are using (the most widely used are Proof of Work and Proof of Stake), resulting in differences in speed, stability, and the level of decentralization.

If the international community is now willing and inclined to collaborate, implementing BCT to comply with the obligations imposed by international treaties could be fruitful and more rapid. Also, the costs of implementing BCT could be borne by governments or by international funds, encouraging private actors to participate in the use of technology. Institutional openness can contribute to technological progress; therefore, an international organization could play a leading role by serving as an example of how to use BCT. In this way, the organization could also increase public trust in the technology. Roger Brownsword goes so far as to suggest setting up an international agency to deal with emerging technologies, with a special focus on legal and regulatory issues (Brownsword 2022). The agency would serve as an intelligence hub and would be the result of a natural evolution from the network of national and regional hubs. This correlates with the author's idea above of building up the use of BCT within the international organizational environment, based on the experience of local or regional private (both individual and corporate) or nongovernmental communities that are already successfully applying the technology.

The disadvantages of BCT are its high costs, the relevance of choosing the right blockchain platform, and the potential for integration problems. Introducing a new technology into an already existing system, or setting up a totally new system or process for that purpose, obviously requires significant investment. Developers need to be paid for their time, and there is also a price for the technology as a product. Training staff, as well as those who will be using the technology, requires much effort and expense. In addition, consulting fees must be paid when resolving the integration of the new technology into the existing system. The cost-effectiveness of using BCT will be evident only on a long-term basis. Also, when choosing the right blockchain platform for a given task, careful consideration must be given in order to avoid any future problems. The platform must suit the requirements of the task, and interoperability must be fulfilled. However, these tasks are usually performed by the software-producing organization contracted for the development of the blockchain (Farshidi et al. 2020). Integration issues – meaning that BCT is usually applied in an already-existing system or must communicate or be compatible with an already-existing technological environment – must be handled as well; this is also the responsibility of the developers or consulting experts. However, governments and international organizations must be aware of the necessity of disclosing and communicating all relevant information regarding the existing technological environment in its widest possible aspect (Rosencrance 2023).

Next, the author demonstrates how, by assisting in the implementation of the treaties of the international law of the sea, BCT can serve the protection of community interests at sea and accelerate the SDGs.

8.4 BLOCKCHAIN TECHNOLOGY IN RESOURCES AND THE ENVIRONMENT

8.4.1 *Conservation of Marine Living Resources*

Ocean policy handles the conservation of marine living resources through planned resource management to prevent overexploitation. These processes include determining the allowable catch and the capacity to harvest natural resources. For monitoring and measuring excess capacity at the international level, clear definitions and measures are required to develop international consensus and cooperation for global and regional plans of action to monitor and reduce excess capacity (Kirkley and Squires 2018). The governments engaged in determining the Total Allowable Catch (TAC) are allocating Individual Fishing Quotas (IFQs) to individual fishers who effectively own this share of the fish stock. If a fish stock increases, governments can increase TACs and fishers can then catch more fish. In the case of Individual Transferable Quotas (ITQs), a fisher can also sell or lease their quota; thus, the value of their "stock" increases with increasing fish stock (Douglas 2018). IFQs are based on the catching history of the individual fishers, meaning that providing data to the governments about the number of fishers' catches is essential in determining IFQs and, therefore, TACs. According to the FAO, less than 40 percent of nations have adequate datasets on what their fishers are catching.

This is especially concerning in developing countries, where, very probably, the fishers are not comfortable with giving access to their fishing history data. In these circumstances, the solutions that blockchain-based projects can provide are of great benefit to ocean governance.

One example is the Fishcoin project, which incentivizes fishers as well as other stakeholders in the fishery supply chain to share data. When they enter data about their catches into the database, they receive a certain amount of cryptocurrency called Fishcoin. Both the cryptocurrency and the activities of entering and sharing data into the system use BCT. Through the widespread adaptation of Fishcoin or similar projects, data-sharing can be not only encouraged but also used as a tool for combating illegal fishing by giving credibility only to those catches registered in the project databases.

Another example is the World Wildlife Foundation's blockchain project From Bait to Plate, which aims to track tuna catches with the assistance of BCT. Fish caught are tagged with Radio Frequency Identification and allocated a QR code, allowing them to be traced to the final retail delivery. Thanks to the benefits of the BCT, tuna-fishing could be more controlled and its sustainability could be achieved (Velasco González-Camino 2019). In this way, the legality of the catch can be ensured and proved in a trusted way to the consumer. Shermin Voshmgir, a blockchain expert and social scientist, called this project the best practice approach to the implementation of blockchain in supply chains in the context of developing countries (Voshmgir et al. 2019). However, it should be noted that when applying BCT in different projects, different types of technologies should be chosen and adapted, using different platforms, and the forms of data collection shall be adjusted to the level of traceability (Pita and Costa 2023).

8.4.2 *Protection of the Marine Environment*

When we think about the protection of the marine environment, the most obvious use of BCT is tracking and tracing the pollution itself. This tool can be used for most types of marine pollution, whether originating from land, vessels, or seabed activities or from dumping at sea. Sensing pollution at its source – either with various sensing devices or, according to the recent trends, with autonomous robots (Islam et al. 2020) – and then entering the sensing data into BCT-based databases allow the use of BCT for tracking and tracing the waste from its source to the disposal. The life cycle and journey of the waste, which has been entered into a digital record created in that way, can then be traced and controlled easily. The same method might be applied to the plastic debris removed from the ocean to ensure traceability and transparency through its journey to the disposal site. The benefits of blockchain – such as the formalization of the recycling profession, the creation of economic benefits, global cooperation, the introduction of digital currency systems, increased transaction security, and a transparent and efficient recycling chain – in marine debris management have already been studied and proven (Gong et al. 2022).

The blockchain-based project called ReSea uses the above method, with local collectors of plastic waste entering data into the system by using their smartphones. The Project Plastic Bank identifies the places in the world that are the largest sources of land-based plastic pollution and incentivizes local individuals to gather plastic materials and exchange them for money and access to social benefits. Diatom DAO is a community-driven decentralized autonomous organization (DAO) aiming to help reduce the plastic in oceans and, in this way, contribute to the protection of the marine environment. The blockchain-based project is incentivizing individuals and organizations by providing them with tokenized Plastic Removal Credits for proven plastic removal. These tokens can then be bought by governments or institutions to offset their carbon footprint. Finally, the funds collected in this way are used to fund projects that aim to remove plastic from the oceans (Diordievic n.d.). One of the most innovative aspects of the project is that the plastic removed is classified and the tokens provided as incentives are distributed according to that classification. In this way, fair distribution is guaranteed.

8.4.3 *Conservation of Marine Biological Diversity*

In the field of the conservation of marine biological diversity, BCT could be applied in the surveillance of MPAs. BCT applications are already used in monitoring systems, and scholars are suggesting applying the technology for environmental monitoring. The advantage of using BCT in maritime monitoring systems is that, because the technology is secure, it resolves the cybersecurity issue faced by traditional technologies. BCT also ensures the integrity, authenticity, and availability of relevant navigation data (Freire et al. 2022). The COVID-19 pandemic has proven that MPA management needs to be supported by innovative technologies, tools, and ethical financing mechanisms that are not only effective but also resilient (Phua et al. 2021). Dominic Waughray, the head of the World Economic Forum's Centre for Global Public Goods, has argued that blockchain could help to enforce the new High Seas Treaty by tracking fishing on the high seas and identifying illegal behavior (Scruggs 2018). These improvements are also necessary for achieving SDG 14. In March 2018, the Blockchain Commission and the UN Development Programme issued a white paper titled "The Future Is Decentralised: Block Chains, Distributed Ledgers, & the Future of Sustainable Development" (Wigley and Cary 2017). The paper recognized that BCT-based pilot projects have demonstrated the viability and benefits of employing the technology for the public good and that BCT can, therefore, be a valuable tool for governments, regulators, private companies, and civil society to establish trust, tackle corruption, and distribute resources. Consequently, it is an appropriate tool for accelerating the achievement of SDGs. As other scholars have argued, the history of biodiversity governance demonstrates the limited efficacy of conventional solutions and the lack of sufficiently powerful political coalitions to address the root causes of biodiversity loss. History also suggests that technological evolution is to a certain degree inevitable. In addition, technologies can catalyze structural social, political, and economic change, often in surprising ways (Rabitz et al. 2022). Therefore, the use of new technologies, including BCT, should be introduced into environmental protection areas, like the conservation of marine biodiversity, through only after careful consideration and thorough technical and technological discussions and tests.

Two projects serve as examples of applying BCT to the implementation of obligations imposed on States by international treaties. Both examples are already working: the electronic bill of lading has been widely accepted among members of the international community, while the electronic CITES permission is still awaiting approval.

8.4.4 *Electronic Data Interchange*

Traditionally, bills of lading are paper documents for goods transported via shipping, based on which the possessor can demand delivery of the goods. Besides being a title, a bill of lading also serves as a receipt for the goods and the contract of carriage of goods by sea. Bills of lading constitute a template that contains data and information about the contracting parties, the shipment, and the goods. It must be signed by the shipper, in case it is required by the master, and later by the receiver. The preparation, signature, and transfer of the document, when it is paper-based, entail the risk of fraud, manipulation, human error, theft, loss, and, in many cases, delays in delivery. Article 8 of the Rotterdam Rules (UNGA 2009)[12] allows transporting the documents under the Convention in an electronic record should the carrier and the shipper consent to doing so. A digitalized version of the bill of lading – the electronic bill of lading (eB/L) – executes an electronic data interchange, sending data from one computer to another. The eB/L uses BCT to store the information and data entered and contained therein. The data and information are the same as in the paper-based form, as are the functions and purposes. However, the method of transmission is automatic in the case of eB/L. Legally, both versions have the same effect, but eB/L has many advantages compared to the traditional paper form. Due to its electronic nature and its use of BCT, eB/L is more secure and efficient. It is easier to track, its cost are lower, it has lower environmental impact, and it ensures easier compliance with regulatory obligations. It must be emphasized that blockchain systems can improve the process of data exchange in a way traditional systems

[12] United Nations Convention on Contracts for the International Carriage of Goods Wholly or Partly by Sea, December 11, 2008 (Rotterdam Rules).

cannot. Article 14(3) of the Hamburg Rules[13] also allows the electronic signature of the bill of lading. Literally, there is no legal obstacle in the relevant international maritime law to the use of eB/Ls. Consequently, eB/Ls have already been used and accepted as a practical solution that is more secure, reliable, rapid, and, most importantly, decentralized, allowing the interchange of data contained in the bill of lading without the need for intervention by any other party. The States allowing and benefiting from eB/Ls (such as Denmark, Estonia, Finland, France, Greece, Italy, the Korean Republic, the Netherlands, Norway, Spain, and Switzerland) are recognizing and regulating their use in the maritime industry in their national legislations. In doing so, they are accepting eB/Ls as valid and enforceable (Zhu et al. 2022). Stakeholders of the supply chain (such as freight forwarders, shippers, ports and terminals, intermodal operators, ocean carriers, brokers, and government authorities) enjoy secure, transparent, and immediate data transfer through the eB/L. The information shared can easily be tracked and stored, with triggers for immediate action when and if necessary throughout the shipment's journey. Thus, eB/L is a relevant example of when and how the international legal obligation can be implemented successfully with the assistance of BCT.

BIMCO (Baltic and International Maritime Council), one of the largest shipping associations in the world, has developed and published an eB/L (eB/L Standard) for the bulk shipping sector. Historically, the possibility of using eB/Ls has been present in the industry for more than two decades, but the obstacles (mainly the lack of interoperability) that prevented its use could not be overcome. Setting up a standard for the eB/L means that the users of such a standard can enjoy the smooth transmission of their eB/Ls through the available platforms.

According to Ali Abbas Khayoon Al-Naseri, electronic transport records can perform the first two functions of traditional paper bills of lading – that is, as receipts for goods and as containing or evidencing the contract of carriage of goods under the Rotterdam Rules. He also concludes in his PhD thesis that negotiable eB/Ls or electronic transport records can function as documents of title that are equivalent to negotiable paper bills of lading under the Rotterdam Rules and other model laws and contract forms (Al-Naseri 2020, 247–248).

8.4.5 *Electronic Permitting*

According to the Convention on International Trade in Endangered Species of Wild Fauna and Flora (CITES),[14] the international trade (export, import, reexport, and introduction from the sea) of the endangered species listed in its Annexes I–III is

[13] United Nations Convention on the Carriage of Goods by Sea, March 31, 1978, 1695 UNTS 3 (Hamburg Rules).

[14] Convention on International Trade in Endangered Species of Wild Fauna and Flora, March 3, 1973, 993 UNTS 243 (CITES).

subject to a permit procedure. The difference between the species included in the Annexes is the level and extension of their endangerment. The contracting parties to the Convention are obliged to designate management authorities to deal with the administration of the permits. The system is aimed at restricting the international trade of endangered plants and animals to duly justified reasons (for example, scientific purposes or exhibition) and, in other cases, ensuring that specimens have been obtained legally and that their survival is being guaranteed. The CITES permit procedures form a complex system for which the conditions and requirements are laid down in the Convention itself. The export and reexport permits, for example, can be obtained only where an import permit has already been issued, which guarantees that the condition for the issuance of the export permit has been met. Originally and traditionally, the acquisition and issuance of CITES permits have been performed on paper, and the possession and representation of those paper-based documents during border control or official inspections were necessary for the execution of the trade. The idea of an electronic CITES Permit System (eCITES) has been accepted by the Conference of the Parties in Resolution 12.3 (CITES COP 2022), on permits and certificates, and its implementation has been elaborated in several other resolutions and decisions. The underlying motivation is a smoother and more transparent implementation of the Convention. The BCT provides a secure solution for cooperation and rapid information exchange among all stakeholders and eases the work of the national governance in combating illegal trade. The framework of eCITES, as an online permit system, has already been detailed and is operational. The contracting parties have already begun its implementation, with some of them partially introducing the framework. The Secretariat of the Convention manages the digital toolkit for implementing the system.

The eCITES governance is a perfect example of how administrative procedures that aim to implement an international treaty can be managed by harnessing the power of emerging technologies. The governance is provided by a so-called Intersessional Working Group on Electronic Systems and Information Technology, and a Task Force has been established to share experiences and information related to the piloting and testing of eCITES. The standard implementation approach is stipulated in the eCITES Implementation Framework, which provides guidance for country managers to implement the system locally. Moreover, the toolkit is available for ensuring harmonious formats, protocols, and standards within the system. In addition, the Secretariat provides advisory services and support for the implementation of eCITES, subject to the availability of funding.

Because of its partial implementation, eCITES still awaits the approval of the international community. However, its practical solution can be used as an analogy for the permitting system under the international law of the sea. It is important to mention here that the acceptance of the technology can be strengthened if BCT is supported in more than one field of international law, with its use and application becoming more widespread. This would entail the significance and acceptance of

BCT becoming stronger in the implementation of international treaties. One step forward in raising trust in the system was achieved on April 2, 2024, when the CITES Secretariat received the prestigious Trade Facilitation Innovation Award from the Asia Pacific Trade Facilitation Forum in recognition of the Convention's electronic permitting systems. The Secretariat highlighted the comprehensive set of standards, tools, and guidance for eCITES implementation and its benefits to the parties. According to the Secretariat, along with other benefits, eCITES has contributed to the SDGs – specifically SDG 13 (Climate Action), SDG 14 (Life Below Water), SDG15 (Life on Land), and SDG17 (Partnerships for the Goals) – by increasing access to reliable wildlife data; improving sustainability, legality, and traceability of wildlife trade; and enhancing economic opportunities for Indigenous peoples and local communities involved in trade.

8.5 LEGAL AND REGULATORY CHALLENGES

How the BCT is designed and implemented influences the type of situation to which it is applied. The diversity of possible applications entails that BCT can raise many different legal issues, both international and domestic. The use of BCT is encouraged only where the end product (database or software) or the process is legally valid and enforceable. Widespread exploitation of BCT would be supported where digital documents are acceptable – not only in business but also, for example, before courts and government authorities. The legal route for achieving this is twofold: setting up an international legal framework for regulating technology and its use, and/or implementing domestic laws and regulations. As seen in the previous chapters, some international treaties reference the use of electronic means of recording and signature, and national laws have begun to regulate crypto assets. However, BCT itself, for the time being, does not have any specific international treaty or domestic legal regulation. Some scholars even claim that it merely subsists outside of the legal realm, which raises several questions and concerns (De Filippi et al. 2022).

First, in order to provide regulatory certainty, all technicalities of BCT should be listed and understood by the regulators so that they are able to draft relevant legislation. Considering the rapid developments and constant changes in technology, this is almost – if not completely – impossible. Therefore, regulators face the same problem as with any other emerging technology. However, this should not be an obstacle to regulation. It is enough counterargument simply to refer to the recent adoption of the world's first comprehensive AI law, the European Union's Artificial Intelligence Act,[15] which, although applicable only at the regional level, is nonetheless a key milestone in the possibility of drafting and gaining acceptance, not to

[15] Regulation (EU) 2024/1689 of the European Parliament and of the Council of June 13, 2024, laying down harmonized rules on AI and amending Regulations (EC) No 300/2008, (EU)

mention the harmonization of the regulation of emerging technologies among several national jurisdictions.

Another obstacle limiting the use of BCT is the lack of admissibility of the data and information stored in the blockchain as evidence in litigation processes before courts (Berto 2019) or in other official procedures before authorities. According to both common law and continental law countries, most States are inclined to accept BCT data as evidence due to the trend of digital transformation in judicial administration worldwide. Consequently, in both criminal investigations (Li et al. 2021) and civil procedures, the data and information stored in the blockchain might be used as evidence. However, the legal validation of this practice should be under domestic laws, which obviously would be encouraged where the international legal instruments also recognize BCT as a safe and trustable technology.

Because the data and information stored on the ledger are accessible to all stakeholders (anybody in public blockchain, and users with permissions in private blockchain), data privacy and data security, along with the protection of intellectual property, are valid legal concerns. These issues might be solved by ensuring that the system is technically secure and that the data entered into the public ledger do not contain confidential or legally protected information. With private or permissioned blockchain, the appropriate identification and strict permission rules need to apply to ensure that no unauthorized persons have access to the information stored on the blockchain.

As a solution to overcome the legal challenges of BCT, a regional hub – the European Blockchain Regulatory Sandbox (EBRS) – was created by the European Commission with the purpose of initiating regulatory dialogues to increase legal certainty for innovative blockchain solutions. The EBRS, which is open to EU member States and to Norway and Liechtenstein, is funded by the Digital Europe Programme. Companies, NGOs, and even public bodies might apply to participate. The program runs from 2023 to 2026, supporting twenty projects annually – including public sector use cases on the European Blockchain Services Infrastructure. Projects are chosen through calls for expressions of interest. The partnership cooperates closely with other EU initiatives, such as the EU Digital Finance Platform and the AI Sandboxes. Legal advice and regulatory guidance are given to members. The program also aims to identify and communicate best practices.

The European Commission's third report on EU Blockchain Ecosystem Developments (EUBOF 2024) details significant growth in blockchain applications across various sectors, including finance, education, government services, and supply chain management. Particularly noteworthy is the adoption of blockchain in national infrastructures and public services, where countries such as Estonia and

No 167/2013, (EU) No 168/2013, (EU) 2018/858, (EU) 2018/1139, and (EU) 2019/2144 and Directives 2014/90/EU, (EU) 2016/797, and (EU) 2020/1828 (Artificial Intelligence Act).

Lithuania have emerged as leaders. These nations have integrated BCT into government operations to enhance efficiency, transparency, and public trust.

Considering the legal challenges, the question of whether we need new international agreements for BCT is unavoidable. It is beyond any doubt that a general framework agreement would be useful to stipulate the importance and declare the legality of BCT. However, the lack of such an international treaty should not be an obstacle to applying the technology. National laws could and should deal with the legal rules to be applied for the BCT. Until then, soft law and best practices should provide enough guidance for allowing the safe and fruitful use of BCT.

8.6 CONCLUSION

As is obvious from the above examples, the conservation of marine living resources, the protection of the marine environment, and the conservation of marine biological diversity can benefit from the innovative solutions introduced by BCT, which has the ability to reduce the burden of documentation, ensure security and safety of data, eliminate fraud and human errors in processes, and avoid delays. Marine conservation and global seafood production networks have a trust problem (Howson 2020). Through BCT, transparency is ensured when tracking fishing and any other activities throughout the whole supply chain. In dealing manually with the data and documentation that must be handled during international transactions, numerous actions must be repeated and the involvement of many different parties is unavoidable. In addition, the supervision of those documents and processes significantly slows down transactions. The use of BCT and other emerging technologies can assist in speeding up transactions along the whole supply and value chain, as well as providing for the security and safety of data, ensuring the rapid sharing of information in such a way that it contributes to efficient, trustable, and transparent processes. Contrary to manual systems, blockchain platforms are decentralized, which results in a system where all stakeholders (shipping companies, fisheries organizations, port authorities, and regulatory authorities) can access the same information instantly when they are registered in the ledger (Mumtaz et al. 2024). Through this practice, not only accountability but also sustainability can be ensured, because the whole net is built up in a more secure and reliable way. Moreover, within regional fisheries organizations that play a crucial role in the conservation of marine resources, monetary incentives can be provided for encouraging positive environmental behavior. In addition, blockchain-based financing might also be used for secure, transparent, and trustable peer-to-peer financing in such a way that combating illegal fishing can also benefit from the technology (Pfreundt 2018).

One other significant aspect of BCT is its rapidity. When one enters data into the system, it becomes immediately accessible to other stakeholders. This feature can be especially important in the event of an incident – for example, if a dangerous substance is dumped into the sea – or a natural disaster, when a rapid response might be crucial in saving living creatures or preventing or eliminating the harm caused. International transactions can also benefit from this feature, as can value chains, where production, transport, and various stages of the supply chain can access all data entered without any delay. Performing these activities manually and through burdensome documentation, and under human supervision and control, impedes the rapid actions required by the circumstances in order to mitigate the consequences of an incident (Berman et al. 2020).

Based on the obligations prescribed by the UNCLOS and other instruments of the international law of the sea, and taking into consideration the cases above, it is the author's opinion that BCT might be used within the following areas to ensure a more rapid, cost-effective, and trustworthy solution for complying with the given obligation:

- the conservation of marine living resources:
  - allocating TACs;
  - collecting and verifying data and information;
  - monitoring compliance with the agreed rules, standards, and conservation measures;
  - providing monetary incentives to regional coastal communities for encouraging positive behaviors; and
  - peer-to-peer financing;
- the protection of the marine environment:
  - registering and entering pollution data;
  - monitoring waste disposal activities at the source of pollution;
  - tracking systems for waste management on ships in order to control dumping at sea; and
  - setting up a harmonized reporting system; and
- the conservation of marine biological diversity:
  - conducting surveillance and management of MPAs.

Through application of BCT when implementing international law of the sea instruments, the conservation and sustainable use of the oceans and their resources – and "the future we want" – will be enhanced and accelerated. The advantages of BCT outweigh its disadvantages, making it an extraordinary tool for protecting the community interests at sea and for supporting the sustainable development of ocean governance. All three elements of the protection of the community interests at sea that have been analyzed in this chapter – the conservation of marine living resources, the protection of the marine environment, and the conservation of marine biological diversity – can benefit from the technology. The legal and regulatory challenges of BCT can be overcome, and although they should be considered carefully during the use of BCT, they should not be obstacles to its use. The author concludes that to harness the power of BCT, a new international agreement would be useful. However, the lack of such an agreement should not delay the use of the technology, since national rules and best practices could provide proper guidance and safeguards for the international community.

REFERENCES

Al-Naseri, Ali Abbas Khayoon. 2020. "The Legal Recognition of Electronic Bills of Lading." PhD diss., World Maritime University.

Baktygul, Koshzhanova. 2023. "International Law in the Era of Blockchain: Law Semiotics." *International Journal for the Semiotics of Law* 36: 2305–2322.

Berman, Ivan, Enrica Zereik, Aleksandr Kapitonov, Fabio Bonsignorio, Alisher Khassanov, Aziza Oripova, Sergei Lonshakov, and Vitaly Bulatov. 2020. "Trustable Environmental Monitoring by Means of Sensors Networks on Swarming Autonomous Marine Vessels and Distributed Ledger Technology." *Frontiers in Robotics and AI* 7: 70.

Berto, Rebecca. 2019. "Blockchain Records: Is the Evidence Admissible? A Challenge for European Member States." *Civil Procedure Review* 10 (3): 49–66.

Brownsword, Roger. 2022. *Rethinking Law, Regulation, and Technology*. Edward Elgar.

Buckup, Sebastian, and Dominic Waughray. 2020. "How to Reverse the World's Trust Deficit Disorder." *Foreign Policy*, January 16. https://foreignpolicy.com/2020/01/16/public-private-partnership-wef-davos-world-trust-deficit-disorder/.

CITES COP (CITES Conference of the Parties). 2022. "Permits and Certificates." Conf. 12.3 (Rev. CoP19).

De Filippi, Primavera, Morshed Mannan, and Wessel Reijers. 2022. "The Alegality of Blockchain Technology." *Policy and Society* 41 (3): 358–372.

Diordievic, Ivan. n.d. "Diatom DAO Review: Ocean Depollution Powered by DAOs." *Unblock*. https://unblock.net/diatom-dao-review/.

Douglas, Alistair. 2018. "Rights to Fish & Data Rights: How Blockchain Technologies Could Help." *Medium*, July 13. https://medium.com/eachmile/rights-to-fish-data-rights-how-blockchain-technologies-could-help-95823bb5eb19.

Dumitriu, Petru. 2020. "Blockchain Applications in the United Nations System: Towards a State of Readiness: Report of the Joint Inspection Unit." JIU/REP/2020/7.

EUBOF (European Blockchain Observatory and Forum). 2024. *EU Blockchain Ecosystem Developments* 3.

FAO (Food and Agriculture Organization of the United Nations). 2022. *The State of World Fisheries and Aquacultures*.

Farshidi, Siamak, Slinger Jansen, Sergio España, and Jacco Verkleij. 2020. "Decision Support for Blockchain Platform Selection: Three Industry Case Studies." *IEEE Transactions on Engineering Management* 67 (4): 1109–1128.

Freire, Warlley Paulo, Wilson S. Melo, Jr., Vinicius D. do Nascimento, Paulo R. M. Nascimento, and Alan Oliveira de Sá. 2022. "Towards a Secure and Scalable Maritime Monitoring System Using Blockchain and Low-Cost IoT Technology." *Sensors* 22 (13): 4895.

Gong, Yu, Yang Wang, Regina Frei, Bill Wang, and Changping Zhao. 2022. "Blockchain Application in Circular Marine Plastic Debris Management." *Industrial Marketing Management* 102: 164–176.

Howson, Peter. 2020. "Building Trust and Equity in Marine Conservation and Fisheries Supply Chain Management with Blockchain." *Marine Policy* 115: 103873.

IBM. n.d. "Benefits of Blockchain." www.ibm.com/topics/benefits-of-blockchain#:~:text=By%20greatly%20reducing%20paperwork%20and,or%20middlemen%20to%20verify%20transactions.

Islam, Anik, Kazi Sadia, Md Masuduzzaman, and Soo Young Shin. 2020. "BUMAR: A Blockchain-Empowered UAV-Assisted Smart Surveillance Architecture for Marine Areas." *ICCA 2020: Proceedings of the International Conference on Computing Advancements*, Article No. 7.

Kirkley, James E., and Dale Squires. 2018. "Capacity and Capacity Utilization in Fishing Industries." *VIMS Books and Book Chapters* 61.

Kosolapova, Elena, and Lynn Wagner. 2025. "2025: Advancing the Pact for the Future as Nations United." IISD, January 15. https://sdg.iisd.org/commentary/policy-briefs/2025-advancing-the-pact-for-the-future-as-nations-united/.

Li, Meng, Chhagan Lal, Mauro Conti, and Donghui Hu. 2021. "LEChain: A Blockchain-Based Lawful Evidence Management Scheme for Digital Forensics." *Future Generation Computer Systems* 115: 406–420.

Mumtaz, Ubaid Ullah, Paul Bergey, and Nicholas Letch. 2024. "Assessing the Role of Blockchain Technology for Marine Bunkering Operations: A Case Study of Task Technology Fit." *Marine Policy* 159: 105909.

Pfreundt, Ulrike. 2018. "How to Harness Blockchain Technology for Marine Conservation." Institute of Environmental Engineering, Swiss Federal Institute of Technology.

Phua, Carol, Dominic Andradi-Brown, Sangeeta Mangubhai, Gabby N. Ahmadia, Shauna L. Mahajan, Kirk Larsen, Stephen Friel, Russell Reichelt, Marc Hockings, David Gill, Laura Veverka, Richard Anderson, Lovasoa Cédrique Augustave, Awaludinnoer Ahmad, Tadzio Bervoets, Kitty Brayne, Rili Djohani, Joan Kawaka, Fabian Kyne, January Ndagala, Jenny Oates, Kennedy Osuka, Mosor Prvan, Nirmal Shah, Fabio Vallarola, Lauren Wenzel, Hesti Widodo, and Sue Wells. 2021. "Marine Protected and Conserved Areas in the Time of COVID." *Parks* 27 (Special Issue): 85–102.

Pita, Cristina, and Gisela Costa. 2023. *Report on the Main Impediments and Potential Incentives for Seafood Blockchain Deployment*. Sea2See.

PwC (PricewaterhouseCoopers). 2020. "Time for Trust: The Trillion-Dollar Reasons to Rethink Blockchain." www.pwc.com.cy/en/issues/assets/blockchain-time-for-trust.pdf.

Rabitz, Florian, Jesse L. Reynolds, and Elsa Tsioumani. 2022. "Emerging Technologies in Biodiversity Governance: Gaps and Opportunities for Transformative Governance." In *Transforming Biodiversity Governance*, edited by Ingrid J. Visseren-Hamakers and Marcel T. J. Kok. Cambridge University Press.

Rosencrance, Linda. 2023. "Why Blockchain Projects Fail and How Companies Can Succeed." *Technopedia*, September 29. www.techopedia.com/why-blockchain-projects-fail-and-how-companies-can-succeed.

Scruggs, Gregory. 2018. "How Blockchain and AI Can Help to Protect the Oceans." *World Economic Forum*. www.weforum.org/stories/2018/12/blockchain-ai-hailed-as-new-tools-to-protect-high-seas/.

Shoker, Ali. 2021. "Blockchain Technology as a Means of Sustainable Development." *One Earth* 4 (6): 795–800.

Tanaka, Yoshiumi. 2019. *The International Law of the Sea*. 3rd ed. Cambridge University Press.

UN (United Nations). 1973. "Report of the United Nations Conference on the Human Environment, Stockholm, 5–16 June 1972." A/CONF.48/14/Rev.1 (1973).

UNDESA (United Nations Department of Economic and Social Affairs). n.d. "14 Conserve and Sustainably Use the Oceans, Seas and Marine Resources for Sustainable Development." https://sdgs.un.org/goals/goal14.

UNESCO. n.d. "10 Challenges." Ocean Decade. https://oceandecade.org/challenges/.

UNGA (United Nations General Assembly). 2009. "United Nations Convention on Contracts for the International Carriage of Goods Wholly or Partly by Sea." A/RES/63/122 (February 2, 2009).

2024. "Oceans and the Law of the Sea: Report of the Secretary-General." A5/62/Add.1 (August 18, 2004).

Velasco González-Camino, Andrea. 2019. *Blockchain: Aplicación a la pesca de atún*. Universidad Pontificia Comillas.

Voshmgir, Shermin, Martin Wildenberg, Christian Rammel, and Tatjana Novakovic. 2019. "Sustainable Development Report: Blockchain, the Web3 & the SDGs." Working Paper Series 7464, WU Vienna University of Economics and Business, Institute for Cryptoeconomics.

WCED (World Commission on Environment and Development). 1987. *Our Common Future*. Oxford University Press.

Wigley, Bob, and Nicolas Cary. 2017. "The Future Is Decentralised: Block Chains, Distributed Ledgers, & the Future of Sustainable Development." Blockchain Commission and UN Development Programme.

Zhu, Xiaohao, Zhipeng Cui, and Pengfei Zhang. 2022. "The Role of Electronic Bill of Lading and Challenges to the Current Legal Framework." *Journal of Shipping and Ocean Engineering* 12: 19–26.

Zou, Keyuan, and Yen-Chiang Chang. 2023. "Preserving Community Interests in Ocean Governance towards Sustainability: An Editorial Note." *Sustainability* 15 (22): 15894.

9

Seabed-Mining Technology and the Precautionary Approach

Digvijay Rewatkar

9.1 INTRODUCTION

The issue of deep-seabed mining has lately evoked polarized positions, which is no surprise given that the history of seabed mining was also rife with contrasting positions during negotiations for the United Nations Convention on the Law of the Sea (UNCLOS).[1] At the Law of the Sea Conferences, the lack of information on technological developments and pressures for the reallocation of resources were foremost among the factors influencing the negotiations. Today, the specter of seabed mining evokes a different sense of polarization along the lines of environmental protection. Before we delve further into the details of the negotiation and technologies, it is essential to orient understanding about the minerals and their locations to better contextualize the issue.

From a geological perspective, the seabed can be classified into three areas: (1) the continental shelf where the depths are less than 200 m; (2) the continental slope indicating the transition from shallow waters to the deep sea; and (3) abyssal plains, which are generally vast areas at depths of 4,000 m. From a zonal perspective, deep-seabed mining takes place in areas beyond national jurisdiction and includes the seabed and ocean floor and subsoil thereof, often categorized as the "Area" (UNCLOS, Article 1(1)(1)). Within the Area, what captured the imagination of the negotiators and holds the most interest are resources, which include all solid, liquid, or gaseous mineral resources in situ or beneath the seabed, including polymetallic nodules (UNCLOS, Article 133(a)).

Subsequently, as deep-sea exploration evolved, polymetallic sulfides and cobalt-rich ferromanganese crusts were discovered within the diverse geography of the Area. To summarize their locations, polymetallic nodules – which by current estimates are in abundance – are found in the abyssal plains; polymetallic sulfides are found near hydrothermal vents; and the cobalt-rich ferromanganese crusts are

[1] UNCLOS, December 10, 1982, 1833 UNTS 397.

found on seamounts. All are formed due to highly specialized and prolonged geological processes. Each of these complex polymetallic ores contains a rich chemistry of minerals – such as copper, manganese, cobalt, zinc, nickel, platinum, and rare earth elements – and is often found in grades higher compared to land-based sources (ISA 2021).[2] As to the scale of resources, mining across 4.5 million square kilometers of the Clarion-Clipperton Zone – an area encompassing 1.5 percent of the world's abyssal plains – could yield approximately 34 billion wet metric tons of nodules containing 6 billion tons of manganese, 270 million tons of nickel, 234 million tons of copper, and 46 million tons of cobalt (ISA 2021).

However, today the discourses on seabed mining are polarized, given its potential impact on the marine environment. For instance, seabed mining in the Clarion-Clipperton Zone would create sediment plumes and noise pollution across an area three times larger, affecting the entire 4,500-m water column and impacting around 6,000,000 cubic kilometers of the ocean (Amon et al. 2022). Paradoxically, the minerals outlined above are also serendipitously essential for the green transition, and the rising demand for green technologies is expected to drive demands for these minerals further, with projections suggesting that the demand for cobalt could increase by 460 percent, nickel by 99 percent, and rare earth elements by 37 percent by 2050 (Herrington 2021).

This highlights the paradox of mitigating climate change through the adoption of green technologies and the reduction of environmental damage that could result from seabed mining. It underscores the critical need for a balanced approach, one that weighs the need for resource extraction against the imperative to protect deep-sea ecosystems. The questions this chapter asks are these: What is the technology necessary, and being developed, to undertake seabed mining with an application of the precautionary approach? What are the legal and regulatory dimensions governing the development and use of technology? The chapter explores the state of seabed-mining technology at the time of the UNCLOS negotiations and its evolution to the present. However, the chapter does not delve into discussions of thresholds and acceptable-harm parameters, as these are currently ongoing at the International Seabed Authority (ISA).

In the following sections, the chapter will explore how such a balance might be achieved, at least within the technology and regulatory framework that could reconcile these competing demands. Since technology is the pivotal factor in achieving a balance between resource extraction and environmental protection, the chapter will investigate the scope of seabed-mining technology within the framework of international law. Section 9.2 will deconstruct the negotiating history of the seabed-mining regime through the lens of technology. Section 9.3 will develop the precautionary approach, which was in the early stages of development

[2] For polymetallic sulfides, polymetallic nodules, and cobalt-rich ferromanganese crusts respectively, see ISA (2021, 34, 42, 50).

at the time of negotiations, and its influence on seabed-mining technology, including measures concerning technology. Section 9.4 will outline the different seabed-mining systems and subsystems currently in development and their impacts on the proximate environments. In conclusion, Section 9.5 will assess the challenges associated with the interface of technology with the precautionary approach.

9.2 SEABED-MINING TECHNOLOGY THROUGH THE NEGOTIATIONS OF UNCLOS

Concerns surrounding seabed-mining technology consistently remained a thematic discussion within the ambit of negotiations for UNCLOS. Interest in its economic potential considerably grew in the 1960s, when John L. Mero described the potential wealth of the ocean in the form of polymetallic nodules. However, the early stages of the negotiations had a pervading sense of uncertainty, owing to the lack of foreseeability or the lack of information about technological developments (Buderi and Caron 1985, 88–95). The deep-seabed-mining technology had received a disproportionate amount of attention among all marine technologies and was strongly politicized in the "North–South" conflict as the symbol of technology gap between the developed and developing States (Boczek 1982, 5). Further, several factors, such as the common heritage principle or the New International Economic Order, interceded the development of the negotiations and influenced the regulatory approaches to seabed technology.

9.2.1 *The Proposal by Arvid Pardo on the Common Heritage of Mankind and the Ad Hoc Seabed Committee*

In 1967, Arvid Pardo, the Maltese Ambassador to the United Nations, made an impassioned plea to the twenty-second General Assembly to address the risk of inequity emerging from the advanced technological capabilities of developed States to explore and exploit the seabed and prevent its national appropriation (UNGA 1967b, paras. 46–55, 1967c). While many assumptions embedded within his speech lacked proportion in the perceptions surrounding the mining of seabed minerals, his plea succeeded in achieving two critical objectives: the nonmilitarization of the seabed (UNGA 1967b, paras. 46–55; Schmidt 1989, 22–25), and the elucidation of the common heritage of mankind (UNGA 1967c, paras. 8–10; Li 1994) approach, capturing the imagination of the developing world as a principled means of accessing this mineral wealth. To this end, it was proposed that an international body be created that would balance the security and economic needs of States and ensure that the activities in the Area would conform to the proposed treaty (UNCA 1967c, paras. 8–10; Akaha 1985, 60).

Pardo's plea succeeded in drawing the focus of the delegates on the risks and opportunities the seabed offered, and led to the creation of the Ad Hoc Seabed

Committee in 1967 (UNGA 1967a). The deliberations of the Ad Hoc Seabed Committee culminated in four resolutions (UNGA 1968). These resolutions created the Committee on the Peaceful Uses of the Sea-Bed and the Ocean Floor beyond the Limits of National Jurisdiction (Seabed Committee) to study, inter alia, the ways and means to promote the exploitation and use of resources through international cooperation on the foreseeable development of technology through international machinery while also studying the harmful effects of such exploitation activities on the seabed, water column, and adjacent coasts (UNGA 1968, A, para. 2(b)).

9.2.2 *The Seabed Committee, Moratorium Resolution, and 1970 Declaration of Principles*

At the Ad Hoc Seabed Committee, the divergences in approach to the modalities of participation in the future seabed-mining industry had become clearer. On the one hand, the developing countries articulated their proposal with international cooperation and share in the benefits accruing from the progress of modern science and technology as the centerpiece of their demands (UNGA 1969a). The developed countries forwarded a dispassionate proposition whereby "no nation, regardless ... of their technological capability should be denied the opportunity to participate in the exploitation of the seabed" (UNGA 1969a, Annex, 3). Overall, the proposals for the Declaration of Principles articulated the need for making the technology to access the resources of the seabed available to developing States (UNGA 1969a, Annex, 1, 7, 12). Against this backdrop, the Seabed Committee was created with the mandate to elaborate the legal principles; the ways and means of promoting the exploitation of resources, including technological aspects; and the economic implications of such activities (UNGA 1968, B).

Some of the key achievements of the Seabed Committee include the 1969 Moratorium Resolution (UNGA 1969b) and the 1970 Declaration of Principles (UNGA 1970a). The Moratorium Resolution was passed on the initiative of the developing States, which feared a "grab" of the seabed resources before much agreement could be achieved, and simply declared that "States and persons, physical or juridical, are bound to refrain from all activities of exploitation of the resources of the area" (UNGA 1969b). Several developed States objected to the Moratorium Resolution and voted against it, as they feared that it would stifle the technological development necessary for the extraction of resources from the international area (Li 1994, 25).

The Declaration of Principles emerging from the compromises in the Seabed Committee reflected a delicate balance between the developing and developed States (Li 1994, 27). It became the cornerstone for the development of a new international seabed regime (UNGA 1970d, 12). The Declaration also recognized that the seabed resources required the articulation of rules different from the customary rules applicable to the living resources of the high seas (UNGA 1970a, para. 4, preamble para. 3). On seabed-mining technology, divergences remained, with the developing States stressing that States without advanced technology should be involved in, and benefit from, seabed mining (UNGA 1970c), and the developed States favoring nondiscriminatory access to the seabed. Given these divergences, the Seabed Committee could only articulate cooperation on the technical and technological aspects, limited to participation in international cooperation programs for scientific research; the publication and dissemination of research; and strengthening research programs through participation as tenets for the transfer of seabed-mining technology (UNGA 1970a, para. 10(a)–(c)).

It was already realized that the monetary benefits drawn from the mineral resources of the seabed were overstated, and most developing States had a limited interest in gaining access to Western technology and to having their experts trained under an international regime (Anand 1975, 249–250). This Declaration of Principles later proved to be critical, as it found greater resonance after the negotiation culminated at the Third Law of the Sea Conference, and it became clear that provisions related to access to technology could not be implemented in spirit without the cooperation of the developed States. These principles later served as guidance for the conclusion of an international agreement that would regulate activities and implement select obligations with respect to the deep-seabed areas.

9.2.3 *Transfer of Technology in UNCLOS Annex III and the 1994 Implementation Agreement*

The Third Law of the Sea Conference bifurcated the discussion on marine technology across general provisions concerning other marine technology, which was deliberated within Sub-Committee III of the Seabed Committee, becoming Part XIV of UNCLOS. Specific provisions concerning seabed-mining technology fall under the broader theme of the legal regime for the seabed and the ocean floor beyond national jurisdiction and were incorporated into part of Annex III under the basic conditions of prospecting, exploration, and exploitation. These provisions had become a symbol of the North–South controversy and had warranted separate treatment within the negotiations, primarily due to the inextricable link to the questions related to access to the Area (Boczek 1982, 34).

Part XIV of UNCLOS reflects the aspirations of the States to facilitate access to and acquisition of marine technology, including seabed-mining technology for developing States. These provisions broadly appear in three parts: (1) Article 144, outlining the general obligations of the ISA; (2) Articles 273 and 274, outlining the role of the ISA; and (3) Article 5 of Annex III, consisting of detailed obligations for the transfer of technology (TOT) to the Enterprise (discussed below) and developing States. However, the overreaching postulates on TOT proved untenable, leading to some provisions, particularly Article 5 of Annex III, being subsequently abridged through the 1994 Agreement relating to the Implementation of Part XI of UNCLOS (1994 Agreement).[3]

The Seabed Committee had three subcommittees, with Sub-Committee I entrusted with the responsibility for preparing the draft provisions concerning the legal regime of deep-seabed mining. Sub-Committee I discussed TOT with the awareness that such provisions would reflect the progressive development of the law of the sea to be facilitated through international machinery (UNGA 1970b). It was also understood that the scope of such TOT was limited to the contours of "activities in the Area" – that is, the exploration and exploitation of seabed minerals in the Area. The underlying consciousness of TOT was inspired by the call for a New International Economic Order (NIEO; UNGA 1974). The NIEO recognized the entrenched sense of inequity among developing States and called for the development of an international order with embedded principles advancing the balanced development of the international community. A key component of such imbalance was articulated in the form of inequitable access to technological progress, with the NIEO promoting TOT to address this issue (UNGA 1974, para. 4(p)). The emergence of the NIEO and the principles embedded within it led to the development of certain progressive policy objectives within UNCLOS that mirrored those principles and called for increased equity in the development of the seabed-mining regime (UNCLOS, Article 150).

Overall, the developing States were driven by a threefold objective on TOT: (1) guaranteed access to seabed-mining technology; (2) just and reasonable terms and conditions; and (3) improved domestic capabilities, including the training of personnel (Li 1994, 146–149). These principles were later integrated into what became Article 144 of UNCLOS. The key point of difference that existed between the developing and the industrialized States on TOT was perhaps ideological, particularly as technology owned by contractors (private corporations or companies), in view of the developed States, was private property and government interference was not warranted (Boczek 1982, 11).

These divergences manifested more sharply through the negotiations, resulting in the developing States, led by the Group of 77, making ambitious proposals concerning TOT. These proposals centered around strong international machinery (by now, there was agreement that the machinery would be the ISA) acting as a repository from which TOT would be facilitated (Platzöder 1990, vol. XI, 230). The developing States also called for the creation of a dedicated fund to effectuate TOT (UNCLOS III 1975, 198–199) and for the establishment of international centers to provide information on technological markets and to help developing countries reduce the total cost of transferring technology (UNGA 1973, 82). These attempts received limited success in that they succeeded in allocating to the ISA the responsibility for

[3] Agreement relating to the Implementation of Part XI of the United Nations Convention on the Law of the Sea of December 10, 1982, July 28, 1994, 1836 UNTS 3.

facilitating such transfers, and by the mid-1970s, the negotiations had led to the inclusion of Articles 273 and 274 in the Convention.

As negotiations progressed, the 1976 session became a major turning point in the deliberations of the First Committee (Platzöder 1990, vol. VI, 83). As the concerns of the developed States found more accommodation, the TOT obligations of the contractors were weakened, and with the ISA at the center, the seabed-mining regime was redesigned toward a parallel system (UNCLOS III 1976). This led to the conceptualization of the Enterprise, a commercial arm of the ISA that would conduct mining alongside national enterprises or contractors, with industrialized States transferring technology to the Enterprise. It was expected that the Enterprise would obtain technology through the establishment of joint ventures or other forms of contractual agreements with contractors (Li 1994, 170).

With the parallel system in place, the issue of TOT to the Enterprise took center-stage in the First Committee at the Third Law of the Sea Conference. This concession on the part of the developing States led to the framing of the TOT provisions in mandatory terms, with multiple proposals emerging. Most notably, the "Brazil Clause" espoused the TOT from seabed-mining contractors to the Enterprise and to those developing States that secured licenses to mine in the reserved areas with a condition of nontransfer to other developed States (Juda 1979, 236). Another formulation mandated that contractors share the general description of the technology and equipment with the ISA, including subsequent changes and innovations (Juda 1979, 237). Overall both sides succeeded in including provisions favoring their interests, but both were also left dissatisfied with the text. The developed States expressed objections to the inclusion of TOT as a precondition for obtaining a mining contract by the contractors, while the developing States maintained that mandatory TOT was not sufficiently reflected in texts (Boczek 1982, 37–38).

When the Reagan administration took office in the United States in 1981, the new government immediately embarked on a major policy review of the draft Convention. As far as the TOT provisions were concerned, three features were considered unacceptable: (1) the compulsory sale of proprietary information and technology that American companies largely control; (2) guaranteed access for the Enterprise to the privately owned seabed-mining technology and also to the technology used by operators but owned by third parties; and (3) the guarantee that any developing country could have the same access to technology as the Enterprise (Reagan 1982a, 1982b; Schmidt 1989, 22–25). This change of policy led to several amendments to the TOT obligations being proposed by the developed States; however, the Group of 77 was not willing to reopen the negotiations at that stage. Therefore, Article 5 of Annex III was completed without further change.

After the Third Law of the Sea Conference, the final text of the proposed UNCLOS received a lukewarm reception from developed States as aspects of seabed-mining provisions remained overreaching (UNGA 1994, paras. 1–28). Since the adoption of UNCLOS, there have been significant political and economic changes that have had a marked effect on the regime for deep-seabed mining. There was a discernible shift toward a more market-oriented economy. Thus began a series of informal consultations under the aegis of the UN Secretary General on outstanding issues relating to the deep-seabed-mining provisions of UNCLOS. These informal consultations took place in 1990–94, culminating in the 1994 Agreement. The provisions concerning TOT were thereafter abridged. Section 5 of the Annex to the 1994 Agreement straightforwardly indicates that Article 5 of Annex III of UNCLOS will not apply. It provides that TOT will be governed by Article 144 of UNCLOS. The reach of the principles in Section 5 of the Annex of the 1994 Agreement can be interpreted as an attempt to facilitate access for the Enterprise and developing countries to the required technology on fair and reasonable commercial terms and conditions. However, these principles were implemented not through strict obligations on contractors but through cooperation and by following the principles of the market economy.

There was a growing consciousness in the 1990s of the anthropogenic effect on the environment, which led to a discernible shift in the discourse concerning the duty of the ISA and State parties to promote the advancement and transfer of technology with a view to protecting the marine environment and to apply the best available technology or environmentally sound technologies (UN 1992, 34.1, 34.3), although the transfer of such technology for deep-seabed mining did not attract sufficient attention during the Third Law of the Sea Conference.[4] It was understood that there would be rising concern regarding the environmental impact of seabed mining and with assurance that technology does minimal harm to the environment, through both greater scientific knowledge and the transfer of modern technology (Li 1994, 44). This line of argumentation further added to the call for the duty of States and the ISA to help the Enterprise and developing States to access and acquire relevant technology. In this connection, it is worth mentioning the emerging legal principles based on the need for pursuing sustainable development through the operationalization of due-diligence obligations and the precautionary approach.

4 In the Third Committee, some delegates from developing countries linked the issue of TOT to the protection of the marine environment. For instance, the Iraqi representative stated that "making the best use of the seas meant preserving the marine environment, controlling pollution from all sources and controlling the exploitation of marine biological and non-biological resources. That called for efforts by every country, separately or through international organizations, to develop marine technology and facilitate its transfer to countries that needed it, especially the developing countries" (UNCLOS III 1975, 101). The Kenyan representative pointed out that developed countries had the duty to transfer technology "in order to ensure the proper utilization of resources and the protection of the marine environment" (103).

9.3 THE PRECAUTIONARY APPROACH AND THE CURRENT DEBATE

Contemporaneous to the negotiations for UNCLOS, the environmental regime had been evolving simultaneously with some pivotal occasions, such as the 1972 Stockholm Declaration (UN 1972) and the enunciation of the 1992 Rio Principles (UNGA 1992). Those instruments served as the early foundations for the development of an environmental lens for existing and future human activities. They aim to strike a balance between the human yearning for development and economic growth, the imperatives of environmental protection, and the rational management of resources. In this regard, rational planning has been identified as an essential tool for reconciling conflict between the needs of development and the need to protect and improve the environment (UNGA 1992, Principle 14). And, to this end, States must adopt integrated and coordinated approaches to the development of resources so as to ensure compatibility with the protection of the environment (UNGA 1992, Principle 13). The tribunal in the *Ijzeren Rijn Railway* arbitration on the issue of the integration of the protection of the environment to development activities articulated the evolving jurisprudence as reconciliatory when it opined:

> Environmental law and the law on development stand not as alternatives but as mutually reinforcing, integral concepts, which require that where development may cause significant harm to the environment there is a duty to prevent, or at least mitigate, such harm.[5]

The International Court of Justice has reconciled these two elements as follows:

> New norms have to be taken into consideration, and . . . new standards given proper weight, not only when States contemplate new activities but also when continuing with activities begun in the past.[6]

This understanding is embedded within the seabed-mining regime as a key policy imperative for "the orderly, safe and rational management of the resources of the Area, including the efficient conduct of activities in the Area and, in accordance with sound principles of conservation" (UNCLOS, Article 150(b)).

Evolving from this discourse on environmental management, the Rio Principles espouse the precautionary approach, which "shall be widely applied by States according to their capabilities," so that where there are "threats of serious or irreversible damage, lack of full scientific certainty shall not be used as a reason for postponing cost-effective measures to prevent environmental degradation" (UNGA 1992, Principle 15). The precautionary approach raises critical questions related to

5 *Iron Rhine ("Ijzeren Rijn") Railway between the Kingdom of Belgium and the Kingdom of the Netherlands*, Award (Perm. Ct. Arb. 2005), 27 RIAA 35, para. 59.

6 *Gabčíkovo-Nagymaros (Hungary/Slovakia)*, Judgment, 1997 ICJ Rep. 7, para. 140 (September 25).

the viability and feasibility of seabed mining. The uncertainties surrounding the effects of seabed mining on the marine environment have led to calls for a precautionary pause or moratorium. However, a precautionary approach applies in the context of scientific uncertainty and in accordance with the capacities of States. Subsection 9.3.1 will explore best available techniques as a precautionary measure within international law to balance these interests. So, the critical question that emerges is this: How can the objectives sought to be achieved through seabed mining be reconciled with the precautionary approach?

9.3.1 *The Precautionary Approach in Seabed Mining*

The UNCLOS does not refer to the application of the precautionary approach to seabed mining, but the need for marine environmental protection and management is embedded within the Convention, particularly in Part XII and Article 145 of Part XI. Further, the Seabed Disputes Chamber of the International Tribunal for the Law of the Sea (ITLOS), in the Area Advisory Opinion[7] perusing the Nodules and Sulphides Regulations, opined that the sponsoring States "shall apply a precautionary approach, as reflected in Principle 15 of the Rio Declaration" in order "to ensure effective protection for the marine environment from harmful effects which may arise from activities in the Area" (para. 125). In view of the Chamber, "the provisions of the aforementioned Regulations transform this non-binding statement of the precautionary approach in the Rio Declaration into a binding obligation" (para. 127). It is critical to note that while there is a theoretical debate surrounding the legal status of precaution as an "approach" or as a "principle," it has largely appeared as an approach within the literature concerning seabed mining. In addition to the advisory opinion rendered by the Chamber, the Draft Regulations on Exploitation of Mineral Resources in the Area (Draft Mining Code; ISA 2019) refer to the application of the precautionary *approach* both as a "fundamental policy and principle" (Regulation 2) and as a "general obligation" applying to the activities in the Area (Regulation 44).

In the environmental law literature, the term "approach" appears to be less in normative content, leaving scope for the discretion of the States in deciding the scope of precautionary actions (Cançado Trindade 2015). The precautionary approach espouses a normative value as an ethical aspiration (Ali 2022, 157), and operationalizing it in the context of maintaining balance in a complex environment of competing goals requires a policy-oriented approach.[8] Precaution operates as a matrix for conscious and informed decision-making and does not advocate for

[7] *Responsibilities and Obligations of States with Respect to Activities in the Area*, Advisory Opinion of February 1, 2011, ITLOS Rep. 2011 (Area Advisory Opinion).

[8] *Indus Waters Kishenganga Arbitration (Pakistan v. India)*, Final Award (Perm. Ct. Arb. 2013), 31 RIAA 3, para. 112.

indefinite inertia in a world with competing challenges. While it is important to exercise caution, indeterminate precaution must not lead to a paralysis in decision-making (Ali 2022, 157). Currently, the discourse on seabed mining is paralyzed by "what-ifs" and "fear of the unknown." Accordingly, the precautionary approach requires a balance between the use of best available techniques with a view to refining practices through a process of learning while enhancing the ability to detect actual risks of serious environmental harm (Ali 2022). In essence, the precautionary approach calls for a trade-off between the methods through which risk for serious environmental harm can be managed through the use of technology by keeping a balance between anticipating harm and trusting resilience, thereby promoting a certain degree of flexibility (Peel 2004, 491). This distinction in the debate over precaution discloses different attitudes to risk rather than fundamentally different appreciations of the importance of taking scientific uncertainty into account in decision-making (Peel 2004, 500).

In this regard, the relationship of the precautionary approach with the principle of prevention is critical to note. The distinction between prevention and precaution is based on the seriousness of the risk; that is, prevention is a general concept that dictates the general actions of States in terms of environmental protection, and precaution amounts to a reinforcement of the obligation in light of a potentially serious danger that cannot yet be predicted.[9] This approach frames the relationship between prevention and precaution as one of a continuum wherein, as the risk evolves from uncertainty to certainty, the sliding scale of action moves from precaution to prevention. Therefore, it appears that there is scope to identify a risk–reward ratio in seabed-mining activity, and technologies must evolve with the anticipation of harm existing systems will cause. Such an evolutionary understanding is also implicit in the development of the jurisprudence of the precautionary approach and its operationalization.

9.3.1.1 Obligations of Sponsoring States

The Seabed Disputes Chamber in the Area Advisory Opinion approaches the question of the precautionary approach from two prongs. First, it considers applying the precautionary approach to the activities in the Area as a direct obligation of sponsoring States; and second, it links these direct obligations to the due-diligence obligations of States:

> The obligations of sponsoring States are not limited to the due diligence "obligation to ensure." Under the Convention and related instruments, sponsoring States also

[9] *Pulp Mills on the River Uruguay (Argentina v. Uruguay)*, 2010 ICJ Rep. 14, Separate Opinion of Judge Cançado Trindade, para. 112 (April 20); *Whaling in the Antarctic (Australia v. Japan: New Zealand intervening)*, 2014 ICJ Rep. 226, Separate Opinion of Judge Cançado Trindade, para. 64 (March 31).

> have obligations with which they have to comply independently of their obligation to ensure a certain behavior by the sponsored contractor. (para. 121)

In effect, this means that States ought to integrate the precautionary approach in their decision-making on sponsoring activities in the Area and translate such intent through various rules, regulations, procedures, and administrative processes to exercise control and regulate the conduct of sponsored entities (paras. 107, 123). This is particularly critical because the application of the precautionary approach, being a treaty obligation, is binding only on States, and it is through this mechanism that the States must obligate the contractors under their control to apply the precautionary approach.

The Chamber further articulated the circumstances in which a State fails to meet its due-diligence obligation:

> A sponsoring State would not meet its obligation of due diligence if it disregarded risks [arising from scientific uncertainty]. Such disregard would amount to a failure to comply with the precautionary approach. (para. 131)[10]

Therefore, a sponsoring State must continuously manage its compliance with this due-diligence obligation and account for emerging risks to fulfill its obligations. The continuous and evolutionary nature of the due-diligence obligation vis-à-vis the precautionary approach has also been a subject of discussion elsewhere. The International Law Commission has understood the duty of due diligence as not intending to guarantee that significant harm be totally prevented (ILC 2001, 154, paras. 7–8, 1994, Article 7, para. 4). The standard of due diligence against which the conduct of the State of origin should be examined is that which is generally considered to be appropriate and proportional to the degree of risk (ILC 1994, Article 7, para. 4). Therefore, "the State may be responsible … for not enacting necessary legislation, for not enforcing its laws …, or for not preventing or terminating an illegal activity, or for not punishing the person responsible for it" (ILC 1994, Article 7, para. 4). This could be understood to be a learning-by-doing approach, whereby the assessment of the risk and the harm done must be made on a continuous basis, with appropriate mechanisms for the implementation of relevant measures to minimize such harm.

In this respect, due diligence requires States to "ensure" that such activities within their jurisdiction or control do not cause significant adverse effects. This does not mean, however, that due diligence applies solely to private activities, since a State's own activities are also subject to the due-diligence rule.[11] It is an obligation that

[10] See also *Southern Bluefin Tuna (New Zealand v. Japan; Australia v. Japan)*, Provisional Measures, Order of August 27, 1999, ITLOS Rep. 1999, 280 at para. 77.

[11] *Pulp Mills on the River Uruguay (Argentina v. Uruguay)*, 2010 ICJ Rep. 14, paras. 101, 197 (April 20); *Certain Activities Carried Out by Nicaragua in the Border Area (Costa Rica v. Nicaragua)*; *Construction of a Road in Costa Rica along the San Juan River (Nicaragua v. Costa Rica)*, 2015 ICJ Rep. 665, paras. 104, 153, 168, 228 (December 16); *Responsibilities and Obligations of*

entails not only the adoption of appropriate rules and measures but also a certain level of vigilance in their enforcement and the exercise of administrative control applicable to public and private operators – such as the monitoring of activities undertaken by such operators – to safeguard the environment. It also requires considering the context and evolving standards of both regulation and technology (ILC 2021, Guideline 3, 26). This leads to this question: How are States expected to operationalize the precautionary approach in the context of seabed mining?

9.3.1.2 Operationalizing the Precautionary Approach

While it is now established that the precautionary approach is applicable to activities in the Area, this section will delve into understanding how the precautionary approach can be operationalized vis-à-vis these activities. The Seabed Disputes Chamber has provided guidance in this regard:

> The due diligence obligation of the sponsoring States requires them to take *all appropriate measures* to prevent damage that *might result* from the activities of contractors that they sponsor. The [precautionary approach] applies in situations where scientific evidence concerning the scope and potential negative impact of the activity in question is insufficient but where there are *plausible indications of potential risks*. (Area Advisory Opinion, para. 131)

The constitutive elements of the precautionary approach envisaged by ITLOS include the threat of environmental harm, uncertainty, and action. The threat of environmental harm is articulated in the form of damage that "might result" based on "plausible indications of potential risks"; in other words, this broadens the characterization of harm. However, unlike the Rio formulation, which characterizes harm to be serious or irreversible, the Chamber applies the precautionary approach to all "potential negative impacts." Should a State disregard these obligations, it would be in violation of its due-diligence obligations. Further, the obligation of States is qualified by the requirement that they take "appropriate measures" to prevent damage; that is, the standard of "appropriate" has an economic, as well as a social, pragmatic, and ideological character (Johnstone 2015, 117–118).

Finally, the most critical constitutive element of the precautionary approach is the remedial action concerning the prevention of environmental degradation. This addresses the element of the methods through which such precaution can be operationalized. Any remedial action must be effective; that is, it should be capable of achieving the desired level of protection. The aim is to create measures that are specific enough to be clear and meaningful, yet flexible enough to allow for changes

States with Respect to Activities in the Area, Advisory Opinion of February 1, 2011, ITLOS Rep. 2011, 10 at para. 131. See also ILC (2001, para. 97); ILA Study Group (2014, 2016).

when new information becomes available (Cooney and Dickson 2005, 301). Additionally, the precautionary measures must be proportionate to the desired level of protection and are to be evaluated on a case-to-case basis. In this regard, ITLOS has provided meaningful guidance on the proportionality of environmental measures:

> Due diligence is a variable concept. It may change over time as measures considered sufficiently diligent at a certain moment may become not diligent enough in light, for instance, of new scientific or technological knowledge. It may also change in relation to the risks involved in the activity. As regards activities in the Area, it seems reasonable to state that prospecting is, generally speaking, less risky than exploration activities which, in turn, entail less risk than exploitation. Moreover, activities in the Area concerning different kinds of minerals, for example, polymetallic nodules on the one hand and polymetallic sulphides or cobalt rich ferromanganese crusts on the other, may require different standards of diligence. The standard of due diligence has to be more severe for the riskier activities. (Area Advisory Opinion, para. 117)

Consequently, precaution must be translated into concrete policy and management measures that are readily understood, that address the protection problem, and that identify actions to be taken in specific contexts (Jaeckel 2017, 47). On a sliding scale of enhanced protection measures, one of the critical tools for the implementation of the precautionary approach when it comes to exploitation activities is Best Available Techniques (BAT; Trouwborst 2006b, 172–174).

To wrap up this discussion on the precautionary approach, we note that seabed mining carries the potential risk of negative impacts on the marine environment. However, this risk can be mitigated or managed through the implementation of the precautionary approach, inter alia, by taking necessary measures to limit the harm caused by mining. The implementation of such measures calls for innovative technological approaches to limit the harm, including the application of BAT.

9.3.1.3 Scope of Best Available Techniques

BAT are measures closely affiliated with the precautionary approach, both in State practice and in academic writings. In addition, BAT has been set out as a requirement of the precautionary approach in Swedish legislation,[12] German case law (Trouwborst 2006a), and the jurisprudence of the Dutch Council of State.[13] Some regional frameworks also apply the BAT standard to activities such as the 1992 Convention on the Protection of the Marine Environment of the Baltic Sea

[12] Environmental Code of 1998, Article 3(2).

[13] Afdeling Bestuursrechtspraak van de Raad van State, Judgment of April 19, 1996, No. G05.93.2238.

Area (Helsinki Convention),[14] as well as the 1992 Convention for the Protection of the Marine Environment of the North-East Atlantic (OSPAR Convention).[15] The Draft Mining Code also recognizes the application of BAT in carrying out precautionary measures (Regulations 44 and 58). Given that BAT appears only at a draft stage at the moment, the ordinary meaning can be derived by application of the rules of interpretation under Article 31 of the Vienna Convention on the Law of Treaties.[16]

BAT IN INTERNATIONAL LAW. At the outset, it is essential to acknowledge that the concept of "Best Available" is inherently relative and involves a comparative assessment. This was the question before the arbitral tribunal in the UK-Sandeel case, where the tribunal interpreted "'best' [to] be read in the context of 'available [technology]' and not in the absolute sense of the best possible" (UK-Sandeel 2025, 489). It is already established that the technology used must be sensitive to the deep-sea benthic environment and adhere to the precautionary approach. According to the arbitral tribunal it follows that "[available technology] is not limited to [one] that exists at the time …, but extends to [technology] which could reasonably have been [used] at that point in time" (UK-Sandeel 2025, 491). Therefore, seabed-mining contractors must make a reasonable degree of effort to obtain the BAT at the time the mining project is under consideration.

From the vantage point of a project opponent, it may be argued that the technology proposed for seabed mining is not the best available, either because superior technology exists or the current technology is fundamentally flawed. To interpret the view of the arbitral tribunal in the UK-Sandeel case, it does not require the opponent to identify a better technology. Instead, the opponent must demonstrate that the significant flaws in the technology prevent it from meeting the standard of best available technology (UK-Sandeel 2025, 494). Given this understanding of "best available," it is crucial to evaluate how BAT has been considered in international law.

In this regard, the Draft Mining Code borrows the definition of BAT from the OSPAR Convention and defines BAT through key elements such as the "latest stage of development" and "state-of-the-art processes" of "facilities and methods of operation" that are "practically suitable for limiting" environmental harm or pollution. Further, factors such as recent successful trials, technological advances, economic feasibility, time limits for installation, and the impact of technology on the environment are considered as constitutive elements of BAT

[14] Convention on the Protection of the Marine Environment of the Baltic Sea Area, March 22, 1974, 1507 UNTS 166 (Helsinki Convention).

[15] Convention for the Protection of the Marine Environment of the North-East Atlantic, September 22, 1992, 2354 UNTS 67 (OSPAR Convention).

[16] Vienna Convention on the Law of Treaties, May 23, 1969, 1155 UNTS 331.

(OSPAR Convention, Appendix I; Helsinki Convention, Annex II Regulation 3). Additionally, the scope of the term "techniques" includes technologies, albeit with a qualification that they must be accessible to operators and industrially scalable under economically and technically viable conditions.[17] To augment the conditions of general availability of the technology, it also must be effective in achieving a high general level of protection of the environment as a whole.[18] These conventions have an embedded understanding that technology is an evolutionary concept and BAT for a given process or facility will change with time in the light of technological advances, economic and social factors, and changes in scientific knowledge and understanding (OSPAR Convention, Appendix I; Helsinki Convention, Annex II).

Further, BAT has been invoked in two cases: the *MOX Plant* case, in which Ireland alleged that the waste management regime concerning the hazardous activity implemented by the UK was falling short, which could be addressed through the use of currently available technology, and that BAT must be adopted.[19] The arbitral tribunal, however, did not opine on that assertion by Ireland. Further, in the *Pulp Mills* case,[20] Argentina had alleged that by not requiring the Orion Mill to employ BAT, Uruguay had failed to take all measures to prevent pollution.[21] This included the nonimplementation of tertiary treatments of discharges and the lack of an empty emergency basin for discharges, to which Uruguay had contended that its plant used state-of-the-art anti-pollution technology, ensuring that the effluent discharges are among the lowest in the world, including all measures to evolve the technology in response to the harm.[22]

The International Court of Justice, on an assessment of the technology employed in the Orion Mill, found:

> From the point of view of the technology employed and based on . . . the December 2001 Integrated Pollution Prevention and Control Reference Document on Best Available Techniques in the pulp and paper industry of the European Commission there is no evidence to support the claim that the Orion Mill is not BAT-compliant. (para. 225)

[17] Stockholm Convention on Persistent Organic Pollutants, May 22, 2001, 2256 UNTS 119 (POPs Convention), Article 5(f)(iii): "'Available' techniques means those techniques that are accessible to the operator and that are developed on a scale that allows implementation in the relevant industrial sector, under economically and technically viable conditions, taking into consideration the costs and advantages."

[18] POPs Convention, Article 5(f)(iv): "'Best' means most effective in achieving a high general level of protection of the environment as a whole."

[19] *MOX Plant Case (Ireland v. United Kingdom)*, Ireland Memorial (Segment 3), PCA Case No. 2002-01.

[20] *Pulp Mills on the River Uruguay (Argentina v. Uruguay)*, 2010 ICJ Rep. 14 (April 20) (*Pulp Mills*).

[21] *Pulp Mills*, Memorial of Argentina, paras. 5.74–5.76.

[22] *Pulp Mills*, Memorial of Uruguay, para. 4.34.

In effect, the Court makes an assessment based on the availability of the technology and the industry standards prevalent at the time (paras. 224–225)[23] and does not indulge in a hypothetical assessment of what the technology should achieve to reduce or minimize harm. However, for States to be duly diligent, it would be important to inquire whether the technologies are best due to considerations of cost and convenience, or if there have been any improvements in the technology available.[24]

From a reading of the international instruments and the *MOX Plant* and *Pulp Mills* cases, it is conceivable that the use of BAT limits the margin of discretion of State parties concerning the implementation of the obligation to ensure effective protection for the marine environment from harmful effects that may arise from activities in the Area. Arguably, the obligation to use BAT may be a useful tool to specify a standard of due diligence (Tanaka 2006, 563–565). To this extent, the obligation could strengthen the regulation of harmful effects of the activities in the Area. In this regard, the seabed-mining regulations appear to push the boundaries of the limited conception of BAT in international law by devising an iterative process through Environmental Management and Monitoring Plans (EMMP) and Environmental Impact Statements (EIS), which ought to offer a continuous assessment procedure to the technology applied and its impacts. BAT is, therefore, a dynamic standard that evolves on technical, geographical, and economic considerations, and determining an objective BAT standard is difficult.

On an overall assessment of BAT in international law, while States have a due-diligence obligation to enact appropriate rules, regulations, and procedures to mitigate the effects of seabed mining on the environment, in effect, BAT also delegates action to contractors to innovate and develop technology that integrates these mitigating factors. Therefore, while States have a procedural obligation, the substantive obligation to implement the appropriate technology is incumbent upon contractors.

BAT IN THE DRAFT MINING CODE. The Seabed Disputes Chamber has also opined on the burden of implementing the precautionary approach and thereby BAT:

> Equality of treatment between developing and developed sponsoring States is consistent with the need to prevent commercial enterprises based in developed States from setting up companies in developing States, acquiring their nationality and obtaining their sponsorship in the hope of being subjected to less burdensome regulations and controls. (Area Advisory Opinion, para. 159)

[23] See also the Joint Dissenting Opinion of Judges Al-Khasawneh and Simma.
[24] Joint Dissenting Opinion of Judges Al-Khasawneh and Simma.

This statement by the Chamber indicates that, rather than considering the capacity of the State, it prefers to consider the capacity of the contractor to adopt BAT and comply with the environmental standards (Papanicolopolou 2020, 154). In this regard, this chapter focuses only on BAT measures to be implemented on the part of contractors, and not the interface of such obligations vis-à-vis the ISA or sponsoring States.

For BAT to be fully implemented, it must fulfill the constitutive elements of the precautionary approach – that is, environmental harm, uncertainty, and action. The Draft Mining Code takes a progressive approach to BAT and has inculcated more dynamic standards within its Regulations. The draft regulation on exploitation expands upon Article 145 of UNCLOS. It articulates fundamental principles for the effective protection of the marine environment and integrates the precautionary approach, the ecosystem approach, the polluter pays principle, data sharing, accountability and transparency, and effective public participation (Draft Regulation 2(e)(i)–(vii)). The draft regulations outline that the activities in the Area must be conducted efficiently and in a manner that is orderly, safe, and rational in accordance with sound principles of conservation and the avoidance of unnecessary waste (Draft Regulation 2(b)(ii)). They integrate the dynamic nature of the due-diligence obligations and espouse the development of incentive structures to support and enhance the environmental performance of contractors beyond the legal requirements, including through technology development and innovation (Draft Regulation 3(f)(iii) and (vi)). Furthermore, it can be reasonably assumed that the final adopted regulations will reflect a more stringent standard compared to the initial draft language.

Besides the fundamental principles and general obligations, the Draft Mining Code references technology and BAT in three areas: (1) applications for approval of Plans of Work in the form of contracts; (2) reducing the risk of incidents; and (3) the protection and preservation of the marine environment.

Applications for Approval of Plans of Work First, applications for approval of Plans of Work submitted by contractors (Draft Regulation 5(1)) are accompanied by a certificate of sponsorship, which establishes the nationality – that is, the jurisdiction and control of the sponsoring State (Draft Regulation 6). Such applications made with the Secretary General of the ISA include, inter alia, the EIS and EMMPs (Draft Regulation 7(1) and (3)). The EIS entails sharing information concerning the technologies and mining process to be employed, including the likely effects of the technology at the time of recovery of the resources from the seabed (Draft Regulation 7, Annex IV, 3.3.2). The EIS also includes a description and assessment of the likely effect of the mining process on the physiochemical, biological, and socioeconomic environment in the mining area (Draft Regulation 7, Annex IV, 3.3.2). It is also accompanied by the environmental management, monitoring, and reporting requirements, reflecting the environmental policy of the contractor (Draft

Regulation 7, Annex IV, 3.3.2). The EMMP includes an assessment of the potential environmental effects and the significance of the proposed activities on the marine environment, along with a description of mitigation measures, management control procedures and responses, and the necessary risk assessment and management techniques to minimize harm (Draft Regulation 7, Annex VII). The EMMP also includes a description of the technology to be deployed in accordance with good industry practice and BAT (Draft Regulation 7, Annex VII).

Once the application has been made, along with the requisite EIS and EMMP, the Legal and Technical Commission assesses the technical capabilities of the contractors on the basis of the necessary technical and operational capability to carry out the proposed plan of work and the technology and procedures necessary to comply with the terms of the EMMP, including the capability to utilize and apply BAT (Draft Regulation 13(3)(a)–(e)). Such assessment is made against the benchmark of the rules, regulations, and procedures set out by the ISA, in particular the fundamental policies and procedures (Draft Regulation 13(4)(e)).

Reducing the Risk of Incidents A contractor must minimize the risk of incidents as far as reasonably practicable, ensuring that the cost of further risk reduction is not grossly disproportionate to the benefits. This obligation aligns with the principle of due diligence by requiring contractors to continually evaluate and adopt risk reduction measures in accordance with new knowledge, technological advancements, established good industry practice, BAT, and best environmental practices.

Contractors are expected to regularly review their risk management strategies to ensure that they reflect current best practices and evolving standards. In determining whether additional risk reduction measures are feasible, contractors must assess whether the time, cost, and effort involved are justifiable in comparison to the potential benefits, considering best practice risk levels for the specific operations being undertaken. This approach closely replicates the assessment criteria of BAT relied on by the International Court of Justice in the *Pulp Mills* case. It not only fulfills the requirements of due diligence but also provides clear guidance on the scope and extent of contractors' due-diligence obligations (Draft Regulation 32). In order to deal with such contingencies and incidents, the contractors must submit an Emergency Response and Contingency Plan and ensure its implementation in the event of incidents (Draft Regulation 33).

Protection and Preservation of the Marine Environment Finally, Part IV of the draft regulations, on the protection and preservation of the marine environment, creates a binding obligation on the ISA, sponsoring States, and contractors to apply the precautionary approach and BAT in carrying out such measures (Draft Regulation 44). To this end, the ISA is developing environmental standards that provide for the environmental quality objectives, monitoring procedures, and mitigation measures (Draft Regulation 45). The mitigation measures identified in the

EIS as such must limit the harm of seabed mining to acceptable levels (Draft Regulation 47(3)(d)). The procedure to implement such mitigation measures and limit such harm must also be articulated within the EMMPs to manage and confirm that the effects meet the environmental quality objectives and standards for the mining operation. The obligations are not limited and cover the entire gamut of activities, including monitoring the effectiveness of mitigation measures through a defined reporting system and maintaining the currency of that system (Draft Regulations 48(3)(c) and 51(c)).

The due-diligence obligation concerning environmental management is a continuous one, according to the mining code, wherein the contractor is expected to assess the validity and compliance of the mining operation with the EMMP (Draft Regulation 52(1)(a)). The reporting of such performance assessments is submitted to the ISA, along with a periodic review of the performance of the contractor by the Legal and Technical Commission of the ISA with adequate safeguards through independent reviews (Draft Regulation 52(3) and (4)). Should the contactor be assessed to have failed to comply with the terms and conditions of its EMMP, a compliance notice to that effect is issued requiring the contractor to take remedial action (Draft Regulation 103(2)(b)).

The incremental evolution in BAT is also recognized within the Regulations, with research on it funded through the Environmental Compensation Fund (Draft Regulation 55(d)). Based on dynamic feedback through the EMMP (Draft Regulation 52), the plans of work initially approved by the ISA are reviewed at intervals, including assessing the evolution in BAT (Draft Regulation 58(1)(f)). Finally, BAT is also a critical element at the end of the life cycle of a mine and is consistently under review and development for the closure plan of a mining site (Draft Regulation 59(2)(a)).

This leads to the final question: What are the technologies currently under testing and development by contractors to fulfill the obligations associated with BAT, and what is their interface with the surrounding environment? Subsection 9.4 will attempt to give a bird's eye view of the technological landscape and its likely effects. In no way is it an attempt to address this effect comprehensively, as a deeper assessment remains outside the scope of the legal obligations of due diligence. However, the section is aimed at orienting the reader to the effects of such mining.

9.4 KEY SUBSYSTEMS OF SEABED-MINING TECHNOLOGY AND THEIR IMPACTS ON THE MARINE ENVIRONMENT

The seabed-mining operation has three key subsystems to its operation from the surface to the deep seabed. First, the production support vessel (mining ship) hosts all the subsystems and serves as the platform from which the mining operation is conducted. This facility supports the collection, gathering, lifting, and storing of polymetallic ores that are mined and must also perform the initial dewatering or sorting of minerals from the seabed before sending them to a transport ship (Zhang et al. 2025, 14). This platform also hosts all the powering equipment driving the electric generators and dynamic position systems. There are two main types: platform-based, which are simple but need tugboats for relocation; and ship-based, which have self-propulsion, high-power systems and precise positioning. The mining ship generally has ample cargo space for dewatering treatment and mineral storage (Solheim et al. 2022).

Second, the seabed nodule collector (SNC) is an underwater vehicle that moves along the seabed collecting polymetallic nodules. The SNC is launched with the help of a launch-and-recovery system and is lowered to the depths of the oceans. It relates to the mining ship through a large umbilical cable, providing it with power, communication, and control of its movements on the seabed. The SNC is the most critical subsystem, as there are different iterations of this technology being developed by different proprietors to attain maximum efficiency with minimum footprint. An SNC generally includes complex hydraulics, mechanical equipment, and robotic collector arms, and based on its type, it may have varying levels of impact on the benthic environment. The third critical subsystem is the riser airlift system, which is used to inject air to reduce the buoyancy of water and to lift the slurry of crushed polymetallic ores from the mining vehicle on the seabed to the mining ship at the surface.

9.4.1 *Impact of Seabed Mining on the Seafloor*

The main objective of the SNC is to collect polymetallic nodules while adhering to certain environmental, economic, and operational parameters as set out by Part XI and the Mining Code. As a critical subsystem, the SNC consists of a nodule collection system, along with a propulsion system to maneuver on the seabed. The SNC must balance its impact on the benthic environment with its production rate to operate responsibly (De Bruyne et al. 2022). Currently, the SNC has the highest number of information and knowledge gaps, such as the environmental impacts and effects, its response to soil characteristics, trafficability, and nodule collection methodology (De Bruyne et al. 2022).

Another subcomponent of the SNC that is critical in its impact is the nodule collection system, which has two major functions: (1) a pickup function, picking up the nodules at the entrance of the collector by means of an active jet system; and (2) a transport function, transporting the nodules for further handling. Within these two functional categories, parameters can further be categorized as either process control parameters, geometrical parameters, or environmental parameters. It is the trade-offs between these parameters that define the efficiency and effectiveness of the collection system. Currently, mechanical and hydraulic systems are being tested along these parameters. The hydraulic collection method is classified into three types: suction, wall-attached jet, and double-row jet. It impacts the sediment layer less than the mechanical method, which often damages the seabed and causes more sediment suspension (Zhang et al. 2025, 6). Within the mechanical model, multiple prototypes have been tested, including a rotary chain-toothed collecting head (Welling 1981) and a combined comb-like shovel to lift nodules (Handschuh et al. 2001).

The SNC, which has a direct interface with the seafloor, will cause two main types of impact: (1) impact on the seafloor; and (2) benthic plume on the seafloor.

9.4.1.1 Impact on the Seafloor

The SNC has a twofold impact on the seafloor: the disturbance it causes at the time of nodule pick-up, and through its traction movement or driving system. Sea trials found that the hydraulic collection method was more adaptable, efficient, and stable on varied terrain, while the mechanical method consumed less energy. Overall, the hydraulic collection method shows higher reliability and environmental sustainability than the mechanical collection method, though it consumes more energy (Muñoz-Royo et al. 2021).

The second type of impact results from the forward movement of the SNC picking up nodules along with sediments. Further, traction of the nodule collector with the seafloor causes benthic organism mortality. This will impact the area accessible to the flora and fauna on the seafloor, and different technological choices exist, such as the Archimedes screws or the caterpillar's tracks, or noncontact suspended vehicles. It is important to note that, owing to the increased sensitivity to environmental impacts, the concept of an SNC has evolved from passive to active collectors, as the former was deemed inefficient and not in sync with current environmental impact policies (Muñoz-Royo et al. 2021). On an assessment of the principles currently opted by contractors for traction of the SNC on the seafloor, it is largely based on caterpillar tracks (Global Sea Mineral Resources 2018) and noncontact suspended vehicles (BGR 2018; BPC 2024).

For tracked SNCs, the soil characteristics define the designs of tracks. The trade-off to be made is increasing the surface area interface of the tracks and the material used for it. A high-surface-area and lightweight material will minimize sinkage and excessive slip and guarantee maximum traction performances, but will run the risk of a larger area of impact. The SNC traction is designed with a low internal friction angle[25] to minimize harm to seafloor organisms. Instead of relying on friction as do ground vehicles, it primarily depends on the sediment's shear resistance (Liu et al. 2014). A good comparative example in this regard is the Archimedes-screw drivetrain

[25] A "low internal friction angle" means that a material, such as soil or rock, has a low resistance to shearing forces, indicating that its particles easily slide past each other, making it less stable and more prone to failure under stress, compared to a material with a higher internal friction angle; essentially, it signifies a lower capacity to withstand shear forces due to poor particle interlocking (Keaton 2017).

used by the early prototype SNC (by Ocean Minerals Company – OMCO), which created deep furrows of a depth of 80 cm (Jones et al. 2025) in comparison to more recent tracked SNC of Nauru Ocean Resources Inc. (NORI) that have reduced depth of sediment disturbance to 3 cm (Metals Company 2023).

A 2023 study revisiting a 1979 collector test conducted by OMCO showed similar densities of nodule-dwelling macrofauna in disturbed and control areas. However, it concluded that near-complete nodule removal during mining would likely cause further significant reductions in nodule-dwelling macrofauna, as nodules serve as essential habitats for these organisms. The overall densities of megafauna were found to be very low on tracks and significantly different from control areas and pre-collection tests. However, mobile organisms, such as megafauna and macrofauna, had come to inhabit even the most disturbed regions, suggesting resilience. Sessile (immobile) megafauna displayed early stages of reestablishment, though communities differ significantly from those in unaffected areas. The study demonstrates that technological approaches may be effective in mitigating the broader ecological impacts of mining activities on seafloor biota (Jones et al. 2025).

A new generation of technology that is being tested by the German Federal Institute for Geosciences and Natural Resources (BGR) comprises the noncontact suspended SNCs that hover about 50 cm over the seafloor using positive buoyancy (BGR 2024). The key feature of this technology is its use of AI to detect benthic life on the nodules. Due to its precision collection process using robotic arms, it picks nodules with the least disturbance; that is, those with attached or proximal megafauna are avoided. Further, its robotic arms do not pick up or disturb the seafloor sediment, as it penetrates only to the extent of 2–5.5 cm in the seafloor. Importantly, the depth of penetration into the sediment does not mean that the entire sediment above that depth will be picked up; rather, the claws will penetrate into the sediment in order to grab the nodule (BGR 2024). The benefit of the noncontact suspended vehicle is that it has a high collection efficiency, low operational energy consumption, minimal sediment disturbance, and reliable operation (BGR 2024).

9.4.1.2 Impact of the Benthic Plume

Similarly, another component of the SNC that has a direct effect on the marine environment is the collection system, which is also seeing the testing of different methodologies. The collection system either sucks up the nodules from the seafloor or dislodges them from the seafloor using a moving comb or robotic arms. In each of these methodologies, the sediment is dislodged along with the nodules, albeit in different proportions (De Bruyne et al. 2022). These collection activities cumulatively create the benthic plume – that is, the movement of the SNC and the collector stirs up the sediment and the rejected particulate matter from the nodules is also released through a hopper (Berge et al. 1991). Within this benthic plume, larger particles will settle quickly, but finer particles hold the potential to spread over a large area of seabed assisted by currents. These sediments can disturb sensory functions and the assimilation of nutrients in living organisms. They can also bury flora and fauna on the seabed (Berge et al. 1991, 33–34).

While the impacts of suspended noncontact SNCs are rather minimal due to the negligible sediment disturbance (Liu et al. 2014),[26] it is the tracked SNCs that generate benthic sediment plumes and remain the subject of several studies. A 2025 study found that sediment from a nodule collector vehicle at 4 km depth forms a seafloor turbidity current, staying close to the seafloor and not rising into the water column to be carried by ocean currents (Gazis et al. 2025). This study further indicated that sediment particles flocculated rapidly and redeposited quickly (Gazis et al. 2025). One of the key recommendations of the study has been to consider the gradient of the mining site to reduce the impact of gravity-driven turbidity currents and prioritize mining in flat areas (Gazis et al. 2025, 6). Additionally, another study found that sediments from the plume created by the 1979 collector test are not immediately visible but can be detected using photogrammetric measurements of sediment infill (up to around 10 mm) between nodules. This study suggests higher densities of megafauna in these areas compared to undisturbed regions (Jones et al. 2025).

9.4.2 *Impact in the Water Column*

Once collected, the nodules move up the discharge duct and fall into a single trough, called the hopper. Much of the initial pickup water flow is also used to transport the nodules up the duct, flushes through the hopper, and is discharged through the diffusor exhaust. As such, this sediment-laden water is immediately released on the seabed before it enters the subsequent transport and processing systems – that is, the riser airlift system (De Bruyne et al. 2022). During this process, the mineral material will not interact with the water column and will not contribute to any change in the physical or chemical equilibrium in the water column except for accidental leaks. However, the pumps and motors will cause noise and vibrations in the ambient water (De Bruyne et al. 2022, 35).

The riser airlift system can be divided into two types: pneumatic lifting and hydraulic lifting. The pneumatic lifting method works by injecting high-pressure gas into the bottom of the deep-sea-mining pipeline from a surface vessel. This creates an upward flow that transports minerals vertically. The hydraulic lifting method uses a high-lift mixed transport pump in the pipeline center for vertical transportation (She et al. 2022). In this case, the choice of the system will be key to minimize the environmental impacts. The most prevalent method is the use of hydraulic-driven pumps – that is, the airlift system.

[26] The results of the impacts will be released after the tests of Eureka III by BGR.

The airlift system creates low fluid pressure at varying depths of the riser, causing low fluid pressure on the seabed through which the mineral material is transported. Given that the air injections take place in the upper portions, the capacity requirement of the pumps is limited, thereby reducing environmental impacts (Berge et al. 1991). Multiple approaches for lift systems exist; for instance, Japanese researchers conducted research on an eight-stage lifting pump (Yamada and Yamazaki 1998); China adopted a space guide vane centrifugal pump (Kang et al. 2019); and Germany and India have proposed and adopted a plugging-type positive displacement pump lifting system (Kang et al. 2024). Overall, commercial mining systems typically use multiple multistage centrifugal pumps connected in series.

Further, different technologies are being tested with a novel approach. In the Eureka III trials by BGR, the collected nodules are stored in the autonomous SNC based on the suspended noncontact nodule collector, which would be transported back up to the production support vessel once its storage is full, thereby minimizing any environmental impact of the collection process on the water column (DHI 2024).

However, the key impact on the water column takes place at the time of dewatering the mineral material – that is, when the seawater is separated from the nodules collected in the production support vessel. The discharge of the wastewater from this process implies adding a significant volume of water with different physical and chemical characteristics, such as seabed water, sediments, fragments of nodules, and benthic biota from the seabed to the water column (Berge et al. 1991). Also, the temperature of the seabed water is significantly lower than surface-layer water and can have an impact on the surrounding ecosystem where the water is released. However, testing has suggested that the impacts of such variant temperatures are limited, given the ratio of the volume of wastewater released to the seawater, thereby having only local and short-duration impacts (Berge et al. 1991, 37; Muñoz-Royo et al. 2021).

Sediments in the midwater plume would likely be released in the disphotic or aphotic zone to reduce the impact on photosynthesis and vertical migrations (Le et al. 2017). To assess the environmental impact of a midwater plume, two phases must be understood: the dynamic plume phase, occurring near the release before ocean currents take over, setting initial depth and dilution; and the ambient plume phase, involving advection, settling, and turbulent diffusion. The dynamic plume model is well established (Wang and Adams 2016), considering its effect on turbulent entrainment (Devenish et al. 2010). This model was recently used to predict midwater plume properties for nodule mining (Rzezni et al. 2019). A key uncertainty for midwater plumes is the role of flocculation, where particles aggregate into larger flocs. The studies conducted have assumed that flocculation was insignificant for a dynamic plume, treating sediment as a passive tracer (Rzezni et al. 2019). This study used plume-monitoring results to model a twenty-year seabed-mining operation, concluding that midwater plume properties near the discharge can be reliably predicted and sediment aggregation effects are minimal (Muñoz-Royo et al. 2021).

However, more sophisticated data and metrics will be required to assess the impacts of such midwater plumes on marine organisms that move with the ocean in the midwater column (van der Grient and Drazen 2021) and the effects on such mobile and stationary marine organisms due to extended exposure to the sediments near a mining operation (Amon et al. 2016). And, while progress is being made on the understanding of the midwater and benthic ecosystems in the Clarion and Clipperton Fracture Zone, there still exist significant knowledge gaps to inform the setting of environmentally acceptable threshold levels (Muñoz-Royo et al. 2021). The questions that are currently being reflected from an environmental point of view concern the depth at which such wastewater must be released to minimize the impacts concerning such particulate matter, as it runs the risk of reducing visibility for marine organisms and interfering with nutrient assimilation and, potentially, other physical functions, such as respiration, development, growth, and reproduction. Therefore, it has broadly been concluded that releasing the wastewater at a depth beyond the most productive zone of the water column would significantly reduce environmental impacts (Berge et al. 1991, 39).

9.4.3 *Impact on the Surface Water*

The impact of the seabed-mining activity on the surface water would be akin to other uses of the sea, such as shipping. The most significant emissions would be related to the exhaust released by the mining vessel in the atmosphere and the noise and vibrations on the surface water. In this regard, this is a critical area of intersection between the work of the ISA and that of the International Maritime Organization (IMO). The IMO in this regard has a range of regulatory and area-based management tools developed for international shipping that could be useful to enhance the safety of seabed mining. Further, the IMO has extensive regulatory experience that could be useful to the ISA as it continues to develop new regimes, regulations, and guidelines for seabed mining. These include guidelines for the assessment and disposal of wastes, as well as civil liability and compensation schemes for pollution damage to the marine environment developed under various maritime law conventions (ISA and IMO 2019).

On an overall assessment, the most significant environmental impacts from seabed mining will be those caused by the SNC on the seafloor. Different technologies are being tested to minimize that impact. Pioneer Beijing Hi-Tech Development Corporation and BGR are currently testing noncontact suspended nodule collectors. The collection system being tested by BGR involves the use of robotic arms, which, as per the performance parameters, should avoid harm to the living organisms on the seafloor and extensive seafloor damage through traction dynamics (BGR 2018; BPC 2024). However, other contractors are testing SNC technologies that have a greater impact on the seafloor. Insofar as the impacts on the water column are concerned, studies have suggested that the sediment plumes, especially at the seafloor, do not significantly harm the environment and have short-term effects (Metals Company 2023). Further, sediment plumes in the upper reaches of the water column, particularly emerging from wastewater discharges, are also considered to be less significant because wastewater quickly dilutes in the ambient surface water. Thus, any deviation from the normal values for temperature and metal concentrations should be local and short-term transient (De Bruyne et al. 2022). Several tests have shown that particulate matter in the wastewater settles much faster than expected, so that the resultant sediment plume is smaller and less disturbing (De Bruyne et al. 2022, 57).

9.5 CONCLUSION

The evolution of discourses on technology in seabed mining has been a journey marked by significant transformations. Initially, these discussions were deeply entangled in the North–South divide, reflecting the broader geopolitical and economic disparities between the developed and developing nations. Developing countries, often lacking the advanced technological capabilities of their developed counterparts, were concerned about equitable access to the resources and technology needed for seabed mining. This divide was exemplified in the negotiations leading to UNCLOS, where developing States advocated for robust technology transfer provisions to ensure their meaningful participation in seabed-mining activities.

During the early stages of the negotiations, the lack of information on technological advancements and the pressure for resource reallocation were critical factors influencing the discourse. Developed nations, since they possess superior technological capabilities, were perceived as having a distinct advantage in exploiting seabed resources, leading to calls for an international regime to manage and regulate these activities equitably. The adoption of the principle of the common heritage of mankind and the establishment of the ISA were significant milestones in addressing these concerns, aiming to balance the interests of all nations.

As technology has advanced, the focus of the discourse has shifted from geopolitical considerations to environmental sustainability. The realization that seabed mining carries significant risks to the marine environment has driven the development and implementation of stringent environmental standards. The application of the precautionary approach and BAT has become central to the regulatory framework governing seabed mining. These measures are designed to mitigate the environmental impact of mining activities, ensuring that they are conducted responsibly and sustainably.

The ISA, in conjunction with sponsoring States and contractors, has made substantial progress in integrating these environmental principles into the seabed-mining regime. The dynamic nature of BAT, which evolves with technological advancements, ensures that the best possible practices are employed to minimize harm to the marine environment. This adaptive approach is crucial in addressing the inherent uncertainties and potential risks associated with seabed mining.

Additionally, examination of the precautionary approach through the perspective of technology indicates that measures should aim to optimize trade-offs across interconnected risks. Its application should rely on thorough assessments to reduce uncertainty over time. The key question is not whether to adopt the precautionary approach but rather what the appropriate action should be. It is essential to evaluate whether the technology can support seabed mining while protecting the marine environment, rather than simply assessing risks to justify strict restrictions or a ban. It is possible that some technologies in seabed mining may require more caution due to higher uncertainty and potential harm. However, this decision should involve stepwise, scalable, and experimental methods rather than a simple yes-or-no answer.

In conclusion, the evolution of the discourse on technology in seabed mining reflects a significant shift from addressing the North–South divide to fulfilling environmental parameters for deep-sea governance. This transformation underscores the complexities associated with international cooperation on technology transfer, technological innovation, and a commitment to sustainability in harnessing the resources of the deep seabed. As seabed mining moves closer to reality, the continued development and application of advanced technologies, guided by robust regulatory frameworks, will therefore be essential in balancing resource extraction with environmental protection.

REFERENCES

Akaha, Tsuneo. 1985. *Japan in Global Ocean Politics*. University of Hawaii Press.

Ali, Saleem H. 2022. *Earthly Order: How Natural Laws Define Human Life*. Oxford University Press.

Amon, Diva J., Lisa A. Levin, Anna Metaxas, Gavin Mudd, and Craig R. Smith. 2022. "Heading to the Deep End without Knowing How to Swim: Do We Need Deep-Seabed Mining?" *One Earth* 5 (3): 220–223.

Amon, Diva J., Amanda F. Ziegler, Thomas G. Dahlgren, Adrian G. Glover, Aurélie Goineau, Andrew J. Gooday, Helena Wiklund, and Craig R. Smith. 2016. "Insights into the Abundance and Diversity of Abyssal Megafauna in a Polymetallic-Nodule Region in the Eastern Clarion-Clipperton Zone." *Scientific Reports* 6: 30492.

Anand, R. P. 1975. *Legal Regime of the Seabed and the Developing Countries*. Thomson Press.

Berge, Stig, Jan Magne Markussen, Gudmund Vigerust, Thorbjørn Berntsen, and Fridtjof Nansen-stiftelsen på Polhøgda. 1991. *Environmental Consequences of Deep Seabed Mining: Problem Areas and Regulations*. Fridtjof Nansen Institute.

BGR (Federal Institute for Geosciences and Natural Resources). 2018. "Umweltfachliche Stellungnahme. Zum Kollektorkomponententest im Rahmen des Forschungsprojektes 'JPI-Oceans MiningImpact II.'" February.

2024. "Environment Impact Statement for Small-Scale Testing of an AI-Controlled Nodule Harvester in the Eastern BGR Contract Area for the Exploration of Polymetallic Nodules (Clarion-Clipperton Zone)." December.

Boczek, Boleslaw A. 1982. "The Transfer of Marine Technology to Developing Nations in International Law." Law of the Sea Institute Occasional Paper No. 32, University of Hawaii.

BPC (Beijing Pioneer Hi-Tech Development Corporation). 2024. "Environmental Impact Statement." May 1. www.deepseapioneer.com/cn/News/20240430176.html.

Buderi, Charles L. O., and Favid D. Caron, eds. 1985. "Perspectives on U.S. Policy towards the Law of the Sea: Prelude to the Final Session of the Third U.N. Conference on the Law of the Sea." The Law of the Sea Institute Occasional Paper No. 35, University of Hawaii.

Cançado Trindade, Antônio Augusto. 2015. "Principle 15: Precaution." In *The Rio Declaration on Environment and Development: A Commentary*, edited by Jorge E Viñuales. Oxford University Press.

Cooney, Rosie, and Barney Dickson. 2005. "Appendix: Guidelines for Applying the Precautionary Principle to Biodiversity Conservation and Natural Resource Management." In *Biodiversity and the Precautionary Principle: Risk, Uncertainty and Practice in Conservation and Sustainable Use*, edited by Rosie Cooney and Barney Dickson. Earthscan.

De Bruyne, Kris, Harmen Stoffers, Stéphane Flamen, Hendrik De Beuf, Céline Taymans, Samantha Smith, and Kris Van Nijen. 2022. "A Precautionary Approach to Developing Nodule Collector Technology." In *Perspectives on Deep-Sea Mining*, edited by Rahul Sharma. Springer.

Devenish, B. J., G. G. Rooney, H. N. Webster, and D. J. Thomson. 2010. "The Entrainment Rate for Buoyant Plumes in a Crossflow." *Boundary-Layer Meteorology* 134: 411–439.

DHI (DHI Water & Environment). 2024. *Impossible Metals Eureka III Pilot Collector Plume Modeling Study: Final Report.* DHI Ref. No. 41807286.

Gazis, Iason-Zois, Henko de Stigter, Jochen Mohrmann, Karl Heger, Melanie Diaz, Benjamin Gillard, Matthias Baeye, Mario E. Veloso-Alarcón, Kaveh Purkiani, Matthias Haeckel, Annemiek Vink, Laurenz Thomsen, and Jens Greinert. 2025. "Monitoring Benthic Plumes, Sediment Redeposition and Seafloor Imprints Caused by Deep-Sea Polymetallic Nodule Mining." *Nature Communications* 16: 1229.

Global Sea Mineral Resources. 2018. *Environmental Impact Statement: Small-Scale Testing of Nodule Collector Components on the Seafloor of the Clarion-Clipperton Fracture Zone and Its Environmental Impact.* ISA_EIA_2018_GSRNOD2019.

Handschuh, R., H. Grebe, J. Panthel, E. Schulte, B. Wenzlawski, W. Schwarz, M. A. Atmanand, R. Jeyamani, M. A. Shajahan, C. R. Deepak, and M. Ravindran. 2001. "Innovative Deep Ocean Mining Concept Based on Flexible Riser and Self-Propelled Mining Machines." *ISOPE Ocean Mining and Gas Hydrates Symposium*, ISOPE ISOPE-M-01-017.

Herrington, Richard. 2021. "Mining Our Green Future." *Nature Reviews: Materials* 6: 456–458.

ILA (International Law Association) Study Group. 2014. "First Report." March 7.

2016. "Second Report." July.

ILC (International Law Commission). 1994. "Draft Articles on the Law of the Non-Navigational Uses of International Watercourses." Reprinted in *Yearbook of the International Law Commission 1994*, vol. II. A/CN.4/SER.A/1994/Add.l (Part 2).

2001. "Draft Articles on Prevention of Transboundary Harm from Hazardous Activities." Reprinted in *Yearbook of the International Law Commission 2001*, vol. II, pt. 2. A/CN.4/SER.A/2001/Add.1.

2021. "Draft Guidelines on the Protection of the Atmosphere." *Yearbook of the International Law Commission 2021*, vol. II (Part Two). A/CN.4/SER.A/2021/Add.1 (Part 2).

ISA (International Seabed Authority). 2019. "Draft Regulations on Exploitation of Mineral Resources in the Area." ISBA/25/C/WP.1 (March 22, 2019).

2021. "Marine Minerals Resources: Scientific and Technological Advances." ISA Technical Study No. 30.

ISA and IMO (International Seabed Authority and International Maritime Organization). 2019. "Competencies of the International Seabed Authority and the International Maritime Organization in the Context of Activities in the Area." ISA Technical Study No. 25.

Jaeckel, Aline L. 2017. *The International Seabed Authority and the Precautionary Principle: Balancing Deep Seabed Mineral Mining and Marine Environmental Protection*. Vol. 83 of Publications on Ocean Development. Brill Nijhoff.

Johnstone, Rachael Lorna. 2015. *Offshore Oil and Gas Development in the Arctic under International Law: Risk and Responsibility*. Brill Nijhoff.

Jones, Daniel O. B., Maria Belen Arias, Loïc Van Audenhaege, Sabena Blackbird, Corie Boolukos, Guadalupe Bribiesca-Contreras, Jonathan T. Copley, Andrew Dale, Susan Evans, Bethany F. M. Fleming, Andrew R. Gates, Hannah Grant, Mark G. J. Hartl, Veerle A. I. Huvenne, Rachel M. Jeffreys, Pierre Josso, Lucas D. King, Erik Simon-Lledó, Tim Le Bas, Louisa Norman, Bryan O'Malley, Thomas Peacock, Tracy Shimmield, Eva C. D. Stewart, Andrew K. Sweetman, Catherine Wardell, Dmitry Aleynik, and Adrian G. Glover. 2025. "Long-Term Impact and Biological Recovery in a Deep-Sea Mining Track." *Nature* 642: 112–118.

Juda, L. 1979. "UNCLOS III and the New International Economic Order." *Ocean Development and International Law* 7 (3–4): 221–255.

Kang, Yajuan, Shaojun Liu, Weisheng Zou, He Zhao, and Xiaozhou Hu. 2019. "Design and Analysis of an Innovative Deep-Sea Lifting Motor Pump." *Applied Ocean Research* 82: 22–31.

Kang, Yajuan, Kaile Wang, Qiong Hu, and Shaojun Liu. 2024. "Research on a Coupled System Design for Mineral Lifting and Wastewater Drainage in Deep-Sea Mining Applications." *Ocean Engineering* 299: 117260.

Keaton, J. R. 2017. "Angle of Internal Friction." In *Encyclopedia of Engineering Geology*, edited by Peter T. Bobrowsky and Brian Marker. Encyclopedia of Earth Sciences Series. Springer.

Le, Jennifer T., Lisa A. Levin, and Richard T. Carson. 2017. "Incorporating Ecosystem Services into Environmental Management of Deep-Seabed Mining." *Deep Sea Research Part II: Topical Studies in Oceanography* 137: 486–503.

Li, Yuwen. 1994. *Transfer of Technology for Deep Sea-Bed Mining: The 1982 Law of the Sea Convention and Beyond*. Vol. 25 of Publications on Ocean Development. Martinus Nijhoff.

Liu, S. J., C. Liu, and Y. Dai. 2014. "Status and Progress on Researches and Developments of Deep Ocean Mining Equipments." *Journal of Mechanical Engineering* 50 (2): 8–18.

Metals Company. 2023. "TMC Subsidiary NORI Shares Preliminary Findings on Environmental Impacts of Pilot Nodule Collection System Test." The Metals Company, December 14. https://investors.metals.co/news-releases/news-release-details/tmc-subsidiary-nori-shares-preliminary-findings-environmental.

Muñoz-Royo, Carlos, Thomas Peacock, Matthew H. Alford, Jerome A. Smith, Arnaud Le Boyer, Chinmay S. Kulkarni, Pierre F. J. Lermusiaux, Patrick J. Haley Jr., Chris Mirabito, Dayang Wang, E. Eric Adams, Raphael Ouillon, Alexander Breugem,

Boudewijn Decrop, Thijs Lanckriet, Rohit B. Supekar, Andrew J. Rzeznik, Amy Gartman, and Se-Jong Ju. 2021. "Extent of Impact of Deep-Sea Nodule Mining Midwater Plumes Is Influenced by Sediment Loading, Turbulence and Thresholds." *Communications Earth & Environment* 2: 148.

Papanicolopolou, Irini. 2020. "Due Diligence in Law of the Sea." In *Due Diligence in the International Legal Order*, edited by Heike Krieger, Anne Peters, and Leonhard Kreuzer. Oxford University Press.

Peel, Jacqueline. 2004. "Precaution: A Matter of Principle, Approach or Process?" *Melbourne Journal of International Law* 5 (2): 483–501.

Platzöder, Renate. 1990. *The Law of the Sea: Documents, 1983–1989*. Oceana Publications.

Reagan, Ronald. 1982a. "Statement on United States Actions Concerning the Conference on the Law of the Sea." National Archives, Ronald Reagan Presidential Library & Museum, July 9. www.reaganlibrary.gov/research/speeches/70982b.

1982b. "Statement on United States Participation in the Third United Nations Conference on the Law of the Sea." National Archives, Ronald Reagan Presidential Library & Museum, January 29. www.reaganlibrary.gov/research/speeches/12982b.

Rzeznik, Andrew J., Glenn R. Flierl, and Thomas Peacock. 2019. "Model Investigations of Discharge Plumes Generated by Deep-Sea Nodule Mining Operations." *Ocean Engineering* 172: 684–696.

Schmidt, Markus G. 1989. *Common Heritage or Common Burden? The United States Position on the Development of a Regime for Deep Sea-Bed Mining in the Law of the Sea Convention*. Clarendon Press.

Shen, Yijun, Minfang Chen, Yanlian Du, and Meng Li. 2022. "Key Mechanical Issues and Technical Challenges of Deep-Sea Mining Development System." *Mechanics in Engineering* 44 (5): 1005–1020.

Solheim, Astrid V., Per Olaf Brett, Jose Jorge Garcia Agis, Stein Ove Erikstad, and Bjørn Egil Asbjørnslett. 2022. "Technology Transfer in Novel Ship Design: A Deep Seabed Mining Study." *SNAME International Marine Design Conference*, D021S002R001.

Tanaka, Yoshifumi. 2006. "Regulation of Land-Based Marine Pollution in International Law: A Comparative Analysis between Global and Regional Legal Frameworks." *Zeitschrift fur Auslandisches Offentliches Recht und Volkerrecht* 66: 535–574.

Trouwborst, Arie. 2006a. "Precautionary Measures." In *Precautionary Rights and Duties of States*. Brill Nijhoff.

2006b. *Precautionary Rights and Duties of States*. Martinus Nijhoff.

UK-Sandeel. 2025. "The European Union v. the United Kingdom of Great Britain and Northern Ireland." Permanent Court of Arbitration (PCA), March 27, 2025. Case Number 2024-45.

UN (United Nations). 1972. "Report of the United Nations Conference on the Human Environment." Stockholm, June 5–16, 1975. A/CONF.48/14/Rev.1.

1992. *Agenda 21: The United Nations Programme of Action from Rio*. United Nations Conference on Environment and Development.

UNCLOS III (Third United Nations Conference on the Law of the Sea). 1975. "Iraq: Revised Draft Articles on Transfer of Technology." In *Official Records*, vol. IV. United Nations, 2009. A/CONF.62/C.3/L.12/Rev.l (April 24, 1975).

1976. "Revised Single Negotiating Text (Part I)." In *Official Records*, vol. V. United Nations, 2009. A/CONF.62/WP.8/Rev.l (May 6, 1976) (includes resolutions 2467 A, B, C and D).

UNGA (United Nations General Assembly). 1967a. "Examination of the Question of the Reservation Exclusively for Peaceful Purposes of the Sea-Bed and the Ocean Floor, and the Subsoil Thereof, Underlying the High Seas beyond the Limits of Present National Jurisdiction, and the Use of Their Resources in the Interests of Mankind." A RES 2340 (XXII) (December 18, 1967).

1967b. Twenty-Second Session, First Committee, 1515th Meeting. A/C.l/PV.1515 (November 1, 1967).

1967c. Twenty-Second Session, First Committee, 1516th Meeting. A/C.1/PV.1516 (November 1, 1967).

1968. "Examination of the Question of the Reservation Exclusively for Peaceful Purposes of the Sea-Bed and the Ocean Floor, and the Subsoil Thereof, Underlying the High Seas beyond the Limits of Present National Jurisdiction, and the Use of Their Resources in the Interests of Mankind." A/RES/2467(XXIII) (December 21, 1968).

1969a. "Proposals and Views Relating to the Adoption of Principles." Committee on the Peaceful Uses of the Seabed and the Ocean Floor beyond the Limits of National Jurisdiction. Working Paper prepared by the Secretariat, A/AC.138/7 (March 6, 1969).

1969b. "Question of the Reservation Exclusively for Peaceful Purposes of the Sea-Bed and the Ocean Floor, and the Subsoil Thereof, Underlying the High Seas beyond the Limits of Present National Jurisdiction, and the Use of Their Resources in the Interests of Mankind." A/RES/2574(XXIV) D (December 15, 1969).

1970a. "Declaration of Principles Governing the Sea-Bed and the Ocean Floor, and the Subsoil Thereof, beyond the Limits of National Jurisdiction." A/RES/2749(XXV) (December 17, 1970).

1970b. "Reservation Exclusively for Peaceful Purposes of the Sea-Bed and the Ocean Floor, and the Subsoil Thereof, Underlying the High Seas beyond the Limits of Present National Jurisdiction and Use of Their Resources in the Interests of Mankind, and Convening of a Conference on the Law of the Sea." A/RES/2750(XXV) (December 17, 1970).

1970c. Twenty-Fifth Session, First Committee, 1777th Meeting. A/C.1/PV.1777 (November 30, 1970).

1970d. Twenty-Fifth Session, Provisional Verbatim Records. A/C.1/PV.1787 (December 7, 1970).

1973. *Report of the Committee on the Peaceful Uses of the Sea-Bed and the Ocean Floor beyond the Limits of National Jurisdiction*, vol. I. 28 UN GAOR Supp.21 (A/9021).

1974. "Declaration on the Establishment of a New International Economic Order." A/RES/S-6/3201 (May 1, 1974).

1992. "Rio Declaration on Environment and Development." A/CONF.151/26 (Vol. I) (August 12, 1992).

1994. "Consultations of the Secretary-General on Outstanding Issues Relating to the Deep Seabed Mining Provisions of the United Nations Convention on the Law of the Sea: Report of the Secretary-General." A/48/950 (June 9, 1994).

van der Grient, J. M. A., and J. C. Drazen. 2021. "Potential Spatial Intersection between High-Seas Fisheries and Deep-Sea Mining in International Waters." *Marine Policy* 129: 104564.

Wang, Dayang, and E. Eric Adams. 2016. "Intrusion Dynamics of Particle Plumes in Stratified Water with Weak Crossflow: Application to Deep Ocean Blowouts." *Journal of Geophysical Research: Oceans* 121 (6): 3820–3835.

Welling, Conrad G. 1981. "An Advanced Design Deep Sea Mining System." *Offshore Technology Conference*, OTC-4094-MS.

Yamada, H., and T. Yamazaki. 1998. "Japan's Ocean Test of the Nodule Mining System." *ISOPE International Ocean and Polar Engineering Conference*, ISOPE-I-98-003.

Zhang, Qi. Xuguang Chen, Lubao Luan, Fei Sha, and Xuelin Liu. 2025. "Technology and Equipment of Deep-Sea Mining: State of the Art and Perspectives." *Earth Energy Science* 1 (1): 65–84.

PART V

Marine Science and Exploration

10

Sensor Monitoring and Reliable Telecommunications (SMART) Submarine Cables and Marine Scientific Research

Youri van Logchem

10.1 INTRODUCTION

Submarine cables as such are not a new technology. On the contrary, activities related thereto can be considered to be one of the traditional uses of the seas and ocean. Submarine cable activities have occurred since the nineteenth century, when telegraphic cables took center-stage (Ash 2014, 19–39). With time, the usage of submarine cables has significantly expanded. This is in terms of both scale and their emergence in a broader range of contexts, including energy, scientific, and military. Combined with this, the importance of submarine cables has increased to a point where they are now widely considered as critical infrastructure (Lott 2024, 125–128). Among the range of contexts where submarine cables have emerged, fiber-optic cables used for (international) communications have notably risen to prominence, mainly in tandem with the creation of the internet in the 1980s (Davenport 2015a, 61–62). The proper functioning of the global telecommunications network, including the internet and financial and security systems, is inexorably interwoven with submarine fiber-optic cables (Van Logchem 2021a).

A relatively recent technological development, constituting a new use of cables, is to outfit fiber-optic communication cables with oceanographic sensors to collect data on the oceans, environment, and climate change, thereby turning them into Sensor Monitoring and Reliable Telecommunications (SMART) cables (Lentz and Phibbs 2012; You 2010a). This is one of the solutions scientists have devised to improve the state of knowledge relating to the seas and oceans (Carter and Soons 2014, 326–327; Davenport 2015b, 210). Currently, significant gaps remain in our knowledge of the oceans, especially of the deep ocean (Doussis 2017, 87–88). One reason for these gaps is the limitations inherent in other means employed to collect oceanographic data, such as buoys and satellites that cannot collect data below specific depths (Butler 2012, 5; You 2010b).

More information on the marine environment can be obtained through the oceanographic sensors attached to submarine telecommunication cables, which are modified versions of those sensors used in cabled ocean observatories. In this light, the development and deployment of SMART cables should be applauded. The paucity of knowledge about the marine environment affects the accuracy of disaster warnings. It also limits our understanding of the impact of climate change on the oceans, hampering our ability to counter climate change successfully. Societal and scientific benefits are thus associated with SMART cables. Consequently, utilizing the vast infrastructure of submarine communications cables and harnessing them to gather oceanographic data multiplies their functionality. However, several legal issues spring from this multifunctionality. Underlying these issues is that SMART cables combine the *transmission* of voice, video, and data traffic with gathering information on the marine environment. While dual-use cables add an additional tool for oceanographic data collection, they also introduce different legal regimes that do not fully align. More specifically, due to fiber-optic cables being outfitted with this additional functionality, several pertinent issues are presented. First, since SMART cables transmit international communications and collect and transmit oceanographic data, should their usage be considered an activity falling under the legal regimes relating to both cables and marine scientific research (MSR), and thus require coastal State consent, depending on the maritime zone involved? Second, would the collection of data by a submarine telecommunication cable be part of the rights and freedoms relating to transit cables of other States beyond the territorial sea of coastal States? This chapter demonstrates that the answers to these issues are variable in that they depend on the location of the cable and how the cable is being used.

Section 10.1 begins this chapter with setting the scene by sketching the roles of submarine cables and SMART cables. It addresses the relationship of SMART cables to fiber-optic telecommunication cables, where SMART cables can be situated among the different methods for collecting oceanographic data, such as buoys and cabled ocean observatories (these are subsea infrastructures – designed to collect data on the marine environment – that employ submarine cables for the transfer of data and power), and canvasses the range of challenges that may arise around SMART cables. The international legal framework applicable to SMART cables is considered in Section 10.2, which emphasizes the crucial distinction between telecommunication cables that only transit a coastal State's maritime zone and those that make landfall in the State's territory. In broad strokes, where for the laying of landing cables the coastal State has extensive authority, this is significantly reduced for transit cables in a coastal State's exclusive economic zone (EEZ) and on the continental shelf. Then, the focus shifts to the classification of SMART cables in light of the role such cables have in marine data collection. Particular attention is paid to their double function, whereby different legal regimes may be activated: that is, the one applicable to submarine cables and the regime for marine data collection. If it concerns MSR, Part XIII of the 1982 United Nations Convention on the

Law of the Sea (UNCLOS)[1] will be relevant (see Section 10.2.2). Although security concerns apply broadly to cables, including against the backdrop of increasing geopolitical tensions, in the case of SMART cables these concerns may be magnified. Submarine cable security has also taken on urgency after a spate of instances where submarine cables were seemingly intentionally targeted, such as in the Balticconnector incident of October 2023 (Henley and Ambrose 2023). Security-related concerns over telecommunication cables and SMART cables take center-stage in Section 10.3. The chapter concludes in Section 10.4 with thoughts on how to deal with emerging legal challenges and the future of SMART cables.

10.1.1 *Background on Submarine Cables*

Submarine cables are either placed on or buried in the seabed. They are roughly a few centimeters in width. Their width and footprint will increase if cables are installed on the seabed with an extra layer of protection composed of a gel-like substance, which is encased in a copper or aluminum tube, followed by layers of steel wires for strength. The entire cable is then covered with a polyethylene sheath for insulation and waterproofing. These features may double the size of the cable (Carter et al. 2009, 8). For fiber-optic telecommunication cables to be turned into SMART cables, the cable repeaters will have to be modified in a way that enables them to collect data. On a side note, cable repeaters are an integral part of a cable and a key ingredient in international fiber-optic cable systems, as they provide the necessary boost to signals transmitted through cables, which will lose their strength and quality over distance. The repeaters in fiber-optic cables have sufficient "space to integrate the temperature, salinity and pressure sensors" (You 2010b, 4), meaning that neither the appearance nor the size of SMART cables is different from that of their non-SMART counterparts. Particularly when located in relative proximity to the coast, submarine cables are buried in the subsoil (Ash 2014, 35), using remotely operated vehicles. This makes them less vulnerable to damage from competing activities, such as fishing, that tend to intensify as one approaches the coast (Section 10.3). Although cables are considered largely environmentally benign, some concerns have been raised over the resulting disturbance to the marine environment if they are buried in the seabed (Carter et al. 2009, 33).

Today, the use of submarine cables is pervasive for international communications – the high-speed transmission of voice, video, and data traffic (Carter et al. 2009, 8). The reliance on submarine cables in international communications continues to grow (*The Economist* 2016, 16). The lynchpin role of submarine cables in communications is illustrated by the fact that approximately 400 cables (making up over 500 individual cable systems) snaking around most of the globe are responsible for about 97 percent of international communications (UNGA 2011, 2023, 125;

[1] UNCLOS, December 10, 1982, 1833 UNTS 397.

Burnett et al. 2014b, 4).[2] This stands in stark contrast to a popular misperception that such communications are conducted primarily using satellites in outer space (Burnett et al. 2014b, 3).

Submarine telecommunication cables have a long pedigree, having first emerged in the nineteenth century (Ash 2014, 20). Then, in line with the state of the technology, it was telegraphic cables that reflected the state of the art (Ash 2014, 20–28). After the submarine telegraphic cable fell into disuse in the 1930s, a new era of telephone cables dawned, with the laying of two such cables between Scotland and Newfoundland (Ash 2014, 28–33). The next phase for submarine cables followed after satellites had risen to prominence in the 1970s and 1980s as the main means for providing international communications (Carter et al. 2009, 15). The discovery of fiber-optic cables in 1966 (Ash 2014, 33), which subsequently were introduced into a marine environment in 1986 (Ash 2014, 34), ultimately eliminated satellites as the main means of international communication. Their downfall was buoyed by the creation of the internet in 1982 and the subsequent combining of that technology with the use of submarine cables, which has changed the face of telecommunications.

Outside of the communications context, submarine cables serve different purposes as well, including the transport of electrical power from one location to another and the collection and transmission of military and oceanographic data (see Section 10.2.2). Submarine cables are in use in the context of the collection of oceanographic data, albeit to that exclusive aim, which sets them apart from most SMART cables (see Section 10.1.2). As a further refinement, MSR cables can be employed for a single purpose (that is, collection of oceanographic data or transmission of such data), or they can combine the two, both collecting and transmitting scientific data. Submarine telecommunication cables have had the role of transporting oceanographic data that was collected through alternative means for data collection as part of an MSR project. Data obtained through cabled ocean observatories are especially relevant in this context (Carter and Soons 2014, 328–332). Cabled observatories come in a variety of shapes and forms and offer different levels of complexity, ranging from oceanographic mooring to complex observatory systems that rely extensively on cables through which power and communications are simultaneously provided. These systems enable the collected data to be transferred instantly to an onshore facility (Carter and Soons 2014, 328–332). In this vein, the NEPTUNE system, which is a regional cabled observatory system in the waters off the coast of Canada, is underpinned by close to 1,000 km of cable for the combined purpose of transmitting data and providing power (Ocean Networks Canada n.d.). Although such cabled systems employ communications technology in a data collection context, they fall short of the integration that is perceived with SMART cables,

[2] UN General Assembly Resolution 65/37 recognizes that "fibre optic submarine cables transmit most of the world's data and communications and, hence, are vitally important to the global economy and the national security of all States" (UNGA 2011, 3).

which have a data collection functionality. Another use of submarine cables is that they have been outfitted with the capacity to conduct MSR actively in the past; this is thus beyond functioning as a means for transporting data. Their use in data collection dates to the second half of the twentieth century, when cables were used to measure ocean currents (Carter and Soons 2014, 325). As time progressed, submarine cables came to underpin other scientific uses as well, including measuring ocean temperatures and gathering information pertinent to natural hazard detection (Carter and Soons 2014, 325). Nonetheless, significant gaps remain in our knowledge of the seas and oceans, which has spurred researchers to find new solutions to close those gaps (Carter and Soons 2014, 325). Against this background, SMART cables have emerged as the new frontier in oceanographic data collection. In some ways, SMART cables are similar to those MSR cables, combining the functions of oceanographic data collection and the transmission of such data, but one important difference lies in that this is a secondary function to providing international communications.

10.1.2 *SMART Cables*

In general, equipping submarine cables with sensors is not a new phenomenon. In such a vein, power cables have been outfitted with sensors since the 1980s to measure ocean temperature (Agarwala 2019, 54). The idea of equipping telecommunication cables with oceanographic sensors took root even earlier. More specifically, Japanese scientists modified analogue cables with sensing technology for earthquake and tsunami detection and warning in 1979 (Howe et al. 2019, 16). In the wake of the Tohoku earthquake and tsunami in 2011, this range of seismic observatories employing sensing technology (that is, seismic and pressure sensors) in communication cables has further expanded off the coast of Japan. While these "SMART cables" involved repurposed analogue communication cables, there are different variants of such cables, however, which leads to the question of their definition. Different terminology is used in the literature to refer to a fiber-optic submarine cable that collects and transmits oceanographic data. This includes "green cable" (Agarwala 2019, 50), "telecom-marine data cable" (Bressie 2012, 1), and "SMART cable" (1–2) – the last of which is discussed in this chapter.

Irrespective of nomenclature, reference is made to the same phenomenon: that is, the outfitting of fiber-optic telecommunication cables with sensors, which enables the cable to measure "ocean temperature and salinity, pressure and acceleration" (Carter and Soons 2014, 327). Fiber-optic telecommunication cables can be modified in three ways to collect data, whereby they take on the features of a SMART cable. First, akin to the example of the seismic observatories created off the coast of Japan, redundant cables can have a new life by repurposing these exclusively for data collection and transmission (a). Second, telecommunication cables already in place and involved in the transmission of international communications can be outfitted with oceanographic sensors to collect data on the marine environment and to then transmit it through the same communications cable (b). Third, new fiber-optic communication cables that have yet to be installed can be purposely designed with these oceanographic sensors included in their repeaters (c) (Davenport 2015b, 244). It is mainly with variants (b) and (c) that this chapter is concerned, as through their modification they become genuine dual-use cables. Due to their dual function, they also raise the most legal challenges (see Section 10.2).

Two of the main benefits of SMART cables are that they can collect information at great depths and at a relatively low cost (Howe et al. 2019, 1–2). Through their use, an improved understanding of the (marine) environment can be obtained. More oceanographic data translates into gaining a better understanding of the climate and oceans (Agarwala 2019, 51, 54–55). This benefits science and, in turn, helps in the fight against climate change and in the accuracy of disaster warnings. Beyond that, SMART cables are a relatively easy and inexpensive way to achieve this. For example, the oceanographic sensors included in the repeaters of fiber-optic cables are modifications of off-the-shelf technology used in cabled ocean observatories (Howe et al. 2019, 2). Beyond that, if active telecommunication cables are equipped with sensors, this avoids having to build dedicated ocean observatories that similarly rely on cables for data transmission and power supply. Technological challenges arise in outfitting fiber-optic cables with oceanographic sensors, however. For example, in installing this technology in long(er) cable routes, including those exceeding 2,500 km, and ensuring that the lifespan of a SMART cable extends about twenty-five years, which would be the same as for its non-SMART counterparts (Howe et al. 2019, 14–17). SMART cables enable significantly more data to be collected, but this performance comes with an important caveat. The resulting picture will continue to exhibit informational gaps, as some parts of the seas are unserved by cables or are covered only to a limited extent. This somewhat uneven distribution of telecommunication cables around the globe would tilt the scales on oceanographic collection in favor of the northern hemisphere, which has a denser cable network (Carter and Soons 2014, 328). The advent of SMART cables would thus not render obsolete other means of obtaining oceanographic data. To provide the fullest picture, the information obtained via SMART cables requires integration with "information gathered from other observation sites" (Carter and Soons 2014, 328), including by satellites, ships, buoys, and observatories (Howe et al. 2019, 3).

10.1.3 *Views of the Cable Industry on SMART Cables*

Despite the scientific and societal benefits associated with SMART cables, some hurdles do exist, which may limit the further rollout of this innovation. Before delving into these hurdles, it requires mention that most activities related to submarine telecommunication cables are undertaken by private actors. By that same token, State involvement is usually limited. More specifically, the industry is composed of three completely or partly privatized actors: the owners of submarine cables, which are generally individual or a consortium of telecommunication carriers (for example, AT&T, Google, and Singapore Telecommunications Limited); those that install cables on or in the seabed (for example, Tyco Telecommunications); and cable maritime route surveyors (Davenport 2012, 202; Van Logchem 2014). It is rare for a submarine cable system to be owned by a single company, as often consortia ranging from six to twenty companies will own parts of a cable system. Furthermore, the consortia divide the bandwidth by divisible rights, apportioning the cable based on the investment in the project. Their bottom line is financial, and in line with this, their modus operandi is geared toward keeping the cable system operational and minimizing coastal State interference (Van Logchem 2014, 113–114). For example, this aspect is already visible in the inception of a cable system. In the determination of a cable route, the cable industry will exert significant effort to identify and, if feasible, avoid those sea areas that carry the risk of damaging cables (Evans and Page 2014, 97–98).

Against this background, the views of the industry on SMART cables take on particular urgency. On the positive side, adding sensors to a cable improves the ability to monitor its integrity remotely as well; a cable without sensors does not have the capacity to detect external hazards. A further benefit for the cable industry is that the data collected by the sensors may illuminate natural hazards, which could help improve cable resilience. Industry recognizes these benefits, as some of its members, including TE SubCom, have expressed interest in SMART cable systems (Subsea World News 2017). At the same time, the industry has some concerns over SMART cables, which may well outweigh their benefits (Bressie 2012, 21). The industry is particularly worried about negative impacts on the delivery of international communications bandwidth if cables used to this specific aim are outfitted with oceanographic sensors (Bressie 2012, 21). Once a telecommunication cable is modified, whereby it is changed into a dual-use cable used for data collection as well, coastal States may use this as a jurisdictional hook to expand their reach over cables (Bressie 2012, 24–25). One example of a State that reportedly opposes giving active telecommunication cables a role in scientific data collection is Japan (Palmer-Felgate 2016). Beyond that, coastal States exercising excessive jurisdiction over telecommunication cables are already a recurring theme, without sensors having been added to these cables (Bressie 2012, 3, 24). This is visible, for example, in the contexts of the delineation of transit cable routes and with regard to the laying or repairing of transit cables in the EEZ or on the continental shelf over which some coastal States assume jurisdiction, despite this lacking a basis in UNCLOS (Van Logchem 2014, 110).

A further concern of the industry centers around security, which may be enhanced when cables are equipped with the capacity to monitor their surroundings, including revealing nearby ship information (see Section 10.3). This aspect may provide additional encouragement to coastal States to assert jurisdiction over SMART cables. Other questions will have to be answered as well before the telecommunication industry widely embraces SMART cables. For example, who will pay for outfitting fiber-optic cables with oceanographic sensors (Agarwala 2019, 50)? Who will be liable for the costs of repair and any additional damage if the sensors interfere with the proper functioning of the cable? There is also the question of ownership of the collected data (Howe et al. 2019, 17–18). As data is collected through cables that are privately owned, such data would be proprietary, placing ownership with the cable owners. But there is another important driver behind how warmly SMART cables will be embraced by industry and that is whether "a business case can be made" for cable owners (Bressie 2012, 3, 25).

Despite the potential challenges associated with SMART cables, they are already being piloted in practice. Examples in this respect are a cable system (SMART Atlantic CAM) connecting the Portuguese mainland to the Azores and Madeira respectively, and the SMART cable lying between the neighboring small island States of Vanuatu and New Caledonia (SMART Cables n.d.). A common feature of these projects is that they sidestep many of the more difficult questions – for example, by avoiding coastal States that have not agreed to the SMART cable route through their maritime zones or because the network is underpinned by an agreement between the States to have the SMART cable system run between their coasts.

10.2 SMART CABLES: A CLASSIFICATION CONUNDRUM?

From a legal perspective, one of the main conundrums is the dual-use nature of SMART cables. Tied to this, the issue arises whether they are subject to one or two legal regimes. Should these dual uses of oceanographic data collection and transmission, and of providing international communication, be treated on an equal footing, rendering the cable subject to both the cable regime and the MSR regime? Or, rather, considering that data collection is an added functionality of a submarine cable that is primarily used for telecommunications, would it be merely subject to the set of rules pertaining to submarine cables? At first glance, the latter line of argument may be difficult to uphold, considering that a single-purpose cable used for international communications is modified to enable it to exercise the secondary function of data collection that may be tantamount to MSR (a), or when a new fiber-optic communication cable is installed with oceanographic sensors (b) (see Section 10.1.2). Connected to this, the aspect of data collection is unrelated to the ability of the cable to transmit international communications, which renders it seemingly difficult for SMART cables not to be perceived as subject to a dual regime. Before addressing where SMART cables fit under the international legal framework (Section 10.2.3), it is necessary to lay out both regimes.

10.2.1 *The International Legal Framework Relating to Submarine Cables*

An international element is required for the international legal framework relating to submarine cables to enter the picture. Usually this occurs because the cable passes through different maritime areas or zones of one or more coastal States. Submarine cables require a starting point and an end point from landing stations ashore. International cable systems require landing stations in the land territories of different coastal States. Before these stations are reached, submarine cables may transit maritime areas that are part of a coastal State's territory and where it has sovereignty (archipelagic waters, internal waters, or the territorial sea); those areas that are subject to functional coastal State jurisdiction (the contiguous zone, the EEZ, and the continental shelf); areas beyond coastal State jurisdiction (the high seas and the international deep-seabed area); or a combination thereof. Depending on the submarine cable segment involved, the applicable international legal rules and the extent of coastal State authority vary.

Submarine cables are regulated by four international legal instruments: the 1958 Geneva Conventions on the Continental Shelf[3] and the High Seas,[4] UNCLOS, and the Convention for the Protection of Submarine Telegraph Cables (1884 Cable Convention).[5] Only the last of these is specifically designed for dealing with telegraphic cables, regulating them in the narrow context of their protection. Particularly relevant for States, however, is UNCLOS. That Convention has attracted close to universal participation, and its provisions on submarine cables have virtually all obtained customary status (Carter and Soons 2014, 332). This is because those provisions on cables in the 1958 Conventions on the High Seas and the Continental Shelf, which UNCLOS replicates, were already considered customary (Davenport 2012, 203). As background, when UNCLOS was negotiated at the Third Law of the Sea Conference, the use of submarine cables was on the decline owing to the increased use of satellites, which were cheaper and more reliable at that time (Carter et al. 2009, 15). This changed after the final text of UNCLOS had been agreed upon in 1982. The real watershed moment came the following year, in 1983, with the creation of the internet (Ash 2014, 34). Fiber-optic cables and the internet became inexorably intertwined in that, through these cables, virtually all the video, voice, and data traffic for the internet were transmitted (see Section 10.1.1). A general implicit reference to the significance of submarine communication cables in UNCLOS can be distilled from one of the aims in the preamble: to strengthen "a legal order for the seas and oceans which will facilitate international communication."

A key aspect of the legal rules for submarine cables is whether they land on an island or mainland territory of a coastal State. If such landfall is made by a cable in its territory, a coastal State has significantly greater authority over it than if it merely passes offshore. The extent of this authority would then not be confined to the cable

3 Convention of the Continental Shelf, April 29, 1958, 499 UNTS 311.

4 Convention on the High Seas, April 29, 1958, 450 UNTS 11.

5 Convention for the Protection of Submarine Telegraph Cables, March 14, 1884, TS 380 (1884 Cable Convention).

segments physically located in its territory, including the territorial sea. This is an automatic corollary to the requirement that cables making a landing in the territory of the coastal State have its consent. To exercise that authority, coastal States may impose certain conditions on the cable and its landing, such as compliance with regulations on the route the cable takes, as well as associated environmental and labor laws. The effect of this is that the set conditions can also relate to those segments of cable systems that are in the EEZ, on the continental shelf, and possibly even beyond (Carter and Soons 2014, 335).

In this light, the provisions of UNCLOS are largely tailored to submarine cables that only pass through a coastal State's maritime zones without making a landfall. The precise rights and obligations of States concerning transit cables vary with the maritime zone involved. For maritime areas that are part of the coastal State's territory (that is, internal waters, archipelagic waters, and the territorial sea), the legal framework for submarine cables is straightforward: the coastal State has full regulatory authority over the laying, maintaining, and repairing of cables within these areas (Articles 2 and 49). This latter provision relating to archipelagic waters must be read in conjunction with Article 51, which provides that archipelagic States must respect in situ transit cables by allowing their repair, maintenance, and possible replacement upon receipt of notice. Coastal State authority applies in maritime zones under the coastal State's sovereignty, regardless of how the cable is classified or its function. A clear picture also emerges for cables transiting areas beyond coastal State jurisdiction, such as the high seas and the international deep seabed. Article 87(1)(c) of UNCLOS grants all States the freedom to lay transit submarine cables in these areas, subject to Part VI of the Convention. That right is further strengthened in Article 112(1). While not explicitly mentioned in Article 87 or 112, repairing and maintaining transit submarine cables, including cable route surveying, are covered by the freedom of the high seas (Van Logchem 2014, 111–112). This view is based on the assumption that repair and maintenance are essential to the lawful use of the sea and inseparable from the freedom to lay transit submarine cables (Van Logchem 2014, 109, 112). A related question is whether attaching oceanographic sensors to submarine cables, which adds the functionality of data collection, could be considered part of the freedom to lay such cables (Strati 2011). This question is further addressed in Section 10.2.3.

Regarding areas within coastal State jurisdiction (that is, the EEZ and the continental shelf), the international legal regime on submarine cables is more complex. Article 58(1) of UNCLOS grants the right to lay cables in these zones, but with certain limitations. The right to lay cables only applies to those transiting the EEZ or the continental shelf without making landfall. Although Article 79(1) of UNCLOS is silent on the right to repair and maintain transit cables, these have to be viewed as activities inherent in the right to lay such cables. Beyond that, in Article 79(2) and (5) there is explicit reference, respectively, to the maintenance and repair of in situ cables. Rights related to transit submarine cables must be exercised with due regard for in situ cables and pipelines and in a way that does not hamper their repair (UNCLOS, Article 79(5); Van Logchem 2014, 110, 118). A similar obligation of due regard in exercising cable rights in the EEZ and on the continental shelf flows from Article 58(3). This provision imposes on all States – which also extends to private actors engaged in cable activities (Van Logchem 2014, 100, 118) – an obligation to comply with laws and regulations of coastal States that are adopted in accordance with Part V of UNCLOS. Particularly relevant for cables are Article 79(2) and (4) (paragraph 3 is concerned with the delineation of pipelines), which allows for limitations to be imposed by coastal States on the right to lay transit cables of other States.

According to Article 79(2) of UNCLOS, the coastal State retains the option to take reasonable measures necessary to protect the exploratory and exploitation rights it has with regard to the continental shelf and any resources contained therein. Measures that would likely fall under this heading are those geared toward prohibiting cable laying in environmentally sensitive areas or areas reserved for hydrocarbon exploitation (Van Logchem 2014, 109). It follows from the same paragraph that coastal States cannot adopt regulations for pollution control in connection with cables located on their continental shelf; the background to reserving this right to pipelines lies in the fact that cables have virtually no detrimental impact on the marine environment (Carter et al. 2014). Article 79(4) states that Part VI leaves untouched that the coastal State can set conditions for cables that enter its territory. However, there are differing opinions on how much room Article 79(2) and (4) leaves for the coastal State to take measures that impose limitations on the right to lay transit submarine cables. The main bone of contention is whether the coastal State's authority goes beyond setting conditions related to natural resources over which the State has sovereign rights (Beckman 2010, 6, 7; Davenport 2015b, 220–222). A general limitation is that measures taken may not amount to the right to lay, maintain, and repair submarine cables being effectively impossible to exercise (Van Logchem 2014, 109).

There is little attempt in UNCLOS to distinguish between different types of submarine cables, suggesting that its provisions apply to the full range of cables (Burnett 2006, 232; Nandan and Rosenne 1993, 270; Takei 2012, 207–208). Only Article 113 specifies its scope of application to extend only to certain types of cables – that is, high-voltage power cables and telegraphic and telephonic communication cables. Despite the provisions in UNCLOS applying to cables broadly, specific types of cables will be subject to another set of rules due to their use and location, pursuant to which the coastal State may assume jurisdiction. For example, if a submarine cable is used for the sole purpose of transmitting data gathered through an MSR project in relation to the continental shelf, it would be under coastal State jurisdiction, and coastal State consent would be required prior to the cable being laid, in accordance with Article 246(1) of UNCLOS. The same analysis would apply by analogy to an out-of-service telecommunication cable that is modified to collect oceanographic data (variant (a) in Section 10.1.2), which may convert it to an MSR activity in the process.

Another example is a telecommunication or power cable connecting different installations on the coastal State's continental shelf. Due to the direct link with the exercise of sovereign rights it has over natural resources and their exploitation, this author suggests that the cable would fall under coastal State authority (UNCLOS, Article 79(4); Davenport 2015b, 222–223). Outside of cables making a landfall and the limitations allowed for under UNCLOS, coastal States cannot assume jurisdiction over activities related to transit cables in the EEZ or on the continental shelf. However, in certain respects, the practice of some coastal States has moved in the opposite direction, in that they claim to have jurisdiction over the laying, maintaining, and repairing of transit submarine cables on the continental shelf (Ford-Ramsden and Davenport 2014, 146–151). Limitations imposed by coastal States on the right to conduct activities in the EEZ and on the continental shelf related to transit telecommunication cables are a thorn in the side of industry. A main concern is that multiplying the functionality of active telecommunication cables will lead to coastal States increasingly exerting jurisdiction over cable-related activities, whereby further complications are layered onto existing ones (Bressie 2012, 24).

10.2.2 *Marine Data Collection*

Marine data collection encompasses a variety of activities conducted to the common aim of enhancing the knowledge of the marine environment (Roach 2007, 542). These activities fall into different categories and include activities conducted in the framework of MSR, operational oceanography, hydrographic surveys, and military surveys (Van Logchem 2021b). Depending on the activity data collected, it may be subject to the rules in Part XIII of UNCLOS. Complicating matters is that UNCLOS does not define MSR in Part XIII, nor anywhere else in the text for that matter. Several attempts by States participating in the Third Law of the Sea Conference to include a definition of MSR during the negotiations for the Convention failed, and States failed to reach an agreement (Soons 1982, 199; Walker 2012, 241–245). Attention was rather directed at designing the substantive rules pertaining to MSR, whereby its contours would be illuminated in the process and alleviate the need for States to agree on a generally accepted definition – or so was the thinking (Soons 1982, 123–124). Nonetheless, in the absence of an express definition, much ink has been spilled on how to define MSR. The absence of a definition in UNCLOS has been lamented, including because that it would lie at the roots of the divergent State practice that emerged around MSR/oceanographic data collection and for the difficulties it has created for the employment of SMART cables (see, for example, Davenport 2015b, 249–250). Differences as to what constitutes MSR have ranged from States that fall on the extreme end of the spectrum – claiming that all forms of marine data collection fall within the jurisdiction of coastal States, including operational oceanography and hydrographic or military surveying – to, on the other end, coastal States that view their jurisdiction as being limited to MSR proper (Churchill et al. 2022, 783–787).

Nonetheless, irrespective of the lack of a universally accepted definition of MSR and divergent State practice, the contours of what constitutes MSR are increasingly clear. An MSR activity is generally understood to have two components: first, the research activity is aimed at furthering the knowledge of humankind on the marine environment; and, second, the results are publicly disseminated (Soons 1982, 124). Activities meeting this definition are within the authority of the coastal State, insofar as they occur within maritime zones over which it has sovereignty or jurisdiction. More specifically, the resulting picture is that MSR within the extent of the territorial sea is predicated on coastal State consent (UNCLOS, Article 245). This is further corroborated by Article 19(2)(j) of UNCLOS, which identifies the passage of a ship becoming non-innocent if it is involved in research or survey activities. Data that is gathered in passage for the sake of safe navigation of the ship (for example, the use of sonar to obtain information on ocean currents) remains beyond the reach of this provision (Soons 1982, 149).

The conduct of MSR in the EEZ and on the continental shelf, as in the territorial sea, is subject to the consent of coastal States (UNCLOS, Articles 56(1)(b) and 246). Another similarity between the territorial sea and the EEZ/continental shelf is that the coastal State can impose conditions on the initiation and conduct of MSR projects. However, UNCLOS draws a distinction between two types of MSR projects in the EEZ and on the continental shelf: first, those projects for which the coastal State shall normally give its consent when a detailed application is made at least six months before the start of the project (Articles 248 and 249); and, second, MSR projects for which there is discretionary autonomy for the State to withhold its consent. In the latter case, a coastal State may, inter alia, exercise its discretion to withhold consent to MSR projects in the EEZ/continental shelf that hold significance for the exploration and exploitation of natural resources (Article 246(5)(a)), or envision the emplacement or operation of installations and structures (Article 246(5)(c)), or if the research involves drilling or setting off of explosives (Article 246(5)(b)). For all the categories of MSR, States seeking consent to conduct activities to this end will be under the additional obligations laid down in Articles 248 and 249 of UNCLOS. This includes offering the coastal State the opportunity to be part of the MSR project (Article 249(1)(a)) and making the collected information available as soon as practically possible (Article 249(1)(e)).

On the high seas, there is the right for all States to conduct MSR projects (Article 87(1)(f)), subject to the two parts of UNCLOS dealing with the continental shelf (Part VI) and MSR (Part XIII). Along similar lines, in the international seabed area, States and competent international organizations have the right to conduct MSR. This aligns with Part XI of UNCLOS, particularly Article 143, which requires MSR projects to be for peaceful purposes and to benefit all humankind. Beyond these two requirements, in both the high seas and the international seabed area, the right to conduct MSR has to be exercised with due regard to the rights of other States and other activities occurring in the international seabed area (Article 87(2)). Of further relevance is Article 258, which is concerned with the deployment of research installations or equipment in the marine environment. This provision may apply to SMART cables, due to the similarities they bear to installations in terms of their relative permanency (see Section 10.2.3).

From the range of activities falling within the ambit of marine data collection, could oceanographic data collection be an alternative categorization for SMART cables (Davenport 2015b, 224)? Two components are attached to "operational oceanography": it must involve the routine collection of oceanographic data, which subsequently is made immediately and generally available. It may be defined as follows: "an activity of systematic and long-term routine measurements of the seas and oceans and atmosphere, and their rapid interpretation and dissemination" (Davenport 2015b, 234). Although the obtained data may produce knowledge similar to the data gathered under the umbrella of an MSR project, in that it benefits humankind as a whole, the main usage of operational oceanographic data is in the realm of the safety of navigation (Kraska 2024, 44–45). Beyond that, general controversy surrounds this category of oceanographic data collection, or – as it is regularly referred to – operational oceanography. One main issue is whether this routine collection of oceanographic data is really an MSR activity in disguise (Mateos and Gorina-Ysern 2010; Whomersley 2021, 29). These differences were mirrored in the practice of States in relation to the "Argo Project" pursuant to which several thousands of monitoring devices that gathered marine meteorological data were deployed on the high seas (Davenport 2015b, 234–235). However, as these devices freely drifted throughout the sea, they sometimes entered into the EEZs of coastal States. Some coastal States were concerned and deemed them to be engaging in MSR, for which coastal State consent is required (Mateos and Gorina-Ysern 2010). Both the controversial status of the collection of oceanographic data (whether or not it qualifies as MSR) and the specifics of SMART cables put into doubt whether they can be easily brought under this rubric. This is because the data collected through these SMART cables is not immediately disseminated, and nor is it collected with the explicit aim of enhancing the safety of navigation. Another aspect that makes it difficult to bring SMART cables under the reach of this "operational oceanography" is that, in contrast to ships or floating equipment routinely collecting data, SMART cables are of a more permanent character, as they are on the seafloor. All this points in the direction that, from the range of activities that equally fall within the scope of marine data collection, SMART cables are an MSR activity (Carter and Soons 2014, 335).

10.2.3 *The Future of SMART Cables*

A logical corollary to SMART cables being a technological development that came after UNCLOS is that none of its provisions have been specifically tailored to this type of cable. This does not render UNCLOS inconsequential, however, as it has the capacity to continue to apply to new technological developments. The legal regimes in Parts VI and XIII are relevant to SMART cables (Strati 2011). SMART cables are in situ in the marine environment and have this same environment as their object on which to collect data, beyond transporting international communications, which clearly raises the specter that they fall within coastal State jurisdiction, depending on their location.

More specifically, on the high seas and in the international seabed area, there exist the two freedoms to lay transit cables (UNCLOS, Article 87) and conduct activities in the framework of MSR (Articles 87(1)(f), 256, and 257). By the same token, coastal States cannot claim jurisdiction over SMART cables. Rather, the jurisdictional competence lies with "the national State of the entity laying or using the cable" (Carter and Soons 2014, 336). In stark contrast, in areas that are part of the territory of the coastal State (internal waters, archipelagic waters, and the territorial sea), both the conduct of MSR and submarine cable activities fall within the sovereignty of the coastal State, allowing it to regulate SMART cables in a way it sees fit (Carter and Soons 2014, 334).

It is a tale of different worlds colliding for SMART cables that *transit* a coastal State's EEZ or continental shelf. While submarine cables transiting the EEZ or continental shelf are largely placed outside the jurisdiction of the coastal State, apart from some limitations related to natural resources, MSR in the EEZ and on the continental shelf falls under the jurisdictional competence of the coastal State (see Sections 10.2.1 and 10.2.2).

Further, an argument has been made that if a submarine cable placed on the seabed collects data (that is, if it is a SMART cable), besides constituting MSR, it falls in the specific category of MSR projects for which the coastal State concerned would have the discretionary autonomy to withhold its consent when an application to that end is made (Carter and Soons 2014, 335). At the root of this argument lies an assumed similarity between a SMART cable and a structure: that is, their "semi-permanent character," which would bring it under the reach of Article 246(5)(c) of UNCLOS (Carter and Soons 2014, 335). This argument that the cable has to be considered a structure has been extended by analogy to cables that collect data landing on shore or entering a coastal State's territorial sea. If SMART cables would be considered a research structure, and given that they are placed on the seabed to remain in place for a longer period of time, the coastal State would have exclusive jurisdiction over the cables by way of Articles 60 and 80 of UNCLOS. Nonetheless, different views have been held in this regard, with Bressie assuming that definite judgment around the status of SMART cables as being also subject to the MSR regime cannot be made based on UNCLOS (Bressie 2012, 20). Underpinning this argument is the failure of UNCLOS to address the precise meaning of both "MSR" and a "submarine cable," leaving the status of the latter up in the air in the absence of judicial pronouncement and/or customary international law having developed in either direction (Bressie 2012, 20).

As a general rule of thumb, legal difficulties and uncertainty tend to come to the forefront for SMART cables in the EEZ and concerning the continental shelf. By way of contrast, MSR is a high-seas freedom beyond areas of national jurisdiction. The argument that outfitting cables with sensors is absorbed by the freedom to lay transit submarine cables under Article 87 of UNCLOS, which by way of Article 58(1) of UNCLOS similarly applies in the EEZ, has little merit, particularly if account is taken of the fact that the oceanographic sensors are purposely added to telecommunication cables to provide them with the added functionality of data collection, which is a fundamentally different activity from transporting international communications. Attaching sensors is also not entangled with the right to lay transit cables in a way the two could not be seen in isolation, as is, for example, the case with repairing or maintaining a transit cable, or conducting a cable route survey prior thereto, which are all necessary components to be able to exercise this right. Viewed in this light, nor can the attaching of oceanographic sensors to telecommunication cables located in the EEZ be seen as a use related to the operation of such cables (UNCLOS, Article 58(1); Strati 2011). Considering the above, the *de lege lata* suggests that MSR is the most proper categorization for SMART cables, whereby a need for obtaining coastal State consent is activated prior to their employment in certain parts of the seas (Carter and Soons 2014, 335).

10.3 THE PROTECTION OF SMART CABLES: NEW WINE IN OLD WINESKINS?

Submarine cables are inherently vulnerable because of their design, being just a few centimeters in width and made of fiberglass encased by plastic (Carter et al. 2009, 8). This is reflected in submarine cable protection being a topic whose relevance coincides with the inception of cables in the nineteenth century (Wargo and Davenport 2014, 255). Cables within shallower waters with depths of less than 100 m are especially vulnerable, since human activity tends to intensify there (Aw 2024, 136). To avoid such waters completely is impossible, as landfall must be made somewhere; therefore, cables are often provided with a layer of additional encasement and buried into the subsoil. At the same time, cable breaks are not isolated to shallow waters, although those are more infrequent. An example is the breakage of a fiber-optic cable located in deeper waters that connect the Shetland Islands to the Faroe Islands, which is part of the SHEFA-2 system, in 2022 (Van Logchem 2022). Beyond the territorial sea, cables are more regularly placed directly on the seabed, which is mostly for reasons of cost and the lesser likelihood of accidentally damaging these cables (Carter et al. 2009, 30–31).

Different degrees of damage can be identified when a cable exhibits a fault, ranging from minor damage to its outer insulation to the full breakage of a submarine cable (Wargo and Davenport 2014, 256). Cable faults are ordinary occurrences during a cable's life cycle, which is normally around twenty to twenty-five years (Rapp 2010). Most cable faults can be retraced to forces lying outside the cable. Two sources of cable fault fall into this category: first, those that result from human activity; and, second, those caused by natural events (for example, earthquakes and undersea tectonic movements). An example of a natural event is a rockfall in the Congo Canyon off the west coast of Africa in 2023, which damaged three telecommunication cables, affecting connectivity in several States (*The Continent* 2023). Natural events make up about 10 percent of cases where a cable has suffered injury (Carter 2014, 238). Although more infrequent, their impact on cables tends to be significant, regularly wiping out large numbers of cables simultaneously. The Hengchun earthquake of 2006 illustrates this, as eight cables were cut, which affected several States (China, Japan, Singapore, and South Korea) for a prolonged period of time (ICPC 2009).

A logical corollary to the fact that only 10 percent of cable damage is the result of natural causes is that most damage results from human activity, particularly bottom fishing and anchoring (Wargo and Davenport 2014, 257). The risks associated with anchoring rose to the fore in 2007 and 2008. Then, the Straits of Malacca and Singapore filled up with ships for which there was a dearth of work because of grim economic tidings. To avoid having to pay fees, several ships began anchoring outside of the designated zones, causing around twenty cable faults in these straits (Wargo and Davenport 2014, 257–258). Theft of submarine cables, because of their concentrations of copper, poses another threat. When, in 2007, fishing trawlers flying the Vietnamese flag removed 180 km of submarine cable with the aim of selling it on the black market, internet connection within Vietnam was seriously affected. It took over three months before the cable was restored to operation, which came at great cost, with estimations ranging from US$5.8 million to US$8 million (Raha and Raju 2021, 3).

A further refinement is that the damage to cables due to human causes may be accidental or intentional. Although of late there is a tendency, especially in media, to ascribe cable damage automatically to malignant intent, it can be difficult to conclude this with certainty. In this vein, after the breakage of two cable segments of the same cable system, SHEFA-2, within a timespan of a few months in 2022, theories soon emerged that the cables were willfully damaged (Van Logchem 2022). Contrary to this, the cable owner indicated that the cables broke because of either harsher weather conditions or the extensive fishing activity within the North Sea (Van Logchem 2022). Admittedly, in other similar events there was probably foul play at hand. An example is the submarine cables providing internet connectivity to the Taiwanese Matsu Islands that have ended up cut with peculiar frequency and regularity. Because in these instances there is at least the suspicion of cables being intentionally targeted, the security angle for States is clearly brought into focus. Connected to this, such events have placed the issue of their legal protection, or arguably the lack thereof, into the limelight (see Section 10.3.1).

If a telecommunication cable exhibits a fault, the aspects of rerouting data traffic and the need for physical repair of the cable come into play. Rerouting is a common feature in the continuous provision of international communications by cable operators. If cable systems lack sufficient resiliency, rerouting data traffic away from the damaged cable may be impossible. For example, following the occurrence of a volcanic eruption in 2022, the sole cable on which the island State of Tonga is virtually dependent for maintaining its international communications broke, which isolated Tonga from the rest of the world (Seselja and Ewart 2022). Other small island States, including Kiribati, are similarly reliant on an individual cable (Guilfoyle et al. 2022, 659–660). Despite their resiliency, if too many cables of the same system are simultaneously incapacitated, data transmission might still be severely impacted. In this light, to ensure resiliency of cable systems, the cable(s) exhibiting fault must be repaired in a timely fashion. The logic behind this is simple: while the cable is out of order, it cannot fulfill its backup role for when another cable, part of the same cable system, exhibits a fault.

Repair operations require the cable to be physically retrieved from the seabed and loaded onto a cable ship. Typically such repair operations last between one and two weeks. Only a small number of companies have the necessary means, including cable ships, for such repair operations (Ford-Ramsden and Burnett 2014, 155). Complicating matters further is the fact that some time may lapse before the necessary State authorizations are in place and repairs can begin. Reasons for this include the procedures certain coastal States have in place for when a fault occurs in a cable located within their maritime zones. Following the Hengchun earthquake, for instance, repairing the damaged cables was complicated and severely delayed by lengthy and multiple permit requirements (Van Logchem 2014, 113). Whether the possibility to make repairs is entwined with obtaining coastal State authorization varies with where the transit cable is located. Only repair operations conducted within maritime areas where the coastal State has sovereignty (that is, internal waters, the territorial sea, and archipelagic waters) would require consent according to international law. However, certain States – including China, India, and Vietnam (Aw 2024, 137–138) – have regulations and laws on the books that require prior permission before the necessary repair works to a damaged transit telecommunication cable lying on the continental shelf can be made (Ford-Ramsden and Burnett 2014, 169; Van Logchem 2014, 113). The permission requirement set by China and India is underpinned by security concerns.

Cable protection is a theme whose relevance cuts across the full spectrum of submarine cables. However, perceivably, SMART cables come with added security concerns, because they may serve as sensors for military purposes. For example, the obtained information could shine a light on ship location, which carries security or military implications. In this light, SMART cables may rise higher on the list of targets by those of ill-will and intent. This will raise not only the specter of sabotage but also generate coastal state countermeasures to ensure offshore security.

10.3.1 *A Flawed International Legal Regime?*

Given their critical nature, also for society, submarine telecommunication cables require adequate protection (Beckman 2014, 281; UNGA 2011, 121, 2023, 125).

Irrespective of it being mostly private actors who conduct activities related to such cables, States retain a critical role in this respect. Among others, they have the responsibility to ensure that cable systems are sufficiently resilient, that such systems meet safety and security requirements, and that repairs can be made as swiftly as possible when such infrastructure is damaged. The need for State involvement has become only more pressing with submarine cables increasingly being viewed through the specter of security. As discussed in Section 10.3, this security angle for States is clearly brought into focus, as instances are on the rise where there is at least the suspicion of cables being intentionally targeted – for example, in the Taiwan Strait. Another example is the Balticconnector incident of 2023, when several submarine telecommunication cables were cut by the *NewNew Polar Bear*, flying the flag of Hong Kong (Ringbom and Lott 2024, 155). But is the international legal framework adequately equipped for ensuring their protection?

A key feature of the international legal framework pertaining to the protection of submarine telecommunication cables is that it is antiquated (Beckman 2010, 7; Takei 2012, 207–208; Van Logchem 2021a). There is a handful of provisions in UNCLOS on cable protection in the EEZ and the high seas – that is, Articles 113–115. These provisions have their roots in the 1884 Cable Convention, which marks the birth of the legal regime for the protection of submarine cables. The 1884 Cable Convention bears the hallmarks of its time, among which is its focus on telegraphic cables. It formed the culmination of several diplomatic efforts that began in earnest in 1882, which was when cables were first laid on the seabed (Burnett et al. 2014a, 65). Under the 1884 Cable Convention, competing fishing activities taking place outside the "territorial waters" of coastal States were recognized as one of the preeminent threats to cables. The 1884 Cable Convention is unique, being the only international treaty exclusively concerned with submarine cables. However, it cannot be considered overly successful, as only forty States became parties to it. Despite its limited success in attracting State participation, the 1884 Cable Convention has shaped the subsequent direction of the international law on the protection of submarine cables. This is reflected in the fact that the relevant provisions in UNCLOS (Articles 113–115) are lifted almost verbatim from the 1884 Cable Convention.

The scope of application of Articles 113–115 of UNCLOS on cable protection is limited to areas lying beyond the extent of the territorial sea. As a corollary, UNCLOS does not contain a provision obligating coastal States to adopt laws and regulations to protect submarine cables within their territory, including in port or in the territorial sea. It has been alleged that this was underpinned by the thinking at the Third Law of the Sea Conference that there was no need to introduce a provision on cable protection in the territorial sea, as States themselves would recognize the importance of properly regulating this domestically (Beckman 2014, 287). Contrary to expectations, however, this has not been reflected in the practice of all States (Beckman 2014, 287).

Under Article 113, the breaking or injuring of a submarine cable located beneath the high seas (or the continental shelf/EEZ) through willful or culpable negligence is addressed. It places the burden of regulation on the flag state or on a State that otherwise has jurisdiction over the persons involved. Conduct that is calculated or likely to result in the breaking or injuring of a submarine cable is also caught under this provision. This is an innovation in UNCLOS, as the provisions developed along similar lines in both the 1884 Cable Convention (Article II) and the 1958 Convention on the High Seas (Article 27) lack this language. In its commentary to Article 62 of the 1956 Draft Articles on the Law of the Sea, whose content resembles Article 113 of UNCLOS, the International Law Commission indicated that a precondition for culpable negligence is that the damaged cable has been clearly marked on charts (ILC 1956, 294). From Article 114 of UNCLOS flows the obligation for States to regulate when, in the laying or repairing of a new submarine cable, a break or injury is caused to an in situ submarine cable for which the owner of the new cable is liable. The extent of liability is confined to the repair costs of the damaged cable; for other types of damage, no civil liability exists. Article 115 of UNCLOS approaches the issue from a different angle: that is, if, in attempting to avoid damaging a submarine cable, an anchor, net, or fishing gear must be sacrificed, the cable owner, assuming that it has "taken all reasonable precautionary measures," will be indemnified.

Different weaknesses around cable protection arise depending on whether it involves maritime areas that are within functional coastal State jurisdiction (the EEZ and the continental shelf) or under coastal State sovereignty – for example, the territorial sea. Because coastal States enjoy sovereignty over their territory, various options to protect cables are part of their arsenal in the territorial sea, including designating areas where ships cannot anchor, or setting a cable burial requirement. The other side of the sovereignty coin is that States are not obligated to exercise any of the powers they have by international law, leaving this to their own discretion. As many of these cables in the territorial sea are likely to make a landfall, coastal States have an interest in ensuring that these cables enjoy adequate protection.

Outside the territorial sea, the picture fundamentally changes, in that more emphasis is placed on what often will be the role of the flag State. Tied to this, the challenges that have arisen in respect of flag State jurisdiction and control, including around flags of convenience, rise to the fore (Van Logchem 2023, 421–428). Despite the obligations in Articles 113–115 of UNCLOS to introduce domestic legislation, State practice differs on this point. Relevant laws may not exist; or, alternatively, if laws are on the books, they may exhibit deficiencies or be out of pace with the present times (House of Lords 2022, 77; Wargo and Davenport 2014, 262–263). Another issue is whether these laws are actually enforced by, for example, flag States, as significant strides would be made if the existing law was "effectively implemented and enforced by all States" (Mensah 2015, 739).

10.4 CONCLUSION

By incorporating oceanographic sensors into fiber-optic telecommunication cables, significantly more oceanographic data could be collected than before with relative ease and at a low cost. This is enabled by the vast network of telecommunication cables that underpins the continuous flow of international voice and data traffic. The oceanographic sensors gather information on the climate and the oceans (for example, to measure changes in water temperature or sea-level rise) and for predicting natural disasters (for example, tsunamis and earthquakes). Attempts to improve matters on both fronts are hampered by the fact that the oceans remain poorly understood, especially the deep-ocean environment. The dearth of available data on the oceans affects, inter alia, how disasters, such as underwater earthquakes, can be predicted reliably. However, SMART cables are not a panacea for plugging the full scientific knowledge gap that exists today. While the global network is extensive, most submarine cables are located in the northern hemisphere. SMART cables thus complement (not replace) other means of oceanographic data collection (Howe et al. 2019, 3).

SMART cables fall into three categories: (a) out-of-service telecommunication cables that are repurposed for data collection and transmission; (b) in situ and active telecommunication cables that are outfitted with oceanographic sensors; and (c) new cables that have the built-in dual function of transmitting international communications and oceanographic data collection. Depending on the type of SMART cable involved, different legal challenges and uncertainties emerge. On the low end of the spectrum are out-of-use service telecommunication cables, which are repurposed to exclusively collect and transmit oceanographic data (category (a)). Their exclusive usage in this context would render them MSR cables. At the high end of the spectrum are the two other categories of SMART cables.

An important variable in this regard is, however, whether the SMART cable is to make a landfall. If so, and irrespective of whether one adheres to the view of these cables being subject to the MSR regime, the laying of the cable concerned would fall under the authority of the coastal State. In a general sense, the picture that emerges for SMART cables, both landing and transiting ones, is that there will be coastal State authority (see Section 10.2.1) in those maritime areas where the coastal State has sovereignty (in internal waters, archipelagic waters, and the territorial sea) over cables and MSR (as well as other types of marine data collection). Most of the difficulties arise when SMART cables *transit* the EEZ or the continental shelf. Behind this lies the fact that SMART cables combine two aspects that are either beyond (the fact of being transit telecommunication cables) or within (the MSR component) coastal State jurisdiction.

Due to this duality, the data collection component must be viewed as separate from the right to lay, repair, or maintain transit submarine cables. To paraphrase the language of UNCLOS, attaching oceanographic sensors to active telecommunication cables – whereby they also actively collect data – cannot be interpreted as inherent to the freedom of laying transit submarine cables. Rather, due to its MSR component, which is a layer added to a telecommunications cable, SMART cables are subject to two contending legal regimes. Thus, within the EEZ and on the continental shelf, SMART cables are subject to coastal State consent, having to be considered as activity conducted in the framework of MSR (Burnett 2011). And a good argument can be made – as discussed in Section 10.2.3 – that there is discretion for the coastal State to withhold consent based on SMART cable systems being akin to a semi-permanent structure on the seabed (UNCLOS, Article 258). On the converse, beyond maritime areas where the coastal State has jurisdiction – that is, in the high seas and the international deep seabed – the freedoms to lay transit cables and to conduct MSR simultaneously exist, enabling SMART cables to be freely employed there.

But in which direction does the pendulum swing for SMART cables? As a positive, they allow the scientific opportunity to gain a better understanding of the (marine) environment that leads to significant societal benefit. However, care must be taken not to put into jeopardy the primary function telecommunication cables fulfill. Concerns of this nature are echoed by the submarine cable industry, which is the main background to SMART cables receiving a more lukewarm response from industry (Davenport 2015b, 247). Keeping fiber-optic cables operational is key for the functioning of the global telecommunications network (for example, the internet, or financial and security systems; Carter et al. 2009, 8). Despite there being a clear scientific imperative, the concomitant international legal dimension makes it difficult at times fully to tap the promise that SMART cables hold, scientifically speaking. The severity of some of these challenges will render the general idea behind turning telecommunication cables into SMART cables – whereby the full force of this vast offshore communication infrastructure can be harnessed for oceanographic data collection – closer to a pipedream. At the core of the difficulties that arise is their dual use, because of which SMART cables, depending on their specifics and location, are subject to two conflicting legal regimes. This clash of regimes is particularly visible for SMART cables that are intended to *transit* a coastal State's EEZ or continental shelf, with there being the freedom to lay transit submarine telecommunication cables in these areas (see Section 10.2.1). A contrary picture emerges for MSR in the EEZ and on the continental shelf, which are under coastal State jurisdiction (see Section 10.2.2). Linked to this, such assertions of coastal state jurisdiction based on SMART cables being MSR cables create difficulty in conducting activities related to telecommunication cables for the industry (see Section 10.2.3).

While the view that SMART cables are subject to the MSR regime is not devoid of controversy, it is clear that different legal arguments are garnered in support of whether SMART cables are, or are not, subject to the MSR regime, beyond the cable regime. These divergent views may be mirrored in the practice of States, and concerns around coastal States expanding their jurisdictional reach as a result are unlikely to be imaginary (Davenport 2015b, 247). In such a vein, Japan would be against the deployment of SMART cables (Palmer-Felgate 2016). Other States may be more receptive to SMART cables, due to the direct benefits that would be generated from their employment – for instance, small island States that are particularly affected by climate change or vulnerable to natural disasters. Divergent State practice can hamper the widespread introduction of SMART cables. As an alternative, a more watered-down approach to the use of SMART cables – one that is built around pragmatism – seems to be the way forward (Howe et al. 2019, 19). Its specifics are tailored in a way that either avoids or addresses the complex legal challenges and uncertainties. This would have to include avoiding the EEZs or continental shelves of those coastal States that consider SMART cables to be subject to the MSR regime, or that have not explicitly agreed to a SMART cable system. Although the future of SMART cables is not necessarily bleak, at present it is laden with some uncertainties and legal challenges that single-use cables do not face.

REFERENCES

Agarwala, Nitin. 2019. "'Green Cables': Development, Opportunities and Legal Challenges: Part I." *Maritime Affairs: Journal of the National Maritime Foundation of India* 15 (1): 49–62.

Ash, Stewart. 2014. "The Development of Submarine Cables." In *Submarine Cables: The Handbook of Law and Policy*, edited by Douglas R. Burnett, Robert Beckman, and Tara M. Davenport. Martinus Nijhoff.

Aw, Stephany. 2024. "Coastal State Duties in the Repair of Submarine Cables." *International Journal of Marine and Coastal Law* 39: 132–156.

Beckman, Robert. 2010. "Submarine Cables: A Critically Important but Neglected Area of the Law of the Sea." *International Conference of the International Society of International Law on Legal Regimes of Sea, Air, Space and Antarctica*, January 15–17.

2014. "Protecting Submarine Cables from Intentional Damage: The Security Gap." In *Submarine Cables: The Handbook of Law and Policy*, edited by Douglas R. Burnett, Robert Beckman, and Tara M. Davenport. Martinus Nijhoff.

Bressie, Kent. 2012. *Using Submarine Cables for Climate Monitoring and Disaster Warning: Opportunities and Legal Challenges*. UNESCO/IOC, WMO, and ITO.

Burnett, Douglas R. 2006. "International Law Considerations for Owners and Operators of Cabled and Buoy Observatories." *IEEE Journal of Oceanic Engineering* 31 (1): 230–235.

2011. "Understanding the Differences under UNCLOS between Submarine Cables and Marine Scientific Research." ITU Workshop, September 9.

2021. "Submarine Cable Security and International Law." *International Law Studies* 97: 1661–1662.

Burnett, Douglas, Tara Davenport, and Robert Beckman. 2014a. "Overview of the International Legal Regime Governing Submarine Cables." In *Submarine Cables: The Handbook of Law and Policy*, edited by Douglas R. Burnett, Robert Beckman, and Tara M. Davenport. Martinus Nijhoff.

2014b. "Why Submarine Cables?" In *Submarine Cables: The Handbook of Law and Policy*, edited by Douglas R. Burnett, Robert Beckman, and Tara M. Davenport. Martinus Nijhoff.

Butler, Rhett. 2012. *Using Submarine Cables for Climate Monitoring and Disaster Warning: Strategy and Roadmap*. UNESCO/IOC, WMO, and ITO.

Carter, Lionel. 2014. "Submarine Cables and Natural Hazards." In *Submarine Cables: The Handbook of Law and Policy*, edited by Douglas R. Burnett, Robert Beckman, and Tara M. Davenport. Martinus Nijhoff.

Carter, Lionel, Douglas Burnett, and Tara Davenport. 2014 "The Relationship between Submarine Cables and the Marine Environment" In *Submarine Cables: The Handbook of Law and Policy*, edited by Douglas R. Burnett, Robert Beckman, and Tara M. Davenport. Martinus Nijhoff.

Carter, Lionel, Douglas Burnett, Stephen Drew, Graham Marle, Lonnie Hagadorn, Deborah Bartlett-McNeil, and Nigel Irvine. 2009. *Submarine Cables and the Oceans: Connecting the World.* UNEP-WCMC Biodiversity Series No. 31. ICPC/UNEP/UNEP-WCMC.

Carter, Lionel, and Alfred H. A. Soons. 2014. "Marine Scientific Research Cables." In *Submarine Cables: The Handbook of Law and Policy*, edited by Douglas R. Burnett, Robert Beckman, and Tara M. Davenport. Martinus Nijhoff.

Churchill, Robin, Vaughan Lowe, and Amy Sander. 2022. *The Law of the Sea*. 4th ed. Manchester University Press.

Continent, The. 2023. "Down to the Wire: The Ship Fixing Our Internet." *The Continent*, November 25. https://continent.substack.com/p/down-to-the-wire-the-ship-fixing.

Davenport, Tara. 2012. "Submarine Communications Cables and Law of the Sea: Problems in Law and Practice." *Ocean Development & International Law* 43 (3): 201–242.

2015a. "Submarine Cables, Cybersecurity and International Law: An Intersectional Analysis." *Catholic University Journal of Law and Technology* 24 (1): Article 4.

2015b. "Submarine Communications Cables and Science: A New Frontier in Ocean Governance?" In *Science, Technology, and New Challenges to Ocean Law*, edited by Harry N. Schreiber, James Kraska, and Moon-Sang Kwon. Martinus Nijhoff.

Doussis, Emmanuella. 2017. "Marine Scientific Research: Taking Stock and Looking Ahead." In *The Future of the Law of the Sea*, edited by Gemma Andreone. Springer.

The Economist. 2016. "The See-Through Sea." July 14.

Evans, Graham, and Monique Page. 2014. "The Planning and Surveying of Submarine Cable Routes." In *Submarine Cables: The Handbook of Law and Policy*, edited by Douglas R. Burnett, Robert Beckman, and Tara M. Davenport. Martinus Nijhoff.

Ford-Ramsden, Keith, and Douglas Burnett. 2014. "Submarine Cable Repair and Maintenance." In *Submarine Cables: The Handbook of Law and Policy*, edited by Douglas R. Burnett, Robert Beckman, and Tara M. Davenport. Martinus Nijhoff.

Ford-Ramsden, Keith, and Tara Davenport. 2014. "The Manufacture and Laying of Submarine Cables." In *Submarine Cables: The Handbook of Law and Policy*, edited by Douglas R. Burnett, Robert Beckman, and Tara M. Davenport. Martinus Nijhoff.

Guilfoyle, Douglas, Tamsin Phillipa Paige, and Rob McLaughlin. 2022. "The Final Frontier of Cyberspace: The Seabed beyond National Jurisdiction and the Protection of Submarine Cables." *International & Comparative Law Quarterly* 71 (3): 657–696.

Henley, Jon, and Jill Ambrose. 2023. "Undersea Pipeline Damage Appears to Be Deliberate, Says Finland." *The Guardian*, October 11.

House of Lords. 2022. "International Relations and Defence Committee, 2nd Report of Session 2021–22." *UNCLOS: the Law of the Sea in the 21st Century*. HL Paper 159.

Howe, Bruce M., Brian K. Arbic, Jérome Aucan, Christopher R. Barnes, Nigel Bayliff, Nathan Becker, Rhett Butler, Laurie Doyle, Shane Elipot, Gregory C. Johnson, Felix Landerer, Stephen Lentz, Douglas S. Luther, Malte Müller, John Mariano, Kate Panayotou, Charlotte Rowe, Hiroshi Ota, Y. Tony Song, Maik Thomas, Preston N.

Thomas, Philip Thompson, Frederik Tilmann, Tobias Weber, and Stuart Weinstein. 2019. "SMART Cables for Observing the Global Ocean: Science and Implementation." *Frontiers in Marine Science* 6: Article 424.

ICPC (International Cable Protection Committee). 2009. "Submarine Cable Network Security." APEC, April 13.

ILC (International Law Commission). 1956. "Report of the International Law Commission Covering the Work of Its Eighth Session." A/3159. Reprinted in *Yearbook of the International Law Commission* 1956, vol. II. A/CN.4/SER.A/1956/Add.l.

Kraska, James. 2024. "Marine Data Collection outside the MSR Regime." In *Viability of UNCLOS amid Emerging Global Maritime Challenges*, edited by Lan Anh T. Nguyen and Hai Dang Vu. Springer.

Lentz, Stephen, and Peter Phibbs. 2012. *Using Submarine Cables for Climate Monitoring and Disaster Warning: Engineering Feasibility Study*. UNESCO/IOC, WMO, and ITO.

Lott, Alexander. 2023. "Maritime Security in the Baltic and Japanese Straits from the Perspective of EEZ Corridors." *Ocean Development & International Law* 54 (3): 327–348.

2024. "The Protection of Critical Undersea Infrastructure within and beyond the Limits of the Territorial Sea under the Jus ad Bellum and Jus in Bello." In *Maritime Security Law in Hybrid Warfare*, edited by Alexander Lott. Brill Nijhoff.

Mateos, Aurora, and Montserrat Gorina-Ysern. 2010. "Climate Change and Guidelines for Argo Profiling Float Deployment on the High Seas." *ASIL Insights* 14 (8). www.asil.org/insights/volume/14/issue/8/climate-change-and-guidelines-argo-profiling-float-deployment-high-seas.

Mensah, Thomas A. 2015. "Submarine Cables and the International Law of the Sea." In *Law of the Sea, from Grotius to the International Tribunal for the Law of the Sea: Liber Amicorum Judge Hugo Caminos*, edited by Lilian del Castillo. Brill Nijhoff.

Nandan, Satya N., and Shabtai Rosenne. 1993. *United Nations Convention on the Law of the Sea 1982: A Commentary*, vol. II. Martinus Nijhoff.

Ocean Networks Canada. n.d. www.neptunecanada.com.

Palmer-Felgate, Andy. 2016. "A Cable Owners Perspective on SMART Cables." SMART Cable Systems: Latest Developments and Designing the Wet Demonstrator Project, Dubai, April 17–18.

Raha, Utpal Kumar, and K. D. Raju. 2021. *Submarine Cables Protection and Regulations: A Comparative Analysis and Model Framework*. Springer.

Rapp, Ronald J. 2010. "Submarine Cables: Critical Infrastructure Supplier Perspective." *Annual COLP Conference*, May 21.

Ringbom, Henrik, and Alexander Lott. 2024. "Sabotage of Critical Offshore Infrastructure: A Case Study of the Balticconnector Incident." In *Maritime Security Law in Hybrid Warfare*, edited by Alexander Lott. Brill Nijhoff.

Roach, J. Ashley. 2007. "Defining Scientific Research: Marine Data Collection." In *Law, Science and Ocean Management*, edited by Myron H. Nordquist, Ronán Long, Tomas Heidar, and John Norton Moore. Martinus Nijhoff.

Seselja, Edwina, and Richard Ewart. 2022. "Tonga Reconnects with Outside World after Data Cable Cut Off by Volcanic Eruption." *ABC News*, February 22. www.abc.net.au/news/2022-02-22/tongas-internet-cable-restored/100846976.

SMART Cables. n.d. www.smartcables.org/systems.

Soons, Alfred H. A. 1982. *Marine Scientific Research and the Law of the Sea*. Kluwer.

Strati, Anastasia. 2011. "The Law: Existing Rules and New Challenges." Green Standards Week Workshop on Submarine Cables for Ocean/Climate Monitoring and Disaster Warning: Science, Engineering, Business and Law, Rome, September 9.

Subsea World News. 2017. "Novacavi Builds New Cable for Subsea Monitoring." May 18. https://subseaworldnews.com/2017/05/18/novacavi-builds-new-cable-for-subsea-monitoring/.

Takei, Yoshinobu. 2012. "Law and Policy for International Submarine Cables: An Asia-Pacific Perspective." *Asian Journal of International Law* 2: 205–233.

UNGA (United Nations General Assembly). 2011. "Oceans and the Law of the Sea." A/RES/65/37 (March 17, 2011).

2023. "Oceans and the Law of the Sea." A/RES/78/69 (December 11, 2023).

Van Logchem, Youri. 2014. "Submarine Telecommunication Cables in Disputed Maritime Areas." *Ocean Development & International Law* 45 (1): 108–111.

2021a. "Corrected Oral Evidence: UNCLOS: Fit for Purpose in the 21st Century?" House of Lords, International Relations and Defence Committee, November 3.

2021b. *The Rights and Obligations of States in Disputed Maritime Areas*. Cambridge University Press.

2022. "Protecting Submarine Cables: Two Submarine Telecommunication Cables Break Off the Shetland Coast." *IISTL Blog*, November 15. https://iistl.blog/2022/11/15/protecting-submarine-cables-two-submarine-telecommunication-cables-break-off-the-shetland-coast/.

2023. "Law of the Sea and International Maritime Law." In *Elgar Encyclopedia of Comparative Law*, edited by Jan M. Smits, Jaakko Husa, Catherine Valcke, and Madalena Narciso. Edgar Elgar.

Walker, George K. 2012. *Definitions for the Law of the Sea: Terms Not Defined by the 1982 Convention*. Martinus Nijhoff.

Wargo, Robert, and Tara Davenport. 2014. "Protecting Submarine Cables from Competing Uses." In *Submarine Cables: The Handbook of Law and Policy*, edited by Douglas R. Burnett, Robert Beckman, and Tara M. Davenport. Martinus Nijhoff.

Whomersley, Christopher. 2021. "What Is and What Is Not Covered by Part XIII of UNCLOS?" In *Marine Scientific Research, New Marine Technologies and the Law of the Sea*, edited by Keyuan Zou and Anastasia Telesetsky. Brill Nijhoff.

You, Yuzhu. 2010a. "Harnessing Telecoms Cables for Science." *Nature* 466: 690–691.

2010b. "Using Submarine Communications Networks to Monitor the Climate: ITU-T Technology Watch Report." November.

11

Advances in Underwater Archaeology

Natalia Perez

11.1 INTRODUCTION

There are numerous objects scattered across the seabed that have previously been inaccessible due to their remoteness and the challenging environment of the deep ocean. Shipwrecks have been found and studied over hundreds of years, and objects found onboard shipwrecks have revealed facets of human history and heritage. While shipwrecks and sites have continued to be found over time, UNESCO estimates that approximately 3 million shipwrecks are still left to be discovered across different parts of the ocean (UNESCO 2007). These shipwrecks often include warships, as a result of the First and Second World Wars, which may be located within the coastal State waters. Questions surrounding ownership arise from the discovery and preservation of, and access to, shipwrecks. There is also the issue of enforcing preservation and the study of wreck sites located throughout different maritime zones, as compared to excavation for commercial purposes. Existing instruments are assessed toward the question of ownership, including the United Nations Convention on the Law of the Sea (UNCLOS)[1] and the Convention on the Protection of the Underwater Cultural Heritage (CPUCH).[2] Each of these international agreements discusses the topic of underwater archaeology, as well as the role of flag States and coastal States.

The aim of this chapter is to consider how emerging technologies in the field of underwater archaeology have led to impacts or questions pertaining to the discovery and ownership of shipwrecks located in maritime zones distinct from the flag State of the sunken vessel. An area to consider is the purpose of access and interest in ownership over shipwrecks. Are there interests in conducting remote studies of shipwrecks due to their cultural and historical significance? Are financial gains from

[1] UNCLOS, December 10, 1982, 1833 UNTS 397.

[2] Convention on the Protection of the Underwater Cultural Heritage, November 2, 2001, 2562 UNTS 3 (CPUCH).

materials and objects found in the debris field area surrounding the shipwreck a potential concern for the coastal State? These questions will provide a lens through which to analyze primary authority and management over the discovery of shipwrecks across the various maritime zones.

First, the chapter analyzes the current state of underwater archaeology and advances in the use of technologies, including how these innovations have altered the course of underwater archaeology. Next, it discusses the relevant articles of UNCLOS – Articles 33, 149, and 303 – and their applicability to the ownership of sunken vessels. The chapter then considers CPUCH, particularly with regard to how it is distinct from UNCLOS in addressing shipwrecks as gravesites. The designation and enforcement of a shipwreck as a gravesite can limit access by commercial divers, along with enhancing cooperation between States. This analysis is followed by cases pertaining to the interaction of flag States and coastal States over the sovereign immunity of sunken warships located within the territorial sea, the exclusive economic zone (EEZ), and the deep-seabed Area. In conclusion, given the expanding nature of emerging technologies used in underwater archaeology, the chapter presents recommendations to consider.

11.2 UNDERWATER ARCHAEOLOGICAL METHODS

A common thread across disciplines in archaeology is the aim of uncovering stories from the past and gaining a deeper understanding of ancient cultures (Memet 2008). This overlaps with goals that drive innovation within deep ocean exploration. The study of shipwrecks presents a particular case to analyze between the convergence of advanced technologies, marine scientific study, and the legal implications of foreign State interactions across maritime zones.

Underwater archaeology encompasses numerous phases, with the focus of this chapter being on the initial stages of discovery, excavation, and preservation. Through focusing on these stages, it is possible to assess how technologies aimed at finding and mapping shipwrecks interact with the legal frameworks governing archaeological objects found at sea. There are several methods through which studies are conducted to better understand a shipwreck. These can include the presence of physical divers, depending on the depth, to record information. Technical divers are able to dive into shipwrecks to a depth of up to and exceeding 90 m without putting themselves in physical danger due to water pressure, darkness, and the potential for disorientation (Bradley 2023). Scientific and commercial diving can be utilized within archaeological sites and shipwrecks located within the territorial sea for both research and tourism purposes.

It can become challenging to conduct studies without the use of advanced technologies when considering shipwrecks in deeper water beyond the territorial sea. This is an area where the use of remotely operated vehicles (ROVs), autonomous underwater vehicles (AUVs), unmanned surface vehicles (USVs), and sonar technologies becomes integral to the discovery and study of shipwrecks. Meanwhile, the use of these advanced technologies introduces legal implications distinct from those associated with archaeological studies conducted by sole divers. This includes questions on the role of robotic technologies in assessing wrecks belonging to a flag State distinct from the waters in which it was found, along with questions on balancing commercial interests with the cultural preservation of shipwrecks.

Once a shipwreck has been discovered and identified, there is the question of which State has the primary role in decisions regarding future study, removal, and actions taken that impact the wreck and the surrounding environment. States may become interested in a historic shipwreck for a variety of reasons, including the location where it was discovered, the original owner of the vessel, whether there were crew on board at the time of the sinking who were from a particular State, or if there are contents found surrounding the vessel that were originally from a separate State, thus potentially leading to a cultural heritage claim. It becomes important to consider how different countries may interact with the discovery of new shipwrecks when there are overlapping claims to ownership and access.

This interaction between States can be seen through multiple cases, one of the most recent being that of the galleon *San José*, discovered within the Colombian territorial sea, where there are claims from three States, a private company, and Indigenous groups to the shipwreck and objects found nearby (Zenkiewicz and Wasilewski 2019). The *San José* highlights various ways in which shipwrecks are perceived, including their underwater cultural heritage and how they can influence the actions of States. This case is described in greater detail below, including how UNCLOS and CPUCH play a role in designating jurisdiction over shipwrecks found within various maritime zones.

11.2.1 *Shipwrecks and Cultural Heritage*

Shipwrecks can offer a vast amount of information to those with the capabilities, time, and resources to conduct archaeological studies. With the advancement of technology, scientific expeditions have searched shipwrecks for signs of potentially polluting substances, the presence of marine organisms, and to gain an understanding of past human behavior (NOAA 2024b). Given that shipwrecks are often accidental, they offer a view into the social, cultural, and economic aspects of past experiences at a specific moment in time (NOAA 2024b). This means that those conducting archaeological studies of warships can also gain knowledge of their past armament and military history (Hayden 2023). Marine archaeologists have described shipwrecks as time capsules through which careful study can allow access to previously inaccessible stories and artifacts. Depending on the wreck site, tangible items may provide a cultural link to a State other than the vessel's flag State. This introduces an added layer, given that a separate State may have an interest in the recovery of items through a cultural link, an interest in the preservation of the items, or an interest in the management and decisions regarding the wreck site.

The discovery of shipwrecks is not always the result of planned activities. Often, shipwrecks are located accidentally during environmental monitoring studies or as a serendipitous occurrence. There are times when it is necessary to conduct studies to gain a better understanding of certain landscapes ahead of a project, such as mapping exercises for underwater cables and offshore wind projects, in order to assess the potential for damage (Pater 2020). There have been instances where shipwrecks off the coast of a country have been stumbled upon during unrelated activities. The role of the coastal State remains the same regardless of whether a shipwreck was discovered through a planned archaeological expedition with appropriate permits, or accidentally without the proper equipment or resources. This is important to note, since States may consider shipwrecks to hold valuable cultural heritage significance, which can then alter the original scope of a project, or the role of all States involved with the shipwreck. Environmental assessments is one type of activity through which shipwrecks can be discovered, although, should a shipwreck be discovered by government or military vessels, States are not obligated to share that information under Article 13 of CPUCH, which states:

> Warships and other government ships or military aircraft with sovereign immunity, operated for non-commercial purposes, undertaking their normal mode of operations, and not engaged in activities directed at underwater cultural heritage, shall not be obliged to report discoveries of underwater cultural heritage under Articles 9, 10, 11 and 12 of this Convention.

The discovery of a shipwreck can not only lead to a plethora of information; it can also be culturally significant for numerous States; it can help gain knowledge about a particular time in history; and it can offer acknowledgment of a final resting site. The exemption of government ships from alerting a coastal State of an underwater cultural heritage discovery can be an area for further study, as it potentially limits coastal State access, future studies, and security.

Meanwhile, discoveries of shipwrecks in an area where there are planned activities involve a question as to whether consent from the flag State of the sunken vessel – if it is different from that of the coastal State – would be required to move forward with such activities. Expanding coastal projects can include "trawling, dredging, offshore oil and gas explorations and port construction," which may place undiscovered shipwrecks at greater vulnerability from destruction (Ridwan 2019, 1623). The discovery of shipwrecks within the territorial sea, contiguous zone, or EEZ that have separate flag and coastal States can lead to discussions over activities that may interact with the shipwreck and surrounding ecosystem. As highlighted, "once a site or its artifacts are damaged or haphazardly removed, there is no way to access its information and recreate the story it might have told" (NOAA n.d.). The importance of cultural heritage connects to the untold stories that each shipwreck inherently contains. One shipwreck may hold significance for numerous States, and it is important to consider how States interact through existing international legal agreements, such as UNCLOS and CPUCH, when it comes to newly discovered shipwrecks with links to more than one State. The following section will discuss the role of emerging technologies in greater depth, followed by an analysis bridging cultural heritage and the ownership of shipwrecks.

11.3 TECHNOLOGIES TO LOCATE AND STUDY SHIPWRECKS

In order to discuss legal interactions over the management of shipwrecks found within various maritime zones, it is important first to review technological advancements used within underwater archaeology. There have been noticeable changes over the years as technological innovations have created opportunities to explore deeper areas of the ocean and previously inaccessible sites. Emerging technologies within underwater archaeology can be divided into separate groups: those used to locate new sites and objects, those used to assist in gathering and documenting artifacts, and those used to study images captured from the sites. There are distinct ways in which these technologies intertwine with the law of the sea, although they all in some way can cause shifts to interpretations under UNCLOS.

11.3.1 *Side-Scan Sonar*

One technology to consider is the use of side-scan sonar. The application of side-scan sonar for underwater archaeological purposes has been actively used in the field since the 1960s (Goncharov 2016). As this technology has continued to develop, it has become an increasingly important tool for the field of underwater archaeology. Side-scan sonar works by emitting and receiving acoustic pulses to aid in mapping the seafloor (NOAA 2002). These acoustic pulses can be emitted at different frequencies, ranging from 50 to 500 kilohertz, depending on the necessary breath and clarity (NOAA 2002). The pulses captured through this method are then used to create an image of the seafloor with shipwrecks and sites appearing in a darker shade than the seabed. One of the benefits of side-scan sonar is its ability to create 3D images of shipwrecks (Goncharov 2016). It is also considered to be a less costly alternative to robotic technologies.

Scholars have noted the possible growth of side-scan sonar to continue developing through the use of global positioning systems for higher navigation and geographic references (Goncharov 2016). One consideration between the use of side-scan sonar and global positioning systems to aid in the discovery of shipwrecks is the potential for conflict over access to the precise coordinates of a shipwreck. There are cases where multiple States having access to shipwreck coordinates could be considered potentially problematic, such as that of the *San José*, where Colombia has decided to keep private the precise coordinates of the shipwreck for security purposes. Another case involves the location of a French warship within US territorial waters (Gates 2019) that was kept hidden. Similarly, the location of the *Geldermalsen* shipwreck has yet to be released publicly for fear of potential looting (Looram et al. 2024). These cases highlight how certain technologies used to locate and study shipwrecks can introduce potential security risks over sharing geographic details.

There have also been studies that take side-scan sonar a step further through its interaction with AI to detect shipwrecks from side-scan sonar imagery. A study conducted by the University of Michigan, AI4Shipwrecks, considers how machine learning can be utilized to uncover shipwrecks from side-scan sonar data (Sheppard et al. 2024). The use of AI may impact the amount of time necessary to identify shipwrecks, which can heighten interactions between underwater archaeology, UNCLOS, and CPUCH, as will be discussed in the following sections.

11.3.2 *ROVs, AUVs, and USVs*

Another technique to consider is the use of USVs, ROVs, and AUVs (NOAA 2024a). While side-scan sonar is a widely used technology within underwater archaeology, it is often deployed through the use of an USV. It is beneficial to cover how these technologies can aid in the discovery and study of shipwrecks.

USVs are used within multiple fields for numerous purposes, and they can be used to reach depths of up to 6,000 m (Merkusheva 2020). While the depth an unmanned vehicle can reach is impressive, it is also rare for an archaeological study to be completed within a single expedition, as it is common for teams to return to the same shipwreck multiple times to conduct studies and gain a better understanding of the area. Archaeological studies often include multiple AUVs and ROVs during a single mission, which can be costly but effective (Merkusheva 2020).

A specific case of the effective use of AUVs in locating wrecks is the discovery of the ARA *San Juan* submarine in 2018. The private company Ocean Infinity successfully located the wreck using five AUVs and two ROVs connected to a research vessel (Song 2023). The search for the submarine included collaboration between nineteen countries, and the official identification of the submarine was made through the use of an ROV (Villán 2019). While the submarine discovered in this case would not fall under CPUCH's 100-year time period in order to be designated a protected site, it is acknowledged as a memorial by Argentine officials. The submarine wreck site was found approximately 600 km east of Comodoro Rivadavia, off the coast of Argentina (Ocean Robotics 2018). This highlights Argentina's role as the flag State of the submarine, with the absence of a separate coastal State given that the wreck was found within the high seas. This case provides an example of international collaboration in locating a potential wreck in times of stress and emergency, which differs from planned archaeological studies, although both include the use of highly advanced technologies.

USVs, ROVs, and AUVs introduce another issue to consider with legal implications distinct from the use of side-scan sonar and imaging technologies. This is centered on the fact that USVs, ROVs, and AUVs can increase human activity within previously challenging environments. It is worth noting the potential damage to archaeologically significant sites and wrecks caused by these vehicles, which can be explored in greater depth through additional research. USVs have been used in tandem with manned vehicles for the discovery of different shipwrecks through "launching, recovery, positioning, battery charging, and data transfer" (Zwolak et al. 2020, 6). A goal of combining these technologies is to increase the level of coverage to be studied and maximize the study area (Roman and Mather 2010). It is beneficial to maximize the study area, as it can present additional information, although it may be questionable from a legal perspective should the proposed study expand into multiple maritime zones.

There is also the issue of the amount of time it takes to conduct an effective study when using USVs and ROVs (Roman and Mather 2010). Advantages of using robotic vehicles include their ability to "carry cameras, video cameras and acoustic sensors to take optical and acoustic images of the site" (Conte et al. 2009, 177). This reduces the instances of physical divers needed to survey a site, and while costly, it can provide highly accurate data over a larger area (Conte et al. 2009, 177). USVs and autonomous vehicles also fall under a distinct legal area compared to research vessels under UNCLOS. A limitation to the use of these technologies is within shallow waters, where they may not be as beneficial as in deep waters (Goncharov 2016). An increasing number of expedition teams continue to employ multiple ROVs and AUVs for their efficiency, accuracy, timeliness, and ability to view and recover items from depths inaccessible to humans. Subsea vehicles allow for the potential of human interaction, although this presents changes that were not in practice at the time of the creation of Articles 149 and 303 of UNCLOS. These types of technologies have become standard practice for locating shipwrecks within deeper waters, and it will be important to ensure that existing practices over the legality of accessing shipwrecks in foreign waters continue to emphasize the importance of underwater cultural heritage and the preservation of wrecks.

11.3.3 *3D Imaging and Photogrammetry*

Three-dimensional images of the seafloor, in addition to containing outlines of shipwrecks, can be beneficial for coastal States in gaining access to a better understanding of the topography of their coastal waters. In addition to side-scan sonar, there have been innovations in the use of other 3D laser and scanning technologies (McCarthy et al. 2019). Three-dimensional scanning systems have played a role in the documentation of cultural heritage, which may work in tandem with CPUCH (Bräuer-Burchardt et al. 2023). The combined use of side-scan sonar and 3D scanning technology has made it possible to create more accurate documentation of objects on the seabed (Bräuer-Burchardt et al. 2023). The use of traditional sonar technology helps create an image of the seabed. However, scholars have noted that "these shipwrecks on the seafloor usually appear as low elevation – high texture seabed features, such as many other small seabed features, with the wooden frame most often disintegrated and the cargo, mainly amphorae, dispersed around the wreck" (Ferentinos et al. 2020, 7). The material with which the vessels were built also impacts their visibility when documented through 3D imaging technology.

Additional advancements in this area have centered on ways to capture images with greater clarity to aid in the identification of vessels and artifacts. Three-dimensional images as a result of side-scan sonar are helpful in capturing more detailed information for shipwrecks on the seabed, as compared to other versions of sonar technologies. Advanced photogrammetry has aided researchers in studying deepwater sites after returning to shore in order to identify and differentiate between objects to determine the flag State of origin, as was seen through the discovery of the US submarine S-28 (Hydro-International 2020).

ROVs, AUVs, USVs, sonar, and 3D imaging technologies can shift parts of the archaeological study of shipwrecks by decreasing the amount of time required at sea and increasing access to more accurate data. However, discussing how this interacts with UNCLOS and CPUCH is important, since these regimes include distinct rights and access with regard to archaeological objects.

11.4 INTERNATIONAL REGIMES

This section builds on the use of technologies by discussing the role of UNCLOS and CPUCH within underwater archaeology, shipwrecks, and State responsibility.

11.4.1 *United Nations Convention on the Law of the Sea*

UNCLOS references underwater archaeology within Articles 149 and 303. Each article centers on the role of States pertaining to objects of an archaeological or historical nature found within different maritime zones. Articles 33 and 303 focus on activities within the territorial sea and the contiguous zone, while Article 149 focuses on the Area. There is a noticeable gap regarding archaeological objects found within the EEZ.

Article 303 ("Archaeological and historical objects found at sea") states in part:

1. States have the duty to protect objects of an archaeological and historical nature found at sea and shall cooperate for this purpose.
2. In order to control traffic in such objects, the coastal State may, in applying article 33, presume that their removal from the seabed in the zone referred to in that article without its approval would result in an infringement within its territory or territorial sea of the laws and regulations referred to in that article.

While Article 303 does not directly reference shipwrecks, it can be expected that shipwrecks would fall under the phrase "objects of an archaeological and historical nature," although there is no clear definition of what is considered to be an object of an archaeological nature. A focus is placed on the removal of objects from the seabed, and the article does not suggest other areas of importance, such as the examination of underwater objects. There is no direct mention of the role of the flag State concerning archaeological objects, as only the coastal State is referenced regarding its sovereignty over the waters in which the objects are located.

The focus on the control of traffic for the removal of objects hints at the likelihood of there being interest in the found objects from multiple States. The reference to Article 33, which focuses on the contiguous zone, notes that objects taken from this area without the consent of the coastal State would equal infringement upon their sovereign rights. This encompasses shipwrecks found within the territorial sea and contiguous zone, although there is a noticeable gap concerning the EEZ. The lack of a clear designation of rights for flag States and coastal States over shipwrecks found within the EEZ is an area to consider with the increasing number of shipwreck discoveries within this area.

Contrary to CPUCH, UNCLOS does not set a specific time period for the designation of shipwrecks as being archaeologically or historically significant. CPUCH states that an object must be underwater for a minimum of 100 years in order to be considered underwater cultural heritage and available for protective measures. Scholars have discussed whether UNCLOS can be interpreted to include a time period of 50, 100, or 200 years for objects to be considered archaeologically significant, based on time periods included within domestic instruments (Cottrell 1994).

Article 149 ("Archaeological and historical objects") states:

> All objects of an archaeological and historical nature found in the Area shall be preserved or disposed of for the benefit of mankind as a whole, particular regard being paid to the preferential rights of the State or country of origin, or the State of cultural origin, or the State of historical and archaeological origin.

Thus, Article 149 includes three potential States that could have preferential rights over archaeological objects: the State of origin, the State of cultural origin, and the State of historical and archaeological origin. It is worth considering when and how these States may be distinct, as scholars have noted that there is no clear hierarchy within this Article to designate which States would gain ownership in the event that multiple States are involved (Henn 2012). Scholars have argued that the use of the phrase "for the benefit of mankind as a whole" leads to an interpretation that underwater wrecks have "a commonness of ownership and benefit of shipwrecks with archaeological significance" (Cottrell 1994). It echoes the goal of Article 303 in the preservation of objects, although there are no in-depth details concerning how objects should be preserved or disposed of. Scholars have also mentioned that "preferential rights suggest that one nation has a priority, but that there are simultaneous rights in other nations" (Cottrell 1994). This connects to the idea that multiple States can have a role in, and active claims to, shipwrecks located outside of their national waters. However, Article 149 centers only on objects found within the Area, which encompasses the seabed beyond the continental shelf. When considering a map of the maritime zones referenced in UNCLOS, the Area would include not objects located within the EEZ but rather those below the water column of the high seas. The number of shipwrecks to be discovered may continue to increase in future years due to technological advancements in exploring the deep ocean. It is, therefore, helpful to consider the potential interaction between the State of origin, the State of cultural origin, and the State of historical or archaeological origin for vessels located and identified within multiple maritime zones.

Articles 33, 303, and 149 offer guidance for States to consider when making decisions on activities related to underwater sites or shipwrecks of historical or cultural interest. The overarching aim centers on collaboration to conserve, protect, or dispose of archaeologically significant objects and artifacts. An example of effective international collaboration can be seen through the discovery of the *Titanic* shipwreck. The UK was the original flag State of the *Titanic*, which was discovered by a team of divers within the high seas, off the coast of Canada in the North Atlantic. This is a well-known and much-studied case, leading to changes in international legislation, such as through the Safety of Life at Sea Convention.[3] The discovery of the *Titanic* shipwreck was possible through the use of *Argo*, an unmanned vehicle capable of reaching depths of up to 6,000 m and capturing images in challenging environments, as well as other deep-sea exploration technologies (WHOI 2024). However, it is significant that it was discovered within the high seas, as most newly discovered shipwrecks tend to be located within coastal waters.

Overlapping interests in ownership and preferential rights may be heightened when shipwrecks are thought to have precious gems, jewels, and stones on board. While all shipwrecks can be considered to hold significant cultural heritage for a variety of reasons, the presence of cargo and artifacts may affect how they are viewed by States. There are conflicting flag State and coastal State claims to the *San José* shipwreck by Colombia, Spain, Peru, a private company from the US, and Indigenous groups from Bolivia. Each of these States cites distinct reasonings for its claims to ownership over the artifacts surrounding the shipwreck. Colombia centers its claim on the fact that the shipwreck is located within Colombian waters and is part of its cultural heritage (Tumin and Glatsky 2024). Meanwhile, Spain claims that it should have access to the shipwreck since it is the original flag State, it has sovereign immunity, and it is the resting site of more than 600 Spanish sailors. Peru and several Indigenous groups claim ownership over the artifacts surrounding the shipwreck, given that colonial powers took the gold, silver, and emeralds from

[3] International Convention for the Safety of Life at Sea, November 1, 1974, 1184 UNTS 2.

Peruvian, Bolivian, and Colombian mines worked by Indigenous people (Pinedo 2024). A private salvage company based in the US claims ownership over content found on board given its claim to have discovered the shipwreck in 1980, years ahead of the discovery by the Colombian Navy. Sections of these differing claims have been taken to the Permanent Court of Arbitration, particularly cases between Colombia, Spain, and the US (Chen and Rios 2024). This case highlights how the State of origin, the State of cultural origin, and the State of historical and archaeological origin have placed claims over the wreck. Article 149 mentions preferential rights, although there is insufficient expansion on these rights to gain a clear understanding of how they would impact a State's claims.

This issue is further complicated by the fact that Colombia has not ratified CPUCH, while Spain has urged that the *San José* be considered as a protected site given its role as a resting place. This leads into the question of how technologies, and the inherent increased access, impact the designation and enforcement of shipwrecks as gravesites. While shipwrecks can be thought of as gravesites, they are also considered homes to marine ecosystems, materials to be exploited, and locations for potential bilateral cooperation or conflict. UNCLOS addresses a starting point for objects found within the territorial sea, the contiguous zone, and the Area, yet it leaves vague aspects of the management and ownership of shipwrecks. CPUCH was designed to resolve some of the uncertainty, but it has not been universally accepted.

11.4.2 *Convention on the Protection of the Underwater Cultural Heritage*

CPUCH, which entered into force in 2009, currently has eighty-one State parties. While fewer States have ratified CPUCH as compared to UNCLOS, the Convention continues to be relevant when it comes to the protection of the underwater cultural heritage. CPUCH has aided in the protection and preservation of shipwrecks and archaeologically significant sites across various areas of the ocean. One of its main focuses is the preservation of underwater cultural heritage, which is defined in Article 1(1)(a):

> "Underwater cultural heritage" means all traces of human existence having a cultural, historical or archaeological character which have been partially or totally under water, periodically or continuously, for at least 100 years.

This Convention differs from UNCLOS in that it provides greater details on archaeologically significant objects, including a specified time period for which an object must be underwater in order to be considered underwater cultural heritage. The 100-year time period can aid in the designation of warships as underwater cultural heritage when more than one State is involved. There are existing domestic regulations governing the protection of shipwrecks, whether due to their understanding as gravesites or to the goal of limiting disturbance, and

CPUCH serves to fill a gap in the management of shipwrecks that may involve multiple States. These issues become more complex as conflicts over the ownership of shipwrecks and their designation as gravesites arise, and when the States involved have not formally adopted the Convention.

In addition, underwater cultural heritage can be separated into tangible and intangible heritage. Shipwrecks and artifacts are considered tangible pieces of underwater cultural heritage, while intangible heritage would include oral stories and traditions passed down through generations (Micronesia 2024). Scholars have referenced how finding the location of certain shipwrecks originated through local knowledge and stories from fishermen and local inhabitants (Finney n.d.). Local knowledge, combined with the technological capabilities of ROVs and AUVs, has led to the discovery of several wrecks. The argument in favor of the role of intangible cultural heritage as related to shipwrecks touches on the importance of oral stories in the discovery stage. This differs from UNCLOS, which does not reference tangible or intangible underwater cultural heritage when considering archaeological objects.

Article 7(3) of CPUCH states:

> Within their archipelagic waters and territorial sea, in the exercise of their sovereignty and in recognition of general practice among States, States Parties, with a view to cooperating on the best methods of protecting State vessels and aircraft, should inform the flag State Party to this Convention and, if applicable, other States with a verifiable link, especially a cultural, historical or archaeological link, with respect to the discovery of such identifiable State vessels and aircraft.

The role of the coastal State, as referenced in Article 7, is to inform the flag State of the discovery of an identifiable vessel within its territorial sea. There are no additional details provided on the continued role of the coastal State, such as to alert the flag State of future proposed activities that may impact the vessel. This can be challenging if the coastal State would need authorization from the flag State prior to conducting activities that may interfere with the sunken vessel. Balancing these varied interests over shipwrecks across maritime zones is important to ensure that wrecks are not unintentionally disturbed.

In addition to the enforcement of guidelines for known wrecks, it is also imperative to have oversight by the coastal State over expeditions to uncover potential wrecks. There have been cases where private divers have found shipwrecks within coastal waters and did not alert the national government as necessary under international customary law and domestic policy in certain States. In France, a group of commercial divers located the wreck of the *Prince de Conty* off the coast of the island Belle-Île-en-Mer in 1974, yet did not alert the French authorities of the wreck, preferring to keep it hidden (Mashberg 2022). Years later, gold ingots recovered from the wreck were located in the US marketplace and were returned to France (Mashberg 2022). The decision to return the ingots to France came as a result of the ship being flagged to France and being located within French territorial waters.

However, China placed a claim to the ingots, citing that they were part of Chinese cultural heritage as they had originated from China (Mashberg 2022). This shows the contrast in access to objects from shipwrecks from a maritime zone sovereignty claim compared to a cultural heritage claim. UNCLOS and CPUCH include sections that focus on the duty to alert the flag State should an object originally belonging to that State be discovered and identified. This assumes that the coastal State is involved in activities taking place over a shipwreck; however, with the role of ROVs and AUVs in accessing deepwater environments, there is the potential for the flag State to be the primary authority of the research expedition over sunken warships, with participation from other States. This leads to a question concerning the interaction and the duty of the flag State to alert the coastal State over data and objects discovered on warships.

11.5 FLAG STATE AND COASTAL STATE JURISDICTION OVER SHIPWRECKS

An instance of effective collaboration between the flag State and the coastal State over the management of a warship in foreign waters is the case of *La Trinité*. The French warship was discovered within US territorial waters off the coast of Florida in 2016. The wreckage was claimed by both the French government – arguing that it has jurisdiction over the ship because it was a French naval vessel – and a private US salvage company, arguing ownership through the discovery. The wreck was stated to belong to the French, given its position as a warship (Blanc 2023). Yet, there were discussions between Florida and France over management efforts to preserve the cultural heritage of the shipwreck and recover certain artifacts to be placed in a museum for public access (Soergel 2018). Both parties formally signed a Declaration of Intention, which noted that France has sole ownership over the shipwreck and authority over decisions and activities that would impact access to the wreck. Meanwhile, authorities from Florida agreed to conduct routine patrols of the wreck, with fines imposed should any artifacts be taken from the wreck without prior authorization (Florida Department of State 2018).

This type of bilateral agreement heightens the role of CPUCH through additional decisive actions to be taken toward the management of underwater cultural heritage. Bilateral agreements where the flag State has authority over activities, and the coastal State has authority in governing management efforts, can be effective in preserving shipwrecks and their cultural heritage. This can increase the necessary lines of communication between both States involved in claiming aspects of the shipwreck. As expressed in previous cases, there can also be a cultural claim for objects found on shipwrecks from the State of origin. Along with imaging technologies used to map shipwrecks, these same techniques can be utilized to identify States of origin. The CPUCH highlights States of origin for their part in creating cultural links. However, whether to use technological resources to identify States of origin for the objects discovered may be the decision of the flag State or coastal State involved in locating the wreck.

The case of *La Trinité* is an example of effective joint management over a warship from one State found within the territorial sea of a different State. Reaching this level of collaboration depends on several factors, and the CPUCH is one factor that can serve as a reference for the protection of sunken vessels. The CPUCH also outlines a process for research studies to gain access to protected sites under strict guidelines. States have distinct processes for how researchers gain access to known shipwrecks or access to explore a State's coastal waters for archaeological studies. This is rooted within domestic policies, as States have different priorities and concerns over access to shipwrecks, whether national or foreign, within their waters. This can make the process for managing wrecks unclear, especially those that involve more than one State and which are located outside of the territorial sea. Clear standards on the management of foreign-flagged shipwrecks can limit the potential of destruction and increase broader knowledge of the seabed, the marine environment, and cultural heritage associated with the wreck.

Disputes over a shipwreck are evident when it comes to ownership over its contents; over its designation and enforcement as a protected site, such as a gravesite; and over the cultural heritage tied to the loss of the vessel. The types of questions and data that researchers are able to gain from shipwrecks have expanded over time, concurrent with the advancement of technologies. For example, there have been studies on wooden frames discovered on shipwrecks to study their place of origin, as well as on the microbial organisms found on shipwrecks that have been submerged for years (Paxton et al. 2024). The type of information gained from studying shipwrecks is only possible if research teams are able to gain access to shipwreck sites.

11.5.1 *Sovereign Immunity of Sunken Warships*

The final element to discuss concerning the interaction of UNCLOS, CPUCH, and advancements in underwater archaeology focuses on the role of the sovereign immunity of sunken warships. As previously discussed, warships constitute a large number of recently discovered shipwrecks. Compared to other vessels used for commercial purposes, warships can have distinct legal protections (Dromgoole 2013). One of these distinctions is the sovereign immunity of the flag State over warships, which would be applicable irrespective of the maritime zone in which a warship was discovered.

Archaeologists are able to identify the original flag State of a sunken vessel based on access to historical logs, photographic evidence, and scientific testing to discover the State of origin. Through the use of photogrammetry, side-scan sonar, and other techniques, practitioners are able to gain clearer data to aid in the identification of sunken vessels. However, certain vessels may be difficult to identify based on environmental factors and the condition of the vessel. Scholars have mentioned the possibility of private salvage claims in instances where a ship is no longer able to be identified, and no flag State can be appropriately notified.

There is the potential for flag State jurisdiction over shipwrecks that have been successfully identified as warships under the principle of sovereign immunity. Scholarly discussions have considered whether sunken warships apply under the role of sovereign immunity, since they are no longer operating under the command of a captain or a crew and are incapable of navigation (Oyama n.d.). This position stems from Article 29 of UNCLOS, which centers on the definition of warships:

> For the purposes of this Convention, "warship" means a ship belonging to the armed forces of a State bearing the external marks distinguishing such ships of its nationality, under the command of an officer duly commissioned by the government of the State and whose name appears in the appropriate service list or its equivalent, and manned by a crew which is under regular armed forces discipline.

The argument that sovereign immunity does not apply to sunken warships highlights the fact that sunken warships are not under the command of an officer or crew. However, State practice has shown that States often consider their sunken warships to be under their jurisdiction through sovereign immunity and their designation as war graves (Ronzitti 2011). There are scholars who support the view of sunken warships as being under the sovereign immunity of the flag State until the flag State has explicitly renounced its jurisdiction over the vessel (Ronzitti 2011). The application of sovereign immunity could place a right of access to the flag State, although it is likely that the coastal State would need to provide its consent if the shipwreck were located within its territorial sea, contiguous zone, or EEZ (Dromgoole 2013).

The coastal State is mentioned in Articles 149 and 303 of UNCLOS as having sovereign rights over objects of an archaeological and historical nature found within its waters. The CPUCH similarly gives rights of access to the coastal State. It then becomes important to consider the interaction between the coastal State and the flag State in cases that involve sunken warships if both have certain competing rights of access.

States have been able to manage shipwrecks effectively through bilateral agreements – as seen in the case of the HMAS *Perth*, an Australian warship located off the coast of Indonesia, by creating a conservation zone over the warship (Pearson 2023). Bilateral agreements between flag States and coastal States to create joint management plans over historic wrecks have been an effective measure and may be beneficial moving forward, as States continue to collaborate to conduct scientific studies of shipwrecks. The creation of a preservation zone surrounding US warships found off the coast of France has also been effective in preventing further damage (Mirasola 2016).

11.5.2 *Shipwrecks as Gravesites*

Aside from the application of sovereign immunity, sunken warships and vessels may also simultaneously be gravesites. Increased access to shipwrecks means that there can be additional instances of disturbances that can interact with ethical concerns over shipwrecks as gravesites. It may be clear to acknowledge shipwrecks as gravesites considering those who perished with the ship; however, in practice, it can be difficult to enforce the idea of a sunken vessel as a gravesite without tangible evidence (Forrest 2003). Wrecks that have been submerged for years experience changes due to the environment, which may make it more difficult to identify exact objects or human remains. The use of robotic technologies and advanced imaging mechanisms can aid in capturing and verifying objects of an archaeological nature on the seabed without the need for retrieval. Without coastal State monitoring and patrol programs, it becomes difficult to enforce the management of underwater shipwrecks as gravesites to avoid disruption from commercial divers, tourism, and other actors.

Effective cases of the protection of shipwrecks as gravesites from unauthorized excavation use several types of mechanisms to surveil the area surrounding the shipwreck. This can be more imperative when it concerns wrecks that could cause damage to the surrounding environment if they are disturbed. The UNCLOS does not make direct reference to shipwrecks as potential gravesites, although Article 2(9) of CPUCH provides that States "shall ensure that proper respect is given to all human remains located in maritime waters." Scholars have noted the discussion over the respectful treatment of shipwrecks as gravesites as a complex and challenging area (Delgado and Varmer 2014). The designation of a shipwreck as a protected gravesite can potentially impact further studies of the surrounding area and likely requires consent and collaboration between the various States involved. The definition of respectful treatment of shipwrecks is important, as technological advancements balance between assisting in uncovering data and not causing disruption to the site. An example is the expanding use of environmental DNA testing, which has been employed on skeletal remains discovered within the Antikythera shipwreck (Lewis 2016). The results of the environmental DNA testing can reveal aspects of the lives of sailors at the time of the sinking, as well as additional details about the State of origin (Briggs 2020). The Antikythera shipwreck involved a Greek vessel that was located within Greek waters off the coast of Crete (Theodoulou 2015). This lessened the number of States involved in the management and ownership of the vessel, since it was discovered within the territorial sea of the original flag State.

Meanwhile, the management of sunken shipwrecks within the EEZ of a separate State can affect a number of decisions stemming from the ownership of the sunken vessel. For example, a State may decide to take action against a shipwreck that is considered a potentially polluting wreck, as well as making decisions concerning the removal of artifacts or other materials on board. Without clear ownership over a shipwreck, it can be hard to determine the correct authority to enforce actions that impact the wreck site, the surrounding marine environment, and the cultural connection to local inhabitants. It can be a timely process, involving national policies, to consider the wreck of a warship as protected within a foreign State's EEZ, although this has been successfully negotiated through the wrecks of the HMCS *Guysborough* and the HMCS *Athabaskan* – Canadian warships located within the French EEZ (House of Commons, Canada 2018).

While UNCLOS and CPUCH are significant in deciding the role of flag States and coastal States regarding archaeological objects, there is a noticeable gap in the enforcement of protected shipwrecks as gravesites. Domestic legislation assists in filling these gaps with regard to shipwrecks flagged to the original State in whose waters they were located. This leaves a question concerning the ownership and enforcement of certain policies over wrecks outside of the national waters of their flag State. Several national policies surround State action over shipwrecks; these vary across States with distinct maritime histories, resources, and objectives. Examples of domestic policies concerning shipwrecks in foreign or international waters include the Abandoned Shipwreck Act of 1987 and the Sunken Military Craft Act of 2004 in the US, and the Protection of Military Remains Act 1986 in the UK (National Park Service 2023).

While regulations vary by country, most States that are heavily involved in archaeological research also have strict application processes and permits necessary for projects to move forward. Some States encourage the participation of a government official on board the archaeological research vessel to ensure that it is conducted according to plan. Other States, such as those that did not have active vessels at the time of the First and Second World Wars, may not have such an interest in accessing and studying foreign vessels. There have been cases where third parties, such as those outside of the flag State and the coastal State, have been involved in the disruption of wreck sites without the prior consent of the flag State or the coastal State. In these instances, it is important to consider how neither State was made aware of those activities until after the artifacts were taken and in transit, as is the case of the HMAS *Perth* (Hosty 2022).

Shipwrecks can also be potentially exposed to access by divers within the territorial sea. There have been cases of commercial divers excavating wreckage sites following the successful discovery of shipwrecks within different areas of the ocean, as seen in the case of the HMS *Repulse* and the HMS *Prince of Wales* (Grammaticas 2023). Shipwrecks are often exploited for their metal and other parts without regard to their applicability as marine conservation zones or gravesites. This can cause tension between the flag State of the vessel that has been excavated and the coastal State in whose waters the operations took place. Meanwhile, in instances where flag States and coastal States are working collaboratively toward the protection of a shipwreck, this can be derailed by actions taken by private companies contrary to the goal of protecting underwater cultural heritage. It is then difficult to consider the applicability of UNCLOS or CPUCH in safeguarding sites of archaeological importance from unauthorized excavation.

A case of competing interests over a shipwreck and its artifacts can be seen in the shipwrecks found by Enigma Recoveries off the coast of Cyprus and Lebanon. Enigma Recoveries used ROVs to excavate more than 588 artifacts from the wreck sites (Milmo 2016). These were then confiscated by officials from Cyprus, claiming that the wrecks were located within its waters. However, the private company claimed that the location of the wrecks is within the high seas between Cyprus and Lebanon (Maritime Executive 2020). The excavation was only possible due to the use of ROVs, and this sheds light on the importance of maritime boundaries when deciding ownership and access to shipwrecks. Along with technological advancements to study and preserve shipwrecks, there have been advancements that have led to a potential increase in tourism and commercial diving over shipwrecks. This is an area to consider for future research concerning legal access to shipwrecks in foreign waters by commercial divers and tourists (Ferentinos et al. 2020).

11.6 CONCLUSION

The aim of this chapter was to cover the distinctions between flag State and coastal State with regard to access to shipwrecks, including those under sovereign immunity, and the potential avenues for effective management. The increasing discovery and identification of shipwrecks across different maritime zones is possible due to advancements in underwater imaging technology, AUVs, the use of AI, environmental DNA testing, and other more specified deep-ocean techniques. Shipwrecks can connect to various States for multiple reasons highlighted in UNCLOS and CPUCH, such as States of origin, States of cultural origin, and States of archaeological or historical origin. While shipwrecks can be gravesites and war memorials, they can also hold tangible and intangible cultural heritage that can offer historical importance for different States. The status of the sunken ship, the location where it was discovered, and its interaction with the surrounding environment can play a role in how it is managed and protected in future instances.

There have been examples of international collaboration in the discovery of new shipwrecks, such as through the joint Skerki Bank archaeological expedition (UNESCO 2023). This project, which includes participation by Algeria, Croatia, Egypt, France, Italy, Morocco, Spain, and Tunisia, takes place in “Italian territorial waters, under the coordination of Italy, and then in Tunisian territorial waters under the coordination of Tunisia” (UNESCO 2023). It also includes the use of two ROVs to study shipwrecks within the Skerki Bank. The advancement of certain technologies has made these interactions more crucial, as some States may have access to specific technologies that other States may be lacking. The UNCLOS places a level of significance on States to collaborate in the preservation of shipwrecks and sites, but it is worth considering the role of UNCLOS when there are competing claims on excavating shipwrecks for commercial purposes, aside from cultural preservation. This can involve interests in exploring and excavating underwater wrecks to gain access to valuable objects, which is in contrast to the goal of collaboration and preservation referenced within international agreements.

The difference in national policies over sunken warships, combined with gaps in the enforcement of protection over sunken vessels across the EEZ and advancements in surveying techniques, makes it critical to address ahead of the continued discovery of shipwrecks at greater depths and in areas farther from the coast. Technological innovations have assisted in gaining information from underwater wrecks and in the identification of sunken vessels, which is likely to continue to increase in the future as new questions are considered concerning shipwrecks that remain to be discovered. While archaeological studies are conducted, ensuring effective collaboration across flag States and coastal States over management and access to deepwater shipwrecks will be important.

REFERENCES

Blanc, Sébastien. 2023. "France Wins Suit over History-Making Shipwreck off US Coast." *Barron's*, October 8. www.barrons.com/news/france-wins-suit-over-history-making-shipwreck-off-us-coast-af1399aa.

Bradley, Ryan. 2023. "Technical Diving." NOAA Ocean Exploration. https://oceanexplorer.noaa.gov/technology/technical/technical.html.

Bräuer-Burchardt, Christian, Christoph Munkelt, MichCael Bleier, Matthias Heinze, Ingo Gebhart, Peter Kühmstedt, and Gunther Notni. 2023. "Underwater 3D Scanning System for Cultural Heritage Documentation." *Remote Sensing* 15 (7). https://doi.org/10.3390/rs15071864.

Briggs, Lisa. 2020. "Ancient DNA Research in Maritime and Underwater Archaeology: Pitfalls, Promise, and Future Directions." *Open Quaternary* 6 (1): 3.

Chen, Heather, and Michael Rios. 2024. "Colombia Launches Expedition to Explore 300-Year-Old Spanish Shipwreck Filled with Sunken Treasure." *CNN*, May 22. www.cnn.com/2024/05/22/travel/san-jose-colombia-shipwreck-expedition-discovery-intl-hnk/index.html.

Conte, G., L. Gambella, D. Scaradozzi, and S. Zanoli. 2009. "Underwater Vehicle Technology in the European Research Project VENUS." *International Journal of the Society for Underwater Technology* 28 (4): 175–185.

Cottrell, Anne M. 1994. "The Law of the Sea and International Marine Archaeology: Abandoning Admiralty Law to Protect Historic Shipwrecks." *Fordham International Law Journal* 17 (3): 667–725.

Delgado, James, and Ole Varmer. 2014. "The Public Importance of World War I Shipwrecks: Why a State Should Care and the Challenges of Protection." In *Underwater Cultural Heritage from World War I: Proceedings of the Scientific Conference on the Occasion of the Centenary of World War I*, edited by Ulrike Guérin, Arturo Rey da Silva, and Lucas Simonds. UNESCO.

Dromgoole, Sarah. 2013. *Sunken Warships and Other State Vessels and Aircraft*. Cambridge University Press.

Ferentinos, George, Elias Fakiris, Dimitrios Christodoulou, Maria Geraga, Xenophontas Dimas, Nikos Georgiou, Stavroula Kordella, George Papatheodorou, Michalis Prevenios, and Makis Sotiropoulos. 2020 "Optimal Sidescan Sonar and Subbottom Profiler Surveying of Ancient Wrecks: The 'Fiskardo' Wreck, Kefallinia Island, Ionian Sea." *Journal of Archaeological Science* 113 (5): 105032.

Finney, Suzanne S. n.d. "The Intangible Underwater: Integrating Intangible Cultural Heritage into the Study of Underwater Cultural Heritage Sites." Museum of Underwater Archaeology.

Florida Department of State. 2018. "Republic of France and State of Florida Sign Declaration of Intention to Embark on a Historic Partnership to Research and Preserve the Trinité Shipwreck." Press Release, December 21.

Forrest, Craig. 2003. "An International Perspective on Sunken State Vessels as Underwater Cultural Heritage." *Ocean Development & International Law* 34 (1): 41–57.

Gates, Megan. 2019. "Who Owns the San Jose Galleon?" *ASIS International*, July 1. www.asisonline.org/security-management-magazine/articles/2019/07/who-owns-the-san-jose-galleon/.

Goncharov, A. E. 2016. "Prospects for Using Sonar for Underwater Archeology on the Yenisei: Surveying a Nineteenth Century Shipwreck." *IOP Conference Series: Materials Science and Engineering* 155: 012037.

Grammaticas, Damian. 2023. "Ministry of Defence Condemns 'Desecration' of Royal Navy Wrecks." *BBC*, May 26. www.bbc.com/news/uk-politics-65724795.

Hayden, Ben. 2023. "Deep Sea Surveys of Three Shipwrecks from Battle of Midway." *WorkBoat*, September 25. www.workboat.com/technology/deep-sea-surveys-of-three-shipwrecks-from-battle-of-midway.

Henn, Cathryn. 2012. "The Trouble with Treasure: Historic Shipwrecks Discovered in International Waters." *University of Miami International and Comparative Law Review* 141 (2): 1–57.

Hosty, Kieran. 2022. *The Sad Fate of HMAS Perth (I)*. Australian National Maritime Museum.

House of Commons, Canada. 2018. *Canada's Ocean War Graves: Report of the Standing Committee on Transport, Infrastructure and Communities*. May.

Hydro-International. 2020. "How Robotic Technology Officially Identified the World War II Submarine S-28 Grave-Site." Hydro-International, August 24. www.hydro-international.com/content/article/how-robotic-technology-officially-identified-the-world-war-ii-submarine-s-28-gravesite.

Lewis, Danny. 2016. "Skeleton Pulled from the Antikythera Shipwreck Could Give Clues to Life Aboard the Vessel." *Smithsonian Magazine*, September 20. www.smithsonianmag.com/smart-news/skeleton-could-unlock-new-details-about-life-aboard-antikythera-shipwreck-180960515/.

Looram, Charlotte Papillaud, and Jade Lindley. 2024. "Preventing and Protecting against Underwater Cultural Heritage Crime." *Frontiers in Conservation Science* 5: 1–11.

Maritime Executive. 2020. "Cypriot Officials, Wreck Hunters Dispute Title to Ancient Artifacts." May 15. https://maritime-executive.com/article/cypriot-officials-wreck-hunters-dispute-title-to-ancient-artifacts.

Mashberg, Tom. 2022. "Gold Ingots from Eighteenth-Century Shipwreck Returned to France." *New York Times*, March 2. www.nytimes.com/2022/03/02/arts/design/china-france-gold-ingots.html.

McCarthy, John, Jonathan Benjamin, Trevor Winton, and Wendy van Duivenvoorde. 2019. "The Rise of 3D in Maritime Archaeology." In *3D Recording and Interpretation for*

Maritime Archaeology, edited by John K. McCarthy, Jonathan Benjamin, Trevor Winton, and Wendy van Duivenvoorde. Vol. 31 of Coastal Research Library. Springer.

Memet, Jean-Bernard. 2008. “Conservation of Underwater Cultural Heritage: Characteristics and New Technologies.” *Museum International* 60 (4): 42–49.

Merkusheva, Daria. 2020. “7 New Technologies to Find Sunken Ships.” ASME, February 26. www.asme.org/topics-resources/content/7-new-technologies-to-find-sunken-ships.

Micronesia (Delegation of the Federated States of Micronesia). 2024. “Briefing Note for Thematic Discussion on ‘Intangible Cultural Heritage Definition.’” February 29.

Milmo, Cahal. 2016. “Odyssey Explorer: Cyprus to Examine Suspect Cargo of Antiquities from Offshore Supply Ship.” *Independent*, January 1. www.independent.co.uk/news/world/europe/odyssey-explorer-cyprus-to-examine-suspect-cargo-of-antiquities-from-offshore-supply-ship-a6816691.html.

Mirasola, Christopher. 2016. “Swimming against the Tide: Colombia’s Claim to a Shipwreck and Sunken Treasure.” *Harvard Law Journal*, January 26. https://journals.law.harvard.edu/ilj/2016/01/swimming-against-the-tide-colombias-claim-to-a-shipwreck-and-sunken-treasure/.

National Park Service. 2023. “Sunken Military Craft Act of 2004.” www.nps.gov/subjects/archeology/sunken-military-craft-act.htm.

NOAA (National Oceanic and Atmospheric Administration). 2002. “Side-Scan Sonar.” NOAA Ocean Exploration. https://oceanexplorer.noaa.gov/technology/sonar/side-scan.html.

2024a. “Maritime Archaeology.” Stellwagen Bank National Marine Sanctuary. https://stellwagen.noaa.gov/maritime/archaeology.html.

2024b. “Why Do We Study Shipwrecks?” NOAA Ocean Exploration. https://oceanexplorer.noaa.gov/facts/whyshipwrecks.html.

n.d. “Underwater Archaeology.” NOAA Marine Protected Areas. https://marineprotectedareas.noaa.gov/toolkit/underwater-archaeology.html.

Ocean Robotics. 2018. “Ocean Infinity Locates the Missing Argentinian Submarine, ARA San Juan.” November 19. https://oceanroboticsplanet.com/ocean-infinity-locates-the-missing-argentinian-submarine-ara-san-juan-19-11-2018.

Oyama, Kaè. n.d. “Legal Status of Sunken State Vessels and Sovereign Immunity.” Museum of Underwater Archaeology.

Pater, Christopher. 2020. “Seabed Infrastructure Projects, Underwater Cultural Heritage and the Environmental Assessment Process: The UK Example.” In *The Archaeology of Europe’s Drowned Landscapes*, edited by Geoff Bailey, Nena Galanidou, Hans Peeters, Hauke Jöns, and Moritz Mennenga. Vol. 35 of Coastal Research Library. Springer.

Paxton, Avery B., Christopher McGonigle, Melanie Damour, Georgia Holly, Alicia Caporaso, Peter B. Campbell, Kirstin S. Meyer-Kaiser, Leila J. Hamdan, Calvin H. Mires, and J. Christopher Taylor. 2024. “Shipwreck Ecology: Understanding the Function and Processes from Microbes to Megafauna.” *BioScience* 74 (1): 12–24.

Pearson, Natali. 2023. “Too Little, Too Late? Redefining the Legacy of HMAS *Perth* (I), an Australian Warship Sunk in Indonesian Waters.” *Historical Archaeology* 57: 169–187.

Pinedo, Emma. 2024. “Indigenous Groups Claim Stake in Sunken Spanish Ship, Cargo off Colombia.” *Reuters*, May 10. www.reuters.com/world/americas/indigenous-groups-claim-stake-sunken-spanish-ship-cargo-off-colombia-2024-05-10/.

Ridwan, Nia Naelul Hasanah. 2019. “Vulnerability of Shipwreck Sites in Indonesian Waters.” *Current Science* 117 (10): 1623.

Roman, C. and R. Mather. 2010. “Autonomous Underwater Vehicles as Tools for Deep Submergence Archaeology Submergence Archaeology.” *Journal of Engineering for the Maritime Environment* 224 (4): 327–340.

Ronzitti, Natalino. 2011. “The Legal Regime of Wrecks of Warships and Other State-Owned Ships in International Law.” *Yearbook of the Institute of International Law* 74: 133–177.

Sheppard, A., A. V. Sethuraman, O. Bagoren, Christopher Pinnow, Jamey Anderson, Timothy C. Havens, and Katherine A. Skinner. 2024. “Machine Learning for Shipwreck Segmentation from Side Scan Sonar Imagery: Dataset and Benchmark.” AI4Shipwrecks Dataset, University of Michigan, Deep Blue Data.

Soergel, Matt. 2018. “Public Will Get to See Wreckage of Sixteenth-Century French Fleet.” *Florida-Times Union*, December 27. www.jacksonville.com/story/news/state/2018/12/27/france-and-florida-agree-wreckage-of-doomed-16th-century-french-fleet-should-be-public-exhibit/6189778007/.

Song, Andrew. 2023. “Submarine Rescue Forensics: Lessons from the Ara San Juan (S-42) Tragedy.” CIMSEC, November 11. https://cimsec.org/submarine-rescue-forensics-lessons-from-the-ara-san-juan-s-42-tragedy/.

Theodoulou, Theotokis. 2015. “Overview of Underwater Archaeological Research with Advanced Technologies in Greece.” In *Best Practices of GeoInformatic Technologies for the Mapping of Archaeolandscapes*, edited by Apostolos Sarris. Archaeopress Archaeology.

Tumin, Remy, and Genevieve Glatsky. 2024. “A Treasure May Be off the Coast of Colombia, but Who Can Claim It?” *New York Times*, March 25. www.nytimes.com/2023/11/10/world/americas/san-jose-galleon-shipwreck-treasure.html.

UNESCO (United Nations Educational, Scientific and Cultural Organization). 2007. *The UNESCO Convention on the Protection of the Underwater Cultural Heritage*. UNESCO.

2023. “Archeological Expedition to Explore Shipwrecks in the Skerki Bank.” April 4. www.unesco.org/en/articles/archeological-expedition-explore-shipwrecks-skerki-bank.

Villán, José Luis. 2019. “The Tragic Loss of ARA San Juan.” US Naval Institute, March. www.usni.org/magazines/proceedings/2019/march/tragic-loss-ara-san-juan.

WHOI (Woods Hole Oceanographic Institution). 2024. “Ships & Technology Used during the *Titanic* Expeditions.” Woods Hole Oceanographic Institution. www.whoi.edu/know-your-ocean/ocean-topics/ocean-human-lives/underwater-archaeology/rms-titanic/ships-technology-used-during-the-titanic-expeditions.

Zenkiewicz, Maciej, and Tadeusz Wasilewski. 2019. “The Galleon ‘San Jose.’ Almost Four Decades of Legal Struggles on the National and International Plane.” *Comparative Law Review* 22: 319–342.

Zwolak, Karolina, Rochelle Wigley, Aileen Bohan, Yulia Zarayskaya, Evgenia Bazhenova, Wetherbee Dorshow, Masanao Sumiyoshi, Seeboruth Sattiabaruth, Jaya Roperez, Alison Proctor, Craig Wallace, Hadar Sade, Tomer Ketter, Benjamin Simpson, Neil Tinmouth, Robin Falconer, Ivan Ryzhov, and Mohamed Elsaied Abou-Mahmoud. 2020. “The Autonomous Underwater Vehicle Integrated with the Unmanned Surface Vessel Mapping the Southern Ionian Sea. The Winning Technology Solution of the Shell Ocean Discovery XPRIZE.” *Remote Sensing* 12 (8). https://doi.org/10.3390/rs12081344.

PART VI

Maritime Security and Naval Threats

12

Floating Nuclear Power Plants, Nonproliferation Norms, and the Law of the Sea

Marc Fialkoff

12.1 INTRODUCTION

In his opening remarks to the International Atomic Energy Agency's (IAEA) *2023 Symposium on the Benefits and Challenges to Floating Nuclear Power Plants*, Director General Rafael Mariano Grossi acknowledged the active interest by countries in deploying floating nuclear power plants (FNPPs) but cautioned that "safeguards and the international legal and regulatory implications needed to be thoroughly analyzed" in discussions about FNPP deployments (Ashton 2023). The complexity surrounding FNPPs goes well beyond technical designs or applications; rather, the challenges are in their classification and categorization under international law and how international norms – such as those in nuclear law, maritime law, and the law of the sea – apply to the variety of deployment scenarios being considered.

With the deployment of FNPPs beyond territorial waters to support the efforts of the offshore oil and gas industries in decarbonizing their energy needs, an emerging challenge is the relationship between nuclear nonproliferation norms and their impact within the exclusive economic zone (EEZ). Under Article 55 of the United Nations Convention on the Law of the Sea (UNCLOS),[1] the EEZ is defined as "an area beyond and adjacent to the territorial sea, subject to the specific legal regime established in this Part, under which the rights and jurisdiction of the coastal State and the rights and freedoms of other States are governed by the relevant provisions of this Convention." In his book *Building a New Legal Order for the Oceans*, Ambassador Tommy Koh explains that one of the outstanding questions relating to the EEZ is its legal status, which has implications for the application of nonproliferation norms such as nuclear security and nuclear safeguards (Koh 2020,

The author would like to dedicate this chapter to the memory of his mother, Wendy Sue Fialkoff.
This submission was written by the author acting in his own independent capacity and not on behalf of UTBattelle, LLC, or its affiliates or successors.

[1] UNCLOS, December 10, 1982, 1833 UNTS 397.

324). If the EEZ is an extension of the national jurisdiction of a coastal State, does the coastal State's nonproliferation framework apply, or is the EEZ akin to the high seas, where the coastal State commands lesser sovereignty, creating a void for nonproliferation norms?

Current international discourse on FNPPs within the EEZ or the high seas focuses on their transit through these zones from a supplier State to a host State and the transport security considerations for ensuring that nuclear material is neither stolen nor sabotaged. Insofar as prior analysis has highlighted the intersection of the law-of-the-sea principles of innocent passage and freedom of navigation for FNPPs through different maritime zones, these analyses do not address deployment and long-term operation within the EEZ and the application of nuclear nonproliferation norms of the host or supplier State (Bernini 2022, 109). Deploying FNPPs in the EEZ raises questions about their regulation under various nuclear law frameworks, including the imposition of the appropriate nuclear security regime and appropriate nuclear safeguards obligations. Fundamental to this is the question of jurisdiction, control, and sovereignty over the FNPP outside the territorial waters of the hosting coastal State and the intersectionality of nuclear law with that of the jurisdictional considerations embedded within maritime law and the law of the sea regime.

FNPP deployment in the EEZ or the high seas puts the FNPP squarely at the intersection of overlapping regimes, where concepts of jurisdiction, control, territorial integrity, and sovereignty are fundamental, driving the inquiry about which regulatory framework applies. For example, with respect to the application of nuclear security, under the Amendment to the Convention on the Physical Protection of Nuclear Material (ACPPNM),[2] Fundamental Principle A of Article 2A(3) stipulates that "the responsibility for the establishment, implementation and maintenance of a physical protection regime within a State rests entirely with that State." From this provision, the State in which nuclear material[3] is located is

[2] Amendment to the Convention on the Physical Protection of Nuclear Material, July 8, 2005, 3132 UNTS 174 (ACPPNM).

[3] For the purposes of nuclear security, "nuclear material" is defined as "material listed in the table on the categorization of nuclear material, including the material listed in its footnotes, in Section 4 of IAEA Nuclear Security Series No. 13, Nuclear Security Recommendations on Physical Protection of Nuclear Material and Nuclear Facilities (INFCIRC/225/Revision 5)" (IAEA 2022a, 137). The definition of "nuclear material" also includes "any material that is either special fissionable material or source material as defined in Article XX of the IAEA Statute" (138). "Special fissionable material" as defined is "plutonium-239; uranium-233; *uranium enriched in the isotopes 235 or 233*; any material containing one or more of the foregoing; and such other fissionable material as the [IAEA] Board of Governors shall from time to time determine; but not including *source material*" (139). "Source material" is defined as "*Uranium* containing the mixture of isotopes occurring in nature; *uranium* depleted in the isotope 235; thorium; any of the foregoing in the form of metal, alloy, chemical compound, or concentrate; any other material containing one or more of the foregoing in such concentration as the [IAEA] Board of Governors shall from time to time determine; and such other material as the [IAEA] Board of Governors shall from time to time determine" (139).

responsible for establishing and maintaining a nuclear security regime, including effective regulatory controls such as licensing, inspections, enforcement, and the promulgation of regulations to support the nuclear security regime (Stoiber et al. 2003, 28–31). Similar to nuclear security, nuclear safeguards – another pillar of nuclear law – require States to establish controls over nuclear material[4] to ensure that they are using the material for peaceful purposes. Under the Basic Undertaking described in IAEA Information Circular 153 (Corrected) (INFCIRC/153 (corr.)), which serves as the basis for many of the Comprehensive Safeguards Agreements (CSAs) between the IAEA and IAEA member States, an agreement "should contain, in accordance with Article III.1 of the Treaty on the Non-Proliferation of Nuclear Weapons, an undertaking by the State to accept safeguards, in accordance with the terms of the Agreement, on all source or special fissionable material in all peaceful nuclear activities within its territory, under its jurisdiction or carried out under its control anywhere" (IAEA 1972, 1).

Like the ACPPNM, the Basic Undertaking in INFCIRC/153 (corr.) and CSAs with the abovementioned provision introduce a jurisdictional question, explicit in that it identifies territory, jurisdiction, or control anywhere within the contracting State. This reinforces the question posed by Koh about whether the EEZ is an extension of a coastal State's national jurisdiction (and, therefore, safeguards would apply in the EEZ). When these regimes intersect with the flag State jurisdiction for vessels and the ambiguity about the extent of control for coastal States in the EEZ, novel questions arise about who and under whose regulatory frameworks FNPPs operate.

This chapter explores the alignment of UNCLOS with the principles of maritime law – namely, the relationship between UNCLOS, flag State jurisdiction, and nonproliferation norms for the deployment of FNPPs in the EEZ. Applying prior work that establishes FNPPs as "installations" when fixed (Bernini 2022, 129), such installations would be regulated under the host coastal State's regulatory framework, including its nuclear security and nuclear safeguards requirements.[5] Under this interpretation, coastal States would have responsibility for ensuring that the highest standards of nuclear security and safeguards are applied to deployed FNPPs while maintaining their commitment to their obligations under the law of the sea. FNPP deployment would raise novel operational questions, but, ultimately, FNPPs

4 For the purposes of nuclear safeguards, "nuclear material" is defined as "any source or any special fissionable as defined in Article XX of the [IAEA] Statute. The term source material shall not be interpreted as applying to ore or ore residue. Any determination by the Board under Article XX of the Statute after the entry into force of this Agreement which adds to the materials considered to be source material or special fissionable material shall have effect under this agreement only upon acceptance by the State" (IAEA 1972, 28).

5 Leopardi explains that the "lawfulness of the installation of an [Ocean Nuclear Power Plant] … depends upon authorization by the coastal state" (Leopardi 2024, 11). Richards proposes coastal state jurisdiction over oil rigs in the EEZ as installations and falling under coastal state jurisdiction according to Article 56 of UNCLOS (Richards 2011, 408).

deployed to support offshore oil and gas production would be viewed as installations when fixed, regardless of their vessel status, under both nuclear law and the law of the sea, enabling the coastal State to implement robust nuclear security and safeguards requirements.

12.2 DEPLOYMENT OF FNPPS OUTSIDE TERRITORIAL WATERS

At the time of writing, the only currently operating FNPP is the *Akademik Lomonosov*, located in Pevek, Russia; however, before the construction, deployment, and commissioning of the *Akademik Lomonosov*, discussions about the siting of FNPPs both within and beyond territorial waters took place in the early 1970s. The same questions regarding the law of the sea are being asked today as were asked back then. In 1974, a study conducted by Oak Ridge National Laboratory (ORNL) and the University of California, Los Angeles (UCLA) investigated the initial feasibility of the construction and operation of an FNPP within the 3-mile territorial limit of the US (Hammond and Okrent 1974, 136). The ORNL and UCLA studied different platform configurations for FNPPs, including barge-type structures, semi-submersible oil-drilling platforms, and multipoint mooring structures, as well as the various safety and geographic considerations for their deployment (Hammond and Okrent 1974, 133).

Additionally, the ORNL and UCLA study surveyed the domestic and international legal landscape for the deployment of FNPPs within and beyond territorial waters (Hammond and Okrent 1974, 136). This work recognized that the siting of an "offshore nuclear power station" would fall into "different classes depending not on the depth of the water but on how far the station is from the coastline" (Hammond and Okrent 1974, 136). The analysis parsed the jurisdictional issues with siting an FNPP within State waters, which are those waters from the coastline to approximately 3 nautical miles, and the overlap with federal jurisdiction (Hammond and Okrent 1974, 136). This work went beyond 3 nautical miles to address the federal jurisdiction controls out to 12 nautical miles (Hammond and Okrent 1974, 136). Beyond the 12-nautical-mile mark, the authors identified ambiguities within both US law and the international law of the sea framework at the time for understanding the rights and responsibilities involved with FNPP deployment (Hammond and Okrent 1974, 136). At the time, their analysis did not identify specific nonproliferation frameworks, except for acknowledging the need to protect against possible sabotage of the FNPP (Hammond and Okrent 1974, 136). When the ORNL and UCLA conducted their study in 1974, neither the Convention on the Physical Protection of Nuclear Material (CPPNM)[6] nor the Non-Proliferation Treaty (NPT)[7] existed. The sole concern outside of nuclear safety

[6] Convention on the Physical Protection of Nuclear Material, October 26, 1979, 1456 UNTS 246 (CPPNM).

[7] Treaty on the Non-Proliferation of Nuclear Weapons, July 1, 1968, 729 UNTS 161 (NPT).

was the identification of a possible sabotage attempt against the nuclear power plant (Hammond and Okrent 1974, 136).

Around the same time as the ORNL and UCLA study, the US Nuclear Regulatory Commission considered a licensing application for the construction of FNPPs off the coast of Jacksonville, Florida, with subsequent siting and deployment of FNPPs off the coast of New Jersey (OTA 1976, 197). In 1976, the Office of Technology Assessment (OTA) reported on the US Nuclear Regulatory Commission's analysis and the siting, deployment, and regulatory considerations for an FNPP deployment off the coast of New Jersey, specifically identifying that the power plant will be inside the 3-nautical-mile limit. This would place it fully under federal and State jurisdiction, consistent with the findings of the ORNL and UCLA study (OTA 1976, 207). The OTA study did conclude that the FNPP would be segregated from major shipping traffic, specifically the Atlantic coastal shipping lanes (OTA 1976, 207).

The ORNL and UCLA study and the OTA analysis focused primarily on the domestic deployment of FNPPs in the US. In contrast to the OTA study, which focused solely on the siting of the FNPP within the 3-nautical-mile limit, the ORNL and UCLA study acknowledged the different maritime zones, drawing the conclusion that further research was needed to understand FNPP deployment in international waters (Hammond and Okrent 1974, 136). In contrast, Marlowe Blake's 1978 analysis of FNPP deployment on the high seas considers FNPPs deployed in the high seas and the implications of the international law of the sea, including environmental protection and fisheries management (Blake 1978, 197–199). Blake begins with the New Jersey deployment of a possible FNPP but then examines the possibility of FNPPs in the high seas beyond New Jersey, though the context and rationale for the extension of FNPPs to the high seas only went so far as to postulate: "Is FNPP deployment considered a 'reasonable use' of the High Seas?" (Blake 1978, 197–199). Blake's legal analysis for FNPP deployment and the reasonableness of such use of the high seas are discussed later. This early analysis highlights that such questions were already being asked and are resurfacing today.

Although prior and current applications include electrical power production for communities and district heating, FNPPs are also being considered to support decarbonization efforts across multiple sectors, including the offshore oil and gas industry (World Nuclear News 2023). As part of its 2021 study "Rethinking Deployment Scenarios for Advanced Reactors," the Electric Power Research Institute (EPRI) analyzed the use of FNPPs in various offshore production supply chains, including ammonia production, commercial airline fuel production, desalinization of water, and support to the offshore oil and gas industry (EPRI 2021). Focusing on offshore oil and gas production, EPRI's report highlighted the modularity of the oil and gas industry infrastructure, and this modularity increases the possibility for interfacing and integrating with small modular reactors or FNPPs that could be deployed to support offshore oil and gas extraction (EPRI 2021, 8).

Additional research by Bernini confirmed EPRI's analysis that FNPPs could be used to support offshore oil and gas extraction (Bernini 2022, 109). Specific examples cited by Bernini include the 2014 memorandum on the construction of an FNPP between Rosatom subsidiary Rosatom Overseas and China's National Nuclear Cooperation (Bernini 2022, 114, citing World Nuclear News 2016). Additionally, Zou et al. demonstrated the configuration for deployment of an FNPP with an offshore oil rig, including the stand-off distance and safety distances between the FNPP, the oil rig, and associated infrastructure nearby (Zou et al. 2021). However, in their analysis, they noted that there are no international regulations for the emergency planning or restricted areas surrounding marine reactors (Zou et al. 2021). Consistent with such analysis, China's General Nuclear Power Group signed a strategic cooperation agreement with China National Offshore Oil Corporation in 2016, proposing to use FNPPs to support China's oil exploration in the Bohai Sea and the South China Sea (Bernini 2022, 114–115; see also Peachey 2016).

Because of the strong emphasis on decarbonization across multiple sectors, FNPP deployment outside territorial waters may become more prevalent. FNPP may support activities including oil and gas extraction, power generation to remote communities such as in the Arctic and remote islands, and the desalination of water. The use of FNPPs beyond a coastal State's territorial waters revisits the questions posed by the ORNL and UCLA study, as well as Blake's cautionary words about whether they represent a reasonable use of the high seas (Blake 1978, 199; Hammond and Okrent 1974, 136). This issue leads to further questions about the classification and categorization of FNPPs within the international legal frameworks, for both nuclear law and maritime law, leading to what has been described as lacunae across multiple legal domains (Steding 2004).

12.3 GORDIAN KNOT OF DEFINING WHAT IS AN FNPP

FNPPs have been in existence in one form or another for the past fifty years, yet the international community has yet to achieve consensus about what comprises an FNPP. The challenge of defining what an FNPP is sits at the center of the proverbial Gordian knot of nuclear law and maritime law, with each legal domain bringing ambiguity to the discussion. For example, within the *IAEA Nuclear Safety and Security Glossary* (IAEA 2022a), there is no formal definition of a "nuclear power plant."[8] Likewise, within maritime law and UNCLOS, the terms "ship" and "vessel" are used interchangeably, with no consensus on what constitutes a vessel (Walker and Noyes 2002).

[8] The term "nuclear power plant" can be found in the *IAEA Nuclear Safety and Security Glossary* under the broader terms "facilities" and "nuclear installation" as examples of what can constitute each concept (IAEA 2022a). However, in the *IAEA Safeguards Glossary: 2022 Edition*, there is no mention of "nuclear power plant" under the term "facility" (IAEA 2022b).

In the current international discussion, identifying whether an FNPP is a vessel, cargo, or a facility, or some combination of the three, will instruct the rights, responsibilities, and corresponding nonproliferation measures associated with FNPPs and their operation under the law. However, even saying "the law" is ambiguous because the FNPP will operate across and within multiple legal regimes, including nuclear law, maritime law, and the law of the sea regime. What Bernini describes as "legal conundrums" for the status of FNPPs under nuclear and maritime law, in fact, presents foundational challenges to their deployment and operation within the UNCLOS framework (Bernini 2022, 120–121). Specific to nuclear security and nuclear safeguards, determining whether the FNPP is a vessel, or an installation, would add additional complexity about who is in control of the FNPP from the perspective of flag State jurisdiction and the applicable legal and regulatory framework.

FNPPs do not operate in a vacuum or in isolation from the greater discussion occurring on advanced nuclear reactors. In 2013, the IAEA explained, in its report *Legal and Institutional Issues of Transportable Nuclear Power Plants: A Preliminary Study*, that FNPPs are part of a larger class of small modular reactors known as transportable nuclear power plants (TNPPs; IAEA 2013a). In that report, the IAEA defined a TNPP as "a factory manufactured, transportable and/or relocatable nuclear power plant which, when fueled, is capable of producing final energy products such as electricity, heat, and desalinated water" (IAEA 2013a). Important for this discussion is a subsequent sentence of the definition developed by the IAEA: "The TNPP is physically transportable *but is not designed* to either produce energy during transportation or provide energy for the transportation itself" (IAEA 2013a, emphasis added). This second element of the definition highlights that the reactor on TNPPs, including on FNPPs, is for energy production, not for the structure itself: the reactor is intended to support shoreside or other activities.

12.3.1 *Evolution of the FNPP: From Breakwaters to Barges*

One of the challenges with defining an FNPP is that the designs for FNPPs have evolved over the years. Starting with the MH-1A (more commonly known as the USS *Sturgis*), the first barge-mounted nuclear power plant in 1966, FNPP designs evolved to resemble land-based nuclear power plants with buildings and freestanding structures (Honerlah 2014, 3). In the ORNL and UCLA siting analysis for FNPPs, the authors identified five different platform support arrangements for FNPPs: (1) barge structures, (2) semisubmersible oil-drilling platforms, (3) the Mohole type, (4) tension leg platforms, and (5) two-barge assemblies (Hammond and Okrent 1974, 133). The 1974 analysis did not define what an FNPP was, but it did identify the safety elements for the operation of the station when deployed within US territorial waters.

Likewise, the 1976 OTA analysis explained the process for constructing the FNPP (OTA 1976, 197–198). According to the analysis, the power plant would be assembled in a shipyard near Jacksonville, Florida (OTA 1976, 197). The plant being developed by Offshore Power Systems at the time would have been a steel barge with a honeycomb frame of watertight compartments (OTA 1976, 197). Mounted on top of the barge structure would be a pressurized water reactor, including steam turbines, generators, and office buildings (OTA 1976, 197). Once construction was completed at the shipyard, the power plants would be towed from Florida to their location off the coast of New Jersey, where they would be sealed in the breakwater, surrounded by concrete caissons (OTA 1976, 198). The supply chain for the Offshore Power Systems FNPP entailed the components being transported from Florida to New Jersey, with its ultimate assembly offshore at the location of deployment. In effect, the barge structures acted as a base for the nuclear reactor and auxiliary structures.

When the 2013 IAEA study on institutional and legal issues for TNPPs was drafted, the report did not comment on the legal status of TNPPs. It did not address the sufficiency or adequacy of either nuclear law or maritime law for FNPPs. During the 2023 IAEA *Symposium on the Benefits and Challenges of Floating Nuclear Power Plants*, the Russian Federation explained its regulatory framework for licensing FNPPs (Salnikova 2023, 10). Under Russian law, the licensee needs to acquire a license from the Russian nuclear regulator (Rostekhnadzor) and certificates from the Russian maritime regulator (Rosmorrechflot; Salnikova 2023, 10). Additionally, the FNPP, under Russian law, is included on the Russian International List of Ships and is registered under the flag of the Russian Federation by the Russian Maritime Register of Shipping (Salnikova 2023, 10; see also Nikitin and Andreyev 2011, 1, 10–12). Although the Russian Federation identifies FNPPs as vessels according to Russian law because of their experience with nuclear reactors powering icebreakers via means of propulsion, the international community has not arrived at a consensus for the classification of FNPPs.

The lack of a taxonomy for FNPPs creates a question about which international organization – the IAEA or the International Maritime Organization (IMO) – is responsible for developing appropriate standards and requirements for the operation of FNPPs. Further complicating this is the fact that deployment location of the FNPP would be governed by the law of the sea regime under UNCLOS. This creates a point within three legal domains where the FNPP must be triangulated to understand how it will be governed, but this can only occur after it can be discerned how the FNPP is classified. The following discussion highlights ongoing discussions by the international community with respect to FNPPs and developing a framework for understanding what they are and, subsequently, how they are to be governed.

12.3.2 *Possible Classification and Associated Legal Frameworks for FNPPs*

This section uses the 2013 IAEA report *Legal and Institutional Issues of Transportable Nuclear Power Plants: A Preliminary Study* as a starting point for a contemporary analysis on FNPPs and their classification. The IAEA's report does not address whether an FNPP is cargo, a vessel, a facility, or some permutation of those possibilities. From 2013, the scholarship on the classification of FNPPs slowly began to focus on these possibilities and associated frameworks.[9] Current work by the IAEA is trying to understand and evaluate the legal and technical impacts of the various possible classifications, with each being reviewed against both nuclear and maritime legal instruments to understand its applicability and alignment with these regimes (IAEA 2023a).

12.3.2.1 FNPPs as Cargo

As a starting point, FNPPs could be classified as cargo, and existing international frameworks under the auspices of the IAEA and the IMO could be applied, namely the IAEA's Regulations for the Safe Transport of Radioactive Material (commonly referred to as SSR-6 (Rev. 2)) (IAEA 2025) because the FNPP, while transport is not active and in essence, is moving either irradiated or fresh nuclear fuel. Additionally, the IMO provisions found in the International Maritime Dangerous Goods Code (IMDG Code; IMO 2022), made under the Safety of Life at Sea Convention (SOLAS),[10] would apply coextensively to those recommendations found in SSR-6 (Rev. 2).

If FNPPs are treated as cargo, there are two scenarios for their transport: first, the FNPP superstructure could be transported without the nuclear material on board, with the nuclear material loaded into the reactor when the FNPP is deployed within the coastal State. In this scenario, the FNPP superstructure would not have nuclear material on board, and the nuclear material would be transported separately, which aligns with provisions of national laws applying SSR-6 (Rev. 2) and the IMDG Code, respectively. Alternatively, the second scenario would have nuclear fuel loaded into the FNPP during outfitting, and the FNPP superstructure and fuel would be transported together to the host location. Under that scenario, there are two sub-scenarios to consider. If the fuel in the reactor is unirradiated, this would constitute a fresh fuel shipment and would be transported in alignment with the provisions of national law applying both IAEA and IMO requirements as adopted by the contracting State. However, if the fuel is loaded into the reactor during outfitting and testing, this would present problems aligning with SSR-6 (Rev. 2) and the IMDG Code because the nuclear material is irradiated and not transported in a certified

9 Popov analogizes FNPPs to nuclear vessels and Russia's experience with regulating nuclear icebreakers (Popov 2022, 47–48); Fialkoff analyzes FNPP classification from the perspective of nuclear security and maritime security (Fialkoff 2020); and Molinari reviews existing maritime law instruments to determine whether an FNPP is a vessel and applying a case-by-case approach for FNPP classification (Molinari 2020).

10 International Convention for the Safety of Life at Sea, November 1, 1974, 1184 UNTS 2 (SOLAS).

package. This specific scenario was addressed during the IAEA's 2023 symposium. In its presentation, the IAEA's Transport Safety Unit explained that SSR-6 (Rev. 1) was designed for the transport of radioactive materials in packages and that FNPPs with irradiated fuel on board were not envisaged by SSR-6 (Rev. 1) or associated guidance (IAEA 2023a). The initial conclusion drawn by the unit head of the Transport Safety Unit was that the transport of fresh and irradiated fuel in-core would not be in a compliant SSR-6 (Rev. 1) package (IAEA 2023a).

Although the IAEA is undertaking ongoing work through a Department of Nuclear Safety and Nuclear Security-wide study about design safety and security considerations for FNPPs, questions persist. The primary concern with applying SSR-6 (Rev. 2) and the IMDG Code is that if loaded into the reactor, the fuel could not be transported in a compliant package and the guides and subsequent national laws would not be applicable. In the alternative, an argument has been made that if the material in the FNPP is not in conformity with national transport safety regulations, the special arrangement provision in SSR-6 (Rev. 2), paragraph 310, could be used (IAEA 2025, 17). Under the special arrangement provision:

> *Consignments* for which conformity with the other provisions of these Regulations is impracticable shall not be transported except under *special arrangement*. Provided the competent authority is satisfied that conformity with the other provisions of these Regulations is impracticable and that the requisite standards of safety established by these Regulations have been demonstrated through means alternative to the other provisions of these Regulations, the *competent authority* may approve *special arrangement* transport operations for a single *consignment* or a planned series of multiple consignments. The overall level of safety in transport shall be at least equivalent to that which would be provided if all the applicable requirements in these Regulations had been met. For *consignments* of this type, *multilateral approval* shall be required. (IAEA 2025, 17)

In their work on developing a risk-informed regulatory framework for microreactor transportation packages, Coles et al. discussed the special arrangement approach and noted that multilateral approval would be required if a special arrangement were to be used for microreactor international transport (Coles et al. 2021, 25). This could be problematic, because all countries where the microreactor – or in this case an FNPP – would transit would need to approve the transit through territorial waters, and such approvals are not guaranteed.

12.3.2.2 FNPPs as Vessels

Because of its experience with nuclear vessels in its icebreaker fleet, the Russian Federation is already classifying FNPPs as vessels. Under Russian law, for an FNPP operating within Russian territorial waters, any possible international voyage of the FNPP would conflict with international maritime law, specifically SOLAS. In its presentation during the FNPP symposium held in 2023, the IMO presented two threshold questions about the applicability of SOLAS to FNPPs (Nironen 2023, 5). First, under regulation 1(a) of Chapter I of the Annex to the Convention, SOLAS would only apply to those ships engaged in an international voyage, with an "international voyage" defined as "a voyage from a country to which the present Convention applies to a port outside such country, or conversely" (Nironen 2023, 5). If FNPPs are constructed and deployed in the same country, then the provisions of SOLAS would not be applicable because an international voyage has not occurred. More specific to the vessel question, regulation 3(a)(iii) of Chapter I provides the scope of application of SOLAS to those ships propelled by mechanical means (Nironen 2023, 6). The IMO representative suggested the following question: "What is the [a]pplication of SOLAS to floating nuclear power plants not propelled by mechanical means (for example, FNPPs towed by tugs)?" (Nironen 2023, 6). This presents a threshold question about whether an FNPP with no means of propulsion other than support by towage would qualify as a vessel for the provisions of SOLAS and whether the Convention's safety provisions would be applicable.

During the FNPP symposium, the representative from the World Nuclear Transport Institute introduced the proposition that the Code of Safety for Nuclear Merchant Ships, IMO Resolution A.491(XII) (IMO 1981), could be revised to incorporate FNPPs into it as part of a technology-agnostic approach to civilian nuclear maritime applications (Chaplin 2023, 5). Resolution A.491(XII) is a supplement to Chapter VIII of SOLAS, which outlines the requirements for nuclear ships. Here "nuclear ships" are defined as ships "provided with a nuclear power plant" (Nironen 2023, 11). In contrast to the SOLAS definition, Resolution A.491(XII) defines "nuclear ships" as any merchant ships "the normal mode of propulsion of which is based upon nuclear energy and whose characteristics are those of conventional displacement ships."

Although the World Nuclear Transport Institute and other organizations are exploring efforts to modernize Resolution A.491(XII) to incorporate FNPPs and the broader framework provided by SOLAS, such analysis should be tempered to consider nonproliferation impacts.[11] The Resolution is a code for safety. In its current formulation, it does not address nuclear security, with only one provision addressing the security of the ship and the physical protection of the fissile materials (IAEA 2023c, 50). Resolution A.491(XII) neither speaks to broader nuclear security considerations nor references the ACPPNM. It is important to temper any revision of A.491(XII) to acknowledge the mandates of the IMO – namely, that the IMO deals with matters of maritime transport and is mainly involved in the development of international regulations, based on proposals by its member States (Nironen 2023,

[11] The IAEA explains that for "the purpose of nuclear liability instruments," transport of the FNPP (containing fresh or spent fuel) "can be considered as a transport of 'nuclear material' just as any other transport of such material." Likewise, the FNPP in a fixed position "would fall under the definition of a 'nuclear installation'" (IAEA 2023c, 42).

2). A revision of the code to include FNPPs could have unintended consequences, such as an implicit bestowment of vessel status on FNPPs and the registration of FNPPs under flag State jurisdiction, presenting unique nonproliferation challenges.

FLAG STATE JURISDICTION AND FNPPS. If FNPPs are classified as vessels, they would enjoy the trappings of being a vessel and they would operate under the flag of the country under which they are registered. Broadly, when a vessel is registered under a flag State, that State grants nationality to the vessel, meaning that the State has "exclusive jurisdiction over the vessel on the high seas to the extent permitted by international law" (Anderson 1996, 140). The reason that vessels are flagged is to ensure that every vessel operating in the maritime domain does so under some regulatory framework or national system of laws (Anderson 1996, 141). Vessels without flags are perceived as dangerous to the international order and as "international pariahs" with no right to navigate freely on the high seas (Anderson 1996, 142).[12]

For the Russian example, the FNPP would be registered as a Russian vessel under the Russian Maritime Register of Shipping and operate accordingly under the laws of the Russian Federation (Salnikova 2023, 10). The connection of a flag and, by extension, nationality and the protection of the laws of the registering State reinforce the "legal fiction" that vessels maintain a "separate personality," which, according to Anderson, can be sued in an *in rem* proceeding in many jurisdictions regardless of ownership (Anderson 1996, 145).

When discussing vessel registration and establishing flag State jurisdiction over FNPPs, there is a nuclear equity that must be considered if FNPPs are granted flag State jurisdiction. Conferral of flag State jurisdiction on an FNPP would link the flag State's nuclear regime and subsequent obligations, including safety, security, and safeguards, to the FNPP's operation. When deployed outside the flag State's territorial waters, flag State jurisdiction would apply, although this may run contrary to the principles of nonproliferation because nuclear security obligations typically apply to the State where the nuclear material resides (ACPPNM, Article 2A(3), Fundamental Principle A). In the 2013 report on legal and institutional issues for TNPPs, the IAEA broached the subject of using bilateral agreements to try and establish long-term framework agreements for TNPP deployments, though the report did not address concerns such as the overlap between flag State jurisdiction and the obligations and responsibilities of coastal States under various nuclear law instruments (IAEA 2013a, 59). The issue of flag State jurisdiction and the creation of a separate personality for FNPPs operating under such flags represent challenges to nonproliferation objectives because, at the core of such objectives, regulatory controls are established by the State where the material is present.

[12] Anderson cites *United States v. Mariano-Garcia*, 679 F.2d 1373, 1382 (11th Cir. 1982) (Anderson 1996, 142).

An extension of the vessel discussion applies to the control and jurisdiction of oil rigs. According to Richards, deepwater oil rigs are treated similarly to vessels; they are flagged similarly to vessels, with the flag State having exclusive national jurisdiction over their operation in the EEZ and the high seas (Richards 2011, 388). Although FNPPs have been compared to offshore energy platforms, a similar analysis about jurisdiction controls would follow if an FNPP were treated as a deepwater energy platform, with the same rules applying as if the FNPP were treated as a vessel (Richards 2011, 388–389).[13]

12.3.2.3 FNPPs as Facilities

A final possibility for the classification of FNPPs would be to classify them as facilities; however, for the purposes of nuclear law, this presents a unique problem because FNPPs are specifically excluded from a basic nuclear law instrument, the Convention on Nuclear Safety.[14] Article 2(i) of that Convention explicitly defines a nuclear installation as "any land-based civil nuclear power plant under [the contracting party's] jurisdiction." The Convention excludes FNPPs because they are not land-based reactors, but the IAEA proposed that in reporting on the safety of other types of civilian nuclear reactors, FNPPs may fall under this as voluntary practice for their alignment to safety principles (IAEA 2023c, 7, citing IAEA 2018a). In a similar presentation, the IAEA's Office of Legal Affairs explained that for the purposes of nuclear liability instruments, when the FNPP is in a fixed position, whether docked or anchored to the seabed, it would be viewed as a nuclear installation for nuclear liability purposes (IAEA 2023c, 42).

In comparison to nuclear safety and nuclear security, nuclear safeguards define "facility" more broadly, and the reactor alone would be defined as a facility under nuclear safeguards (IAEA 1972, 27). In INFCIRC/153 (corr.), which is titled "The Structure and Content of Agreements between the Agency [IAEA] and States Required in Connection with the Treaty on the Non-Proliferation of Nuclear Weapons," "facility" is defined as: (a) "a reactor, a critical facility, a conversion plant, a fabrication plant, a reprocessing plant, an isotope separation plant or a separate storage installation"; or (b) "any location where *nuclear material* in amounts greater than one *effective kilogram* is customarily used" (IAEA 1972, para. 106). In Section 12.4, the application of nuclear safeguards, specifically the provisions of the Basic Undertaking, highlights the challenges if an FNPP is classified as a vessel for the purposes of maritime law. When the FNPP must be under safeguards, the question arises of whose safeguards obligations apply. This

[13] Richards highlights the consequences of limited regulatory authority of a coastal state with regard to a deepwater oil rig operating in the EEZ and the potential environmental and economic disaster if an oil rig were experiencing an accident (Richards 2011, 388–389).

[14] Convention on Nuclear Safety, September 20, 1994, 1963 UNTS 317.

becomes further complicated when the FNPP flag State is a nuclear weapon State (NWS), and the coastal State where the FNPP is operating is a nonnuclear weapon State (NNWS).

12.4 NONPROLIFERATION NORMS AND THEIR ROLE IN FNPP GOVERNANCE UNDER UNCLOS

The principles established under nuclear nonproliferation instruments, including the NPT, CPPNM, and ACPPNM, do not stop at the coastline but permeate through the maritime zones established under UNCLOS. As Laura Rockwood, former section head for Non-Proliferation and Policy Making in the Office of Legal Affairs at the IAEA, explained: "The nuclear non-proliferation regime is a complex of varied and evolving instruments and measures intended to deter and detect the proliferation of nuclear weapons. It includes, *inter alia*, global and regional treaties on non-proliferation, export controls, [and] physical protection" (Rockwood 2022, 357). Herbach goes further to acknowledge that the "interconnectedness of nuclear security and non-proliferation is clear," with each being "founded on dealing with the risk of nuclear material being diverted to non-peaceful purposes" (Herbach 2021, 45). The challenge observed with the deployment of FNPPs into the EEZ of coastal States is that the deployment of fixed nuclear installations in these zones expands the application of nonproliferation norms beyond traditional approaches that have primarily focused on the transport of nuclear materials. Through the lens of the law of the sea regime, the EEZ is seeing an intensifying zonation compared to what was previously envisioned under UNCLOS (Ryan 2019, 10170). Included in this intensifying zonation are maritime security and, by extension, national security considerations that begin to pull the EEZ further under a coastal State's exclusive national jurisdiction (at least in theory; Ryan 2019, 10170).

For FNPPs, there are two questions: How far do the nonproliferation obligations of coastal States reach into the EEZ? And how are nonproliferation obligations balanced with the interests of coastal States if an FNPP is flagged and operating under the nonproliferation requirements of the flagging State? These questions were posed during the IAEA FNPP symposium in November 2023 (IAEA 2023b, 3:55:56). In response, an IAEA representative from the Office of Legal Affairs explained that, with respect to CSAs, it is a "principle of international law, this is an agreement between a state and us, the international organization [IAEA], and territorial scope of application is determined by the state" (IAEA 2023b, 3:56:18). When further elaborating on the jurisdiction considerations in relation to UNCLOS, the IAEA representative explained that "maritime territories are defined in accordance with UNCLOS by the States parties" and that "if a State with a Comprehensive Safeguards Agreement [CSA] decides to operate a TNPP in its territorial waters or contiguous zone, the State must inform the Agency [IAEA] accordingly and provide information on the design and nuclear material used in reactor" (IAEA 2023b, 3:56:26–3:56:34). For the EEZ, the IAEA representative concluded that "it's for the State to decide [on the EEZ] and the State to take into consideration relevant provisions of the UN Convention on the Law of the Sea of 1982" (IAEA 2023b, 3:57:00).

In its statement, the IAEA identifies the need for the State to identify within the CSA the scope of territorial application for consideration of safeguards and, by extension, nuclear security; however, in both cases, FNPP deployment and the extension of nonproliferation norms may yield questions about whether such an extension further brings the EEZ under the exclusive national jurisdiction of the coastal State. This section explores some of the specific contours of the intersection of nonproliferation norms with the law of the sea regime and provides a theory for the extension of nonproliferation norms that aligns with the jurisdictional thresholds established under UNCLOS.

12.4.1 *UNCLOS and Its Role in FNPP Governance*

UNCLOS has been described as "a constitution for the oceans," providing guidance on rights, responsibilities, and activities that can be conducted within the maritime zones established under the Convention (Koh 2020, 93). Within Part 5 of UNCLOS, Article 55 defines the EEZ as "an area beyond and adjacent to the territorial sea, subject to the specific legal regime established in this Part, under which the rights and jurisdiction of the coastal State and the rights and freedoms of other States are governed by the relevant provisions of this Convention." Article 56 establishes the rights and jurisdictional duties of coastal States to include sovereign rights for the exploration, exploitation, conservation, and management of living and nonliving organisms within the water column, seabed, and subsoil. Further, Article 56 enables the coastal State to establish sovereignty over activities that are for the economic exploitation and exploration of the zone. Examples provided in Article 56 include energy production from the water currents or the wind. Although nuclear energy is not mentioned in this article, paragraph (1)(b)(i) provides jurisdiction for coastal States over "the establishment and use of artificial islands, *installations* and structures" (emphasis added). The paragraph offers a link to subsequent analyses describing FNPPs as installations under nuclear law instruments and develops an argument for coastal States to enable their nonproliferation obligations to reach FNPPs while operating in the EEZ.

With the exception of contemporary research focused on the transport of FNPPs and the role of UNCLOS, prior work has focused primarily on the reasonableness of FNPPs being used in the high seas under the 1958 Geneva Convention on the High Seas.[15] Blake's analysis challenged the "reasonableness" of deploying

[15] Convention on the High Seas, April 29, 1958, 450 UNTS 11. For contemporary analysis of UNCLOS and FNPPs, see Bernini (2022, 124–125); IAEA (2013a, 77); but see Blake (1978, 197–199).

FNPPs[16] on the high seas because, under his analysis, FNPPs will not only appropriate space for their operation but also appropriate resources that will have direct long-term pollution effects on the marine environment (Blake 1978, 224). Blake's theory was that the FNPP operation would directly interfere with the fishing freedoms provided under the high seas conventions and impact fish catchments to the extent that such diminishment in fishing due to pollution would lead to unreasonable use of the high seas (Blake 1978, 224). Blake's analysis does consider the security implications for deployment on the high seas as a means for relieving US dependence on foreign energy, although his security analysis focuses on energy security rather than nonproliferation considerations (Blake 1978, 223–224).[17]

Contemporary analysis of FNPP operation under the UNCLOS regime has primarily focused on the transport of FNPPs through the various maritime zones instead of their operation in the EEZ. For example, in the 2013 IAEA report on TNPPs, UNCLOS is examined primarily through the lens of innocent passage and freedom of navigation for a TNPP, with transport, rather than operation, being the primary focus of the analysis (IAEA 2013a, 77). Throughout the analysis, UNCLOS is viewed through the lens of transport, with no consideration for the jurisdictional limits established under the regime and how TNPP deployment in one of the maritime zones would influence obligations and the implementation of various nuclear law instruments. Likewise, Bernini's analysis of small modular reactors and TNPPs under the law of the sea regime focused on two specific elements. First, Bernini examined the ship-versus-installation question, applying UNCLOS and SOLAS to identify where TNPPs, specifically FNPPs, would qualify under the various regimes (Bernini 2022, 121–124). Second, and similar to the 2013 IAEA report, her analysis of the UNCLOS regime and FNPPs focused on navigation rights for the transiting of FNPPs, in contrast to deployment within the zones (Bernini 2022, 124–125). Bernini's analysis goes further to link the UNCLOS analysis to civil liability for nuclear damage, drawing this conclusion based on IAEA deliberations of the International Group on Nuclear Liability (INLEX; Bernini 2022, 129). Under INLEX's interpretation, if the TNPP is in a fixed position, it is considered a nuclear installation for the purposes of civil liability and nuclear liability instruments (Bernini 2022, 129). This interpretation provides more support to establish how nonproliferation obligations would apply to FNPPs in the EEZ and whose obligations would also apply.

[16] While Blake uses "floating nuclear plants," the contemporary term used to describe the technology is "floating nuclear power plants." For the purposes of this chapter, the terms are synonymous but reflect those used by the authors at the time of the writing of their respective works.

[17] However, note that at the time Blake authored his article, neither the NTP nor the CPPNM had been adopted, so nonproliferation considerations were in their infancy.

12.4.2 *Nonproliferation Norms and Their Relationship to the Law of the Sea and FNPPs*

Nuclear security and nuclear safeguards are inextricably linked by their shared goal of preventing nuclear material from being used for non-peaceful purposes either by non-State or State actors. According to Herbach, the legal framework for nuclear security that evolved from the nuclear nonproliferation regime started with the adoption and entry into force of the NPT (Herbach 2021, 7). Important to nuclear security and nuclear safeguards is the establishment of regulatory controls, responsibility, and accounting for nuclear material. Although both nuclear security and nuclear safeguards are essential to nonproliferation and greater arms control frameworks, it is important to differentiate their objectives and goals.

For both nuclear safeguards and nuclear security, FNPPs present challenges for identification, application, and implementation. Under both regimes, FNPPs require States to revert to basic questions about who is in control and which law applies to deployment. These questions are further complicated by FNPP deployment in the EEZ, where the coastal State has limited legal competence in contrast to a flag State (if the FNPP is registered).

12.4.2.1 Nuclear Safeguards

One of the primary competencies of the IAEA is the administration of safeguards, as outlined in Article XII of the IAEA Statute.[18] Among the obligations under that Article, the IAEA is permitted to examine designs of equipment and facilities and to send inspectors to a State to access locations where fissionable material is present. According to the IAEA, safeguards are a set of technical measures that are applied by the IAEA on nuclear facilities and material. Through these technical measures, the IAEA seeks to verify independently a State's legal obligation that nuclear facilities are not misused and nuclear material is not diverted from peaceful uses. States accept these measures through the conclusion of safeguards agreements (IAEA 2023d).

With respect to nuclear safeguards, the focus is at the State level, and agreements between the IAEA and the State ensure that nuclear material under the State's control and jurisdiction, or within the State's territory, is accounted for and can be verified as being used for peaceful purposes. At a minimum, the Statute provides a legal framework in tandem with the NPT for establishing the IAEA as the international organization for concluding safeguards agreements with States, authorizing it to send inspectors to ensure compliance with those agreements.

[18] Statute of the International Atomic Energy Agency, October 26, 1956, 276 UNTS 3.

NPT IMPLICATIONS. In furtherance of nonproliferation objectives, the NPT establishes the international framework for States to possess nuclear material and their obligations under the Treaty. For FNPPs, Article IV(1) of the NPT enables States "to develop research, production and use of nuclear energy for peaceful purposes without discrimination," with FNPPs falling within the scope of this provision although not explicitly identified. Article IV(2) goes further to enable and promote the transfer of nuclear materials to NNWS as long as those materials are transferred for peaceful purposes. Accordingly, Article III(1) of the NPT requires that NNWS accept safeguards and enter into safeguards agreements with the IAEA in alignment with the NPT and the IAEA Statute, but this should not conflict with their right to use nuclear material for peaceful purposes per Article IV.

For safeguards, as identified by the IAEA in its 2013 report, FNPPs present unique challenges, especially if they are exported from one country to another and depending on whether the exporting country and the receiving country are NWS or NNWS.[19] The analysis provided by the IAEA report outlined the obligation for the construction and operation by either the NWS or the NNWS, including export and the requirement for safeguards, but the report is unclear about implementation for the extraterritorial deployment of FNPPs in which the FNPP is flagged under an exporting State's maritime law and is operating in a coastal State's territory.

Subsequently, during the 2023 FNPP symposium, the Department of Safeguards presented on the IAEA's preparation for FNPPs, including the challenges associated with nuclear material accountancy for material placed in a reactor before inspection, remote locations impacting data transmission for verification, and training for inspectors (Newton 2023, 2–5). One of the challenges acknowledged by the Department of Safeguards was the portability of FNPPs and the need for understanding the legal implications with respect to the NPT and safeguards agreements established between the IAEA and the State (Newton 2023, 2–5), However, for FNPPs, the question becomes the IAEA and which State? Is it the coastal State, the FNPP-supplying State, or some combination (Popov 2022)?

CSAS AND THE ADDITIONAL PROTOCOL. Under Article III of the NPT and Article XII of the IAEA Statute, NNWS must enter into CSAs with the IAEA. Using INFCIRC/153 (corr.) as a model, States negotiate their CSAs with the IAEA to be in compliance with their treaty obligations. Although the 2013 IAEA report does discuss the specific implementation of articles from INFCIRC/153 (corr.) with respect to ensuring that FNPPs are under safeguards, the report overlooks a jurisdictional question fundamental to understanding whose safeguards obligations apply (IAEA 2013a, 25–31). Paragraph 1 of INFCIRC/153 (corr.), also known as the Basic Undertaking, outlines that the State undertakes to accept safeguards "on all source or special fissionable material in all peaceful nuclear activities *within its territory*,

[19] For discussion on safeguards scenarios, see IAEA (2013a, 25–31).

under its jurisdiction or carried out under its control anywhere, for the exclusive purpose of verifying that such material is not diverted to nuclear weapons or other nuclear explosive devices" (IAEA 1972, 1, emphasis added). When applied to FNPPs, this raises a question about which of the three conditions takes priority. Does the territorial location of the FNPP, the jurisdiction (to include flag State jurisdiction), or the physical control of the FNPP determine whose safeguards obligations apply? The second "or" in the Basic Undertaking creates ambiguity. However, during the FNPP symposium, the IAEA's Office of Legal Affairs indicated that the CSA would be based on the scope of territorial application as outlined both in agreement with the IAEA and in accordance with UNCLOS. This would indicate that, at least at the negotiation stage between the IAEA and the State, the territorial scope of application for safeguards should be established to include the maritime zones as outlined in UNCLOS.

At least for the purposes of the CSA and subsequently for the Additional Protocol, which provided additional requirements and obligations for NNWS, the gravamen is also whether territorial integrity, jurisdiction, or control takes priority for establishing safeguards obligations. This creates inherent vagueness between the coastal State that will have a territorial claim and the flag State; subsequently, there is a jurisdictional question about who exhibits control (whether manifested as physical or custodial control) of the FNPP. At present, the IAEA has not provided guidance on how to interpret the Basic Undertaking and any priority of territory, jurisdiction, or control for FNPPs. As far as the 2013 IAEA report and the conclusions drawn from the Department of Safeguards and the Office of Legal Affairs indicate, safeguards will apply to FNPPs; however, it is still unclear whose safeguards regime applies and how the respective obligations should be implemented.

12.4.3.2 Nuclear Security

In contrast to safeguards, where the focus is on ensuring that State actors use nuclear materials peacefully and that NNWS do not divert nuclear material for nuclear weapons, "nuclear security" is "the prevention and detection of, and *response* to, criminal or intentional unauthorized acts involved or directed at *nuclear material, other radioactive material, associated facilities* or *associated activities*" (IAEA 2022a, 140). For nuclear security, the focus is the prevention, detection, and response to non-State actors attempting to steal or sabotage nuclear and other radioactive materials.

CONVENTION ON THE PHYSICAL PROTECTION OF NUCLEAR MATERIAL AND ITS AMENDMENT. Although Herbach points to a constellation of treaties, agreements, and conventions focused on the prevention of terrorism, including nuclear terrorism, the only instrument focused on ensuring the physical protection of nuclear material for civilian application is the ACPPNM (Herbach 2021, 64). The original focus of the CPPNM was the physical protection of nuclear material during international transport (Drobysz 2022, 343). With the ACPPNM, the scope of application expanded to include the physical protection of nuclear material in use, storage, and both international and domestic transport, with transport including domestic and international transport (Newton 2023, 2–5).

To further support State parties to the ACPPNM with implementing their obligations, Article 2A(3) outlines twelve fundamental principles to support the development of a nuclear security regime. Each of these fundamental principles in practice applies to the deployment of FNPPs; however, with the intersection to the UNCLOS regime, specific fundamental principles present novel questions about their application and subsequent implementation to FNPP deployments in a coastal State's EEZ. For example, as noted above, Fundamental Principle A clearly states that "the responsibility for the establishment, implementation and maintenance of a physical protection regime within a State rests entirely with that State." This principle is further elaborated upon in the IAEA's Nuclear Security Series No. 20, "Objective and Essential Elements of a State's Nuclear Security Regime" (IAEA 2013b, 4). This publication is nonbinding guidance that supports IAEA member States with the implementation of their obligations under the ACPPNM. Specifically, Essential Element 1 of Nuclear Security Series No. 20 expands upon the language used in Fundamental Principle A of the ACPPNM and adds "under a State's jurisdiction" (IAEA 2013b, 4). This presents similar questions with respect to a State's jurisdiction over an FNPP. Is it the coastal State's jurisdiction or that of the flag State? Complicating this inquiry are the UNCLOS zones, where a coastal State would have exclusive jurisdiction in the territorial zone compared to the EEZ. Additionally, Fundamental Principle C identifies the State as being responsible for establishing and maintaining a legislative and regulatory framework to govern the physical protection of nuclear material; however, which regulatory framework applies to FNPPs comes into question, depending on whether the coastal State's jurisdiction applies or if flag State jurisdiction and nuclear security laws and regulations apply.

For nuclear security, the question of jurisdiction is not abstract as far as identifying who is responsible for the nuclear security of the FNPP, but it has practical implications – for example, in response to a nuclear security event. Fundamental Principle K of the ACPPNM discusses the need for contingency plans to respond to the unauthorized removal of nuclear material or the sabotage of nuclear facilities or material. However, what does the response look like in the event of a nuclear security event on an FNPP located in the EEZ? In his analysis on the international frameworks governing the response to incidents involving FNPPs, Karcz identifies the myriad of nuclear law instruments, including the CPPNM and ACPPNM, the Convention on Early Notification of a Nuclear Accident, and the Convention on Assistance in the Case of a Nuclear Accident or Radiological Emergency (Karcz 2023, 45–51). Karcz's analysis provided a case study for a nuclear security response to a sabotage event of an FNPP with radiological release; however, the location of the

FNPP in his scenario is at a port facility where the FNPP is deployed extraterritorially (Karcz 2023, 55). His conclusion from this case study was that the ACPPNM, the Early Notification Convention, and the Assistance Convention would be "triggered immediately" with no order for activation (Karcz 2023, 55). If the scenario was changed for deployment in the EEZ, would the flag State for the FNPP be the triggering State, or would the coastal State be able to initiate, and who would manage incident response in the EEZ? The analysis does not address jurisdictional variances caused by the UNCLOS maritime zones. Karcz asks if a "jurisdictional decay" occurs for a nuclear security event depending on whether the security event occurs in the territorial waters compared to the contiguous zone or the EEZ. Although timely, Karcz's analysis highlights the need for greater understanding and analysis of the response to nuclear security outside territorial waters and the span of control exercised by coastal States in responding to nuclear security and nuclear safety events if FNPPs are to be deployed in the EEZ.

12.5 MUTUALLY REINFORCING REGIMES: NONPROLIFERATION AND THE LAW OF THE SEA

In both nonproliferation and the law of the sea regimes, a central tenet that can be drawn is the need for control, whether regulatory control of nuclear material or the establishment of jurisdiction as highlighted under the UNCLOS regime. FNPPs illuminate a challenge with establishing who is in charge, primarily from the lens of jurisdiction, and whose legal regime applies. Although some contend that FNPPs and States that register FNPPs under their flag are bound by UNCLOS, such an analysis is highly dependent on the location of the FNPP and whether coastal State law applies or that of the flag State (Steding 2004, 732–737).[20] As an annex to the 2013 IAEA TNPP report, the IAEA did consider the role of bilateral agreements as a mechanism to facilitate the deployment of TNPPs and, by extension, FNPPs (IAEA 2013a, 59). Under this mechanism, the role of bilateral agreements included "an overarching long-term framework agreement covering nuclear cooperation in general, supplemented by one or several detailed agreements or memoranda of understanding specifically related to the technical and legal requirements of the supply of a TNPP" (IAEA 2013a, 59). The concern with bilateral agreements is that when the bilateral agreement seeks either to divest a country of nonproliferation obligations or responsibilities or to exclude the FNPP from regulatory controls of the coastal State, the bilateral agreement could be viewed as a vehicle to circumvent obligations or divest security or safeguards obligations to the State supplying the FNPP. Divesting

[20] According to Steding's reading of UNCLOS, FNPPs are vessels and therefore subject the FNPP and the Russian Federation to the obligations as described in UNCLOS. However, Steding's analysis is focused primarily on environmental impacts and managing pollution from the FNPP compared to nonproliferation (Steding 2004, 732–737).

such responsibility would not only undermine efforts at universalization but also cause turmoil to key tenets of both nuclear security and nuclear safeguards frameworks.

In the alternative, prior research into the relationship between oil rigs and their responsibilities to coastal States when operating in the EEZ provides a seamless parallel for possible arrangements for FNPPs to operate in the EEZ and with respect to nonproliferation obligations (Richards 2011, 408). Richards's analysis that oil rigs operating in the EEZ should be construed as facilities when fixed establishes them as installations under Article 56 of UNCLOS (Richards 2011, 408). As a result of this classification, the coastal State can exert jurisdiction over the oil rig commensurate with Article 56 of UNCLOS (Richards 2011, 408).

If the same logic that Richards applies to oil rigs is applied to FNPPs, the following conclusions can be drawn. First, such an interpretation of FNPPs as installations when fixed would be consistent with the INLEX decision discussed by Bernini in her analysis of small modular reactors and TNPPs operating under the UNCLOS regime (Bernini 2022, 129).[21] Once the FNPP is determined to be an installation, regardless of the flag registration, the coastal State would in theory be able to extend its nonproliferation obligations over an FNPP operating within its EEZ. This is confirmed by Leopardi's conclusion that an Ocean Nuclear Power Plant (ONPP) would be authorized by the coastal State (Leopardi 2024, 11). In practice, this would include the FNPP being included under the coastal State's CSA and Additional Protocol for safeguards purposes. For the purposes of nuclear security, the FNPP would conform to the legislative and regulatory requirements of the host State rather than the supplier State.[22] This would also include obligations under other counterterrorism agreements, such as the International Convention for the Suppression of Acts of Nuclear Terrorism[23] and the Protocol for the Suppression of Unlawful Acts against the Safety of Fixed Platforms Located on the Continental Shelf.[24]

Such an approach would elevate the question raised by Koh: What is the extent of national jurisdiction over the EEZ? Is the concept of intensification of maritime zones, as discussed by Ryan, just a logical outgrowth of an ever-growing use case for

[21] INLEX concluded at its May 2018 meeting that "a transportable TNPP in a fixed position (that is, in the case of a floating reactor, anchored to the seabed or the shore, and attached to shore by power lines) would fall under the definition of a 'nuclear installation [reactor]'" (Bernini 2022, 129).

[22] Leopardi, in contrast, analyzes only the maritime security instruments for the security of ONPPs, including the Convention for the Suppression of Unlawful Acts against the Safety of Maritime Navigation, March 10, 1988, 1678 UNTS 221 and the Protocol for the Suppression of Unlawful Acts against the Safety of Fixed Platforms Located on the Continental Shelf, March 10, 1988, 1678 UNTS 304, but not analyzing the ACPPNM with respect to ONPPs (Leopardi 2024, 24–26).

[23] International Convention for the Suppression of Acts of Nuclear Terrorism, April 13, 2005, 2445 UNTS 89.

[24] Protocol for the Suppression of Unlawful Acts against the Safety of Fixed Platforms Located on the Continental Shelf, March 10, 1988, 1678 UNTS 304.

the EEZ? To answer Koh's question, the extension of nonproliferation objectives and aims to the EEZ is not an encroachment on the EEZ but rather a recognition to have "peace at sea." Consequently, the extension of nonproliferation norms to the EEZ is necessary.[25] Such uses of the sea as FNPP deployments reinforce the UNCLOS regime by promoting the rule of law, both in the context of the law of the sea and in ensuring that nonproliferation objectives and obligations are managed, maintained, and strengthened.

12.6 CONCLUSION

The deployment of FNPPs in the EEZ highlights the complexity of overlapping regimes and resorts back to basic questions about which law applies and who is in control of the FNPP. When trying to reconcile how FNPPs will operate under the UNCLOS regime, there is inherent divergence in the ancient traditions of maritime law and the law of the sea with the advancement of nuclear technology. With efforts toward decarbonization entering the maritime domain, the challenge will be how to prepare for coming change to ensure that the world is ready for FNPPs and can be confident that the cornerstones of nuclear nonproliferation are in place.

This chapter highlights the many ways the law of the sea, nuclear nonproliferation, and the advancement of nuclear technology converge. Although the concept of FNPPs is now more than fifty years old, their development in the 1960s and 1970s came at a time when the nonproliferation regimes were in their infancy or did not exist. Fifty years later, FNPPs are reemerging, now with more mature nuclear nonproliferation regimes and technologies, but countries are still seeking answers about how to ensure that FNPPs do not become targets of malicious actors or are not diverted by States for non-peaceful purposes. In this regard, both the law of the sea regime and safeguards and security requirements are striving to answer questions that are still unresolved. At a time when nuclear technology is expanding its application to the oceans, whether through decarbonizing shipping or supporting carbon reduction for offshore oil and gas industries, "a clear roadmap is needed" (Chambers 2024). The core issue for FNPPs is ensuring that wherever an FNPP is deployed, whether in the territorial sea or to the outer edges of the EEZ, nonproliferation norms are maintained. In all instances, it is unclear what that looks like, especially when overlapping or competing jurisdictional considerations from the coastal State and the flag State exist. Reconciling those claims is key to legal clarity. This chapter provides a framework for such a reconciliation in which the FNPP, when fixed in the EEZ, is treated as an installation and, for the purposes of UNCLOS and nonproliferation regimes, is the

[25] Koh describes the role of UNCLOS in establishing peace at sea. Under his assessment, UNCLOS promotes peace at sea in three ways: (1) establishing a new, fair, and equitable world order for the oceans; (2) promoting the rule of law; and (3) promoting peaceful dispute resolution (Koh 2020, 149).

responsibility of the coastal State. On the other hand, an unfixed FNPP remains solely the responsibility of the flag State if indeed the power plant is a ship or a vessel. A floating nuclear device is also under the responsibility of the State that launched it.

FNPPs are currently in the eye of the storm, charting their course not just through their role in a decarbonized economy, and they are plying through centuries of maritime law, the law of the sea, and nuclear law instruments to find a safe and secure future. If FNPPs can ford the gap between the law of the sea and nonproliferation regimes, a new order is foreseeable that highlights the opportunities of the sea with reemerging technological possibilities.

REFERENCES

Anderson, H. Edwin, III. 1996. "The Nationality of Ships and Flags of Convenience: Economics, Politics, and Alternatives." *Tulane Maritime Law Journal* 21: 139–170.

Ashton, Lucy. 2023. "Floating Nuclear Power Plants: Benefits and Challenges Discussed at IAEA Symposium." IAEA, November 21. www.iaea.org/newscenter/news/floating-nuclear-power-plants-benefits-and-challenges-discussed-at-iaea-symposium.

Bernini, Elena. 2022. "Small Modular Reactors and Transportable Nuclear Power Plants." In *Emerging Technology and the Law of the Sea*, edited by James Kraska and Young Kil Park. Cambridge University Press.

Blake, Marlowe J. 1978. "Floating Nuclear Plants: A 'Reasonable Use' of the High Seas?" *California Western International Law Journal* 8 (2): 191–227.

Chambers, Sam. 2024. "International Atomic Energy Agency Head Calls for a Roadmap for Nuclear Energy at Sea." *Splash* 247. https://splash247.com/international-atomic-energy-agency-head-calls-for-a-roadmap-for-nuclear-energy-at-sea/.

Chaplin, Simon. 2023. *IAEA International Symposium on the Deployment of Floating Nuclear Power Plants*, November 14–15, World Nuclear Transport Institute.

Coles, Garill, Steven Short, Steven Maheras, and Harold Adkins. 2021. *Proposed Risk-Informed Regulatory Framework for Approval of Microreactor Transportation Packages.* Pacific Northwest National Laboratory, PNNL-31867.

Drobysz, Sonia. 2022. "Nuclear Security: Physical Protection, Illicit Trafficking and Nuclear Terrorism." In *Principles and Practice of International Nuclear Law*, edited by Kimberly Sexton Nick and Stephen G. Burns. Nuclear Energy Agency, OECD.

EPRI (Electric Power Research Institute). 2021. *Rethinking Deployment Scenarios for Advanced Reactors.* Technical Brief: Advanced Nuclear Technology, December.

Fialkoff, Marc Richard. 2020. "The Floating Chameleon: Floating Nuclear Power Plants and the Nexus of Maritime and Nuclear Security Law." *Journal of Maritime Law and Commerce* 51 (2): 103–147.

Hammond, R. Philip, and David Okrent. 1974. "Deepwater Siting of Floating Nuclear Power Plants." *Annals of Nuclear Science and Engineering* 1 (2): 129–138.

Herbach, Jonathan. 2021. *International Arms Control Law and the Prevention of Nuclear Terrorism*. Elgar International Law.

Honerlah, Hans B. 2014. *Sturgis MH-1A Decommissioning Project Summary*. US Army Corps of Engineers.

IAEA (International Atomic Energy Agency). 1972. "The Structure and Content of Agreements between the Agency and States Required in Connection with the Treaty on the Non-Proliferation of Nuclear Weapons." INFCIRC/153 (Corrected).

2013a. *Legal and Institutional Issues of Transportable Nuclear Power Plants: A Preliminary Study*. IAEA Nuclear Energy Series No. NG-T-3.5.

2013b. *Objective and Essential Elements of a State's Nuclear Security Regime*. IAEA Nuclear Security Series No. 20.

2018a. "Guidelines Regarding National Reports under the Convention on Nuclear Safety." INFCIRC/572/Rev.6 (January 19, 2018).

2018b. *Regulations for the Safe Transport of Radioactive Material: 2018 Edition*. No. SSR-6 (Rev. 1).

2022a. *IAEA Nuclear Safety and Security Glossary: Terminology Used in Nuclear Safety, Nuclear Security, Radiation Protection and Emergency Preparedness and Response*. IAEA.

2022b. *IAEA Safeguards Glossary: 2022 Edition*. IAEA.

2023a. "IAEA Floating Nuclear Power Plant Activities: High Level Overview." *IAEA International Symposium on the Deployment of Floating Nuclear Power Plants*, November 14–15.

2023b. *International Symposium on the Deployment of Floating Nuclear Power Plants (FNPP 2023)*, November 14, 2023/CN-330. https://streaming.iaea.org/24399.

2023c. *Legal Considerations for Floating Nuclear Power Plants: International Symposium on the Deployment of Floating Nuclear Power Plants: Benefits and Challenges*. IAEA Office of Legal Affairs.

2023d. "Safeguards Explained." www.iaea.org/topics/safeguards-explained.

2025. *Regulations for the Safe Transport of Radioactive Material: 2025 Edition*. No. SSR-6 (Rev. 2).

IMO (International Maritime Organization). 1982. "Code of Safety for Nuclear Merchant Ships." A XII/Res.491 (November 19, 1981).

2022. *International Maritime Dangerous Goods (IMDG) Code, Amendment 41–22*.

Karcz, Jason. 2023. "Responding to the Call: Assessing International Legal Frameworks for Response to Incidents Involving Floating Nuclear Power Plants." *Nuclear Law Bulletin* 1 (110): 37–58.

Kindt, John Warren. 1983. "Floating Nuclear Power Plants, US and International Regulations." *Marine Policy* 7 (2): 90–100.

Koh, Tommy. 2020. *Building a New Legal Order for the Oceans*. National University of Singapore Press.

Leopardi, Martin Ratcovich. 2024. "International Law and Ocean Nuclear Power Plants in the Arctic." *International Journal of Marine and Coastal Law* 39 (4): 712–741.

Molinari, Elia. 2020. "A New Vessel on the Block: How the Law of the Sea Applies to Floating Nuclear Power Plants." Master's thesis, Arctic University of Norway.

Newton, Traci. 2023. "Safeguards by Design: Preparing for FNPPs." *International Symposium on the Deployment of Floating Nuclear Power Plants*, November 14–15.

Nironen, Antti. 2023. "Application of Key IMO Instruments to Floating Nuclear Power Plants?" *IAEA International Symposium on the Deployment of Floating Nuclear Power Plants*, November 14–15, International Maritime Organization.

Nikitin, Alexander, and Leonid Andreyev. 2011. *Floating Nuclear Power Plants: Bellona Report*. Bellona.

OTA (Office of Technology Assessment). 1976. *Coastal Effects of Offshore Energy Systems: An Assessment of Oil and Gas Systems, Deepwater Ports, and Nuclear Powerplants off the Coast of New Jersey and Delaware*. Congress of the United States.

Peachey, Caroline. 2016. "More Progress on China FNPP." *Nuclear Engineering International*, January 29. www.neimagazine.com/news/more-progress-on-chinese-fnpp-4795667/.

Popov, Andrey. 2022. "Russian Vision of the Problems and Prospects of the International Legal Framework in the Context of Small Modular Reactors and Transportable Nuclear Power Units." In *Nuclear Law: The Great Debate*, edited by IAEA. Asser Press.

Richards, Rebecca K. 2011. "Deepwater Mobile Oil Rigs in the Exclusive Economic Zone and the Uncertainty of Coastal Jurisdiction." *Journal of International Business and Law* 10 (2): 387–411.

Rockwood, Laura. 2022. "The IAEA Safeguards System." In *Principles and Practice of International Nuclear Law*, edited by Kimberly Sexton Nick and Stephen G. Burns. Nuclear Energy Agency, OECD.

Ryan, Barry J. 2019. "The Disciplined Sea: A History of Maritime Security and Zonation." *International Affairs* 95 (5): 1055–1073.

Salnikova, Nadezhda. 2023. "Floating Nuclear Power Units Technologies for Russian and Foreign Markets." IAEA *International Symposium on the Deployment of Floating Nuclear Power Plants*, November 14–15, Afrikantov OKBM JSC.

Steding, Douglas John. 2004. "Russian Floating Nuclear Reactors: Lacunae in Current International Environmental and Maritime Law and the Need for Proactive International Cooperation on the Development of Sustainable Energy Sources." *Pacific Rim Law & Policy Journal* 13 (3): 711–742.

Stoiber, Carlton, Alec Baer, Norbert Pelzer, and Wolfram Tonhauser. 2003. *Handbook on Nuclear Law*. IAEA.

Walker, George K., and John E. Noyes. 2002. "Definitions for the 1982 Law of the Sea Convention: Part II." *California Western International Law Journal* 33 (2): 191–324.

World Nuclear News. 2016. "Russia and China Outline Expanded Cooperation." November 8. https://world-nuclear-news.org/Articles/Russia-and-China-outline-expanded-cooperation.

2023. "Floating Nuclear Power Plant Set for First Refuelling." October 13. www.world-nuclear-news.org/Articles/Floating-nuclear-power-plant-set-for-first-refuell.

Zou, S. F., D.X. Gong, J. Song, J Zhao, and X. H. Zhang. 2021. "Study of Thermal Supply Mode of Floating Nuclear Power Plant in Offshore Oil and Gas Fields." *IOP Conference Series: Earth and Environmental Science* 701: 012017.

13

National Security Challenges to Implementing the BBNJ Regime on Marine Genetic Resources

James Kraska

13.1 INTRODUCTION

Two issues arising from the new high seas regime on marine genetic resources (MGR) may stymie State ratification and impede effective implementation. The MGR regime is the cornerstone of the 2023 High Seas Treaty (UN 2023), formally titled the Agreement under the United Nations Convention on the Law of the Sea on the Conservation and Sustainable Use of Marine Biological Diversity of Areas beyond National Jurisdiction.[1] On June 19, 2023, a UN conference adopted the Treaty as part of a package of measures to protect biodiversity in areas beyond national jurisdiction (BBNJ). The Treaty is designed to provide access and benefits mainly for MGR to developing States. State parties are required to provide complete transparency for MGR research through an online portal. The principal feature of the Treaty, however, may also pose its most significant challenge to implementation because the required transparency bypasses intellectual property rights (IPRs) and may require the disclosure of biological research that implicates national security.

The regime does not protect IPR at all, thereby reducing incentives for advancing marine science and biotechnology on the high seas. Since advanced States conduct most MGR research, the lack of IPR protection makes the High Seas Treaty less likely to achieve full and energetic implementation. The Treaty also does not exempt specific national security research conducted on the high seas. Developed States are engaged in deep-sea biotechnology research for national defense, and the lack of exemption for most of these activities may weaken their resolve to implement the Treaty. These two issues may undermine the goal of attracting a large number of developed States to join the Treaty, thereby making it successful. Without the most

[1] Agreement under the United Nations Convention on the Law of the Sea on the Conservation and Sustainable Use of Marine Biological Diversity of Areas beyond National Jurisdiction, A/CONF.232/2023/4 (June 19, 2023) (High Seas Treaty).

technologically advanced States, the MGR regime will be unable to fulfill its vision of providing access and benefits to developing States.

This chapter proposes that the Conference of the Parties should address these shortcomings. There are two fixes the Conference could undertake once convened to encourage more developed States to join the Treaty. First, the type of access and benefits of MGR that flow to developing States could be formalized and oriented toward monetary contributions for capacity-building and technology transfer, rather than complete disclosure of market-sensitive IPR. The financial contributions may be complemented with in-kind contributions to the Global South, consistent with existing IPR. This approach safeguards IPR to encourage participation while also ensuring that benefits accrue to developing States. Second, the military activities exemption in the Treaty applies to research conducted on the high seas by warships and other public vessels. Yet a substantial amount of biological research at sea is funded through grants from the Office of Naval Research (ONR) and the Defense Advanced Research Projects Agency (DARPA), and carried out by civilian oceanographic vessels. The military activities exemption should be interpreted broadly to include this type of research that is funded by the armed forces, even if it is not conducted on board a warship.

13.2 MARINE GENETIC RESOURCES

Marine biotechnology is a growing economic sector, with companies investing in new commercial products and medical treatments derived from marine genetics. MGR may be used in commercial, industrial, and manufacturing applications in healthcare, including for treating cancer and understanding the role of inflammation (Leary et al. 2009, 186–187). For example, drugs developed from marine organisms include remdesivir to fight COVID-19 and azidothymidine (AZT), the first approved treatment for HIV (Heffernan 2022).

The High Seas Treaty defines MGR as "any material of marine plant, animal, microbial or other origin containing functional units of heredity of actual or potential value" (Article 1(8)). This definition does not include genetic material or digital information derived from fish or other living marine resources.

Finding and utilizing MGR requires advanced oceanographic technology and sophisticated integration of marine scientific research and biotechnology. Only the wealthiest States have the industrial base and technological capability to find and exploit MGR and produce digital data – called digital sequence information (DSI) – from them. The Treaty seeks to distribute or "share" access to and benefits of MGR and DSI throughout the world, especially inuring to the benefit of developing States. This goal has both an economic component to help accelerate the development of the Global South and an ethical component of distributive justice to atone for the perception that developed States rose to power through colonialism and the postcolonial exploitation of developing States. The effort to transform the maritime segment of biotechnology, however, skirts over the market incentive for companies to fund MGR and DSI research if they are required to give away their IPR. Furthermore, the unintended consequence of radical transparency on MGR is that marine genetic research related to military and security purposes is placed at risk. In the US, for example, ONR and DARPA fund significant amounts of marine scientific research. Much of this research is open source and unclassified, but with an eye toward military applications. Some research is classified. Under BBNJ, details on the research of these programs must be made globally transparent in a step-by-step fashion, from the initial stages to the research findings, including the sharing of DSI. These requirements imperil national security.

Section 13.3 explores the progressive emergence of the High Seas Treaty and its various key definitions, as well as the Treaty's structure and various constructive ambiguities. The section discusses the tensions in State views that went into, and resulted in, the Treaty conceptions of MGR and DSI, which must be uploaded to a comprehensive, globally transparent online Clearing House Mechanism (ClHM).

Next, Section 13.4 underscores the remaining and critical problem of IPR by discussing the debate over the status of a treaty that contains no provision on the issue. Without robust IPR protections, the ClHM may reduce investments and risk-taking by the US marine biotechnology industry, perhaps putting jobs at risk and generating less science. The failure of the Treaty to protect IPR weakens American and allied biotechnology industries by compelling them to subsidize the rest of the world through transparency of their research, which will inevitably reduce their competitive posture and the economic prosperity of the States that fund such research. The exact requirements for complete transparency of all MGR damage national security, including homeland defensive biosecurity and biological applications that give US and allied forces an edge in advanced warfare. These shortfalls likely imperil any effort by States with advanced biotechnology sectors to ratify the Treaty. The flaws in the MGR framework mean that the US and its alliance partners are likely unable to comply with the Treaty's requirements to share their most advanced research without undermining economic prosperity and national security.

Section 13.5 contextualizes the High Seas Treaty by considering the role of MGR research in national security. The ClHM's laudable goal of transparency appears inconsistent with research and development of MGR for national defense, particularly in biological warfare defense and the application of bioelectrical organisms in undersea warfare. The US and its allies are pursuing this type of research to counter the People's Republic of China. The Treaty's provisions on exempting warships from the provisions of MGR are insufficient to cover these defensive equities. The Conference of the Parties, however, would be positioned to adopt an elastic interpretation of the warship exemption that may weaken US preparations for biological attack and biodefenses and would risk exposing military and intelligence research programs aimed at maintaining America's competitive advantage.

13.3 THE HIGH SEAS TREATY

The High Seas Treaty emerged from a twenty-year process to progressively develop the law to fill perceived gaps in the United Nations Convention on the Law of the Sea (UNCLOS).[2] The Convention was innovative in creating the 200-mile exclusive economic zone (EEZ) to bring living and nonliving resources under coastal State management. This solution was designed to address the "tragedy of the commons," in which resources are overexploited because no single State has control over them (Hardin 1968). Whereas the resources of the EEZ immediately fell under the sovereign rights and jurisdiction of coastal States, it was apparent that ocean governance on the high seas was underdeveloped. While UNCLOS entered into force in 1994, member States were putting the final touches on the 1995 High Seas Fish Stocks Agreement to regulate stocks that moved back and forth between the high seas and a coastal State's EEZ, or between EEZs.[3] The 1994 Implementation Agreement on deep-seabed mining was negotiated to amend the provisions on seabed mining in UNCLOS. It was the first implementing agreement under the Convention,[4] the second being the High Seas Fish Stocks Agreement. Although the High Seas Fish Stocks Agreement has helped bring high-seas fisheries under more effective management, the areas beyond national jurisdiction continue to lack strong protections for resource conservation and international marine environmental law. The High Seas Treaty was designed to address the protection of high-seas biodiversity and to strengthen the weak provisions on marine technology transfer in Part XI of UNCLOS. Along the way, the management of MGR captured the process and became the flagship issue of the negotiations.

The High Seas Treaty is the third implementing agreement under UNCLOS.[5] Because the formal name is too long to be catchy, the effort was, for most of the past two decades, called "biodiversity beyond national jurisdiction" or "BBNJ." More recently, some proponents have settled on the name "High Seas Treaty." While the need to protect high-seas biodiversity is pressing and universally accepted, the provisions on the transfer of marine technology and MGR broadly divide along a Global North–South divide. The wealthy developed States are active in MGR research, and the Global South seeks access and benefits to these new riches of the sea. In a 2018 study of 38 million records of genetic sequences associated with

[2] UNCLOS, December 10, 1982, 1833 UNTS 397.

[3] Agreement for the Implementation of the Provisions of the United Nations Convention on the Law of the Sea of December 10, 1982, Relating to the Conservation and Management of Straddling Fish Stocks and Highly Migratory Fish Stocks, December 4, 1995, 2167 UNTS 3.

[4] Agreement Relating to the Implementation of Part XI of the United Nations Convention on the Law of the Sea of December 10, 1982, July 28, 1994, 1836 UNTS 3 (Implementation Agreement)

[5] The High Seas Treaty stands alongside the 1994 Implementation Agreement on Part XI for seabed mining and the 1995 High Seas Fish Stocks Agreement, which also implement UNCLOS.

patents, entities located in just three developed States were responsible for more than 74 percent of all the patents related to MGR: Germany (49 percent), the US (13 percent), and Japan (12 percent; Blasiak et al. 2018, 1, 2). Ninety-eight percent of the patents in ocean genetics were registered by entities in just ten States. Hence, the MGR provisions in the Treaty are imbued with a sense of fulfilling postcolonial debts or advancing social justice for the least developed States. The Global South extracted new commitments on MGR and technology from the developed States in exchange for two major parts that support a stronger framework to protect marine biodiversity on the high seas. First, the Treaty contains provisions to advance the use and transparency of environmental impact assessments (EIAs) for activities on the high seas. The provisions on EIAs build upon the weaker requirements already contained in UNCLOS (Articles 204–206). Second, the Treaty provides a process for creating additional marine protected areas on the high seas to provide special protection for designated areas. This process complements existing routes for designating special areas under the various annexes of the Marine Pollution Convention[6] and through the adoption process at the International Maritime Organization on particularly sensitive sea areas (IMO 2006, n.d.).

The elements of the High Seas Treaty designed to protect BBNJ gained widespread support. They were of particular interest to the developed States, increasingly concerned with the relationships among ocean health, climate change, and the global biosphere. On the other hand, the developing States focused on obtaining access and benefit-sharing for Western MGR and the transfer of advanced marine technology. In fact, the provisions regulating MGR constitute the core of the new Treaty, as they are the most transformative and impose tangible costs on States that provide access and benefits to other States.

13.3.1 *Two Treaties Fused*

The High Seas Treaty may be thought of as two separate agreements fused. There are four parts to the Treaty. Part II regulates MGR, while Part III regulates marine protected areas, which are referred to as area-based management tools (ABMTs). Part IV addresses EIAs and progressively develops the requirements in UNCLOS for conducting environmental assessments of activities that may adversely affect the marine environment (Articles 204–206). Part V focuses on capacity-building and technology transfer (CB&TT). These four distinct parts reflect two treaties conjoined at birth, with Part III (ABMT) and Part IV (EIAs) providing tangible new protocols to protect the marine environment. Western governments mainly pursued these two parts. Part II (MGR) and Part V (CB&TT) are based on the transfer of

6 International Convention for the Prevention of Pollution from Ships, November 2, 1973, 1340 UNTS 184.

TABLE 13.1 *Final Statements at the Resumed Fifth Session upon adoption of the High Seas Treaty (IISD 2023, 1, 7).*

State(s)	Emphasis in Final Statement
India	MGR and CB&TT
Core Latin America Group	MGR
The Netherlands	EIAs and marine protected areas
Norway	One of the few outliers among developed States, mentioned fair access and benefit-sharing from MGR, plus fisheries
The UK and China	Kunming-Montreal Global Biodiversity Framework under the Convention on Biological Diversity, including the 30×30 target for ABMT
Russia	Opposed the adoption of the High Seas Treaty and warned of "astronomical amounts of money" that would be required to implement the Treaty

advanced maritime biotechnology and marine technology from the developed world to the developing States. These provisions satisfied the Global South.

This division in North–South interests was reflected in the statements of governments upon the adoption of the instrument, when States uniformly stressed either side of this equation. A sample of statements is reflected in Table 13.1.

13.3.2 *Constructive Ambiguities*

Articles 9–16 of the High Seas Treaty aim to equitably share benefits arising from activities with respect to MGR and DSI for the conservation and sustainable use of BBNJ and to build the scientific and industrial capacity of developing States. Yet, even by the Further Resumed Fifth Session of the Intergovernmental Conference held from February 20 to March 3, 2023, there was little agreement on what this meant. Upon the adoption of the Treaty at the Further Resumed Fifth Session, the delegate from Iceland declared that "nothing has been protected yet, no benefits have been shared" (IISD 2023, 1, 7). Eritrea emphasized that there are "constructive ambiguities" in the Treaty, including on how to meet the 30×30 target for protecting 30 percent of the high seas with marine protected areas by 2030 and how best to ensure the fair and equitable sharing of benefits derived from MGR (IISD 2023, 6). The Russian Federation "lamented that many key issues in the text had not been resolved, including how the creation of a hierarchical structure [will operate alongside] existing, relevant, international organizations," such as the World Intellectual Property Organization (WIPO; IISD 2023, 3). The Natural Resources Defense Council, speaking for the fifty-one-member High Seas Alliance, lauded the Treaty as a historic agreement for the millions who depend on the ocean for their survival, but then noted that "now the real work begins" (IISD 2023, 8). Within the excitement that marked the completion of the Treaty, this remark reflects the sentiment that, on the core issues, the Treaty's completion was really an agreement to keep negotiating at the Conference of the Parties. The hopes for the Treaty are as grand as they are divergent, and no one has a roadmap to reconcile the competing visions. Proponents are invested in future Conferences of the Parties to figure all this out, and it is uncertain whether the aspirations can ever be fully realized.

13.3.3 *Marine Genetic Resources and Digital Sequence Information*

Determining the legal status of MGR was the most challenging issue in the BBNJ process and the High Seas Treaty. States have competing ideas on how to treat MGR and DSI in areas beyond national jurisdiction. The Treaty states that parties shall be guided by the principle of the common heritage of humankind (Article 7(b)). But the Treaty does not explicitly describe MGR as the common heritage of humankind, although Part II establishes an access and benefit-sharing regime for MGR through a "Clearing-House Mechanism" or internet portal (Articles 9–16). States are required to register their MGR and DSI research and, through the online portal, provide detailed notifications of prospecting and exploration activities and discoveries related to marine genetics (Article 12). These requirements include cataloging physical materials associated with MGR and divulging DSI that would permit another user to reconstruct the genetics (Article 12).[7]

Like UNCLOS, the High Seas Treaty relied on a process of constructive ambiguity to reach agreement on some of its most basic terms through text and definitions that are inherently vague. The Treaty also regulates DSI but does not define that term. There have been years of discussions on what might constitute DSI in other multilateral environmental forums, especially meetings of the Convention on Biological Diversity,[8] but the term has not been defined through those processes either. A study commissioned by the Conference of the Parties to the Convention on Biological Diversity provided the following range of what data are included in DSI:

- Group 1 – Narrow definition consisting of DNA and RNA;
- Group 2 – Intermediate definition consisting of DNA, RNA, and proteins;
- Group 3 – Intermediate definition consisting of DNA, RNA, proteins, and metabolites; and

[7] Part II of the High Seas Treaty is also focused on building capacity in developing States, particularly the LDCs, landlocked developing countries, geographically disadvantaged States, SIDS, coastal African States, archipelagic States, and developing middle-income countries: Article 9(b). Further, Part II seeks to generate knowledge and understanding about MGR, DSI, and the development and transfer of marine technology under the Treaty: Article 9(c)–(d).

[8] Convention on Biological Diversity, June 5, 1992, 1760 UNTS 79.

- Group 4 – Broad definition favored by the G77, which includes DNA, RNA, protein, metabolites, traditional knowledge, and ecological interactions (Houssen et al. 2020, 32).

There were significant discussions on the issue at the BBNJ intergovernmental conference, although States did not reach consensus. Yet, requirements for the disclosure of DSI repeatedly appear in the High Seas Treaty because developing countries considered open access to the underlying digital data of marine genetic organisms to be as important as access to the physical specimens to fulfil their vision of access and benefit-sharing. Among scientific communities, the term "DSI" is generally considered a policy rather than a scientific term.

The key question in the entire High Seas Treaty is to what extent MGRs are considered the common heritage of humankind subject to a global regulatory scheme, versus freely available resources in the global commons as part of the freedom of the seas. Pursuant to the Treaty, seven entities under the jurisdiction of a party are relevant stakeholders:

1. academic and research institutions, with the Treaty providing a basis for States to exclude the most cutting-edge and consequential MGR and DSI because they support biotechnology industries; furthermore, the US approach to research is through grants to individual scientists who use, store, or transfer organisms collected in BBNJ, generate and/or use DSI on MGR of BBNJ, or engage in sample collection activities in BBNJ (Article 11);
2. businesses that house scientists who use, store, or transfer organisms collected in BBNJ, generate and/or use DSI on MGR of BBNJ, or engage in sample collection activities in BBNJ (Article 11);
3. institutions and businesses that are interested in utilizing traditional knowledge of Indigenous peoples and local communities (Article 13);
4. Indigenous peoples and local communities that may hold relevant traditional knowledge associated with MGR in BBNJ databases, maintained at the national and international levels (Article 13);
5. repositories, including collections (such as natural museums) and gene banks (Article 51(3)(c));
6. countries that ratify the Treaty; and
7. The Conference of the Parties (see, for example, Article 14(1)) and the access and benefit-sharing committee (Article 15) of the Treaty.

All State parties may conduct MGR and DSI activities on the high seas (Article 11(1)). In situ, these activities shall be carried out with due regard for the interests of other States in areas beyond national jurisdiction (Article 11(3)). Parties "shall endeavour to cooperate" through specific modalities, including the ClHM under Article 51 (Article 11(3)). The Group of 77 supported a notification system that applies both pre- and post-cruise to marine scientific research, including research externally funded by ONR or the National Science Foundation. Toward this end, States must take the necessary measures to ensure that information is provided to the ClHM (Article 12(1)). Notification to the ClHM shall be made six months before in situ collection and shall include the nature of the objectives of the collection, the scope of the research, the geographic area covered by the research, and a summary of the scientific methods to be applied (Article 11(2)). The information shall also include a data management plan. Upon notification, the ClHM shall generate a BBNJ "standardized batch identifier" to track the MGR (Article 12(3)). Once the standardized batch identifier is generated, State parties shall provide additional information, including the database where the DSI or MGR are deposited or held, details on the geographic area where they were collected, and updates to the data management plan (Article 12(5)). The batch identifier shall be attached to any utilization of these resources, including commercial applications (Article 12(8)). This includes the use of the standardized batch identifier for publications, granted patents, product development, and product sales. The regulations apply to the utilization of MGR and DSI collected or generated before the High Seas Treaty enters into force.

No State may claim or exercise sovereignty or sovereign rights over MGR in BBNJ, even if the work is done on board a vessel (Article 11(4)). Collection in situ does not constitute a legal basis for any claim over the marine environment or its resources (Article 11(5)). The benefits that flow from the resources "shall be shared in a fair and equitable manner" (Article 14(1)). Benefits may be either monetary or nonmonetary. Parties shall adopt the legislative, administrative, or policy measures to ensure that the MGR and DSI are "deposited in publicly accessible repositories and databases, maintained either nationally or internationally, no later than three years from the start of such utilization, or as soon as they become available" (Article 14(3)).

Monetary benefits shall be shared fairly and equitably through the financial mechanism set forth in Article 52 (Article 14(5)). States shall make annual contributions to the special fund in Article 52, with a party's contribution constituting 50 percent of the assessed contribution to the budget adopted by the Conference of the Parties (Articles 14(6) and 47(6)). The payments shall be made as milestone payments; payments related to the commercialization of productions; a tiered fee paid periodically; or other forms of monetary payments (Article 14(7)). The structure for actual payments of monetary benefits remains somewhat elusive, and developed States strongly supported the application of nonmonetary benefits.

Nonmonetary benefits appear preferred by the terms of the Treaty. They include access to samples of MGR and DSI, open access to "findable, accessible, interoperable and reusable (FAIR) scientific data in accordance with current international practice and open and responsible data governance," data associated with the standardized batch identifier in publicly searchable and accessible forms, the transfer of marine technologies in accordance with Part V of the Treaty, capacity-building, and technical cooperation (Article 14(2)). The Treaty established an access and benefit-sharing committee to develop guidelines and provide transparency for the fair and equitable sharing of monetary and nonmonetary benefits (Article 15(1)). The committee also may make recommendations to the Conference of the Parties (Article 15(3)).

The ClHM is the key component for the monitoring and transparency of activities relating to MGR and DSI (Articles 16(1) and 36(2)). States must submit EIAs to the ClHM promptly when the activity in situ "may cause substantial pollution of or significant and harmful changes to the marine environment" (Article 28(2)). EIAs are published through the ClHM (Article 29(5)). Drafts of EIAs shall be placed on the ClHM and made available for public comment and consultation, which also provides an opportunity for the Scientific and Technical Body to consider and evaluate the report (Article 33(3)). On the other hand, if a party determines that an EIA is not required for the planned activity, it shall provide this determination and supporting information to the ClHM (Article 30(1)(a)(i)).

13.4 THE LINGERING PROBLEM OF IPRS

The High Seas Treaty's requirements for States to reveal and share MGR encroach on existing national and international IPR by requiring radical transparency of all marine genetic science and technology conducted beyond national jurisdiction (the high seas). The Treaty requires State parties to provide details of MGR and related marine scientific research through an online internet portal, the ClHM, to be shared with the rest of the world under the theory that all humankind has an interest in, and indeed rights to, the data.

Rules to protect IPR never made it into the final text, and the problem was swept under the rug in the final push to get an agreement at any cost. The High Seas Treaty would require the emerging US marine biotechnology industry to share its IPR and trade secrets with the rest of the world. Foreign companies can leverage research and compete in global markets without funding their own programmatic research. The lack of IPR protections alone poses a potentially insurmountable obstacle to developed States becoming parties, but the Treaty has even greater strategic implications for economic and national security. The same provisions in the Treaty that require States to reveal and share MGR through the ClHM weaken the US economy and undermine national security. These provisions reflect a regime complexity that merges the Treaty with IPR treaties, making the entire architecture virtually impenetrable (Blasiak et al. 2020, 588). Literally no one knows how they will interact.

Delegates considered IPR in a draft Article 12, but the provision was cut. It was not included in the Treaty to avoid undermining the objectives of fair and equitable sharing of benefits. Insistence on a strict IPR regime could also undercut the effective implementation of traceability, which is essential to determine where on the high seas the MGR material or DSI originated. Throughout the negotiations, IPRs were regarded as "something of an outcast" (Thambisetty 2022, 3). Some States opposed including IPR in the High Seas Treaty, expressing concerns about the risks posed by the fragmentary nature of the obligations, the relationship between patents and territoriality, and the need to disclose the origin of MGR. There was a division between the developed States, which emphasized the incentive function of IPR, and the Global South, which was more interested in IPR's allocative function as a source of development. The IPR issue was a fulcrum for success or failure, so it was deferred, presumably to be addressed by the Conference of the Parties after entry into force. As explained by Professor Siva Thambisetty:

> The central problem in the negotiations is a lack of quid pro quo to heighten the IP elements. On the one hand, the status quo is favourable to those who engage in [marine scientific research] – so there is no political will on their part to change that. On the other hand, keeping existing arrangements on IP, minus mitigating measures, is almost certain to exacerbate the technological gap between developed and developing countries even further, and goes against growing domestic and international policy critiques of such IPR regimes – so accepting the status quo around intellectual property as fait accompli hits at the very need for this instrument. (Thambisetty 2022, 3, footnote omitted)

There are existing models that adopt a flexible approach to IPR that could fulfil the mandate of the High Seas Treaty. These models may be adopted, but would require specially designed provisions to accommodate the Treaty's unique transparency mechanisms. Developing countries generally have greater latitude under WIPO and the 1995 Agreement on Trade-Related Aspects of Intellectual Property Rights (TRIPS),[9] administered by the World Trade Organization. TRIPS reflects different IPR standards across socioeconomic levels. It requires States to comply with the provisions of the Paris Convention for the Protection of Industrial Property[10] and the Berne Convention for the Protection of Literary and Artistic Works.[11] The latter has exceptions for "moral rights," which permit developing States under certain conditions to limit the right of reproduction (Article 6*bis*). However, TRIPS explicitly excludes these moral rights exceptions from its member compliance requirements (Article 9(1)).

[9] Agreement on Trade-Related Aspects of Intellectual Property Rights, April 15, 1994, 33 ILM 81 (TRIPS).

[10] Paris Convention for the Protection of Industrial Property, March 20, 1883, 828 UNTS 305 (last revised July 14, 1967) (Paris Convention).

[11] Berne Convention for the Protection of Literary and Artistic Works, September 9, 1886, 1161 UNTS 3 (last revised July 24, 1971). Articles 1–12 and 19 of the Paris Convention are incorporated into Article 2(1) of TRIPS. The Berne Convention (except for Article 6*bis*) is incorporated into Article 9(1) of TRIPS.

TRIPS recognizes Special and Differential Treatment (SDT) for developing and least developed countries. These provisions grant longer transition periods, providing more time for developing States to implement TRIPS-compliant laws. For example, least developed countries have an extended deadline for pharmaceutical patents until 2034. TRIPS also allows these countries to tailor their IP laws to their level of development, needs, and capacity to enforce IPR protections. These States may adopt weaker enforcement requirements to prioritize other socioeconomic goals – such as access to education, health, and technology transfer – over strict IPR enforcement. Compulsory licenses may be issued on patented products without the consent of the patent holder, especially in cases of national emergency. Public health exceptions are among the most compelling areas, with fewer IPR restrictions for developing States, and these are likely to be a feature of MGR research. Under the 2001 Doha Declaration on the TRIPS Agreement and Public Health (WTO 2001), developing States may issue compulsory licenses to produce generic versions of patented drugs during a health crisis. The licenses permit the production of more affordable medications to address diseases such as HIV/AIDS, tuberculosis, and malaria. Developing countries are also entitled to parallel importing, which allows them to import protected goods from States where they are sold at lower prices, bypassing restrictive IP rules. Favorable IPR terms may also be adopted in the agricultural sector to provide quick access to seeds and plant varieties. TRIPS includes provisions that encourage developed countries to promote technology transfer to the least developed States (Article 66(2)).

WIPO has assisted developing States in implementing the rules and exceptions to IPR, and we may expect that the High Seas Treaty will offer the same tailored aid, primarily through the ClHM. Since MGRs have potential applications in biotechnology and pharmaceuticals for developing new drugs, enzymes, and bio-based products, the issue of IPR will persist. The key concerns revolve around how States should balance the protection of IPR with the need for fair access to and benefit-sharing from MGR under the new Treaty. The fair and equitable sharing of benefits arising from the use of MGR is the cornerstone of the Treaty. Without the effective implementation of that vision, the Treaty will not succeed. The Global South is particularly focused on this issue, and the implementation of the Treaty hinges on this central goal.

The challenge for BBNJ, however, is how developed States and corporate investors in the developed world can remain incentivized without IPR protections. Unlike TRIPS, which provides special dispensation to developing States and least developed countries, MGR and DSI data under the High Seas Treaty must be uploaded to the ClHM for all States – including competitors in the developed world – to use. The Treaty requires complete transparency in research and development of MGR, including the disclosure of where the resources are collected and how they are being commercialized. This system is designed to ensure accountability in the exploration and exploitation of resources and to drive benefit-sharing.

How may access and benefits flow to developing States while still maintaining a competitive edge against other developed States? The Treaty establishes mechanisms for sharing both monetary and nonmonetary benefits. Monetary benefits include revenues from commercial products derived from MGR, while nonmonetary benefits may include access to research, technology transfer, and capacity-building efforts. Monetary benefits seem to be the easiest way to share the bounty of MGR with the Global South, although developed States seek to grow their own organic research and development enterprise and therefore prefer nonmonetary benefits.

13.4.1 *The Nagoya Protocol Model*

The Nagoya Protocol[12] is a supplementary agreement to the Convention on Biological Diversity, focusing on the fair and equitable sharing of benefits arising from the utilization of genetic resources. It was adopted in 2010 in Nagoya, Japan, and entered into force on October 12, 2014. The Protocol is a key international agreement designed to ensure that countries and communities that provide genetic resources receive a fair share of the benefits from their use, while also promoting biodiversity conservation and sustainable development. The High Seas Treaty draws inspiration from the Nagoya Protocol, which applies to genetic resources within national jurisdictions. The Treaty seeks to extend similar principles to the high seas, ensuring that IPRs do not undermine benefit-sharing obligations. The Protocol promotes the equitable sharing of benefits derived from the use of genetic resources within national jurisdiction, including from plants, animals, and microorganisms. This genetic material has applications in biotechnology, pharmaceuticals, and agriculture. The Protocol operates on the principle that States have sovereign rights over their genetic resources. Researchers or companies can gain access to genetic resources from biodiversity-rich States through prior informed consent and pursuant to negotiated mutually agreed terms. When a company, researcher, or institution uses genetic resources for commercial or noncommercial purposes, the benefits arising from this use must be shared with the State of origin and/or Indigenous communities that provide the resource. Such benefits may be monetary, such as royalties, license fees, or profit-sharing from a commercial product, or nonmonetary, such as technology transfer, research collaboration, and capacity-building.

The High Seas Treaty does not contain provisions on IPR, although the Treaty states that it must not undermine existing international legal regimes. The debate over "not undermining" relevant frameworks and bodies was a recurring theme throughout the negotiation process. The provision on "not undermin[ing]" is

[12] Nagoya Protocol on Access to Genetic Resources and the Fair and Equitable Sharing of Benefits Arising from Their Utilization to the Convention on Biological Diversity, October 29, 2010, 30008 UNTS 3.

included in the Treaty (Article 5). Still, many delegates argue for further clarification and for a standard definition to be agreed upon as implementation begins. One delegate remarked: "The sooner we clarify this notorious 'not-undermining provision,' the better for the Ocean and for all of us" (IISD 2023, 10).

Developed States may seek to preserve their advantage in these areas, and this would require the enforcement of IPR. The lack of protection in this area may make it impossible for many States to join or effectively implement the Treaty. Whether the US becomes a party or not, however, US companies with a presence in the foreign markets of Treaty parties will be subject to the new regime. This reality guided US efforts in the Intergovernmental Conference and will continue to be the major issue for the US, whether it is a party or nonparty to the Treaty.

While sharing marine scientific research knowhow and technology with developing States is an admirable goal, the ClHM may have the opposite effect by reducing investments and risk-taking by the US marine biotechnology industry. Patents and IPR enable the life science industry to engage in the risky process of developing drugs and other products, putting their capital at risk in search of a reward.[13] The MGR requirements appear to assume that advances in biotechnology on the high seas will be made by scientific consortia or government-funded basic science programs. In such cases, sharing the results of the scientific program is a subsidy to the rest of the world funded by the governments of developed States. If private industry is funding the science, the transfer payment is made by private corporations that, unlike the US government, must realize profits to stay in business, pay their employees, and continue funding research. Forcing these companies to divulge their IP may weaken them, put jobs at risk, and lead to less science.

The idea that States and companies that discover MGR on the high seas have a duty to share their innovations with the developing world gained traction in 2014. The Nagoya Protocol called for the treatment of MGR in a globally transparent manner that would permit access and the sharing of benefits (COP 2010).[14] The Ad Hoc Open-Ended Informal Working Group held meetings between 2006 and 2015 (UN 2015), and the High Seas Treaty negotiations began in earnest in 2018 (UN n.d.). Normative questions circulated throughout the process, such as what was owed by the developed world to the developing world, whether sharing MGR would benefit the developing world, and whether benefits could be shared at an acceptable cost to induce the developed world to participate. In the end, the North wanted an environmental agreement, and the South wanted marine and biotechnology. The

[13] A similar case was made against the waiver of IPR protections for COVID-19 therapies (Pooley 2024).

[14] In addition to the Convention on Biological Diversity, MGR have been a feature of discussions at the International Seabed Authority, the United Nations Informal Consultative Process on Oceans and the Law of the Sea, and the UN General Assembly debates on oceans and the law of the sea.

fear of failure drove both sides to sweep aside doubts about the Treaty's practicality, with IPR being the most obvious casualty. The IPR issue was known but ignored.

The Global South can access and benefit from MGR and marine technologies produced by Western States. The costs of transferring technology to them are borne by Western States and businesses that share (give away) their IP. The provisions are unworkable in a globalized market economy and are inconsistent with the WIPO regime. This conclusion was well known during the negotiations. Still, apparently idealism overcame practicality, and the issue of IPR protections was quietly bypassed. Those chickens have yet to come home to roost. Biosecurity is the next shoe to drop.

13.5 THE UNEXPECTED PROBLEM OF NATIONAL SECURITY

The transparency requirements for MGR and DSI in the High Seas Treaty implicate national security research on biological defense and emerging technologies that anticipate the use of biological organisms in naval operations. The Conference of the Parties may address the challenges in this area after entry into force. Adjusting and expanding the interpretation of the exemption for military activities may be required to entice States to implement the Treaty. Biosecurity concerns and the use of marine organisms in naval operations were beyond the negotiators' imagination, but these security technologies may have profound consequences for the Treaty's viability. Biosecurity considerations were neglected because the world was in a very different place in the early 2000s, when the BBNJ process began. By 2023, when the final text of the High Seas Treaty was adopted, strategic and economic competition made it more difficult to achieve collective action. Furthermore, the Treaty was always considered an environmental treaty. Hence, the negotiators and experts leading national delegations approached it from that epistemological perspective, rather than focusing on its ramifications for national security.

Two related changes in the international security environment require a reset of the thinking on MGR and require action by the Conference of the Parties before implementation would be widespread and effective among the most developed States. The first is that, unlike in the early 2000s, there is consensus in the US, and increasingly in the West, Japan, Australia, and elsewhere, that China poses a geostrategic threat rather than simply a market competitor. The peace and goodwill of the end of the Cold War have entirely run their course. China has replaced its "peaceful rise" campaign of the early 2000s with new challenges to the international order. The second significant change is the COVID-19 pandemic, which has heightened global sensitivity to biological security and the importance of biotechnology. Neither of these two trends was anticipated when the BBNJ negotiations began twenty years ago. Yet both trends have reset the national security chessboard, making the MGR provisions of the High Seas Treaty more challenging to implement.

The shift in US thinking to consider Beijing not just as a competitor but as an all-spectrum threat began in the last years of the Obama administration and continued through the Biden administration and have accelerated in the second Trump administration.. There is now a bipartisan belief that China is a threat to the rules-based international order. Emerging technology is "the fulcrum of U.S.-China competition" (Strobel 2023). For example, the 2017 US National Security Strategy states:

> For decades, U.S. policy was rooted in the belief that support for China's rise and for its integration into the post-war international order would liberalize China. Contrary to our hopes, China expanded its power at the expense of others' sovereignty. China gathers and exploits data on an unrivalled scale and spreads features of its authoritarian system, including corruption and the use of surveillance. It is building the most capable and well-funded military in the world, after our own. Its nuclear arsenal is growing and diversifying. Part of China's military modernization and economic expansion is due to its access to the U.S. innovation economy, including America's world-class universities. (White House 2017)

Lawmakers on both sides of the aisle believe that China is harvesting American technology and innovation, threatening economic and national security (Trump White House 2020). Robert C. O'Brien, Trump's National Security Advisor, called China a predatory power and the "threat of the century" (Hepher 2020). The Biden administration advanced those same themes. On this issue, the position of the 2022 Biden–Harris National Security Strategy was virtually indistinguishable from that of its predecessor:

> The PRC is the only competitor with both the intent to reshape the international order and, increasingly, the economic, diplomatic, military, and technological power to do it. Beijing has ambitions to expand its sphere of influence in the Indo-Pacific and become the world's leading power. It is using its technological capacity and increasing influence over international institutions to create more permissive conditions for its own authoritarian model, and to mold global technology use and norms to privilege its interests and values. Beijing frequently uses its economic power to coerce countries. It benefits from the openness of the international economy while limiting access to its domestic market, and it seeks to make the world more dependent on the PRC while reducing its own dependence on the world. (White House 2022, 23)

The Biden–Harris administration warned that China is the "pacing challenge" (White House 2022, 20, 22). The administration even extended the protectionism of US technology-intensive industries, surprising allies (Duehren and Mackrael 2024). The US CHIPS Act,[15] a cornerstone of Biden–Harris industrial policy, is a manifestation of this sense of the military risk associated with the technological rivalry with China (Swanson 2022, 15). China swiftly retaliated against the CHIPS

[15] CHIPS and Science Act of 2022, Public Law 117–167 (August 9, 2022).

Act by restricting the export of gallium and germanium, two minerals used in the technology industry (Areddy and Hua 2023). After the early 2023 incident of a Chinese spy balloon overflying the US, the Biden–Harris administration used even stronger words, warning that China was a threat to "our sovereignty" (Politi and Fedor 2023). Like his predecessor, Biden named China the greatest danger to American security, supply chains, and technology partnerships. The US and its allies are engaged in a struggle with authoritarian regimes to maintain the lead in advanced technologies – everything from AI to synthetic biology (Strobel 2023). The backbone of the provisions on MGR, and indeed the entire High Seas Treaty, is the transparency of marine biotechnology, which appears incompatible with US industrial and military security.

While the hallmark of the High Seas Treaty is the ClHM, transparency, shared access, and equitable benefits, the realities of the current world include deglobalization, the internalization of supply chains, and restrictions on sharing emerging technologies, from semiconductors to quantum key communications (White House 2023). Biotechnology is likely to follow the same course as other advanced technologies, such as semiconductor chips, diluting the goals of the ClHM. In short, the ClHM flies against the zeitgeist of the time, which is a product of great-power competition that did not fully manifest until about 2017. The pandemic only reinforced the economic and security trends. These developments cast doubt on the willingness of the most powerful States either to join the Treaty or, if they do, to implement its terms in the comprehensive manner envisioned by the Treaty and the ClHM.

Mindful of the China threat and the risk of another pandemic, the US and its allies are working to internalize research, development, and production of innovative, high-end, value-added technologies to gain greater economic autonomy and national security. While fissures in economic globalization emerged during the first Trump administration, they accelerated more recently, becoming a bipartisan feature of American politics and deepening economic protectionism. The US is not alone in these views. In Europe, these same trends toward economic security contributed to the Brexit movement and accelerated with the war in Ukraine and EU sanctions against Russia (Benson et al. 2024). Similarly, Japan has awakened to the threat from China. In 2021, Japan and the US singled out China as a threat to the international order in a joint statement (Siripala 2021). The National Security Strategy of Japan states that "China has intensified its attempts to unilaterally change the status quo by force" (NSC Japan 2022). Forming a trifecta, the US, the EU, and Japan are now energized against the technological threat of China, with other allies, especially in East Asia, also viewing China as a threat (European Council 2022; Jozuka and Essig 2022; Silver et al. 2023).

The US signed the High Seas Treaty on September 20, 2023, stating that it may expand marine-protected areas to protect biodiversity (Blinken 2023). With that signature, the US acquired duties under the Vienna Convention on the Law of

Treaties not to act inconsistently with the "object and purpose" of the Treaty.[16] But the core provisions of the Treaty regulate the discovery and exploitation of MGR. They are not directly related to protecting marine biodiversity, and yet they have significant implications for the US biotechnology sector and national security that are not widely appreciated.

The Treaty will require ONR and DARPA to disclose their programs and discoveries in high-seas biotechnology and share them with potential adversaries. The Department of Defense is studying how these genetic organisms and digital genomics may provide insights into biodefense for homeland security, and how they can be manipulated at the molecular and organism levels to accomplish national security missions, such as aiding the hunt for enemy submarines.[17] Marine scientific research involving genetic organisms also may be used to strengthen biological warfare defenses, not a trivial consideration in a post-COVID-19 world. Likewise, marine biotechnology has applications for a range of naval activities, from submarine detection to underwater communications.

13.5.1 *National Security*

Three aspects of national security are put at risk by the High Seas Treaty's provisions on MGR. First, although the Treaty does have an exemption for military activities, it is narrowly construed. Notably, it would not exempt marine science funded by ONR or DARPA that is conducted by civilian scientists aboard civilian or government oceanographic ships. Second, the Treaty weakens US efforts to understand and prepare for biological attack and to strengthen biodefense by making public research derived from high-seas genetic organisms. Third, the Treaty risks exposing military and intelligence research programs aimed at enhancing the position of US forces in future armed conflicts, such as bioengineered organisms that can help locate enemy submarines or facilitate communication with friendly swarms of autonomous underwater vehicles. These three issues are discussed below.

[16] Vienna Convention on the Law of Treaties, May 23, 1969, 1155 UNTS 331.

[17] The Defense Science Board Task Force on Biology notes: "Genomics and bioinformatics could lead to tailored and personalized training, enhancing warfighter performance. Genome editing could lead to manipulation of higher organisms to improve or create combat-relevant characteristics. Synthetic biology could lead to advanced materials with special properties that improve warfighter and weapon system survivability, enable novel combat capabilities, and reduce costs and manufacturing time for materiel. Novel ways of tagging, tracking, and locating using synthetic biology and biosensors could improve intelligence, surveillance, reconnaissance, and targeting. Advances in immunology and new biological materials could transform vaccine development and enhance resilience of soldiers in environments with dangerous pathogens. Better understanding and monitoring of the microbiome can help ensure the health of warfighters in stressful environments and under difficult conditions" (Defense Science Board 2020, [1]).

13.5.1.1 Military Activities Exemption

The High Seas Treaty states: "The obligations in [Part II concerning MGR] shall not apply to a Party's military activities, including military activities by government vessels and aircraft engaged in non-commercial service" (Article 10(3)). "Military activities" are not defined in the Treaty. Still, past practice suggests that they could include a broad remit for national security research, homeland security, intelligence, and related research and development, such as biotechnology and pharmaceutical research for biological weapons defense and response. Earlier, the Treaty states that it "does not apply to any warship, military aircraft or naval auxiliary" (Article 4). Even so, each party "shall ensure, by the adoption of appropriate measures not impairing the operations or operational capabilities of such vessels or aircraft owned or operated by it, that such vessels or aircraft act in a manner consistent, so far as is reasonable and practicable, with this Agreement" (Article 4). To the extent that the "military activities" are defined broadly, MGR provisions become weaker. The problem, however, is that military activities are exempt only when conducted from a government vessel or aircraft. In contrast, most of the research undertaken by ONR and DARPA is carried out on civilian oceanographic vessels and in university laboratories. Part II (on MGR) applies to "other vessels or aircraft owned or operated by a Party and used, for the time being, only on government non-commercial service" (Article 4). This provision means that other government vessels, such as those operated by the National Oceanic and Atmospheric Administration, are covered by the Treaty.

13.5.1.2 Homeland Biosecurity

The COVID-19 pandemic refocused the US on the need to contend with diffuse biological threats and, indeed, to explore the science behind the terrifying prospect of biological warfare (Healey 2022; Lyon 2021). The COVID-19 pandemic, which originated in China in late 2019, has heightened concern about the development of biological warfare agents and reopened dormant biodefense research. The US intelligence community is split on the virus's origin, with both natural and laboratory-leak theories plausible (BBC 2023; Manson 2021). Regardless of its source, the pandemic underscored the vulnerability of global economic prosperity to pathogens, and understanding this threat vector is now a significant concern (Gordon and Forrest 2022).

The US Department of Defense has embarked on building expertise in defensive biotechnology. Although research to defend against biological attack is not unlawful and complies with the Biological Weapons Convention,[18] it stands to reason that

[18] Convention on the Prohibition of the Development, Production, and Stockpiling of Bacteriological (Biological) and Toxin Weapons and on Their Destruction, April 10, 1972, 1015 UNTS 163.

some of the technology could be weaponized or used to counter defensive responses if it fell into the wrong hands (Reeves et al. 2018). While pockets and individuals of excellence are sprinkled throughout the Department, as a whole the Pentagon lacks expertise, connections, and investments in life sciences and technology to the same extent as in areas such as computer science and aerospace technologies (Evans 2020). It is unlikely that the US will invest heavily in biosciences only to put it all online under the High Seas Treaty's transparency regime outlined in Part II and the ClHM framework in Article 51. At best, the US might participate through token reporting on a limited number of MGR and DSI initiatives. Furthermore, while the rules for implementing the Treaty may be ironed out in the Conference of the Parties, there is little to lend confidence that the Conference will fare better than the Intergovernmental Conference did in creating greater precision or fidelity in the rules.

13.5.1.3 Naval Biotechnology

Finally, perhaps the most significant challenge to national security posed by the High Seas Treaty is that it would require complete transparency into a variety of marine biogenetic research sponsored by the Navy but conducted from non-warship platforms. The US military is interested in genome sequencing, bioinformatics, genome editing, synthetic biology, new materials, immunology, the microbiome, and neuroscience (Defense Science Board 2020, 1).

DARPA is at the forefront of US biosecurity. A relatively flat organization with six technical program offices, DARPA is focused on homeland defense with programs to strengthen "active bio-surveillance and bio threat countermeasures" (DARPA 2019, 9). The program managers have great autonomy and are empowered to take risks on innovative ideas (Gallo 2021, 4–6). In the context of the High Seas Treaty, DARPA's Biological Technologies Office is responsible for the "development and use of biotechnology for technological advantage, including neurotechnology, human-machine interface, human performance, infectious disease, and synthetic biology R&D programs" (Gallo 2021, 3).

The US is exploring the use of engineered marine organisms for a variety of tactical roles, including living camouflage, new drugs to help members of the armed forces survive harsh environments, and self-healing paint (Bird et al. 2021). The Department of Defense sponsors a program called Applied Research for the Advancement of Science and Technology Priorities Program on Synthetic Biology for Military Environments (Alia-Novobilski 2017). The cross-service program is focused on keeping US advantages in areas such as quantum computing and bioengineering. For example, Naval Research Laboratory scientists are working on electroactive bacteria and miniaturized, potentially high-throughput bioelectrochemical platforms (Yates et al. 2021). One program is exploring the development of environmental "chassis" microbes to deliver "robust performance" outside the laboratory (US GAO 2018, 27). Navy scientists are also working on using common marine microorganisms that might be genetically engineered into living tripwires to signal the passage of enemy submarines, underwater vessels, or even divers. Scientists are exploring whether the genetic makeup of an abundant sea organism, such as *Marinobacter*, can be altered to make it respond to substances left by enemy vessels, divers, or equipment (Tucker 2018). These could be metals, fuel exhaust, human DNA, or some molecule not naturally found in the ocean but associated with diesel-powered submarines (Tucker 2018). The reaction could take the form of electron loss, which could be detectable to friendly submarine drones or prepositioned equipment on the seabed (Tucker 2018). Naval Research Laboratory researcher Sarah Glaven said at an event at the Johns Hopkins University's Applied Physics Lab: "In an engineered context, we might take the ability of the microbes to give up electrons, then use [those electrons] to talk to something like an autonomous vehicle. Then you can start imagining that you can create an electrical signal when the bacteria encounter some molecule in their environment" (Tucker 2018).

13.6 CONCLUSION

From the beginning of the negotiations, the US and many developed States were somewhat circumspect about the lack of IPR protections in the High Seas Treaty, much as they had been skeptical of Part XI on deep-seabed mining in UNCLOS until the Implementation Agreement was adopted in 1994. In that case, UNCLOS received its sixtieth instrument of ratification on November 16, 1993, and was set to enter into force on November 16, 1994 (Article 308). Yet Iceland (June 1, 1985) was the only developed State to have ratified UNCLOS. Australia (October 5, 1994) and Germany (October 14, 1994) joined only after the implementing agreement had addressed the interests of the developed States. We are at a similar crossroads with the High Seas Treaty, at which developed States may be deterred from joining or fully implementing it because of weaknesses in the IPR regime and the narrowly drawn warship exemption.

The US asserted:

> We do not interpret anything in this Agreement as authorizing or permitting any waiver or undermining of existing intellectual property rights and obligations under international or national law; requiring mandatory disclosure of trade secrets, protected undisclosed or confidential information; requiring mandatory disclosure in patent applications of the origin or source of marine genetic resources; or requiring compulsory licenses. (UNGA 2023, 113)

It is unclear under what conditions the US Senate would render advice and consent for presidential ratification of the High Seas Treaty, given the inability to accede to UNCLOS itself. If the US becomes a party to the new treaty, it will have to adopt implementing legislation applicable to US companies to enable them to participate in the access and benefit-sharing regime. It appears unlikely that the US and other developed States can paper over the conflict between the Treaty and the global framework for the protection of IPR or accept the risks to bio-naval research and development once they become manifest. As with the original Part XI, applicable to deep-seabed mining in 1982, the number of ratifications is key to the Treaty's entry into force, but the quality is equally important. If major actors in high-seas activities – such as the US, Japan, and Germany – do not join the High Seas Treaty because of concerns over IPR and national security, its effectiveness will be severely compromised.

REFERENCES

Alia-Novobilski, Marisa. 2017. "Tri-Service Effort Leverages Synthetic Biology Expertise to Address Future Warfighter Needs." Wright-Patterson AFB, September 27. www.wpafb.af.mil/News/Article-Display/Article/1326042/tri-service-effort-leverages-synthetic-biology-expertise-to-address-future-warf/.

Areddy, James T., and Sha Hua. 2023. "China Restricts Exports of Two Minerals Used in High-Performance Chips." *Wall Street Journal*, July 4. www.wsj.com/articles/china-restricts-exports-of-two-metals-used-in-high-performance-chips-a649402b.

BBC (British Broadcasting Corporation). 2023. "Intelligence Report Says US Split on COVID-19 Origins." June 24. www.bbc.com/news/world-us-canada-66005240.

Benson, Emily, Federico Steinberg, and Pau Alvarez-Aragones. 2024. "The European Union's Economic Security Strategy Update." Center for Strategic & International Studies, January 26. www.csis.org/analysis/european-unions-economic-security-strategy-update.

Bird, Lina J., Biki B. Kundu, Tanya Tschirhart, Anna D. Corts, Lin Su, Jeffrey A. Gralnick, Caroline M. Ajo-Franklin, and Sarah M. Glaven. 2021. "Engineering Wired Life: Synthetic Biology for Electroactive Bacteria." *ACS Synthetic Biology* 10 (11): 2808–2823.

Blasiak, Robert, Jean-Baptiste Jouffray, Colette C. C. Wabnitz, Emma Sundström, and Henrik Österblom. 2018. "Corporate Control and Global Governance of Marine Genetic Resources." *Science Advances* 4 (6): eaar5237.

Blasiak, Robert, R. Wynberg, K. Grorud-Colvert, S. Thambisetty, N. M. Bandarra, A. V. M. Canario, J. da Silva, C. M. Duarte, M. Jaspars, A. Rogers, K. Sink, and C. C. C. Wabnitz. 2020. "The Ocean Genome and Future Prospects for Conservation and Equity." *Nature Sustainability* 3: 588–596.

Blinken, Antony J. 2023. "Signing of the High Seas Treaty." Press Statement, US Department of State, September 21.

COP (Conference of the Parties to the Convention on Biological Diversity). 2010. "Decision Adopted by the Conference of the Parties to the Convention on Biological Diversity at Its Tenth Meeting." UNEP/CBD/COP/DEC/X/1 (October 29, 2010).

DARPA (Defense Advanced Research Projects Agency). 2019. *Creating Technology Breakthroughs and New Capabilities for National Security*. DARPA.

Defense Science Board. 2020. *Task Force on Biology: Final Report*.

Duehren, Andrew, and Kim Mackrael. 2024. "'What the Hell?' Europe Chafes at America's Protectionist Tilt." *Wall Street Journal*, January 29. www.wsj.com/politics/policy/us-europe-trade-relations-849fe23a?mod = hp_lead_pos10.

European Council. 2022. "Joint Statement EU-Japan Summit 2022." Press Release, May 12. www.consilium.europa.eu/en/press/press-releases/2022/05/12/joint-statement-eu-japan-summit-2022/.

Evans, Eric. 2020. *Memorandum for Under Secretary of Defense of Research and Engineering: Final Report of the Defense Science Board (DSB) Task Force on Biology.*

Gallo, Marcy E. 2021. "Defense Advanced Research Projects Agency: Overview and Issues for Congress." Congressional Research Service, R45088.

Gordon, Michael R., and Brett Forrest. 2022. "U.S. Defense Strategy Casts China as Greatest Danger to American Security." *Wall Street Journal*, October 27. www.wsj.com/articles/u-s-defense-strategy-casts-china-as-greatest-danger-to-american-security-11666885023.

Hardin, Garrett. 1968. "The Tragedy of the Commons: The Population Problem Has No Technical Solution; It Requires a Fundamental Extension in Morality." *Science* 162 (3859): 1243–1248.

Healey, Meredith. 2022. "Pandemic Chaos Proves the World Isn't Prepared for Biological Warfare, Experts Say." *CBC News*, April 24. www.cbc.ca/news/politics/biowarfare-bio weapon-covid-pandemic-1.6427565.

Heffernan, Olive. 2022. "Who Owns the Ocean's Genes? Tension on the High Seas." *Scientific American*, September 12. www.scientificamerican.com/article/who-owns-the-ocean-rsquo-s-genes-tension-on-the-high-seas/.

Hepher, Tim. 2020. "Trump's Security Adviser Says: China Is the Threat of the Century." *Reuters*, October 22. www.reuters.com/article/idUSKBN2770EC/.

Houssen, Wael, Rodrigo Sara, and Marcel Jaspars. 2020. "Digital Sequence Information on Genetic Resources: Concept, Scope and Current Use." CBD/DSI/AHTEG/2020/1/3, Annex (January 29, 2020).

IISD (International Institute for Sustainable Development). 2023. "Summary of the Further Resumed Fifth Session of the Intergovernmental Conference to Adopt an International Legally Binding Instrument Under the UN Convention on the Law of the Sea on the Conservation and Sustainable Use of Marine Biodiversity of Areas Beyond National Jurisdiction: 19–20 June 2023." *Earth Negotiations Bulletin* 25 (252), June 23.

IMO (International Maritime Organization). 2006. "Revised Guidelines for the Identification and Designation of Particularly Sensitive Sea Areas." A 24/Res.982 (February 6, 2006).

n.d. "Special Areas under MARPOL." www.imo.org/en/OurWork/Environment/Pages/Special-Areas-Marpol.aspx.

Jozuka, Emiko, and Blake Essig. 2022. "Japan Turns Away from Post-WWII Pacifism as China Threat Grows." *CNN*, May 21. www.cnn.com/2022/05/21/asia/japan-us-alliance-quad-summit-defense-hnk-dst-intl/index.html.

Leary, David, Marjo K. Vierros, Gwenaëlle Hamon, Salvatore Arico, and Catherine Monagle. 2009. "Marine Genetic Resources: A Review of Scientific and Commercial Interest." *Marine Policy* 33 (2): 183–194.

Lyon, Regan F. 2021. "The COVID-19 Response Has Uncovered and Increased Our Vulnerability to Biological Warfare." *Military Medicine* 186 (7–8): 193–196.

Manson, Katrina. 2021. "US Intelligence Split over COVID-19 Lab-Leak Theory." *Financial Times*, May 27. www.ft.com/content/8e023b1b-8e43-4ba9-81a7-9d65c0e4b020.

NSC Japan (National Security Council of Japan). 2022. "National Security Strategy of Japan."

Politi, James, and Lauren Fedor. 2023. "Joe Biden Warns China over Threats to US Sovereignty in State of the Union Address." *Financial Times*, February 7. www.ft.com/content/63d9325d-3eff-46e3-9077-c0c3589dd20d.

Pooley, James. 2024. "Opinion: Sharing COVID Therapy Secrets Is a Trojan Horse That Would Gut U.S. Biotech." *Wall Street Journal*, January 6. www.wsj.com/articles/WP-MKTW-0002846886?mod = article_recs_pos3_sb_hp&next_redirect = true.

Reeves, R. G., S. Voeneky, D. Caetano-Anollés, F. Beck, and C. Boët. 2018. "Agricultural Research, or a New Bioweapon System?" *Science* 362 (6410): 35–37.

Silver, Laura, Christine Huang, and Laura Clancy. 2023. "In East Asia, Many People See China's Power and Influence as a Major Threat." Pew Research Center, December 5. www.pewresearch.org/short-reads/2023/12/05/in-east-asia-many-people-see-chinas-power-and-influence-as-a-major-threat/.

Siripala, Thisanka. 2021. "US and Japan Name China as Threat to International Order." *The Diplomat*, March 17. https://thediplomat.com/2021/03/us-and-japan-name-china-as-threat-to-international-order/.

Strobel, Warren P. 2023. "American Spies Confront a New, Formidable China." *Wall Street Journal*, December 26. www.wsj.com/politics/national-security/american-spies-confront-a-new-formidable-china-5c384370?mod = hp_trending_now_article_pos2.

Swanson, Ana. 2022. "Biden Administration Clamps Down on China's Access to Chip Technology." *New York Times*, October 7. www.nytimes.com/2022/10/07/business/economy/biden-chip-technology.html.

Thambisetty, Siva. 2022. "Intellectual Property and Marine Genetic Resources: Navigating Articles 10–13 in the BBNJ Draft Treaty." London School of Economics and Political Science, Policy Briefing 48.

Trump White House. 2020. "President Donald J. Trump Is Protecting America from China's Efforts to Steal Technology and Intellectual Property." Fact Sheet, May 29. https://trumpwhitehouse.archives.gov/briefings-statements/president-donald-j-trump-protecting-america-chinas-efforts-steal-technology-intellectual-property/.

Tucker, Patrick. 2018. "The US Military Is Genetically Engineering New Life Forms to Detect Enemy Subs." *Defense One*, December 1. www.defenseone.com/technology/2018/12/us-military-genetically-engineering-new-life-forms-detect-enemy-subs/153200/.

UN (United Nations). 2015. "Ad Hoc Open-Ended Informal Working Group to Study Issues Relating to the Conservation and Sustainable Use of Marine Biological Diversity beyond Areas of National Jurisdiction." United Nations Division for Ocean Affairs and the Law of the Sea, March 13. www.un.org/depts/los/biodiversityworkinggroup/biodiversityworkinggroup.htm.

2023. "UN Delegates Reach Historic Agreement on Protecting Marine Biodiversity in International Waters." *UN News*, March 5. https://news.un.org/en/story/2023/03/1134157.

n.d. "Intergovernmental Conference on an International Legally Binding Instrument under the United Nations Convention on the Law of the Sea on the Conservation and Sustainable Use of Marine Biological Diversity of Areas beyond National Jurisdiction (General Assembly Resolution 72/249)." Intergovernmental Conference on Marine Biodiversity of Areas beyond National Jurisdiction. www.un.org/bbnj/.

UNGA (United Nations General Assembly). 2023. "Compilation of Statements Made by Delegations under Item 5, 'General Exchange of Views,' at the Further Resumed Fifth Session of the Intergovernmental Conference on an International Legally Binding Instrument under the United Nations Convention on the Law of the Sea on the Conservation and Sustainable Use of Marine Biological Diversity of Areas beyond National Jurisdiction, as Submitted by 30 June 2023." A/CONF.232/2023/INF.5 (August 3, 2023).

US GAO (United States Government Accountability Office). 2018. "Science and Technology: Considerations for Maintaining U.S. Competitiveness in Quantum Computing, Synthetic

Biology, and Other Potentially Transformational Research Areas." GAO-18-656 (September 26, 2018).
White House. 2017. "National Security Strategy of the United States of America." December.
2022. "National Security Strategy." October.
2023. "Fact Sheet: President Biden Announces New Actions to Strengthen America's Supply Chains, Lower Costs for Families, and Secure Key Sectors." Press Release, November 27.
WTO (World Trade Organization). 2001. "Declaration on the Trips Agreement and Public Health." WT/MIN(01)/DEC/2 (November 20, 2001).
Yates, Matthew D., Lina J. Bird, Brian J. Eddie, Elizabeth L. Onderko, Christopher A. Voigt, and Sarah M. Glaven. 2021. "Nanoliter Scale Electrochemistry of Natural and Engineered Electroactive Bacteria." *Bioelectrochemistry* 137: 107644.

Conclusion

This volume explored some of the most essential transformative marine technologies and the law of the sea, including how ports accommodate autonomous ships, the use of autonomous ships as time charterparties, the interface between AI and seafarers, attributing "conduct" of autonomous surface ships to ship masters, the normative and doctrinal dimensions of shipping decarbonization at the IMO, protection against maritime cyber threats, satellite vessel tracking, blockchain in commercial shipping, seabed mining and underwater archeology innovations, SMART submarine communications cables, and the lacunae of IPRs in the governance of marine genetic resources in the 2023 High Seas Treaty.

Chapter 1, by Dr. Murat Sümer, maps the relationship between Maritime Autonomous Surface Ships (MASS), particularly remotely controlled ships (RCS), and port State jurisdiction (PSJ). Removing human operators on ships and in ports represents a paradigm shift in marine technology, challenging established frameworks under the law of the sea. RCS highlights how technological innovations necessitate adaptations in international maritime law to ensure navigational safety, environmental protection, and compliance with global standards.

Ports, as gateways to international trade, handle over 80 percent of global commerce and are integral to State sovereignty under the UNCLOS. UNCLOS, while silent on explicit definitions of "port" or "port State," affirms in Article 8 complete territorial jurisdiction over internal waters, including ports. This sovereignty allows port States to regulate foreign vessels voluntarily entering their facilities, encompassing inspections, detentions, and denial of access. The International Maritime Organization (IMO) serves as the oversight body for the International Convention for the Safety of Life at Sea (SOLAS 1974), the International Convention for the Prevention of Pollution from Ships (MARPOL 73/78), and the International Convention on Standards of Training, Certification and Watchkeeping for Seafarers (STCW, 1978). These treaties emphasize "no more favorable treatment" clauses to enforce standards universally, even on nonparty flag States.

Historically, PSJ evolved from customary law restrictions in the pre-1970s era to a robust mechanism in the 1980s, bolstered by UNCLOS and regional memoranda, such as the Paris MoU. This evolution addresses flag State inadequacies, positioning port States as supplementary enforcers. Marine technology introduces novel jurisdictional tensions for RCS, which are classified under IMO's MASS degrees three and four, and are operated from remote operations centers (ROCs). Devoid of onboard crew, RCS rely on remote masters and AI-driven systems for navigation, but UNCLOS was drafted for manned vessels. His chapter suggests that the flexible "rules of reference" system in UNCLOS (e.g., Articles 211, 218, 219) can accommodate RCS by incorporating the IMO's Generally Accepted International Rules and Standards (GAIRS), treating them as "ships" at the discretion of the flag State (Article 91).

Key challenges arise from ROC locations. If situated outside the flag State's territory, effective flag State jurisdiction (FSJ) under Article 94 may be compromised due to overlapping sovereignties, potentially violating UNCLOS obligations for control over vessels. The chapter proposes extending the jurisdiction of the International Tribunal for the Law of the Sea (ITLOS) from viewing the ship as a unit (e.g., M/V Saiga (No. 2) and M/V Virginia G) to include ROCs as integral components, akin to a ship. This change could mitigate jurisdictional gaps, supplemented by enhanced PSJ through port State control (PSC) inspections of ROCs, especially if digitized certificates and remote audits were adopted through the IMO's Facilitation Committee guidelines.

Access to ports for RCS is not a right but a privilege (UNCLOS Article 25(2)). States may impose construction, design, equipment, and manning (CDEM) standards in ports, provided they are nondiscriminatory and publicly announced (UNCLOS, Article 211(3)). Potential extraterritorial effects may conflict with WTO principles, such as GATT's freedom of transit, thereby risking the establishment of trade barriers. To incentivize skeptical port States, the chapter advocates compulsory pilotage for RCS in port approaches, leveraging local expertise to address high-traffic hazards. While IMO avoids comprehensive pilotage regulation due to regional variances, the draft MASS Code could mandate it for safety, aligning with SOLAS and environmental protections in UNCLOS (Article 211(4)).

PSC emerges as a critical compliance tool, evolving from inspections focused on construction, design, equipping, and manning to broader scopes that include human elements and cybersecurity. For RCS, PSC could extend to ROC verifications, ensuring alignment with ISM Code equivalents, such as the proposed Remote Operations Management (ROM) systems.

RCS integration hinges on harmonizing marine technology with the law of the sea. While flag States retain primary responsibility, the expanding role of port States serves as a safety net against jurisdictional fragmentation. Achieving consensus at IMO is imperative to prevent fragmentation and foster safe, sustainable, and autonomous shipping without hampering global trade. The universal application of a MASS Code can guide IMO decisions. This framework not only upholds the evolutionary spirit of UNCLOS but also positions port States as pivotal guardians in the era of remote maritime operations.

In Chapter 2, Ceren Cerit Dindar examines how time charterparty agreements interact with MASS. Charterparty contracts license the temporary use of vessels. The applicability of time charterparties to autonomous ships necessitates adaptations in standard forms, such as the New York Produce Exchange (NYPE) 2015, to align with advancements in AI, remote operations, and dynamic autonomy levels.

Fully autonomous ships operate without onboard crews, relying on ROCs for monitoring, control, and intervention. Marine technology enables seamless transitions between remote and fully autonomous modes, as seen in vessels. One of them is *Yara Birkeland*, an autonomous 120-TEU container ship that carries cargo between ports at Herøya and Brevik in Norway. The development of the MASS Code aims to address navigational safety, but private contractual law, governed predominantly by English principles, must evolve concurrently.

Time charterparties, unlike bareboat charters, allocate possession and operational control to shipowners while granting charterers commercial employment rights. For MASS, ROCs, and vessel personnel, arrangements should be made by shipowners or third-party managers (e.g., through BIMCO's AUTOSHIPMAN form), preserving the charter's essence. Key obligations necessitate revisions: Shipowners must ensure seaworthiness, encompassing ROC infrastructure, cybersecurity, and AI systems, which extend traditional duties under NYPE Clause 2. Under the NYPE form (Clause 2), items such as port charges and usual expenses shall be for the charterers' account. To mitigate breaches, descriptive clauses (preamble and Annex A) should incorporate autonomy capabilities, such as automated cargo-handling.

Charterers' obligations, including compliance with safe port warranties (NYPE Clause 6), necessitate a redefinition of "safety" to encompass digital resilience against cyber threats, compatible automated berthing infrastructure, and real-time data integration. Ports deemed unsafe due to persistent technological deficiencies (e.g., inadequate V2X communication) could trigger liability. Off-hire provisions require expansion to cover ROC failures, software glitches, or connectivity issues, potentially with *de minimis* thresholds to avoid disputes over minor disruptions.

Ultimately, while freedom of contract allows amendments, standardized updates to NYPE forms are essential to prevent fragmentation. This evolution harmonizes the benefits of marine technology while emphasizing uniform standards in the law of the sea. MASS integration is ensured without compromising global trade or liability regimes. As IMO progresses in developing the MASS Code, charterparty law must adapt to foster innovation while upholding navigational freedoms under UNCLOS.

In Chapter 3, Khanssa Lagdami explored AI at sea. The integration of AI into marine technology is reshaping the maritime industry, enhancing operational efficiency, safety, and sustainability while posing significant challenges to the law of the sea and labor regulations. Her chapter examines AI applications in shipping, such as autonomous navigation, predictive maintenance, voyage optimization, and cybersecurity. The application of AI in these roles has implications for seafarers. Adaptive legal frameworks will have to be crafted under UNCLOS, the Maritime Labour Convention (MLC, 2006), and STCW, 1978.

Marine technology advancements, including MASS, leverage AI for real-time data processing from sensors, big data analytics, and machine learning to enable collision avoidance, route optimization, and energy management. Projects like Yara Birkeland exemplify degree-three autonomy (remotely controlled without an onboard crew), which reduces human error and fuel consumption. However, these innovations disrupt traditional seafaring roles, potentially displacing low-skilled jobs while creating demand for upskilled positions in ROCs. Studies suggest AI will redefine rather than eliminate seafarer roles, necessitating competencies in data analysis, AI oversight, and cybersecurity.

Flag State responsibility (UNCLOS, Article 94) requires reassessment for AI-driven vessels, where liability for accidents complicates attribution among human operators, software developers, and flag States. For example, sensor degradation or algorithmic failures may lead to collisions. The IMO addresses this dilemma through its E-Navigation Strategy (MSC.1/Circ.1595) and the ongoing development of the MASS Code. This framework aims to harmonize AI integration with safety and environmental protections, potentially mandating human oversight at high autonomy levels to align with navigational freedoms and pollution-prevention duties (UNCLOS, Articles 87 and 192–194).

Labor law implications are profound. AI surveillance via digital monitoring raises concerns over privacy, technostress, and occupational safety and health. The MLC's provisions on working hours, rest, and repatriation (Regulations 2.3–2.5) may not adequately cover shore-based remote operators, prompting calls for amendments to prevent excessive monitoring and to ensure the right to disconnect. STCW revisions are essential to incorporate AI-related training, focusing on competencies for MASS degrees one to four. The EU AI Act (Regulation (EU) 2024/1689), which entered into force in August 2024 and will be fully applicable by August 2026, classifies maritime AI as high risk. This designation mandates transparency, data governance, and human oversight. This aligns with the MASS Code, which requires EU-linked vessels to comply with bias mitigation and cybersecurity protocols, potentially influencing global standards through collaboration with IMO member States.

Challenges include cybersecurity vulnerabilities, as evidenced by breaches such as the NotPetya attack on Maersk in 2017, and data leakage risks, underscoring the need to align with the General Data Protection Regulation (GDPR) to protect seafarers' personal data. Opportunities lie in the ethical deployment of AI, fostering human–AI collaboration to enhance safety without exacerbating isolation or mental health issues aboard ships.

While AI propels marine technology toward decarbonization and efficiency, aligning with the sustainable use mandate in UNCLOS, it demands evolutionary reforms in maritime labor laws. International cooperation, including tripartite ILO–IMO dialogues, is vital to safeguard seafarers, prevent fragmentation, and ensure an equitable technological transition, striking a balance between innovation and human-centric principles.

Maral Javidbakht considered the attribution of conduct for MASS in Chapter 4. The emergence of MASS represents a transformative leap in marine technology, enabling vessels to operate with varying degrees of human independence through sensors, AI algorithms, and ROCs. Her chapter examines the attribution of MASS shipmasters' conduct to flag States under the law of the sea, emphasizing that technological advancements do not erode traditional accountability.

Marine technology allows shipmasters to retain overall command remotely, even in high-autonomy scenarios (IMO MASS degrees 3–4). In such cases, navigational and operational duties may be conducted via ROCs. However, international law rejects masterless navigation. Shipmasters must remain human, exercising overriding authority for safety (e.g., SOLAS, UNCLOS Article 98). UNCLOS treats ships as units (ITLOS jurisprudence in M/V Saiga (No. 2)), linking masters to flag States jurisdictionally, irrespective of location (Article 94). MASS qualify as "ships" under UNCLOS, subject to flag State obligations for effective control and due diligence in preventing wrongful acts.

Attribution is reflected in the rules of the Articles on Responsibility of States for Internationally Wrongful Acts. For government-operated MASS, masters are de jure organs (Article 4), and their conduct is directly attributable to the flag State. For privately operated vessels, attribution arises if the master exercises governmental functions (Article 5) or acts under flag State instructions/effective control (Article 8). Remote locations pose enforcement challenges – for example, extraterritorial ROCs – but do not negate attributability, as jurisdiction stems from the ship's flag, not its physical presence. Flag States bear due-diligence duties to ensure that masters comply (UNCLOS Articles 94, 217), with breaches attributable to State omission if preventive measures are not taken. Ultimately, MASS integration requires harmonized marine technology in accordance with the principles of the law of the sea. While AI reduces the need for onboard human roles, human masters safeguard predictability and safety. Flag States must enhance due diligence – for example, cybersecurity for ROCs – to avert responsibility gaps, thereby fostering innovation without compromising navigational freedoms or environmental protections under UNCLOS.

In Chapter 5, Sindhura Polepalli adds normative concepts of justice and equity to the discussion of shipping decarbonization. The imperative for decarbonization in international shipping is closely tied to advancements in marine technology and evolving interpretations of the law of the sea. Her chapter critiques the sector's transition toward net-zero greenhouse gas (GHG) emissions by mid-century, emphasizing procedural and legal disparities hindering a "just and equitable transition" (JET).

Shipping handles over 80 percent of global trade but relies on fossil fuels, contributing 3 percent of anthropogenic GHG emissions. Maritime emissions are projected to grow by 90–130 percent of these figures by 2050, compared to 2008 levels. Marine technology innovations – such as zero-emission vessels (ZEVs), alternative fuels (e.g., ammonia, hydrogen), energy-efficient designs, and digital optimization tools – offer pathways to reduce carbon intensity. However, adoption of these "green" technologies requires equitable global frameworks to avoid exacerbating vulnerabilities in developing States.

UNCLOS frames anthropogenic GHGs as marine pollution (Article 194(1)), obliging States to prevent, reduce, and control emissions with due diligence and a precautionary approach. The International Tribunal for the Law of the Sea's (ITLOS) Advisory Opinion of May 21, 2024, reinforces this duty, linking UNCLOS obligations to the Paris Agreement's 1.5°C goal and invoking the concept of common but differentiated responsibilities and respective capabilities (CBDR-RC). ITLOS mandates assistance from developed States to developing States – those with lesser capabilities (Articles 202–203). This mandate ensures continuous support until parity is achieved. This human-centric lens addresses the risks posed by climate change, including sea level rise that impacts Small Island Developing States (SIDS) and Least Developed Countries (LDCs).

As the competent international organization, the IMO stewards sector-specific measures via the Marine Environment Protection Committee (MEPC). The 2023 Revised IMO Strategy on Reduction of GHG Emissions from Ships targets a 20–30 percent reduction in vessel source emissions by 2030, a 70–80 percent reduction by 2040, and net-zero emissions by 2050. Short-term measures under MARPOL Annex VI, such as the Energy Efficiency Existing Ship Index (EEXI) and Carbon Intensity Indicator (CII), leverage marine technology to achieve a 40 percent reduction in carbon intensity from 2008 baselines. However, mid-term proposals, including a GHG Fuel Standard (GFS), universal levies, and emissions trading systems, reveal gaps. The Comprehensive Impact Assessment (CIA) highlights the disproportionate burdens on developing fleets, yet it lacks transparency and broad stakeholder input.

To address these challenges, SIDS advocate revenue recycling for adaptation. Developed States push levies under the polluter-pays principle. These are often flag-neutral but ignore the nuances of CBDR-RC. Hybrid mechanisms, such as feebates that incentivize ZEVs, integrate marine technology (e.g., onboard carbon capture) but risk trade distortions without equitable revenue distribution. As of August 2025, the IMO approved the Net-Zero Framework in April (MEPC 83), which combines GFS with economic incentives, was slated for formal adoption in October 2025, and is expected to enter into force in 2027. This advances UNCLOS obligations, but critiques persist, including from the US Federal Maritime Commission on economic impacts.

The chapter urges reforms – including revising IMO member State groupings, explicitly embedding the polluter-pays principle, and elevating JET to the Legal Committee – to harmonize marine technology deployment with law of the sea principles. Without addressing CBDR-RC and assistance obligations, decarbonization risks perpetuating inequities and contravening UNCLOS's mandate for sustainable ocean governance. Ultimately, JET demands leadership from developed States, public–private partnerships for technology transfer, and inclusive coalitions to foster resilient, low-carbon shipping ecosystems.

Many of the technologies for shipping and autonomous vessels require reliable communications between the ship and shore, between the ship and other instruments or devices in the water, and within the ship. Raul "Pete" Pedrozo explores the vulnerability of these communications in Chapter 6. Maritime cyber threats, particularly the jamming and spoofing of Global Navigation Satellite Systems (GNSS), pose escalating risks to navigation reliant on marine technology, undermining safety and efficiency in international shipping. This chapter examines vulnerabilities in systems such as GPS, GLONASS, BeiDou, and Galileo, which provide critical Position, Navigation, and Timing (PNT) data. Low-power GNSS signals are susceptible to intentional interference, which can degrade accuracy, integrity, continuity, and availability. Malign actors – primarily China, Iran, Russia, and North Korea – employ electronic warfare to disrupt commercial vessels, with incidents surging: over 5,800 vessels affected in Q2 2025 alone, including persistent Baltic jamming attributed to Russia, Persian Gulf AIS spoofing since mid-2025, and disruptions during the Israel–Iran conflict impacting nearly 1,000 ships daily. Such attacks, often near oil terminals or conflict zones, compromise safety under UNCLOS, which mandates pollution prevention and navigational freedoms (Articles 192–194).

UNCLOS implicitly requires States to ensure navigational safety (SOLAS integration), while ITU Radio Regulations prohibit harmful interference in navigation. Jamming and spoofing are violations of these duties. The IMO addresses these issues through the Maritime Safety Committee, which has established guidelines (MSC.1/Circ.1526) and adopted Resolution A.1045(27), which urges resilient PNT. In March 2025, IMO, ICAO, and ITU issued a joint statement expressing "grave concern" over rising incidents, calling for safeguards to protect radionavigation services. US measures, including DHS advisories and NCAGS reporting, emphasize the use of real-time alerts and multilayered defenses.

Marine technology mitigations include enhanced receivers, encrypted Satellite Time and Location (STL) signals offering 30–50 m accuracy, eLoran backups, and anti-jamming antennas such as the Veripos GAJT-710MS. Emerging innovations, such as laser-based positioning (e.g., CyScan GeoLock) and quantum navigation, may bolster resilience. In 2025, the US Space Force's X-37B mission tested quantum sensors for GPS-free PNT and laser communications, while Q-CTRL's gravimetric trials and French/Chinese laser systems may advance secure, high-bandwidth alternatives. Quantum clocks promise orders-of-magnitude precision.

Ultimately, resilient PNT architectures must integrate defense-in-depth and cybersecurity to uphold the rules reflected in UNCLOS. As cyber threats proliferate, international cooperation must evolve to prevent navigational disruptions and ensure safe, spoof-proof maritime operations amid geopolitical tensions.

There is a fusion of space and ocean technologies. In Chapter 7, Richard Kilpatrick discusses space-based vessel tracking and its impact on maritime operations. Vessel-tracking innovations represent a convergence of marine technology advancements and evolving obligations under the law of the sea, enhancing maritime domain awareness while introducing new vulnerabilities. His chapter traces the evolution from early twentieth-century radio communications, which were codified in the 1914 SOLAS Convention following the Titanic disaster, to the Global Maritime Distress and Safety System (GMDSS) in 1988. Contemporary tools, such as the Automatic Identification System (AIS) and Long-Range Identification and Tracking (LRIT), now rely on space-based satellites. These SOLAS-mandated systems (1974, as amended) integrate satellite infrastructure for real-time PNT, aligning with navigational safety imperatives (UNCLOS, Articles 94, 98) and IMO guidelines (MSC.1/Circ.1307).

Contemporary marine technology leverages AI, machine learning, and satellite imagery to process AIS data, which is cross-referenced with radar and drone data. This combination enables better detection of "dark" vessels evading tracking through spoofing or deactivation. As of August 2025, innovations include blockchain for secure cargo tracking, AI-driven analytics for sustainability (e.g., wind-powered vessels), and autonomous ship operations, as highlighted in the MASS Code developments. These tools bolster enforcement against IUU fishing, sanctions evasion, and maritime piracy and terrorism, and support pollution prevention (UNCLOS, Article 194) and flag State duties.

However, enhanced transparency risks misuse. Houthi militants, for example, have exploited AIS for targeting and sinking vessels and hijacking others. This action prompted US advisories (MARAD, March 2025) recommending AIS deactivation in high-risk areas, which has to be reconciled with SOLAS mandates for continuous broadcasting, except in the event of security threats. IMO guidelines and flag State rules must strike a balance between transparency and protection, potentially by using encrypted signals or selective data sharing. Evolving threats require standards aligned with UNCLOS and harmonized with IMO AIS guidelines. As AI and quantum navigation advance, vessel tracking promises safer oceans but necessitates ethical safeguards against exploitation, ensuring equitable maritime governance.

In Chapter 8, Krisztina Tilinger unpacks how blockchain interacts with the law of the sea. Blockchain technology (BCT), as an innovative marine technology, intersects with the law of the sea to advance sustainable ocean governance, aligning with UN SDG 14 and UNCLOS. The oceans absorb 23 percent of anthropogenic CO_2 emissions and are vital for regulating the climate and supporting biodiversity, yet face threats from pollution, overfishing, and climate change. UNCLOS mandates the conservation of marine living resources (Articles 61–62), environmental protection (Part XII), and the preservation of biodiversity (Article 194), emphasizing community interests over State-centric exploitation.

BCT's decentralized, distributed, and immutable ledger ensures data authenticity, reducing fraud, bureaucracy, and costs while enhancing trust in public administration. UN recommendations advocate for BCT integration in achieving the SDGs, with applications in commodity tracking, refugee aid, and peer-to-peer financing. In ocean governance, BCT enables transparent total allowable catch (TAC) allocation, real-time pollution monitoring, MARPOL-compliant waste management tracking, and marine protected area (MPA) surveillance via smart contracts and token incentives for sustainable practices.

Challenges to broader integration of BCT include high energy consumption, scalability issues, legal recognition as evidence, and data privacy under GDPR equivalents. The EU's 2023 European Blockchain Regulatory Sandbox (EBRS) addresses these through regulatory dialogues, with the 2025 *EU Blockchain Ecosystem Report* highlighting growth in finance, government, and supply chains, led by Estonia and Lithuania. As of August 2025, advancements include the UN Ocean Conference's "Digital Oceans" agenda and side events, such as Sea2See's blockchain-based seafood transparency, alongside Ocean Protocol's mid-year updates that enhance data monetization for marine research. BCT harmonizes marine technology with UNCLOS, promoting equitable resource use without the need for new treaties, as national laws and best practices are sufficient. By automating compliance and incentivizing conservation, BCT accelerates SDG 14, striking a balance between innovation and environmental stewardship to achieve resilient oceans.

Chapter 10 by Digvijay Rewatkar examines seabed-mining technology and its material impact on implementing the precautionary approach. Seabed-mining technology intersects critically with the law of the sea, balancing resource extraction in Part XI with environmental safeguards in Part XII of UNCLOS. His chapter examines how States may use technology to access minerals in the Area beyond national jurisdiction. Seabed minerals include cobalt, nickel, and rare earth elements. Projections indicate that demand will surge by 2050. Risks associated with seabed mining include sediment plumes, noise pollution, and loss of biodiversity and habitat. Marine technology may help mitigate these risks.

The UNCLOS negotiations from 1973 to 1982 reflected a North–South divide, with developing States advocating technology transfer under the common heritage principle (UNCLOS, Article 136) amid technological uncertainties. The precautionary approach, initially nascent but formalized in Principle 15 of the Rio Declaration (1992), mandates risk aversion when scientific uncertainty persists (UNCLOS Articles 145, 194). The International Seabed Authority (ISA), established under UNCLOS Part XI, operationalizes this normative approach in its Draft Exploitation Regulations, emphasizing best available technology (BAT) and environmental impact assessments (EIAs) to minimize harm.

Marine technology advancements include collector systems for nodules (e.g., suspended noncontact robotics by Beijing Pioneer and BGR, reducing seafloor traction), cutters for sulfides/crusts (e.g., Patania II), and riser-lift systems for ore transport. Impacts on the marine environment appear to vary. Benthic disturbances destroy habitats, mid-water plumes affect nutrient cycles and respiration, and surface emissions mimic shipping pollution. Studies post-2024 collector tests (e.g., NORI-D) show short-term plume dilution, but knowledge gaps in mid-water ecosystems persist.

The forthcoming Mining Code incorporates precautionary measures, such as adaptive management and regional environmental plans, for the Clarion-Clipperton Zone. Meanwhile, thirty-four States, including France and Chile, have called for a moratorium on commercial exploitation. Challenges include the dynamic evolution of BAT, uncertainty about how to implement equitable tech transfer (UNCLOS Article 144), and how to integrate the BBNJ treaty into planning and operations. Seabed-mining technology must align with the evolutionary framework of UNCLOS, prioritizing precaution to reconcile mineral needs with the integrity of ecosystems. Scalable, experimental approaches could optimize trade-offs, fostering sustainable deep-sea governance amidst climate imperatives.

In Chapter 10, Youri van Logchem analyzes the relationship between Sensor Monitoring and Reliable Telecommunications (SMART) submarine communications cables and the legal regime governing marine scientific research. SMART cables exemplify innovative marine technology, integrating oceanographic sensors into submarine fiber-optic cables to enhance data collection on climate change, aquatic environments, and disaster warnings. His chapter uncovers the dual functionality of SMART cables, which transmit international communications while gathering environmental data. This dual purpose may create tension between the cable regime and the rules for marine scientific research (MSR) in UNCLOS.

Submarine cables carry approximately 99 percent of the world's global data traffic. SMART systems retrofit existing cables or design new ones with sensors (e.g., accelerometers, pressure gauges) for real-time monitoring of seismic activity, tsunamis, and ocean warming, thereby addressing deep-ocean knowledge gaps that are unattainable via buoys or satellites. Under UNCLOS, cable laying is a high-seas freedom (Article 87), with coastal States exercising limited jurisdiction in the exclusive economic zone (EEZ) and on the continental shelf (Articles 58, 79). However, SMART cable data collection may activate the MSR regime in Part XIII, requiring coastal consent in the EEZ and on the continental shelf (Article 246). Transit cables (nonlanding) may evade full coastal State jurisdiction, but sensor integration may classify their activity as MSR. Coastal State sovereignty applies in territorial seas (Article 2). Security concerns abound. Following the attack on the Nord Stream pipeline and the associated cable damage, concern has grown that SMART cable data could be at risk. Routing on the high seas or through stable, consenting States may reduce the conflicts among the different legal regimes.

In Chapter 11, Natalia Perez examines advances in underwater archaeology and their implications for the regime under UNCLOS. UNCLOS addresses archaeological objects at sea, including in the contiguous zone (Article 33), the Area (Article 149), and general duties of States (Article 303). UNESCO estimates that there are 3 million undiscovered wrecks, including many warships, in foreign waters, prompting debates over flag State versus coastal State rights. Technical and information breakthroughs in underwater archaeology are transforming the discovery, study, and preservation of shipwrecks. As more finds are discovered, questions have arisen about ownership, sovereign immunity, and cultural heritage. Technologies like remotely operated vehicles (ROVs), autonomous underwater vehicles (AUVs), unmanned surface vehicles (USVs), and sonar-enabled deep-sea exploration beyond diver limits (e.g., 90 m) facilitate noninvasive imaging and eDNA analysis for historical insights. The 2001 UNESCO Convention on the Protection of Underwater Cultural Heritage (UCH) prohibits commercial exploitation, designates wrecks as gravesites, and mandates in situ preservation.

Marine technology democratizes access but risks the looting of sunken wrecks. The UNCLOS and UNESCO frameworks should evolve to promote equitable governance, prioritizing cooperation and technology transfer (UNCLOS Article 202). This approach strikes a balance between heritage preservation and innovation, thereby preventing commercial overreach in contested areas.

Chapter 12 by Marc Fialkoff turns toward the legal regime of Floating Nuclear Power Plants (FNPPs) and the law of the sea. FNPPs embody cutting-edge marine technology, enabling decarbonized energy for offshore platforms subject to complex, intersecting regimes under the law of the sea and nuclear nonproliferation. His chapter examines jurisdictional ambiguities in EEZ deployments, reconciling the sui generis nature of the EEZ (Article 55) with IAEA safeguards and the Amendment to the Convention on the Physical Protection of Nuclear Material (ACPPNM).

In the EEZ, UNCLOS balances coastal rights (Article 56) and high-seas freedoms (Article 58), classifying FNPPs as ships, installations, or artificial islands, depending on the circumstances. Fixed FNPPs may qualify as installations (Article 60), thereby extending coastal jurisdiction for nonproliferation purposes, including Comprehensive Safeguards Agreements (CSAs) under NPT Article III and nuclear security, as per ACPPNM Principle 2A(3). Disputes continue to surround FNPP, especially their use within foreign EEZs. Some proposals advocate for coastal responsibility for fixed FNPPs, which attempts to align UNCLOS evolution with the peaceful use (Article IV) provisions of the NPT. Harmonizing regimes ensures nonproliferation without impeding maritime innovation, fostering sustainable ocean energy amid climate imperatives.

In Chapter 13, James Kraska questions whether the regime for marine genetic resources (MGR) in the 2023 BBNJ agreement is sufficient to protect legal rights to intellectual property or naval technology. MGR encompasses genetic material from marine organisms with potential market or naval value. For example, marine genetic resources have been used in biotechnology to develop pharmaceuticals such as remdesivir. These organic materials require advanced marine technology for collection. This technology includes deep-sea submersibles, genomic sequencing, and AI-driven analysis, which is predominantly held by developed States. These new technologies are not unrelated to military risk at sea.

Under UNCLOS, high-seas freedoms (Article 87) evolve through BBNJ to balance exploitation with conservation (Articles 192–194). This has imposed notification, assessment, and equitable sharing obligations without protecting IPRs. This transparency risks exposing proprietary data, thereby deterring innovation in marine technology sectors, such as synthetic biology. National security concerns are also present. DARPA and the Office of Naval Research (ONR) fund civilian vessels for bio-naval research to detect underwater threats. Related research would be posted on the ClHM. Although the BBNJ Agreement exempts warships, this may nevertheless conflict with UNCLOS's military exemptions under Article 298(1)(b).

To enhance implementation, the Conference of the Parties (COP) should prioritize monetary/in-kind benefits (e.g., capacity-building funds) over full disclosure of research on the ClHM. This approach would preserve IPR to incentivize participation without compromising distributive justice. Furthermore, broadening the warship exemptions to include defense-funded research aligns with UNCLOS's structure, which favors sovereign immunity.

* * *

The chapters in this volume illuminate the dynamic interplay between advances in marine technology and the law of the sea, navigating challenges ranging from autonomous shipping to deep-sea resource governance. Collectively, these chapters highlight the potential of marine technology to revolutionize shipping, exploration, and sustainability while also exposing legal fissures in jurisdiction, equity, and security. UNCLOS's evolutionary spirit must adapt to foster innovation without exacerbating divides, ensuring that benefits like enhanced safety and biodiversity protection accrue globally.

Future marine technologies warrant exploration in quantum navigation for spoof-proof PNT, AI-driven predictive maintenance for zero-emission vessels, hydrogen/ammonia fuels for decarbonized propulsion, deep-sea robotics with bio-inspired designs for minimally invasive mining, and integrated ocean observatories using blockchain-secured IoT for real-time biodiversity monitoring. These could align with the IMO's MASS Code and BBNJ, promoting equitable and secure ocean stewardship.

Marine technology cannot be categorized into a single basket. It is more accurate to refer to "marine technologies," each with its own ecosystem of hardware and software and distinct yet overlapping legal regimes. Furthermore, the international maritime law applicable to each technology must be considered within the context of its use. Commercial uses, government uses, and marine scientific research purposes are each discrete activities with specific legal regimes. This means that future lines of inquiry focused on the intersection of marine technology and the law of the sea might fragment into separate epistemological communities. On the other hand, there are benefits to selecting the most critical or transformative technologies and testing their application to legal regimes that evolve more slowly. This cross-pollination yields insights across subfields of ocean law and policy.

Index

www.ingramcontent.com/pod-product-compliance
Lightning Source LLC
Chambersburg PA
CBHW070245020426
42255CB00004B/277